Comanche Dictionary and Grammar
Second Edition

SIL International®
Publications in Linguistics
92

This Comanche dictionary is based on research drawn from the files of the late Elliot Canonge which he initiated in the early 1940s under the auspices of the Summer Institute of Linguistics. Dr. Robinson has rescued and enhanced this important body of data which spans traditional and contemporary varieties of Comanche speech styles and four geographically identifiable dialects. The Comanche-English section of the work, as complete as current sources permit, constitutes the central portion of the dictionary, but an English-Comanche section indexes Comanche entries to aid in locating Comanche forms from the point of view of their English equivalents. In turn, Dr. Armagost's provision of an introductory exploration of Comanche morphology and syntax further enhances this volume as an important contribution to our knowledge of this branch of the Uto-Aztecan family of languages.

Series Editors

Virgil Poulter
University of Texas at Arlington

William R. Merrifield
SIL International®

Volume Editors

Alan C. Wares
Mickey Brussow

Iris M. Wares

Consulting Editors

Doris A. Bartholomew
Pamela M. Bendor-Samuel
Desmond C. Derbyshire
Robert A. Dooley
Jerold A. Edmondson

Austin Hale
Robert E. Longacre
Eugene E. Loos
Kenneth L. Pike
Viola G. Waterhouse

Production Staff

Bonnie Brown, Managing Editor
Judy Benjamin, Compositor
Patrick Gourley, Cover design
Wekeah Bradley and Ron Burgess, Drawings

Comanche Dictionary and Grammar
Second Edition

Lila Wistrand-Robinson
and
James Armagost

SIL International®
Dallas, Texas

Copies of this and other publications of SIL International® may be obtained from:

SIL International Publications
7500 W. Camp Wisdom Road
Dallas, TX 75236-5629

Voice: 972-708-7404
Fax: 972-708-7363
publications_intl@sil.org
www.ethnologue.com/bookstore.asp

Contents

Elliott Donton Canonge

1921 - 1971
Friend of the Comanches

Mary Redbird

Artist Wekeah Bradley
with daughter Hawana

Eva Tooahnipah

Mary Wahkinney
and May Wanqua

Ron Burgess, artist

Rev. & Mrs. Ned Timbo

Eva Watchetaker

Daisy Waters

George Smith
Watchetaker

Acknowledgments

This Comanche-English dictionary and grammar is an outgrowth of the work of the late Elliott Canonge, whose field work was done between 1945 and 1963 under the auspices of the Summer Institute of Linguistics. Various SIL scholars influenced him in the analysis of the Comanche vowel system described in his 1957 article Voiceless vowels in Comanche. His Comanche Texts, first published in 1958, includes in the appendix a list of words retrieved from the text materials by computer. Since his dictionary file of approximately 3500 words was not available to the public, his widow gave permission for it to be edited and published.

Through Kansas State University, a grant was received for this purpose from the National Endowment for the Humanities (Project 1366) for a fourteen-month period during 1978 and 1979, eight months covering only half-time work. The grant period included nine weeks of fieldwork in Oklahoma, consulting with fluent speakers of Comanche and checking both Canonge's list and words encountered in previous bibliographic research. The language associates were Felix Kowena, Mary Redbird, Daisy Waters, Ned Timbo, Mary Wahkinney, Eva Tooahnipah, Watchetaker, and Maude Blevins. Consulting sessions were recorded on audio tape and archived at Kansas State University.

The dictionary portion of this study and recent fieldwork associated with it are primarily the work of Lila Wistrand-Robinson, but SIL editor Iris Wares needs also to be mentioned and thanked for her indefatigable work in preparing this part of the volume for publication. James Armagost, of Kansas State University, became associated with the project in connection with the NEH grant and is primarily responsible for the grammar portion of the study.

Sketches are the work of talented Comanche artists Weckeah Bradley and Ron Burgess.

Finally, we wish to acknowledge the work of the editorial staff of SIL's Academic Publications Department (currently called Global Publishing Services) and its computer operators in preparing this volume for publication.

Lila Wistrand-Robinson
James Armagost
June, 1990

Preface

The Comanche people are at present located around Walters, Cache, and Lawton, in the State of Oklahoma. They seem to have originated in the Southwest, although at one time they lived and ranged from the Northwest Coast, down the Pacific Coast, and across to what is now Oklahoma, Texas, and Mexico. They moved back and forth in the latter area until the coming of white colonists in the eighteenth and nineteenth centuries. This dark and painful period was marked by the needless slaughter of the Comanche people, who fought relentlessly for their land and their rights; but they were unable to gain the victory. Land was bought and fenced off, and buffalo were slaughtered until the days of the massive hunts came to a close, bringing to an end the traditional, nomadic Comanche way of life.

Sent to English-language schools, where they were punished for speaking their own language, many Comanche students lost proficiency in their native tongue. With the coming of compulsory education, English gradually became the first language of recent generations of Comanche children. Cultural changes took place in Indian schools where children in dormitories away from home were required to wear clothing and eat food of the white men. In spite of this, present-day Comanches have preserved many aspects of their native culture, some of which have been recorded in this dictionary.

The Comanche language is a member of the Uto-Aztecan language family, Numic branch, and Shoshone group. Other Uto-Aztecan groups are Piman and Nahuatlan. Shoshone is the nearest sister language, so closely related that a Comanche speaker immediately recognizes the similarity when he hears it spoken. Other members of the Shoshonean group are Hopi, Northern and Southern Paiute, Snake, and Ute. Also related are Papago, Mono, and Tubatulabal in the Southwest. Finally, in Mexico are Yaqui-Mayo, Huichol, Cora, Tarahumara, and the various dialects of Nahuatl or Aztec, completing the Uto-Aztecan language family.

This volume is designed not only to record and preserve Comanche speech but also to help younger generations of Comanches learn about their history and culture. For this reason, names of outstanding Comanche tribal members have been included, as well as historical dates, fauna and flora of the area, and facts about cultural artifacts and their use or construction.

Comanche words are listed in the Comanche-English dictionary (Part I) along with dialectal variants, grammatical categories, simple etymologies, and illustrative sentences. The reader may use the dictionary to find linguistic, historical, or cultural information, or to look for particular Comanche words with their accompanying information.

Following Part I there are five appendixes listing fauna (animals, birds, reptiles, fish, and insects), flora, body parts, months of the year, and personal names. Appendix E has been included here by request as a reference for finding names for Comanche children. Trees and plants listed in Appendix B are a key to the ecological setting of the Comanches and to many of the medicinal plants used in Comanche culture. Some items in this list include scientific names for more specific identification.

The English-Comanche lexicon (Part II), is a reference to Comanche terms for speakers of English. Each English word is followed by corresponding Comanche words or phrases. To find a particular Comanche entry, one may use the lexicon first and then go to the dictionary to find a more complete explanation of a Comanche word.

By use of the dictionary and the grammar (Part III) in conjunction with the narratives in Comanche Texts, a student should be able to gain a rudimentary knowledge of the language.

A brief bibliography lists books and articles on the history, culture, language, and linguistic studies of Comanche.

Abbreviations

A	accusative		DA	daughter
ABS	absolutive		DAT	dative
ABSTR	abstract		DECL	declarative
AFF	affirmative		DEF	definite
AG	agentive		DEM	demonstrative
AJ	adjective		DERIV	derivational
ALL	allative		DIR	direction
AN	animate		DO	definite object
ARCH	archaic		DS	different subject
AUG	augmentative		DUR	durative
AUX	subordinate verb		DV	ditransitive verb
AV	adverb		EMPH	emphasis
BEN	benefactive		ENGL	English
BR	brother		EVID	evidential
C	Comanche		EXCL	exclamation
C&J	Carlson and Jones		FA	father
CAUS	causative		G	genitive
cf.	compare		HU	husband
CMPL	completive		HUM	human
CO	coreferential		!	imperative
COG	cognate		I	inclusive
CONT	continuative		IMM	immediate
CTR	contrast		INAN	inanimate
D	dual		INCEP	inceptive
D1	immediate proximal		INDEF	indefinite
D2	removed proximal		INFER	inference
D3	immediate distal		INSTR	instrument
D4	removed distal		INTENS	intensifier
D5	scattered		INTERJ	interjection

IO	indirect object	QUES	interrogative
IRREG	irregular	QUOT	quotative
IV	intransitive verb	RDP	reduplication
K	Kwahere (dialect)	REAL	realized
L	locative	RECIP	reciprocal
M	manner	REF	reference (to)
MEAS	measure	REFL	reflexive
MO	mother	REL	relative clause
MV	main verb		marker
N	nominative	REP	repetitive
N	Nookoni (dialect)	S	singular
NEC	necessity	SB	sibling
NEG	negative	SEP	separate
NOM	nominal	SH	Shoshone
NONHUM	nonhuman	SO	son
NP	noun phrase	SP	Spanish
NTOP	nontopic	sp.	species
NUM	numeral	SS	same subject
O	Ohnono (dialect)	ST	stative
OBJ	object	SUBJ	subject
OBL	obligation	T	time
P	Pehnanɨɨ (dialect)	TMP	temporary
P	plural	TOP0	topic
PART	partitive	TV	transitive verb
PERS	person/personal	UNR	unrealized
PFX	prefix	UNSP	unspecified referent
PN	pronoun	VB	verbalizer
PO	possessor	VOC	vocative
PPL	participle	VP	verb phrase
PREP	preposition	W	Wia?nɨɨ (dialect)
PROG	progressive	WI	wife
PST	narrative past	Y	Yapai?nɨɨ (dialect)
PUA	Proto-Uto-Aztecan	X	exclusive
Q	quantifier	?	analysis unknown

Part I

Comanche-English Dictionary

Introduction

1. Entries. Comanche entry words are printed in boldface type at the left-hand margin of each column. For easy reference, the first word on each page also appears at the left-hand margin at the top of the page, and the last word on the page appears on the same line at the right-hand margin. Instead of pronunciation being indicated in each entry, a guide to pronunciation is presented immediately following this preface. Unless otherwise marked, all entries are singular; verbs are cited with the progressive suffix *-tʉ* or *-rʉ*.

Many Comanche nouns have a long form, such as *aawo* 'cup, vessel, container', and a shortened form, such as *awo*, which combines with other lexical roots to form compounds, such as *awo noʔo* 'armadillo' and *awo tahwi* 'cupboard'. Such long and short forms are often listed separately in the dictionary in their normal alphabetical order, but are cross-referenced to each other. The reader should beware that separately-listed combining forms are sometimes labeled as prefixes to indicate their dependent character, even though they are more properly lexical rather than inflectional from a strictly linguistic point of view.

Alphabetic order is the same as in English except that voiceless (underlined) vowels are ordered immediately after their voiced counterparts, the sixth vowel *ʉ*, and glottal stop *(ʔ)* is placed at the end of the alphabet, following *y*.

As is customary in other dictionaries, word space takes precedence over consonants or vowels so that the open compound precedes the closed sequence in alphabetic order. Once again, the reader needs to beware that more work needs to be done to define the rules of word formation for Comanche, especially in respect to compounding of lexical material. It is not at all clear how open and closed compounds should be treated and we are aware that this matter is not handled with complete consistency in these pages. Some compounds are left open, with word space, others are closed, without word space. Earlier versions of this manuscript employed hyphen for some compounds but these were edited out for lack of firm guidelines regarding their use.

2. Variants.   Variations in pronunciation or meaning, as spoken by different Comanche clans, are indicated by abbreviations of clan names. These variants are not otherwise listed in the dictionary. Most of the entries originally collected by Canonge came from the *Wia?nʉʉ* (W) 'worn-away people' of the Walters area (also called *Mahnenʉʉ*). Wistrand-Robinson's word checking took place chiefly with members of the *Kwahare* (K) 'antelope' clan in the Cache and Lawton areas of Oklahoma. She did brief checking, also, with four other groups. The *Yapai?nʉʉ* (Y) 'root-eaters' (reportedly named because they ate roots in the winter months when nothing else was available) roamed the Arkansas River valley in earlier times. The *Pehnanʉʉ* (P) were so named because a deer reportedly went through their camp at one time and the people shouted so much that the deer died of fright. They are located ten miles west of Duncan, Oklahoma, which is also called Comanche City. Brief checks also took place with the *Noyʉhkanʉʉ* or *Nookoni* (N) 'wanderers', located between the Red River and the Peace River, and with the *Ohnono* (O) clan in the Lawton area, yielding a few variants from each of these groups.

3. Case and number.   Following a main entry with or without dialectal variants, there may be special accusative or plural forms listed for a noun or verb. Singular (sg) or plural (pl) marking follows forms to which they apply. Examples of separate forms for singular and plural subjects are:

> **ʉhpʉitʉ** (v) *pl* ʉhkooitʉ   sleep.
> **okweetʉ** (v) *pl* o?okwetʉ   flow.

Examples of verbs with separate forms for singular and plural objects are:

> **pa?wʉhtiarʉ** *(v, sg obj)*, *pl obj* **pawʉ?weniitʉ**   baptize.
> **tʉkʉhpehkarʉ***(v, sg obj)*, *pl obj* **tʉkʉwasʉrʉ**   kill for food.

4. Grammatical Classification.   Only a very broad grammatical classification of Comanche words is attempted in the dictionary. Consult the grammar for more details.

5. Definitions.   Definitions include basic meanings in concise form, and may include scientific names for specificity of fauna and flora. The denotata of kinship terms are abbreviated as in the list of abbreviations that accompanies the grammar.

Some archaic definitions, marked arch, are included where these have been identified, in order to document this information; e.g.,

namuwoo, (n, arch) husband.

6. Etymologies. For some dictionary entries, simple morphological analyses are given in terms of the literal meaning of separate morphemes comprising a total entry. These analyses take two forms, as follows:

awo nohi? (n) dice game (*lit* playing container; refers to bowl or containerused in playing dice).

keto?kapaa (n) kerosene [**ke** not + *to?ka* dark + **paa** liquid].

7. Examples. Example sentences of two types are presented—those given by Comanche language associates, and sentences taken from Canonge's *Comanche Texts*. Numbers in parentheses after an illustrative sentence refer to page number and sentence number in *Comanche Texts*; e.g. 115:3 refers to page 115, sentence 3 in *texts*.

8. Cross Reference. As an additional aid in locating dialectal variants or related words, many entries are cross-referenced.

Guide to Pronunciation

The Comanche alphabet, consisting of six vowels and twelve consonants, is as follows, with vowels having both voiced and voiceless realizations. These occur in the following order:

a a̱ b e e̱ h i i̱ k m n o o̱ p r s t u u̱ ʉ ʉ̱ w y ʔ

Single vowels are pronounced as follows:

		Examples:	
a	as in *a* of *father*	*ma*	'my, his'
e	as in *ei* of *eight*	*ke*	'no'
i	as in *ee* of *see*	*hini*	'what?'
o	as in *o* of *go*	*ahó*	'hello, thank you
u	as in *oo* of *boot*	*hubiyaʔ*	'song, hymn'
ʉ	as *u* with the lips spread; not found in English.	*sʉmʉʔ*	'one'

Long vowels are written as a sequence of two like vowels, as in *aa* or *ee*. They are pronounced like simple vowels, but are longer in duration. Examples:

haa	'yes'
ma eeko	'his tongue'
marii	'them'
noobi	'hill'
pimorooʔ	'cow'
yuupʉ	'fat (person)'
ʉnʉʉʔ	'insect, bug'

Voiceless (or whispered) vowels in Comanche are underlined. Examples:

7

a̱	*kasa̱*	'wing'	o	*aawo̱*	'cup, vessel'
e̱	*taabe̱*	'sun'	u̱	*yuhu̱*	'fat, grease'
i̱	*noo'bi̱*	'hill, knoll'	u̱	*nakwu̱si?*	'pumpkin'

Stress is marked (´) when it does not fall on the first syllable and yet is primary stress, and marked (`) when it is secondary stress. Examples:

aakáa?	'devil's horn'	*amawóo?a-paa*	'apple juice
atakwásu̱?	'corn soup'	*na?bukuwàa?a-nábaa*	'gasoline'
pasawí?oo?	'frog'	*pòhotu̱-na?su̱kía*	'heavy shawl'

In shorter words, the stress on the first syllable usually becomes secondary to the marked primary stress, as a rule of thumb. On compounds, the relationship between the two words may cause the stress to fall on either the first or on the second word of the compound.

Consonants:

b	made with air blown lightly through slightly parted lips,		
	or like English *v* in 'a van'	*tabe*	'sun'
h	as in *h* of *hot*	*husi̱*	'cactus'
k	as in *k* of *ski* (unaspirated)	*kaku?*	'grandmother'
m	as in *m* of *move*	*moowi?*	'lariat'
n	as in *n* of *no*	*ma nami?*	'his sister'
p	as in *p* of *spin* (unaspirated)	*ma puuku̱*	'his horse'
r	as in *tt* of *batter*	*nu̱ ara?*	'my uncle'
s	as in *s* of *sun*	*ma so?o*	'his cheek'
t	as in *t* of *stop* (unaspirated)	*tabe*	'sun'
w	as in *w* of *wish*	*wahi*	'cedar'
y	as in *y* of *you*	*yuyu*	'grease'
?	as in *oh?oh*, where air is cut off in the throat		
	between syllables (glottal stop)	*po?a?*	'skin, bark'

Combinations of the above consonants which should be noted are:

| kw | as in *qu* of *quick* | *ma kwahi* | 'his back' |
| ts | as in *ts* of *beets* | *tseena?* | 'wolf' |

In the Kwahare band and a few other bands, word-medial gw occurs, as follows:

| gw | as in *gu* of *guano* | *nigwaitu̱* | 'ask for' |

Preaspiration and preglottalization of certain consonants occur word-medially, as follows:

hn	aworahna	'cupboard'	?n	sʉsʉmʉ?nʉʉ	'some'
hk	eka-huhkupʉ	'cardinal'	?b	hunu?bi?	'creek'
hp	ekasahpana?	'soldier'	?w	ta?wo?i?	'gun'
ht	ahotabeni̱htʉ	'thanksgiving'	?r	eka?e?ree	'swamp rabbit'

Comanche-English Dictionary

A

aa (n) animal horn. **ekakuura?aa** young buffalo's horn. *See* **na?aa.**

aahe, ahe (interj) I claim it! (said when claiming coup in time past).

aakaa?, ahkaa? (n) banana (domestic fruit introduced; so named because it appeared similar to native plant, devil's horn).

aakáa?, ahkáa? (n) devil's horn, devil's claw (native weed: grows in barnyard or where cattle are fed; has edible black seeds).

aakáa?

aakwusitu (v), *pl* **aakwusina** sneeze.

aamuyake? (n) horn (wind instrument). *See* **woinu.**

aanatsihtuye? (n) animal horn comb, horn brush.

aatakíi?, ahtakíi? (n) grasshopper (small species).

aatamúu?, ahtamúu? (n) grasshopper (large, no wings).

aawo (n) cup, vessel, container; *arch* basket. **Nu pia? tsa? aawo makotsetu.** My mother is washing dishes. *See* **awo-.**

aawui utama?, aakwuhtama? (n) yarn (*lit* tie horn; *arch* used for braiding men's hair).

aawusipu, aakwusipu (n) braid.

aawusitu, aakwusi?aru (v) braid.

ahna (n) underarm, armpit, side of chest. *See* **ana-,** anatukate.

ahó (adv) thank you, hello. *See* **ura.**

ahotabenihtu (n) thanksgiving, prayer of thanks.

Ahotabenihtu mua (n) November (Thanksgiving month).

ahpu? (n), *acc* **ahpu?a** father.

ahra (n) jaw.

ahweniitu (v) root around (as a hog). *See* **muwainitu.**

ahwepu (n) tuber (any food dug up from soil). *See* **totohtu,**

to?roponii?, ta?wahkóo?,
payaape, tutupi̲tu̲.

ai (interj) Expression of disgust.

aibuniitu̲, ahi?bu̲niitu̲ P (v)
destroy, waste, torment.

aihinahanitu̲, aikuhaniitu̲
(v) sin (do evil, do wrong).
Aihinahaniitu̲. He did something
bad.

aikurekwatu̲ (v) curse (use profane
language).

aimi?aru̲ (v), *pl* **wahkami?aru̲** lope,
trot, move in slow motion. **Aru̲ka
tsa? aimi?aru̲.** The deer is loping.
See **pohyami?aru̲.**

aitu̲ (adj) bad, wicked, evil. **Uru̲
tsa? aitu̲.** That (over there) is no
good. *See* **tu̲tsu̲, kesuatu̲.**

ai?bihinu̲u̲sukatu̲ (adj)
discouraged, downhearted. *See*
narahtokwetu̲.

akwaru̲tu̲ (v), *pl* **akwaru̲?ru̲kina**
belch, burp.

akwaru̲? (n) belch, burp.

ama- (pfx) underarm to waist, side
of chest. *See* **ahna, ana-.**

amawóo (n) apple (*lit* wormy
chest[?]). *Pyrus malus* L.

amawóo?a pàa (n) sweet cider,
apple juice.

amawosa (n) pocket (*lit* underarm
bag).

amawo?a? po?a? (n) apple skin.

amawu̲nu̲tu̲ (v) suffer chest pain
(have pneumonia in side of chest).
See **tu̲?inawu̲nu̲ru̲.**

aná, anáa (interj) ouch!
(exclamation when suffering
physical pain other than burn).

ana-, ahna (n) underarm, armpit.

anáabi, anabi (n) one hill. *See*
ku?ebi, nookaru̲ru̲.

anahabiniitu̲ (v) seek (vision quest;
seek power or blessing by fasting
on a mountain).

anakwanare? (n) gourd (wild taxon;
lit underarm odor). *Cucurbita
foetida* (wild gourd having strong
odor similar to garlic).

anapu̲hu̲, anapu̲, ahnapu̲ (n)
underarm hair (*lit* underarm fuzz).

anatukate, ahnatukate (n) armpit.
See **ahma.**

ania, ani̲a (n) mane. **tu̲hu̲ya ania**
horse mane.

anikwita mi?aru̲ (v) roll along (as a
ball); tumble, summersault (turn a
flip). *See* **nakkuminooru̲.**

anitu̲ (v, hum subj), *pl* **aaneru̲** give
up exhausted, die in accident;
nonhum subj fall over (as a plant).

ani̲kuura? (n) ant.

ani̲mui (n) housefly.

ani̲mui wasu̲ (n) fly spray (*lit* fly
kill).

ani̲mui wu̲htokwe?a? (n) flyswatter
(*lit* thing with which to hit and
kill flies).

arai, ahrai W, P, **ahra?i** (n) bridle
(*lit* for the jaw).

arakwu̲?u̲tu̲ (n) marriage of uncle
and niece.

arapu̲, ahrapu̲ W, P (n) jaw.

aratsi? (n) wheel game (the wheel is
a willow rim with rawhide spokes
radiating from a rawhide circle
a half-inch in diameter in the
middle; a special throwing arrow
is used).

aratuhku, ahraruhku (n) jowl meat
(meat of jaw).

ara? (n) uncle (mother's brother,
father's brother), niece, nephew
(man's sister's child).

Arʉka páaʔ (name) Deer-water (a Comanche chief).

arʉka tuhku K, O, P (n) deer meat.

arʉkáa kuhma (n) buck (single male deer).

arʉkáa rʉhkapʉ, W arʉkáa tʉhkapʉ Y (n) deer meat, deer food **K, O.**

arʉkaʔ (n), *acc* **arʉkaʔa** deer.

arʉkaʔ nʉkuhma (n) buck (male deer leading herd of does).

ata-, atah-, atʉ- (adj) different, other, another. **Atʉma.** It is a different one.

atabaroʔitʉ (v) rise, swell (tend to flood; as water in a creek or river). *See* **paroʔikitʉ.**

atabitsi W (n) foreigner (other than of Comanche origin).

atabitsʉnoi (n) button snakeroot. *Liatris punetata* Hook (roots chewed for juice; also used as remedy).

atahunubi, atʉhunuʔbi P (n) tributary, branch of a creek, fork of a stream. *See* **nabatai.**

Atakʉni, Ata kahni (name) Lone-tipi (person).

atakwáʔsʉʔ (n) quick-cook corn soup (made of fresh, roasted, dried corn with meat, bones added).

atakwaʔsʉʔaipʉ (n) quick-dried corn, roasted corn.

atakwaʔsʉʔaitʉ (v) roast corn (quick-dry corn over fire). **Atakwaʔsʉʔaitʉ ma.** He is making quick-dried corn.

atanaʔi (n) foreigner, *adj* **atanaitʉ** foreign.

atapu, atahpu K, atapuku Y (adv man) doing differently, doing another way. **Atapuku ma nahaniitʉ.** He is fixing it another way.

ataʔokwetʉ (v) overflow (flowing over banks, as a creek), *adj* **ataʔokwetʉ** overflow.

Atsabiʔ (name) Creator, Holy Spirit (name of deity).

atʉrʉ (adj) different, wrong one. **Atʉrʉ ma.** It is the wrong one.

atʉrʉʉ (n) others.

atʉsokoobi, atʉhʉsokoobi (n) foreign country.

awerʉ, ahwetʉ (v) dig up (as roots). **Paapasi ahwetʉ.** He is digging potatoes.

awi-, ahwi- (v) miss aim. **Pʉhimataka ma tsaʔ u ahwinu.** He just barely missed it. *See* **tsimiʔakʉrʉ.**

awo- (pfx) cup, vessel, container. *See* **aawo.**

awomakotse (n) dishwasher (person who washes dishes).

awomakotserʉ (v) wash dishes.

awonohiʔ (n) dice game (*lit* playing container; refers to bowl or container used in playing Indian dice).

awonoʔoʔ (n) armadillo (*lit* carries its own container).

awotsawʉniʔitʉ, awotsawʉni-tsiitʉ (v) set the table.

awomatsumaʔ (n) teatowel, dishtowel, towel.

aworahna (n), *pl* **aworahniʔi** cupboard (*lit* shelf or box for dishes).

E

ebi- (pfx) blue.

ebihuutsuuʔ (n) bluejay, bluebird.

ebikahni, ebikʉni (n) plaster (*lit* blue house).

ebikuyuutsi? (n) roadrunner, chaparral cock (*lit* blue quail). *Geococcyx californianus* (of the cuckoo family).

ebimuura ya?ke? (n) bullfrog. *Rana catesbiana* (*lit* gray mule that cries). *See* **pasawí?oo?.**

ebimuutaroo?, ebimuhtaroo? K (n) mountain boomer (type of lizard).

ebipaboko?ai? P (n) mountain boomer (type of lizard).

ebipitʉ, ebipi̱tʉ (adj) blue-gray, light blue.

ebitotsiya? (n) Texas thistle. *Cirsium texanum.*

ebi̱ wʉmi̱na? (n) influenza, flu (*lit* blue illness).

ebu (dem pro) different, various directions.

eebi, ehbi (adj) blue.

eetʉ, etʉ- (n) bow for shooting arrows, bois d'arc wood for archery bows.

ehka, eeka (dem adj, acc sg scattered) those.

eka-, ekʉ- (pfx) red color.

ekaamawoo?, ekaamagwoo? (n) crab apple (*lit* red apple). *Malus* spp. *See* **tʉe amawóo?.**

ekae?ree W (n) swamp rabbit. *Lagomorpha* (species with red color on forehead). *See* **ta?wokina?e?reeka.**

Ekahohtʉpahi hunu?bi (n) Red River (*lit* red bank river).

ekahuukupʉ, ekahuhkupʉ (n) red soil (with iron content). *See* **eka sokoobi.**

ekakuhtabearʉ (v) shine red (give forth a red light as from fire or sun).

Eka kura (name) Red-buffalo (person).

ekakúura? (n) buffalo calf (*lit* red buffalo).

ekakuyáa? (n) jack (in card game; *lit* redhead).

ekakʉma? (n) bay horse (reddish brown male).

ekakwitse?e (n), *pl* **ekakwitsibai?etʉ** lightning flash.

ekakwitse?erʉ (v), *pl* **ekakwitsimi?arʉ** discharge a flash of lightning.

ekamitsáa?, ekamitsonaa? (n) cactus (*lit* red hackberry).

Ekamurawa (name) Red-crooked-nose (person).

ekamurora?i huupi (n) redbud (*lit* red-bursting tree). *Cercis canadensis.* L.

ekanarʉmʉʉ? (n) red store, trading post (type of store for Indians in earlier years).

ekanatsʉ, eka naropa? (n) eriogonum root (*lit* red medicine). *Eriogonum longifolium* Nutt. (used for treating stomach trouble).

ekapaa, ekahpaa (n) wine (*lit* red juice).

ekapia?, ekahpia? (n) sorrel mare (*lit* red female).

ekaohapitʉ (adj) orange (*lit* red-yellow). *See* **ohaekapitʉ.**

ekapokopi, ekapokòo? (n) yaupon holly (*lit* red berries). *Ilex omitoria* sp? (leaves used for making a type of tea).

ekapokopi (n) strawberry. *Fragaria vesca* L.

ekapuhihwi (n) gold, money, coins. *See* **puhihwi.**

ekapusi?a̱, ekapusi? (n) flea (*lit* red louse).

ekasahpana? (n) soldier (*lit* red chested; early Spanish uniforms had red sashes). *See* **taibo ekᵾsahpana?.**

ekasokoobi (n) red soil. *See* **eka huukupᵾ.**

ekasonipᵾ (n) grass, little bluestem (*lit* red stem). *Andropogon scoparius* Michx. (grass makes good pastures; stems used as switches in sweat lodge; ashes from stems used for treating syphilitic sores [C & J]).

ekatasia, ekatᵾsi?a, tasia (n) measles (*lit* red bumps).

ekatotsa̱ (n) bank of stream, river bank (*lit* red gully).

ekatseena? (n) red fox. *Vulpes* sp. *See* **kᵾ?kwᵾria?, tseena?.**

ekatsiira?, ekahtsiira? (n) red pepper. *Piper Cayenne.*

ekatᵾᵾpi (n) red brick, red rock.

ekaᵾnᵾᵾ (n) red ant (*lit* red insect).

ekaᵾnᵾᵾ?a tᵾhka?eetᵾ (n) anteater.

ekawaapi̱, ekawaapᵾ (n) juniper, red cedar. **Juniperus virginiana** (fruits eaten; smoke from leaves used in purifying).

ekawehaarᵾ (v) burn red, turn red hot.

Ekawokani (name) Red-young- man (person).

ekawoni (n) smartweed. *Polygonum* (digs into flesh and burns; saliva causes it to release hold for removal).

ekawᵾkwiapᵾ (n) blister (*lit* red raw place). **Nᵾ nape tsa? eka wᵾkwiapᵾ.** My foot is blistered.

ekawᵾpisi̱ K, ekawipᵾsa? P (n) rouge (made from a type of red sandstone; can be mixed with tallow or tree sap as a salve).

ekabapi̱ (n) redheaded buzzard (*lit* redhead). *Buteo* sp.

ekahkoni (n) Indian breadroot. *Psoralea hypogeae* Nutt. [?] (roots used for food; eaten raw).

ekahwi (adj) gold color, shiny. *See* **puhihwi.**

ekapi̱, ekapitᵾ (adj) red.

ekapisa? (n) rouge (*lit* red powder; made from a type of red sandstone).

ekapo?, ekapoho (n) mescal bean. *Sophora secundiflora* (bake beans in oven, drill holes for stringing as ornaments; used for decoration or ceremonies).

ekayᵾ?yᵾ?ka? (n) jelly (*lit* quivering red [substance]).

eka?otᵾ, ekapisiapᵾ (n, adj) pink.

eka̱huutsu?, ekahuhkupᵾ (n) cardinal, redbird.

eka̱sahpana? paraiboo? (n) army officer (*lit* soldier chief).

eko-, eeko, eeko̱ (n) tongue.

ekotᵾwᵾni? (n) glottis.

ekotᵾyaipᵾ (n) tongue-tied person.

ekwakᵾᵾpi?, egwakᵾᵾpi? (n) ground squirrel.

ekwi (n) fish.

ekwipisa̱? (n) red rock.

ekwᵾsibeniitᵾ (v) lick (with tongue).

emᵾahkatᵾ (v, adj) to deceive, deceptive.

emᵾahkatᵾ, emᵾaro?i̱katᵾ (adj) mischievous, deceitful, lunatic (beyond reason or advising).

Esahibi (name) Wolf-drinking (historical personage; a brave warrior and leader).

Esatai (name) Little-wolf (person).

esi- (pfx) gray.

esiebipitu (adj) lavender (*lit* gray-blue).

esiekapitu (adj) pale pink (*lit* gray-red).

Esihabiitu (name) Gray-streak, Gray-flat-lying-object (former Comanche chief).

esi inapu (n) dried meat, jerky (very dry). *See* **inapu**.

esikakwo?a, eshi kawo?a, (n) gray face (used in making fun of someone or in name calling).

Esikono (name) Gray-box (war chief of Antelope Eaters around 1836–1916; moved to live west of Old Post Oak Mission in Oklahoma before the time of the roads).

esikooitu (v, pl) faint repeatedly, convulse. *See* **esi tuyaitu**.

esikuhma? (n) horse (gray male).

esimuura? (n) mule (*lit* gray mule).

esinabuniitu (adj) appear gray. *See* **esitsunu?iitu**.

esinuuhparabi (n) loco weed. *Astragalus* sp.

esipia? (n) gray mare.

esipipikuuru (v) murmur, mumble (*lit* make strange or unclear sounds).

esipohoobi, esipohobi (n) sage (white, lobed cudweed). *Artemisia ludoviciana* Nutt. (multipurpose medicine to cure mental trouble, cold, backache, liver disorders, kidney problems).

Esitami? (name) Asetammy (*lit* gray brother; person).

Esitohi? (n) Milky Way (name of distant stars).

esitoyaabi (n) gray mountain.

Esitoyanuu (n) Mexicans captured by the Comanches (named for the Esitoya mountains).

Esitoya? (n), *pl* **esitoyapitu** mountains east of El Paso, Texas.

esitsunu?iitu (v) gray appearance. *See* **esi nabuniitu**.

esituyaitu (v) faint, convulse (*lit* death gray). *See* **esi kooitu**.

esiunuu? (n) elephant (*lit* gray animal).

esiwana?uhu, esikwaha?hu (n) blanket (cotton bed blanket).

esipitu (adj) gray, slate color.

Esunapu (name) Asenap (*lit* gray foot).

etuhuupi (n) osage orange, hedge apple, bois d'arc wood. **Maclura pomifera** [Raf.] Schn.

etusikawo?aru W (v) accuse someone of being gray-faced.

etuu (dem adj, nom pl scattered) those.

etusipu (n) ashes.

ewa kuupi? (n) ground squirrel (*lit* striped squirrel).

e?bootsiaru (v) mildew, decay, rot.

e?bootsia? (n) mildew, decay, rot.

e?muaru (v) go crazy, act without self-dignity (ref. to women).

e?rée (n) forehead.

H

haa (interj) yes.

haahpi (adj) prone position, lying down.

haahpitu (v, inan subj), *pl* **haniòkatuisituated**, lying somewhere; *pl, anim subj* **kwabi** lie down, stretch out. **Habiitu nu**.

I am lying down. **Kima habikị.**
Come lie down (48:20).

haakarṳ (v), *pl* **hakaakarṳ** find
room for someone or something.

haapane, hahpane, hahpaniitṳ O
(n) level valley.

habiitṳ (v) sleep, lie down.

habikṳni, habikahni (n) bedroom,
sleeping quarters (*lit* night
dwelling), night cradleboard
(baby's cradleboard is of simple
construction of hide laced up,
sometimes with padding, for baby
to sleep by mother's side).

habikṳno? (n) day cradleboard
(used to transport baby on
mother's back). *See* **waakohno.**

habikṳno?

X wehki'aɪ

habikwạsuu, habikwạsu?u W (n)
nightgown, pajamas (*lit* night
dress).

hagwoitṳ W (adj) loose.

hahka (dem pro, acc sg) whom.

haipia? (n) opposite-sex sibling-in-
law (BrWi, WiSs, BrWiSs, SsHu,
HuBr, SsHuBr), opposite-sex cross
cousin (parallel or cross).

haitsíi (n voc) dear friend.

haitsị (n) same-sex friend, same-sex
cousin (parallel or cross).

haitsị ihtaipṳ (n) former friend
(*lit* thrown away; one who is no
longer a friend).

haitsị wihtaitṳ (v) disown a friend
(give up a friendship).

hakaapu, hakahpu (adv
interrog) which way? where to?
Hakaaputu surṳ mi?ai? Which
way is that one going?

hakai (adv interrog, state of being)
how? **Hakai ṳnṳ nṳṳsuka?** How
do you feel?

hakani (adv interrog, manner)
how?. **Hakani ṳnṳ nahanṳ?**
What happened to you? (*lit* what
way did you become?).

hakaniiku, hakanihkṳ (adv
interrog) what way? how?
Hakanihku ṳnṳ ma poomia?
How are you writing this?

hakani?yṳ, hakani?yutṳ (adv
interrog) why? **Hakani?yutṳ ṳnṳ
sinihku tai hanịtṳni?** Why are
you telling us to do it this way?

hakarṳ (pro interrog, nom) who?
which? *pl* **hakarṳṳ. Hakarṳ
narṳmṳkahtu mi?ai?** Who is
going to town?

hakṳse? (adv interrog, loc) where?

hakṳ, hakṳrṳ (adv interrog) where?
what place?

hani- (pfx) maize, corn, ear of corn.

haníibị (n) corn, maize, ear of corn
(sweet or field corn). *See* **nṳmṳ
hani.**

hanikotsapṳ (n) cornmeal mush.

hanikwasṳkṳrṳ (v) toast corn, roast
corn. *See* **atakwa?sṳ?aitṳ.**

haninookopṳ, haninohkopṳ (n)
corn bread.

hanitusupʉ (n) ground corn, cornmeal.

haniwoʔora K, hanibitawoʔoraa W, O (n) corncob.

hani buhipʉ (n) corn shucks, corn leaves.

hanipʉ (n) prepared food.

hanisahoba, hanisahuupa (n) corn soup (not quick-cook type).

Hanitaibo (n) Corn People (Comanche band).

hanitʉ (v), *pl* **hanikatʉ** do, fix, repair.

hanitʉnirʉ (v) order, command (*lit* tell to do, give orders).

hapianaʔ, hapinna (n) suspenders.

haya kwasikʉ (adv) at last. *See* **kwasikʉ.**

hayarokwetʉ (num) four.

haʔii (interj) Oh, my! (used by women only). *See* **ʉbia.**

haʔnii (n) beaver.

haʔwoʔitʉ, haʔwokahtʉ (adj) hollow, loose (not tight).

hehékitʉ (v, anim subj) pant, breathe heavily. **Orʉ sarii tsaʔ hehékʉka.** The dog is panting.

hehekʉbʉniitʉ (v) pant with tongue hanging down, pant heavily.

hekwiʔ, hehkwiʔ (n) spleen.

hibiawo (n) drinking cup.

hibikahti (n) cup.

hibikʉtʉ (v) water an animal. **Sariiʔa ma hibikʉtui.** He will give water to the dog.

hibikʉtʉ (v) drink alcoholic beverage (be made drunk).

hibipʉ, hibitʉ (n) drunk person, intoxicated person.

hibipʉ, hibitʉ, hibihkatʉ O (adj) drunk, intoxicated. *See* **kwinumapʉ.**

hibitʉ (v) drink. **Paa nʉʔ hibitʉ.** I am drinking water.

hihini (n) thing.

hiitooʔ K, N (n) meadowlark, field lark. *See* **ohanʉnapʉ.**

Hiitooʔ K, N (name) Meadowlark, Field-lark (personal name).

himakʉ (pro interrog, acc) with what? on what? **Himakʉ nahaniitʉ?** On what (am I) going to attach (it)?

himataaka, himatakʉ W (adv man) barely. **Orʉ tsaʔ nabokoʔa himataka miʔarʉ.** That car is just barely going.

himaʔarʉ (v, pl), *sg* **yaarʉ** pick up several objects, take several objects. **mahimamiarʉ** keep on taking objects.

himaʔikarʉ (v), *pl* **himawekwiitʉ** carry in.

himiitʉ, himikatʉ (v, pl) give several objects. *See* **utʉkatʉ.**

hina (interrog pro, acc) what? **Hina mʉnʉ hanibʉi niʔ?** What are you all doing so much? (5:3). *See* **hini.**

hinanahimitʉ (v, pl obj) exchange gifts. *See* **naʔuhturʉ.**

hinanahimitʉ waipʉ (n) gift-exchanging partner (woman).

hini, hiini (pro interrog, nom) what? **Osʉ hini ohto huhkúwʉnʉkinạ?** What is that coming stirring up dust along there? (7:38). *See* **hina.**

hipaʔa (adv interrog) on what?

hipeʔ (adv interrog) when? **Hipe tanʉ piarʉkarʉ?** When are we having thanksgiving (prayer)?

hipekaʔi (num interrog) how many? how much?

hipetʉ (num interrog) how many? how much? **Hipetʉ itʉ nawe hʉpai?** How much does this cost?

hipʉ (adj) possessed, owned, belonging to. **Okǫ ma hipʉ.** It belongs to that person (over there).

hipʉkatʉ (v) own, possess. **Sariia hipʉkatʉ nʉ.** I own the dog. *See* **mahípurumʉtʉ.**

hiʔoo- (pfx) ref. to sunflowers.

hiʔookwanaʔ (n) sunflower salve (cold remedy for nose and throat; contains eucalyptol and mint; *lit* sunflower odor).

hiʔoosanahkòo (n) weed wax (plant from whose sap chewing gum was made).

hiʔoopi̱, hiʔohpi̱ (n) sunflower stalk or plant.

hiʔoopi̱taohayaa, hiʔopi̱tatotsiyaa (n) sunflower head.

homo-, homobi (n) powder, flour.

homobi saapi̱, homobi sahpi̱ (n) face powder (*lit* powder-paint).

homopisarʉ (v) powder the body, flour, powder something (powder the body with talcum powder).

homoketʉmaʔ (n) powdery (fine and dry).

homonabi̱sakatʉ (v) apply powder to oneself.

homonutsaitʉ (v) crumble (like dust). *See* **mahomonutsarʉ, tahhomonutsarʉ.**

homopʉ (n) powder, flour. *See* **pisahpi̱.**

homorohtíaʔ (n) packaged flour (*lit* bread flour; packaged wheat flour).

homorosoʔyokiʔ (n) talcum powder.

hooki̱ (n), *pl* **poʔropʉnʉʉ, poʔroʔnʉʉhog.** *See* **mubi̱poʔrooʔ.**

hooki̱ tʉʉhtʉmapʉ (n) hog-pen fence. *See* **poʔro tʉhtʉmapʉ.**

hoora (n) hole dug in soil.

horarʉ (v) dig a hole. *See* **tʉhorarʉ.**

hoʔaitʉ, hoekwarʉ (v) hunt (look for prey). **Wasapeʔa u hoekwai.** He went hunting for a bear.

hoʔaniitʉ (v) sneak around, spy on, look for. **Ohkanʉ usukwaitʉ u hoʔaniitʉ.** I have found what I have been looking for. *See* **kuhiyarʉ.**

hoʔyopitʉ (v) ill (feel malaise). *See* **kehoʔyopitʉ.**

hoʔyopi̱ (adj) sickly, ill.

hoʔyopipʉ (adj) uneven, inexact.

hu- (pfx) ref. to tree, wood, stick. *See* **huu-.**

huaawo, huakwo, huagwo (n) mortar. *See* **huuaawo.**

huba (n) coffee.

huba aawoʔ (n) coffeepot.

huba aikʉtʉ (v) brew coffee (boil coffee). **Tai huba aikʉtʉ mʉ.** I am boiling some coffee for us.

huba aitʉ (v) make coffee.

hubebitʉ (v) drink coffee.

hubinitʉ (v) groan, cry out.

hubiyaarʉ (v) cry, yell noisily.

hubiya piayakeetʉ (n) death wail.

hubiyaa piayakeetʉ, hubiha piayaketʉ (v) cry loudly, wail.

hubiyairʉ (v) make noise yelling.

hubiyaʔ (n) song, hymn (*lit* sounds mournful, like crying).

hubʉhkaʔ (n) illness (the type a child contracts).

huhku-, huuku- (pfx) ref. to dust.

huhkukwʉnʉrʉ (v) blow dust, dust storm. *See* **huukunatsirʉ, huuku kwʉmʉrʉ.**

huhkupʉ (n) dust.

humasᵾapᵾ (n) domestic tree.

hunakᵾ (post) outside, before, in front of.

hunakᵾ, hunakwᵾ, huukᵾ, huʔnakwᵾ (post) outside. **hunakᵾhu** toward the outside. **hunakwᵾhi** from outside.

hunuʔbᵢ (n) creek, stream. *See* **okwèetᵾ**.

hupᵢmiʔarᵾ (v) back up, go backwards.

husᵢ (n) cactus. *Cactaceae* sp. (edible and used as medicine), peyote (hallucinogenic drug for ceremonies).

huu-, huupᵢ, huuhpᵢ, huh- (n) tree, wood. *See* **hu-, tuhhuuʔ**.

huu aawo (n) mortar, barrel, wooden vessel (*arch* sandrock in natural bowl shape used with a pestle). *See* **huaawo**.

huubaʔ (n) coffee (*lit* tree water).

huuhimarᵾ (v, pl obj), *sg* **huuyaarᵾ** possess sticks.

Huuhunuʔbᵢ (n) Timber Creek.

Huuhwiya, Huwiya (name) Refuse-to-come (a medicine man who refused to attend the council at Fort Sill).

Huuhʔinᵾᵾ (n) Timber People (Comanche band, Southern Comanches).

huukabatᵾ, huhkabatᵾ (n) woods, clump of trees. *See* **soohuuhpᵢ**.

huukisaakitᵾ (v) hear or make noise in timber.

huukonoʔitᵾ (n) natural windbreak.

huukᵾ, huhkᵾ (n) collarbone. *See* **sihkupᵾ**.

huukukatᵾ, huhkukatᵾ (adj) dusty (be dusty).

huukukwᵾmᵾrᵾ (v) blow dust. *See* **huhkukwᵾnᵾrᵾ**.

huukumatsumarᵾ, huhkumatsu-marᵾ (v) dust off by hand.

huukunatsirᵾ, huhkunatsirᵾ (v) blow dust. *See* **huhkukwᵾnᵾrᵾ**.

huukunatsirᵾ, huhkunatsirᵾ (v) dust off.

huukunaʔ (n) match (to strike for fire).

huukunᵾetᵾ, huhkunᵾetᵾ (v) blow dust.

huukupᵾ, huhkupᵾ (n) dust.

huukᵾmuyakeʔ, huhkᵾ muyakeʔ (n) whistle (made of collarbone or substitute; used by medicine men).

huukᵾhᵾnᵾrᵾ, huhkuwᵾnᵾrᵾ (v) dust storm, raise dust, stir up dust.

huumaraʔ, huhmaraʔ (n) falcon. *Falco* sp.

huunakarᵾʔ (n) wooden bench.

huunaroʔiʔ (n) ladder, stairs.

huunarᵾmᵾᵾʔ (n) lumberyard (*lit* wood store).

huunatsihtuʔyeʔ, huu natsihtᵾʔyeʔ (n) wooden comb.

huunaʔ (n) groundhog, woodchuck.

huupi kasamawᵾ (adj), *pl* **huupi-takobiʔi** battered tree (as by winds).

huupi poʔaʔ (n) tree bark.

huupisoʔnaʔaitᵾ (v) make a bird nest. *See* **pisonaʔaitᵾ**.

huupita homoketᵾ (n) sawdust (*lit* tree powder). *See* **huupita pisonᵢ, huutusupᵾ**.

huupita kwiita, huupi kwiita (n) tree stump. *See* **huupita tᵾrahna**.

huupita mooka (n) tree limb.

huupita pisonᵢ (n) sawdust. *See* **huupita homoketᵾ**.

huupita po?a (n) tree bark.

huupita turahna (n) tree root, stump. *See* **huupita kwiita.**

huupitan pihnàa, hupitan sanahpi (n) rosin (*lit* juice of a tree).

huupihnàa (n) syrup, molasses, sugar cane.

huusibe? (n) drawknife, wood plane, peeling tool (cobbler's tool, modern carpenter's tool; *arch* artifact used by early Comanches to peel bark off trees).

huutsi piahpu? (n) daughter-in- law (SoWi, SbSoWi).

huutsihkaa?, huutsihka?a (n) two-man handsaw. *See* **mo?o huutsihka?a?.**

huutsika?aru (v) saw something with a saw.

huutsiyaa? (n) teepee pole (holds flap on top of teepee; *lit* pole-that-holds-up).

huutsi, huhtsi (n) paternal grand-mother, woman's agnatic grand-child.

huutsi piahpu, hutsi piahpu (n) daughter-in-law (of man or woman).

huutsúu, huhtsúa? (n) bird (general term).

huutsú?a kàhni (n) bird nest, birdhouse, sensitive pea (*lit* bird house). *Cassia nictitana.*

huutsú?a pisoo?ni (n) bird nest (so named for strings, rags, etc. used in building it).

huutsú?a tuahkapu (n) sumac. *Rhus* sp. (*lit* bird food).

huutubu?itu W (adj) slender (*lit* like a tree).

huutunaakatu K (adj) slender (*lit* like a tree is straight).

huutusupu W (n) sawdust (*lit* wood ground up). *See* **huupita homoketu, huupita pisoni.**

huuturohpako?i?i (n) wooden mallet.

Huuwuhtukwa? (name) Take-a-stick-and-hit-someone (person).

huuyaaru (v), *pl* **huuhimaru** possess, carry a stick.

huuyukkwi? (n), *pl* **huu yukkwu?nuu** lumberman, white man (from homesteaders' practice of making log cabins).

huwabo?kóo? (n) wild currant, mulberry, huckleberry. *Ribes odoratum* Wendl.

huyuba?atu, huyubatu (adj) oblong, long and flat. *See* **piahuyubatu.**

huyuni (adj) oval.

hua- (pfx) ref. to fish or fishing.

huahuupi, huaana huupu (n) fishing pole.

huaru (v) to trap, to fish.

Huaru u. He is fishing.

huaru? (n) trap (general term for all traps).

huato (n) fish (unknown species).

huawapi, tahuawapi (n), *pl* **hua?etu** fisherman, trapper.

hua? W, **hua?eetu** K (n) fish hook.

hubi, huubi, hubi waipu (n) middle-aged woman (grown, possibly heavy-set).

hubi tsiitsi?, huubi tsihtsi? (n) elderly woman (little old lady).

huhkiapu (n) shadow.

huhkunaru, nuhkunaru (v) cover something. **Sonipu tsa? nuhkunaru.** The hay is covered. *See* **wuhkunaru.**

huhtsawukatu (v) feel cool.

huitsi, huihtutsi (num) a few, a little bit. See tutaatu.

Hukiyani (name) Carrying-her-sunshade (person).

hukiai (n) umbrella.

hukiku (n) shade. See huuki.

hukitu (adj) shaded.

hunu- (pfx) ref. to thinness.

hunupoʔaʔ (n) human skin. See mapóʔaʔ.

hunubi pokaaʔ (n) bat (lit thin cockleburr).

hunuketu, huʔnuketu (adj) thin (as thin paper or onion skin). See tapituhtsi.

huu (num interrog) how many? Unu huu tomopu? How old are you?

huu, huutu (num) a few; n huututsi just a few. Huututsi maʔ. There are just a few.

huukatu, hukatu, hukai (v, inan subj) cool off (as food).

huukiaʔ, hukiapu (n) shadow. Ma huukiaʔ tsaʔ mamaʔaitu usúni. His shadow is always with him.

huukina huupi (n) poles for constructing brush arbor.

huukiʔaitu (n) brush arbor (usually made of horseweed, blackjack oak, or willow branches). See sonihuuki.

huukiʔaiʔ (n) umbrella.

huuki (n) shade. huukiku in the shade. See hukiku.

huunu? (n) porcupine (lit thin, for thin quills). See yuhnu.

huusu (num) a few times. Nah huusu uruu maʔaipisikwanuuʔii ma. He slid with them just a few times.

huutsaʔwetu, huutsaʔwuru (v, hum subj) cool off.

huutsaʔwu miʔaru (v) go on vacation (lit go to cool off).

huutsipu, huhtsipu (n) saliva. See kupisiʔ.

Huwuni (name) Dawn (person).

huwuni (n time) dawn. See kuhu wunukatu, tosa huwunikatuma?.

huʔniipu? (n) hiccough.

huʔniitu, huuʔnitu (v), pl huʔnipubu hiccough.

Huʔnipitu (name) Hiccough-daughter (person).

I

ibu (adv dem, prox) this direction. Ibu nu miaruʔi. I will go this direction.

ibuʔikuru (v) fill (cause to be full). See pawusaʔnaitu.

ibuʔitu (v) filled to the brim. See paa maʔibuʔikutu.

ibuniitu, ipuniitu (v) come this way.

Idahi (n) Snakes (Athapascan name for the Comanches—their enemies).

ihka (pro dem, prox acc sg) this. Ihka masukaa. Feel this (60:22). Ihka puni tuihú. Look at this, friend (41:7).

Ihtataʔo (n) Burned Meat (small Comanche band that became extinct).

ikaru (v), pl wekwiitu, wekwimiʔaru enter. Itu tsaʔ ikaruʔi. This person is going to enter. Tenahpuʔ tsaʔ ikahkii. The man came in. See sutenaʔikuru.

iki (adv dem, prox) here. Iki tanu yukwi. Let's sit here (60:16).

ikuhu to here.

inaaru, inasu (adj compar) younger than, smaller than. **Ma tami?a inasu ma.** He is younger than his brother.

inakwata, inagwata, inawaata, inawata, inawàata (n) meat-drying A-frame (poles for preparing jerky).

inakwu (adv dem, prox) this direction. **Inakwuhi nu? puniwatu?i.** I will go to look in this direction (104:11).

inapu (n), *acc* inapa jerky, jerked meat. *See* **esiinapu.**

inaru (n) meat jerky, jerked meat.

ina?etu (v) jerk meat, hang meat up to dry (one step in the process of making jerky). **Situ wa?ihpu? ma ina?etu.** This woman prepares jerky.

Isananaka?, Isunanika (n) Howling-coyote, Echo-of-the-wolf-howl (star name; former chief and one of the signers of the Medicine Lodge Treaty).

isananarumu?ipu? (n) gossip.

isanaramu?itu? (n) one who gossips.

isapu, ishapu? (n) lie, liar. *See* **naya?isa?aitu, kaawosa.**

Isatekwa (name) Liar, Lie-talk (person).

isawasu? (n) pesticide, poison.

isawasu wanakotse? (n) lye (*lit* soap poison).

Isawura (name) Crazy-bear (person).

isa?aitu (v) lie (tell an untruth).

Ishatai (name) Coyote-droppings (Comanche messiah who predicted Coggia's Comet to last for five days and to be followed by drought; he instituted Sun Dance in 1874).

isu (pro dem, prox acc sg) this. **Isu hakuku u yaa?i?** Where was this you took? (82:22).

itsa, itsee (n) snake root, church root. *Liatris* sp. (from Mexico; good for curing asthma or emphysema; rub on legs to repel rattlesnakes). *See* **timuihu?.**

itsaraitu unua kahni (n) den, animal hole.

itsina, itsini (n, acc) agent, Indian agent (fr Engl *agency*).

itu (pro dem, prox nom sg), *pl* **ituu** this. **Paakuhu tsa? itu nuhi tsayuma?i.** This one made us fall in the water.

itukwu (pro dem, prox nom du) these two. **Itukwu tsa? nikwanarukwu.** These two have been talking.

iyaa?itu (v) watch for (be a guard). **Suru tsa? tabeni ma naharu?iha iyaa?itu.** That one watches for when it will be noon.

i?a (adv loc, prox) somewhere (near). **I?a tsa? miibe?tu haniitu.** There is a meeting someplace close by.

K

kaabehkaru, kaabehkatu (v) trick, fool, deceive, cheat, play dead. **Ke nu bumi kaabehka- wa?itu.** I can't be cheated myself (11:30).

kaahaniitu (v) fool, deceive, cheat.

Kaaiwanuu (n) Kiowa people.

kaakwakuru, kaakaku (v) defeat by cheating, win in a contest by cheating. **Numasu u kaakwakui.** I beat you by cheating.

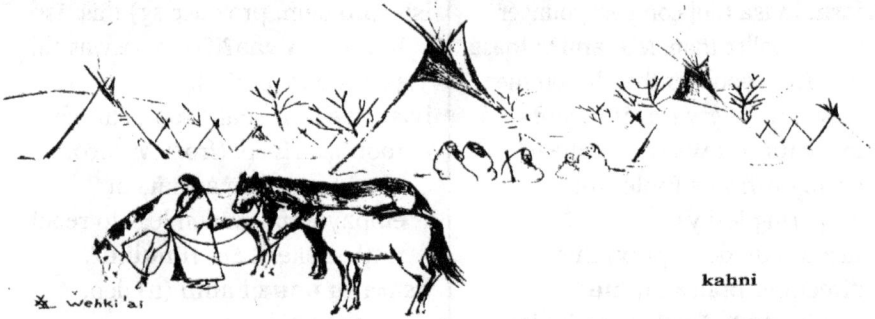

kahni

kaanatsaka?uhtupu̧ (n) one who betrays.

kaanatsaka?uhturu̧ (v) betray someone.

kaasuaru̧ (v), *pl* **kaayu̧kwiitu̧** intend to deceive or cheat, pretend (even if not successful), kid around. *See* **nohitekwaru̧.**

Kaatu̧, Katinu̧ (n) God.

kaawosa̧ (n) fox, jackal; liar, dishonest person, shyster. *See* **isapu̧?.**

kaayu̧kwi̧tu̧ (adj) cheater.

kabitsi̧ (n) cabbage.

kabu̧ru̧u̧? (n) sheep.

kabu̧ru̧u̧?a tua (n) lamb (*lit* sheep child).

kabu̧ru̧u̧?a pu̧hu̧ (n) sheep wool.

kabu̧ru̧?a tahkoni wapi̧ (n) shepherd (hired sheep lord).

kabu̧ru̧u̧ tu̧hkapu̧ (n) mutton (*lit* sheep meat).

kah- (pfx) house, teepee, room, home.

kahku?e (n) smoke hole (in teepees), upper story, upstairs (in any house or building). *See* **kahniku?e.**

kahni, -ku̧ni (n) house, teepee, room, home. **Situ̧kwu̧ pu̧hu̧ kahni betu mi?aru̧.** These two are going toward their house.

kahni (n) house. *See* **puku kahni.**

kahni ku?e (n) housetop, smoke hole. *See* **ku?e, kahku?e.**

kahni mi?a (v) visit, go visiting (*lit* house go).

kahni nasiyuuki? K (n) shingle.

kahni tai (n) room, cave. *See* **taina.**

kahni tu̧banaa (n) wall (of house). *See* **tu̧banaa?.**

kahni tu̧bitsika? K (n) trailer house. [**kahni** house + **tu̧** (unspec) + **bitsika?** pulled]. *See* **tu̧biyaaku̧?.**

kahni busi̧?a (n) house bug of any kind, bedbug (*lit* house louse).

kahni nahu̧u̧ki (n) porch (*lit* house shade).

kahnitaiku̧ (n) tunnel, burrow. **Tu̧?rikuu tsa? pu̧ kahnitaiku̧ ikanu̧.** The prairie dog went into his burrow.

kahnitu̧eka (n) Indian paintbrush. *Scrophulariaceae Castilleja indivisa.*

kahni?aitu̧ (v) build a house, construct a house or other building. **Kahni?aitu̧ ma.** He is building a house.

kahni̧ ebi̧ (n) W plaster; K house paint.

kahni̧ tu̧boopu̧, kahni̧ tu̧bana ru̧boopu̧ (n) wallpaper.

kahpe (n) bed.

Kahpewai (name) No-bed (person).

kahpinakwu (adv) west (*lit* bed-behind; since teepees faced east).

kahtui? (n) neighbor (*lit* house friend). **Nu kah?tui? tsa? nu makai.** My neighbor has given me some food.

kahtu (v) sit, live. **Tutaatu kuyuutsi? tsa? su?na sonikku kahtu.** A little quail is sitting somewhere there in the grass.

Kahúu nihku pipikure (name) Squeaky-like-a-mouse (person). *See* **Pipiku?.**

kahúu pipikuniitu, kahúu pipikuru (v) squeak (as a mouse).

kahúu pumata huaru? (n) mousetrap, rattrap.

kahúu?, kahhúu? (n) house mouse.

kaku? (n) maternal grandmother, maternal great aunt, woman's uterine grandchild.

kamakuna W, **kamakunua** K (n) loved one, beloved.

kamakuru (v) love (want someone to remain present). **Unu nu kamakunu?** Do you love me?

kamatu (v) taste. **Tsaa ma? kamatu.** It tastes good. **Moha ma? kamatu.** It tastes sour, bitter, acid. **Otu ma? kamatu.** It tastes neither sweet nor sour.

kamúuta? (n) sweet potato.

kanaba?aitu (adj) stand tall, tall and slender. **Tenahpu? oru kanabawunu.** That man is tall and slender. *See* **huutubu?itu.**

kanabuutsi?, kanabuhtsi? (n) thin person.

karukatu (v, adj), *pl* **yukwi mi?aru** sit down, stay; *adj* **yukwiitu** seated.

karukuru, karuukukatu (v), *pl* **yukwikukatuset** up (as a teepee);

cook, boil food. **Pihuura nu karuukukatu.** I am cooking beans.

karuuru (adj) stationary (remaining in place).

kasabipikuru, kasapiipikuru (v) flap wings, whir (make wing noises while flying).

kasamaaru (n) club (of playing cards).

kasamawuru (v, adj) batter; battered (as by wind). **Huuhpi kasa?mawuru.** The tree is battered (by the wind).

kasaráiboo? (n) angel (*lit* winged stranger).

kasa (n) wing.

kasakatu (adj) winged. **Situ kwasinaboo? kasakatu mawakatu yutsuhkina.** This snake having wings came flying towards him (27:6).

katakakitu W, **katatakitu** K, **O** (v) woman's whoop (cry of excitement).

katsonakwu (n) rear, rump.

kawonokatu (n) street (*lit* wolf separate camp).

kawohwitu (v) ring (as a bell). **Kawohwitu.** It is ringing (*lit* it is belling). *See* **tu?tsayaketu.**

kawohwi? (n) bell. **Kawohwi? tsa? yakeetu.** The bell is ringing (*lit* bell is crying).

ka?amooru (v) lap with the tongue (as a dog laps water).

ka?i (n) forehead.

ka?ibuhu, ka?ibuu (n) eyebrow (*lit* forehead fuzz). *See* **puhu.**

Ka?mutuhi? W, Kamuru?i? K (name) Looking-from-side-to-side (person).

ka?ra?áa?, ka?ara?áa? (n) tick.

ka?wekịtʉ (adj compar) greater than. **I ka?wekịtʉ.** This is greater.

ka?witsetʉ K, **kawʉtʉ?itʉ** W (v) shake head in disagreement.

ka?witʉ (v, hum subj) hold council, gather together. **Ka?witʉ urʉ.** They are gathering (to hold council).

ke-, kee (pfx) no, negative.

Ketokwe hina haniitʉ (name) Satan, devil (*lit* not exact whatever do). *See* **Tuhkwasi taiboo?.**

Kebakowe? (name) Coyote (*lit* does-not-go-in-water; nickname for Coyote).

kebayʉmʉkitʉ (adj) quiet (not moving), still (unmoving). **Paa tsa? kebayʉmʉkikatʉ.** The water is (very) still.

kebisa?makarʉ, kepịsa?makarʉ (v) encourage, strengthen.

Kehaitsipaapị (name) Bald (*lit* without hair).

kehe, kehena (num) nothing.

kehewa?itʉ (v) be missing, exhaust supply, run short. **Urʉʉ kahninʉʉ kehewa?ị.** Their teepees were gone (37:8).

keho?yopịtʉ, keóyo?bahtʉ (adj) healthy, whole. *See* **kenama?ʉbʉ?itʉ.**

kekʉnabeniitʉ (v) leave person alone, stop quarreling (*lit* stop biting; used when person is aggravated).

kemabana?itʉ (v) reject, dislike, lack knowledge of. **Kema mabana?itʉ.** He doesn't like anything. **Ke hina mabana?itʉ.** He doesn't know how to do anything.

kemahpʉ?arʉ, kemahpʉ?a (v, adj) fail to do something, unable to do something (even though one has the desire to comply). *See* **tsuhitʉ.**

kemakʉmapʉ, kemakʉmahpʉ (adj) dulled edge, dulled. *See* **kʉmakwa?i.**

kemarʉkwịsʉ (adv time) soon. *See* **miitụtsi.**

kemenikwitʉ W, **keme?oniikwitʉ** K (v, adj) reject someone, rejected.

kemi?arʉtatsino (n) north star (*lit* not-moving star).

kenama?ʉbʉ?itʉ (adj) healthy, well (not sickly). *See* **nama?abʉ.**

kenanawatsitʉ, kenanakwatsitʉ (adj) clear, plain, understood. *See* **nanawatsikarʉ.**

kenaninabenitʉ (adj) distraught, continue uncontrollably (unable to stop when one should, as talking or crying).

kenatsʉwitʉ (adj) weak.

kenawʉnʉrʉ, kenagwʉnʉrʉ (adj) be in deep water (*lit* cannot stand up; as in water over one's head).

keno, kenu (n) hillside, hill.

kesósoorʉ (adj nonhum) tame, gentle.

kesósoorʉ (adj, human) humble, calm, relaxed.

kesuatʉ (adj) mean, rough. *See* **aitʉ, tʉtsʉ-.**

Kesʉ (adv) never.

keta? (neg) Don't! (used in commands). **Keta? tekwaarʉ.** Don't talk!

ketekwa (adj) dumb (unable to speak).

ketokwetʉ (adj) deficient, not good enough.

keto?kapaa (n) kerosene [ke not + to?ka dark + paa liquid]. *See* tuka?anabaa.

Ketse na?bo (name) Painted- feather (*lit* striped wing).

ketsihanabenitu (adj) starving (extremely hungry; without food).

ketunabunitu (adj) dark, darken (be dark, get dark).

ketunakatu (adj) deaf, disobedient. *See* tunakatu.

kewáhabahku (adv) doubtless, surely.

kewesikatu, kewesiketu (adj) straight (not curly).

kewesiketu (adv) be straight (not curled, unable to curl). Kewesiketu u. It won't curl.

keyu K (adv time) late, tardy (after the appointed time). Keyu u? pitui. He arrived late.

keyu?u, keyuu W (adv time) late.

kia (adv) maybe, perhaps (expresses wonder, doubt, inquisitiveness). Nah kia u? po?ayaahkwa?i. Guess it just blew away (49:29). *See* suukutsa?noo.

kiahbitu (v, pl), *sg* to?ibitu come out at a particular place.

kibo?aru (v) peel off skin, skin something. *See* kwuru?aru.

kihtsi? (adv time) now (right now), immediately. Ukihtsi nu? mi?aru. I am going right now. *See* meeku.

kii (n) corner.

kiinaboo (n) diamond (in playing cards, *lit* striped or spotted corner).

kiipu (n) elbow.

kimaru (v), *pl* sumunokima come. Situkuse? tutaatu tuinuhpu? mawakatu kimaru. This little boy is coming toward her (82:16).

Kiyu (name) Horseback (person).

ki?aru (v) cut something.

ko- (pfx) ref. to cut.

kobe-, koobe (n) face. Uruu pia? tsa? u kobekuhu wihii. Their mother threw it in his face (17:24).

kobe kiihtu?eka? W, kobe wihtu?eka? K (n) face cream.

kobe matsuma? (n) towel, face towel (*lit* face-wiping cloth).

kobe nabo? K (n) camera (*lit* face marking). *See* numiboo?etu.

kobe tsa?nika? (n) mask, false face (*lit* face loincloth).

Kohi (name) Narrow-gut (person).

kohikamutu (v) suffer abdominal pain.

kohikamukatu (n) stomach ache, intestinal flu.

kohinehkitu (v) wear something around the waist (men's apparel only).

kohinehki?, kohineeki? (n) belt, G-string. *See* tsa?nika?.

Kohitu se?tanuku (name) Sitting-bear (Comanche chief about 1821–1871).

kohi, kohhi? (n) small intestine, waist area, abdomen.

koho?aaitu (v) harvest. U koho?aiitu?i u. He will harvest corn (cut ears).

kohpapu (n), *pl* kohbiapu broken object.

kohparu (v), *pl* kohbi?aitu, wuhkobi? break up. Huupita kohbiaru. (It) is breaking up trees.

kohpooru (v) brand (mark with heat). *See* tsihpooru.

kohtoo rꙮnahpꙮ (n) fireman (one who puts out fires).

kohtoo wapi̱ (n) fire-builder (one who builds fires).

kohtoopꙮ (n) fire, heat of fire.

kohtóorꙮ (v) build a fire. **Surꙮꙮ tsaʔ wihnu pia kohtóoi.** Then they made a big fire.

kohtsáarꙮ (v) stew, cook (as apples or corn mush).

kohtsáaʔ, kohtsapꙮ, kohtsaarꙮ (n) cooked cereal, stewed food. *See* **tꙮkarꙮkꙮpꙮ.**

kokáaʔ (n), du **kokáaʔnꙮkwꙮ,** pl **kokáanꙮ** guinea fowl. *Numido meleagris.*

kokoráʔa (n) chicken.

kokoráʔa kahni (n) chicken coop.

kokoráʔa kuhma W, **kokoráʔa nꙮꙮahpꙮ** K (n) rooster.

kokoráʔa nooyo̱ (n, arch) chicken egg.

kokoráʔa aràhimaʔetꙮ, kokoraʔa ʔatahimaʔetꙮ (n) chicken hawk.

kokoráʔa arꙮhtꙮmaʔ, kokoraʔa arꙮhtꙮmapꙮ (n) chicken wire (*lit* chicken's fence).

kokoráʔa atùapꙮ (n, modern) chicken egg (*lit* chicken child).

kokoráʔa pokopi̱ (n) egg (*lit* chicken fruit).

kokoráʔa tasiʔa (n) chicken pox (*lit* chicken rash).

kokoráʔa yaketꙮ K (v) cluck (as a hen), crow (as a rooster).

Komanche, Comanche (n) Those-who-are-always-against.

kono-, konóopꙮ (n) firewood (load of, stacked in place).

kono honiitꙮ (v), *pl* **kono hoyꙮkatꙮ** bring back firewood.

kono miʔarꙮ (v) fetch firewood.

kono honiitꙮ

konóorꙮ (v) bring in firewood.

koobetꙮ (adj) be hard and brittle (as leather curls in fire).

kooipꙮ (n), **pl kooi- pꙮnꙮꙮ** dead person.

kooitꙮ (v, pl) to die. *See* **tꙮyaaitꙮ.**

koonitꙮ (v) turn around. **Ibꙮ niitꙮ kooni.** Turn this way.

kooniʔetꙮ (v) turn around.

koono̱, kohno̱, -kꙮno (n) cradle, box, container, resting place.

kooʔ (n) mush, cornmeal mush.

kooʔitꙮ (v) cut up something, slice, chop.

korohko̱ (n) necktie. *See* **yuʔakorohko̱.**

korohko̱rꙮ (v) wear something around the neck.

koropitꙮ, korꙮpitꙮ (adj) brown, khaki, tan, dust-colored, beige.

kotsana (n) flank of living animal, hindquarter. *See* **tohoobe̱.**

koʔabitsipꙮ (n) cheese (*lit* cut milk).

koʔitꙮ (v), *pl* **koyama-** return, come back.

Kuhiyai (name) Peeping-from-behind-tree (person).

kuhiyarꙮ (v) peep at, spy on someone. *See* **hoʔaniitꙮ.**

kuhkerꙮ (v) chop firewood.

kuhkuparɨ (v), *pl* kuhtokwe kill
with heat, cremate, burn to death
accidentally.

kuhkwarɨkitɨ (v, adj) take a steam
bath, bathed.

kuhma (n) male, man.

kuhmaru (v) marry (of a woman).

kuhmito?ai? (n) popcorn (*lit* heated
turns inside out).

kuhnu?itɨ W (v, adj) boil, boiled.

kuhparɨ (adj) melted.

kuhpawikɨ?itɨ (v) melt something
(as in rendering lard). *See*
yuhukarɨ, ku?okwerɨ.

kuhpitsɨni?arɨ W, **kuhpitsoonitɨ**
K (v) render lard, fry out fat. *See*
yuhukarɨ.

kuhporákitɨ (v) crackle, make
popping noise. *See* **kukɨbihkutɨ.**

kuhpuru?airɨ (v) pop on someone,
splatter. *See* **puruarɨ.**

kuhpuru?aitɨ (adj) splattered.

kuhtabearɨ (v) flash (as a light).

kuhtakwitsoo?nitɨ W,
kuhtso?okitɨ, kuhtsookitɨ K (v)
wrinkle, wither, shrivel up from
heat.

kuhtsahwirɨ (v) throw into the fire,
burn something up.

kuhtsiyarɨ (v, sg obj), *pl obj*
kuhtsihimaarɨ roast on a stick
(make a shish kebob) [**kuhtsu**
cow + **hima?arɨ** pick up (pl)].

kuhtsu pokàa? (n) cocklebur, burr
(*lit* cow berry).

kuhtsu taibo napɨ (n) cowboy
boots.

kuhtsu taibo nohhiitɨ W (n)
rodeo (**lit** cowboy play). *See*
tukumakwɨyetɨ?.

kuhtsu taibo? (n) cowboy,
cattleman.

kuhtsu tɨbini? (n) horned toad.

Kuhtsu tɨhka (n) Buffalo Eaters
(middle Comanche band in
western Oklahoma along the
Canadian River and north of it;
said to have left the northwest for
Colorado, Kansas, New Mexico,
Oklahoma, and Texas about 900
A.D.).

Kuhtsu kwi?ta (name) Cow-dung
(person).

Kuhtsuna kwahipɨ (name) Buffalo-
hump (Comanche chief of earlier
years).

Kuhtsunu kwahipɨ (name) One-
who-rides-buffalo (Comanche
chief of early years).

kuhtsu? W (n) cow. *See* **kuutsu?.**

kuhtsu?maru (v) burn down (*lit*
finished by fire).

kuhtsɨnikɨrɨ (v) heat something.

kuhtsɨni? (n) fever (*lit* going
through heat).

kuhtsɨnitɨ (adj) be feverish (have
a fever).

Kuhtu (name) Coals-in-a-wood-fire.

kuhtu tɨkɨmanirɨ K (v) cook over
charcoal, barbecue.

kuhtuubi K (n) charcoal.

kuhtɨyarɨ (v) burn oneself to
death, self-immolate.

kuitsi (n) throat.

kuitsɨkwaitɨ K (v) gag oneself (by
putting something in the throat).

kuitsɨmarɨkitɨ (adj) strangled.

kuitsɨmarɨkɨtɨ (v) strangle
someone.

kuitsɨsɨatɨ, kuitsɨatɨ (v) have a
sore throat.

kuitsɨtsɨwoirɨ W (v) gag (put a
finger down the throat to induce
vomiting).

kuitsitukwuni, kuitsituwunu? (n) adam's apple. *See* **pia kuitsi?.**

Kukapu (name) Cooks-dried-meat (person).

kukubihkutu (v) crackle, pop, sizzle. *See* **kuhporákitu.**

kukumepu (n) parched corn, toasted maize.

kukumeru (v) parch corn.

kukume?awe (n) skillet (used for parching corn). **Nu kukume?awetuku nu? nasuwatsi?.** I lost my skillet (122:20).

kumahpu?, kuhmapu? (n) husband. **U kumahpu? tsa? hunu?betu aainukwa.** Her husband loped off toward the creek.

kuma?omeru, kutsaniru (v) stir up fire.

kumiitsanatsu (n) milkweed. *Asclepiadaceae.*

kuna-, kuuna (n) firewood.

kunapiso?ni (n) wood shavings, chips (*lit* firewood nest).

kunawaikina pu?e (n) railroad tracks (*lit* firewood wagon road).

kunawaikinu, kunawaikina (n) train, railroad car (*lit* firewood wagon).

kunawobipuuku (n) train, railroad car.

kunakuaru K (v), *pl* **kunakuu?e-taruappear,** bob up, protrude. *See* **kuro?itu.**

kunanatsu (n) prickly ash, toothache tree. *Zanthoxylum americanum* Mill (has yellow roots; grows in sandy soil; grind bark with prehistoric bones as medicine for arthritis, fever, sore throat, and toothache). *See* **tupinatsu.**

kuna na?mahpee? (n) lightning bug (*lit* firewood ball).

Kuna?itu? (n) Onion Creek, Texas (*lit* firewood rock; named for volcanic plug located on south bank of creek).

kuparu (v) cut something or someone down.

kupisaru (v) dry by heating (as on a stove) [**kuh-** fire + **pisa-** dry].

kupisi, kubisi (n) brain.

kupisinamaya, kupisimawa (n) croton weed (leaves mixed with animal brains for use in tanning hides). *Croton monanthogynus* Michx.

kupisi?aru (v) rub with brains (one of last steps in tanning a hide).

kupitaru (v) light a lamp or fire, throw a light on something.

kupita? (n) light, lamp, flashlight. *See* **tuka?.**

kuputsaru (v) explode from heat, burst from overheating.

kuro?itu W (v), *pl* **kunakuu?itu** appear, bob up, protrude. *See* **kunakuaru.**

Kurupitsoni (name) Looks-brown (person).

kuruupe (n) opening in clothing.

kusi- (pfx) ref. to gray color of ashes. *See* **kusipu.**

kusiebipitu (adj) K light blue; **W** lavender.

kusikwa?aa? (n) crane (*lit* gray thing that flaps wings). *See* **pa?atoyokatu huutsuu?.**

kusikwi?ii? (n) Mexican blanket (gray-blue, previously issued by government to Native Americans); **W** blue-gray bird (sp. unknown).

kusimuura (n) donkey (*lit* gray mule).

kusinʉʉhparabi (n) gray-colored plant (sp. unknown).

Kusiokwe (n) Pecos River (*lit* gray stream).

kusisai? (n) small gray bird (generally found around cattle; sp. unkown).

kusisʉkʉi, kusi sʉkʉ (n) fall plum. Prunussp. (fruits either eaten fresh or dried and stored for later use; *lit* gray plum). *See* **yusʉkʉ**.

kusipi̱ W, kusipi̱tʉ K (adj) gray, light blue.

kusipʉ (n) ashes.

kusitekwarʉ, kusihtakwarʉ (v) whistle.

kusiwʉhpima W (v) roast in ashes (formerly made bread or cooked meat by placing in coals, covering with ashes). **Surii kusiwʉhpimanu ma.** He roasted them in the ashes.

kusiwʉʉnʉ (n) shrub (similar to sage tree; grows by river; used as medicine; sp. unknown).

kusiyuna? (n) shovel (for ashes). *See* **tʉtsiyuna?**.

kusuatʉ (v) warm (feel warm from weather).

kusʉwetʉ, kusʉkwetʉ (v) radiate heat, blow heat toward one.

kutsani, kutsuhpi̱ (n) fire poker.

kutsihpʉ? (n) donkey (*lit* fire end).

Kutsiokwe (n) Peace River (*lit* clear water).

kutsiyaapʉ (n) shish kebob.

kutsi?omo (n) shin or shin bone.

kutsi?wobi? (n) donkey (*lit* fire-end-board or hoof).

kutsi̱tonarʉ (v), *pl obj* **kutsi̱towakarʉ** set on fire, burn.

kutʉhorapʉ W, kutóorapʉ K (n) fireplace, hearth, fire hole.

kutʉhorarʉ, kutoorarʉ (v) dig a fire hole. **Nʉ pia? tsa? wihnu nʉmi kutʉhórakʉ?eeyʉ.** My mother then would dig a fire hole for us (109:6).

kutʉhubihtaa ohweetʉ (n) coal mine.

kutʉhuubi̱ W, kutuubʉ K (n) coal.

kutʉhuyuna? W, kutʉʉyuna? K (n) coal shovel.

kuuma, kuhma (n) male animal.

kuumabaitʉ, kuhmabai (v) be married, have a husband.

kuumarurʉ, kuhmarukatʉ (v) marry a man.

kuupʉ (n) cache (food stored by animals or birds).

kuura (n) pack rat.

kuurʉ (v) cache (storage of food by animals or birds).

kuutsu? K (n), *pl* **kuutsuhnanʉʉ** cow, cattle. *See* **kuhtsu?**.

kuwaaitʉ (v) dry up.

kuwikʉsii (n) pony tail.

kuwo?nepʉ (n) hollow, burned out tree trunk.

kuwʉhora?, kuhwora? (n) hoe, mattock.

kuyaarʉ, kuyaami?arʉ (v) carry on the head.

kuya?akatʉ (adj) afraid, scared, frightened. **Sitʉ tʉse? wa?ihpʉ? tʉbitsi kuya?anu̱.** This woman was really scared (52:19). *See* **wʉ?yʉrʉhkikatʉ**.

kuya?arʉ (v) frighten.

kuyúusi?, kuyúutsi? (n) quail. *See* **tʉebasuu?**.

kuyu?nii, kuyuníi? (n), *pl* **kuyuníi?nʉʉ**, *acc pl* **kuyuníi?a** turkey.

Kuyuníi?nʉʉ pisikwanuu?i.
The turkeys were sliding (5:1).
tosa kuynii? white turkey,
eka kuyunii? red turkey, **tuu
kuyunii?** black turkey.

ku?e (n) top, summit, on top of.

ku?ebi, ku?ekarʉ (n) hill, peak
(standing alone). *See* **anáabi.**

Ku?e kwʉsih taibo? (n) Chinese (*lit*
spinner-braided foreigners).

ku?e kwʉsi? (n) spinner (hair style;
braid from top or back of head;
style worn by early Comanches and
other Native American peoples).

**ku?e naba wʉhtia, ku?e nabaa
kwʉhtia** (v) baptize by sprinkling
(*lit* to pour out water on top).

ku?e tsasimapʉ (n) scalp (war
trophy).

ku?e tsasimarʉ (v) scalp someone.

ku?e wóo? (n) dove, pigeon (*lit* top
moaning, moaning on top). *See*
pasahòo, taibo huutsuu?.

ku?e wʉnʉrʉ, ku?e kwʉnʉ (v)
buck off, pitch off (as does a
horse).

ku?hiboo?, ku?hiboorʉ (n) nurse
cape (dress with a large round
collar).

ku?inapʉ (n), *acc* **ku?inapʉha**
roasted meat (possibly jerked).
**Suhka pʉ ku?inapʉha u?
tsayumi?ii.** He took off his
roasted meat (7:39). *See*
tʉkwʉsʉkʉpʉ?.

ku?inarʉ (v) roast meat over fire or
dry it for jerky, barbecue.

ku?inawaata, ku?inakwaata (n)
grill, barbecue grate.

ku?miitsa (n) wart.

ku?nikakʉrʉ (v), **pl obj kuwekwa
kʉrʉ** rope someone or something

while moving. **Tʉnahpʉ tsa?
pimoroo?a tua?a ku?nikakʉi.**
The man roped the calf.

ku?nikarʉ, kuwekwarʉ (v) slip a
rope around something.

ku?nika? (n) mourning cape (worn by
mother or grandmother of deceased;
so named because of tightness on
the neck of the wearer).

ku?nuitʉ (v) to swallow.

ku?okwerʉ W (v) render lard (*lit*
with heat liquify). *See* **yuhukarʉ,
kuhpitsʉni?arʉ.**

ku?tsiyaarʉ (v), *pl obj* **ku?tsihi-
marʉ** roast on sticks. **Pʉʉ
kohtoopʉba?a urʉʉ u ku?tsi-
yaa?eeyʉ.** They roasted it over
their fire on sticks (73:10).

kʉarʉ (v), *pl* **to?itʉ** escape, come
out, climb out.

kʉayʉka?etʉ W (v) ride horseback.
See **tʉhʉyakarʉ.**

kʉayʉka?etʉ   🦌 wehki'ai

kʉbʉráata (adj) tall and slender.

kʉhkarʉ?itʉ (v) bite together.

kʉhkarʉkatʉ (v) bite into and not
turn loose.

kʉhka?arʉ (v) bite off. **Nʉmatitʉ
sʉmʉsʉ piakʉhka?a.** Take a big
bite from me once (22:14).

kʉhkihtserʉ (v) W spit out; K mash
in the mouth.

kʉhkobarʉ (v), *pl obj* **kʉhtokwe** bite to death, break or sever with the teeth. **Itʉ tsaʔ ihka kʉhkobaʔi.** He broke this with his teeth. *See* **kʉnutsanʉ.**

kʉhkwatuubirʉ K, kʉhtsobokikatʉ W (v) roll in the mouth.

kʉhkwibikitʉ (v) quiver (lips), chatter (teeth). *See* **sʉhkwibitʉ, kʉʉhtarakii.**

kʉhkwitsitʉ (v), *pl* **kʉhtoroki, kʉhtoromi** grit the teeth, clack the teeth (once, or many times as does a hog).

kʉhpararʉ (v) straighten something (holding in mouth, as an arrow shaft).

kʉhparoʔaitʉ K, kʉhparʉʉbʉrʉ W (v) moisten in the mouth.

kʉhpitsoonitʉ (v) grind (with teeth), extract juice (by mouth).

kʉhpohtorʉ (v) burst with the mouth, pop with the mouth (as chewing gum).

kʉhpomarʉ (v) trim, prune (to shape a tree). **Huupihta mooke kʉhpomai.** (He) trimmed the branches of the tree. *See* **wʉhʉwʉʔniitʉ, wʉʔyʉkwitʉ, kʉmakoorʉ.**

kʉhpomiʔitʉ (v) W chew up fine; K bite off.

kʉhporokitʉ (v) grit the teeth, grind the teeth.

kʉhpunitʉ (v) taste, try out. *See* **kʉʔkwiyarʉ.**

kʉhtáa mubitaiʔ (n) hickory (*lit* hard shelled; named for the nut).

kʉhtáa nuʔyaʔa W, kʉhtaa nuhye K (n) racer snake.

kʉhtáaku (adv) tightly. **Mʉʉ kahni nʉʉʔka kʉhtáaku tsahtʉmiʔinʉ.**

All of you shut your house tightly (3:7).

kʉhtáatʉ (adj) strong, tight, hard.

kʉhtabai (n) pecan.

kʉhtáanʉetʉ (v) storm, blow hard. **Sukʉhu sitʉ urii kʉhtáanʉenʉ.** This (wind) blew hard on them there (53:26).

kʉhtoponarʉ W, kʉhtoponirʉ K (v) make round with the mouth.

kʉhtoʔyarʉ K (v) unwrap something with the mouth.

kʉhtsakarʉ (v) catch something with the mouth. **Kʉhtsakaʔaitʉ ma.** He is catching something with his mouth.

kʉhtsayaʔyaʔkeʔ (n, arch) coyote (*lit* yowling animal). *See* **kʉʔkwʉriaʔ.**

kʉhtsiarʉ (v), *pl* **kʉsoʔi** bite (mainly used in speaking of dogs or babies who bite). **Sitʉ kwasi- nabooʔ ubinai u kʉhtsianʉʉ.** This snake bit him from behind (27:9).

kʉhtsuukarʉ (v) close the mouth.

kʉhtsuʔmarʉ (v) eat up, finish off by eating. **Pihuura tsaʔ kʉhtsuʔmai nʉ.** I ate up all the beans.

kʉhtsʉtsʉʉʔniʔ (n) poisonous wild onion (**lit** cause teeth to clench). *Allium* sp.? (similar to large wild onion). *See* **kʉʉkạ.**

kʉhtʉkʉtoʔipʉ, kʉhtoʔipʉ (n) leftover food (something from mouth). **Pʉʉ kʉhtoʔipʉha urʉʉ sitii tʉrʉeʔtii makamaʔeeyʉ.** They fed their leftovers to these children (74:14).

kʉhʉwʉnʉkatʉ (n) dawn (before sunup). *See* **hʉwʉni.**

kʉhyaarʉ (v), *pl obj* **kʉhhimarʉ** take something in the mouth.

kɨkɨbɨraakwaʔsiʔ (n) scissortail, fork-tailed flycatcher. *Muscivora fortificata.*

kɨmakoorɨ (v) trim, prune (as to shape a tree). **U kɨmakooʔi ɨ.** He trimmed it. *See* **kɨhpomarɨ.**

kɨmakwaʔi, kɨmakwai, kɨmawahtɨ (adj) dull **nahu kɨmakwaʔi** dull knife. *See* **kemakɨmapɨ.**

kɨmapɨ (n) sharpened edge, knife edge, can opener.

kɨmaʔ (adv loc) beside, along the edge of.

kɨmaʔkɨ (post) beside.

kɨmaʔrɨ (post) alongside.

kɨminarɨ (v) break something, break a bone (using instrument).

kɨmiʔakɨrɨ (v) send (make go by talking; talk someone into going, persuade someone to go).

kɨnabenitɨ (v) bite (as an insect).

kɨnorɨ (v) graze (eat grass, as cattle do).

kɨnuaitɨ (v) move something with the mouth.

kɨnutsarɨ (v) break up with the teeth. *See* **kɨhkobarɨ.**

kɨnuʔ (n) paternal grandfather, paternal great uncle; man's agnatic grandchild, man's agnatic grandnephew.

kɨpisoʔaitɨ K, kɨpɨhisoʔaitɨ W (v) anger someone, annoy. *See* **mahrubɨhkaitɨ.**

kɨpisiʔ, kɨpɨsiʔ (n) saliva. *See* **huutsipɨ, tusi-.**

kɨpɨtsarɨ (v) break open with the teeth.

kɨrahúuʔ K, kɨʔraʔhúuʔ W (n) hackberry. *Celtis occidentalis var. canina.* Raf. (used to cure diarrhea).

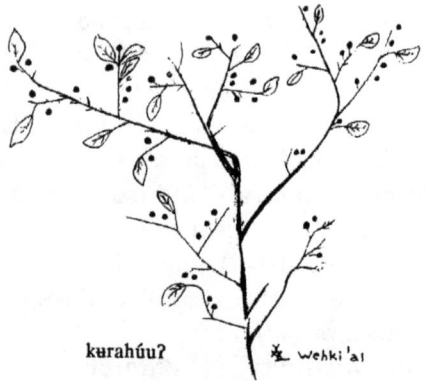

kɨrahúuʔ   ⅄ wehki'aɪ

kɨriata (n) yellow pond lily. *Nymphaea advena* Ait.? (roots boiled and eaten).

kɨrɨʔatsi (n) yellow lotus. *Nelumbo luteo* [Willd.] Pers.? (roots boiled or eaten raw; nutritious).

kɨsarɨ (v) open the mouth.

kɨsiʔkwarɨ (v) tear with the teeth.

kɨsukarɨ (v) taste. **Pokopihta u kɨsukai.** He tasted the fruit.

kɨtáatɨ, kɨhtaatɨ (adj) tight, strong, hard.

kɨtsuʔtsuʔkitɨ, kɨtsɨbarɨ (v) squeak, creak (make squeak as a floor or shoes).

Kɨtsɨkwipɨ (name) Chew-up (person).

kɨtsɨbakitɨ (v) bite together.

kɨtsɨkwetɨ (v) chew. *See* **kɨyuʔnetɨ.**

kɨtsɨweʔ (n) chewing gum.

kɨtu (adv) yesterday.

kɨtubarɨ W, kɨtɨrɨkwaitɨ K (v) click, snap (make snapping sound as a trigger).

kɨtɨbarɨ (v) crack with the teeth.

kɨɨhtarakiitɨ (v) chatter the teeth. *See* **kɨhkwibikitɨ.**

kɨɨkanarɨhkaʔ (n) wild onion (roots roasted in coals and eaten).

kʉʉka̱, kʉka (n), *acc pl* **kʉʉkewild**
onion. *Allium* sp. (edible root). *See*
kʉhtsʉtsʉʉhni?.

kʉʉkʉme?, kʉhkʉme? (n) stranger.
(archany nonkinsman).

kʉʉtsi̱ (n) wisdom tooth.

kʉwokarʉ, kʉhpiwokarʉ (v) drag
something (by mouth). **Sarii
tsa? u kʉhpiwokarʉ.** The dog is
dragging it (by its mouth).

kʉyu?netʉ (v) chew. *See*
kʉtsʉkwetʉ.

kʉ?kwiyarʉ (v) nibble, taste (eat a
small amount). *See* **kʉhpunitʉ.**

kʉ?kwʉriarʉ (v) dribble, spill (from
the mouth). *See* **kʉ?okwetʉ.**

kʉ?kwʉria? (n) fox, coyote. *See*
**kaawosa̱, oha ahnakatʉ,
kʉhtsaya?ya?ke?.**

kʉ?okwetʉ (v) slobber, dribble from
the mouth. *See* **kʉ?kwʉriarʉ.**

kʉ?tseena (n), *pl* **kʉtseenanʉʉ**
fox, wolf, coyote (long form). *See*
tseena?, kʉhtsaya?ya?ke?.

kʉ?urʉ (v) have hope. **Nʉ kʉ?urʉ
suni.** I hope it is like that. **Kʉ?urʉ
hai.** I do hope so.

kʉ?wikeetʉ (v) shake something
(holding it in the mouth). **Sarii
tsa? tabukina?a kʉ?wikeetʉ.**
The dog is shaking the rabbit
(with his mouth).

kʉ?wonʉhʉbai (n, arch) handcar.

kʉ?wʉnʉbaa?i̱, kʉ?wʉnʉhʉbai
(n) railroad handcar. *See* **pi?yʉpʉ
káa?i̱.**

kwaabih kahni (n) rooming house.

kwabarʉ, kwabatʉ (v) hug,
squeeze, carry in the arms. *See*
toyokwabarʉ.

kwabitʉ (v, pl), *sg* **habiitʉ** lie
down.

Kwahari tʉhka, Kwaharʉnʉʉ (n)
Antelope Eaters (Comanche band
now located in Cache and Lawton,
OK; said to have originated in
1100 A.D. from the Tejas (tʉhka)
group, Deer Hunters).

kwahi (n) back (of person or
animal).

kwahi kupi̱si̱ (n) spinal cord
(excluding any bones).

kwahi noorʉ (v) carry on the back,
backpack.

kwahinupʉ (n) spine, backbone.

kwahiporopʉ, kwahiwo?oraa (n)
spinal column, backbone.

Kwahira (name) Robe-on-his-back
(person).

kwahisiapʉ (n) covetous person.

kwahisi?a (v) covet, envy another
person. *See* **nasuyaketʉ.**

kwahitsuhni̱ (n) vertebra (one bone
of the backbone).

kwahitʉki? (n) saddle blanket.

kwahtsʉ W (n), *acc* **kwahtsʉna**
rib.

kwakurʉ K (v) defeat, win over
someone. *See* **tahni?arʉ.**

Kwana (name) Quanah Parker
(Comanche chief, eldest son of
Narua and Nokona; born in 1847,
was the last war chief of the
Comanches; died in 1911).

Kwana kuhtsu paa? (n) Rio Grande
(*lit* stinking buffalo river; named
in Comanche for dead buffalo
killed by the Comanches because
they crossed the river and could
not be driven back).

Kwana pekwasʉ (n) Rio Frio (*lit*
stinking fish river; named in
Comanche for dead fish in dried
water holes).

kwanaru̱ (v) have odor, have bad odor, *modern* smell good. **Totsiyaa tsa? tsaa kwanaru̱.** The flower smells good (has pleasant odor).

kwanu?itu̱ K, kwa?nu?itu̱ W (v) throw body on the ground, squat. *See* **wu̱nu̱hkaru̱ru̱.**

Kwaru̱ (n) Comanche band (*lit* loud-speaking people; located in Cache-Lawton area).

kwasi- (pfx) ref. to animal tail.

kwasi nu̱ru̱u̱?wu̱? (n) snapping turtle. *Chelydra serpentina. See* **pa?kwaku̱me.**

kwasi taiboo? (n) monkey (*lit* tailed foreigner).

kwasi taiboo?a na?ku̱htabai (n) coconut (*lit* monkey pecan).

kwasi taiboo?a tu̱hkapu̱ (n) coconut (*lit* monkey food).

kwasi tona? (n) scorpion (*lit* stinging tail, or tail that stings).

Kwasia (name) Eagle-tail-feather (person).

kwasiku̱ (adv time) last, next time. *See* **hayakwasiku̱.**

kwasinaboo pekwi (n) eel (*lit* snake fish).

kwasinaboo wu̱hkitsu?tsu?ikatu̱ (n) rattlesnake. *See* **wu̱htsabeyakatu̱.**

kwasinaboo? (n) snake (general term). **Situ̱ kwasinaboo? ubinai u ku̱htsianu̱.** The snake bit him from behind (27:9).

kwasinaboo?a tu̱ahkapu̱ (n) tomato, *arch* goat rue (*lit* snake food). *Leguminosae Tephrosia virginiana.*

kwasi (n) animal tail.

kwasu?u sakweni, kwasu?u tohtsana? (n) clothes hanger.

kwasu?ukatu̱ K, kwasu?u tuaru̱ W (v) own an article of clothing.

Kwasu?ukatu̱ nu̱. I have a dress.

kwasu?u̱ (n) dress, shirt, coat. *See* **tenahpu̱?a kwasu?u̱.**

kwasu?u̱ tu̱mu̱u̱ru̱ (v) buy an article of clothing.

kwasu̱ku̱pu̱ (n) cooked food.

kwasu̱ku̱ru̱ (v) roast food, fry meat or vegetables.

kwasu̱pu̱ (adj) ripe.

kwasu̱tu̱ (v) cook. **Suru̱ u kwasu̱hka, pu̱ tu̱ru̱e?tii nimainu̱.** When it was cooked, he called his children.

kwetu̱sapu̱, kwetsapu̱ N (adj) unfriendly. *See* **nakahanupu̱.**

kwetu̱suaku̱ru̱ W, kwetu̱sa?itu̱ K (v) ignore, reject. **U kwetu̱sua-ku̱tu̱ nu̱.** I am ignoring him.

kwe?yaru̱ (v, nonhum subj) shed (as a tree sheds leaves).

kwe?yu̱ku̱ sohóobi (n) silver maple (*lit* shedding cottonwood).

kwe?yu̱katu̱ (v, hum subj) tire out. **Oha ahnakatu̱ tsa? kwe?- yu̱katu̱.** Coyote is tired out (10:23).

kwibihpikitu̱ W, kwibibikitu̱ K (v) tremble. *See* **su̱hkwibitu̱.**

kwibukitu̱ (v) lash (as hard rain or hail), switch, whip. **Nu̱ tua?a nu̱ kwibukii.** I switched my boy. *See* **tu̱kwibukiitu̱.**

kwihitu̱ (v) throw overhand.

kwihnai (n) eagle (considered sacred). *See* **piakwihnai.**

kwihne kahpinakwu̱ (n) northwest.

kwihne muhyu̱nakwu̱ (n) northeast.

Kwihne tosabitu̱ (name) White-eagle (person).

kwihnenakwu̱ (n) north (*lit* cold direction).

kwihnai

kwihnerʉ (v) be cold, turn cold (weather).

kwihne? (n) wintertime.

kwiipʉsiarʉ (v) tan a hide (by smoke).

kwiisuatʉ W (adj) foggy. *See* **pakʉnaikatʉ**.

kwiita (n) buttocks.

kwiita, kwitakʉ P (n, nonhum sub) bottom.

kwiitsʉba?itʉ (v) dart, flash, flicker (as a snake's tongue).

kwinumakatʉ (adj) dizzy.

kwinumapʉ (n) drunk, intoxicated person. *See* **hibipʉ**.

kwinumarʉ (v) make dizzy.

kwinumasuarʉ (v) feel faint. *See* **sua watsikatʉ**.

kwinu?yarʉ (v) spin around, turn around. *See* **natsahkwinu?itʉ**.

kwipunarʉ (v) twist. *See* **makwipunarʉ**.

kwipʉ, kwiipʉ (n) smoke.

kwipʉsiapʉ (n) palomino horse (smoked-tan color).

kwisihka (adj) tangled. *See* **sakwʉsikʉtʉ**.

kwisihkarʉ (v) make, cause to tangle.

kwisikatʉ K (v) tangle, braid. **Wanaramu tsa? kwisikatʉ.** The thread is tangled. *See* **kwʉsipʉ**.

kwita maropona (n) doodlebug, sowbug (*lit* excrement roller).

kwitapʉ (n) feces, excrement.

kwitatsi (n) large intestine.

kwitso?aitʉ (v) recover (get well, improve in health).

kwitso?arʉ (v) save, rescue (as from a tragedy). *See* **makwitso- ?arʉ, wʉhkwitso?arʉ**.

kwitsunairʉ (v) twist the body. *See* **nʉʉkwitsʉnarʉ**.

Kwi?ena mʉa (n) September.

kwʉhti? (n) wounded person (from gunshot).

kwʉhʉniwaitʉ, kwʉhʉnikwaitʉ (v) propose marriage (ask a girl for her hand; ask parents for hand of their daughter).

kwʉhʉpʉ, kwʉʉpʉ (n) captive (must have possessor). **nʉ kwʉhʉpʉ** my captive.

kwʉhʉrʉ (v) arrest, capture, catch.

kwʉhʉ? (n) wife.

kwʉrʉ?arʉ (v) peel off (as skin, fruit peeling, furniture finish). *See* **kiabo?arʉ**.

kwʉsiberʉ W (v) brush off. *See* **wʉsiberʉ**.

kwʉsipʉ W (adj) tangled, braided. *See* **kwisirʉ**.

kwʉʉhtikʉrʉ, kwʉtikʉrʉ (v), *pl* **kwʉtikukʉrʉ** shoot something.

kwʉʉhturʉ (v) marry (take a wife). **U kwʉʉhturu?i nʉ.** I will marry her.

kwʉʉhtʉkatʉ W, K, kwʉʉkatʉ P (adj) married (of a man). *See* **kumahpʉ?**.

M

ma (pro, 3rd prox acc sg) him, her, it. **Ma marɰkɰtsi, nɰ ma tɰhkaru?i̱.** After finishing it, I will eat it.

maa (adv dem, prox) with or on someone or something [**ma** (dem) + **ma** on, with]. **Sitɰɰ maa yɰkwihkatɰ.** These ones are sitting on it (120:14).

maaitɰ (adv dem, prox) at or to someone or something [**ma** (dem) + **metɰ** at, to]. **Wakare?ee? maaitɰ yahnéeyɰ.** The turtle is laughing at him (10:26).

maatu (adv dem, prox) up to or onto someone or something [**ma** (dem) + **matu** up to, onto]. **Sitɰɰ kwasinaboo? maatu tunehtsɰnɰ.** This snake ran up to him (35:10).

mabáaku?neetɰ (adj) baptized (*lit* hands put under water).

mabáa?aitɰ (adj) watered, moistened.

mabararɰ (v) massage, press down, rub medicine on body. *See* **narɰ?ekarɰ.**

mabarɰ W (v) knead, mix. *See* **tɰmabarɰ.**

mabasahtɰkitɰ K (v) sit in sun to dry. *See* **pasahtahtɰkitɰ.**

maba?isokitɰ (adj) dampened, sponged. *See* **pa?i̱soketɰ.**

mabekakɰrɰ W (v) pay medicine man. *See* **tɰmabekarɰ.**

mabe?akatɰ W (adj) parted (hair).

mabihtɰ?uyarɰ (v) exchange one item for another (*lit* with hands give back).

mabiso?àitɰ (adj) angry, angered.

mabisukiitɰ (adj) crushed into small pieces.

mabitsiarɰ (v) respect, honor, care for (*lit* take hand). *See* **maritsiakatɰ.**

mabitsoorɰ (v) press down with hands to expel water.

mabohto, mabohto?itɰ (v) snap fingers.

mabo?ayarɰ (v) take off, be carried away by wind, blew away. **Yɰtsɰnohi?a mabo?oyanɰ.** The kite flew.

mabunihkarɰ (v) tempt or test someone (*lit* see hand).

mabɰarɰ (v) release from hands.

mahbotsetɰ, mahpotse (v) push away (jerk hand away from body).

mahiko?itɰ (v) return from warpath. **Hayarokwetɰɰ tuibihtsi?anɰɰ mahíko?ika̱.** Four young men were returning from the warpath (93:1).

mahimi?arɰ (v) go on warpath.

mahípɰrɰmɰrɰ (v) buy for oneself, possess (hold in hand).

mahípɰrɰmɰtɰ (v) possess (hold in hand). *See* **hipɰkatɰ.**

mahiyaitɰ (v) reach out, offer hand. **U hina mahiyai nɰ.** I am reaching for it. *See* **makwɰbɰtsɰrɰ.**

mahiyarɰ (v) swear, take oath (ref. to holding up hand). **Mahi- yarɰ nɰ.** I am taking an oath.

mahka (pro, 3rd prox acc sg) him, her, it.

mahkarɰ W (v) hitch up (as horse and buggy). *See* **nomohkarɰ.**

mahkɰkitɰ K (v) drive in animals (*lit* cause to come in).

mahkɰrɰ W (v) drive up animals.

mahkʉsuwaitʉ (v) drive along or away.

mahkwʉmarʉ (v) loosen with hands, unwrap.

mahoinitʉ (v) go in circles, encircle.

mahomonutsarʉ (v) crumble to powder (with hands), mash into small particles. *See* **manutsaʔarʉ, tahhomonutsarʉ, homonuhtsaitʉ.**

mahooikatʉ (adj) stalked, ambushed.

mahorarʉ (v) scoop up, dig (with hands). *See* **tsahhorarʉ.**

mahri (pro, 3rd prox acc du) two of them.

mahrubʉhkaitʉ (v) anger someone. *See* **kʉpisoʔaitʉ.**

mahrʉ (pro, 3rd prox nom du) of two of them. **Sitʉkʉseʔ wihnu mahrʉmaʔai.** This one then went with them (two).

mahtokooʔ (n) thumb (*lit* hand grandfather).

mahtokwʉnaitʉ K, mahtokwʉnʉ-ʔitʉ W (v) lean on something, rest on something (as a broom against or on a wall). **Huunaroʔiʔ mahtu namahtokwʉnʉka.** A ladder was leaning along it (92:10).

mahtsokaitʉ (v) close the hand. **Nʉ moʔe nʉ matsokai.** I closed my hand. *See* **moʔo-.**

mahtsukitʉ (v) close someone's hand.

mahtuaʔ (n) little finger.

mahtʉpináaʔ K (n) middle finger. *See* **masʉwʉhkiʔ.**

mahuihkatʉ, mahwikatʉ (adj) pushed over, knocked over.

mahuinoorʉ (v) come slowly (*lit* come walking being pushed).

mahuyubakatʉ (adj) oblong (formed by rolling between the hands).

mahuʔnetʉ (v) crawl on hands and knees (pulling forward with the hands). *See* **wʉhuʔnerʉ, tahuʔnerʉ.**

mahʉrʉhwakatʉ (adj) opened [**mahʉ**- push + **tʉhwaʔ** open].

mahyarʉ (v) defile, break a taboo, law, treaty. **Marii mahyaʔi marʉ.** They broke the treaty against them.

maihtʉkʉ (adv man) openly, plainly.

makaarʉ (v) feed. **Nʉ maaka!** Feed me!

makahtʉnikatʉ (v) tell to feed [**maka**- feed + **tʉni**- tell].

makamaitʉ (v) wait for someone.

makamʉkarʉ (v) ambush. *See* **tʉkamʉrʉ.**

makaʔmukitʉ (v) prepare for (as a room for a guest). **Marʉʉ nanawaʔihpʉʔanʉʉ sihka tʉha tsaaku makaʔmukiʉ.** Their womenfolk prepared this meat good (69:9).

makitsarʉ (v) mash, squash, hand grind.

makitsetʉ (adj) squashed, mashed.

makoobikatʉ (adj) broken up.

makoʔitʉ (v) regain possession (get something back).

makuhpʉkatʉ (adj) strangled, choked.

Makutabai (name) dog hero (notorious in tales).

makuyaʔaitʉ (adj) frightened. *See* **wʉʔyʉrʉhkikatʉ.**

makʉetʉ W (v) refuse, prohibit.

makʉma?aitʉ (adj) sharpened.

makʉnaitʉ (v) hold down with hand (as in catching animal).

makʉ (adv dem, prox) right here. **Sitʉwʉ tsa? makʉ pitʉnʉ.** These two arrived here (115:3).

makʉtserʉ, makiitsetʉ (v) mash. **Nʉ mo?o ma makʉtsenʉ.** I mashed it with my hands. *See* **mapi̱tserʉ.**

makwatubiitʉ (adj) folded, rolled up.

makwarʉ (v) feel around (with hands). *See* **mawa-.**

makwe (n) back of the hand.

makwihtserʉ (v) persecute, afflict.

makwineetʉ, makwineerʉ (v) wipe off with the hand.

makwipunarʉ K, makwʉpetʉ W (v) twist, crease with the hands (as a rope). *See* **takwʉperʉ, kwipunarʉ.**

makwitso?aitʉ (v) save someone, rescue, prevent someone's death. **Nʉmatu to?i̱tsi ʉnʉ, nʉ makwitso?ainʉ.** Coming out onto me, you saved me (105:28). *See* **kwitso?arʉ.**

makwiyetʉ, makwʉyeerʉ (v, adj) chase someone, chased.

makwi?numaitʉ (v) be made dizzy, made drunk, intoxicated. **Po?saba tsa? ma makwi?numai.** The whiskey made him drunk.

makwi̱teerʉ (v) strip off (as seeds from a plant).

makwʉbʉtsʉrʉ W (v) reach for (with hand). *See* **mahiyaitʉ, marurʉ?arʉ.**

makwʉmutsiarʉ (v) sharpen an edge [ma- (dem) + kwʉ- edge + mutsia sharpen].

makwʉri?aikatʉ (adj) spilled accidentally.

makwʉrʉ?eka? W (n) hand lotion (*lit* something spilled on the hand). *See* **mo?okwitʉ?eka?.**

makwʉ?netʉ (v) rub lightly, touch lightly with the hand.

makwʉ?nikʉtʉ K (v) smooth (with hand).

makwʉ?nikʉ W (n) tire, wheel. *See* **na?bukuwà?a narahpaana̱.**

makwʉsaitʉ (v) open the hand.

makwʉsà? (n) sleeve.

makwʉsetʉ (adj) sprained.

makwʉsikʉkatʉ (adj) tangled by hand.

mamámutsiakatʉ (adj) formed to a point (by hand, as in greenware).

mamamʉekatʉ (adj) delayed, detained.

mamárʉmarʉ (v) close up, cover (as with a lid).

mami?akʉtʉ (v) operate manually. *See* **nʉʉmi?akʉrʉ.**

mamutsiakatʉ (adj) sharpened to a point.

mamutsiarʉ (v) make pointed. **Ma mamutsiarʉ ma?.** He is sharpening it to a point. *See* **manutsiarʉ.**

mamʉsuakatʉ K (adj) prohibited, taboo.

manáawʉnʉ?etʉ (v) incite to rear up.

manahkerʉ (v) measure. **U manahkeki u.** He came to measure it. *See* **tʉmanahketʉ.**

manakʉarʉ (v, sg obj), *pl obj* **manakʉʉ?irʉ** cause to protrude). **Sitʉ wakare?ee? u kwasitaka etʉsipʉka manakʉʉ?ikʉnʉ.** This turtle made just their tails stick out of (*lit* at) the fire (10:22).

manakwų K, manaanakwų W
(adv loc) far away (long distance,
on the other side). **Surɨɨkųse?
manakwųhi tuuʔeeyų.** Those
(people) carried water far (81:2).

mananaaʔwaihkarɨ (v) wait
on, care for, entertain, extend
hospitality to a guest.

manawɨnɨkatų (adj) reared up,
standing on hind feet (as a horse
or bear).

manaʔkoroomitɨ (v) K cover the
head (as with a cloth); W cover
something over.

manekihtɨʔ (num) full house in
card game, arch five.

manímɨarɨ (v) blame, criticize,
find fault.

manitɨ (v) cross over (as a river or
bridge). **Manituʔi ma.** He will
cross over.

manookatų (adj) carried on back.

manoorɨ (v) carry, haul in a vehicle
(give someone a lift).

manuarɨ W (v) rake together. *See*
marɨʔokitɨ.

manutsaʔarɨ W (v) break up,
crumble (with the hands). *See*
homonuhtsaitɨ, tahnutsaʔerɨ.

manutsiarɨ W (v) form into a point
(as greenware). *See* **mamutsiarɨ.**

manųkikɨrɨ, manųkikɨrɨ (v,
sg obj), *pl* **objmanurakɨ-** shoo
away (make something run). *See*
tanųkikɨtɨ.

manɨɨsukaarɨ (v) excite, give
sensation (cause good or bad
feeling in body or spirit).

manɨɨtsikwaʔ W (n) pain, ache.

manɨɨʔmaitɨ (v) tire of
something. *See* **wɨʔtsikwarɨ,
nakɨnɨɨʔmaitų.**

manųarɨ (v) raise someone, rear a
child.

manųkɨtų (adj) pressed down,
packed in tightly.

manųsutarɨ (v) surrender (give up
to a victor).

manųsutaʔaitɨ (v) surrender
someone.

manųsuʔnarɨ W (v) tame a wild
thing.

mapaanaʔ (n) palm reader,
fortuneteller. *See* **nipųkaaʔeetɨ.**

mapaana (n) palm of hand.

mapitserɨ (v) mash up something.
See **makųtserɨ.**

mapóʔaʔ (n) human skin. *See* **hɨnɨ
poʔaʔ.**

mapɨhų, mapɨhų (n) hair on lower
arm or hand (*lit* arm fuzz).

mapųnukeerɨ (v) polish by hand.
See **tapųnukeerɨ.**

mapɨtsarɨ (v) burst open, break
open (with hand).

marahpunihkatų (adj) tried on, tested.

marátųbaitɨ (v), *pl* **maráhtataʔi-**
crack something (with hand). *See*
marɨbarɨ.

marebunitɨ (v) cure partially
through touch. **Ma marebuni nɨ.**
I made him better.

marii (pro, 3rd prox acc pl) them.
Marii punihtsi ma ikahkį. Looking at them, he came in. **Marii
ɨkɨniwɨnɨka, marɨɨkųhu
kɨahkį.** As they just spoke,
something bright came out in
sight (86:15).

maritsiakatų (adj) honored,
respected. *See* **mabitsiarɨ.**

marohtɨmarɨ (v) close up with
hand (put on lid) [ma- hand +
tohtɨma- close up].

maropoʔnaru (v), *pl obj*
maropoʔniʔitu roll around, coil
(by hand). **U sumurayuʔnetsi
uruu, u maroponiʔinu.**
Completely pounding it, they
made balls of it (116:17).

maropoʔniʔipu (n) round object
(formed by hand). *See* **tohto-
ponitu.**

marukaru (v) quench by hand, snuff
out.

maruruʔaru (v) reach for, stretch
out arm. **Waʔihpuʔ maruruʔah-
tsi huabokooʔa pomanu.**
The woman, stretching out her
arm, picked a huckleberry. *See*
mahiyaitu, makwubutsuru.

marua (n) herd.

Maruhke (n) Eating-tribe (Shoshoni
band; Snake People).

marukaru (v) finish (by hand).
Soone nu marukai. I finished
(making) the quilt.

marukitu (v) touch (with hand).
Numa ma maruki. He touched me.

marukiʔnetu (v) flatten something
(with hand, as a tortilla; *lit* cause
to be flat).

marumabunipu (n) tested item,
tried item.

marumaru (v) close, cover (with lid,
as a box).

marui muru (v) buy something.

marupisuʔaru W (v) unfold (by hand)
[ma- hand + tupuisuʔa unfold].

marurooniitu K (adj) braced,
supported. *See* **tohturooniitu.**

maruroonitu (v) brace (by hand)
[ma- hand + turooni- brace].

maruu (pro, 3rd prox gen pl) their
maruu paraibooʔ their chief
(70:11).

maruuʔnitu (v) beg.

maruʔokitu K (v) rake together. *See*
manuaru.

marubaru (v) crack something with
hands. *See* **marátubaitu.**

maruhnikatu (v) respect someone.

masiito (n) fingernail.

masitotsaru W (v) pinch (*lit* take
hold with the fingernail).

masiʔwaru (v) tear (by hand), *adj*
masikwaitu torn (by hand).

masuabetaitu (v) learn by
experience, know by experience.
See **suabetai.**

masukaaru (v) feel, touch (with the
hand) [ma- hand + suka- touch].

masutsaru (v) offer someone help.

masuyakeru (v) be tempted, suffer
temptation (by something one is
handling).

masuyuʔikaru K (v) tame an
animal, break a horse. **Tenahpuʔ
tsaʔ pu puuki masuyui.** The man
tamed his horse.

masuʔnaitu K (v) rub the wrong
way (as of fur). *See* **masuroonitu.**

masuʔneru (v) rub applying
pressure with the hands.

masuʔwaʔnekitu (v) dog paddle,
paddle water, waddle or move
clumsily. **Sarii masuʔwaʔnekitu.**
The dog is swimming (dog
paddling). *See* **paruhparu.**

masuapu W (n) home-grown garden
product.

masuaru W (v) raise garden
product.

masuroonitu W (v) rub the wrong
way (as of fur). *See* **masuʔnaitu.**

masusuʔnitu (v) numb the hand
[ma- hand + susuʔni numb]. *See*
tsasusuʔnikatu.

masɨwɨhki? (n) fingers (including thumb).

masɨwɨhki? W (n) middle finger. *See* **mahtɨpįnáa?.**

matsaaihkakurɨ (v) lead along (as horse or blind person). *See* **tsakami?arɨ.**

matsáapikaarɨ (v) pull to make noise (as a bell rope).

matsáhtsurɨ (v) squeeze hand.

matsákwɨnɨkɨrɨ (v) help up from sitting to standing position (by the hand).

matsarɨ W (v) grasp (with hand).

matsáyɨtsɨrɨ (v) help up (from lying to sitting position (by the hand).

matsíhtuyeetɨ P (v) comb someone's hair.

matsi?okwɨkatɨ (adj) hand gathered (as with a needle).

matsobokɨkatɨ (adj) rolled (by hand).

matsokatɨ (adj) held (in hand).

matsumarɨ (v) wipe.

matsuma? (n) cloth (piece of fabric).

matsurɨ (v) nudge, pinch.

matsɨkikatɨ (adj) tight (on the hand) [**ma-** hand + **tsɨki-** tight].

matsɨbakikatɨ (adj) glued, pasted, sealed.

matųwetų (v) limp (human, or front leg of animal). *See* **pitųwetɨ.**

matɨhwarɨ (v) open something (as a door).

matɨsohpe? (n) wildcat.

mawa- (pfx) feel around with hand. *See* **makwarɨ.**

mawaatsą (n) rib.

mawakatu (adv dem, prox) toward someone or something.

mawo?a?aiyu (n) cement.

mawɨmerɨ (v) hurt someone (make suffer).

mayaketɨ (v) play instrument (with hands) [**ma-** hand + **yake-** cry].

mayake? (n) piano.

mayɨ?yɨrɨ (v) hand jerk, hand twitch.

ma? (pro, 3rd prox nom sg) he, she, it. **Nɨ tohtɨkwai ma?.** He hit me.

ma?aikɨrɨ (v) row (as a boat), push something that rolls. *See* **wɨ?aikɨrɨ, tsi?aikɨrɨ.**

ma?itsa?bɨkatɨ (adj) cramped hand, paralyzed hand. *See* **sɨkwe tɨyai.**

ma?kwe?yarɨ (v) lose something from hand or wrist.

ma?nika? (n, arch) finger ring. *See* **mo?otsi?nika?.**

ma?nɨ sarii? (n) dachshund (*lit* short-legged dog).

ma?ohta?aitɨ (v) hill up (put soil around base of plant). *See* **wɨno?karɨrɨ.**

ma?okwerɨ (v) milk something, squeeze to a head (*lit* cause to flow, as a boil). *See* **tɨma?okwetɨ.**

ma?omerɨ (v) stir up fire.

ma?urarɨ (v) find something with the hand [**ma-** hand + **ura** find]. *See* **urarɨ.**

ma?wiitsa (n) wrist.

ma?wikarɨ, ma?wikerɨ (v) push, shove. *See* **wɨtsɨkitɨ.**

ma?witsohko (n) bracelet [**ma?wiitsa** wrist + **tsoohko** bead].

ma?wɨminarɨ (v) reach out and touch. *See* **wɨminarɨ.**

ma?wɨtsa ro?ponitɨ (v) have cramp in hand).

maʔyꭒkwiitꭒ (v) fix up, set up, doll up someone. *See* **namaʔyꭒkwitꭒ**.

maʔyꭒneetꭒ (v) entertain (make smile or laugh). **Ohnaʔa maʔyꭒneetꭒ u.** He made the baby laugh.

me, meh (quotative particle, indicates something spoken). **Surꭒkꭒseʔ ohaʔahnakatꭒ, 'Mꭒi nahubiyaaruʔi̱ nꭒʔ me urii niikwiiyꭒ.'** 'I'll sing for you,' said the coyote. (3:6).

meeku (adv time) right now. **Mee-ku takwꭒ nararꭒꭒna̱.** Now let us two run a race (9:8). *See* **kihtsiʔ**.

miakꭒrꭒ (v) run after, chase.

miakꭒtꭒ K (v) chase. **U miakꭒi, tꭒhꭒyabai.** He chased him on horseback.

miarꭒ, miʔarꭒ (v) go. **Ma piaʔ pꭒhi muhnehtsi miʔanꭒ.** His mother went leading them (81:9).

miibeʔtꭒ, miihbeʔtꭒ (adv loc) farther along, adv time temporarily.

miihtsi̱ (n) ankle.

miitꭒtsi̱, miihtsiʔ (adv loc) near, adv time soon, shortly. *See* **kemarꭒkwi̱sꭒ**.

mitsokokꭒkatꭒ (adj) sleepy.

mitsonaaʔ (n) southern hackberry. *Celtis laevigata* [Willd.]

mitꭒkoʔo (n) roof of mouth.

moha-, moha (adj) sour, bitter, acidic.

mohakamarꭒ (v) taste sour, bitter, acid.

mohatsi̱ (adv intens) very. **Mohatsi̱kuna sꭒsuatꭒ nꭒ.** I am very cold *See* **nohi**.

mohatsꭒkuekapitꭒ (adj) bright red.

mohtoʔa (n) K pimple; **mohtoʔa** W rash (red bumps on skin).

momꭒsaka (n) fire-tender in a peyote meeting.

monahpꭒʔ (n), *pl* **nonanꭒꭒ** son-in-law (DaHu, SbDaHu).

monꭒ ohni (n) tuberculosis.

mooka (n), *acc* **mooke** branch (of plant). **huupita mooka** tree branch.

mookꭒsꭒaitꭒ (v) branch out.

moonꭒʔꭒakatꭒ (adj) cancerous, chronic.

mootekwoʔpꭒ (n) sign language (*lit* hand talk).

moowiʔ (n) lariat (*lit* hand rope; made of plaited rawhide for roping).

MooʔwetꭒŢ (name) No-hand (person).

Mopai (name) Owl (person).

Mota, Tatseni (name) Lee Motah (b. Nov. 12, 1911).

motso sariiʔ (n) poodle (*lit* bearded dog).

motso taibooʔ (n) bearded white man.

motso̱, motso- (n) beard.

moyaʔitꭒ (v) slander (speak against someone).

moʔo (n), *acc* **moʔe** hand. **Nꭒ moʔe nꭒ matsukai.** I closed my hand.

moʔo huutsihkaʔaʔ (n) handsaw, ripsaw. *See* **huutsihkaaʔ**.

moʔo kwitꭒʔekaʔ K (n) hand lotion (*lit* hand ointment). *See* **makwꭒrꭒʔekaʔ**.

moʔo narꭒso (n) glove (*lit* hand sack).

moʔo rꭒbooʔ (n) typewriter (*lit* hand writer).

moʔo tsaaitꭒ (v) hold hands.

mo?o tsi?nika? (n, modern) finger ring. *See* **ma?nika?.**

mo?o wuhtamaru (v) hobble an animal, handcuff a person.

mo?o wuhtama? (n) a hobble (tied on animal).

mo?obe? (num) five. **Suru kuse? mo?obe?kaa u mi?a?i tomonu.** That one went for five years (85:3).

Mo?pi tsokopu (name) Old-owl (former Comanche chief).

mu-, mubi (n) nose. *See* **muhbi.**

mubitai, mu?bitai, mu?bitai huuhpi (n) walnut. *Juglans regia* L. (nuts eaten, leaves used to treat ringworm).

mubi po?roo ruhkapu W (n) pork (*lit* pig meat). *See* **po?ro ruhkapu.**

mubi po?roo ruhtuma? W (n) hog fence.

mubi po?roo? (n) pig, hog.

mubi po?ro?a po?aa W (n) pork rind.

mubi sarii? (n) greyhound (*lit* nose dog).

mubisitu (v) blow the nose. **Keta?-ka mubisituu.** Don't blow your noses (127:7). *See* **wumupusitu.**

mubi tsoo?nitu (v) suck (as on candy; *lit* draw up the nose).

mubi tsoo?ni? (n) candy sucker. *See* **mukwite?.**

mubohtohkipu (n) bubble, balloon.

mubohtohkiru (v) inflate (as a balloon). *See* **pohtokuru.**

mubohtohkitu (v) inflate (form bubbles). *See* **pohtohkitu.**

mubora?itu (v) bud.

mubutsaakatu (n) bloom (*lit* blown up, burst).

muhasuaru, muhakatsu?aitu K, **muhabuni** W (v) frown.

muhatsi (adj) bright. **Muhatsiku kupitakatu.** The light is bright.

muhbi, muubi, mubi, mu- (n) nose.

muhibitu (v) inhale deeply through nose, breathe through nose.

muhkaru W (v) hook something.

muhnemi?aru (v) lead others (as horse leads other horses).

muhnetu, muuneru (v) proceed ahead, precede someone (be in the lead).

muhpe? (n) hoe (heavy type). **Suruu wa?ihpuanuu puu muhpe?ma?ai paakuhu weenu.** Those women went down in the water with their hoes (127:6). *See* **to?tsimuhpe?.**

muhpoo kahni wanapu K, **muh-poo wanapu** W (n) mosquito net.

muhraa?ipu, muhraipu (n) kiss.

muhraru (v) kiss someone.

muhwitu K (v) throw with nose or mouth. *See* **mukwubuaru.**

muhyu nakwu (n) east (cardinal direction) [**muhyu** doorway + **nakwu** direction] (Comanche dwellings were traditionally oriented to face the rising sun).

muhyu (n) doorway. **Surukwu uhru kahni muhyuhkutu ku?inubuni.** Those two were roasting much out from their teepee door (105:23). *See* **namuhyu, natsahtuma?.**

mukuhparu W (v) gore someone.

mukwihteru (v) suck on something (one time).

mukwite? (n) lollypop, candy sucker. *See* **mubitsoo?ni?.**

mukwo (n voc) husband. *See* **kwuuhtukatu.**

Mukwooru (name) Spirit-talker (civil chief who attended the San Antonio Council House meeting in 1840).

mukwubuaru W (v) throw with nose or mouth. *See* **muhwitu.**

mukwuru W, **mukwutikuru** K (v) gore, butt (as with horns).

mumutsi?, muumutsi? (n) soap-weed, yucca, beargrass (roots used as soap and to cure ulcers). *Yucca louisianensis* Trelease.

munaikiyutu W (v) be ahead of. **Sarii tsa? tenahpu? munaiki-yutu.** The dog is in front of the man.

munakuaitu (v) poke out nose [**mu-** nose + **na-** (refl) + **kua** come out].

munakwu (adv loc) ahead, in front of. **Sarii tsa? tenahpu? muna-kwu.** The dog is ahead of the man.

munua? (n) hog, pig (*lit* moves something with nose). *See* **po?ro?.**

muparai habinitu K, **muhpa?a-raitu** W (adj) lying face-downward, lying in prone position.

mupitsi (n) giant (mythical hero).

mupitsuha pisahpi W, **mupitsa-pisahpi** K (n fungus) mushroom, puffball, devil's snuffbox.

mupitsuha tunowapi W (n) camel (*lit* giant packhorse).

mupihabiitu (adj) bent over.

mupihabiru (v) bend over (as a tree limb).

Mura hunu?bi (n) Pease River (*lit* mule creek).

Mura kwitapu (name) Mule-dung (former Comanche chief).

murora?ipu W, **muruhrapu** K (n) bud of a plant or tree.

muruahwunuru (v) point out something (with lower lip or chin).

murukaru (v) extinguish (blow out), quench a fire.

muru?itu (v) overflow. **Hunu?bi tsa? muru?i.** The creek overflowed. *See* **paru?itu.**

musasuaru (v) worry (be concerned). *See* **pisukwitaru.**

musoopitu (v) suck on body to draw out pain (as traditionally practiced by Comanche healers).

mutsi- (pfx) point, pointed.

mutsikwà?aa? (n) mosquito (*lit* pointed thing that awkwardly flaps wings).

mutsi atsamukwe? (n) wild grape (winter variety). *See* **natsamukwe?.**

mutsikuni, mutsikahni (n) wigwam (made of curved sticks) [**mutsi** point + **kahni** house].

mutsimuhpe? (n) pick (a tool; *lit* pointed hoe).

mutsipu (n) sharp-pointed object (as an ice pick).

mutsiwahtu, mutsikwahtu (adj) dull (unpointed).

mutsonoo?itu (v) pull someone's beard.

mutsu?itu (v), *pl* **mutsi?itu** dive (as into water).

mutusiberu (v) shave someone.

muunanahwenuru W, **muuna-hweru** K (v) hoot (as an owl).

muura? (n) mule.

muutsi, mutsi- (n) point (tapering end). *See* **puha kahni muutsi.**

muu yakenitu (v) moo (as a cow) [**muu** moo + **yake** cry].

muuyaketʉ (v) make music, play a wind instrument. *See* **yaketʉ, muyakeʔ**.

muwainitʉ K (v) root around (as a hog). *See* **ahwenitʉ**.

muwarʉ W (v) follow scent, smell around (as a dog does). *See* **ʉkwisʉʔninitʉ**.

muwoʔneʔ (n) termites [**mu-** nose + **woʔne-** make holes]. *See* **wobi muwoʔneʔ**.

muyakeʔ (n) music of any kind, sounding of a horn. *See* **muuyaketʉ**.

muyʉʉʔwʉrʉ (v) bend over [**mu-** head + **yʉʉwʉ-** go down].

muʔibuikʉrʉ (v) fill up (*lit* to the mouth fill up, as to fill a bucket).

muʔkwipunaʔ (n) elephant (ref. to trunk).

muʔwoo (n) grown man, adult male.

muʔyanesuarʉ (v) grin, smile [**mu-** mouth + **yahne-** laugh + **sua-** feel].

mʉa (n) moon, month.

mʉahtabebaʔitʉ (adj) have moonlight.

mʉakatʉ (n) moonlight.

mʉarʉboopʉ (n) calendar (*lit* month paper).

mʉhʉ (pro, 2nd gen du) of you two.

mʉi (pro, 2nd acc pl) you. **Hakani mʉi naahkaku maʔ paroʔikitʉ.** As you (pl) were continuing, somehow the water rose (122:15).

mʉkwʉ, mʉhʉ (pro, 2nd nom du) you two. **Hina mʉkwʉ?** What do you two (want)?

mʉmi (pro, 2nd acc pl) you.

mʉmʉ, mʉʉ (pro, 2nd gen pl) your. **Mʉmʉmaʔai nʉʔ pisikwa-nuuʔii.** I slid with you (pl).

mʉnitʉ (v) unable (though willing and agreeable). **Pʉʉ muhyi urʉʉ mʉninʉ.** They were unable to do (open) their door (4:17).

mʉnʉ, mʉnʉ (pro, 2nd nom pl) you. **Mʉnʉkia nʉkʉbʉni?** Are you (pl) dancing? (3:4).

mʉroʔitʉ (v) bob up.

mʉʉ (pro, 2nd gen pl) your. **mʉʉ hipʉ** your things. *Also* **mʉmʉ**.

mʉʉrʉ (v) do to, treat, control someone. **Hakani ʉ mʉʉruʔi?** What shall I do with you?

mʉʉrʉʔikatʉ (v) feel pity. **Tʉtaa marii mʉʉrʉʔikatʉ mʉ.** I feel pity for them.

mʉʉwarʉʔitʉ (v) perplexed (not knowing what to do with something).

N

na- (pfx, reflexive).

naabaitʉ, naahbaihtʉ (num) six.

naabia, nahbiʔa (n) male kinsman.

naahábitʉ (v), *pl* **naahkwabika-** continue lying down.

naahkarʉ (v) hire, continue doing something.

naanaarʉ, nahnaarʉ (v) grow in height and health.

naape (n) foot, lower leg. *See* **nape-**.

nabaa (n) oil, gasoline. *See* **naʔbukuwàaʔ nábaa, nahyʉ**.

nabaai tokwaaitʉ (n) oil well [**nabaa** oil + **tokwaaitʉ** looked for in ground]. *See* **tukaʔanabaa**.

nabaaka (n) bullet [**na-** (refl) + **paaka** arrow].

nabakʉtʉ (v) commit suicide.

Nabakwuhtiapu (n), *pl*
Nabakwuhti- apunuu Christian,
baptized one.

nabana?aitu (adj) conceited.

nabatai K (n) tributary, creek
branch. *See* **atahunubi.**

nabawuhtiaru (v) immerse oneself
in water.

nabehkakuru (v, sg obj), *pl obj*
nakwusukuru cause to be
killed.

nabihtawuna (n) beginning, start.

nabikapu (n) leather, leather
harness (*lit* leather item).

nabimaru (adj) covered (having a
cover).

nabinai tuboopu (n) deed or title to
land.

nabinaihkatu (adj) chosen.

nabinaru (v) choose, pick out.

nabina?etu (v) save, store away.

nabiso?aru (v) puncture oneself
with something.

nabitukuru (v) war, battle with
weapons.

nabitubunitu (v) look behind
oneself.

nabi?aaikunakaru K, nabi?aiku?
W (n) rocking chair.

nabi?atsikatu (adj) taboo.

naboo-, nabooru (adj) marked,
striped, spotted.

naboohmatusohpe? W (n) leopard
(*lit* spotted wildcat). *See* **nabooh
toyaruhku?, toyaruhku?.**

naboohmura? (n) zebra (*lit* striped
mule).

Naboohnuu (n) Navaho people;
Athapascans (former enemies of
the Comanches).

naboohroya ruhku? K (n) leopard
(*lit* carrying spots underneath).

See **toya ruhku?, nabooh
matusohpe?.**

Naboohroya? N (n) Navaho
Mountain (named after the
Navaho people).

naboopu (n) picture [**na-** (refl) +
poo- write].

naboopuha naro?nika? (n) picture
frame [**naboopu** picture + **-ha**
(acc) + **na-** (refl) + **to?nikaa-**
put away].

naboopuha naruso (n) picture
frame [**naboopu** picture + **-ha**
(acc) + **naruso** sack].

naboopuha pukurato?nika?i? (n)
picture frame.

naboo? K (n) pencil, marking
instrument. *See* **tuboo?.**

nabo? (n) marking.

nabo?aa W (n) shingle, siding,
covering.

nabuihwunutu W, nabui?wunetu
K (v) examine oneself, check over
one's appearance.

nabunitu (v) look at oneself, appear
(as to dress) [**na-** (refl) + **puni**
see]. **Nohi? tsaa nabuniyu nuu.** I
look very nice (32:12).

nabuni? (n) mirror, looking glass
[**na-** (refl) + **puni-** see].

nabusa? (n) chain.

nabusi?aketu (v) delouse (look for
head lice on one another).

nabusa nabikapu, nabusa
narumuhku (n) harness (chain)
[**nabusa?** chain + **narumuhku**
harness].

nabusi?aipu (n) dream.

nabusi?aitu (v) dream.

nabuesu (adv time) early (ahead of
time). **Nabuesu namaka? muki!**
Get ready ahead of time!

nabɨkapɨ W, nɨpɨkapɨ K, N (n) grave, burial mound.

nagwee, naʔwée? (n) ford, river crossing. *See* **puʔe nagwe.**

nah (adv) just. **Tanɨwitsa nah paakɨhu ma wihinɨ.** We should just throw him in the water (16:20).

naha-, nah- (pfx, reciprocal) with each other, together.

nahabitɨtɨ (v) come onto someone, happen to be somewhere.

nahamuhkɨ K (n) safety pin, diaper pin, pin. *See* **naʔhɨmuhkɨ.**

nahaniitɨ (v), *pl* **nayɨkwiitɨ** continue, go along. **Suni urii nayɨkwibɨniku, ɨ Oha ahnakatɨ ɨrɨɨkɨ bitɨnɨ.** They continued much that way; Coyote arrived among them (3:3).

nahapɨ (n) happening, event.

naharɨ (v) happen, become, continue (*lit* how did you become?). **Hakani ɨnɨ nahánɨ?** What happened to you? (6:14).

nahawaruʔikatɨ (adj) needy, hard up.

nahayaʔni (adv compar) worse (when previously not too bad). **Nahayaʔni ma nɨsukatɨ.** She is getting worse.

nahimiitɨ (v) exchange gifts (give gifts to each other).

nahkabaʔitɨ (adj) rejected, refused (said of a person).

nahkɨepɨ K (n) stingy person.

nahkɨsuaberɨ (v) understand someone.

nahmakutɨ (v) compare one thing with another.

nahmaʔai (adv) together (with each other).

nahnamiʔarɨ (v, anim subj) grow.

nahnapɨ (n), *pl* **nanɨnapɨrɨɨ** eldest child, grown son or daughter, adult kinsman.

nahnia (n) name.

nahnia makarɨ (v) name someone. *See* **nihakɨrɨ, makaarɨ.**

nahnɨmiitɨ (v) walk around. **Nɨʔ nahnɨmiitɨ.** I have been walking around.

nahohiyaitɨ (v) hurt oneself. *See* **namarɨnitɨ, nahuhyaitɨ.**

nahorapɨ (n) hole dug by man.

nahotsaʔmaʔ, nahotsaʔamaʔ (n) horse blanket, saddle blanket.

nahoʔyopɨkurɨ (v) mark inexactly (slightly above or below the proper mark).

nahuahtsitɨ, nahutsitɨ W (n) sigh. *See* **nasuawɨhkitɨ.**

nahúbiniitɨ (v) groan. **Surɨkɨseʔ wihnu nahubiniiyɨ.** Then that one was groaning (5–6:12).

nahubiyaarɨ (v) sing a song for someone. **Mɨi nahubiyaaruʔi nɨʔ.** I will sing for you (pl) (3:6).

nahuhyaitɨ W (v) hurt oneself. *See* **nahohiyaitɨ, namarɨnitɨ.**

nahuuʔ W, nahhooʔ K (n) knife, drawing knife.

nahɨyatɨ, naʔɨyatɨ N (adj) sloping, slanting.

nahweakutɨ W (v) burn oneself.

nahyemiʔarɨ (v) go live with in-laws.

nahyɨ (n) oil. *See* **naʔbukuwàʔa nahyɨ.**

naiya (adv time) often, frequently.

naiʔbi, naiʔpi N (n) young woman (to about fifteen years old).

nakaaʔaitɨ, nakaʔaitɨ (adj) false, hypocritical.

nakabarʉ (v) reject a person.
nakahanupʉ W (n) unfriendliness.
See **kwetʉsapʉ**.

nai?bi

nakamabitsiahkatʉ (adj) attentive
(paying attention).
nakarʉ W (v) hear. *See* **tʉnakarʉ**.
nakarʉ? W (n) chair. *See*
wobinakarʉ?.
nakarʉ?karʉ (v) sit down.
nakatsʉhetʉ, nakatseetʉ (v) smoke
ritually (to seek medicine).
nakị (n) ear.
nakị hiikatʉ K (v) heed, listen with
attention.
nakị kwiitạ (n) K back part of ear
cartilage; W ear lobe.
nakị oonạ (n) ear wax (*lit* ear salt).
nakị sarii? (n) hound dog (*lit* ear
dog).
nakị tai?, nakị tóone N (n) lizard
(long variety; *lit* large earholes).
nakị toonʉkatʉ K, **nakị
toona** N (n) pierced ear. *See*
nanakịtonapʉ.
nakị tsa?nika? (n) earring (*lit*
entered into the ear).
nakị wʉnʉkatʉ (adj) have an earache.
nakkuminoorʉ (v) somersault. *See*
anikwitami?arʉ.

**nakkʉtaba?i, na?kʉtabai huuhpi,
na?kʉta?i? huuhpị** (n) pecan.
Carya illinoensis [Wang.] **K.
Koch.** (nuts eaten, leaves used
in treating ringworm and also as
black stain [C & J]).
nakobe matsuma? (n) face towel
[**na-** (refl) + **kobe** face +
matsuma? wiper].
nakobe tsa?nika? (n) halter
[**na-** (refl) + **kobe** face +
tsa?nikatʉput down].
nakohpoopʉ K (n) brand
(identifying animal's owner).
nakohpoopʉ W (n) printed material.
nakohtóo? (n) stove (*lit* possession
for fire).
nakoo?ipʉ (n) pieces (anything cut
into pieces, as dried fruit or nuts)
[**na-** (refl) + **koo?i** cut + **-pʉ**
(nom)].
nakuhkwarakitʉ (v) steam bathe
(take a steam bath).
nakuhkwaraki? K (n) sweat bath,
steam bath (steam made by
throwing water on hot rocks).
nakutịsị, nakutʉsị (n) gunpowder.
nakutʉkʉna? (n) heated rock (used
like heating pad to ease pain).
nakuyaarʉ (n) grass fire, prairie
fire, fire.
nakʉahkatʉ (adj) protruding.
nakʉakitʉ (v) appear (come in
sight, become visible).
nakʉhkuparʉ (v) eat oneself to
death, drink oneself to death.
nakʉmʉʉ?etʉ W (adj) turned.
nakʉhitʉ (v) listen. *See* **tʉnakiitʉ**.
nakʉhoorʉ (v) eavesdrop,
overhear.
nakʉhoowaaitʉ (n) eavesdropper,
sneaky person.

nakᵤkatᵤ (adj) attentive, listening.

nakᵤnikatᵤ waikina̱, nakᵤni waikina̱ (n) covered wagon (*lit* wagon made into a home).

nakᵤnᵤᵤʔmaitᵤ (adj) discouraged, tired of something. *See* **narahtokwetᵤ, manᵤᵤʔmai.**

nakᵤwiyakᵤrᵤ K (v) burn oneself.

nakwiita̱ (n) saucer [**na-** (refl) + **kwiita̱** bottom].

nakwᵤsi tsaʔnikaʔ (n) saddle strap (*lit* that which is put on the tail; flank girth, passes under tail of horse).

nakwᵤsipᵤ (n) dried pumpkin (dried and braided for winter use) [**na-** (refl) + **kwᵤsipᵤ** braided].

nakwᵤsiʔ (n) pumpkin.

nakwᵤsᵤkᵤrᵤ (v, pl) kill several persons. *See* **nabehkakᵤrᵤ.**

namabeʔahkapᵤ (n) part (in the hair).

namabimarᵤ (v) put away, hide something (put food in oven).

namabitsiapᵤ (n) care for oneself.

namabitsooni sonihpᵤ (n) mesquite weed. *Leguminoseae.*

namabitsooʔni (n) mesquite. *Prosopis glandulosa* Torr. (meal from pods eaten; leaves used to neutralize stomach acidity [C & J]; wash mesquite and make sugar from it, mixing with patsokwe; mixture is called patso). *See* **wohiʔhuu, natsohkweʔ.**

namabunitᵤ (v) practice something.

namahkaʔmukitᵤ (adj) complete, prepared. *See* **namakaʔmukitᵤ.**

namahkiapᵤ W (n) cut on hand.

namahku (n), acc namahkui, *acc pl* **namahkunii** clothes (any wearing apparel), household goods, personal belongings.

namahtowᵤnarᵤ (v, sg obj), *pl obj* **namahtowᵤniʔitᵤlean** something. **Huunaroʔiʔ maktu namaahtowᵤnᵤka̱.** A ladder stood leaning along it.

namahyaʔ (n) baking powder.

namakaʔmukitᵤ (v) prepare oneself (get oneself ready). **Meekuka namakaʔmuki̱.** Now everyone get ready (70:11–12). *See* **namahkaʔmukitᵤ.**

namakupakᵤrᵤ (v) work someone to death.

namakupᵤkatᵤ (adj) overworked, worked to death.

namakᵤmaʔaipᵤ (n) sharpened item.

namakᵤnᵤmapᵤ (n) tired person, sore person.

namakwatubiitᵤ (v) fold over, wrap, roll up. *See* **tahkwatúubitᵤ, tᵤmakwatᵤbiʔetarᵤ.**

namakweyaipᵤ (n) exhausted person or animal.

namaminaitᵤ (v) sprain or break hand or lower arm.

namamiʔakᵤ (interj, byword) That's life!

namamohkarᵤ, nanomohkarᵤ (adj) hitched (as animals).

namamᵤsurᵤ (v) prohibit.

namanahkeetᵤ W (v) parade (as Native Americans went from camp to camp in full dress before leaving on a trip). *See* **wᵤhabitᵤ.**

namanahkitᵤ (v) measure oneself.

namanakwᵤ K (adv loc) separated by great distance.

namanoke (interj, byword) It is worse!

namanuhkitʉ (v), *pl* **namanuraarʉ** run away afraid, flee from.

namaroʔihkatʉ (n) discarded thing.

namaroʔitʉ (v) discard something, escape from somewhere (get rid of something). *See* **tsahwitʉ**.

namarunehtsʉrʉ, namarunetsʉ (v) run to something through fear, flee from.

namarʉkapʉ (n) finished item.

namarʉnitʉ K (v) hurt oneself, to wound. *See* **nahohiyaitʉ, nahuhyaitʉ**.

namaʔabʉ (n), *pl* **namaʔʉbʉnʉʉ-mʉ** sickly person. *See* **kenama ʔʉbʉʔitʉ**.

namaʔyʉkwitʉ (v) primp. *See* **maʔyʉkwiitʉ**.

namewatsʉkwitʉ (num) eight.

nami?

nami? (n) younger sister.

namotʉsibetʉ, namutʉsibe (v) shave oneself.

namotʉsibeʔ (n) handkerchief (*lit* nose wiper).

namoʔo kotsetʉ (v) wash hand.

namoʔo matsumaʔ (n) napkin [**moʔo** hand + **matsuma** wipe].

namuhkarʉ (v) fasten on harness.

namuhyʉ (n) doorway. *See* **muhyʉ, natsahtʉmaʔ**.

namutsonoʔitʉ (v) pull own beard.

namutsoraʔ (n) bridle bit (*lit* object held in mouth).

namuwoo, namʉwoo (n, arch) husband.

namʉsuʔnetʉ (v) rub hands together.

namʉnewapi (n) leader, important man.

namʉsi (adv) hurriedly, quickly. **Namʉsi kohtoohtsika tai maaka.** Quickly making us a fire, feed us (85:9).

namʉsi buhihwi tekwapʉ (n) telegram (*lit* quick money word).

namʉsohi, namʉsoi (adv time) immediately, right now.

namʉsohitʉ (v) hurry up (make haste). **Namʉsohiika!** Hurry up! (85:11).

namʉsokoopʉ (n) buried person or thing.

namʉsoapʉ (n) clothing, apparel.

namʉsoarʉ (v) change clothes, dress (get dressed).

nana- (pfx) through, throughout.

nanáarʉmuʔi tʉboopʉ (n) story- book [**na-** (refl) + **narʉmuʔipʉ** tell story + **tʉboo** paper]. *See* **narʉmuʔi tʉboopʉ**.

nanaarʉʉmoa (adj) marvelous, wonderful.

nanabuni saawʉʔ (n) window screen.

nanabuni tsahparaʔ (n) window blind.

nanabuni wanapʉ K (n) curtain (*lit* window cloth).

nanabuni wanatsahparaʔ W (n) curtain (*lit* window cloth spread out).

nanabuni? (n) window [**nana-** through + **buni** see].

nanahbiso?aitụ (adv) slow-moving.

nanahtenanʉʉ (n) menfolk, husbands.

nanakatso?arʉ (v) splice (*lit* do through the end).

nanakịtonapụ (n) pierced ear (*lit* pierced through). *See* **nakị- toonʉkatụ.**

nanakukʉtʉ (v) judge (*lit* talk through in behalf of).

nanakuya?arʉ (adj) fearful, odd, queer, strange (*lit* scared through; said of people).

nanakụhurʉ (v) gamble (*lit* burned through). *See* **wanarohpetitʉ.**

nanakwʉʉhtʉ (v) marry each other (get married). **Nanakwʉʉhtu?i urʉ.** They are getting married.

nanakwʉʉrʉ (v) marry someone (perform the marriage ceremony).

nanakwụhʉ W, **nanakwụnʉkwụ** K (n) married couple.

nanamʉ?aitʉ K, **nanamʉanoorʉ** W (v) stall (delay oneself).

nanamụsu? (n) in-law.

nananịsuyake (adj, pl) pretty.

nananʉʉ?maitʉ (v) tire oneself, exhaust oneself (become exhausted). *See* **narahkupaitʉ.**

nanapunipụ (n) footprint. *See* **napụ, narapunipụ.**

nanarʉna?itʉ (v, arch) run a race.

nanawatsikarʉ (v) misunderstand statement. *See* **kenanawatsitʉ.**

nanawa?ihpʉ?anii (n, acc pl) women.

nanawa?ihpʉ?anʉ W (n), *acc pl* **na?kwa?ihpʉ?a** womenfolk (man speaking).

nana?atahpu na?ha? rʉʉpị (n) diamond (*lit* different flashes rock).

nana?atanaikị, nana?atahpoto K (adv dir) from different directions.

nana?ataputụ (adj) different kinds. *See* **nanịsusumatụ.**

Nana?butitʉikatụ mʉa (n) March (*lit* hot-or-cold month).

nana?isa nayʉkwi tʉkwụ (v) flirt with each other.

nanihkanuitʉ (v) clear throat.

nanihkuparʉ (v), *pl* **nanihtokwe-** laugh heartily.

naníhpana?aitʉ (v) boast, brag on oneself. *See* **nihpana?aitụ.**

nanihpu?e?aikʉpụ K (n) pact, treaty, tradition. *See* **pu?e?aikʉpụ.**

naníhtsawa?itʉ (v) ask for help, request something. *See* **nigwaitụ.**

nanihtʉbinitʉ (v) ask permission.

nanika?witʉ (v) meet to suggest something.

nanimaa?ʉbʉ?ikʉtʉ (v) ask, plead, beseech.

nanina?ukitʉ (v) rejoice verbally.

nanipu?e?aitʉ, nani?atsiitʉ (v) make an agreement or contract). **Nʉmʉnʉʉ paraibonʉi ʉ?aii nanipu?e?aitʉ.** The Comanches made an agreement with the government.

nanípʉka (n) guess-over-the-hill (game played by boys).

nanitsʉwakatụ K (adj) quarrelsome, argumentative.

naniyo?naitʉ K (v) riot (have a commotion).

nani?emʉahpʉ aitʉ (v) blaspheme (say what one does not mean).

nani?ookitʉ (v) try (bring to trial as in court).

nani?ookị taiboo? (n) lawyer (*lit* trial white man).

nani?uru?aitu (v) counsel, advise. *See* **tusu?uru?**.

nani?wiketu W (v) quarrel, argue. **Nani?wiketu marukwu.** They are arguing.

nani?yusukaitu W (n) commotion.

nanisuabeta?aitu (v) introduce oneself (make oneself known). *See* **natsahpunitu**.

nanisusumatu (adj) different kinds. *See* **nana?ataputu**.

nanisutaikutu (v) intercede, pray for someone.

nanisutaitu, nanusutai (v) pray.

nanisuwukaitu (n) spirit, marvel, miracle.

nanisuwukaitu (adj) spirited, marvelous, wonderful (having a spirit). *See* **suyoro?akapu**.

nanohmunu wapi K (n) officer, leader.

nanoomanitu (v) harness something (as an animal).

nano?onai (adv dir) from all directions.

nanusutsawaitu (adj) faithful.

nanuuhtupuka? (n) buckle, button, hook. *See* **natsweni?**.

nanuwoku (n) payment of damages (usually paid in horses, guns, blankets, or clothing in the old days).

nanuso?iitu W, **nanuso?otu** K (adj) busy.

nanusu?uyaatu (adj) laughingstock, ridiculous.

naparukitu (v) soak oneself in water.

napatawi?aitu (adj) wornout (shoes).

napiso?aitu (adj) slow [**na-** (refl) + **piso-** angry + **ai-** made to be].

napisaru (v) paint oneself, make up oneself (apply make-up).

napiso?akatu (adj) punctured (by object, in buttocks area).

napu-, nape- (pfx) ref. to foot and lower leg, shoes. *See* **naape**.

napu (n) shoe, footprint, trail. *See* **nanapunipu**.

napu makaru (v) give away moccasins.

napu narawuna? (n) shoe nail [**napu** shoe + **na-** (refl) + **roobuna?** stake].

napu rahpaana (n) shoe sole [**napu** shoe + **tahpaana** sole]. *See* **narahpaana**.

napu rurawuna? (n) shoe nail [**napu** shoe + **turawuna?** nail].

napu ru?eka? (n) shoe polish [**napu** shoe + **tu?eka?** paint].

napu saaru (adj) laced, strung.

napu soona (n) floor (*lit* shoe quilt).

napu tsakwusa? (n) shoelace, shoestring [**napu** shoe + **tsakwusa?** string].

napubosaru (v) fasten with shoelace.

napubosa? (n) shoehook, shoelace.

napuhu (n) trail.

napuhu mi?aru (v) trail (follow a trail closely).

nara- (pfx) ref. to foot or lower leg.

naraaiku? (n) bicycle (*lit* item for feet to make lope). *See* **ta?aikutu**.

narabee?aitu (v) take an oath.

narabu (n, voc) old man (familiar joking term).

narahka?witu (v) congregate, gather together. *See* **uhoika?wutu**.

narahki?apu (n) a cut on the foot, foot wound.

narahkooni wapi W (n) shepherd.

narahkupaitu (v) exhaust oneself, give up. *See* **nananui u?maitu.**

narahpaana (n) shoe sole. *See* **napurahpaana.**

narahpana? (n) tire (of wheel).

narahpomi?itu (adj) (divided into groups.

narahpunipu (n) footwear tried on, attempt (anything).

narahtokwetu (adj) discouraged, downhearted. *See* **nakunuu?-maitu, ai?bihinuusukatu.**

narahtsukikatu, narahtsukikatu (adj) crowded together (as people in a room).

narahtukii? (n) stirrup (*lit* item to put foot in). *See* **ta?nika?.**

naraketorootu (n) haircut (hair cut short).

narakotseru (v) wash feet.

narakwusakatu napu, narakwisa napi (n) cowboy boots.

naraminaitu K (v) sprain ankle.

naraminaitu W (v) break at joint of foot.

narapunipu (n) footprint. *See* **nanapunipu, napu.**

nararunaru (v) gamble over some type of competition. **Meeku takwu maba?atu nararuuna.** Now let us two run a race over it (to see who will win) (9:8).

narawekwi kahni (n) jail, prison.

narawuhtama? (n) garter (*lit* item one ties on the leg).

narayaakupu (n) pound (unit of weight).

narayaakuru (v) weigh something.

narayaaku? (n) scale (for weighing).

nara?okatu (adj) bunched up, pounded, dried.

nara?uraitu (v) meet, encounter someone.

nara?urakutu (v) learn, find out for oneself.

nara?woru K (v) scratch, rub with foot (as to relieve itch).

narenahpu? (n), *pl* **nanahtenanuu** man's male kinsman.

nariso?aru W (v) give an enema (insert something into rectum).

narohkwuri?etu (adj) spilled.

narohparu (v) fight hand-to-hand, wrestle.

narohtsanaru (adj) hanging, hung up.

narohtuma? (n) can, lid, canned goods.

narominaitu (v) break at joint of body (as elbow or knee).

naromunitu (v) lack (run short of something), outrun someone.

naropusaru (adj), *pl* **naropusi?i** beaded.

naro?ikahni K (n) bathroom (*lit* defecating house).

naro?itu (v) defecate.

naro?i? (n) ladder, stairs.

naro?toneetsi? (n) throwing arrows (up to distance of two hundred yards).

Narua, Nadua (n) Cynthia Ann Parker (white girl captured by Comanches in 1836; after being taken back to the whites, she died grieving for her Comanche family).

narubunitu (v) run a race.

naruituahkaru (v) help one another.

narureru (v) stretch arms or body (as when one has been sitting for a long period).

narutsa?i (n, voc) old lady (husband's term for wife).

naruahweru (v) confess (tell on oneself).

naruahwuku (n) bride.

narubahkaru , naruba?eru (v) bet on something.

narubuni?etu? (n) racer (person who races).

naruhkapu (n) partly eaten food.

naruhka? (n) groceries.

naruhka?ruaru, naruhka?rumuu (v) buy or otherwise receive groceries.

naruhka? sokoobi (n) vegetable garden. *See* **tumusua sokobi.**

naruhka?tsu?maru (v) run out of groceries.

narukitu (adj), *pl* **naruni?i** placed, put in place.

narukuyunapu (n) tale, fairy story. *See* **narumu?ipu.**

narukuyunu ruboopu (n) history (*lit* story on paper).

narumakaru (v) pay with money.

naruma?eru (v) exchange.

Narumi? (name) Lord, Master (name used for deity).

narumuhku (n) bridle reins, harness.

narumu?ikatu (v) tell, relate. **Ma haitsinii nu narumu?ikatu.** I am telling his friends. *See* **tu?aweru.**

narumu?ipu (n) story, tale. *See* **narukuyunapu.**

narumu?i tuboopu (n) newspaper, storybook. *See* **nanáarumu?i tuboopu.**

narumuuru (v) trade, sell to one another, exchange. **Pu oyoru? ma narumuuru.** They are selling their clothes to one another.

narumuu? (n) town, store.

narunoo bapi, narunoo paapi (n) saddle horn.

narunookatu unuu (n) camel [**narunookatu** have a saddle + **unuu** animal].

narunoo? (n) packsaddle.

narunoo? namuku (n) saddle strap (that which passes around the girth).

narunoo?ro?yaru, (v) *pl* **narunoo? roo?itu** (v) unsaddle a horse.

narunoo?rukitu (v), *pl* **narunoo? tahni?ru** saddle up.

narurunitu (v, arch) hold races.

naru?ekaru (v) massage, apply medicine. **Natusu?u naru?ekai nu.** I rubbed medicine (on him). *See* **mabararu.**

naru?uyapu (adj) mean, dangerous.

naru?uyu kuhtsuni? (n) typhoid fever (*lit* dangerous fever).

naru?uyu tasi?a (n) smallpox (*lit* dangerous spots).

naru?uyu uu?a? (n) chronic sore, cancer, lesion.

naruso, naruso (n) bag, sack.

naruso?ipu (n) tanned hide, process of tanning a hide.

nasaanuto?itu (v) rust, rust out; *adj* rusted, rusted out.

nasaapu (n) boiled food.

nasaa?wu? K (n) screen door.

nasaa?wu? W (n) bedspring, window screen.

nasanopi K, nasaanuto?ipu W (n) rust.

naséka (n) persimmon. *Diospyros virginiana* L. (fruit eaten fresh or dried).

nasiyuuki? (n), **kahni si?yuki** roofing shingles [**na-** (refl) + **si?yuki?** overlap].

nasuawʉhkitʉ K (v) sigh, breathe deeply while awake. *See* **nahuahtsitʉ, ʉsuaketʉ.**

nasukoo?i kahni (n) sweathouse [**nasukoo?i** sweat + **kahni** house].

nasukoo?itʉ (v) steam bathe (take a sauna, sweat bath).

nasukoo?i? (n) sweat bath, sauna.

nasupetipʉ K (n) faithful person, dependable person. *See* **nasutsawaitʉ.**

nasupetitʉ (v) hope in, depend on someone.

nasupeti? (n) hope.

nasupʉ K (n) ground up object. *See* **tusupʉ.**

nasutamakʉrʉ W (v) remind someone.

nasutamʉ habitʉ (v) rest pensively, lie down and think.

nasutamʉ wʉminaitʉ K (v) break a bone.

nasutamʉ wʉminaitʉ W (v) fall short.

nasutamʉkatʉ tamai, nasutamarʉ (v) think about something, remember. *See* **sukwʉkitʉ.**

nasutarʉ (v) surrender, give up.

nasutsa akwarʉ K (v) show off, act pretentious. **Iima nʉ? nasutsa akwatu?i.** I am going to show off with this.

nasutsarʉ (v) display (show off something).

nasutsawaitʉ W (adj) faithful, dependable. *See* **nasupetipʉ.**

nasuwatsi (v) lose something.

nasuwatsipʉ (adj) forgotten.

nasuwatsirʉ (v) forget. **Nʉ nisuwatsipʉha nʉ ninʉsutamakʉbʉni.** You (pl)

remind me a lot of the one I had forgotten (8:43).

nasuwʉhkitʉ (v) lose faith in someone.

nasuyaketʉ (v) covet, wish for, lust for, admire.

nasúyake? K (n) lust.

nasu?aitʉ? (n) shame.

nasu?aitʉ (adj) ashamed, bashful.

nasu?ana (adv compar) terrible, much worse (when previously already bad). **Nasu?ana u nʉsukatʉ.** He is feeling much worse.

nasʉki?apʉ (adj) fringed.

nasʉsʉa?eetʉ, nasʉseetʉ (adj) nasty, dirty, no good. *See* **tuhtsaipʉ.**

Natai (n) Proud (or arrogant) People (Wichita name for the Comanches of Tejas.

natsa (interj) no matter! (related to remonstrance or accusation).

natsaakʉsi, natsaakwʉsi (n) sneezeweed. *Helenium micro-cephalum* Gray (yellow flowers; to induce sneezing, to cure headache, or expel afterbirth [C & J]).

natsaaturu?itʉ? (n) tug-of-war (*lit* pulling against one another).

natsahki?apʉ (n) cut, gash.

natsahki?arʉ (v) cut oneself, gash oneself, wound oneself.

natsahkupʉkatʉ (v) pull oneself down.

natsahkupʉkatʉ (v) scratch (digging into skin).

natsahkweniitʉ (adj) hung up, hanging.

natsahkwe?yarʉ (v), *pl* **natsah kwe?yu?itʉ** undress, disrobe. *See* **tsahkwe?yarʉ.**

natsahkwine? (n) automatic pistol (*lit* spins to wound).

natsahkwinu?itʉ (v, adj) spin around, spun. *See* **kwinu?yarʉ.**

natsahpunitʉ (v) test something; introduce oneself (to someone) [**na-** (refl) + **tsah-** hand + **puni** see]. *See* **nanisuabeta?aitʉ.**

natsahto?itʉ (v) pull oneself up.

natsahtsiaitʉ (v) scratch oneself.

natsahtʉma? K (n) door, doorway. *See* **namuhyʉ, muhyʉ.**

natsahwi?etʉ (v) open of its own accord. **Pʉnʉsʉ tsa? natsahwi-?etʉ.** It opens itself.

natsaka?uhtu?etʉ (v) betray someone.

natsaka?uhtu?etʉ? (n) traitor, betrayer.

natsakwenitʉ (v) swing back and forth.

natsakwʉsa? (n) zipper (anything that closes by pulling up on handle).

natsakwʉsikʉ? (n) laced object (anything that laces up).

natsamarʉ (v) accuse someone, complain about someone, exaggerate (woman's word).

natsamarʉnitʉ (adj, hum) strained.

natsaminaitʉ (v) dislocate (pull out of joint of own accord).

natsaminarʉ (v) disjoint (pull out of joint on purpose).

natsamukwe? (n) wild grape. *Vitis* sp. *See* **mutsinatsamukwe?.**

natsamukwe?a paa (n) wine, grape juice.

natsamukwe?a sʉʉki (n) grapevine.

natsamʉritʉ, natsamʉrihitʉ (v) turn over.

natsanahaatʉ (adj) persistent.

natsanʉhkʉ? (n) saddle girth.

natsawenitʉ (v) hang (suspended off ground), swing. **Kakwohwi tsa? natswenihkatʉ.** The bell is hanging.

natsaweni? (n) hanger, hook.

natsawo?nitʉ (v) scratch an itch. *See* **tsakwo?nerʉ.**

natsawʉnʉkatʉ (adj) situated, set in place (as a lamp).

natsawʉnʉrʉ (v) set something in place.

natsayaa ruka? K, **natsayaahkatʉ tuka?** W (n) lantern, lamp (carried by handle). *See* **tuka?.**

natsayaarʉ (v) carry by the handle.

L wehki'ai

natsa?ani?

natsa?ani? (n) four-wheeled hack, two-seated buggy (*lit* fold back, since top folded back). *See* **wobipuukʉ.**

natsa?nikarʉ (v) wear something.

natsihpara? (n) ventilator at top of teepee (opened to allow smoke to escape; closed to keep out the cold).

natsihpe?akarʉ (v) part hair (using special Comanche instrument for that purpose). **Wa?ipʉ tsa? natsihpe?akaarʉ.** The woman parted her hair with the hair-parter.

natsihpe?aka? (n) hair-parter (wooden artifact used by Comanches to part hair).

natsihpusa? (n) buckle that is buckled.

natsihtóo mi?aru (v) walk away (using walking cane).

natsihtóo nooru (v) walk with cane.

natsihtóo? K (n) cane, staff, crutch. *See* **tu?ehkooi?.**

natsihtóo?etu (n) double ball (variation of shinny or lacrosse).

natsihtóo?itu (v) play lacrosse.

natsihtu?yeetu (v) comb hair.

natsihtu?ye? (n) comb, hairbrush. *See* **puhihwi natsihtu?ye?.**

natsihtuma? (n) padlock. *See* **tutsihtuma?.**

natsihtupuka? (n) brooch, decorative pin.

natsimina? (n) joint.

natsinaro?ikutu (v) give oneself an enema.

natsinuhkuru (v) cram into limited space. *See* **tsinukuru.**

natsiwekwa? (n) spur [na- (refl) + tsi pointed + wekwa- jab].

natsohkwe? (n) mesquite [na- (refl) + tsohkwe- pound fine]. *See* **namabitsoo?ni, wohi?huu.**

natsomu (n) dried plum.

natsuwukai (adj) odd, strange (not like others). **Nenahpu tsa? natsuwukai?aru.** The man is odd.

natsu taibo? K (n) medical doctor (*lit* medicine man). *See* **natusu?upuha raiboo?.**

natsuwi (n) strength.

natsuwitumaka?eetu (v) strengthen, encourage. **Ta?ahpu tsa? natsuwitumaka?etu.** God gives us strength.

natsuwitu (adj) strong physically. **natsuwitu tenahpu?** strong man. **Noha u natsuwitu.** He was strong (previously but not now). He used to be strong.

Natumuu pa?i huna? (n) north fork of Red River (at Traders Spring, Okla.; *lit* trading river).

natusu?u narumuu? (n) drugstore (*lit* medicine store).

natusakuna (n) rawhide wardrobe case (envelope-shaped, laced at edges; with fold-over, tie-down flap; the best suit of clothing was kept in this bag).

natusu?u puha raiboo? W (n) doctor (*lit* medicine-power man). *See* **natsu taibo?.**

natusu?u (n) medicine. *See* **puha.**

natusu?u kahni (n) hospital, drugstore (*lit* medicine house). *See* **wuminaa kahni.**

nawohani (n) maize (cross between Indian corn and white corn). *Zea mays* L.

nawoo?i, nahwooi- (v, pl), *sg* **yaketu** cry.

nawo?oru (adj) striped.

nawuhkobaitu (v) break bone. **Nu ome nawuhkobai.** I broke my leg.

Naya (name) Slope (person).

nayaaru, nagyaaru (v) trail a human or an animal. **Tenahpu tsa? aruka?a naayaaru.** The man is trailing the deer. *See* **tunahyaru.**

nayanohitekwaru? (n) joker (person who jokes frequently).

naya?isa?aitu (n) liar (person who likes to spread stories). *See* **isapu?.**

nayukwiitu (v, pl), *sg* **nahanitu** continue along, move on. **Suni ?uri nayukwitu u?.** They moved on there.

nayuì wokwe (n) cactus (small species; sometimes difficult to see as it blends with the soil). *Mammalaria* sp.

naʔa- (pfx, reciprocal).

naʔaa (n) buffalo horn case (used for storing fire-making drills). *See* **aa.**

naʔahnia K, naʔahnia N (n) palomino horse (*lit* that which wallows).

naʔakutu (v) meet, come together.

naʔanampu (n) in-law.

naʔanitu (v), *pl* **naʔaniʔitu** wallow, roll over or around (animal action).

naʔata W, naʔatanakwu K (adv loc) separated but in same general area.

naʔatsiyaaʔ (n) seesaw, teeter-totter.

naʔaʔtsomeʔ (n) dried plum. *See* **kusisukui.**

naʔaruruuʔ (n) fist fight.

naʔarutu W (v) fight, hit with fists.

naʔbekoʔaru (adj) parted, separated (as clouds part or break up).

naʔbukuwàaʔ (n) automobile [**na-** (refl) + **puku** horse + **waa** horn sound].

naʔbukuwáaʔ kahni (n) garage (*lit* automobile house).

naʔbukuwàaʔa nábaa (n) gasoline (for automobiles). *See* **nabaa.**

naʔbukuwàaʔa nahyu (n) motor oil. *See* **nabaa.**

naʔbukuwàaʔa narahpaana W, naʔbukuwàʔa tahpaana K (n) automobile tire. *See* **makwuʔniku.**

naʔbutikumakatu tuuhkaʔaaʔ (n) double-bladed axe. *See* **tuuhkaʔaʔ.**

naʔhumuhku W (n) safety pin. *See* **nahamuhku.**

naʔisahanitu W (v) commit adultery.

naʔiyaitu (v) watch oneself.

naʔisa suakutu (v) **K** want to flirt; **W** flirt with someone.

naʔisa yukwitu K (v) flirt with someone (not reciprocated). **Naiʔbi tsaʔ naʔisa yukwiituʔ.** The young woman is flirting (with no response).

naʔmahpeʔeʔ, naʔmahpeeʔ (n) ball (*lit* object thrown by hand; used to play game of jacks).

naʔnia (n) buckskin horse.

naʔnohneʔeyuʔ (n) archaic game.

naʔnubeʔ (adj) divided evenly.

naʔnumu (n) female kinsman.

naʔnuumu (n) kinsman, descendant. *See* **nuhmabina.**

naʔokitu (v) rejoice.

naʔokusuaru (v) feel happy.

naʔomo, naʔoomo (n) wheel.

naʔomo nasuwuhkiʔ (n) spoke of wheel.

naʔoyorumakaru K (v) exchange several gift items.

naʔraibooʔ (n) slave, tenant (*lit* possession of white man).

naʔrubomitu (v) divide, break up under own volition.

naʔrubomitu (adj) divided, broken up.

naʔsuhpeeʔ (n) ball (small, Native-American football) [**na-** (refl) + **suh** kick + **peeʔ** fall].

naʔsuhpeʔetu (n) Native-American ball game.

naʔsukiaʔ (n) fringes, shawl with fringes. *See* **pohotu naʔsukiaʔ, tapi naʔsukiaʔ.**

na?tsiyaa? (n) seesaw, teeter- totter [**na-** (refl) + **tsiyaa-** throw one].

na?tsi?aiku? (n) baby buggy.

na?uhturu W (v, sg obj), *pl obj* **hinanahimiitu** exchange gifts.

na?uyubuti W, **na?uyubetotu** K (adv dir) down, downward.

na?uyatu (adj) slanting, sloping.

na?wa?ihpu? (n) man's female kinsman. *See* **wa?ihpu?**.

na?wee?, nagwee (n) ford, wagon crossing. *See* **pu?e nagwe**.

na?wekitu? (n) hide-and-seek.

na?wosa (n) drawer. *See* **ooyoru tahna**.

na?yunehtu? W (n) shield.

na?yunetu (v, pl), *sg* **yahneetu** laugh.

na?yuwetu (v) play hand games.

nehki wuhtupuka? (n) belt buckle.

nehki W, **nehki?** K (n) belt.

ni- (pfx) ref. to speech.

nigwaitu K, **nikwaitu** W (v) request something. *See* **nani̇htsawa?itu**.

nigwatsukatu (v) stutter.

nikwekwitu (v, pl), *sg* **ni?ika?itu** invite someone in.

nihakuru (v) name someone, read (as a book). *See* **nahniamakaru**.

nihkwibihbikitu (v) tremble in speech (as when about to cry, or when elderly).

nihmakwihtseru (v), *pl* **nihmakwih- tseyuru** call down, rebuke, scold.

nihpana?aitu (v) brag on someone, praise someone. *See* **nani̇hpana?aitu, pana?aitu**.

nihpitukuru (v) coax someone.

nihpu?aitu (v) stop talking.

nihto?itu (v) ban, order to leave. **Puhi tua?a u nihto?itu.** He is ordering their son to leave.

nihto?itu (v) sing a song, sing out.

nihtsamu?itu (v) agree to a pro- posal, nod the head in agreement. **Tenahpu tsa? pu miaru?iha uri nihtsamu?i.** The man promised them that he would go.

nihtunetsaru (v) pester someone (keep talking in a manner which disturbs). *See* **nimusasuaru**.

nihtunetsu?itu (v) urge on, encourage to go on.

nihtunetsukatue? (n) a bore (one who pesters by talk).

nihtubunioru (v) waken by speaking to someone.

niikwiitu (v) speak to, address (used with me). **Oha ahnakatu, 'Mui nahubiyaaru?i nu?,' me urii niikwiiyu.** Coyote said to them, 'I will sing for you all.'

niipuni-, nihpunitu (v) ask (to persuade someone to do something).

nikwukitu (v) inquire (ask around to procure information).

nimabunikutu (v) explain, instruct (tell to do). *See* **nitsubunikutu**.

nimaihkana? (n) called one.

nimaikatu (v) call to someone. **Wa?ipu tsa? pu kumapu?a nimaikatu.** The woman called to her husband.

nimakabaitu (v) reject someone.

nimaka?mukitu (v) make a plan. *See* **su?atsitu**.

nimakwihtsetu (v) say mean things, talk tough, fuss at someone.

nimamusukutu, nimamusuitu (v) say no to someone, refuse.

nimarukaitu (v) finish telling.

nimoya?ekuru (v) forbid, prohibit (tell not to do).

nimɨɨmiʔarɨ W (v) pass word on, gossip.

nimɨsasuarɨ (v) annoy, harass by chatter, pester by talk. **Tɨepɨrɨ tsaʔ nimɨsasuarɨ.** The child annoyed (us) by his talk. *See* **nihtunetsarɨ.**

ninabitsiarɨ, nimabitsiarɨ (v) order sternly, speak firmly.

ninakabarɨ (v) refuse to accept someone, reject man as husband.

ninakabaʔikɨtɨ (v) prohibit, warn (tell someone not to do something wrong).

ninakabaʔitɨ (n) rejected person.

Ninakabaʔiʔ (name) Refusing (person).

ninakɨakɨrɨ W (v) give notice, tip off.

ninɨkitɨ W (v) compare with something.

ninɨsuabitarɨ K (v) advise, inform (let someone know something).

ninɨsupetitɨ (v) appease, gratify.

ninɨsutamakɨtɨ (v) reminded orally (remember by something someone says).

Nipanɨɨ (n) Eastern Apaches (Ipa's People; fought the Comanches in battle on E. Red River; the Apaches were routed).

nipɨkaaʔeetɨ (n) fortuneteller, shaman. *See* **nɨminipɨkaʔ, mapaanaʔ, tɨnipɨkawapi.**

nipɨkarɨ (v) tell a fortune. **Nɨ nipɨkaai u.** He told my fortune. *See* **nɨnipɨkarɨ.**

nipɨyerɨ (v) sing one song after another (in succession).

nisuabetarɨ (v) K explain something, teach someone something; W introduce someone.

nisutaitɨ (v) pet, stroke. **Sariiʔa nisutaiʔi.** He petted his dog. *See* **tohtarakiʔarɨ.**

nisuyakeetɨ (v) tempt by describing something.

nisuʔuyaitɨ W (v) jeer, mock (make fun of). *See* **usúʔuyaʔitɨ.**

nitsɨbahikɨʔitɨ (v) persuade someone to do something, talk someone into something.

nitsɨbunikɨtɨ (v) explain, instruct (cause to know). *See* **nimabunikɨtɨ.**

nitɨsuʔnai wapi (n) mediator, go-between.

niwatsiʔaikɨʔitɨ (v) hold back information, keep quiet.

niwɨnɨrɨ (v, pl), **sg tekwarɨ** talk to someone.

niyakekɨtɨ (v) imitate a cry, make a birdcall. **Huutsuʔa niyakekɨi u.** He imitated the bird cry.

niyukarɨrɨ W, **niyunahkarɨ** K (v) quiet someone (command to neither move nor talk).

niʔatsiwapiʔ (n) commander. *See* **tɨni atsɨkatɨʔ.**

niʔatsiitɨ (v) advise, order, command.

niʔemɨabɨnitɨ (v) rave, speak irrationally (as when one is delirious or near death).

niʔheʔbunitɨ (v) insult, taunt, berate someone falsely.

niʔikaʔitɨ (v), *pl* **nigwekwitɨ** invite into home or room. **Mari nigwekwi nɨʔ.** I invited them to come in.

niʔtsuʔnarɨ (v) forgive, quiet by speech. *See* **tɨsuʔnarɨ.**

niʔwatsɨkatɨʔ (n) error in speech.

niʔwikerɨ (v) scold someone.

ni?wiketʉ (v) quarrel with someone. **Nani?wiketʉ marʉkwʉ.** The two of them are quarreling.

ni?woso?arʉ (v) berate someone.

ni?yʉsʉkaitʉ (v) disturb, create a commotion, upset people by bad tidings.

nobʉahraitʉ (v) abandon someone, leave someone behind.

noha (adv) nearly, almost, used to. **Noha u? nʉ kwʉhʉru?i.** He almost caught me. (105:28). **Noha nʉ mi?arʉ.** I was going (but did not).

nohabitʉ (n) hen (clucker), setting hen.

nohabi suwaitʉ (v) want to lay an egg. *See* **suwai.**

nohi (adv) very. **nohi tʉtaatʉ taa haitsiour** very small friend. *See* **mohatsi.**

nohi?nuraarʉ (v) run around and play.

nohitʉetʉ (n) doll (*lit* toy child).

nohiwaikinʉ, nohi wobipuku (n) toy wagon.

nohihtaiboo?nʉʉ (n pl) circus, circus people (*lit* playing white men).

nohitekwarʉ (v) fool someone, joke, pretend, make-believe. *See* **kaasuarʉ.**

nohitʉ (v) play (make fun of), ridicule. **Nahruku nʉmi nohiti.** That one is just playing with us (making fun of us) (8:44). *See* **tʉnimakwihtserʉ.**

nohi? (n) plaything, toy.

nohko aawo? K (n) oven (*lit* biscuit container).

nohko aawo (n) oven for baking biscuits. *See* **pʉkʉra nohko?ena.**

nohkopʉ (n) biscuit.

nohkorʉ (v) bake biscuits.

nohrʉna? (n) bedstead.

nohrʉna saawʉ, nohna saawʉ? (n) bedspring.

nohrʉnaarʉ (v) make a bed.

noka?itʉ (v) move off to live separately, camp apart from the main group.

nokimarʉ (v) come moving along. *See* **nora?wʉarʉ.**

Nokoni (n) Comanche band (located between Red River and Peace River).

nomi?arʉ (v), *pl* **sʉmʉnomi?aru** move away (change residence).

nomohkarʉ (v) hitch up horses and buggy, hook up doubletrees on buggy. *See* **mahkarʉ.**

nomʉnewapi W (n) officer, leader.

nonanʉʉ (n pl), *sg* **monahpʉ?** sons-in-law.

noo (adv) sure, particular, definite. **Obotika hunu?ruti noo hina puhwaihbʉʉni.** Over there along the creek look for a particular thing (6:24).

noo- (pfx) hill, knoll; ref. to hauling.

noohkirʉ (v) haul in. *See* **noopitʉ.**

nookarʉrʉ (n) one hill standing alone. *See* **anáabi.**

Nookoni, Nocona, Peta Nokona (name) Wanderer (Comanche chief, Kwana Parker's father; died in 1860 on Mule Creek).

nookwarʉ, nookwai (v) carry away, haul away.

noomanitʉ (v) carry across.

noona K, noopʉ W (n) load.

noonʉmi?arʉ (v) move from place to place. *See* **noyʉkarʉ.**

noopitʉ (v) haul in, arrive carrying something. *See* **noohkirʉ, pitʉnu.**

noorɯ (v) to haul away. **Ohka tanɯ tuhkanáaiʔ tenahpɯʔa tɯmɯsɯapɯ kahti noohtsi.** Let's carry off some of that Wichita man's crop (77:7).

nooyo (n) egg.

norawɯʔaitɯ (v) move away.

noraʔwɯarɯ W, **noragwɯarɯ** K (v) go moving along. *See* **nokimarɯ.**

noroʔyarɯ (v), *pl* **noroʔitɯ** unhitch a horse. **Pɯ puukuniʔ u noroʔitɯ.** He unhitched his horses. *See* **toʔyarɯ.**

norɯbakitɯ (v), *pl* **tɯbakitɯ** pack. **Norɯbakị u kimai.** She packed and came on.

norɯnaarɯ (v) make a bed.

norɯnapɯ (n) bed (made up with linens).

notsaʔkaarɯ (v) take women along, allow women to accompany. **Notsaʔkaa miʔarɯ saʔ.** He is taking women along.

notsaʔkaʔ (n) partner, friend, sweetheart, spouse. **Sɯmɯʔ tuibihtsiʔ pɯ notsaʔkaʔmaʔai paʔanai urii puniʔi.** One young man with his sweetheart saw them (70:21). *See* **tɯhtɯiʔ, tɯɯʔurapɯ.**

noyotsoʔmẹ tabuʔ (n) Easter rabbit [**noyotsoʔme** Easter + **taabu** rabbit].

noyoʔna ohapịyuna (n) egg yolk.

Noyɯhkanɯɯ, Nookoni (n) Roamers, Wanderers (band of middle Comanches; formerly located in Peace River region of Texas; now located between Lawton and Richard's Spur).

noyɯkarɯ (v) wander from place to place, roam. *See* **noonɯmiʔararɯ.**

noyɯkaʔ (n) roamer, vagabond.

noʔa-, noʔapɯ (adj) pregnant.

noʔa nohkopɯ (n) pie (*lit* pregnant biscuit).

noʔitɯ (v) pluck out something, pick a bird of its feathers. **pɯhɯ noʔitɯ** pluck eyebrows.

noʔwosarɯ (adj) hunchback.

noʔyaikɯtɯ (v) boil, steam. **Huba tai noʔyaikɯ.** Boil us some coffee. **Paapasi tɯ noʔyaikɯɯtɯ.** The potatoes are boiling.

nuarɯ (v) slide, move over. **Pɯnɯsɯ uʔ nuai.** He moved over. *See* **pisikwanúuʔitɯ.**

nuhkitɯ (v) run, run away. **Ohaahnakatɯ makuhpa nuhkínu.** Coyote ran ahead of him (10:18). *See* **pɯanuhkitɯ, wenuʔnukịmi- ʔarɯ.**

nuhtsairɯ (v) stoop, bend over. **Tenahpu tsaʔ nuhtsai.** The man is stooped. **Huupi tsaʔ nuhtsarɯ.** The tree (limb) broke off.

nuhtsaitɯ (adj) crumbled.

nuhtsapɯ (adj) bent over, broken (as a fallen tree), stooped (as the elderly). *See* **tumuurɯ.**

nuhyaʔ (n, arch) snake of any species.

nuhyimiʔarɯ W, **nuhyinoorɯ** K (v) crawl like a snake.

nuhyɯyukitɯ, nuhyukitɯ (v) rotate, change from one position to another. **Woʔaruhkapɯha tsaʔ nuhyɯyukitɯ.** She poured the rice from one pan to another.

nunurawɯtɯ (v) run away one by one. **Nɯmɯnɯɯ tsaʔ nunurawɯtɯ.** The Comanches ran off one by one.

nunuraʔwɯʔ, nunurakwɯ (n) movie (that which runs and runs).

nuraakitʉ (v) come running. **Sitʉʉ siʔana nuraakii.** These came running here somewhere.

nʉ (pro, 1st excl gen sg) my.

nʉbawʉhtiawapi (n) baptizer (one who baptizes).

nʉbawʉhtiarʉ (v) baptize someone.

nʉe (pro 1st acc sg) me.

nʉemaitʉ (v) cease blowing, become calm.

nʉena (n) wind. **Ma nʉena tsaʔ aitʉ.** The wind is not good.

Nʉena (name) Wind (person).

Nʉenuhkiki (name) Wind-running-here (woman's name).

nʉepi (n) tornado, wind storm. **Nʉepi tsaʔ tamʉku kimarʉ.** The storm is coming to us.

nʉetʉ (v) blow (as wind). **Kʉhta ma nʉetʉ.** The wind is blowing hard.

Nʉetʉtsi (name) Blowing-wind (person).

nʉetʉ (n) wind, breeze.

nʉhkana W, **nʉhkarʉ** K (n) powwow, dance.

nʉhkarʉ (v) dance. **Tai nʉhka-rʉʔika.** Let's dance (3:8).

nʉhkiʔapʉ (n) a cut.

nʉhmabina (n) descendants.

nʉhpopiʔ, nʉhpopiwiyaaʔ (n) jumping rope.

nʉhtsikwarʉ (v) labor in child-birth, body pain. **Nʉ nape tsaʔ nʉhtsowarʉ.** My foot is hurting (paining me). See **nʉʉtsikwarʉ.**

nʉkuwʉmiʔarʉ (v) clabber, curdle.

nʉkuʔwʉpʉ (n) clabber. **pitsipʉha nʉkuʔwʉpʉ** clabbered milk. See **nʉtsʉʔwʉpa pitsipʉ.**

nʉkʉta (n) goose, *pl* **nʉkʉtanʉʉ** geese.

nʉkʉrʉ (v) dance. **Surʉʉ kʉseʔ nʉkʉbʉniyʉ.** They danced much.

nʉmamoʔoʔ (n) raccoon. See **paruukuʔ.**

nʉmi (pro, 1st pl excl acc) us, people.

nʉmi booʔetʉ W (n) camera. See **pʉhtu kunʉmʉ tʉbooʔena, kobenaboʔ.**

nʉmi himaʔetʉ (n) policeman, sheriff, lawman (*lit* one who catches us). See **tʉʉhtamʉh raiboʔ.**

nʉmi makwinumaʔetʉ pahmu (n) marijuana cigarette.

nʉmi makwinumaʔetʉʔ (n) marijuana (*lit* that which makes us dizzy).

nʉmi nipʉkaʔ K (n) fortuneteller [**nʉmi-** us + **nipʉ-** tell fortunes + **-ʔ** (nom sg)]. See **nipʉkaaʔeetʉ.**

nʉmi nooʔetʉ, nʉnʉmi nooʔetʉʉ (n) bus, taxi (*lit* that which carries people on its back).

nʉmi tsaʔʉbʉikʉʔeetʉ (n) ether (*lit* that which makes people sleep).

nʉmirʉ (v), *pl* **yʉkarʉ** able to walk, move around (as a child learning or a person who has been ill).

nʉmʉ (pro, 1st pl excl gen) our; *n* The Comanche People, *pl* **Nʉmʉnʉʉ.** (Whites use the alternate names **Nʉmʉ, Nʉʉmʉ, Nerm, Nimma.**)

nʉmʉ haahkanaʔ (n), *pl* **nʉmʉ nahkanʉʉ** family, relatives.

nʉmʉ hani (n) maize, Indian corn, squaw corn (blue kernel with long, narrow cob). *Zea mays* L. See **haniibi.**

nʉmʉ kuhtsuʔ (n) buffalo (*lit* our cow).

numu kuhtsuʔ

numu maʔtsaʔbahkiʔ (n) lizard (clings to skin).

numu narumuuʔ (n) trading post, Indian store.

numu nohkopu (n) Indian corncake, biscuit.

numu paraiboʔ (n) Indian agent.

numu renahpuʔ (n) Comanche man.

numu tsuhni (n) Comanche bones [numu our + tsuhni bones].

numuwahtu (n) prairie (open, uninhabited land). See puhuwahtu.

numu kutsu tuhkapu (n) buffalo meat. Numu kuhtsu tuhkapu tsaʔ tuhkaru. I eat buffalo meat.

numukuni, numu kahni (n) teepee, skins or other covering for teepees (lit our dwelling).

numunainaʔ (n) life (must occur with possessor). nu numunainaʔmy life, ta numunainaʔ anyone's life.

numunaitu (v) acculturate as a Comanche (live as a Comanche).

numunakaru (v) own a home.

numu napu (n) moccasin (lit our shoe). See taʔseʔyukuʔ.

numunetu (v) dwell, live somewhere.

numu rekwaku wapi (n) interpreter of Comanche. See tekwaku wapi.

numu ruaitu (v) Comanche-born. Tuinuhpu tsaʔ numu ruai. A Comanche baby boy was born.

Numu ruibetsu (name) She-invites-her-relatives (person).

numu ruibihtsiʔ (n) Comanche young man.

numu ruborapu K (n) present generation (present living ones; lit our born-ones). See puhkura nahanu, uku numunuu.

numu ruboraru (adj) procreated by us (born of Comanche parents).

numu ruhorapu (n) creation (lit created from heaven).

numu rusaasi (n) Comanche perfume plant (leaves are used as perfume). See tusaasi.

numuʔaraʔ (n voc) lover (used between parties to an extra-marital affair).

nuna wuhtupuka? (n) buckle.

nuna karukuʔ K (n) brooch (ornament worn on chest).

Nunapi (n) little people similar to elves.

nunapu (n) chest (of the body).

nunatsiʔnikaʔ (n) jewelry (pinned on or with a stickpin).

nuníhkooniru (v) send word to someone to return.

nunipukaru (v) guess, tell fortunes. See nipukaru.

nunooru (v) carry on back.

nunu (pro, 1st pl excl nom) we.

nunu puhiʔ, nunuphi (n) midget, troll (lives in rocky hill). See pue tuyaaiʔ.

nunubetu (adj) fit (proper size). Nu napu tsaʔ nunubetu. My shoes fit.

nunumuni tuhtsu (adv man) badly, wrong. Nunumuni tuhtsu unu

hina haniyu. You really do things wrongly.

nɨnɨʔitɨ (v) stop following someone, slow down what one is doing.

nɨnɨʔyɨwiʔ W, nɨnɨyɨʔwoʔ K (n) alligator (*lit* that which swallows people).

nɨpetsɨʔ (n) wife. **Nɨpetsɨʔa pitɨi u.** He brought the girl (wife) home.

nɨpetsɨʔitɨ (v) get engaged to be married, lead away a wife, get married. **Orɨ tsaʔ nɨpetsɨì.** He is getting married.

nɨpɨkapɨ K, N, W (n) grave.

nɨpɨkapɨ K, W (n) graveyard.

nɨpɨkarɨ (v) bury someone. **Nɨ nɨbahaʔa nɨpɨkai.** I buried my nephew.

nɨpɨkarɨɨʔ (n) funeral, burial ceremony.

nɨpɨkɨ sokoobi (n) cemetery, graveyard.

nɨrɨaʔwekɨʔ, nɨrɨahwekɨʔ (n) bride (one who has been given away in marriage).

nɨtsɨʔwɨpa pitsipɨ K (n) buttermilk, clabbered milk. *See* **nɨkuʔwɨpɨ.**

nɨtɨhyoi wapi, nɨtɨhyɨi wapi (n) messenger, angel.

nɨɨsihwaʔitɨ (v) tear skin.

nɨɨbanikatɨ (v, hum subj) lean against something.

nɨɨhkiʔyuʔitɨ (v) mutilate oneself, hack oneself (self-mutilation in mourning death of a loved one).

nɨɨhkupatɨ (v) trip and fall. *See* **nɨɨhpisiʔmaitɨ.**

nɨɨhkwitubitɨ (v) wrap around and around (as yarn on a ball).

nɨɨhpisiʔmaitɨ (v) trip and fall. *See* **nɨɨhkupatɨ.**

nɨɨhtamiʔitɨ (adj) wrapped and tied up.

nɨɨhtaʔneerɨ (v) brush something off of oneself.

nɨɨhtokaʔeʔ (n) muscle (*lit* that of oneself which is cut; refers to ancient custom of self-mutilation for the dead).

nɨɨhtonitɨ (v) strut, display (mating ritual of animals).

nɨɨhtoʔitɨ (v) mount on horseback.

nɨɨhtsiʔaitɨ (v) split of own accord.

nɨɨhtɨmaʔ (n) fence.

nɨɨhtɨpikaʔ (n) button, harness buckle.

nɨɨhtɨʔekaʔ (n) petroleum jelly, personal ointment. *See* **tsiʔwɨnɨɨ tɨʔekaʔ.**

nɨɨhɨhtsaʔwɨʔ (n) fan (of any kind; *lit* that with which to make oneself feel cool).

nɨɨkiʔaitɨ (v) cut oneself.

nɨɨkitseʔ (n) a bruise.

nɨɨkɨnarɨ (v) cover over (place cover over the top of something).

nɨɨkwenitɨ (v) hang oneself.

nɨɨkwitsɨnarɨ (v) twist oneself. *See* **kwitsunairɨ.**

nɨɨminaitɨ (v) break bone (arm or leg).

nɨɨmiʔakɨrɨ (v) operate manually (as lawnmower or wheelbarrow). *See* **mamiʔakɨtɨ.**

nɨɨmɨ (n) liver (requires possessor). **nɨ nɨɨmɨmy liver, u nɨɨmɨ marɨkwɨ two livers.**

nɨɨpearɨ (v, sg obj), *pl obj* **nɨɨpiyuʔitɨ** chip off (one, many chips).

nʉʉpitua? (n) sash, band (for supporting baby on back).

nʉʉpʉrʉsuanʉpurʉ (v) unravel something.

nʉʉpʉrʉsuarʉ (v) unravel of own accord. *See* **pʉrʉsu?arʉ.**

nʉʉpʉtsapʉ (n) surgery, surgical operation.

nʉʉsoo?, nʉʉsoo kahni (n) canvas tent.

nʉʉsoo?etʉ (v) hang over something, lean over something.

nʉʉsukatʉ (adj) puny, sickly.

nʉʉti?akatʉ (v) spill of own accord.

nʉʉti?arʉ (v) spill something.

nʉʉtsikwarʉ K (v) ache, give pain (with aching member as subject). **Nʉ papi tsa? nʉʉtsikwarʉ.** My head aches (*lit* my head aches). *See* **nʉhtsikwarʉ.**

nʉʉtsʉke? (n) haircut.

nʉʉtsʉketʉ (v) get a haircut.

nʉʉtsʉkʉnarʉ (adj) tied up.

nʉʉ?kwipunarʉ (v) twist oneself around something.

nʉʉ?maitʉ (v) tire out, become lazy.

nʉʉ?nʉarʉ (v) rise from seated position.

nʉʉ?wikeetʉ (v) shake something off. *See* **sʉʉta?ni?arʉ.**

nʉ? (pro, 1st nom sg) I.

nʉ?ʉnehki K (n) belt (for waist).

nʉ?ʉhpee? (n) baseball.

nʉ?ʉnehki?a nanʉʉtʉpika? W (n) belt buckle.

nʉ?ʉnehkikatʉ? (adj) belted, sash (*lit* wearing something around the waist).

O

obutʉma? (n) upriver.

oha- (pfx) ref. to yellow color.

ohaahnakatʉ W (n) fox, coyote (*lit* yellow under arms). **Ohaahnakatʉ urʉʉkʉ pitʉnʉ.** Coyote arrived among them (3:3). *See* **kʉ?kwʉria?.**

ohaekapitʉ (adj) orange (*lit* yellow-red). W (n) bay horse (light bay color). *See* **ekaohapitʉ, ohapitʉʉ.**

ohaeka? K (n) bay horse (light bay color).

ohahuupi (n) osage orange, bois d'arc tree. Maclura pomifera (Raf.) Schneider (bows manufactured from branches; roots used in treatment of eye disease).

ohahʉkwʉnikatʉ, oha hʉwʉni? (adj) early, before dawn, early dawn (*lit* yellow horizon).

ohanʉnapʉ W (n) field lark, meadowlark. Sturnella (*lit* yellow breast). *See* **hiitoo?.**

ohawaikina (n) streetcar, trolley (*lit* yellow wagon).

Ohawasápe (name) Yellow-bear (Comanche chief).

Ohawʉnʉ (name) Yellow-steps (person).

ohahkuyaa? (n) king in playing-card deck (**lit** yellow head holding; for crown on king's head).

ohahpitʉ sʉkʉ?kamatʉ W (n) lemon (*lit* yellow sour-tasting).

ohahpiyaa? (n) bumblebee (*lit* carrying yellow on its back).

ohahpokopi K, **ohapitʉ pokopi** W (n) domestic carrot (*lit* yellow fruit).

ohahpuhihwi (n) copper (*lit* yellow metal).

ohahtuhkapu (n) domestic carrot.

ohakuhtsuni (n) yellow fever.

Ohapia (name) Bay-mare (person).

ohapi (adj) yellow.

ohapi, ohape (n, acc) watermelon (yellow variety).

ohapituu, ohapitua pokopi (n) orange (citrus fruit). *See* **ohaekapitu**.

ohápituuʔa takaʔ W (n) grapefruit (*lit* kinsman of orange). *See* **pia ohapitu**.

Ohapitu kwahi (name) Yellow-back (person).

ohasuhuubi (n) black willow. *Salix nigra* Marsh (*lit* yellow willow; for yellow tinge of bark; ashes used to treat sore eyes).

ohayaaʔ (n) sunflower. *Helianthus* sp. (yellow flower of any kind).

ohinibetutu (adv dir) left (to the left). *See* **tubitsi petutu**.

ohinikatu (adj) left-handed. *See* **tubitsikatu**.

ohininakwu (adv loc) at or to the left side. *See* **tubitsinakwu**.

ohka, ohko (pro dem, dist acc sg) him, her.

ohnáakuno? (n) cradle (*lit* baby container).

ohnaʔa noruhnaaʔ (n) baby crib, baby bed.

ohnaʔaʔ (n) baby (girl or boy).

ohnitu (v) cough.

ohpepu (n) tear.

ohpetoʔikaru (v) eyes water, tears flow.

ohta- (pfx) ref. to dirt, soil.

ohta kahni W (n) storm cellar, adobe house, cyclone cellar (*lit* dirt house). *See* **sekwikuni**.

ohtakatu (adj) earth-covered (as a cellar).

ohtapii (n) dirt, soil.

ohútuki, ohútukoi (n) flank (animal side; part from which Comanches remove sinew for sewing hides).

oihtuyaitu (v) choke to death by rope around the neck. *See* **tsaʔoibehkatu**.

okweetu (v) flow. **Hunuʔbi tsaʔ kuhta okwetu.** The river flowed fast.

okwèetu (n) creek, stream, small river. *See* **hunuʔbiʔ**.

okwehkwatu (v) float away. **Taa tuhkapuruku tsaʔ okwehkwaʔi.** Our meat floated away (123:24). *See* **sumu okwetu**.

omo-, oomo (n) lower leg (from the knee down).

omotoi (n) pipe stem (straight leg bone used as stem).

ona- (pfx) ref. to salt.

Onawai (name) Salt-worn-out (person).

onaabi (n) salt.

onaʔaitu (v) salt something (*lit* make to be salty). **Tuhkapuha onaaʔaitu nu?.** I salted the food.

Ononuu, Ohnonuu (n) Hill People (Comanche band that lived in area of Cyril, Okla.)

onoʔitu (adj), *pl* oʔonokawutu crooked. **Puʔe tsaʔ onoʔitu.** The path (is) crooked.

ooibehkaru (v) hang someone with a rope.

ooyoru tahna (n) drawer, dresser drawer. *See* **naʔwosa**.

ooʔitu (v) vomit.

ooʔru W, **oʔyoru** K, N (n), *acc pl* **ooʔri** clothing, apparel, belongings of any type. **Marʉʉ oo?rʉ o?okwenunạ.** Their clothes were floating (122:19).

oo?rʉ kahni W, **o?yorʉ kahni** K (n) clothes closet.

oo?rʉ tani?i?, o?yorʉ tahna? (n) bureau (for clothes), chest of drawers.

oo?rʉ tohtsana? W (n) clothes hanger.

oo?rʉ tʉtsịhtu?ye? W, **o?yorʉ natsihtuye?** K (n) clothes brush.

oo?rʉ tohtsani?i?ana huuhpi (n) clothesline pole.

orʉ (pro dem, 3rd dist nom sg) he, she, it.

otʉ- (pfx) K beige, brown; W brown. *See* **otʉpịtʉ.**

otʉhtʉ mapo?akatʉ (adj) brown-skinned.

otʉpịtʉ (adj) K beige; W brown.

otʉ aawọ (n) bottle (*lit* brown container).

otʉ kamaitʉ (v) bland (taste neither sweet nor sour).

otʉ kʉma? W (n) sorrel horse, chestnut-brown horse.

Otʉ kwasu (name) Brown-robe (person).

otʉ kwasʉkʉrʉ (v) brown the food, cook something brown (well done; almost burned).

otʉ mitsonaa? (n) soapberry (*lit* brown blackberry). *Sapindus Drummondii* H. and A. (stems used for making arrows for aratsi game).

otʉ nohkopʉ W (n) cookies (*lit* brown biscuits). *See* **pihná nohkopʉ.**

otʉ peena (n) wasp, yellow jacket (*lit* brown sugar-eaters).

otʉ pihnàa? W (n) brown sugar.

otʉ suakatʉ (adj) stingy (*lit* think brown).

otʉ tohtía? (n) cookie (gingersnap(s); *lit* brown bread).

owóora (n) tree trunk (main body of the tree).

oyo-, oyʉ, oyètʉ, oyo?kọ (num) all.

oyóotʉ? (n) parfleche, meat bag (bag made of rawhide).

oyorʉ tʉmarʉ (v) buy clothing.

oyo?rʉ ka?wekịtʉ (adj) above everything, more than anything.

oyo?rʉtu (adv loc) throughout a location.

o?oo? (n) owl (horned or long-eared).

o?yʉ?sʉ (adv time) every time.

P

pa- W (pfx) ref. to water.

paa (n) water. *See* **tuupʉ.**

paa kʉa?etʉ (v) drip water. **Nʉ pui tsa? paa kʉa?eetʉ.** My eye waters (once in a while).

paa ma?ibu?ikʉtʉ K (v) fill with water. *See* **ibu?ikʉrʉ, pawʉsa?naitʉ.**

paa mutsaa? (n) bend in river (*lit* water's elbow).

Paa roponi (name) See-how-deep-the-water-is (person).

paa tsoko (n) otter [**paa** water + **tsoko-** old one].

Paa tsokotubʉtʉ (name) Black-otter (person).

Paa tso?ko (name) Otter (*lit* water-old; person).

paa tʉpʉnaatʉ? W, **paa tʉpʉnaatʉ** K (n) island.

paabitsanitʉ (v) strangle on water, choke. *See* **pitsanitʉ**.

paai, pai, bai (n) vein.

paaka, paka (n) arrow.

paakipʉ, pahkipʉ (n) dried cowhide, leather.

paanʉ (n) loaf of bread.

paapasi, papasi (n) wild potato, Irish potato. *Convolvulaceae* (tuber eaten raw or cooked).

paapi (n) head. *See* **papi-**.

paasitsi (n) sleet (*lit* water sailing).

pabi? (n) elder brother.

pabo- (pfx) clear, transparent.

pabo taiboo? (n) white man.

pabo tuhku (n) hindquarter, light meat, thigh meat.

paboka?aitʉ (adj) clear (as glass).

paboko, pabokohi (n) large intestine (*lit* light or clear intestine).

paboko aawo (n) drinking glass, jar, vase, bottle.

pabokopitʉ (adj) crystal clear, transparent (free from cloudiness or stain).

paboko?ai

paboko?ai (n) lizard (timber variety).

pabopitʉ (adj) blond, light-complected. **Waipʉ tsa? pabopitʉ.** The woman has a light complexion. *name* **Pabopitʉ** Light-complected (person).

paha piahpʉ (n) sister-in-law (of a woman).

pahabitʉ (v), *pl* **pakwabitʉ** bathe, swim. **Pibia kwasinaboo? mawakatu pakwabihkwaina.** Big snakes are swimming around toward her (52:18). *See* **tapʉhabi**.

pahabi aawo (n) bathtub (*lit* swimming container).

pahabi kahni W (n) bathroom.

paha? (n) father's sister; woman's brother's child (either sex).

pahibahtʉ (adj) three separated groups. **Pahibahku nʉ? marahni?i.** I laid them out in three separate piles.

pahibahtʉnʉnʉ (n) three separate families, three groups of people.

pahihtʉ (adj) three.

pahitʉ (v), *pl* **yumarʉ** fall off, be born, drop off (as leaves from a tree).

pahki wiyaa? (n) rawhide rope.

pahkipʉ (n) rawhide ready to use. *See* **ʉhtaayu?**.

pahmo namahya (n) sumac (*lit* tobacco mixer). *Anacardiaceae* sp. (mixed with tobacco to smoke; cannot be smoked alone; clears sinuses).

pahmu (n) tobacco.

pahna?aitʉ (v) treat with respect. **Sʉmʉ?a pahna?aitʉ.** He treats someone with respect.

paho ʉmarʉ, pahoopi (n) hail.

pahorapʉ (n) water well, well.

pahparatsihkweetʉ W (adj) bright, shiny.

pahparatsihkwetʉ tʉʉpi (n) diamond (*lit* shiny stone).

pahpatsohkitʉ (v) drip.

pahtsi (adj) smooth, slick.

pahtsi bapikatʉ K (adj) bald headed (*lit* smooth headed).

pahtsi kaburuu? (n) slick-haired goat (*lit* smooth goat).

Pahtsi ketu (name) Smooth (person).

pahtsi ku?e (n) bald head (*lit* smooth top).

pahtsi kwasi (n) opossum (*lit* slick tail).

pahtsi kwasi tukahpu (n) mulberries (*lit* opossum food).

pahtsi mubitai, paatsi mubitai? (n) hickory (*lit* smooth walnut; used for barbecuing).

pahtsi no?itu (v) pluck a bird clean of feathers. *See* **puhu no?itu.**

pahtsi okwe? (n) clear stream (*lit* clear-flowing; spring-fed stream).

pai (n, acc) water. *See* **paa.**

paihtsi (adj) shrunken. **Paihtsi ma? nahai pumi nu kotsehka.** When I washed it, it shrank.

Pai paka pia huna? (n) Pedernales River (*lit* arrowhead river; riverbed contains flint for making arrowheads).

pai tusi?itu K (v) spit out liquid. *See* **tusitu.**

paiyapi (n) plant with edible fruit (name unknown; grows in Apache, Okla. area; seeds not swallowed; roots roasted or boiled and eaten).

paka tuu?ru? (n) dragonfly (*lit* stretches itself arrow-like).

Pakawa (name) Kills-something (person).

pakawkoko?, pakokoko (n) prairie chicken.

pakeeso, pakeetso (n) purple prairie clover. *Petalostemum purpureum* (Vent.) Rydb. (roots chewed have sweet taste).

Pakekuni, Pake kahni (name) Dry-teepee (person).

pakuyu?atu (adj) lukewarm.

paku?neru (v) duck head under water. *See* **tsahpaaku?nikaru.**

pakunaikatu (adj) foggy. *See* **kwiisuatu.**

pakuuka (n) wild onion, swamp weed (*lit* water onion). *Allium* sp. (bulbs roasted and eaten).

paku?nuapu, pakunaipu (n) fog.

pakusiiwunuru (v) drool.

pakwaruhtukitu W (v) gargle (with water or other liquid). *See* **wuhkwaru?rukitu.**

pakwa?nuaru (v) splash into water.

pakwihtsikuru, pawihtsikuru (v) splash water on, dampen.

pakwu?su?mitu (adj) filled with water by drinking. *See* **wutsu?mitu.**

pamukwaru?rukitu (v) bubble in water, make bubbles.

pamuputso?ni, pamuputsoo?nipu (n) swamp.

panaaitu (v) praise (speak well of; personal object obligatory). *See* **nihpana aitu.**

panaaitu (adj) proud.

panatsayaa? (n) blackberry, raspberry.

panatsitoo? (n) oar, canoe paddle (*lit* water stick).

panihputu mabà?atu (adj) high, tall (*lit* upward long).

panimi?aru (v) take someone home as guest, escort a guest some place. **Sumu?a panimi?ai.** He took someone home.

Papitsimina? (n), *pl* **Papitsimina-nuu** Sioux people.

papi (n) head (including face and hair). **Meekuru nu papiba?a**

to?i. Now climb up on my head
(19:12). *See* **paapị**.

papị hʉnʉpoʔa, papị boʔa (n) scalp
(*lit* head skin).

papị kuʔe (n) scalp (*lit* head top).

papị tsaʔnikaʔ (n) wig (*lit* to put on
the head).

papị tsihtʉpʉkaʔ (n) hairpin,
barrette, bobby pin.

papị tsiʔnikaʔ (n) side comb (*lit* to
put in the hair).

papị tsʉnʉʔitʉ (v) tangled hair.

papị wihtʉʔekaʔ (n) hair tonic (*lit*
hair grease).

papị wʉnʉkatʉ (adj) headache.

papị wʉi htamaʔ (n) otter, mink (*lit*
bundled head).

papịkamaitʉ (v) have a headache.
Papịkamai nʉʔ kʉtʉ. I had a
headache yesterday.

papịkamaka natʉsuʔu (n) aspirin
(*lit* headache medicine).

papoosinʉ (adj) soaked thoroughly,
rotting.

papʉsipʉ (adj) rotten. **Kokoraʔa
noyo tsaʔ papʉsipʉ.** The egg was
rotten.

papʉsitʉ (v) rot (become rotten).
Kokoraʔa noyo tsaʔ papʉsituʔi.
The egg will turn rotten.

papʉtsipịtʉ (adj) naked.

paraibo (n) peace chief (family
headman who could become
peace chief for the band).

paraibooʔ (n) chief, officer, agent,
chief wife among multiple wives,
stepmother.

paraimoʔo (n) mole (*lit* upside-
down hands).

paratsihkweʔerʉ (v), *pl* **paratsih-
kweyutʉ** glitter, shimmer.

parawa sʉkʉ (n) late-summer plum.

paroʔikitʉ (v) rise, swell (as a
river or creek). **HunuʔbiÂ tsaʔ
paroʔikitʉ.** The creek is rising.
See **atabaroʔitʉ**.

paruaitʉ (v) flood (cover dry area
with water).

paruhparʉ (v) paddle hands in the
water, dog paddle (*lit* slap water).
See **masuʔwaʔnekitʉ**.

Parukaa, Padouka (n) Comanches
(Siouan name for the Comanche
people).

paruukuʔ, paʔruhkuʔ (n) raccoon,
coon. *See* **nʉmamoʔoʔ**.

Paruwa kuma (name) Bull-elk (war
chief of the Antelope Band).

Paruwa sʉmʉno (name) Ten-elks
(person).

paruʔitʉ (v) flood the riverbank,
overflow the creek bed.
Hunuʔbi tsaʔ paruʔi. The creek
overflowed. *See* **muruʔitʉ**.

parʉa, parʉabi, parʉʉabi (n)
rough-leafed dogwood. *Cornus
asperifolia* Michx. (crossgrain
wood used for making arrow
shafts).

Parʉa kuhma (name) Bull-bear
(strong, fierce man who broke a
black bear's neck with his bare
hands).

parʉa kuhma, parʉʉhya kuhma
(n) bull elk (*lit* male water horse).

parʉa sʉkʉiʔ (n) plum, plum tree.
Prunus sp. (fruit eaten fresh or
dried; dried for later use). *See*
sʉkʉʔi, yusʉkʉ.

parʉbooʔ, parʉbooʔa tʉboʔ (n) ink
pen (*lit* water-writer).

parʉbʉʉʔitʉ (v) soak through (as
water through cloth).

parʉhwimiʔarʉ (v) melt away.

paruhwitu (v) melt.

parukitu (v) soak in water (for period of time).

parukwihtsipu (n, pl) *sg* **suuki** switches (as willow twigs, young and tender). **Situ wa?ihpu? turueh parukwihtsipuha u matsubaki?etu**. This woman sticks it on a little switch.

parutsohpe? (n) spring, spring water.

paruutsi (n) chin.

pasahòo (n) pigeon, dove, wren. *See* **ku?e wóo?**.

pasahtahtukitu W (v), *pl* **pasahtahni?itu** set out to dry, sit in the sun to dry. *See* **mabasahtukitu**.

pasahtohtsanaru (v) hang up to dry.

pasakuru (v) dry something.

pasanuaru (v) recede (go down, as creek after rising).

pasapuni (n) cross-eyed person.

pasapu (n) dry object.

pasaru (v) dry off body, dry out (as wet clothes). *See* **tubitsibasaru**.

Pasawío (name) Big-green-frog (Comanche name for one of E. Canonge's daughters).

pasawí?oo? (n) frog. *See* **pohpi kwáai?, ebi muura ya?ke?**.

pasawi?oo?a huki?ai? (n) mushroom (*lit* frog shade).

pasi waapi (n) sand, fine gravel.

pasibunaru (v) sprinkle (rain), shower (light rain).

Pasiwa huunu?bi, Pasi hunu?bi (n) Sand Creek.

pasiwanooru (v) haul sand.

pasiwanoo? W, **pasiwanookatu** K (n) sand dune, sand hill.

pasiwona puhubi, pasiwunu? bohoobi (n) silvery wormwood.

Artemesia filifolia Torr (velvet-like leaf used as toilet tissue; in bulk used as cushion in teepee or mattress in childbirth).

pasiwunuuru (v) leak (running in a steady stream).

pasoko?aru (v, sg obj), *pl obj* **pasokoo?itu** cover with earth, bury (as in planting potatoes).

pati- (pfx) green.

patiwiaketu, patuiwiakeetu (adj) green (moss-colored).

patowo?nepu (n) eroded soil, washout.

patowo?neru (v) wash out earth, erode.

patsahto?itu (v) pump water (as with a hand pump).

patsahto?i? (n) windmill, water pump (*lit* make water go up).

patsanuaru (v) channel water (by ditches or dam).

patsa?aiku, paatsa?aiku? (n) water pump, pump [**paa** water + **tsa?aiku?** pumper].

patsiketu (adj) slick, smooth.

patsi? (n) eldest sister. **nubatsi** my eldest sister.

patso?, patsokwe (n) mesquite-leaf mixture (mixed with other material having good flavor).

patso?itu (adj) damp, wet. *See* **pa?isoketu**.

patu tsanitu (v), *pl* **patu tsani?eru** snagged (as along water's edge).

paturuyaitu (v), *pl* **patukooitu** drown.

pawahkapu (n) herb (name unknown; grows near creeks).

pawobi puuku W, **pawobi** K (n) boat, canoe [**paa** water + **wobi** board + **puuku** horse].

pawuhpa?itu (v) splash with water, beat on someone with watery object.

pawuhtia wapi (n) baptizer (one who baptizes).

pawuhtumapu (n) dam (*lit* water banked up).

pawunuaru (v) scrub.

pawunua? (n) mop [**paa** water + **wunuai** sweep].

pawupa?itu (v) paddle feet in water (as when swimming).

pawu?we?niitu (adj) sprayed with water.

pawusa?naitu W (v) fill with water. *See* **ibu?ikuru, paa ma?ibu?ikutu.**

payaape, payapi (n) aqueous, wild tuber (grows above water, producing rich-flavored, potato-like tubers in clusters, each about three inches long). *See* **ahwepu.**

payunitu (v) water something, pour water on (from container).

payu?yukatu (adj) softened. *See* **yu?yukaru.**

pa?a- (pfx) long.

pa?a toyokatu huutsuu? K, pa?ati toyopukatu huhtsuu? W (n) crane (bird), stork (*lit* long- neck bird). *See* **kusikwa?aa?.**

pa?abe?nuu (n) triplets.

pa?arai, pa?rai (adv loc) upside down, on opposite side, on back.

pa?arai mo?o (n) woodchuck.

pa?a ruyu?, pa?a to?ayo? (n) giraffe (*lit* long neck).

pa?asu, pa?atusu, pa?atsu (adj) shallow (not deep or thick, as depth of chair or height of stairstep).

pa?atu (adj) long, high.

pa?boosi? (n) water lizard, water dog.

pa?ekusahpana? (n) sailor (*lit* water soldier).

pa?ibuikatu (adj) water-filled.

pa?ikaru (v), *pl* **paa?kwekwi** sink to the bottom in water. **Suru huupi pa?ikaai u?.** That log sank.

pa?isokeru (v) sprinkle, dampen (as clothes to iron). *See* **pi?wu?wenitu.**

pa?itsi?wunuru (adj) short (in stature; *lit* stand short).

pa?isoketu, pa?isoki (adj) wet, soaked. **Aawo tsa? pa?isoki.** The cup got wet. *See* **maba?isokitu, patso?itu.**

pa?ituhtsi? (adj) short (in length).

pa?kwakume, paa kwakume (n) snapping turtle. *Chelydra serpentina* (lives in rivers and streams). *See* **kwasi nuruu?wu?.**

pa?mukusu?aru (v) sprout. **Pihuura tsa? pa?mukusu?ai.** The beans sprouted.

pa?mutsi (n) plant similar to water lily (name unknown; root eaten raw or cooked; have rich, sweet taste).

pa?mutsi?, pa?mutsia (n) saddle (made of animal hip bones covered with wet rawhide which dries to shape; loops gird horse) [**pa?a** high + **mutsi** pointed]. *See* **tumuhku.**

pa?okwetu (v) eyes water heavily, shed many tears. **Nu pui tsa? pa?okweetu.** My eyes are watering heavily.

pa?puhi tuhka? (n) celery.

pa?raihabiitu (v) lie on back. **Situ tenahpu? pu norunapuka**

pa?araihabiitɨ. This man is lying on his back in his bed (99:10).

pa?sa ponii, pa?sah ponii (n) acorn.

pa?sa ponii huupi (n) oak. *Quercus* sp. (acorns eaten; trunks used for fence posts).

pa?sonipɨ (n) weeds.

pa?sɨno?a?, pa?asɨno?a? (n) kangaroo (*lit* shallow pregnancy).

pa?wɨhtakóo? (n) tadpole.

pa?wɨhtaràa?, pakwɨhtaràa? (n) scaffold (from which to hang water containers).

pa?wɨhtɨma? (n) beaver (*lit* makes dams).

pa?wɨtiarɨ (v, sg obj), **pl obj pawɨ?weniitɨ** baptize (pour water on someone); spray water on something (pour water here and there or in one spot).

pa?wɨtɨ (v) dam up (body of water).

pehe, huupipehe (n) seed.

pehkarɨ (v), *pl* **wasɨpɨ** kill. Ihka nɨ? tɨhɨye pehkatɨ. I am killing this horse. *See* **tɨkɨwasɨ?**.

peko?arɨ (v) split open, part (as clouds).

pekwi pɨmata hɨarɨ (n) fish trap.

Pekwi tɨhka (n) Fish Eaters (Comanche band said to have become a separate band around 1200 A.D.)

pekwi tɨhka?, pekwi tɨhka? huutsu (n) kingfisher. *Alcedinidae*.

pekwipɨ (adj) swollen. ku?itsi pekwipɨ swollen throat. Nɨ ku?itsi tsa? pekwikatɨ. My tonsils are swollen.

pekwitɨ (v) swell. U nape tsa? pekwitu?i. His feet are going to swell. **Pekwikatɨ ma?.** It is swollen.

pekwitɨ, peekwi (n), *pl* **sootɨ** peekwi fish (general term). sooka?wɨkatɨ school of fish. Pekwi nɨ? tsapietɨ. I am fishing.

Pena tɨhka (n) Sugar Eaters, Honey Eaters (southern-most Comanche band before and during the migration).

Penanɨɨ (n) Sugar Eaters (Comanche band now at Spur, Okla. and in northern Okla.)

pepikurɨ (n) casino.

pesotái (n) buttonbush. *Cephalanthus occidentalis* L. (wood used to make lacrosse sticks).

peti- (v) drop (let fall).

petihtarɨ (v) throw away, dispose of. Ma petihtai nɨ?. I threw it away. *See* **wihtaitɨ**.

petsɨ kwarɨ (v) invite to go along.

petsɨ mi?arɨ (v) fetch, go to get.

petsɨ pitarɨ (v) go after (to bring back to point of origin).

petɨ toyapɨ K (n) adopted daughter (*lit* daughter to carry).

petɨboopɨ W (n) adopted daughter [**petɨ** daughter + **tɨboopɨ** paper].

petɨ? (n) daughter.

pia (n) mother, mother's sister.

pia (adj) big, large, loud. Su?ana u pia pɨhɨwahtɨkɨ tɨrikuu?nɨɨ sookɨniba?i. Somewhere there in the big prairie, prairie dogs had a town.

pia animui (n) horsefly (*lit* large fly).

pia pɨku rekwarɨ (v) shout (raise voice louder than ordinary speech).

pia utsaatᵾ (adv man) piled badly, disorderly in placement. **Itᵾ tsa? aiku pia utsaatᵾ.** This thing is badly piled.

Pia ᵾtsᵾ?i mᵾa (n) December (*lit* big cold month).

pia baa (n) ocean (*lit* large water).

Pia baa (name) Big-water (Comanche chief who attempted to negotiate prisoner exchange in San Antonio in 1840).

Pia buha rabeni (n) Fourth of July (*lit* big Sunday).

piabᵾ (n) female animal. **kabᵾrᵾ?a piabᵾ** female goat (a nanny goat).

pia huutsuu? (n) eagle (*lit* large bird).

pia huyubatᵾ (adj) oblong. *See* **huyuba?atᵾ.**

pia kahúa (n), *pl* **pibia kahúu** rat, field mouse (*lit* large mouse).

pia kuitsi? (n) adam's apple (*lit* big throat). *See* **kuitsi tᵾkwᵾni.**

pia kᵾsarᵾ (v) open mouth wide.

pia kwihnai (n) eagle. *See* **kwihnai.**

Pia mᵾa (n) July (large month; shortened form of name). *See* **Pᵾmata pia buhha ra?ena mᵾa.**

Pia nᵾ?ᵾpai?i (n) Big-whip (whip-holder at a dance who had the special privilege of stopping a dance to recite a coup; similar to a master of ceremonies).

pia ohapitᵾ K (n) grapefruit (*lit* large yellow). *See* **ohápitᵾᵾ?ataka?.**

Pia opᵾ, Pi?opᵾ (name) (Chief captured by Coronado in 1540.)

Pia pasi hunu?bi (n) Red River (*lit* large sand creek).

pia pᵾhᵾ re?tsi (n) tarantula (*lit* large fuzzy brother-in-law). *See* **pᵾhᵾ re?tsi.**

Piana buni?, Piana ronitᵾ (name) Big-looking-glass (a former Yapai chief).

piana huwai? (n) big doctoring (Beaver ceremony).

piapᵾ (n) giant, large object; *adv* loudly, widely, everywhere.

pia rekwa (v) shout (talk loudly to someone).

pia rᵾnikwᵾtᵾ (v) sing loudly. **Waipᵾ tsa? pia rᵾnikwᵾrᵾ.** The woman is singing loudly [**pia** loud + **tᵾnikwᵾ** sing].

Pia rᵾtsima (name) Big-fall-by-tripping (person).

pia rᵾ?ewo (n) tablespoon. *See* **tᵾe aawo.**

pia tsatuakatᵾ (adj) wide open.

pia tsatuarᵾ (v) open something wide.

pia tseena? (n) wolf (*lit* large fox).

pia tso?nika? (n) headdress, war bonnet (big hat).

pia tᵾbookᵾni (n) college. *See* **tᵾboo kahni.**

pia wekitᵾ (adj) wide, roomy.

pia wᵾ?utsitᵾ (v) pile high, heap up. **Hina ta pia wᵾ?utsi?** What shall we pile up high?

Pibia niwᵾnᵾ?nᵾᵾ (n) Talk Loud (Comanche band).

pihi- (pfx) ref. to heart.

pihikarᵾ (adj) satisfied (*lit* the heart is set; have enough of something).

pihima (v, pl obj), *sg obj* **piyarᵾ** ride double (carry someone behind on horseback).

pihinaboo? (n) heart (in card game; *lit* heart printed).

pihisi?apᵾ (n) cowardly, piker (*lit* heart-chipped-off).

pihiso?ai (adj) vexed, peeved, angry.

pihiso?aitʉ (adj) disturbed, angry.

pihiso?aiwʉnʉrʉ (v) stand angrily, desire not to be disturbed.

pihitsi̱ (adj) greedy.

pihitsi̱naina (n) greed.

pihitsi̱tʉyarʉ (adj) extremely greedy, hoggish.

pihi?a W, **pihi?anʉʉ** K (n, pl), *sg* **tuinahpʉ?** boys.

pihi̱ (n) heart.

pihkarʉ (v), *pl* **pipi̱kutʉ** drumming, ring a bell (make repetitive sound by striking hollow object).

pihka?arʉ (v) break loose (something being pulled from behind).

pihka̱ (n) scar.

pihkobarʉ (v) break something down (as by sitting on it). *See* **pinutsarʉ**.

pihkʉma? K, **pihkʉmaarʉ** W (n) hem (bottom edge of something hanging).

pihnaketʉ, piinakerʉ (v) itch. **Nʉ paapi tsa? piinaketui.** My head will itch.

pihnaaketʉ (adj) itch. **Nʉ mo?o tsa? pihnaaketʉ.** My hand itches.

pihnákamarʉ (adj) taste sweet (have a sweet taste).

pihná nohkopʉ (n) sweet bread, cake, cookies (*lit* sugar biscuit). *See* **otʉ nohkopʉ**.

pihná rʉhkarʉ (v) crave sweets [**pihna?** sweets + **tʉhka** eat].

pihná baa (n) soda pop [**pihnaa** sugar + **paa** water].

pihnáa? W (n) sugar, sweets.

pihpárʉbʉ?ai (adj) wet seat (of pants or dress soaked from inside to outside).

pihpi̱, piipi̱ (n) horsefly.

pihpokaarʉ, piipokarʉ (adj) uneven, fall short (too short or too long). **Ohka tsa? kwasʉ piipokame.** The dress is uneven.

pihpóo?, piipóo? (n) water jug (made of hide or stomach of animal; wet hide is stitched with sinew, then air is blown in while it dries). **Pihpóo? tsa? paa ukupayu?iitʉ.** They carry water in the hide water jug.

pihtsamuu (n) milky-rooted plant.

pihtsakʉ huupi̱, waikina pihtsakʉ huupi̱ (n) singletree.

pihúraa, pihúura? (n) bean.

pihúura huupi (n) catalpa. Catalpa speciosa Warder (*lit* bean tree).

piinaai (n) leftover, remnant saved (as of food or cloth). **wanapʉ piinaimatʉ** leftover piece of cloth.

piitsʉnʉa? (n) straight pin [**pih-** long + **tsʉ?nʉa?** round at end].

pika (n) leather.

pika kwasu? (n) man's buckskin jacket.

pika namʉsoopʉ (n) buckskin clothing (for man, woman, or child).

pikapʉ (n) leather, buckskin, tanned deer hide. *See* **taibo pikapʉ**.

pikʉtsekarʉ (v) crush, mash (as by sitting on something soft).

pikwebuitʉ (v) turn around quickly. **Sarii tsa? piikwebui.** The dog turned around quickly.

pikwʉrʉpʉka? W, **pipʉrʉpʉka?** K (n) diaper (*lit* folded over for the seat).

pikwʉsii? (n) sulky, buggy (two-wheeled vehicle, singletree). **Uba nʉ rʉa pikwʉsii to?inʉ.** There

I climbed into the buggy. *See* **sumasunooi.**

pimimi?aru (v) walk backward, step backward, back up.

pimoroo taiboo? (n) cowboy.

pimoroo? (n), *pl* **pimoroo?nuu** cow. **Su?ana piapuhu pimoróo? kimaayu.** A big cow was coming along the edge of the water (19:1).

pimoroo?a korohko? (n) white elm. *Ulmus americana* L.

pimoroo?a kuhma (n) bull.

pimoroo?a piabu (n) cow.

pimoroo?a tua? (n) calf.

pimoroo?a tuyu?wipu (n) cow's cud.

pimoro?a puhi (n) cowhide, animal hide.

pimunikatu (adj) stuck fast (unable to pull something out).

pinai, binai (post) from behind. **Situkuse? kwasinaboo? u pinai u kuhtsianu.** This snake bit him from behind him (27:9).

pinakutsuru, pinakutsuitu (v) tickle someone.

pinakwu, pinaku (post) behind. **Tuinuhpu tsa? kahni pinaku.** The boy is behind the house.

pinutsaru (v) sit on something breaking it to pieces. *See* **pihkobaru.**

Pipiku? (name) Squeaky (short form of name of Elliot Canonge's son). *See* **Kahúu nihkupipikure.**

pipóhtoru (v) pop (make popping sound by sitting on something).

pisahpi (n) powder. *See* **homopu.**

pisaru (v) make up someone (apply make-up). **Nu takana kobe homopisai.** I powdered my sister's face. **homobisai** apply powder.

pisayu?ne? (n) tin or other shiny metal, jingles (shoe ornaments of metal). **Ma pisayu?ne?ai tanu.** Let's make jingles (shoe ornaments) out of it.

pisi (adj) festering, infected. **Ma?u?a tsa? pisi.** The sore is infected.

pisi (n) pus, infection.

pisi ma?rokóo? (n) rainbow (*lit* infected thumb).

pisi mi?aru (v) infecting (becoming infected).

Pisi narumuu? (n) Cache, Okla. (*lit* rotten store).

pisi wa?kóo? W (n) oyster [**pisi** pus + **wa?kóo?** shell].

pisi wa?rokóo? K (n) oyster [**pisi** smelly + **wa?rokóo?** seashell].

pisibuni? (n) cattail, cat's tail. *Typha latifolia* L.

pisiko?i (v) ride seated on a sled. **Nu kako tsa? pisikooinu.** Grandma went on a sled ride.

pisikwanúu?itu (v) slide down. **Wihnu suru pisikwanúu?inu.** Then that one slid down (5:11). *See* **nuaru.**

pisikwanúu?i? (n) slide.

pisona?aitu (v) build a nest. *See* **huupiso?na?aitu.**

pisoonaru (v) put down something to sit on.

pisóona (n) quilt, 3' by 6' pallet used during peyote meeting.

piso?aru (v) prick someone with something.

Pisu kwá?na? (n) Smeller (somewhat derogatory name given northern band by other bands).

pisukwitaitu (v) squirm, move nervously.

pisukwitakᵾrᵾ (v) interrupt someone because of worry.

pisukwitarᵾ (v) fret, worry, suffer on deathbed. Pᵾ tuabaatᵾ pisukwitai. She is worried about her boy. *See* musasuarᵾ.

pisunarᵾ (v) drag something spread on flat surface. Tᵾʔehwaikina pisunaarᵾ nᵾʔ. I am dragging the small wagon.

pisuníiʔ K (n) skunk (*lit* constant bad odor). *See* pohniʔatsᵢ.

pisuniʔeeyᵾ (n) skunk (*lit* casts off bad odor).

pisuʔnetᵾ (v) rub against something, scratch rear or back against something. Pimoróoʔ tsaʔ pisuʔnetᵾ. The cow is rubbing her rear.

pisuʔniʔ (n) nest. kahúa pisuʔni rat nest.

pisᵾtᵾkitᵾ (v) pace (as a horse). Tᵾhᵾya tsaʔ pisᵾtᵾkitᵾ. The horse is pacing (along).

pitsa miʔarᵾ (v) return, go back (moving away from speaker).

pitsa múu, pihtsa múuʔ (n) legume. *Camote de ratán, Hoffmanseggia Jamesii* T. and G. (*lit* milky roots; tubers eaten).

pitsa nabooʔ K (n) calico horse (*lit* spotted on the hips). *See* tosanaboò.

pitsa ᵾkwakatu kimarᵾ (v) back up, come backwards (movement with back toward speaker).

pitsákarᵾ (v) pull something behind (as a trailer).

pitsakaʔ (n) trailer (anything pulled behind). *See* tᵾbiyaakᵾʔ.

pitsanitᵾ, pitsᵾhanitᵾ (v) choke. Tehahpᵾ tsaʔ pitsanikatᵾ. The man choked. *See* paabitsanitᵾ.

pitsanᵾ tᵾyaitᵾ (v) choke to death. Pitsanᵾ tᵾyaihumiarᵾ maʔ. He is choking to death.

pitsi makatᵾ (v) wean a baby. Nᵾ rᵾʔeti nᵾʔ pitsi makatᵾ. I weaned my baby.

pitsi pᵾha nᵾkuʔwᵾpᵾ (n) clabber, clabbered milk. Nᵾkuʔkwᵾʔimaʔ. It is sour.

pitsi tora, pitsi tohra (n) prickly poppy. *Argemone intermedia* Sweet (used for treating sore eyes).

pitsiiʔ, pᵢtsamᵾ (n) woman's breast.

pitsimai (adj) weaned.

pitsipᵾ, pitsipa (n) milk.

pitsipᵾ pimoróoʔ W (n) milk cow.

pitsipᵾ wihtua (n) milk bucket, milk can.

pitsipᵾha poʔaa (n) cream (*lit* milk's covering).

pitsohka kwaba W, pitsoko kwaaʔbaʔ W (n) turtle (alligator snapping, large water turtle). *Macroclemys temmincki.*

pitsohkorᵾ (v) put on trousers. Tenahpᵾ tsaʔ pitsohkorᵾ. The man put on his trousers.

pitsᵾkwinaʔ (n) apron (worn by Indian women).

pitᵾsᵾ (adv dir) back. Pitᵾsᵾ miʔarᵾ nᵾʔ. I am going back. Pitᵢsᵾ u yaai. He took it back.

pitᵾsᵾ nuʔyeʔ W (n) woodpecker.

pitᵾwetᵾ (v) limp (of human or of hind leg of animal). Tenahpᵾ tsaʔ pitᵾwetᵾ. The man is limping. *See* matᵾwetᵾ.

pitᵾnᵾ (v) arrive, approach someone. Wakareʔeeʔ mawaka pitᵾni. Turtle came up to him. Oha ahnakatᵾ urᵾᵾkᵾ pitᵾni.

Coyote arrived among them. *See*
noopitų.

pitųbarų (v) crack something by
sitting on it.

pitųsohkǫ?, pitsohkǫ? (n)
trousers.

piwokami?arų (v) drag something
along. **Sųmų? tenahpų? pų kahni
wųhpiwokųkatų.** One man is
dragging his teepee (123:21).

piwokarų (v) drag something. *See*
wųhpiwokarų.

piwo?sa wųnarų (v) ache in lower
back, have a backache.

piwo?sa wųnųkatų (v) have a
backache in lower back.

piwo?sa̲, piwo?se (n, acc) hip,
lower back, tailbone. **Nų biwose
nų? mahrųni.** I hurt my hip.

piyarų, piyami?arų (v), *pl*
pihimacarry someone behind on
horseback, ride double.

pi?isųtų (n) pacer (type of horse).
Tųhųya tsa? pi?isųtų. The horse
is a pacer.

**pi?nakwų bųetsų, pi?nakų
pųetsųkų** (adv) day after
tomorrow.

pi?nu?a mi?arų, pignu?a mi?arų
(v) go backwards, go back and
forth or from side to side (as in
wagon).

pi?nu?a? (n) crab (*lit* goes
backward).

pi?onų suakųtų (adj) angry.

**Pi?opų parųba tųyo, Peope
Padiva, Taoyo, Tuyo** (name)
Boy (very young chief of the Fish
Eaters band in earlier years).

pi?to, pi?to?na?i (adj) bobtailed.
Sarii tsa? pi?to. The dog is
bobtailed. **Sųsųmų? kwasinaboo?**

pi?to?na?i̲. Some snakes are
bobtailed (36:16).

pi?tohtsía? W (n) white-tailed deer
(*lit* bob-tailed white spot).

pi?to?arų, pi?to?na?itų (v) bob a
tail, cut off short.

pi?weesu?ru?itų (v) swing sitting
down.

pi?weke mi?arų (v) walk swinging
hips.

pi?wesurúu?i̲? (n) playground
swing [**pi?** backside +
weesuru?ųi swing].

pi?wų?wenitų (v) spill, sprinkle.
Pai u? pi?wų?wenimi?arų. It is
going along sprinkling water (as
city water-sprinkler truck). *See*
pa?isokerų.

pi?wųriarų (v) spill something (by
sitting on or beside it).

pi?yųpų káa?i̲ W (n) railroad
handcar [**pi?yųpų** pumping
motion + **kaa?i** that which does].
See **kų?wųnųbaa?i̲.**

pohbitų, popitų (v), *pl* **pohbiarų**
jump. **Sitų oha ahnakatų
hunu?matu pohpínų.** This coyote
jumped into the creek (14:18, 19).

pohitų (adj) stretched (as a hide).

pohkóo? (n) burrowing owl.

pohni?atsi̲ (n, arch) skunk.
Pohni?atsiha nų? ųkwi. I smell a
skunk. *See* **pisuníi?.**

pohóobi, pohho nųkwų (n)
sagebrush, quinine weed.
Artemisia tridentata Nutt.

pohotatų (adj) thick. **Esiwana tsa?
pohotatų.** The blanket is thick.

pohotų na?sųkía? (n) heavy shawl.
See **na?sųkia?.**

pohpi kwáai? W (n) frog (*lit*
jumping goes). *See* **pasawi?oo?.**

pohtohkikatu (adj) bloated (swelled up from air or gas inside). **Sarii tsa? pohtohkikatu.** The dog is bloated.

pohtokitu (v) puff up, bloat, swell up, rise (as bread dough). **Tohtia tsa? pia pohtokii.** The bread rose high (large). *See* **mubohtohkitu.**

pohtokuru (v) inflate [**pohto** burst + **-ku** (cause)]. *See* **mubohtohkiru.**

pohto?itu (v) burst (break open with a bang).

pohyami?aru (v) run slowly, walk fast, trot. *See* **aimi?aru.**

poiya (n) fever plant (plant whose leaves are used in treatment of fever).

pokaru (v) play poker.

poko ruhka? (n) cucumber (large variety).

pokopi tuaru (v) bear fruit.

pokopi (n) berries, fruit, nuts.

pokopi masuapu (n) orchard, garden.

pomapu (n) picked berries, harvested crop, produce.

pomaru (v) pick fruit, harvest a crop. **Panatsaya nu? pomaru.** I am picking berries. *See* **tubomaru.**

poohkatu, pooru (adj) scattered around (scattered here and there, piece by piece). **Amawóo tsa? poohkatu.** The apples are scattered around. *See* **tsahpo?aru.**

poosubuhkaitu (v) go crazy, have an evil spirit.

poosubukukaitu (adj) berserk, crazed (gone crazy).

Poo?aiku (name) Blow-it-away (person).

poo?sa? (n) crazy person. **Tenahpu tsa? poo?sa?.** The man is crazy. *See* **po?sa.**

poputsanawutu (adj) bumpy (as a road).

porokaru (v) crack (make cracking sound, as knuckles).

porokitu (v) snap (emit snapping sound as of fingers).

posaaki (n) bridge.

Positsu mua (n) February (*lit* sleet month).

poyohkaru (adj) made to trot.

po?aru (v) spread legs out.

po?ayaahkwaru (v) blow away. **Nuetu tsa? u po?ayaaku?i.** The wind is blowing it away (49:29).

po?ayaakutu (v) blow away.

po?aya?eetu (n) thistle (*lit* many blown around). *Cirsium undulatum* Nutt., Spreng.

po?a? (n) bark, cover, skin. *See* **huupi po?a?, hunu po?a?, amawo?a? po?a?, sonabo?a.**

po?hibahpakitu, po?ahibahpakitu (v) wave, flap (in the wind).

po?himaru, po?ahimaru (v) winnow (as to clean grain).

po?oya? (n) blown-away object.

po?ro tuhkapu K (n) pork. *See* **mubipo?roo ruhkapu.**

po?ro tuhtumapu (n) fence of hog pen.

po?ropunuu (n, pl), *sg* **hooki** hogs.

po?ro? (n), *pl* **po?ro?nukwu,** *du* **po?ro?nuupig,** hog, swine. *See* **munua?, hooki.**

po?sa (adj) crazy.

po?sa baa (n) whisky (*lit* crazy water).

po?sa baa kahni (n) saloon.

po?sabihi?a (adj) mischievous.

Pua paatsoko (name) Medicine-otter (person).

puha bahmu?itu (v) smoke during religious ceremony.

puha kahni (n) church, peyote teepee (*lit* medicine house).

puha kahni muutsi (n) steeple. *See* **muutsi.**

puha nabisaru (v) anoint (apply medicine paint).

puha namaka?mukipu (n) medicine outfits (paraphernalia for peyote ceremony; herbs, rattles, gourds). **Situu sumu?oyetu puu puha namaka?mukipuha himanu.** All these ones got their medicine outfits (70:18).

puha natsu W (n) red false mallow (used for reducing swelling). *Malvastrum coccineum* [Pursh.] A. Gray. *See* **yokanatsu?u.**

puha niwunuruu K, **puha niwunuru** W (n) church service.

Puha rabeni (n) Sunday (holy day).

puha raiboo? W, **puha rekwiraiboo?** K (n) preacher, medicine man.

Puha rakatu (n) Sunday (*lit* holy rest).

puha rekwaru W, **puha rekwutsitu** K (v) preach (*lit* speak with power).

Puha rupaanu (n) Lawton, Okla.

Puha rupanaabi (n) Medicine Bluff

Puha ruboopu (n) Bible (*lit* holy writings).

puha tenahpu (n) medicine man, medicine doctor.

puha wuhtitu, puha kwuhtiru (v) bewitch someone.

puhakatu (n) heal-all plant (acts as a stimulant). *Prunella caroliniana*

Mill.; *adj* K **puhakatu,** W **puha namahkukatu** having supernatural power.

Puhawi (name) Medicine-woman (person).

puha?aitu (n) shaman.

puha?aitu (n) prepared medicine, curing ceremony.

puha?aru (v) prepare medicine, hold a curing ceremony for someone.

puha (n) medicine, supernatural power. *See* **natusu?u.**

puhi (n) leaf.

puhi huuba (n) dry tea (*lit* leaf coffee). *See* **puhi tuhpaa.**

puhi huuki (n) brush arbor (*lit* leaf shade). **Puhi huuki puha niwunu uruu.** They had a brush-arbor meeting.

puhi koo?ipu (n) dead grass (burned by the sun).

Puhi mua, Puhhi mua (n) June (leaf month).

puhi taitu (n) K clump of grass; W bush. *See* **puhi topika.**

puhi ta?ara?, puhi ta?raabu (n) poison ivy (*lit* leaf poison). **Anacardiaceae.**

puhí tsawoo? (n) cultivator (*lit* grass scratcher).

puhi tubi, puhi tuhpa K (n) bush clover (beverage made from leaves acts as stimulant). *Lespedeza capitata* Michx.

puhi tuhpaa W (n) liquid tea. *See* **puhi huuba.**

puhi tuhkapu (n) lettuce (*lit* leaf food).

puhi tumakwatubi? (n) leaf wrappers for cigarettes. *See* **tumakwatui.**

puhi turuhka? (n) mistletoe.
Viscum Foradendron sp. (*lit* leaf
thief).

puhi tuyaitu (v), *pl* **puhi koo?i**
choke out, kill by growing over.

puhi tuyaitu (n) dead grass.

puhi yukwitu (v) hoe soil.

puhi yukwitu? (n) hoe (implement).

puhi bihnáa? (n) watermelon.

puhihwi (n) money, gold (*lit* shiny
leaf). **Situ kuse? wihnu ma
kwuhu sooti puhihwipa?i.** This
then his wife had much money
(47:7). *See* **ekapuhihwi.**

puhihwi kahni (n) financial bank
(*lit* money house).

puhihwi naruso W (n) pocketbook,
wallet, coin purse (*lit* money
sack). *See* **puhihwi wosa.**

puhihwi natsihtu?ye? (n)
metal comb, wire brush. *See*
natsihtu?ye?.

puhihwi paraiboo? (n) banker (*lit*
money boss).

puhihwi tekwapuhana huupi (n)
telephone pole (*lit* money talk pole).

puhihwi tekwapu (n) telephone (*lit*
money talk).

puhihwi tuaru (v) get, have money.

puhihwi tuboopu (n) check, bank
draft (for transfer of money).

puhihwi tuuhtumaru (v) put up a
barbed wire fence.

puhihwi tuuhtuma? (n) barbed
wire (*lit* money fence).

puhihwi wehki (v) look for money.
See **wehkinitu.**

puhihwi wosa K (n) woman's purse,
pocketbook. *See* **puhihwi naruso.**

puhihwi yaaru (v), *pl* **puhihwu
himaru** cash a check (receive
money in exchange).

puhihwimaka (v) give money to
someone.

puhihwi ta ahweetu (n) treasure
(*lit* gold dug up).

puhipu (n) leaf (from tree or bush).

**Puhipuha puma oha to?i?ena
mua, Puhipuha** (n) October (leaf
fall month).

puhitookatu (v) graze on turkey
grass.

puhitóo? K (n) turkey.

puhitóo? (n) turkey grass.

puhitopika (n) bush. *See* **puhitaitu.**

puhkapu (adj) ripped, torn.

puhkaru (v) tear something, rip
something.

puhkaru (adj) burst open (as a
cloud).

puhnuketu (adj) slick, smooth,
slippery.

puhwaaitu (v) look for, search
carefully for (search with the
eyes). **Obotika hunu?ruti noo
hina puhwaihbuuni.** Look for
something over the creek (6:24).

puhyunukitu (v) glide, move slowly
(as train moves along track).

pui (n) eye.

pui hwai (adj) blind (sightless).

pui naruso, pui naso (n) eyelid.

pui tsaseni, puitsasena? (n) rye
grass (sharp-edged, used in cutting
cataract from the eye). *Elymus*
sp.(?)

pui tsa?nika? (n) eyeglasses.

puibuutu (v) be sleepy-eyed (have
eyes heavy with sleep).

puibuututu (adj) sleepy.

puih tsahtsuru (v) wink (*lit* squeeze
the eye).

puihtsara? W (n) flank of animal.

puihtsita? K (n) rib area of animal.

puikɨso (n) chigger, redbug.

puiwɨnɨrɨ (v) examine, look over.
See tsaʔatsitɨ.

puiʔ (n) temple (upper side of the
head).

puitɨsii, puʔtɨsii (n) eyelash.

puku, puukɨ (n), acc puki horse.
Tai puku tsakakɨ kwatuʔi nɨʔ.
I will go to lead the horse for us
(43:25). Sitɨ kɨseʔ ma kuma-
hpɨʔ pɨhɨ puki toʔyanɨ. This
her husband unhitched their horse
(48:17).

puku hibikɨʔ (n) water trough.

puku kahni, pukukɨni (n) stable.
See kahni.

puku tsakamiʔarɨ, K puku
tsakɨkarɨ (v) lead a horse.

puku rúaʔ (n) colt (lit horse child).

puku rɨhkaʔ, puku tɨhkaʔ (n)
nosebag.

Pukutsi (n) Crazy Warriors (men
who did everything backward;
similar to the Koshare of Eastern
Pueblo).

Pukuʔa tuaʔ (name) Colt (lit horse
child).

puni kwarɨ (v) visit (go to see).
Uhka tai puni kwatuʔika. We
will (let's) go to see that one
(7:36).

punitɨ (v) see, look at. Sitɨ pia
tɨrahyapɨ ma puninɨ. This big
meatball saw it (23:29).

Punitɨ (name) Looking (person).

pupɨkatɨ (adj) threadbare (thin
cloth).

puruarɨ (v) splatter. Yuhu tsaʔ
puruanɨ. The lard splattered.
Orɨ tsaʔ waipɨʔ ma puruʔai.
That woman splattered it. See
kuhpuruʔairɨ.

pusiaketɨ (v) search for head lice,
delouse.

pusiʔa natsihtuʔyeʔ (n) fine-
toothed comb (lit head louse
comb).

pusiʔa, pusiʔa (n) head louse. See
yupusia.

putsi kwɨtsɨbaitɨ (v) sing high
pitched (as does a woman).

putsi tɨnikwɨyɨ K (adj) high
pitched.

putsi waipɨ (n) trunk of a white,
dead tree. Siʔana putsi waipɨha
soho bokóoʔa wɨnɨku. Here
where a white, dead mulberry tree
is standing (16:13).

puuhkikatɨ (adj) blown out,
extinguished (as a candle).

puuhkitɨ (v) blow breath (blow on
a person in a curing ritual).

puuyaketɨ (n) buzzing sound (made
by a mosquito).

puʔe nagwe (n) wagon crossing. See
nagwe.

Puʔekatɨ (n) Christian (lit one who
has a path). See tɨipuʔe.

puʔeyarɨ (v) follow a road.

puʔeʔaikɨpɨ W (n) tradition. See
nanihpuʔeʔaikɨpɨ.

puʔeʔarɨ (v) construct a road, clear
a path.

puʔe (n) road, trail, path. Puʔetu
nɨʔ miʔarɨ. I am going through
the road. See tɨipuʔe.

puʔiʔ (n) gall bladder.

puʔiʔwɨnɨrɨ (adj) suffer gall-
bladder pain.

pɨ (pro coref, 1st gen sg) his, her, its.

Pɨ tua wɨni kwai (name) Been-to-
see-his-son (person).

Pɨa kwarɨ (n) Desert-in-large-group
(Comanche band now in Walters

area; so named by other group because a large group deserted together).

pʉa miʔarʉ (v) leave someone for good.

pʉa nuhkitʉ (v) run away from somewhere, desert. *See* **nuhkitʉ**.

pʉa watsi (n) wild stallion, horse.

pʉah kwarʉ (v) separate in marriage, leave a spouse.

pʉah taitʉ (v) forsake someone, desert.

pʉah taikatʉ (adj) divorced, separated in marriage.

pʉarʉ (v) turn loose, quit something, cease doing. **Ma pʉaruʔi nʉʔ.** I will let go of him. **Pʉ pahmuʔina uʔ pʉai.** He quit smoking. *See* **tohpʉarʉ**.

pʉe, pʉesʉ (adv time) already.

pʉe nʉmʉ roopʉnʉʉ (n) forefathers (past generations).

pʉe tʉyaaiʔ, pʉeh tʉyaaiʔ (n) ghost, evil spirit (spirit of someone long deceased, invisible but can be heard). *See* **nʉnʉpʉhiʔ**.

pʉesúubeʔ K (n) velvet cloth, work-type handkerchief.

pʉesúubeʔ W (n) nursling, young (as pony, chick, kitten).

pʉetsʉku, pʉetsʉkusʉ (adv) early morning (before sunup). **Situʉkʉseʔ u pʉetsʉku sooyotʉ pitʉsʉ tʉasʉ ukʉhu miʔanʉ.** These ones (who) are many that morning went back again (28:24).

pʉetsʉkunakwʉsa (n, arch) morning.

pʉetʉpʉ (n) elderly woman.

pʉewatsi (adj) wild, untamed.

pʉewatsi kʉʉka (n) wild onion. *See* **kʉhtsʉtsʉʉʔniʔ**.

pʉhetʉ, pʉhhetʉ (adv man) fast, quick.

pʉhimataka (adv man) barely. **Pʉhimataka okʉ pitai.** They barely arrived (in time).

pʉhkai (v) stop crying, hush.

pʉhkaikatʉ (adj) hushed, comforted.

pʉhkaitʉniitʉ W, pʉhkootʉnitʉ K (v) comfort an adult (help someone stop crying).

pʉhkitʉ (v) stop raining. **Pʉhkipʉ ʉmanʉ.** It stopped raining.

pʉhkʉra nahanʉ W (n) present generation. *See* **nʉmʉ rʉborapʉ**.

pʉhkwinuʔitʉ W, pʉkwitsunitʉ K (v, nonhum subj) squirm, wriggle.

pʉhtsapʉ (adj) broken, burst, blown out (as a tire).

pʉhtsarʉ, pʉtsʉharʉ (v) burst, explode (as a balloon). **Surʉ urʉʉ hanipʉ pʉtsʉhánʉ.** Their charge exploded (29:28).

pʉhtsaʔetʉʔ (n) dynamite, explosive. **Situʉkʉseʔ suhka pʉhtsaʔeti ukʉhu haninʉ.** These ones prepared there that explosive (29:26).

pʉhtuku nʉmʉ, tʉbooʔena (n) camera. *See* **tʉbooʔetʉ, kobenaboʔ**.

pʉhtʉ (adj) heavy.

pʉhʉ kabʉrʉʉʔ (n) sheep (*lit* woolly goat).

pʉhʉ kuʔkweʔyaʔ (n) lion (*lit* head covered with hair).

pʉhʉ kwʉsuʔʉ (n) fur coat.

pʉhʉ nʉnapʉ (n) hairy chest, chest hair.

pʉhʉ pusia (n) crab louse (*lit* hair louse). *See* **suhuposía**.

puhu tsahkwe?yaru (v) skin an animal. *See* **wusibo?aru.**

puhu tso?nika? (n) fur hat.

puhuwahtu (n) prairie. *See* **numuwahtu.**

puhu natsu (n) medicinal herb (grows in Mexico; medicinal use to ease pain, lower fever, cure kidney disease).

puhu no?itu (v) pluck a bird clean. *See* **pahtsi no?itu.**

puhu rasoona (n) rug, carpet (*lit* fuzzy floor).

puhu re?tsi (n) brother-in-law, spider (*lit* fuzzy brother-in-law). *See* **pia puhu re?tsi, tetsi.**

puhu rumuihpaa? (n) fur cap. *See* **tumuihpaa?.**

puhu ru?saasi, puhu rutsaasi (n) medicinal herb (has roots with hairs similar to wool; used in mixture for purifying blood).

puhusu?kui (n) peach (fuzzy plum).

puhu? (n) hair fuzz, animal hide, shee wool, hairy vegetation (*lit* hair fuzz).

puka (v) bury (animals or humans).

pukapu (n) lap (of a seated person).

Pukura totsiyaa?ai?eka (n) Decoration Day [**puku-** field + **-ra** (gen) + **totsiyaa?** flowers + **ai** do + **eka** day]. *See* **Totsiyaaih tabenihtu.**

pukuhu, pukhu (n) place known by speaker and hearer. **Pukuhu nu? numinu.** I have been there (speaker and hearer know where).

pukura nohko?ena W (n) oven (*lit* place in which one bakes biscuits). *See* **nohko aawo.**

pukura yukwi?ena W (n) parlor, livingroom (*lit* place in which to sit). *See* **yukwi kahni.**

pumata nookoina (n) wheat flour.

Pumata pia buhha ra?ena mua (n) July (Fourth-of-July month; long form). *See* **Pia mua.**

Pumata waahima?ena mua, Pumata wahi mua (n, month) December (*lit* gift month).

Pumata wanohi?ema mua (n) December (*lit* Christmas-gift month).

punusu (pro, refl) oneself. **punusu habinu** go to bed oneself.

pupa?akura tuboo?ena W (n) desk (*lit* place on which to write). *See* **tubooruhka?.**

pupa?akura turahkwu?ne?ena (n) ironing board (*lit* place on which one irons).

pupe? (adj) complete, fulfilled.

purusu?aru (v) uncoil, unwind, unravel. *See* **wuhpukusuaru, tsahkwumaru.**

puu (pro coref, 3rd gen pl) their.

puu- (pfx) ref. to blood.

puuokwetu (v) bleed, hemmorhage.

puuhibiru (v) partake of Communion.

puuhibitu?itu (n), *pl* **puuhibitu?inunu** Communion (sacrament), Mass (sacrament). *See* **tohtíaruhkapu.**

puuhpi (n) blood.

puupi (n) Communion wine.

puura (n) arm.

puuyu namanahkepu (n) decoy duck (*lit* duck-parading item).

puuyu (n) duck.

Pu?na petu (name) Only-daughter (person).

pu?une W, **pu?ne** K (adv num) only. **pu?ne puuyu** only (one) duck.

S

saa huubạ (n) soup (boiled tree-water).

saabara (n) bedsheet, sheet for bed.

saabe busia (n) body louse (*lit* sleeve louse).

saah totsi baa (n) beer, hard cider (intoxicating drink of any type that foams up; anything that boils up or bubbles up as solder on a hot iron) [**saa-** boil + **totsi** square + **paa** water].

saahtotsitoʔikatɨ (adj) fermented, foaming, frothing at the mouth.

saahtotsitoʔiʔ (n) foam.

saapɨ (n) boiled meat.

saatitamakatɨ (adj), *pl* **tsatsatitamakatɨ** loose tooth, chattering teeth.

saatotsiya (n) flowering plant (*lit* boiling flower).

saatotsiyapɨ (n) potted plant.

saatɨ (v) boil.

saawihtua (n) cooking pot, cauldron (*lit* bucket for boiling).

saaʔarɨ (v) cause to boil.

saaʔwɨ (n) ref. to holes.

saaʔwɨ tɨkɨmaʔaiʔ (n) lace (perforated trimmed edge).

saaʔwɨtɨ (adj) holey (full of holes).

saaʔwɨʔ (n) mesh, sieve, screening.

saaʔwɨ hɨaʔ (n) fishnet.

saaʔwɨ napɨ (n) sandals (*lit* perforated shoes). *See* **waraatsị**.

sahkị (n) canoe.

sahpáanaʔ (n) side of stomach or abdomen (on surface).

sakwɨsikɨtɨ (v) tangle, *adj* tangled. *See* **kwisihkarɨ**.

samohpɨʔ (n), nom *pl* **samonɨɨ**, acc *pl* **samonii** sibling, brother, sister.

sanahkena W, **sanahpị** K (n) sap (of a tree or plant).

sanahkoo kɨyuʔnetɨ (v) chew gum.

sanahkooʔ W, (n) gum; **sanahkooʔa kɨtsɨkwetɨ** K chewing gum. **Usɨ pɨnihku nɨmɨ sanahkóoʔaiʔenạ**. That's the way (we) made our gum (110:21).

Sanah pia (name) (Comanche medicine woman).

Sanah pia ariba (name) (Comanche female chief).

sanahtuʔreʔ (n) snail (*lit* sticky leech).

sanarɨ (v) adhere, stick to.

sanaweha (n) broomweed, mormon tea. *Gutierrezia dranunculoides* [D.C.] Blake (used for making brooms and to cure kidney or bladder trouble and influenza).

Santanta (name) (Comanche chief; mother was Wapɨsoni; went to Washington, D.C.; in 1847, signed German peace treaty).

sapɨ (n) stomach. **Sitɨ kɨseʔ oha ahnakatɨ ma sapɨka ikanɨ**. This coyote entered into her stomach (20:22).

sapɨ (n) ref. to stomach.

sapɨ nɨɨtsikwarɨ (n) stomach ache.

sapɨ wɨnɨkatɨ (n) baby colic, extreme stomach pain.

saraa (adv dir) across (meaning uncertain). **Surɨ kɨseʔ, 'Hinatsa nɨʔ panoo saraa saraa saraaʔ'** That one said, 'What shall I carry across?' (19:3).

Saria Tɨhka, Sata Teichas (n) Dog Eaters (Comanche band that split cir. 1300 A.D. from the Teichas; what is now Texas).

Sarii Tɨhka? (n), *pl* **Sarii Tɨhka?nɨɨ** Cheyenne, Arapaho (*lit* dog eaters).

sarii? (n), *pl* **sarii?nɨɨ,** *pl* **accsarii?nii** dog. **Sitɨɨ kɨse? ma sarii?nɨɨ tɨnayaarɨ.** These his dogs are trailing (91:3). **Sitɨ kɨse? pɨ sarii?nii pianimaiɨ.** This one loudly called (to) his dogs (92:19).

Sata Tejas I, Saria Tɨhka I (name) **Sata Tejas I** (Dog Eaters chief cir. 1689–1693).

Sata Tejas II, Saria Tɨhka II (name) **Sata Tejas II** (Dog Eaters chief cir. 1873–1889).

sekwi (n) ref. to mud.

sekwi bii? (n) second stomach of cow (*lit* mud stomach).

sekwikɨni, sekwɨ kahni K (n) cellar, storm cellar (*lit* mud house). *See* **ohta kahni, sokokɨni.**

sekwi nuyu?itɨ (adj) mud-covered. **Sekwi nuyu?itɨ ɨnɨ.** You are covered with mud.

sekwi sɨhkai, sekwikɨ sɨhkai (adj) stuck in the mud. **Nabukuwaa tsa? sekwi kɨsɨhkai.** The car is stuck in the mud. *See* **yubu tsɨhkatɨ.**

sekwipɨ (n) mud.

sekwitsipuhitsi (n) mud-men (clowns; masked dancers).

seni (adv man) different ways, various ways.

senihtɨhtsi? (n) pitiful, undependable person.

setɨɨ (pro dem, scattered nom pl) those.

seyɨyuki?, ehyɨyuki? (n) ash. *Fraxinus* sp. (name refers to seed pods that rattle in the wind).

sia- (pfx) ref. to feather.

sia sona rɨbaki? (n) feather mattress.

sia tsohpe (n) feather pillow.

siba huupi, siiba huupi K (n) flowering dogwood. *Cornus florida.*

sibepɨ (n) shaving, scraping.

sibe?nikiyutɨ (adv time) from now on. **Tahɨ puhiwihta takwɨ sibe?nikiyutɨ puhihwikahnikɨ tahni?i?etu?i.** From now on we'll put our money in the bank (49:33).

sie (n, acc) feather. **Sie nɨbuni.** I see a feather.

Sihka tabe ke isopɨ (name) This-midday-sun-does-not-tell-a-lie (person).

sihkupɨ W (n) collarbone. *See* **huuku.**

sihkutɨ (adv) from here.

sihwapi (n) torn object.

sihwarɨ (v) tear something. **Ma tsa? sihwa nɨ.** I tore it.

siibarɨ K (v) harrow. *See* **tsatɨsukitɨ.**

siibetɨ (v) shave, scrape off. **Huupita siibetɨ ma?.** He scraped the stick. *See* **wɨhsibetɨ.**

siiko, sikoo? W (n) wild hyacinth. *Camassia esculenta* [Ker.] Robinson? (roots eaten raw [C & J]).

siikɨ (n) navel.

siipɨ? (n) urine.

siitɨ (v) urinate. **Siitu?i nɨ.** I am going to urinate.

sikusarɨ (v) steal. *See* **tɨrɨhkarɨ.**

simuhtarɨ (v) suck through nose (as elephant sucks water, or as insect sucks nectar).

sinihku (adv man) manner (in this way). **Keta? kwasiku sinihku atuhuna nohi?a yaaru.** Next time don't take in this way a stranger's toy (83:32).

situkwu (pro, 3rd prox nom du) these two.

si?aru (v) chip off.

si?ana (pro, 2nd prox acc sg) you.

si?anetu (adv loc, prox) at this point.

si?ba? (n) arrow [**si** feather + **pa** arrow].

soho bokopi (n) hackberry. **Celtis reticulat** Torry.

soho bo?koo? W (n) mulberry. **soho bo?kóo?** mulberry tree. *Morus rubra* L. (fruit eaten; wood used for making bows). **Huuhkaba soho bokóo? wunuru.** In the timber, there is a mulberry tree (16:10).

soho kua?etu totsiyaa? (n) morning glory (*lit* climbing flower). *Convolvulaceaesp.*

soho obi (n) cottonwood. *Populus deltoides* Marsh (thin skin next to bark peeled off and fed to horses to give them endurance).

soho ro?itu (v), *pl* **soho kua** climb up.

soho weeru (v, pl) climb down.

soko (n) land.

sokoba?aihtu (n) nations.

soko bookutu (n) title deed, deed (title to land).

soko kimaru (v), *pl* **soko numitu** come walking (come on foot).

soko naboopu W (n) map (*lit* land picture).

soko rahka?miitsa? (n) cucumber (*lit* ground wart; small, introduced domestic plant).

soko ruboopu (n) geography, map [**soko** land + **tuboopu** paper].

soko rumanahkepu (n) quarter section [**soko** land + **tumanahke**-measure]. *See* **sokotsihka?apu.**

soko rumuru (v) lease land.

soko rutsupu (n) mile.

soko sikusa (n) dandelion (*lit* ground-stealing plant). *Taraxacum officinale* Wiggins (medication for respiratory problems).

soko sikusatotsiya? (n) dandelion flower.

soko tsatuwaru (v) open country to settlement. **kesu ta soko tsatiwaku** before our country was opened.

soko tsihka?apu (n) quartersection of land [**soko** land + **tsihka?a** cut off]. *See* **soko rumanahkepu.**

soko yu?yumuhkuru (v) quake of earth, tremor of earth.

soko yu?yumuhkutu (n) earthquake.

sokobi paa tubinaatu W (n) island (*lit* land in the middle of water).

sokokuni, soko kahni (n) cellar, storm cellar. *See* **sekwikuni.**

sokomi?aru (v) go walking (go on foot). **Sokomi?aru nu?.** am walking (going on foot).

sokoobi (n) land, earth.

sona (n) cloth cover.

sona bo?a (n) quilt top.

sona rubaki?, sonana rubaki? (n) mattress (*lit* stuffed quilt) [**soona** quilt + **tubaki**- stuff].

soni (n) grass.

soni bihnáa? (n) sugar cane.

soni huuki (n) brush arbor, arbor. *See* **huki?aitu.**

soni narúa?, soni narui? (n) oats.

soni narʉso? (n) towsack, gunny sack [**soni** grass + **narʉso̱** sack].

soni nʉʉhtama? K, **sonipʉha nʉʉhtama?** W (n) baling wire [**sonipʉ** grass + **-ha** (acc) + **nʉʉhtama?** tying thing].

soni sokoobi (n) pasture (open grassland).

soni toorʉ (v) graze on grass.

soni tsiyaa? (n) pitchfork [**soni** grass + **tsiyaa?** to pitch].

soni tso?nika? (n) straw hat, hat [**soni** grass + **tso?nika?** hat].

soni tʉhtʉmapʉ (n) fenced pasture [**soni** grass + **tʉhtʉma-** fence + **pʉ** (nom sg)].

soni wiyaa? (n) twine, clothesline rope; arch split root used for weaving baskets.

soni wokweebi (n) grass burr [**soni** grass + **wokweebi** thorn].

soni wʉhpomarʉ (v) mow grass, cut weeds or grass (with hoe or sickle) [**soni** grass + **wʉhpoma** cut down].

soni wʉhpoma? (n) sickle.

soni wʉhtʉmapʉ (n) pasture, feeding lot (around haystack) [**soni** grass + **wʉhtʉmapʉ** fenced place].

soni wʉhtʉma?, soni tʉhtʉma? (n) baling wire, wire [**soni** grass + **wʉhtʉmaa?** bale].

soni wʉtsʉkerʉ (v) mow grass (with lawnmower or tractor).

soni wʉtsʉke? K (n) scythe, lawnmower. *See* **tʉʉtsʉke?**.

sonipʉ (n) grass.

sonitsiima?, sonitsihima? (n) pitchfork [**soni** grass + **tsi** (nom) + **hima** take].

soo (num) many, much.

soo be?sʉ, soo be?sʉkʉ (adv time) many years ago, long ago. **Soo be?sʉkʉ tsa? tʉa su?ana tʉ?rikuu?nʉʉ soo kʉniba?i.** It is said that long ago the prairie dogs had a town somewhere.

soo huuhpi (n) woods, forest (*lit* many trees). *See* **huukabatʉ**.

Soo kʉni? (n) Lawton, OK (*lit* many houses, town; so named by Cache Comanches).

soo mo?o? (n) centipede (*lit* many hands).

soo naahkwetʉ (adj) distant (*lit* a long way off).

soo naboo? (n) printed material [**soo** many + **na** (nom) + **boo** print].

Soo pitenʉ (name) Comes-often (person).

soo tuku, soo tukukʉ (n) flank of animal (*lit* much meat).

soo tʉhimarʉ? (n) coon can, kick-the-can (*lit* many rations).

soo yake? W (n) mockingbird, locust (*lit* always chirping). *See* **tʉnimanahke huutsu?**.

sookʉni, soo kahni (n) town, village. **Tʉ?rʉkuu?nʉʉ sookʉniba?i.** The prairie dogs had a town.

soomo̱ (n) lung.

soona̱ (n) quilt, cloth cover.

sootʉ, sooti (num indef) many, much. **Sooti kʉse? surʉ turʉe?tʉpa?i̱.** That one had many children (15:2). **Sitʉ kʉse? pimoróo? sootʉkʉhu paakʉhu weenʉ.** This cow went down to much water (20:23).

soro?rokitʉ (v) purr (as a cat).

so?o narᵿbaki?, soo narᵿbaki? (n) shotgun (*lit* cheek to put [shells] in).

so?o ruhkᵿ (n) gums (of teeth) [**so?o** cheek + **tuhkᵿ** flesh]. *See* **tamaruhkᵿ**.

so?o tsuhni (n) cheekbone [**so?o** cheek + **tsuhni** bone].

so?o̱ (n) cheek, cheekbone.

sua, suarᵿ (n) mind, breath, soul, thought.

sua kwana̱ (n) breath odor. **aisua kwana̱** bad breath. **tsaa suakwana̱** good-scented breath.

sua soyuraperᵿ (v) allow to rest or cool off.

sua watsikatᵿ (v) faint, become comatose. *See* **esitᵿyaitᵿ, kwinuma̱ suarᵿ**.

sua watsikᵿ (adj) unconscious, comatose.

sua watsitᵿ (v) become insane (lose mind).

sua yurahpitᵿ (v) rest, relax.

suaabe, suabi (n) cross (Christian symbol).

suabetaikatᵿ (adj) conscious, revived (after being knocked out).

suabetaikᵿrᵿ (v) teach, train someone. *See* **tᵿni̱ suabetarᵿ**.

suabetaitᵿ, suabetarᵿ (v) recognize. **Nᵿ suabetainu̱ urᵿa.** He recognized me. *See* **masuabetaitᵿ**.

Suabi puharaibo (n) Catholic person, priest, nun (*lit* holy people of the cross).

suahkena̱ (n) breath.

suahketᵿ (v) breathe. **Kehtaku ma? suahketᵿ.** He is breathing heavily.

suakᵿtᵿ (v) think good thoughts (think well of someone). **Tsaa u suakᵿtᵿ.** He thinks well of him.

suakᵿtᵿaitᵿ (v) sympathize (feel for someone; think of someone a lot).

suana (n) will, soul, thoughts.

suapᵿ (n) thought, sense.

suapᵿwahtᵿ (adj) stupid, senseless. **Urᵿ tsa? sarii suapᵿwahtᵿ.** That dog is stupid.

suatᵿtᵿ (v) think.

sua?sua?miarᵿ (v) breathe heavily, pant.

sua?su?maitᵿ (v) unable to breathe, out of breath, dead. **Suatsu?mai ma?.** He is dead (quit breathing).

sua?su?makatᵿ (adj) breathless, dying one. **Suatsu?makatᵿ ma?.** He is dying (breathing his last).

sube? (conj) both.

sube?sᵿ (adv time) immediately, since then. **Sube?sᵿ kᵿse? suni uhka u mᵿᵿhka, sᵿsᵿmᵿ? kwasinaboo? pi?to?na?i.** Since then when he acted on him that way, some snakes are bobtailed (36:16).

sube?tᵿ, sube?tᵿ (interj) That's all (narrative-closing; end of story). **Tanᵿ usᵿ tsihákwitso?ainu̱. Subetᵿ.** We were saved from hunger by that. That's all (18:36, 37).

suhkapᵿ (n dem, dist acc sg) that one.

Suhta? (n), *pl* Suhta?nᵿᵿ Sioux people.

suhu posía (n) crab louse. *See* **pᵿhᵿ pusia**.

suhurᵿkitᵿ (v) snort.

sukuupᵿ (n) elderly man (over 70 years).

sukwᵿkitᵿ (v) think about, reason. *See* **nasutamakatᵿ**.

suni (adv man) that way. **Keta? kwasikᵿ ᵿ puhiwihta suni**

muuru. Next time don't treat your money that way (49:33).

suniyutu (adv) because (for that reason).

sunihku (adv man) thus.

supana?itu (adj) knowledgeable, knowing. **Ma?noo nu turue?tuhtsin?uu supana?itu.** I wonder what he knows about my children (15:9).

supewaitu (adj) carefree, leisurely.

supikaahkatu (adj) perceptive, aware.

suru (pro dem, dist nom sg) he, she, it.

suruu (pro dem, dist nom pl) those.

sutaaitu (v) bless someone, have mercy.

sutaitu (adj) blessed.

sutena (adv man) forcefully.

sutena betsumiaru (v) lead off by force.

sutena betu (v) take someone by force.

sutena ikuru (v) enter by force. *See* **ikaru.**

sutena karuru (v) force to sit down.

sutenapu (n) stubborn person.

sutsamuru (v) promise.

sutuu?aru (v) find out, notice.

suuta? (n) jack (in playing cards).

suwaitu (v) want, desire, need. **Kahni nu? suwaaitu.** I need a house. **Tsaa nu? naboori kwasu?i suwaaitu.** I want a nice, designed coat (32:8). *See* **nohabi suwaitu.**

suwukaitu (adj) amazing.

suwu?kai (v) be amazed.

suyoro?akapu (adj) wonderful. *See* **nanisuwukaitu.**

suyoro?aru (v) wonder at.

su?ahri (adv loc) along there. **Oha ahnakatu su?ahri tupanakuhi tsa?wo?netu.** Coyote is scratching along there in the bank (16:16).

su?akutu (v) like someone, admire someone. *See* **tokwetutuaru.**

su?atsitu (v) think about something, make a plan. *See* **nimaka?mukitu.**

su?atu (pro indef) another one (not this one).

su?makutu (v) spend money. **Tenahpu tsa? puhiwihta su?makui.**The man is spending money.

su?uraru (v) recall, ponder, search the mind in effort to remember [**su** think + **ura** find].

su?uyaa?aru (v) laugh at, deride. *See* **tuni su?uya?eetu.**

su?uya?i? (n) laughingstock. *See* **usú?ya?itu.**

suatu (v) grow (increase), bloom (bud open), augment in number. **Sonipu tsa? suahkatu.** The grass is growing. **Pimoroonuu tsa? suanu.** The herd of cattle is growing.

suhkwibitu, suhkwibi?bikitu (v) shiver, tremble, quiver. *See* **kuhkwibikitu.**

suhtorokitu W, suwi?no?no?kitu K (v) shiver (from the cold). *See* **tsihturuaru.**

suhtuyaitu (v), *pl* **suhkooi** freeze to death, die of the cold.

suhu, suhuubi (n) willow. *Salix* sp.

suhu aawo (n) basket (woven of willow).

suhu mupitsu (n) screech owl (*lit* willow giant) [**suhuubi** willow + **mupitsi** giant].

suhu tsitsina?, suutsununi (n) willow twigs, arch potato [**suhu** willow + **tsitsina?** root].

suku- (pfx) ref. sour.

suku ka?ma? (n) lemon [**suku** sour + **kama-** taste].

sukubuninitu (v) make a wry face (as from eating something sour or bitter).

suku?i (n) plum (a particular wild variety). *Prunus* spp. **suku?i huuhpi** plum tree. *See* **yusuku, parawa suku, kusi suku, natsomu, parua sukui?.**

sukwe naisu (n) side of an object (front or back).

sukwe tuyai (adj) paralyzed (*lit* nerves dead). *See* **ma?itsa?bukatu.**

sukwe tuyaipu (n) paralyzed person.

sukweebi? (n) fifty cents, half-dollar.

sukweru (adj) half, *n* **sukweebi** end of row or nerve.

sumasu nooi K, sumu?a noo?, suma noo? (n) one-horse buggy, horse-drawn sulky. *See* **pikwusii?.**

Sumonu kuhtsu paa (n) Nueces River (*lit* river of ten buffalo; name derived from a hunting expedition in which ten buffalo were killed).

sumu (num) one; *adv* completely, thoroughly.

sumu kuhtsumai (adj) eaten up completely.

sumu makukatu (adj) complete, thorough.

sumu okwetu (v) float away. *See* **okwehkwatu.**

sumu nokimaru (v, pl), *sg* **kimaru** come (as a group).

sumu nomi?aru (v, pl), *sg* **nomi?aru** move away as a group (abandon a location).

sumu oyetu (pro indef) everyone.

sumu rayu?neru (v) pound completely (as pounding meat).

sumu ruhkaru (v) devour, eat most of something.

sumu sihwaru (v) tear off, rip completely.

sumu susunitu (adj) homogeneous throughout (all the same). *See* **suunitu.**

sumu uhtsumitu (v, pl), *sg* **uhtsumaru** close everyone's eyes (require everyone to close eyes completely).

sumu? (pro indef) one, someone, people. *acc* **sumu?a. sumu?a ka?wikatu** gathering of people, congregation.

sumusu (adv) once, one time.

suroonitu, tasuroonitu (v) bristle (hair), stand hair on end. **Sariia tsa? puhu suroonitu.** The dog's fur bristled.

susuatu (adj) cool, chilly.

susumu? (num indef) one at a time, some. *See* **su?sumu?nuku.**

susu?ana (adv time) sometimes, once in a while.

susu?nikatu (adj) numbness.

susu?nitu (v) numb, feel numb, asleep. *See* **tasusu?nitu, masusu?nitu.**

suu (adv accom) together (said of a group).

suu aniru (v) kick (causing object to bounce away).

suu awo (n) tin cup.

suu potseru (v) kick something away. *See* **suuhpotsukatu.**

suuhkwuhtitu (v) kick.

suuhkwuhtukuru (v) kick something.

suuhpotsukatu (adj) kicked away, discarded by kicking. *See* **suupotseru.**

suuki (n), *pl* parukwihtsipu twig, switch.

suukoitu, suhkoitu K (v) freeze (solids). **Tomatu tsa? suhkoi.** The tomatoes froze.

suuku (adj) sour, acidic.

suukutsa?noo (adv doubt) perhaps, maybe. *See* **kia.**

suumaru, suumanuru (num) ten.

suuma?aitu (v) gather together, congregate. *See* **narahka?witu.**

suuma?okaru (v) call together many people, invite to congregate.

suumu?oku (n) group of people, crowd of people.

suunitu (adj) homogeneous, alike. *See* **sumu susunitu.**

suupetu, suuhpetu (adj) level, even, flattened. **Sokobi tsa? suupetu.** The earth is level.

suuta?ni?aru (v) kick off, shake something off. *See* **nuu?wikeetu.**

suutsunitu (v) chill (have chills), tremble with cold. *See* **suhkwibitu.**

su?sumu?nuku (adv) one at a time. *See* **susumu?.**

T

ta (unspecified subject or possessor).

ta-, tah- (pfx) ref. to foot; ref. to sound *tah* (as in pounding or cracking).

taa (pro, 1st gen du) of us two.

taa- (pfx) ref. to morning.

taabu?kina noyo (n) Easter egg (*lit* rabbit egg).

taahkatu (adj) morning, daytime [*ta* morning + -**katu** have].

taahkitu (adj) dawn. *See* **huwuni.**

taaitu (n) hole (in the ground).

taamahkaru (v) prepare breakfast for someone [**taa-** morning + **mahka** make for].

taama (n) tooth.

taaruhkapu (n) pancakes, cereal [**taa-** morning + **tuhkapu** food].

taaruhkaru (v) eat breakfast (*lit* morning eating).

taatsa, tatsatu (adj) summer season.

taatsukwitu (num) seven.

taayutsutu (v), *pl* taayoritu arise (get up in the morning). **Itu tsa? tenahpu? puetsuku taayutsunu.** This man got up early.

tabahko (n) Indian tobacco. *Rubella Nicotiana rustica* L. (roots cooked with fat to make soup [C & J]; medicinal use to cure asthma, liver ailment, kidney malfunction, influenza, and fever).

tabakoitu (v) split (cause to split). **Ma rabakoi!** Split it! (expression accompanied by blowing toward storm cloud to avoid having storm).

tabe-, taabe (n) sun, day, clock, wristwatch.

Tabe kwi?ne (name) Sun-eagle (Comanche war chief about 1759).

tabe mo?o (n) hour hand (on clock or watch).

Tabe nanika (name) Hears-the-sunrise, Voice-of-the-sunrise (Comanche chief living in 1872).

tabe narumuhku (n) watch chain [**tabe** watch + **narumuhku** harness].

tabetotsiyaa (n) fleabane daisy, clock flower. **Erigeron tenuis** T. and G. (root used as medicine).

tabe wenuaku? (n) watch chain [**tabe** watch + **wenuaku?** hanging down object].

Tabe wunuru (name) Standing-sun (person).

tabe wunu?itu (v) stand in the sun, stand just above the horizon (said of the sun before it sets).

tabe kusuwehkatu (adj) hot day, scorching day.

tabéni (adv) today, morning.

tabe ruhkapu W (n) dinner, lunch.

tabe ruhkaru K (v) eat dinner or lunch [**tabe** sun + **tuhka-** eat].

tabe to?ikitu W (adj), **tabe toi?** K (n) sunrise, sunup.

tabe uhpuitu (v), *pl* **tabe uhkooru** nap (take a nap) [**tabe-** day + **uhpui** sleep].

tabe uhyuh? K, **tabe uhyuihka** W, **tabe uhyyi** (adv) afternoon.

tabé?aitu (v) swear (take an oath), vow (as in court).

tabe?ehi (adv time) late in the day.

tabe?ikai K (n), **tabe?ikaru** W (adj) evening, sunset, sundown.

tabe?ikami?aru (v) sun goes down (setting of the sun).

tabe?ikunakwa? (n) west (*lit* where the sun goes down).

tabú?kina? (n) rabbit. **Soobe?su kutsa? rua piarabú?kina? kahníba?i.** Long ago it is said a big rabbit had a home (15:1).

tabuikatu (n) grief, sadness.

tah- (pfx) foot. *See* **ta-**.

tahbaitu (v) break in pieces. *See* **tahtaba?itu**.

tahhanitu (v) pound on something, hammer something (*lit* make a *tah* noise).

tahhima?eru (v) catch (with claws), grab (with claws).

tahhomonutsaru W (v) crumble to powder with the foot [**tah-** foot + **homo** powder + **nutsa** crumble]. *See* **mahomonutsaru**.

tahi, tahhibatu W, **tahibi** K (adj with inanimate nouns) flat, thin, lightweight. **Tusoona tsa? tahibi.** The plate is flat.

tahipu pekwi (n) flounder (*lit* flat fish). *Pleuronectes genus.*

tahka- (pfx) ref. to ice or snow.

tahka aawo (n) refrigerator, icebox.

Tahka hunu?bi (n) Colorado River (*lit* ice creek).

tahkaaitu (v) cut out of the herd, divide.

tahkabi (n) ice, snow.

tahkamuru (v) stand waiting (for someone or something).

tahkana? (n) spear. *See* **tutsiwaii?**.

Tahkapu (name) Poor-one (person).

tahka we?wenuka? (n) icicle (*lit* ice hanging down).

tahka? (n) arrowhead (*lit* divided, broken).

tahka?ikatu (adj) frozen.

tahka?imiaru (v) freeze (be in the process of freezing).

tahka?umaru (v) snowfall (*lit* snow rains or falls).

tahkitemi?aru (v) slip standing up, slide standing up, skate [**tah-** feet + **kite-** slide + **mi?a-** go]. *See* **tasiko?i?mi?aru**.

tahkobaru, tahkobakatu (v) break off, snap off (with the foot).

tahkoonikaru (v) round up, herd, rustle (as to steal cattle).

tahkoonitu (v) domineer, stop someone by force.

tahkuyaʔaru (v) frighten, make threatening movements (with the foot, as in kicking toward someone).

tahkuaru (v) drive out, force (encourage) to leave (animate subj).

tahkuaru (v) drive away, force away (with the foot).

tahkumaʔaitu (v) sharpen (using a treadle grindstone) [**tah-** foot + **kumaʔaa-** sharpen].

tahkwatúubitu (v) fold (with the foot) [**tah-** foot + **kwatuubituto** fold]. *See* **namakwatubiitu.**

tahkweʔyaru (v), *pl* **tahkweʔyuʔi-** take off a shoe.

tahkwineru W (v) wipe (with the foot or lower end of something).

tahkwumaru (v), *pl* **tahkwumiʔi-** unwrap something (with the foot) [**tah-** foot + **kwuma** unwrap].

tahkwuʔneru (v) iron, press (as of clothing; *lit* rub with a foot).

tahkwuriaru (v) spill something (with foot) [**tah-** foot + **kwuriaru** spilled].

tahma (n), *adj* **tahma roʔikatu** spring season, summer.

tahmai napu (n) deer meat, dried meat, summer-dried meat (butchered and dried in the summer) [**tahma** summer + **inapu** dried meat].

Tahma mua, Kurahmaru mua (n) April (*lit* new-spring month).

Tahma uhuyi (n) August.

tahma yokakeʔ (n) popcorn [**tahma** spring + **yokakeʔ** spongy + **ʔ** (nom sg)].

tahma roʔitu (v) become spring.

tahnaaru (v) plant seeds, sow seeds.

tahnikatu (v) keep an orphan as foster child.

tahniʔaru (v) defeat, overcome, win in a contest against someone. *See* **kwakuru.**

tahnutsaʔeru K (v) crumble (with the foot). *See* **manutsaʔaru.**

tahpáana (n) sole of foot [**tah** foot + **paana** palm].

tahpai (adj) cracked of own accord.

tahpanaʔaaru (v) sole shoes (put soles on shoes) [**tah-** foot + **pana-** sole + **ʔa-** (V)].

tahpapu (n) broken object (as a dish or glass).

tahpararu (v) soften something by trampling on it (Comanches put rawhide or dried meat on a flat surface, covered it, then tramped on it to soften it).

tahparaʔitu (v) align spine, stand on someone's back to ease pain.

tahparu (v) crack something, break something. *See* **tapearu, wutubaru.**

tahpiko? (n) heel of shoe.

tahpomiʔitu (v, pl), *sg* **tsahkokaru** break.

Tahpooku mua (n) March (*lit* cotton-ball month).

tahpookuʔ (n) cottonwood. *See* **weʔyuku sohoobi.**

tahporooru (v) break in pieces, shatter.

tahpunitu (v) try on shoes [**tah-** foot + **puni-** see].

tahtabaʔitu (v) cause to break in pieces. **Ketaʔ ma rahtabaʔitu.** Don't break it to pieces. *See* **tahbaitu.**

tahta?nitʉ (v) shake the foot (as to shake off dust or dirt). *See* **ta?wikitʉ.**

tahta?yʉtʉ, W (v) jerk the lower leg [tah- foot + taa?yʉ- jerk]. *See* **ta?yʉrʉhkitʉ.**

tahtokoo? (n) big toe [tah- foot + to?koo? grandfather].

tahtoorʉ (v) put on shoes.

tahto?itʉ (v) let out (allow to leave, as by opening gate).

tahtsaitʉ (v) catch up with, overtake.

tahtsanitʉ (v) stumble [tah- foot + tsani- hang].

tahtsarʉ (v) raise one leg.

tahtsiarʉ (v) scratch someone (with foot or toes) [tah- foot + tsia- scratch].

tahtsukitʉ (v) erase, wipe away (using foot).

tahtsumarʉ K (v) wipe something off.

tahtsʉkitʉ (adj) crowded while standing (*lit* crowded foot, as in tight shoes).

tahtúa? (n) little toe (*lit* foot child). *See* **tʉeh tahtua?.**

tahtunaabarʉ (v) straighten something wrinkled (using the foot).

tahtʉbunitʉ (v) waken (cause to wake up with heavy steps or noisy walking) [tah- foot + tʉbuni- wake up]. *See* **tʉbunitʉ.**

tahtʉkarʉ (v), pl tahni?itʉ put away, drill in (as seed), keep something. *See* **tʉkarʉ.**

tahtʉkitʉ (v) take away something live.

tahtʉki?i? (n) stool, footstool.

tahtʉkwarʉ (v), *pl* tahpa?itʉ- throw at something.

tahtʉmarʉ (v) close up (nail shut, cover over).

tahtʉpinaa? (n) middle toe [tah foot + tʉpinaa (weki) middle].

tahuhkuwʉnʉrʉ (v) raise dust by walking [ta- foot + huhku- dust + wʉnʉ- stand].

tahu?nerʉ (v) crawl on knees [ta- on knees + hune- crawl]. *See* **mahu?netʉ, wʉhu?nerʉ.**

tahʉ (1st pers pl poss pro) our.

tahʉʉki?aikʉ (n) brush arbor, arbor (*lit* planted shade). *See* **hʉʉki?aitʉ.**

tahwikarʉ (v) earn something. *See* **tʉrahwikatʉ.**

tai (1st pers pl obj pro) us.

taibo bihnaa? (n) cantaloupe (*lit* white man's sugar). **Surʉʉ kʉse? taiboo? bihnáa?a tʉrʉní?inʉ.** Those ones planted cantaloupes (77:2).

taibo ekʉsahpana? (n) soldier (white man) [taibo- white man + ekʉsahpana? red-chested]. *See* **ekasahpana?.**

taibo huutsuu? (n) pigeon (*lit* white man bird). *See* **ku?ewóo?.**

taibo na?seeka? (n) date (*lit* white man persimmon).

taibo pikapʉ (n) leather (commercially prepared; *lit* white man leather). *See* **pikapʉ.**

taibo sʉkʉ?i (n) domestic plum (usually a hybrid) [taibo- white man + sʉ?kʉ?i wild plum].

taiboo? (n) non-Indian, white person. **Sitʉʉ taiboo?nʉʉ tʉbehkapʉha sʉmʉ noohtsi, pʉ kahnikʉhu mi?anʉ.** Carrying off these white men's game, he went home (97:33).

taina (n) hole, cave, room.

takahpʉ (n) poor person.

taka?aitʉ (adj) duplicate (*lit* made a sibling).

taka?arʉ (v) copy, duplicate (*lit* make a sibling).

taka?katʉ (adj) having a sibling (brother, sister, mate).

takoosahpʉ? W, takootsapʉ? K (n) a mix, batter allowed to become set, dough-like batter (as cornmeal, plaster, blacktop road).

takotserʉ (v) wash feet (of someone or something else).

takuhtʉyaaihumi?arʉ (v) thirst to death, die of thirst (suffer great thirst).

takusito?itʉ, takwʉsito?itʉ (v) perspire, sweat.

takʉsuaitʉ (adj) thirst (feel thirsty) [**takʉ** dry + **sua-** feel].

takwainitʉ (v) go on foot to look for [**ta-** foot + **kwai-** go away + **ni** walk].

takwekwitʉ (v, pl obj), *sg obj* **ta?ikʉrʉ** imprison.

takwi- (pfx), *adj* **takwikatʉ** wrinkled. **takwikoobe** wrinkled face; **takwimo?o** wrinkled hand.

takwikakwo?apʉ (n) wrinkled all over.

takwikakwo?arʉ (v) wrinkle something.

takwipʉ (n) person of delicate health, sickly person.

takwitsoo?nimi?arʉ (v) wither, wilt, droop.

takwi?oobitʉ (v) gather (as in sewing).

takwokarʉ W (v) drag something (with the foot).

takwʉkitʉ (v) throw (throw at the foot of something, throw at a line).

takwʉperʉ (v) crease (with the foot). *See* **makwipunarʉ.**

takwʉsaitʉ (v) loosen (with the foot).

takwʉsarʉ (adj) loosened by foot.

takwʉsipʉ (n) perspiration, sweat.

takwʉsiskʉrʉ (v) tangle (with the foot).

tama- (pfx) tooth. *See* **taama.**

tamakotse? (n) toothpaste [**taama** tooth + **kotse?** washer].

tamakwita (n) roots of the teeth [**taama** tooth + **kwiita** bottom].

tamamatsuma? (n) toothbrush [**taama** tooth + **matsuma** wiper].

tamatsa?nika? (n) false teeth, dentures [**taama** tooth + **tsa?nika** put on].

tamanahkerʉ (v) measure (by stepping off a distance) [**ta-** foot + **manahke** measure].

tamanikarʉ (v) drive across (as drive cattle across).

tamanʉʉtsikwatʉ, tamanʉʉsukatʉ (v) suffer from a toothache [**taama** teeth + **nʉʉsukaa** feel].

tamaruhkʉ (n) gums of teeth [**taama** teeth + **tuhkʉ** flesh]. *See* **so?oruhkʉ.**

tamarʉkarʉ (v) graduate (finish high school or college).

tamarʉkʉkatʉ (adj) completed, graduated person.

tamihtsi?benihtsi? (n, voc) dear little brothers (an expression of endearment). **Tamihtsi?benihtʉhtsi?nʉʉ, hina mʉnʉ hanibʉì ni?** Dear little brothers, what are you doing so much? (5:3).

taminaitʉ (v) break at the joint (cause to be broken).

tamiʔ (n) younger brother.

tamu, tamʉ (n) sinew (taken from muscle of beef). **nʉmʉ ramu** Comanche thread.

tamunaikʉmiʔarʉ (v) go on foot to meet someone, meet someone by going on foot.

tamutsoʔi K, tamutʉsoʔi (n) greenbriar. *Smilax bonanox* (leaves used as cigarette wrappers).

Tamutʉsoʔi hunuʔbi (n) Briar Creek.

tamʉkʉrʉ (v) drive animals by force. **Tʉhʉye tamʉkʉ.** Drive the horses up.

tana, tanapʉ (n) knee.

tanatookarʉtʉ (v), *pl* **tanatooyʉkwitʉ** kneel down sitting back on heels. *See* **wʉnʉhkarʉrʉ.**

tanaʔ kuʔe (n) kneecap [**tana** knee + **kuʔe** top].

Taninʉʉ (n) Liver Eaters (band of middle Comanches in Texas located south of the Peace River).

tanisiʔ W, tanʉniʔ K (n) king (in card game).

Tanoyoʔtsoʔmeʔe̱ (n) Easter [**ta-** (unspec) + **noyoʔ** egg + **tsoʔmeʔ** gather].

tanuarʉ (v) push, move something, rake together (with foot).

tanuraakʉtʉ (v) chase away.

tanʉkikʉtʉ (v) shoo (cause to fly away in some way, as to frighten chickens). *See* **manʉkikʉrʉ.**

tanʉʉhkupaitʉ (v) trip someone [**ta-** with foot + **nʉʉhkupai-** made fall].

tanʉʔyʉkitʉ (v) tread heavily, stomp (make sound of running, heavy footsteps).

tanʉkʉtʉ K (v) tamp down (with the feet).

tapearʉ (v) crack something. *See* **tahparʉ.**

taperʉ (v) push, make fall using foot (as push soil into a hole).

tapi wanapʉ K (n) dry goods (*lit* thin cloth, as opposed to sturdy, hand-woven material or buffalo hide). *See* **tarʉwanapi̱.**

tapi naʔsʉkiaʔ (n) lightweight shawl [**tapi̱** flat, thin + **naʔsʉkia** shawl]. *See* **pohotʉ naʔsʉkiaʔ.**

tapisoʔaitʉ W (adj) angered, enraged.

tapi̱koʔ (n) heel of the foot.

tapi̱tʉhtsi (adj) thin (tissuelike), sheer. *See* **hʉnʉketʉ.**

tapʉnukeerʉ W, tapi̱nuketʉ K (v) polish (slick, smooth). *See* **mapʉnukeerʉ.**

tapʉ K, tapʉhʉ W (n) leg hair [**ta-** foot + **pʉhʉ** fuzz].

tapʉhabi (v, sg obj), *pl obj* **tahpakwabi** make swim. *See* **pahabitʉ.**

tapʉherʉ (v, sg obj), *pl obj* **tayu miʔitʉ** drop (let fall), remove, take off (with claws or foot).

tapʉtsaitʉ (v) break open (with the foot), burst (with the foot).

tarʉwanapi̱ W (n) dry goods, material possessions. *See* **tapiwanapʉ.**

tasarʉ (v) step over something (lift foot to step over something).

tasa̱kwʉʉhkiʔ (n) toes.

tasiito̱ (n) toenail, claw, hoof.

tasikoʔiʔmiʔarʉ (v) skate (slide on something while standing on feet). **Kahnikuhu tasiko?imi?a-ru.** He skated to the house. *See* **tahkitemi?aru.**

tasitotsaru W (v) scratch, rub (with foot, as to relieve an itch).

tasi?a? W, **tasi?akoobe** K (n) smallpox, freckles, rash on skin. *See* **tutusa?wutu.**

tasi?kwairu (v) tear with the foot [**ta-** foot + **si?kwa** tear].

tasi?kwaitu (adj) torn by a foot.

tasi?womi?aru (v) walk dragging one foot (as when injured or lame).

tasoni (n, acc) floor, carpet, rug.

tasoona (n, nom) floor, carpet, rug [**ta-** foot + **soona** quilt].

tasukaru (v) touch, feel with foot.

Tasúra (n) That's It, Water Horse Band (a Comanche band).

tasu?netu (v) wipe feet, rub feet [**ta-** foot + **su?ne** rub].

tasukupunitu (v) squint, peep (look through squinted eyes). **Sumu? kuse? uruumatu tasukupuni.** One of them peeped (4:13). *See* **wihtekatu.**

tasukumitu (v) have cold feet [**ta-** feet + **sukumi** become cold].

tasusu?nitu (v) numb, asleep. **Nu napema nu? karu u tasusu?ni.** Sitting on my foot, it became numb. *See* **susu?nitu.**

tatsatu (adj), *n* **taatsa** summertime.

Tatsatu mua, Tatsa mua (n) August (*lit* summer month).

tatsii? (n) nits, lice eggs. **Ma papikuku nu? tatsii punii.** I saw, found lice eggs in her hair.

tatsinuupi (n) star. **Tatsinuupi tsa? tsitsirapuutu.** The star is twinkling, sparkling.

tatsipu (n) sumac (foul, ill-smelling), skunkbush. **Rhus trilobata** Nutt. (bark used in treating colds).

Tatsiwóo (name) Buffalo (person).

tatsukweru (v) mash, crush, smash.

tatuwetu (v) limp (person only). *See* **wihnaitu.**

tatubaru (v) break something. **Ohnaa tsa? nu tusone tatubai.** The baby broke my dish.

tatuke?neru, tanukunuru (v) press something down (with foot) [**ta-** foot + **take?ne** press down].

tawekwitu (adj) penned up, driven into ground (one end). *See* **ta?ikukatu.**

tawiaru W, **turawi?iaru** K (v) wear out shoes.

tawohho (n) enemy tribe (*lit* our enemies). *See* **wohho-.**

tawo?i? K (n) gun (any type), pistol, rifle.

tawunaru (v), *pl* **tawuni?itu** stake down, nail down. **Numukahni u? tawuni?itu.** He staked down the teepee (using several stakes).

tayu?maru (v), *pl* **tayumi?i-** knock something down.

tayu?nekaru (v) pound food. **U sumutayu?netsi, u maroponi?inu.** Completely pounding it, (they) made balls of it (grapes) (116:17).

tayu?neru (v) crush, pound with a pestle (cause to be crushed). **Hanibihta u? tayu?netu.** She pounded the corn (with a pestle).

tayutsuru (v) awaken someone by shouting, speaking (cause someone to get out of bed by shouting or speaking).

Ta?ahpʉ (name) Our Father, Great Spirit (deity).

ta?ahpʉ?a tekwawapi̱ K (n) prophet (one who tells forth a message).

ta?aikʉtʉ (v) pedal (cause to roll by pushing with feet as in pedaling a bicycle) [**ta-** foot + **ai** lope + **kʉ** (caus)]. See **naraaikʉtʉ**.

ta?aikʉtʉ (n) bicycle. See **naraaikʉ?**.

ta?ikʉkatʉ (adj) imprisoned, locked up. See **tawekwitʉ**.

ta?ikʉrʉ (v), pl **takwekwitʉ** pen up animal, lock up someone.

ta?itsa?bʉrʉ W (v) have leg cramp.

ta?ka? (n), pl **ta?ka?nʉʉ** kinsman of either sex.

ta?ka?miitsa? (n) wart.

ta?ki? (n) kidney.

ta?kʉbuu? W, tahkabuu? K (n) slingshot.

ta?nika? W, tahtʉkii? K (n) stirrup [**ta-** foot + NIKA? put through]. See **narahtʉkii?**.

ta?nikʉtʉ (v) insert (put through), nail something.

ta?okitʉ (adj) spilled by someone.

ta?ookitʉ (v) drive together, round up (get together as cattle).

ta?oo? (n) meat (dried and pounded).

ta?se?yukʉ?, ta?si?yuki? (n) man's moccasin (named for the rattle or jingle of tin decorations on buffalo-hide moccasin as man walked). See **nʉmʉnapʉ**.

ta?si?woorʉ (v) paw the earth, scratch up earth.

ta?siwoo rʉhkapʉ W (n) buffalo meat.

ta?si?woo?

ta?siwoo wana?ʉhʉ W, ta?siwoo ʉhʉ K (n) buffalo blanket (soft, tanned hide).

ta?si?woo? (n) buffalo [**ta-** foot + **si?woo** paw earth]. Ta?si?wóo?a mʉʉ tʉbitsi yuhuwehki?ha tai tʉbehkakʉ. Kill us a buffalo that you find (is) really fat (69:4).

ta?urarʉ (v) meet someone. O tsa? wa?ihpʉ? pʉ kumahpʉ?a ra?uranʉ. That woman met her husband.

ta?urʉkarʉ K (v) own something. oyo?ko bʉ ta?urʉkanaall she owns.

ta?urʉkarʉ W (v) deserve, merit. U ra?urʉkatʉ ?u. He deserves it.

ta?wahkóo? W, ta?bahkóo K (n) edible tuber. See **ahwepʉ**.

ta?wairʉ (v) locate something (by feeling around with the foot).

ta?wiitsa̱ (n), du **taa?witsanʉkʉ** calf of leg [**ta-** foot + **wiitsa̱** leg].

ta?wikitʉ (v) shake foot. See **tahta?nitʉ**.

ta?witsa roponiitʉ K (v) have leg cramp (in calf of leg). See **toponitʉ**.

ta?wokinae?ree eka K (n) swamp rabbit. See **ekae?ree**.

ta?wo?ekarʉ (v), pl **ta?kwʉbai-** shoot a gun repeatedly (as a rifle or machine gun).

ta?wo?i? (n), acc ta?wo?i? a
gunshot. Ta?wo?i?a nʉ? nakai. I
heard a gunshot. See tsatʉkarʉ.

ta?yaami?arʉ (v) carry in the claws.

ta?yaahkana? W, ta?yaahkatʉ
K (n) something carried in the
claws.

ta?yʉrʉhkitʉ K (v) jerk the leg. See
tahta?yʉtʉ.

tebuunitʉ (v) recover from illness,
improve in health. Tʉepʉrʉ tsa?
tebuuni. The child got better.

tekwawapi (n) speaker, spokesman.

tekwakʉwapi W, tekwawapi
K, (n) interpreter. Taibo? nʉʉ
u? nʉmʉ tekwawapi. He was
the interpreter of Comanche
for the white man. See nʉmʉ
rekwakʉwapi.

tekwakʉtʉ (v) interpret (lit to help
to speak; speak for someone).
Taibo?nii u? tekwakʉtʉ. He
interpreted for the white men.

tekwapʉ (n) word, speech.

tekwapʉ rʉboopʉ (n) grammar (lit
words on paper).

tekwarʉ (v), pl niwʉnʉrʉ speak,
talk to someone. See yʉkwitʉ.

Tekwitsi M (name) Skinny-and-
wrinkled (person).

tekwʉniwapi (n) a brave, Indian
brave, town crier. Paraibo tsa? u
tekwʉniwapi?ai. The chief made
him a brave.

tekwʉnitʉ (v) announce (as town
crier gives news). Paraibo?a
kimana?u tekwʉni?i. He
announced the chief's coming.

tenahpʉ? W, tʉnahpʉ? K (n) man,
pl tananʉʉ, tenanʉʉ men. Urʉ
tsa? tʉnahpʉ? nʉʉmʉ. That man
is a Comanche.

tenahpʉ?a kwasu?ʉ (n) man's shirt.
See kwasu?ʉ.

tenahpʉ?

Tenebeka, Tʉnʉbekʉ (name) Gets-
to-be-middle-aged-man (a man
who lived in 1872).

tetsi (n) man's brother-in-law. See
pʉhʉre?tsi.

te?animui (n) biting fly.

timʉihʉ? (n) snake root, church
root (from Mexico). Liatris Schreb.
(for curing asthma, emphysema;
rub on legs or feet to repel
rattlesnakes). See itsa.

Tinawa, Tenawa, Tehnahwah
(n) Those-who-stay-downstream
(Comanche band formerly
northeast of the Brazos River and
northwest of the present Dallas-
Fort Worth area).

tiro?woko (n) throwing arrows.

tobo?ihupiitʉ (v) stop (come to a
stop). Kuyuníi?nʉʉ si?ana maba?a
tobo?ihupiitʉ. The turkeys came
to a stop here somewhere by him
(8:41). See wʉnʉhupiitʉ.

toboʔikatʉ (v) stand.

toh- (pfx) ref. to push (with the fist, hand).

tohhobinitʉ, tohnobinitʉ (v) hurt (cause to groan by hitting with fist).

tohhomonutsarʉ W, tuhhumunutsarʉ K (v) crumble, crush in pieces (with fist).

tohkobiʔitʉ (v) break something up. **Huupita maʔ tohkobiʔitʉ.**He is breaking up the wood (into sticks).

tohkonarʉ (v) dig a hole in the ground (as with crowbar or pole).

tohkʉarʉ (v, sg obj), *pl obj* **tohto-ʔitʉ** help to mount. *See* **toʔitʉ.**

tohkweʔyarʉ (v) take off, disassemble, remove (as part from an object).

tohkwʉmarʉ (v) pry open, pound on to open, open forcibly.

toh-, tohmapʉ (n) year.

Tohmʉa (n) January (year month, for beginning a new year) [**tohmapʉ** year + **mʉa** month].

tohoobe̲, tohobe (n) hindquarter, thigh (from knee up), foreleg. *See* **kotsana.**

tohpaakuʔnetʉ W (adj) pushed under water.

tohpakurʉ (v, pl), *sg* **topʉkaarʉ** chisel something, split something.

tohparaarʉ W (v) soften by pounding. *See* **tsohkwe.**

tohpaʔitʉ (v), *pl* **tohtʉkwarʉ** hit with fist, slap with palm of hand, punch. **Ma kobetohpaʔitʉ uʔ.** He hit him on the face.

tohpaʔi̲sokitʉ W (adj) sprinkled.

tohporoorʉ (v) scatter by force. **Haniibita uʔ tohporoʔai.** He scattered the corn.

tohpotsotsii (n) nightshade. *Sola- num* sp [C & J] (used in general tonic and in tuberculosis remedy).

tohpunitʉ (v) test, try out, bargain, make a deal (as in buying or bartering).

tohpʉarʉ (v) stop hitting with fist or palm of hand. *See* **pʉarʉ.**

tohpʉtsaʔitʉ (v) make burst (as a bag). **Wose uʔ tohpʉtsaʔi.** He burst the bag.

tohpʉsakurʉ K (v) dab to wipe or erase, erase. *See* **tohtsomarʉ.**

tohtaniʔitʉ (v) carry and put down.

tohtarakiitʉ (v) pet, stroke.

tohtarakitʉ (v) clap hands [**toh-** hand + **tara-** (sound) + **ki-** say].

tohtarakiʔarʉ (v) knock on door, pet or stroke. *See* **nisutaitʉ.**

tohtía masʉaʔ (n) wheat (grain).

tohtía narʉmʉʉʔ (n) bakery (*lit* bread store).

tohtía narʉso̲ (n) flour sack.

tohtía sonipʉ (n) wheat plant (*lit* bread grass).

tohtía sonipʉha takaʔ (n) rye, barley (*lit* mate to wheat).

tohtía tsasaʔwʉkiʔ (n) flour sifter.

tohtíaʔ (n) bread, tortilla, pancake.

tohtíaʔarʉ (v) bake, make bread.

tohtíaʔ rʉhkapʉ (n) Communion (sacrament), Mass (sacrament). *See* **pʉʉhibituʔitʉ.**

tohtoponitʉ (adj) round, spherical. *See* **maropoʔniʔpʉ.**

tohtopoʔnarʉ (v) roll up with something.

tohtoʔitʉ (v, pl), *sg* **tohkʉarʉ** exit forcibly. *See* **toʔitʉ, kʉarʉ.**

tohtsanarʉ (v), *pl* **tohtsaniʔi** hang up something.

tohtsatsaru (v) move from side to side (as a snake before attack).

tohtsiyu?itu (v) scrape meat from a hide, chisel or split with an axe. *See* **topukaaru.**

tohtsi?aru (v) **K** chisel wood; **W** hit with knuckle or fist.

tohtsomaru W (v) dab to wipe or erase. *See* **tohpusakuru.**

tohtubu?itu (v) drill a hole with an instrument (as into wood or leather with a drill).

tohtuki?aru (v) put something back in place.

tohtukwaru (v, pl), *sg* **tohpa?itu** slap or punch repeatedly.

tohtumapu (adj) closed off, stopped up.

tohtumaru (v), *pl* **tohtumi?itu** stop flow (as of liquid by putting lid on opening).

tohturooniitu W (adj) braced, supported. *See* **maruurooniitu.**

tohturu?aru W (v) rip something. *See* **wuhturu?aru.**

tohtuwaru (v) open something (using an instrument).

tokaru (v) pull off, knock off. *See* **wuhtokaru.**

tokiaru (v) peel off (as tree bark).

tokobo?niitu K (adj) calm, quiet.

toko? (n), *acc* **toko?a** maternal grandfather, man's uterine grandchild.

tokusuakutu (v) trust someone, believe in someone. **U rokusua-kutu nu?.** I believe in him.

tokwaitu (v) excavate, explore for oil, dig (searching in soil).

tokwetabeni (n) noon, midday.

tokwetukan (n), *adj* **tokwehtukanihtu** midnight (at the stroke of midnight).

tokwetukatu (adj) agreeable, approving. **Tokwetukatu u? Cachekahtu mi?aru?i.** She agreed to go to Cache.

tokwetuparu (v) listen (pay attention), obey orders.

tokwetutuaru (v) admire, agree with someone. *See* **su?akutu.**

tokwetu (adj) exact, proper. **Nu napu tsa? tohtokwetu.** My shoes fit just right.

tokwitetu (v) peep into.

tokwuriaitu (v) spill something on purpose.

tokwusikutu (v) tangle something (with the hands).

tokwusuakuna (n) belief, faith.

tokwusuakutu (v) believe something or someone.

tokwuki?aru (v) pitch, throw (something long, as a spear).

tokwuriaru (v) spill out on something, pour on. **Pitsipuha u tokwuriaru.** He poured the milk on it.

tomakwuyetu W (v) chase on horseback.

tominaru (v) break at joint of body.

tomo- (pfx) ref. to sky, cloud.

tomoba?atu (n) sky, heavens [**tomo** cloud + **pa?atu** above].

tomohtoopu W (n) two-year-old item. *See* **wahatomopu.**

tomohtootu W (adj) two years old.

tomoobi (n) clouds, heavens.

tomooru (adj) winter. **Utsui tomooru ma?.** It was a cold winter.

tomopu (n) year. **tomoopu K** (n) cloud, winter, year.

tomotsiaru W (v) sharpen to a point.

tomoyaketu (v) thunder. **Pia tomoyaketu.** It thundered loudly [**tomo-** cloud + **yake** cry].

Tomoʔa tuaʔ (name) Sky-child (person).

tomoakatʉ W (adj) cloudy. **Tomoakatʉ maʔ.** It was a cloudy day. **Tomookati nʉʔ puni.** It is clouded up I see.

tomoʔakitʉ (v) cloud up.

tomʉsiketʉ K (adj) tangled up. **Nʉ paapi tsaʔ tomʉsiketʉ.** My hair is tangled up.

tonarʉ (v), *pl* **towaka-** insect sting, stab, pierce. **Ʉnʉbihnaa nʉ tonaʔi.** The bee stung me.

tonaʔ (n) stinger of an insect.

tonʉkʉrʉ (v) tamp down (with instrument, as with crowbar or pole).

tookaatso, tohkaatso (n) toe.

tooniitʉ (v), *pl* **tooyʉhkatʉ** graze from place to place. **Pimoroonʉʉ tsaʔ nanaʔatanaiki tooyʉhka-tʉʉ.** The cows are grazing in different pastures.

toorʉ W (v) graze.

tooʔitʉ (v, pl), *sg* **toʔyarʉ** unhitch.

Tope (name) Quanah Parker's wife, Tope (died in 1962 at over ninety years of age).

Topehtsi, Topache (name) Pass-it-on (outstanding deacon; a strong Christian man).

topohtʉ (adj) round (ball-like), spherical.

toponi- (pfx) ref. to ball-like.

toponibihuuraʔ (n) pea [**toponi (htʉ)** round + **pihuuraʔ** bean].

toponitʉ K (v) have muscle cramp or spasm (describes knot formed when muscle cramps). **Nʉtawʉ tsaʔ toponi.** My foot muscle cramped. *See* **taʔwitsaroponiitʉ.**

toponiwekị (adj) circular.

Topʉsana (name) Flower (baby of Cynthia Ann Parker; the baby died of white man's disease after being captured with her mother by whites).

topʉ (n), *acc* **topʉha** shield. **Topa uʔyarʉ.** He took a shield.

topʉkaarʉ (v), *pl* **tohpakurʉ, tohpakuʔitʉ** chisel, split (as to split wood). *See* **tohtsiyuʔitʉ.**

topʉsarʉ (v) bead something (do beadwork on an article). **Nʉmʉnapʉha uʔ topʉsarʉ.** She beaded the moccasin.

toroʔihtʉkitʉ (adj) isolated, separated from others.

tosa- (pfx) white, silver.

tosa ekapitʉ W (adj) pink (*lit* white-red).

tosa hʉwʉnikatʉmaʔ, tosa hʉʔwʉnikitʉ (adv) early, before dawn (*lit* white horizon). *See* **hʉwʉni, tsaa nabuni.**

tosa kwanaʔhʉ W, tosa wanahʉ K (n) bedsheet [**tosa** white + **kwanaʔhʉ** blanket].

tosa kwiisuʔ (n) black bird with white wings.

tosa nabooʔ (n) K horse (calico); W horse (paint; white patches on chest and rump) [**tosa** white + **naboo** painted]. *See* **pitsa nabooʔ**

tosa nabunitʉ (v) appear to be white [**tosa-** white + **na** (refl) + **puni** see].

tosa nakaai (n) hawk [**tosa** white + **nakaai** hear].

tosa nʉʉbaaiʔ (n) frost, dew (short form) [**tosa** white + **nʉʉbaaʔi** dew].

tosa nʉʉbaikatʉ (n) frost. **Tosa nʉʉbaikatʉ maʔ.** There is frost.

tosa ohapitu (adj) cream colored (*lit* white-yellow).

tosarai? (n) devil's horse (insect).

tosahpuhihwi (n) silver money, coins [**tosa** white + **puhihwi** money].

tosahtuka? W (n) candle [**tosa** white + **tuka** light].

tosahwi (n) silver.

tosapi K (n), *adj* **tosapitu** W white, silver.

tosa rohtiya? (n) cracker [**tosa** white + **tohtiya?** bread].

tosa seyu?yuki? (n) ash tree. *Fraxinus americana* L.

tosa tukanai huupi (n) white oak.

tosa wahtsuki (n) horseweed.

tosa waikina (n) hack (white two-seated buggy). See **tuwaikina**.

tosa yuhu rukai? K (n) candle [**tosa** white + **yuhhu** lard + **tukai** light].

tosa?   ⚡ wehki'ai

tosa? (n) white horse.

tosiite (n), *acc* **tosíito** hoof (as of cow or horse).

tosi?kwaru (v) tear something (using an instrument, as a knife). **Tuhanitu u puhi tosikwai.** He tore the hide he is skinning.

toso?netu (v) rub off, scrape off.

toso?waitu (v) try or want to hit with fist.

totohtu (n) edible tuber. *See* **ahwepu**.

totsiyaa aawo (n) vase (*lit* flower container).

Totsiyaaih tabenihtu W, **Totsi yaarabenihtu** K (n) Decoration Day, Memorial Day (lit flower day). See **Pukura totsiyaa?ai?eka.**

Totsiyaa mua (n) May (*lit* flower month).

totsiyaa papihtsipu (n) stamen of flower.

totsiyaa patupinaatu, totsiyaa puhhipu (n) flower petal (*lit* flower leaf).

totsiyaa tsakwuna? (n) flower vase (*lit* flowers set out). See **tsakwunaru.**

totsiyaa?, totsiyaapu (n) flower. **Tsaati nu? totsiyaa?a puni.** I see a pretty flower.

totsiyaa?a suuki (n) vine, stem of plant.

totsiyaitu (v) bloom, blossom out.

totsiyakatu (adj) blooming.

totsubakitu (v) hang up. **Naboo?a u totsubakii u?.** He hung the picture.

totubihkuru (v) beat on, knock on, make galloping sound. **Tuhui nu? totubihkunu nahkai.** I hear the horses galloping.

toya, toyaabi (n) mountain.

toyaarukitu W, **toyaakatu** K (v) carry (hold something in lap while riding). **Ohnaa?a u toyaarukitu.** He is holding the baby in his lap.

toyaketu (v) make cry by hitting [**to-** hit + **yake-** cry].

toya ruhku? (n) leopard (*lit* mountain meat). *See* **nabooh roya ruhku?**.

toyarʉ (v), *pl* **tohimarʉ** adopt a child, lift up, carry in arms. **Ohnáa?a ma? toyaai.** She carried the baby (in her arms). **Pʉʉ ohna?nii marʉʉ tohimaʉ.** They carried their babies. *See* **tʉetʉnabinarʉ**.

toyo (n) neck.

toyo kwabarʉ (v) hug (around neck) [**toyo** neck + **kwabe** hug]. **Nʉ kaku tsa? nʉ toyokwabai.** My grandmother hugged me. *See* **kwabarʉ**.

toyo tahka?miitsa̱ (n) sweetbreads (*lit* neck wart).

toyo tsihka?arʉ (v), *pl* **toyo tsihpomarʉ** behead (cutting, as with knife). **Kokora?a?a toyo tsihka?ai.** He cut off the chicken's head.

toyo wʉhka?arʉ (v) behead (chopping, as with axe).

toyopʉ, tooyo̱ (n), *acc* **toyopʉna** neck. **Nʉ toyopʉ tsa? nʉʉtsikwarʉ.** My neck hurts.

toyʉsekaitʉ (v) excite, stir up excitement.

toyʉsʉkai (adj) exciting.

to?aikʉrʉ (v) roll to start something, start (cause to operate with the hand).

to?itʉ (v, pl), *sg* **kʉarʉ** appear, come out. *See* **tohto?itʉ**.

to?i̱ (n), *acc* **to?iha** pipe (for smoking). **Pʉ to?iha u? pahu-mu?itʉ.** He is smoking his pipe.

to?ibitʉ (v), **pl kiahbitʉ** come out at particular place.

to?nikarʉ K (v) put away for safekeeping. *See* **tʉrʉbaki?arʉ**.

to?nikarʉ W (v), *pl* **tʉbakitʉ** load into a container. **maro̱?nikatʉ** put food into mouth.

to?pʉ (n) shield. *See* **topʉ**.

to?roponii? (n) beetlike tuber. *See* **ahwepʉ**.

to?tsimuhpe? (n) mattock, pick for scraping hides (with short cedarwood handle and heavy metal blade). [**to?tsi** chisel + **muhpe** hoe]. *See* **muhpe?**.

to?urarʉ (v) meet someone, find something being looked for. **Pai to?uraai u?.** He found water.

to?wʉmi̱naitʉ (v) fail to reach, fall short.

to?wʉ?wenitʉ (v, pl), *sg* **wʉhtiarʉ** empty into, dump into (pour into different containers).

to?yabaitʉ (v) prick up the ears. **Tʉhʉya tsa? to?yabahkatʉ.** The horse is pricking up its ears.

to?yarʉ W (v), *pl* **too?itʉ** unhitch an animal. **Pʉ puuki u to?yarʉ.** He unhitched his horse. *See* **noro?yarʉ**.

tsaa (adj) good, well. **Surʉse? tsaa kamanʉ.** That tasted good (110:15). **Tsaa nʉ? u mʉʉi.** I made him well, healed him.

tsaa kamarʉ (v) taste good.

tsaa manʉsurʉ (v) please someone (make someone happy, be happy).

tsaa manʉsu?itʉ (adj) pleased.

tsaa marabetoikatʉ K (adj) bright, shiny.

tsaa naahkatʉ (adj) rich. **Orʉ tsa? tʉnahpʉ tsaa naahkatʉ.** That (he) is a rich man.

tsaa nabuni (adv) dawn. *See* **tosa hʉwʉnikatʉma?, hʉwʉni**.

tsaa nabunitʉ (v) dawn (light enough to see). **Tsaa nabunikitʉ maʔ.** It is getting light enough to see.

tsaa nʉʉsukatʉ (adj) happy, rejoicing.

Tsaa tenayakeʔ (name) Good-crier (person).

Tsaa tsopaʔ (name) Easy-to-break (person).

tsaana, tsanani (adv) futilely, emptily (in vain, to no avail).

tsaanahapʉ (n), *acc* **tsaanahapʉha** riches, treasure.

tsaati tamakatʉ W, **tsatsati tamakatʉ** (v) chatter (teeth), quiver (lips).

tsaatʉ (adj) good.

tsaatʉ narʉmuʔipʉ (n) gospel, good news.

tsah- (pfx) ref. to pull (forward or up by hand).

tsahhanitʉ, tsahaniitʉ (v) drive a car or team by hand.

tsahhomonutsarʉ (v) crush, crumble (with both hands).

tsahhorarʉ (v) dig (with the hands). *See* **mahorarʉ.**

tsahhuhyarʉ (v) hurt someone by accident.

tsahhʉkwʉʔniitʉ W, **tsahhʉwʉʔniʔarʉ** K (v) lift up (as to see underneath).

tsahimarʉ (v, pl obj), *sg obj* **tsayarʉ** carry a container by the handle.

tsahkarʉkʉrʉ (v, sg obj), *pl obj* **tsayʉkwikʉ-** set upright, right something.

tsahkaʔarʉ (v, sg obj), *pl obj* **tsah pomiʔitʉ** pull apart, break off (sever a flexible object by hand). **Puibihnáa nʉʔ tsahpomiʔitʉʔi.** I am going to pull watermelons (off the vine).

tsahkítoʔarʉ (v) shell something by hand, peel something. **Ohapitʉa uʔ tsahkitoʔai.** He peeled the orange (with fingers).

tsahkiʔaitʉ (v) cut someone to wound, scratch using an instrument.

tsahkobarʉ (v, sg obj), *pl obj* **tsahkobiʔitʉ** break off, snap off (sever something stiff with hands).

tsahkokarʉ (v, sg obj), *pl obj* **tahpomiʔitʉ** break something up (into fine pieces with foot) [**tah-** foot + **pomi-** break up].

tsahkooʔitʉ (v) cause to return, cause to turn around and come back.

tsahkʉarʉ (v, pl obj), *sg obj* **tsahtoʔitʉ** pull up, force out, take out.

tsahkʉnarʉ (v) sew (primarily by hand though could be by machine).

tsahkwanitʉ (v) claw at something, tear at something.

tsahkwaʔnuʔitʉ (v) throw down a person (as in wrestling).

tsahkweʔyarʉ (v, sg obj), *pl obj* **tsahkweʔyuʔitʉ** undress, disrobe, pull something off or out. *See* **natsahkweʔyarʉ.**

tsahkwitsoʔarʉ (v) save someone's life (by pulling him out of something).

tsahkwʉmarʉ (v, sg obj), *pl obj* **tsahkwʉmiʔitʉ** unwrap, unwind, unlace, loosen, unroll. **Nʉ nahposa nʉʔ tsahkwʉmarʉ.** I am unlacing my shoe. *See* **pʉrʉsuʔarʉ, tsahpekoʔarʉ.**

tsahkwᵾnunúukitᵾ (v) unwind (as thread or yarn). **Nᵾ wanaramị u? tsahkwᵾnanukị.** He unwound my thread.

tsahkwᵾrᵾ?arᵾ (v) skin animal, take off layer. **Arᵾka?a nᵾ? tsahkwᵾrᵾ?arᵾ.** I am skinning the deer. *See* **pᵾhᵾ tsahkwe?yarᵾ.**

tsahnᵾarᵾ (v) lift from a prone position. **Tenahpᵾ tuinahpᵾ?a tsa?nᵾai.** The man helped the boy get up.

tsahpaaku?nikarᵾ (v) duck someone, push someone under water. **Ohka u tsahpaaku?nikatᵾ.** He is ducking her. *See* **paku?nerᵾ.**

tsahpakịtᵾ (v) adhere (stick on), cling to.

tsahpako?arᵾ (v) split, tear apart. **Amawo?a tsahpa?ko?i nᵾ?.** I split the apple in two (with hands).

tsahpakᵾkarᵾ (v) attach (as a postage stamp). **Tsa? tᵾboopᵾ tsahpakᵾkatᵾkwᵾ.** The two pieces of paper are stuck together.

tsahpararᵾ (v) spread out something (as piece of cloth). **Tosakᵾni nᵾ? tsahpararᵾ.** I am stretching out a canvas (on the ground).

tsahparᵾ (v) pull down. **Sooni nᵾ? tsahpe.** I pulled my blanket down.

tsahparᵾ W (v) release (allow someone to go) [**tsah-** pull + **pᵾa?** let loose].

tsahpeko?arᵾ (v) unwrap an object. **Nᵾe tamasursai?a tsahpeko?ai.** I unwrapped my gift. *See* **tsahkwᵾmarᵾ.**

tsahperᵾ (v, sg obj), *pl obj* **tsayuma** tear down (as a building); scatter bundled items (throw groups of items here and there).

tsahpetitᵾ (adj) scattered (bundled items).

tsahpiso?arᵾ (v) anger. **Nᵾ naami? nᵾ? tsahpiso?ai.** My younger sister made me angry.

tsahpitsoorᵾ (v) wring out with hands (as in washing clothes). **Wa?ihpᵾ? tsa? oyo?ri tsahpitsooni.** The woman wrung out the clothes.

tsahpi?erᵾ (v) fish, pull out (fish). **Pekwina nᵾ? tsahpi?eru?i.** I will fish. **Orᵾ tsa? tᵾepᵾ paapasi oko tsahpi?epᵾniitᵾ.** That child is pulling potatoes out of that container.

tsahpohtoorᵾ (v) burst by pulling [**tsah-** pull + **pohto-** burst].

tsahpomi?itᵾ (v, pl) break, pull apart. *See* **tsahka?arᵾ.**

tsahporakitᵾ (v) crack knuckles. **Pᵾ mo?ai u? tsahporakiitᵾ.** He is cracking his knuckles.

tsahporᵾ (v) mark off, make a mark on something. **Ohka nᵾ? sokobitᵾ tsahporu?i.** I am going to mark off that land.

tsahpo?arᵾ, tsahpo?akatᵾ (v) scatter something. **Tuinapᵾ tsa? amawoo?a tsahpo?akatᵾ.** The boy scattered the apples around. *See* **poohkatᵾ.**

tsahpo?tsarᵾ (v, inan obj) jerk something toward oneself, pull a bouncy object [**tsah-** pull + **po?tsa** jerk].

tsahpunitᵾ (v) show someone something (make known to

someone) [**tsah-** pull + **puni** see]. **P<u>u</u> naboohp<u>u</u> tsahpunii.** She is showing her picture.

tsahp<u>u</u>ar<u>u</u> W (v) release (allow someone to go) [**tsah-** pull + **p<u>u</u>a** let loose].

tsahp<u>u</u>k<u>u</u>su?ar<u>u</u> W, tsahp<u>u</u>su?ar<u>u</u> K (v) unfold, take apart, unroll. **tsahp<u>u</u>su?ait<u>u</u>** unfolded (as cloth).

tsahp<u>u</u>yer<u>u</u> (v) pull out of container. **Si?anet<u>u</u> ma kwasimaku marii tsap<u>u</u>yén<u>u</u>.** At this place he pulled them out by their tails (10:20).

tsahp<u>u</u>her<u>u</u>, tsaap<u>u</u>her<u>u</u> (v), *pl* **tsayumi?i** take down off of something, unload. **N<u>u</u> soona tsahp<u>u</u>he.** I pulled down, took down my blanket (off shelf). *See* **tsap<u>u</u>yet<u>u</u>.**

tsahtaaikat<u>u</u> (adj) holey (having hole or holes).

tsahtaik<u>u</u>t<u>u</u> (v) dig, make a hole with hands. **Or<u>u</u> tsa? wa?ip<u>u</u> ohta wanahp<u>u</u> u tsahtaik<u>u</u>t<u>u</u>.** She is making a hole through the material (cloth).

tsahtobar<u>u</u> (v) uproot (pull up by the roots). **S<u>u</u>m<u>u</u>ruku tsa? ma tsahtoba ohka tam<u>u</u>suaka.** Someone uprooted that plant. **P<u>u</u> it<u>u</u>m<u>u</u>s<u>u</u>ap<u>u</u> u? tsahtoba- kat<u>u</u>.** She is uprooting her plant.

tsahtoko?ar<u>u</u> (v) pull bones out of joint.

tsahtopo?nar<u>u</u> (v), *pl* **tsahtoponi- ?it<u>u</u>** roll into a ball (make round).

tsahto?ar<u>u</u> K, tsahtoko?ar<u>u</u> W (v) unseal something, pry up, pull off. **U ku?e tsahto?ar<u>u</u>.** He is unsealing the top. **U ku?e u?**

tsahto?akat<u>u</u>. He is pulling the top off.

tsahto?ir<u>u</u> (v, sg obj), *pl obj* **tsap<u>u</u>yet<u>u</u>** bring out, take out, pull up. **Or<u>u</u> tsahto?i kahnik<u>u</u>- k<u>u</u>.** That man brought that baby out of the house.

tsahto?it<u>u</u> (adj), *pl* **tsahk<u>u</u>ar<u>u</u>** forced out, pulled up.

tsahtsi?ar<u>u</u> (v) scratch leaving a mark. **Wa?oo? n<u>u</u> tsahtsi?ai.** The cat scratched me.

tsahtsukit<u>u</u> (v) close (as to shut a window). **Narabuni u? tsahtsuki.** He closed the window.

tsahtsu?mar<u>u</u> (v) deplete a supply. **Kobe matsuma? tsah- tsu?mai.** He took the last towel.

tsahtukar<u>u</u> (v) unplug to extinguish, to disconnect (as an electric cord). **W** snuff fire with fingers.

tsahtunaabar<u>u</u> (v) straighten (lay out straight). **Ohka n<u>u</u>? huupina tsahtunaabaru?i.** I am going to straighten that wood.

tsahtuneht<u>u</u> (adj) stretched (as a bow), straightened (as an arrow).

tsahturer<u>u</u> (v, sg obj), *pl obj* **tsah- tunehts<u>u</u>t<u>u</u>** pull with full strength, stretch (make tense, as a bow).

tsahtur<u>u</u> (v) stretch something out (as a rope).

tsaht<u>u</u>war<u>u</u>, tsaat<u>u</u>war<u>u</u> (v, sg obj), *pl obj* **tsaht<u>u</u>wa?it<u>u</u>** open something (as a box or trunk), take down a teepee. **Ma tsaat<u>u</u>wa.** Open it. **Mutsik<u>u</u>ni u? tsaht<u>u</u>wai.** He took down the tent.

tsaht<u>u</u>bunit<u>u</u> (v) wake someone. **Or<u>u</u> tsa? tenahp<u>u</u>? t<u>u</u>e?p<u>u</u>ri**

tsahtʉbuni. That man woke the baby. *See* **tʉbunitʉ.**

tsahtʉkitʉ (v, sg obj), *pl obj* **tsahtanʉhiʔitʉ, tsahtahini W,** *pl* **tsahtaniʔitʉ K** set down, put down in place.

tsahtʉmarʉ (v) close (as to close a door). **Tenahpʉ tsahtʉmaruʔi.** The man will close the door.

tsahtʉrʉʔarʉ (v) rip with fingers (as threads or seams).

tsahtʉʔokiʔ K (n) rake. *See* **tʉtsanuaʔ.**

tsahwitʉ (v) open, discard (toss aside). **Ma tsahwituʔi nʉʔ.** I am going to open it. **Ohko tʉboopʉ narʉbakina hunapʉ tsahwi.** He threw that bag of paper trash outside. *See* **namaroʔitʉ.**

tsaiʔwarʉ K (v) tear something (with hands into small pieces).

tsakamiʔarʉ (v, sg obj), *pl obj* **umamiʔarʉ** lead along. **Tʉhʉyʉ uʔ tsakamiʔarʉ.** He led the horse along. *See* **matsaaihkakurʉ.**

tsakarʉ (v) lead a person or an animal.

tsakaʔuhrʉ (v) betray, lead astray.

tsakitsetʉ (v) crush or squash (with the fingers).

tsakʉbitʉkitʉ (v) arrive home (leading a person or an animal).

tsakʉhunitʉ (v, sg obj), *pl obj* **tsakʉhuyʉkʉrʉ** lead up a horse.

tsakwatʉ (v) feel around, grope around (as for something as in the dark). **Pʉ wiyaʔa uʔ tsakwai.** He felt around for his rope.

tsakwenitʉ (v) hang something.

tsakwerʉ (v) help down (as by holding hand). **Waikinbaku uʔ**

tsakwee. He helped her off the wagon.

tsakwipunarʉ (v), *pl* **tsaʔkwitsuniʔitʉ** twist something, screw something in.

tsakwoʔnerʉ (v) scratch an itch. **Nʉ pʉʉrʉ tsakwoʔnetʉ.** I am scratching my arm (where it itches). *See* **natsawoʔnitʉ.**

tsakwʉhburʉ (v) cause to turn something around.

tsakwʉhwitʉ (v) caused to turn around.

tsakwʉnarʉ (v, sg obj), *pl obj* **tsawʉniʔitʉ** set down carefully, lay out (as food on a table). **Iki ma tsakwʉna.** Set it here. *See* **totsiyaa tsakwʉnaʔ.**

tsakwʉkatʉ (v) shoot (let fly with force as a gun or an arrow). *See* **wʉhkikatʉ, tsatʉkarʉ.**

tsakwʉriarʉ (v) knock over and spill accidentally.

tsakwʉsarʉ W, tsikwʉsarʉ K (v) lace up.

tsakwʉsikʉkatʉ K (v) tangle. **Tamu uʔ tsakwʉsikʉkatʉ.** She is tangling the thread.

tsakwʉʔikʉrʉ W (v) tangle something. **Tamu natsakwʉsikʉ.** The thread is tangled.

tsamanirʉ (v) carry across. **Ohka puʔetʉ ma tsamani.** He carried it across the road. **Sʉmʉ tsamani etʉtsi.** Each having carried everything across.

tsamarʉkarʉ (v) finish. **Pʉ tʉtsawo uʔ tsamarʉkai.** He finished plowing. *See* **marʉkarʉ.**

tsaminarʉ (v) disjoint (pull something out of joint). **U moʔi uʔ**

tsaminaruʔi. He will pull his hand out of joint.

tsamiʔakɯrɯ (v) help someone walk. **Ukɯ waʔihpɯ tsamiʔakɯtuʔi nɯʔ.** I will help that woman to walk.

tsamuhraikɯtɯ (v) cause (two others) to kiss. **Orɯ tsaʔ tenahpɯ ohka tuinɯhpaʔa ma tsamuhraikɯi.** The man made the young man kiss her.

tsamukɯsitɯ (v) blow the nose.

tsamupɯsitɯ W (v) cause to sneeze. *See* **tsaʔakɯsitɯ.**

tsamɯsasuakatɯ (adj) worried, caused to worry. **Nɯ ruapɯ nɯ tsamɯsasuakatɯ.** My boy has got me worried.

tsamɯrikarɯ (v) turn something over.

tsanamɯsohnitɯ (v) hurry, cause to hurry.

tsanikatɯ (v) hang suspended. **Nɯ kwasu tsaʔ tsanikatɯ iima.** My dress is hung on, by this thing.

tsanoorɯ (v) pull, pluck (by hand, something growing). **Sonipa uʔ tsanooʔi.** He pulled the grass. **Kokoraʔa pɯhi tsanooʔituʔi.** He will pluck the chicken's feathers.

tsanuarɯ (v) move by hand, pull on something. **Pɯ kune uʔ tsanuaruʔi.** He is going to move his firewood.

tsanutsarɯ (v) break into pieces, break off a piece. **Tohtiya uʔ tsanutsai.** He broke off a piece of bread.

tsanɯmaitɯ (v) lazy.

tsanɯnɯrɯ (v) cause to stop (rein in a horse, wave down a car). *See* **tɯtsanɯnɯʔitɯ.**

tsanɯkɯrɯ (v) buckle or tighten something. **Narɯmuhki uʔ**

tsanɯkɯi. He buckled (or tightened) the harness.

tsapeherɯ, tsaperɯ (v, sg obj), *pl obj* **yumarɯ** jerk down, pull down (make someone fall). **Orɯ tsaʔ nɯ tsaperɯ.** That person made me fall down.

tsapɯsikɯ (n) sensitive briar. *Schrankia* Nutt. (dc.)

tsapɯhesuwarɯ, tsaphesuwarɯ (v) tempt to turn aside (attempt to throw off someone from a goal or purpose).

tsapɯkarɯ, tsasiʔarɯ W (v) split, cut in half. **Huupita nɯʔ tsapɯkaruʔi.** I will split the wood.

tsapɯtsarɯ (v) burst (by applying pressure). **Orɯ tsaʔ nɯ mubohtokiʔ.** That person burst my balloon.

tsapɯyetɯ (v, sg obj), *pl obj* **tsayumiʔi** unload (take down from). **Waikinakahku nasoki uʔ tsapɯyeetɯ.** He took the sack down from the wagon. *See* **tsahpɯherɯ.**

tsasaʔwɯkitɯ (v) sift. **Homopɯha nɯʔ tsasaʔwɯkiitɯ.** I am sifting flour.

tsasaʔwɯkiʔ K, tsasaʔkwɯkiʔ W (n) sieve, flour sifter.

tsasikwaitɯ (adj) torn up completely.

tsasinɯkaarɯ, tsasinakatɯ (v) pull back, scrape, skin. **Nɯ moʔi nɯʔ tsasinɯkatɯ.** I scraped my hand.

tsasoʔarɯ (v) strain out something.

tsasukarɯ (v) feel something, examine (with fingers).

tsasukwarɯ (v) grab for, snatch, sieze. **Ohko puhihwita tsasuwai.** He grabbed for that man's money.

tsasuʔatsitʉ (v) help decide, convince someone. **Nʉ peta nʉʔ tsasuʔatsituʔi u hanituʔiha.** I am trying to help my girl make up her mind what to do.

tsasuʔnerʉ (v) scrape, smooth, soften (as a hide). **Ohka pahkipa tsasuʔne.** He scraped the hide.

tsasʉsʉʔnikatʉ (adj) numb (from cutting off the blood supply). **Nʉ moʔe ʉnʉ masʉsʉʔnikʉkatʉ.** You made my hand numb. **Tsasʉsʉʔni uʔ.** It was numb from squeezing. *See* **sʉsʉʔnitʉ.**

tsatsiaʔ (n) splinter (as of wood).

tsatsubihkurʉ (adj) rattled, rattling.

tsatsʉbipʉkurʉ (v) make something rattle. **Tʉboopʉa uʔ tsatsʉbipʉkurʉ.** He is rattling the paper.

tsatʉkarʉ (v) shoot, propel (as a gun or arrow). **Taʔwoʔa uʔ tsatʉkai.** He shot the gun. *See* **tsakwʉkatʉ, taʔwoʔekarʉ.**

tsatʉkaʔkarʉ (v) shoot a repeating gun. **Taʔwoʔa uʔ tsatʉkaʔkaruʔi.** He will shoot the repeating rifle. *See* **taʔwoʔekarʉ.**

tsatʉsukitʉ (v) harrow, till (loosen soil). **Pʉ sokobita uʔ tsatʉsukii- tʉ.** He is harrowing his ground. *See* **tʉtsatʉsukitʉ, siibarʉ.**

tsawehkwatʉ (v) haul off. **Nah nʉʔ mʉʉ kahnikʉhu ʉ tsaweehkwatuʔi.** I will just haul you off to your camp (39:35).

tsayaketʉ (v) cause to ring. **Kawohwiʔa nʉʔ tsayaketʉ.** I am ringing the bell. *See* **tuʔtsayaketʉ, kawohwitʉ.**

tsayarʉ (v, sg obj), *pl obj* **tsahimarʉ** carry a container by the handle (as by a strap usually on top).

tsayoritʉ (v) rouse, wake up someone.

tsayumarʉ (v) throw down.

tsayumiʔi (v, pl obj), *sg* **tsapʉyetʉ** take down, unload, remove (such as roasted meat from coals). *See* **tsahpʉherʉ.**

tsayʉkwikʉ (v, pl obj), *sg obj* **tsahkarʉkʉrʉ** set up straight.

tsayʉkwitʉ (v) sit straight.

-tsaʔ (enclitic, declarative mode). **Kohtopʉtsaʔ tukamiʔarʉ.** The fire is going out. **itsaʔ nʉ kahni.** This is my house.

tsaʔaikʉrʉ (v) pump (as water). **Pai uʔ tsaʔaikʉtʉʔ paa tsaʔaikʉrukʉ.** He is pumping water from the pump.

tsaʔaikʉrʉ (v) make (animal) lope. **Pʉ puuki uʔ tsaʔaikʉi.** He made his horse lope.

tsaʔakʉsitʉ K (v) sneeze.

tsaʔatsitʉ (v) inspect. **Tʉhʉye uʔ tsaʔatsi.** He inspected the horse. *See* **puiwʉnʉrʉ.**

tsaʔikarʉ (v, sg obj), *pl obj* **tsaʔwekwitʉ** admit (allow to enter). **Urii nʉmʉni tsaʔwekwi.** Let those Comanches in.

tsaʔnikaʔ, tsaʔanikaʔ (n) underwear, G-string, loincloth, jock strap. *See* **kohinehkiʔ.**

tsaʔnikoorʉ (v) put something down.

tsaʔnikʉkatʉ (adj) have underwear on. **Tuinapʉ tsaʔnikʉkatʉ.** The boy is wearing underwear.

tsaʔohkwerʉ (v) drain a liquid (by hand, as by opening a faucet).

Pai nʉʔ tsaʔohkweruʔi. I will drain the water out. **Pai nʉʔ tsaʔohkwetʉ.** I am draining the water.

tsaʔoibehkatʉ (adj) strangled (outside cause, not food). *See* **oihtʉyaitʉ.**

tsaʔokʉrʉ (v) strangle (person or animal).

tsaʔokwetʉ (v) drain. **Paa tsaʔ orʉ tsaʔokwetʉ.** The water is draining.

tsaʔonutsai (adj) bent. **Paka tsaʔ tsaʔonutsai.** The arrow is bent.

tsaʔonutsarʉ (v) bend. **Pʉ pake uʔ tsaʔonutsai.** He bent his arrow.

tsaʔookitʉ (v) bunch up. **Sonipʉ tsaʔookituʔi.** The grass is going to bunch up. **Sonipʉ tsaʔoohkitʉ.** The grass has been raked up.

tsaʔoorʉ (v) rake up, bunch up. **Sonipʉha uʔ tsaʔooruʔi.** He is going to rake the grass. **Sonipʉha uʔ tsaʔookitʉ.** He is raking the grass.

tsaʔrurʉ (v) give (in hanging container).

tsaʔwenitʉ, tsahkwenitʉ W (v) hang up something on a nail or hook.

tsaʔwikiitʉ (v) shake something. **Nʉ saria nʉʔ tsaʔwikiitʉ.** I am shaking my dog.

tsaʔwʉminarʉ (v) fail to reach something. **Tuinapʉ tsaʔ tʉhkaʔ tsaʔwʉmihnai.** The little boy cannot reach the table (top).

tseenaʔ K (n) gray fox, coyote (short form). *See* **ekatseenaʔ, kʉʔtseena.**

tsihakooihkatʉ (v) have famine, drought.

tsihakwitsoʔarʉ (v) save (from starvation). **Sariiʔa nʉʔ tsihamakwitsoʔai.** I saved the dog from starvation.

tsiharʉyaitʉ (v, sg), *pl* **tsihakoorʉ** starve to death. **Tsiharʉyaai humiʔarʉ nʉʔ.** I am about to die of hunger. **Tenahpʉʔ tsaʔ tsiharʉyaai.** The man died of hunger.

tsihasiʔapʉ (n) ravenously hungry person (hungry all the time). **Tuinʉhpʉ tsaʔ tsihasiʔapʉ.** That boy is hungry all the time.

tsihasuarʉ (v) hunger, have an appetite (feel hungry).

tsihhabʉhkamapʉ (n) menopausal woman. **Pʉ tsihabʉhkamapʉ ai.** She has gone through menopause.

tsihhabʉhkamarʉ, tsihhabʉhketʉ (v) menstruate.

tsihimarʉ (v, pl obj), *sg obj* **tsiʔyarʉ** carry something on a stick.

tsihkaʔarʉ (v) cut with a knife. **Tʉhkapa uʔ tsihkaʔarʉ.** She is cutting the meat (with knife).

Tsihkoba, Chikoba (n) Breaks Something (Antelope band).

tsihkwinumai (adj) weak, faint (from hunger).

tsihpeʔakarʉ (v) part hair.

tsihpoma (v, sg obj), *pl obj* **tsihpomiʔitʉ** cut up into pieces, slice. *See* **tʉtsihpomiʔipʉ.**

tseenaʔ

tsihpooru (v) mark something, draw line (using pointed object). **Tuboopuha ma? tsihpooru.** He marked the paper (with pointed object). *See* **kohpooru.**

tsihpuraru (v) ventilate (set up ventilator at top of teepee).

tsihtabo?ikutu (v, pl obj), *sg obj* **wunukuru** insert, set out, transplant. **Kuuke u? tsihtabo?ikutu.** He set out onion plants.

Tsihtara (name) Short-dress (person).

tsihtararu (adj) tall, high up (as a short dress).

tsihto?aru W, **tsihtu?waru** K (v) pry open. **U tsihto?aai u.** He pried it open.

tsihtsirahputu (adj) shiny, sparkling. **Taahka tsihtsirahputu.** The icicle is shiny.

tsihturuaru K (adj, anim) be stiff (inan obj must have **ta-** or **nara-**). **Ma tatsuturua.** Get it stiff. **Tenahpu?a kwasu?u tsa? naratsuturuapu.** The shirt is stiff.

tsihturuaru W (v) shiver from cold, shake from cold. **Tsihturuaru nu?.** I am shivering. *See* **suhtorokitu.**

tsihtu?yeru (v) comb hair, curry animal fur. **Tuewa?ihpu?a nu? tsihtu?yeetu.** I am combing the little girl's hair.

tsihtupukaru (v) pin together. **Wanapunihiu? nahma tsihtupukai.** She pinned the cloth together.

tsihturooru (v) support something (to keep it upright). **Huuhpima u? tsihturooni.** He supported it with a stick.

tsihtu?aweru (v) point (in a direction).

tsihtuwaru (v) unlock. **Natsahtuma ma? tsihtuwai.** He unlocked the door.

tsiikuwitehka? K, **tsikwitehka?** W (n) petroleum jelly (*lit* chapping oil). *See* **tsi?wunuu tu?eka?, nuuhtu?eka?.**

tsiira? (n) chili pepper. **Tsire?a ma? tuhkai.** He ate chili pepper.

tsii?wuweniitu (v) dredge, scoop, shovel out. **Huuhkupa u? tsii?wu?weniitu.** He is shoveling out the dirt.

tsikwainitu, tsiwainitu (v) probe (feel around with something sharp or with a pole).

tsiminaru, tsimino?itu (v) disjoint (separate bones at joint).

tsimi?akuru (v) miss doing (nearly accomplish; almost acquire but lose). **Tuhuye u? tsimiakui.** He almost hit the horse. *See* **awi-.**

tsimuami?aru (v) stagger when walking.

tsinuku (adj) crammed into limited space, squeezed tight, crowded (inanimate item).

tsinukuru (v) cram (crowd something into a limited space). **Pihuura?a kurohkuaawoku u? tsinukui.** He crowded the beans into the jar. *See* **natsinuhkuru.**

tsiperu, tsipeheru (v) unseat, unhorse (cause to fall off, as to unhorse with a spear or lance).

tsisu?waru (v, sg obj), *pl obj* **tsisu?kwa?nekitu** poke, jab.

tsiyaketu (v) hurt someone (make someone cry).

tsiyunaru (v) shovel (carry material on end of something, as a shovel).

Huuhkupa u? tsiyuna?i̱. He is shoveling the dirt (moving it from one location to another).

tsi?aikɨrɨ (v) push something that rolls (as a baby buggy). *See* **ma?aikɨrɨ.**

tsi?nikarɨ (v) insert into something. **Orɨ tsa? aawokṵ wanapɨha tsi?nikai.** He stuck a rag in a bottle.

tsi?wapɨ, tsii?wa (adj) chapped (as rough or cracked skin).

tsi?wapɨ W (n) rough skin, cracked skin.

tsi?wa?itɨ, tsi?kwa?itɨ (v) chap (become rough or cracked). **Nɨ hɨnɨpo?a tsa? tsi?kwa?i.** My skin is chapped.

tsi?wṵnɨɨ tɨ?eka? W (n) petroleum jelly [**tsi?wa?i-** chap + **wɨnɨ-** skin **tɨ?eka-** paint]. *See* **tsiikṵwitehka?, nɨɨhtɨ?eka?.**

tsi?yarɨ (v, sg), *pl* **tsihimarɨ** carry something (object is hanging off the end, as of a stick). **Huuhpima u? wanapɨha tsi?yai.** He carried the cloth on the end of a stick.

tsobokitɨ (v) shake vigorously.

tsohkwe K (v) soften by pounding. *See* **tohparaarɨ.**

tsohkwe? (n) pestle (wooden, with hole in center). **Nɨ tsohkwe?a nɨ? watsikɨi.** I lost my wooden pestle.

tsohpe takwɨnarɨ (v) pound pillowsticks into ground.

tsohpe tawɨna? (n) pillowsticks (two forked sticks pounded into ground at head of the bed for hanging belongings).

tsohpe tɨhka?aa? W, **tsohpi tɨhka?aa?** K (n) hatchet (as for chopping bones or tent stobs). **Tsohpi tɨhka?aa? tsa? kɨhmapɨ.** The hatchet is sharp.

tsohpe (n) pillow. **Tsohpe tsa? kahpeba?atɨ.** The pillow is on the bed.

tsohponiitɨ (v) try on headwear.

tsohtɨkikatɨ (v) lay the head down on something. **Tsohpeba- ?a ma? tsohtɨki̱katɨ.** He lay his head down on the pillow.

tsokwɨkɨɨna? W, tso?kɨna? K (n) scarf, bandana. *See* **wɨhtsohkɨna?.**

tsomo-, tsoomṵ (n) bead.

tsomo korohko (n) bead necklace [**tsoomo** bead + **korohko** necklace]. **Tsomo korohko?ai nɨ?.** I made a necklace.

tsonikarɨ (v, sg obj), *pl obj* **tsowekwatɨ** have a hat. **Sooti ma? tsowekwakatɨ.** She owns many hats.

tsoohpa tsuuni W, tsoo tsuuni K (n) shoulder bone.

tsoo? (n) great grandparent, great grandchild.

tsopekwiiyu W, tsopewiiyṵ K (n) cockscomb (crest on rooster's head).

tsotsomarɨ (v) wipe something with the head.

tsotsoo?ni̱ (n) meningitis. **Wa?ihpɨ tsa? tsotso?ni̱ hanikatɨ.** The woman is ill with meningitis.

tsotso?neetɨ (v) rub head against something. **Kahni tɨbanaakṵ tsotsoneetɨ.** He rubbed his head against the wall.

tso?aahpɨ? (n) granddaughter's husband.

tso?apia? (n) grandson's wife.

tso?apʉ (n) shoulder. **Nʉ tso?apʉ tsa? nʉʉtsikwarʉ.** My shoulder hurts.

tso?meetʉ (v) gather, pick (harvest plant product). **Naakʉtabai?a nʉ? tso?meetʉ.** I am gathering pecans.

tso?mepʉ (n) harvest (picked or gathered items). **Nʉ tso?mepʉ ma?.** That is what I picked (my harvest).

tso?nikarʉ (v) wear a hat, poke head into something (put on a hat). **Tso?nikarʉ ma?.** He is wearing a hat. **Aawokʉ nʉ? tso?nikaai.** I poked my head in a can. See **tʉtso?nikarʉ.**

tso?nika? (n), pl **tsowekwa?** hat.

tso?nʉarʉ (v) lift head, raise head.

tso?wiketʉ (v) shake the head no, oppose something (indicating negative feeling).

tso?yaarʉ (v) carry something on the head. **Otʉaawe tso?yaarʉ.** She is carrying a jar on her head.

tso?yaa? (n) head of hair, hair.

tsuh (interj) yes, now, ready.

tsuhitʉ (v) unable to do something. See **kemahpʉ?arʉ.**

Tsuhni (name) Bone (person).

tsuhni, tsuhni? (n) bone. **Tsuhnipʉ tsa? kohpapʉ.** The bone is broken.

tsuhni bunitʉ, tsuuni bunitʉ (v) glare at (with hateful expression; lit bone look).

tsuhni karʉ (v) sit down quickly (lit bone sit).

tsuhni kwʉnʉrʉ K, **tsuhnisihkwetʉ** W (v) stop suddenly.

tsuhni muyake?, tsuhni pʉmayake? (n) whistle (originally only of bone; now also of wood).

tsuhni tekwarʉ (v, sg), pl **tsuhni niwʉnʉtʉ** curse (lit bone talk; talk mean or rough).

tsuhni wʉminahkatʉ (adj) rheumatic.

tsuhni wʉminakatʉ? (n) rheumatism (lit bone illness).

tsuhnipʉ (n) skull.

tsukuhpʉ? (n) old object, elderly male. **Tsukuhpʉ? tsa? ainʉʉsukatʉ.** The elderly man is ill.

tsunisʉ, tsunʉsʉ (n) certain plant with edible tuber.

tsuwíhnu (expr) doubt the truth of a statement.

tsu?ma, tsu?makʉtʉ (v) finish, use up. **Pihuura tsa? sʉmʉ tsu?mai.** The beans are all gone.

tsʉhkarʉ (v) stuck down in (animate subj). **Tsʉhkai nʉnʉ.** We're stuck. **Tsʉhkami?arʉ nʉnʉ.** We became stuck.

tsʉhkikatʉ (v) crowd with people, fill with people. **Kahni tsa? tsʉhki.** The house is crowded (by many people).

tsʉkikatʉ (adj) crowded into narrow place, stuck between two things.

tsʉmʉkikatʉ (adj) calm spirit, quiet spirit, peaceful spirit.

tsʉʉ?tsʉki? (n) whooping cough.

tsʉ?nitʉ (v) stay late, delay. **Ʉi u? tsʉ?nii.** He stayed too late (longer than he should have).

tsʉ?tsʉkitʉ (v) whoop (cough), cough hard.

tu-, tuh- (pfx) black, dark.

tua boopʉ W (n) adopted son [**tua** son + **boopʉ** paper].

tuakatʉ (v) be in labor, give birth.

tua? (n) son. **Hina ʉnʉ tua??** What son are you? (13:3).

tubokóo (n) thornapple, black haw (local term) [**tu** black + **pokóo?** fruit] *Crataegus* sp. (sweet fruit eaten; inner bark chewed as gum).

tubupokoo (n) chippaberry (black fruit; threshed down from the nine-foot tree; the leaf is about an inch long and thorny; the bark used as chewing gum).

tuhani̱ (n) shadow.

tuhbanatsaya, tuu panatsaya (n) blackberry bush. *Rosaceae* sp.

tuhhu (n) shinbone.

tuhhu rɨhkapɨ (n) bone marrow [**tuhhu** bone + **tɨhkapɨ** meat].

tuhhu rɨhkarɨ (v) eat bone marrow.

tuhhuu? (n) stick for hand game, poker chip.

tuhkanaai kwasu?ṳ (n) undershirt.

tuhkatɨ (adj) deep, down, downward (a hole in ground).

tuhka?naai rekwarɨ (v) speak Wichita language.

Tuhka?naai? (n), *pl* **Tuhka?nai?-nɨɨ**. Wichita people.

tuhka?naai? niwɨnɨ (n) Speakers of Wichita language.

tuhkohhi̱ W, **tuhkoihi̱** (n) intestine.

tuhku tsa?nikapɨ (n) sausage (Kiowa dish of intestine stuffed with meat and juice, then boiled).

tuhkṳ (n) flesh, body, meat.

tuhkṳni, tuukṳni (n) black cradle.

Tuhkwasi taiboo? (n) Satan, devil. *See* **ketokwe hina haniitṳ**.

tuhmeko̱ (n) cricket.

tuhmubitai (n) black walnut. *Juglans nigra* L. (nuts eaten; leaves used for treating ringworm and as an insecticide).

tuhnaséka (n) Mexican persimmon. *Brayodendron texanum* Scheele

(small tree; fruits eaten; serves as opossum or raccoon food).

tuhnatso?me?, tuu natso?me?a (n, acc) prune (*lit* black dried plums). **Tuu natso?me?a nɨ tɨhkai.** I ate prunes.

tuhparokoo?, tuu paroko? (n) water moccasin (snake) [**tuh-** black + **paa** water + **ro** through + **ko** cutter]. **Tuhparokoo? tsa? ma kɨhtsiai.** A water moccasin bit him.

tuhpihhínaboo? (n) spade (in card game) [**tu** black + **pihhi** heart + **nabo?** printed].

tuhpui, tuhpuui (n) pupil of eye. **Tuhpuuiha nɨ? mahrɨni.** I hurt the pupil of my eye.

tuhtahkanaboo?, tuu tahkana-boo? (n) spade (in card game) [**tuu** black + **tahka** arrow + **nabo?** printed].

tuhtaiboo? W, **tuhtenahpɨ** K (n) black person.

tuhtsaipɨ (n) dirty object (unclean). **Wanapɨ tsa? tuhtsaipɨ.** The cloth is dirty. *See* **nasɨsɨa?eetɨ**.

tuhtseena? (n) wolf [**tuh** black + **tseena?** coyote].

tuhu rekwarɨ, tuhu rɨkweerɨ, tuhu rekwaitɨ (v) jerk and slam things in anger, talk rough, act angry (human), growl in anger (animal).

tuhu su?aitɨ (v) feel anger, feel rage.

tuhu yɨkwiitɨ (v) rave (rave madly at someone in anger).

tuhubɨkɨkatɨ (v) become angry at a person. **Pɨ patsia u? tuhubɨkɨkatɨ.** She became angry at her sister.

tuhupi (adj) black. **Tuhupitu
kwasu.** It is a black dress.
Tuhupiti nu kwasukatu. I have a
black dress.

tuhupu (n) mean person or animal
(easily angered).

tuhuupi, tuhu huupi (n) blackjack
oak, barren oak. **Quercus
marilandica** Muench (acorns
eaten; leaves used as cigarette
wrappers [C & J]).

tuhupu (n) hide, raw skin.

tuibihtsi? (n) young man, Indian
brave (warrior).

tuinuhpu?

tuinuhpu? W (n), *pl* **pihi?anuu** K
boy. *See* **pihi?a.**

tuka uhyui (adv) night, early
morning (from midnight to
dawn).

tukaani, tukani (adv) evening,
night. **Tukani humi?aru.** It is
getting dark (82:13).

tukami?aru (v) go out, die out
(said of fire). **Kohtopu tsa?
tukami?aru.** The fire is going out.
See **wuhtukaru.**

Tukanai (n) Caddo people (*lit* night
hunter).

tukanikatu (adj) dark (without
light), unlighted.

tukanitu (adj) be night.

tukaru (v) extinguish (put out a fire
or flame). **Nu?kohtopuha tukai.** I
put out the fire. *See* **wuhtukaru.**

tuka? (n) lamp, light. *See* **kupita?,
natsayaa ruka?.**

tuka?a nabaa (n) kerosene, coal oil,
oil well [**tuka?a** lamp + **nabaa**
oil]. *See* **nabaai tokwaaitu,
keto?kapaa.**

tuka?a nahhuupi (n) lamppost (*lit*
lamp wood).

tuka?a naku?e W, **tuka naku?e** K
(n) lamp chimney, chimney. **Oru
tsa? tuka naku?e puuhtsai.** The
lamp chimney broke (cracked).

tuka?a nawanapi (n) lamp wick.

tuka?ekapitu (adj) red (dark).

tuka?yuwu W (adj) purple.

tukuhputu (adv dir) upward
(limited in distance; not as high
as sky).

tukumakwuyetu? W,
tukuwekwikatu K (n) rodeo. *See*
kuhtsu taibo nohhiitu.

tukunu natsu, tuka natsu (n)
purple coneflower. *Echinacea* sp.
(roots used in treating sore throat
and toothache [C & J]).

tumuukatu (adj) bent down,
stooped.

tumuuru (v) bend down, stoop. *See*
nuhtsapu.

tuna, tunaa (adj) straight. **tuna
wunukatu** stand straight.

tuna wosa (n) war-bonnet bag
(also held feathers, war paint,
brush, and mirror; was of tubular

shape and worn hanging from the waist).

tunehtsꭱrꭱ (v) go on, run to something. **Meeku tunehtsꭱruʔi takwꭱ.** Now we two will run (9:13).

tunꭱhaa (n) cymopterus plant. *Cymopterus acaulis* (Pursh.) Rydberg (rootstocks eaten [C & J]).

tupisinawoniʔ (n) dusk (after sundown).

tupisi kꭱmaʔ (n) bay horse.

tupisibitꭱ (adj) dark color.

tupꭱsꭱnarꭱ (adj) dusk, evening.

turetꭱ (v) stretch.

turuarꭱ (v) bear offspring, lay eggs (give birth to many young).

turuawapi (n) hen, laying hen (as leghorn).

Tusa Kahni (n) Black Houses (name for Wichita people because of black inside fire pits and dark purple color of tents).

tusanahpi (n) tar [tu- black + sanahpꭱbi sap].

tusi, tusipꭱ (n) saliva. *See* **kꭱpisiʔ.**

tusi aawo (n) spittoon, ashtray [tusi (pꭱ) spit + aawo container].

tusitꭱ (v) expectorate, spit. **Sokoko urúsiitꭱ.** He spit on the ground. *See* **paitusiʔitꭱ.**

tusohóʔ (n) elm [tu- black + soho cottonwood + ʔ (nom sg)] *Ulmus fulva* Michx.

Tusohoʔokweʔ (n) Washita River [tusoho elm + okweʔ river]. **Tusohoʔokweʔ tsaʔ paruʔikitꭱ.** The Washita River is rising.

Tusokweʔ K, Tusohoʔkweʔ W (n) Anadarko, Okla. [tusoho elm + kweʔ place].

tusupꭱ W (n) pulverized or grated object, grounds. *See* **nasupꭱ.**

tusurꭱ (v) grind, thresh. **Pꭱ haniibita tusurꭱ.** He ground his corn.

tutupitꭱ (n) wild tuber (dark-skinned root; white inside; grows in field or along pond). *See* **ahwepꭱ.**

tutꭱsawꭱ koobe (n) freckled face (*lit* spotted face).

tutꭱsaʔwꭱtꭱ W, tutꭱsa kawoʔarꭱ (adj) freckled. **Sooti maʔ tutꭱsaʔwꭱtꭱ.** He has many freckles. *See* **tasiʔaʔ.**

tutꭱtsaai wahtꭱ (adj) clean, spotless, pure (in mind and soul; *lit* without spots).

tuu- (pfx) water (in container).

tuuhuniitꭱ W, tuuniitꭱ K (v, sg), *pl* **tuuhuyꭱkarꭱ, tuuyukarꭱ** fetch water.

tuukꭱmiʔarꭱ (v) fetch water for someone.

tuumeʔso (n) young catfish.

tuumoʔtsoʔ (n) fullgrown catfish [tuu water + moʔtsoʔ whiskers].

tuupꭱ (n) water (in container, having been brought in). *See* **paa.**

tuurꭱ (v) draw water. **Hunuʔbikitꭱ u ruurꭱ.** He is drawing water at the stream. **Tuumiʔai uʔ.** He went to draw water.

tuusanahpitꭱ (v) pave a road; adj blacktopped. **Tuusanahpitꭱ maʔ puʔeʔaitꭱ.** He is putting tar on the road.

tuuʔetꭱ, tuuwapi (n) water boy (one who fetches water).

tuuʔre napꭱ (n) galoshes, rubber boots.

tuuʔre tahpikoʔ, (n) rubber heel.

tuꭱnꭱꭱʔ (n) june bug, black beetle [tu- black + ꭱnꭱꭱ bug].

tuwaikina̱ (n) hack, carriage (black top, two-seater). **Tuwaikinapa nʉ? too?i.** I unhitched the black carriage. *See* **tosa waikina̱.**

tuwikaa?, tuhwikaa? (n) raven, crow, blackbird.

tuwokwe (n) goathead (vine with thorns) [**tu-** black + **wokwe** thorn].

tu?amowoo, tʉrʉi amawoo (n) thorn apple, red haw (local popular term). *Crataegus* sp. (fruits eaten [C & J]).

tu?anikuura? (n) wood ant (*lit* black ant).

tu?ebipi̱tʉ (adj) **K** dark blue; **W** purple.

Tu?paapi̱ (name) Black-head (person).

tu?re?, tuu?re? (n) leech, rubber band.

tu?runaasʉ (adj) straighter-than-straight [**tu-** (redup) + **tunaa** straight + **sʉ**].

Tu?runaasʉ (name) Straighter-than-straight (person).

tu?rʉmetʉ (adj) wasted.

tu?tsayaketʉ (v) ring something (as a bell). *See* **tsayaketʉ.**

tʉ- (pfx, unspecified object).

tʉa, -rʉa (quotative adv) it is said that, they say that.

tʉanóo (conj) or.

tʉapako?itʉ (v) split into two parts.

tʉahpi̱ (n) Chickasaw plum. *Prunus angustifolia* Marsh (fruits eaten fresh or stored [C & J]; grown around Anadarko).

tʉasʉ (conj) also, and, again. **Tʉasʉ tʉ?a̱hwe.** Tell it again.

tʉbakitʉ (v, pl obj), *sg obj* **norʉbaki̱tʉ** load items (as into wagon, gun, sack).

tʉbanaa rʉbopʉ (n) wallpaper.

tʉbanaa? (n) wall, edge, cliff. *See* **kahni tʉbanaa.**

tʉbawʉhtia wapi̱ (n) baptizer (one who baptizes) [**tʉ-** (unspec) + **pa** water + **wʉhtia-** put under + **wapi** (nom)].

tʉbehkapʉ (n), *pl* **tʉkwʉsʉ** animal killed or butchered for food.

tʉbehkarʉ (v, sg obj), *pl obj* **tʉkwʉsʉrʉ** butcher an animal. **Pimoroo?a urʉ tʉbehkai.** They butchered the cow. *See* **tʉhaniitʉ.**

tʉbehyaarʉ (v) accuse someone falsely, find fault with someone.

tʉbekwipʉ, tʉbekwi (n) mumps [**tʉ-** (unspec) + **pekwi** swell. **Tʉbekwi̱katʉ u.** He has the mumps.

tʉbinaa?wekitʉ (adj) divided in half.

tʉbinaa?weki̱ (adv) middle. **Pia kwasinaboo? suhka sekwikʉni tʉbi̱naa?weki̱ habitʉ.** A big snake was lying in the middle of that cellar (51:6). num half. **Pʉ puhiwihta ma? tʉbi̱naa?weki̱ti narohtumakʉ tʉki̱nu.** She put half her money in a can (48:10).

tʉbinaa?werʉ (v) divide in half.

tʉbinarʉ (v, sg obj), *pl obj* **tʉrʉbinitʉ** question someone. **U rʉbini u.** He questioned him.

tʉbinitʉ (v) ask a question, question someone. **Nʉsu?a tsa? sʉmʉ?a mʉi tʉbinitu?i̱.** I will ask you one question.

tʉbitsi (adv intens) really, surely. **Tʉbitsiku nʉ? mi?apa su waitʉ.** I really want to go. **Tʉbitsi ʉtsʉi kwihne ma?.** It was really a cold winter.

tʉbitsi basapʉ (adj) dried, dry. *See* **pasapʉ.**

tʉbitsi basarʉ (v) dry something. *See* **pasarʉ.**

tʉbitsikatʉ (adj) right-handed. *See* **ohinikatʉ.**

tʉbitsi petutʉ (adv dir) to the right. *See* **ohinibetutʉ.**

tʉbitsi suarʉ (v) decide, intend.

tʉbitsinakʉkʉrʉ K (v) listen carefully.

tʉbitsinakwʉ (adv loc) right side. *See* **ohininakwʉ.**

tʉbiyaakʉ? W (n) trailer (anything hanging at rear of vehicle). *See* **pitsaka?, kahni tʉbitsika?.**

tʉbitabu?itʉ (adj) blind (unable to see clearly).

tʉbitsiyu (adj) true.

tʉbomarʉ, tʉbumarʉ (v) gather in (as garden produce). *See* **pomarʉ.**

tʉboo kahni (n) school house, building [**tʉboo** writing + **kahni** house]. *See* **pia tʉbookʉni.**

Tʉboo renahpʉ makwe kwi?ena mʉa (n) September (*lit* paper man hand enter month). *See* **Kwi?ena mʉa.**

tʉboo tahni? (n), *pl* **tʉboo tahni?i** postman, mailman (*lit* letter deliver).

tʉboo wapi (n) male teacher (middle and high-school grades).

tʉboo bia? (n) teacher [**tʉboo** write + **pia?** mother].

tʉboo hima?eetʉ K, tʉboo parahni?i?eetʉ W (n) postman, mailman [**tʉboo** letter + **hima** take + **?e** (rep)].

tʉboopʉ (n) letter, paper.

tʉboopʉ kʉni (n) post office (*lit* letter house).

tʉboopʉ wosa W, tʉboo wosa K (n) mailbox. *See* **wosa.**

tʉboorʉ (v) write **Pʉ haitsiha tʉboo?i.** He wrote to his friend.

tʉboo rʉhka? (n) desk (*lit* writing table). *See* **pʉpa?akura tʉbòo?ena.**

tʉboorʉʉ pia? (n) female teacher [**tʉboorʉʉ** students + **pia?** mother] (teaches in elementary grades).

tʉboo? (n) pencil. **Tʉboo?a u? nʉ uhtʉnʉ.** He gave me a pencil. *See* **naboo?.**

tʉboo?etʉ W (n) camera. *See* **kobenabo?**

tʉbora, tʉborakatʉ (adj) born, originated.

tʉbunitʉ (v) wake up, awaken. *See* **tahtʉbunitʉ, tsahtʉbunitʉ.**

tʉbuuhki? (n) bellows, blacksmith's blower.

tʉe (adj) little, small. **Tʉe huupita nʉ? masʉai.** I planted a little tree.

tʉe aawo (n) spoon, teaspoon [**tʉe** little + **aawo** container]. *See* **piarʉ?ewo.**

tʉe amawóo? (n), *pl* **tʉrʉe amawóo?** crab apple. *Pyrus coronaria* L. *See* **eka amawoo?.**

tʉe tʉmakupa? (n) bobcat [**tʉe** little + **tʉmakupa?** panther].

tʉe basuu? W (n) quail. *See* **kuyúusi?, tʉrʉe basuu.**

Tʉe buakʉtʉ (name) Little-medicine (person).

Tʉeh buha rabeni (n) Saturday.

tʉehmahtua? W (n) little finger [**tʉe-** little + **ma** hand + **tua?** child].

tʉehna matsuma? (n) washcloth [**tʉe-** little + **na** (nom) + **matsuma?** wiper].

tʉehpʉʔrʉ (n) child.

tʉeh tahtuaʔ (n) little toe [tʉe little + tah- foot + tuaʔ child]. *See* tahtúaʔ.

tʉe kahuuʔ (n) mouse.

Tʉe kuhtsu (name) Little-buffalo (led a large number of N. Comanches in 1864 attacking in Texas near the Brazos River on Elm Creek, near Fort Belknap; died Oct. 13, 1864; Fehrenbach 1974:453).

tʉe kuyúutsi K (n) quail, partridge (small variety) [tʉe- little + kuyúutsi quail]. *See* tʉrʉe kuʔyuutsi.

tʉetekwʉni wapi (n) Indian brave, brave young man.

tʉetʉnabinarʉ (v) adopt a child. *See* toyarʉ.

tʉetʉtaatʉ kʉʉka (n) wild onion. *Allium* sp. (small, strong like garlic, grows in pastures).

tʉe waikina (n) single buggy (one-seated buggy).

tʉe anikuuraʔ (n) sugar ant (*lit* small ant).

tʉe esi ʉnʉʉ (n) gnat [tʉe little + esi gray + ʉnʉʉ bug].

tʉeʔtʉ (n) child, little one (must have possessor). Nʉ tʉeʔtʉ tsaʔ tʉbooʔ kwai. My child went to school.

tʉhaniitʉ (v) butcher (cut up in pieces). Pimorooʔa uʔ tʉhaniitʉ. He is cutting up the cow. *See* tʉbehkarʉ.

tʉhaʔwokatʉ (adj) hollow.

tʉhhorarʉ (v) dig a hole. tʉʉhtʉmaʔa tʉhhorapʉ dug fencepost hole.

tʉhimana W, tʉhimarʉ K (n) rations. Ke tsaʔ soohi tʉhimarʉ. There were not many rations.

tʉhimaʔetʉ (v) get rations. Tʉhimakwai uʔ. He went to get rations.

tʉhima rabeni (n) ration day (day on which rations were distributed).

tʉhkamarʉ (v) eat up (finish eating completely). Pihuura nʉʔ tʉhkamai. I finished eating beans. Pihuuratsaʔ kʉhtsuʔmai nʉ. I ate up all the beans.

tʉhkanʉmiitʉ (v, sg), *pl* tʉhkayʉkarʉ graze (move about eating).

tʉhkapa (n, acc) meat, food.

tʉhkapa nakoopʉ (n) steak.

tʉhkapa narʉsupʉ W, tʉhkapa nasupʉ K (n) ground meat.

tʉhkapʉ (n) meat, food. Setʉ seʔ nʉʉmʉʔ wihnu tʉhkapʉ tuaʔetʉ. Those Comanche people then got meat (130:13).

tʉhkarʉ (v) eat. Tʉhkaruʔi tanʉ! Let's eat! Ʉ tʉhkaruʔi tanʉ! Eat your food!

tʉhkaʔ (n) fork, table fork.

tʉhkaʔena (n) food.

tʉhkupaʔ (n) billy club.

tʉhnearʉ W, tʉniarʉ K (v) read. Tsaa tʉhneanu. You spoke well (made a speech). Ohka tʉboo pʉha tsaa tʉhnearʉ. You read that letter well.

tʉhoitʉ (v) hunt game. Tabuʔkina nʉʔ tʉhoitʉ. I am hunting rabbits.

tʉhorarʉ (v) dig (with a tool). *See* wʉhhorarʉ, horarʉ.

tʉhoraʔ, tʉhhoraʔ (n) crowbar, posthole digger. *See* tʉkʉh kweʔyaʔ.

tʉhpetʉ (adj, sg), *pl* tʉtʉbetʉ full and running over, overflowing. Aawo tsaʔ tʉhpetʉ. The cup is running over. **Paa tsa? aawo tutubetu.** The jars are full of water.

tuhpo?tse? (n) ball bat [**tuh-** (unspec) + **po?tse?** bouncer].

tuhraniitu K, **tuhhanitu** W (v) pound, hammer. **Ihka nu? tuhraniitu.** I am hammering.

tuhtsohpe?aipu (n) Comanche butter. *See* **tuutsohpepu.**

tuhtsohpe?aru (v) render an animal carcass; make Comanche butter (by boiling crushed bones).

tuhtui? (n) girl friends, partners. *See* **notsa?ka?.**

tuhtukitu (v, sg), *pl* **turuni?itu** plant seed (using a dibble stick).

tuhuya, tuhuuya (n) horse. **Tuhuuya.** I see a horse. **Tuhuhya tsa? toonitu.** The horse is grazing.

tuhuya karu, tuhuya karunitu K (v, sg), *pl* **tuhuya yukwitu** ride horseback. *See* **kuayuka?etu.**

tuhuya

tuhuya natsihtu?ye?, tuhhuya tsihtu?ye?, tuuya tsihtu?ye? (n) currycomb, horse brush. **Oka tuhuya tsihtu?ye? nu uhtu.** Give me that currycomb.

Tuhuyana kwahipu (name) Horseback (Comanche chief).

tuhuya ro?itu (v), *pl* **tuhuya kuaru** climb on horseback (get on a horse; more general term than mount). *See* **tuya to?yeru.**

tuhuyena puni W, **tuhuyena napuni** K (n) horse tracks, hoofprints. **Tuhuyena napuanaai putu nu? mi?ai.** I followed the horse tracks.

tuhubu, tuhpu (n) hide (raw skin).

tuhwaitu (v) come open (when not tightly closed). **Natsahtu matuhwai.** The door came open.

tuhwaru (v) open something. *See* **matuhwaru.**

tuhyetu (v) mail a letter or package, send something or someone. **Ihkana nu? tuhyetu?i.** I am going to send this.

tuhyu (n) motor oil (petroleum). **Nu? tuhyu?uku hani.** I put oil in my car.

tuituaru (v) help someone. **Pu pia?a u? tuituai.** She helped her mother.

tui? (n) friend (of a woman).

tukamuru, tukamukatu (v) ambush (those who lie in wait; source of name Tucumcari, NM). *See* **makamukaru.**

tukaru (v, sg), *pl* **tahni?itu** put away, put in place, bury. **U tukii nu? oku.** I put it up there. *See* **tahtukaru.**

tukarukupu (n) cloth patch, stewed food. *See* **kohtsáa?.**

tukarukuru (v) patch something, cook food, stew food. **Tahpani tukarukui u?.** He patched the tire.

tuka? (n) light, lamp.

tukeh koo?, tukoh koo? (n) scissors [**tukeh-** cut + **koo?** cutter]. *See* **wanakoo?.**

tɨkerɨ (v) hunt (several days from main camp). **Ma tua? tɨkenɨ.** Her son hunted several days from the main camp.

tɨkiihkarɨ (v) board someone, care for needs of someone, keep an orphan as foster child.

tɨkiitɨ K, tɨkɨhnetɨ W (v) lay something down. **Ma tɨɨki!** Put it down!

tɨkohpoopɨ (n) brand.

tɨkohpoo? (n) branding iron [**tɨ-** (unspec) + **koh-** heat + **poo?** marker]. **Tɨkohpoo?a nɨ? tɨmai.** I bought a branding iron.

tɨkotse? K, tɨkotse?eetɨ W (n) washing machine [**tɨ-** (unspec) + **kotse** wash + **?e** (rep)].

tɨkɨ (n) ref. to food.

tɨkɨ ahwerɨ (v) dig edible roots. **Pɨetsɨkusɨ nɨ? tɨkɨ ahwenɨ.** Early this morning I dug something to eat.

tɨkɨ himarɨ (v, pl), *sg* **tɨkɨ yaarɨ** receive food.

tɨkɨ mahnitɨ, tɨkɨ mɨhanitɨ (v) cook for someone (prepare a meal). **Marii tɨɨmahyakɨ!** Cook for them!

tɨkɨ mahya? (n) pepper.

tɨkɨ manipɨ (n) meal (prepared food). **Orɨ tsa? nɨ tɨkɨ manipɨ nɨ yuni.** Let that person bring my meal to me.

tɨkɨ maniwapɨ (n) hired cook (person known for cooking).

tɨkɨ masɨa sokoobi̱ W (n) garden patch, vegetable garden plot. *See* **tɨmɨsɨa sokobi.**

tɨkɨ noopɨ (n), **acc tɨkɨ noopana** lunch (food carried along). **Nɨ rɨkɨ noopana hanikɨi.** She prepared a lunch for me.

tɨkɨ noorɨ (v) carry food (take a lunch along). **Tɨkɨ noo kwatu?i nɨ?.** I am going to take food along.

tɨkɨ soona̱ (n) tablecloth [**tɨkɨ** food + **soona̱** quilt]. **Tɨkɨ soona̱ tɨmɨi nɨ?.** I bought a tablecloth.

tɨkɨ to?ipɨ (n) leftover food [**tɨkɨ-** food + **to?ipɨ** left over]. **Tɨkɨ to?ipɨha nɨnɨ tɨhkai.** We ate the leftover food.

tɨkɨ tsuhmarɨ (v) exhaust food supply, run out of food. **Sɨmɨ tɨkɨ tsuhmai nɨnɨ?.** We are all out of food.

tɨkɨ tusupɨ (n) sausage, ground food of any type.

tɨkɨ tusu? (n) food grinder, grinder.

tɨkɨ tɨmɨɨpɨ (n) groceries, store-bought food. **Tɨkɨ tɨmɨɨrui nɨ?.** I am going to buy some store food.

tɨkɨ wasɨ? (n, sg), *pl* **wasɨpɨ** game (animals killed in the hunt). **Tɨkɨ wasɨi tsa? tɨ oorɨ.** That person killed some game. *See* **pehkarɨ**

tɨkɨ wesipɨ (n) crumbs, scraps (leftovers after a meal) [**tɨkɨ** food + **wesipɨ** toasted]. *See* **tɨkɨ yumapɨ.**

tɨkɨ wɨhpara? K, tɨkɨ kwɨhpara? W (n) apron. **Nɨ tɨkɨ wɨhpara?a nɨ uhta!** Give me my apron!

tɨkɨ wɨhpomi?, tɨkɨ wɨhpoma? (n) cleaver (*lit* food cutter). **Tɨkɨ wɨhpoma? nɨ? su?waitɨ.** I want a cleaver.

tɨkɨ yaarɨ (v, sg), *pl* **tɨkɨ himarɨ** K eat (partake of food); W take to eat.

tɨkɨ yumapɨ (n), *pl* **tɨkɨ yumi?ipɨ** crumbs. **Sarii tsa?**

ohka **tuku yumapuha tuhkai.**
The dog ate those crumbs. *See*
tuku wesipu.

tukuh kaʔaʔ (n) wire pincers
[**tukuh-** bite + **kaʔa-** break off].

tukuh kweʔyaʔ (n) pliers, pincers,
crowbar [**tukuh-** bite + **kweʔyaʔ**
pull out]. *See* **tuhoraʔ.**

tukuh pehkaru (v, sg), *pl* **tuku
wasuru** bag game. **Tuku pehka
kwai uʔ.** He went to bag game.

tukuh pomaʔ (n) wire cutter, pincer
[**tukuh-** bite + **puma-** break in
little pieces].

tukumaʔai (n) ribbon, bias tape (*lit*
edge trim).

tukumaʔaituʔ (n) ambusher; cloth
edged with ribbon or lace.

tukuru (v) cut (with teeth or sharp
edge).

tuku kahni (n) restaurant, eating
place. **Oku nuʔ tuku kahniku
tuhkaruʔi.** I am going to eat over
at that restaurant.

tuku soonaru (v) spread a tablecloth. **Nu bia tsaʔ tuku soonai.**
My mother spread a tablecloth.
**Situu kuseʔ tuku sonutsi puu
tukuh manipuha tsawuniʔinu.**
These ones spreading a cloth, set
out their cooked things (128:17).

tukwibukiitu (v) switch, whip (as to
whip a horse while riding). **Nurua
nuʔ kwibuki.** I switched my boy.
See **kwibukitu.**

tukwita (n) base, bottom. **kahni
tukwitaku** to the base of the
teepee. **Ohka tukwita tsaa
nabuni.** The base of that thing
looks good.

tukwitsunaʔ (n) elephant (described
by its trunk).

tukwuru (v) shoot, propel. **Paka
mua tukwui uʔ.** He shot an arrow.
See **tsatukaru, wuhkikatu.**

tukwusiitu (v) braid, weave. **Kakuʔ
tsaʔ aawo tukwusiitu.** Grandma
is weaving a basket.

tukwusukupuʔ (n) roasted meat.
See **kuʔinapu.**

tukwusukuru (v) roast meat (or any
other food in live coals or on a grill).

tukwusuru (v, pl), *sg* **tubehkaru**
kill, butcher.

tumabaru (v) knead. **Pu tohtía maʔ
tumabaaru.** She kneaded her
bread. *See* **mabaru.**

tumabekaru (v) pay something
to medicine man. **Pahmui ma
tumabekaku!** Give him (pay him)
tobacco now! *See* **mabekakuru.**

tumabisoʔaitu (adj) hateful,
troublesome, ornery.

tumabukweʔ (n) screwdriver [**tu-**
(unspec) + **mabukwerotate**].
Tumabukweʔ maʔ yaakatu. He
has a screwdriver.

tumabunikuru (v) demonstrate,
show how (to do something).
**Puniku ra turapusaʔena ma
tumabuniku.** Show him how to
do beadwork.

tumahkupaʔ (n) panther [**tuma-**
clench + **kupa** smother].
Tumahkupaʔ tsaʔ naruʔyatu. A
panther is dangerous.

tumahyokuru (v) agree to a
statement, listen to someone.

tumakaru, tumaakaru (v) pay
debts. **Pu tubopu ma rumakatu.**
He is paying his bills.

tumakotsetu (v) wash dishes. **Nu
biaʔ tsaʔ aawo tumakotsetu.** My
mother is washing the dishes.

tɨmakɨmaʔaaiʔ (n) stone, whetstone, sandpaper. *See* **tɨpi tɨmatsuneʔ.**

tɨmakɨmaʔarɨ (v) hone, sharpen something.

tɨmakwatuiʔ, tɨmɨkɨtubiʔ, tɨmakwatɨbiʔ (n) cigarette-wrapper plant (when used as cigarette wrappers, odor of burning leaves is sweet, similar to marijuana odor).

tɨmakwatubiʔetarɨ (v) roll up, wrap up (as wrap a package). *See* **namakwatubiitɨ.**

tɨmanahketɨ (v) measure something. **Ika nɨʔ huupita tɨmanahketɨ̯.** I am measuring this tree. *See* **manahkerɨ.**

tɨmanahkeʔ (n) ruler, tape measure, any device used for measuring. **Ohka tɨmanahke nɨ uhtɨ̯.** Give me that ruler.

tɨmanɨkuʔwetɨ (n) cottage cheese.

tɨmaramiitɨ (v) share in, chip in, join in (partnership). **Wahatina ɨ ma tɨmaramituʔi.** I am going to chip in two dollars.

tɨmarɨ (v) W fill something; K cover up (put a lid on). **Ma yaatsi marɨma.** Take it and put a cover on it.

tɨmarɨkarɨ (v) finish (complete a task). **Tabeni nɨnɨ tɨmarɨka-ruʔi.** We will finish at noon.

tɨmarɨmaʔ K (n) lid. *See* **tɨrohtɨmaʔ.**

tɨmarɨɨmaatɨ (num) many, much. **Tɨmarɨɨmaatɨ̯ naʔkɨtabai.** There are many pecans. **Paa tsaʔ tɨmarɨɨmaatɨ̯.** There is a lot of water.

tɨmatsukiʔ (n) screw [tɨ- (unspec) + matsuki- go out of sight].

Tɨmatsukiʔa nɨʔ watsikɨi. I lost the screw. *See* **tɨtsipɨsaʔ.**

tɨmatsumaʔ W, **tɨratsukiʔ** K (n) dishtowel, dustcloth, cloth for wiping [tɨ- (unspec) + matsuma-wipe].

tɨmatsunarɨ (v) file a surface, rasp a surface. **Huupita ɨ tɨmatsunarɨ.** He filed the wood.

tɨmatsuneʔ W, **tɨmatsunaiʔ** K (n) file, rasp. **Pɨ tɨmatsunaiʔ watsikɨi.** He lost his file.

tɨmaya huupi (n) smooth sumac (*lit* mix together). *Rhus glabra* L. (fruit eaten by children; leaves mixed with tobacco for smoking).

tɨmayokɨrɨ (v) trust, obey. **Ohka tɨmayokɨ̯katɨ nɨʔ.** I am trusting that person. **Marɨmayokɨkɨ̯!** Obey him!

tɨmaʔniikarɨ K (v) **tɨmaʔnika- ʔetɨ̯** W (v) insert hand (as into pocket). **Nɨ moʔe nɨ kwasu tɨmaʔnikai.** I put my hand in my pocket.

tɨmaʔokwetɨ (v) milk a cow. **Pɨetsɨkusɨ nɨʔ tɨmaʔookwe.** Early this morning I milked the cow. *See* **maʔokwerɨ.**

tɨmerɨ (v) gamble. **Nɨʔ tɨme-miʔarɨ.** I am going to gamble. *See* **wanarohpetitɨ.**

tɨmoʔo wɨhtamaʔ (n) hobble for a horse (rope or other material to be tied on as hobble).

tɨmuhku (n) Indian-type saddle. **Tɨmuhkukatɨ nɨʔ.** I have an Indian saddle. *See* **paʔmutsiʔ.**

tɨmuihpaaʔ W, **tɨʔmepaaʔ** K (n) cap (billed, as baseball cap). *See* **pɨhɨ rɨmuihpaaʔ.**

tɨmuʔnikatɨ (adj) caught (stuck inside something as in a hole or sack). **Sarii tsa? mubita tumu?nikatu.** The dog's nose is caught.

tumuuru (v) buy, trade. **Kwasu?u tumuumi?aru nu?.** I am going to buy a dress. **Oyo?ru tumuuru nu?.** I am buying clothing.

Tumubo, Timbo (name) Son-ofbull-bear (kindhearted; known for saying, 'If you ever have grandchildren, never let them go hungry.')

tumusua sokobi K (n) garden patch, vegetable garden. **Nu tumusua sokobita unu hanikutui.** You are going to prepare a garden spot for me. *See* **tukumasua sokoobi.**

tumusuapu (n) garden crop, garden product. **Nu rumusuapu tsaa nabuni suakatu.** My crops are growing and looking good.

tumusuaru (v) plant crops, raise a garden. **Tumusu?ai u.** It grew (of plants). **Tumusuru nu?.** I am raising a garden. *See* **tukumasua sokoobi.**

tunahyaru (v) trail something. **Aruka?a tunahyaa mi?aru.** He is going along trailing a deer. *See* **nayaaru.**

tunakaru (v) listen, hear something. **Ohka nu? tunaka?ru?i.** I am going to hear what he is saying. *See* **nakaru.**

tunakatu (n) hearing (having ability to hear).

tunakatu (adj) obedient. *See* **ketunakatu.**

tunakiitu (v) listen, pay attention. **Tunaki kima.** I came to listen. *See* **nakuhi.**

tuni-, tuniru (pfx) authority, rule (govern).

tuniatsikatu? (n) commander. **Tai tuni?atsikatu u?.** He is our commander. *See* **ni?atsiwapi?.**

tunikepisa? (n) spokesman, elocutionist (speaker who strengthens others by his talk). **Taahpu? tsa? nu tunikepisa?.** Our Father (God) is my strength.

tunihpararu (v) plead. **Mi?apuha tunihparaa.** She pleaded to go.

tunikukekitu K, **tuninukekutu** W (v) announce (speak loud and clear).

tunikwuru (v) sing a song. **Puhakuniku u? tunikwuuru.** He is singing in church.

tunimakwihtseru (v) criticize, ridicule (make fun of). *See* **nohitu.**

tunimanahke huutsu? K (n) mockingbird (repeating bird). *See* **soo yake?.**

tunipukawapi W (n) fortuneteller (person with extrasensory perception). *See* **nipukaa?eetu.**

tunisuatu (adj) noisy. **Turu?epuru tumaku tunisuatu.** The children are noisy.

tuniwaitu (v) collect money, dun (to collect payment). **U runiwai kwaú!** Go and collect (the money)!

tuniwaitu? (n) tax collector, bill collector.

tuni?atsiku (n) counselor, adviser (one who gives advice and direction).

tuni?atsitu (v) advise, counsel. **Nu ahpu? tsa? nu tuni?atsitu?i.** My father will give me counsel (my father counsels me).

tunisuabetai wapi W, **tunisua wapi** K (n) teacher.

tunisuabetaru (v) teach something to someone. *See* **suabetaikuru**.

tunisuʔuyaitu, tunisuʔuyaʔeetu (v) mock, laugh at, jeer at (make fun of). **Turueʔpuruu ohka tenahpu sukuhpa tunisuʔuyaitu.** The children are making fun of that man. *See* **usuʔuyaʔitu**.

tunoo kuna waikina K, **tuunooh kuna kwaikina** W (n) freight train [**tuunoo** haul + **kuuna** fire + **waikina** wagon].

tunookatu? (n) camel.

tunoona bukuwaʔ (n) truck (for hauling).

tunoo wapi (n) pack-animal leader. **Nu tunoo wapi tsaʔ tsaa numi muʔheetu.** My pack horse is a good leader.

tunoo waikina (n) truck, wagon [**tunoo** haul + **waikina** wagon].

tunookuru (v) load up (an animal or a vehicle). **Na bukuwaa tunookutu uruu.** They are loading up a car.

tunoomiʔaru (v) pack a load on foot.

tunoopu W, **tunooku** K (n) pack for an animal (loaded and ready to go).

tunooru (v) carry load (on back). **Huupitoo uʔ tunooru.** He is carrying a load of firewood. **Pu ohnaa waakune tunooru.** She is carrying her baby on her back.

tunooʔ (n) saddlebag (double satchel thrown over saddle to carry bedding or food for travel).

Tuoyobisesu (name) Chief Comanche-dog-soldiers.

Tupanai (name) Cliff (person).

tupánaʔ (n) creek bank, incline.

tupe (n) mouth, lips. *See* **tuupe**.

tupe tsahkweʔyaru (v) unbridle a horse (take off bridle and bit).

tupe tsaʔnikaru (v) bridle a horse.

tupe tsaʔnikaʔ (n) bridle [**tupe-** mouth + **tsaʔnikaʔ** hook on].

tupe wihtuaʔ (n) bucket with spout [**tupe-** mouth + **wihtuaʔ** bucket].

tupehemiʔaru (v, an subj) fall off. *See* **tupuheru**.

tupi (n) stone, rock. *See* **tuupi**.

tupi aawo (n) crock, jug (stone container). **Nu tupi aawo tsaʔ soo toomoopu.** My crock is very old.

tupi kuni (n) stone or brick house, jail, prison [**tuupi** stone + **kahni** house].

Tupi kuniʔ (name) Stonehouse (person).

tupi natsu (n) medicinal plant (*lit* rock medicine; a bug mixes sunflower rosin with a secretion, then leaves it on the fork of this weed; the rosin mixture was put in a buckskin amulet and worn to keep one from having bad dreams or to keep evil spirits away from a baby). *See* **kunanatsu**.

tupi pabokoʔaai W, **tupi paboko** K (n) rock lizard [**tuupi** stone + **paboko** clear].

tupi táhparu (v, sg), *pl* **tupi táhpaʔitu** stone someone (throw stones at someone or something). **U rupi tahpaʔi uʔ.** They stoned him.

tupi tumatsuneʔ (n) whetstone, sandpaper. *See* **tumakuma?aaiʔ**.

Tupi wunu (name) Rocky-creek (person).

tupi puʔe (n) surfaced road (gravel or concrete). *See* **puʔe**.

tʉpi simuhta? (n) moth (large species) [**tʉpi-** rock + **simuhta** nose].

tʉpi sokoobi W, **tʉpi sokoona** K (n) rocky ground.

tʉpunirʉ (v) look at, watch (as at a show). *See* **watsi puniitʉ.**

tʉpuuni (n) picture.

tʉpuuni yʉ?yʉmuhku? K (n) movie [**tʉpuuni** picture + **yʉyʉmuhku?** move].

tʉpʉherʉ W, **tʉpeherʉ, tʉpherʉ** K (v) fall off or away from. *See* **tʉpehemi?arʉ.**

tʉpʉnaatʉ (adv loc) middle, center (in the middle).

tʉpʉsi kʉma? (n) sorrel horse (of yellowish or reddish-brown color).

tʉrah kwʉ?nerʉ K (v) iron clothing (*lit* rub with foot).

tʉrah kwʉ?ne? (n) iron, flatiron (for ironing clothes).

tʉrahnai?itʉ (v) drill a field (plant a field by machine).

tʉrahnarʉ (v) plant by hand (sow crops or garden by hand).

tʉrahnirʉ (v) cut down (as to fell a tree).

tʉrahtsuki? K (n) eraser [**tʉra-** press + **tsuki-** rub].

tʉrahwikatʉ (v) win a prize, earn something. *See* **tahwikarʉ.**

tʉrahyapʉ (n) meatball (Comanche-style; prepared of dry, pounded meat mixed with grease and sugar).

tʉrahyarʉ (v) meatball preparation (mix sugar, grease, and pounded meat together forming meatballs). **Nʉ bia? tsa? tʉrahyarʉ.** My mother is making meatballs.

tʉraka?aitʉ (adj) increasing numerically, augmenting in quantity.

tʉrana (n) *pl* **tʉrananai** root.

tʉrana?ipʉ (n) marrow (cooked out from bones).

tʉrana?itʉ (v) cook out marrow from bones.

tʉrana (n) leg bones, marrow bones (marrow is taken to make meatballs eaten at peyote breakfast).

tʉranʉ (n) breadroot, Indian bread.

tʉrape suwaitʉ (v) tempt one to sin.

tʉrapehekatʉ (n) sinner (fallen one).

tʉrapʉtsarʉ W (v) puncture a tire, blow out a tire.

tʉrawʉnarʉ K, **tʉrakwʉnarʉ** W (v) stake something, nail something. **Wobita u tawʉnai.** He nailed the board.

tʉrawʉna? K, **tʉrakwʉna?** W (n) tent pin, stake, nail. **Tʉrawʉna-?a tso?me.** Pick up the stake.

tʉrayaa sarii (n) bloodhound. **Tʉrayaa sarii u hipʉkatʉ.** He has a bloodhound.

tʉrayu?nepʉ (n) pounded meat.

tʉrayu?nerʉ (v) pound meat.

tʉrayu?ne?, tʉraiyu?ne? (n) wooden pestle (made of hardwood tree knot, used for pounding meat or corn). **Pʉʉ tʉrayu?ne?a yaahtsi, uma u tayu?nenʉ.** Taking their pestle, with it they pounded it (116:16).

tʉroh pakʉ?i? (n) wedge.

tʉrohtsanitʉ (v) hang something (with a clothespin or on a hook).

tʉrohtsani?i? (n) clothesline, hook, nail.

tᵾrohtᵾbᵾʔiʔ (n) auger bit, bit used
for boring holes (as in a hide).

tᵾrohtᵾmapᵾ (n) canned food.
**Sᵾᵾkᵾi tohtᵾmapa nᵾʔ
suʔwaitᵾ.** I want (a jar of) canned
plums.

tᵾrohtᵾmaʔ (n) lid (*lit* close the
neck). *See* tᵾmarᵾmaʔ.

tᵾrohtᵾwaʔ (n) can opener
[**tᵾro-** lid + **tohtᵾwa-** open by
punching].

tᵾrokuriapᵾ K (n) garbage. *See*
tᵾtsakwᵾriapᵾ.

tᵾrokwᵾsuakᵾtᵾ (adj) believer. **Ta
Ahpᵾʔa u tᵾrokwᵾsuakᵾtᵾ.** She
believes in Our Father God.

tᵾropᵾsapᵾʔ (n) beadwork.

tᵾropᵾsarᵾ (v) bead something.
Nᵾmᵾ napᵾha tᵾropᵾsai. She
beaded the moccasins.

tᵾroʔnikarᵾ (v) put something into
the mouth.

tᵾrᵾbakiʔarᵾ (v) load into.
Waikina u tᵾrᵾbaki. He loaded
the wagon. *See* toʔnikarᵾ.

tᵾrᵾbinitᵾ (v) ask a question.

tᵾrᵾe, tᵾrᵾeʔtᵾ, tᵾrᵾeʔti (n, acc)
child.

tᵾrᵾe kuʔyuutsi (n) quail. *See* tᵾe
kuyúutsi.

tᵾrᵾe basuu K (n) quail. **Lophortyx**
sp. *See* tᵾe basuu.

tᵾrᵾehpᵾ (n), nom *pl*
tᵾrᵾehpᵾʔrᵾᵾ, *acc pl*
tᵾrᵾehpᵾʔrii child, children.

tᵾrᵾetᵾparᵾ (v) have children.

tᵾrᵾetᵾsuarᵾ (v) care for child (like
a mother).

tᵾrᵾhkarᵾ (v) steal. **Puhihwihta u
tᵾrᵾhkai.** He stole the money. *See*
sikusarᵾ.

tᵾrᵾhkaʔ (n) thief.

tᵾrᵾkᵾ kahni (n) den of thieves,
house of thieves.

tᵾrᵾkwobamᵾ (n) sneezeweed.
Helenium autumnale L. (used in
bath to treat fever [C & J]).

tᵾrᵾnirᵾ (v) ask for something.
Kokoraʔa u tᵾrᵾni. He asked for
a chicken.

tᵾrᵾtsᵾpᵾ (n) number, group of
figures (Arabic numerals).

tᵾrᵾtsᵾrᵾ (v) count something
(unspecified) [**tᵾ** (unspec) +
tᵾtsᵾ count].

tᵾrᵾʔai waipᵾ (n) working woman.

tᵾrᵾʔai wapi (n) workman,
servant, renter, hired hand, clerk,
disciple.

tᵾrᵾʔaipᵾʔ (n) work.

tᵾrᵾʔaitᵾ, tᵾrᵾʔarᵾ (v) do work.
Lawtontsa tᵾrᵾʔaitᵾ. He is
working in Lawton.

tᵾrᵾʔawe wapi W (n) prophet (one
who proclaims a message).

tᵾrᵾʔekarᵾ (v) paint something, *adj*
painted.

tᵾrᵾʔekaʔ (n) paint. *See* tᵾʔekaʔ.

tᵾrᵾhaniʔ W, tᵾhraniʔ K (n)
hammer. **Nᵾrᵾhaniʔa nᵾ
yaanᵾki.** You must bring back my
hammer.

tᵾrᵾnapᵾ (n) planted crops.

tᵾrᵾnarᵾ (v) plant (sow seed using a
planting machine).

tᵾrᵾnaʔ (n, sg), *pl* tᵾrᵾniʔiʔ planter,
seeder (machine for sowing seed).

tᵾrᵾniʔitᵾ (v, pl), *sg* tᵾhtᵾkitᵾ
plant seed (using a dibble stick).

tᵾsáarᵾ (v) dye something
(nonspecific color). **Wanapa
tᵾsaarᵾ.** She dyed the cloth. **U
rᵾsaai u.** He dyed it. **ekᵾsaʔarᵾ**
dye red, **ebisaʔarᵾ** dye blue.

tɨsaasi̱ (n) Indian perfume plant, sage. Tɨsaasi̱kinɨ nɨ himinu̱. Give me some sage. *See* numɨ rɨsaasi̱.

tɨsaaʔ (n) dye (nonspecific color). Ekatɨsaaʔ nɨʔ suʔwitu̱. I want red dye.

tɨsibetɨ (v) plane something smooth. Huupihta tɨsibeʔi tsaaku̱. He planed the wood good (smooth).

tɨsibeʔ (n) carpenter's plane (tool for smoothing wood).

tɨsoona, tɨsoona̱ (n), *acc* tɨso- one pan, dishpan, plate. Tɨsoone nɨʔ kotse. I washed the pan.

tɨsoyuni (n) grinding stone, sifter.

tɨsoʔarɨ (v) tan a hide.

tɨsoʔipɨʔ (n) tanned hide.

tɨsutaibitsi̱ (n) mercy, pity, meekness. Tɨsutaibitsi̱ maʔoorɨ. That person is merciful.

tɨsutaikatɨ (v) pity, befriend (treat with kindness). Tsukuhpa ohka tɨsutaikatɨ uʔ. He has pity on that old man.

tɨsuwaʔitɨ (adj) jealous (of husband or wife, unspec object).

tɨsuʔatsipɨ (n) judicial power, power, will, authority.

tɨsuʔatsi̱katɨ (v) think about something. Nɨ biaʔ nɨʔ tɨsuʔatsi̱katɨ. I am thinking about my mother. Tɨsuʔatsi nɨʔi miʔarɨ. I think I will go.

tɨsuʔatsi̱tɨ (v) have authority, have power. Tsaa u tɨsuʔatsitɨ. He has good power.

tɨsuʔnarɨ (v) forgive, pardon. Nɨ tɨsuʔnai uʔ. He forgave me. *See* niʔtsuʔnarɨ.

tɨsuʔnarɨ (v) quiet down, calm down (become quiet).

tɨsuʔɨrɨ (v) give counsel, advise. Nɨroko tsaʔ tsaa tɨsuʔɨrɨ. Grandpa gives good advice. *See* naniʔɨruʔaitɨ.

tɨsuʔɨrɨʔ (n) wisdom, counsel, kind thoughts.

tɨtaatɨ (adj) small size, unworthy, pitied. Tɨtaatɨwe u! She's pitiful!

tɨtaatɨ (num, indef) small quantity. *See* huitsi.

tɨtsahkɨnarɨ (v) sew (on a sewing machine). Pɨ tɨtsahkɨna ɨhtuku̱ uʔ. She sewed through it.

tɨtsahkɨnaʔ (n) sewing machine.

tɨtsahtɨʔoorɨ (v) rake something.

Tɨtsakana (n) Sewers (derogatory group name).

tɨtsakɨnaha yuhu (n) sewing machine oil.

tɨtsakwoo raibooʔ (n) white farmer. Nɨ ahpɨʔ tɨtsakwo raiboeetɨ. My father farmed for a living.

tɨtsakwoopɨ (n) plowed field.

tɨtsakwɨɨriapɨ W (n) garbage. *See* tɨrokuriapu.

tɨtsakwɨriapɨ K (n) trash.

Tɨtsanoo yehkɨ (n) Comanche band.

tɨtsanuaʔ (n) rake (garden tool). *See* tsahtɨʔokiʔ.

tɨtsanɨnɨʔitɨ (v, adj) stop (as a team of horses); stopped, halted (from a buggy or from horseback). *See* tsanɨnɨrɨ.

tɨtsapara huupi (n) clothesline pole.

tɨtsatɨki̱ʔ (n) harrow (cultivating implement).

tɨtsatɨsukitɨ (v, adj) harrow, harrowed (break up or pulverize soil). *See* tsatɨsukiitu̱.

tɨtsaʔookiʔ (n) hay rake (farm implement).

tʉtsaʔwooʔ K, tʉtsakwooʔ W (n) plow.

tʉtsaʔworʉ, tʉtsakworʉ (v, unspec obj) plow soil. **Pʉ sokoni u tsaʔwoi.** He plowed his ground.

tʉtsihkaʔarʉ (v, sg obj), *pl obj* **tʉtsihpomiʔitʉ** cut off, cut up. **Pʉ paapi uʔ tsihpomai.** She cut her hair. **Tʉtsipomiʔi uʔ.** She cut them (the hairs).

tʉtsihpetiʔ (n) spade (garden tool).

tʉtsihpomiʔipʉ (n) object cut into pieces. *See* **tsihpoma.**

tʉtsihtsukaʔ (n) index finger.

tʉtsihtʉmaʔ (n) key, lock (*lit* close with something pointed).

tʉtsihtʉrʉ (v) padlock something.

tʉtsikwʉsarʉ (v) swindle, cheat (take against someone's will). **Naiʔbihta uʔ tʉtsikwʉsai.** He beat him out of that girl.

tʉtsipʉsaʔ, tʉʉhtsipʉsaʔ (n) screw. *See* **tʉmatsukiʔ.**

tʉtsiwaiiʔ K, tʉtsikwaiiʔ W (n) spear, sword [tʉ- (unspec) + tsiʔwai- probe with long pole]. *See* **tahkanaʔ.**

tʉtsiyaaʔ W (n) pitchfork [tʉ- (unspec) + tsiya- pick up with long pole].

tʉtsiyunarʉ (v, unspec obj) shovel something. **Tʉtsiyunarʉ uʔ.** He is shoveling (unspec object).

tʉtsiyunaʔ (n) shovel. *See* **kusiyunaʔ.**

tʉtsiyunaʔ K (n) spade.

tʉtsiyuʔiʔ (n) chisel (tool).

tʉtsoʔnikarʉ (v) poke head into something (unspec obj) [tʉ- (unspec) + tsoʔnika poke head in]. **Tʉtsoʔnikaai uʔ.** He poked his head into something. *See* **tsoʔnikarʉ.**

tʉtsuʔmapʉ (n) broke financially, penniless.

tʉtsʉ-, tʉhtsʉ (adj) cruel, mean, ugly, bad. *See* **kesuatʉ, aitʉ.**

tʉtsʉ narʉmiʔitʉ (v) gossip, tell off-color stories [**tʉtsʉ-** bad + **narʉmu-** tell story].

tʉtsʉ puhaʔ (n) witch doctor [**tʉtsʉ-** bad + **puha** medicine]. **Tʉtsʉ puha uʔ umikwai.** He went to see a witch doctor.

tʉtsʉrʉ (v) count definite objects.

tʉtsʉhanitʉ (v, unspec obj) drive, handle, manage (as to drive a vehicle or ride a horse) [**tʉ-** (unspec) + **tsahani** handle].

tʉtʉbetʉ (adj, pl), *sg* **tʉhpetʉ** full.

tʉtʉsuana (n) evil spirit, unclean spirit.

tʉʉhkaʔarʉ (v, sg), *pl* **tʉʉhpomiʔitʉ** chop. **Tʉʉhkaʔama uʔ tʉʉhkaʔarʉ.** He is chopping with an axe.

tʉʉhkaʔaʔ (n) axe. *See* **naʔbutikʉmakatʉ tʉʉhkaʔaaʔ.**

tʉʉhkonarʉ (v, unspec obj) sharpen a cutting edge, croak (as of a frog). **Tʉʉhkonaai uʔ.** He sharpened it something. **Pasawio tsaʔ tʉʉhkonarʉ.** The frog croaked.

tʉʉhkoʔneʔ (n) a steel tool (as implement for sharpening knives).

tʉʉhtamaʔ (n) string, yarn, ties. **Tʉʉhtama nʉʔ.** I saw some yarn. *See* **wʉhtamaʔ.**

tʉʉhtamʉh raiboʔ, tʉʉhtʉmʉ raibooʔ, tʉhtamʉ raiboʔ (n) policeman, sheriff (*lit* man who ties us up). **Tʉʉhtamʉh raibooʔ tsaʔ pite.** The policeman drove up. *See* **nʉmi himaʔetʉ.**

tʉʉhtsohpeʔ (n) congealed bone
marrow. **Tʉʉhtsohpe tʉsai
uʔ.** She cooked congealed bone
marrow (prepared it).

tʉʉhtʉmapʉha tʉrawʉnaʔ (n), *pl*
tʉʉtʉmapa narawʉniʔi fence
staples.

tʉʉhtʉmapʉ K (n) fence. **tʉʉhtʉmapʉ nahhuupi** fence post.

tʉʉhtʉmarʉ (v, unspec) fence
something. **Tʉʉhtʉmai uʔ.**
He fenced something. *See*
wʉhtʉmarʉ.

tʉʉmooi, tʉʉmoanʉ (adj)
surprised, amazed.

tʉʉnoo ʉnʉʉʔ K (n) camel. *See*
ʉnʉʔa pʉnʉsʉ narʉnooʔ- katʉ.

tʉʉnua (n) broom grass. *Gramineae*
(one of the kinds of grasses used
to make brooms).

tʉʉnuarʉ (v, unspec obj) sweep
something. **Tʉʉnuaʔi uʔ.**
She swept. *def obj* **Tasoneʔ
wʉʉnuarʉ.** She is sweeping the
floor.

tʉʉnuaʔ (n) broom. **Tʉʉnua tʉmʉi
nʉʔ.** I brought a broom.

tʉʉnuaʔ, tʉʉnua masʉaʔ (n)
broom corn. *Sorghum vulgare* Pers.
[**tʉʉnua-** sweep + **masʉaʔ** corn].

tʉʉpe (n) mouth, lips. **Nʉ tʉʉpe
tsaʔ tsiiwa.** My lips are chapped.

tʉʉpi (n) stone, rock. **Tʉʉpiʔa u
wihi.** He threw a stone. *See* **tʉpi.**

tʉʉtsohpepʉ (n) Indian butter
(skimmed grease).

tʉʉtsʉkeʔ W (n) lawnmower,
scythe. *See* **soniwʉtsʉkeʔ.**

tʉʉtsʉkʉnarʉ (v, unspec obj) tie
up a horse (particular horse
unspecified). **Tʉʉtsʉkʉnai uʔ.** He
tied up a horse.

tʉʉyʉ mutsoraʔ K (n) bridle bit.

tʉʉʔurapʉ W, K (n) sweetheart,
lover, boy friend (of a woman).
See **notsaʔkaʔ.**

tʉwoorʉ W (v) go hunting (go on a
hunting trip involving the whole
camp).

tʉyaaitʉ (v, sg), *pl* **kooitʉ** die.
Tenahpʉʔ tsaʔ tʉyaai. The man
died.

tʉyai waikina K (n) hearse.

tʉyaipʉ kohno (n) casket (*lit* death
box).

tʉyaipʉ, tʉyaiʔ K (n) corpse, dead
body. **Tʉyaipʉ tsaʔ puʔekʉ
habiitʉ.** The corpse was lying in
the road.

tʉyaipʉha nooʔeeʔtʉ (n) W hearse,
K undertaker. **tʉyaipʉ nooetʉʔ** K
hearse.

tʉyatoʔyerʉ (v) mount a horse. *See*
tʉhʉyaroʔitʉ.

tʉyumarʉ (v) fall into something.
Ʉmapakʉ tʉyumai. He fell into
the pond.

tʉyuwarʉ (v) swallow something. **Pai
u tʉyuwi.** He swallowed water.

tʉyʉkwipʉ (n) actions (behavior).
Suni uʔ tʉyʉkwitʉ. That is the
way she behaves.

tʉʔaape (n) voice.

tʉʔape nanakarʉ (v) echo.
**Hapanitʉkʉtʉ tʉʔape nanakaʔi
uʔ.** It echoed in the valley.

tʉʔasʉitʉ (v) freeze (liquid). **Paa
tsaʔ tʉʔasʉi.** The water froze.

tʉʔawetʉ (v) tell. **Hakʉ surʉ
pokopi ʉ tʉʔawenạ?** Where is
that fruit you told of? (16:12). *See*
narʉmuʔikatʉ.

tʉʔawekʉʉkarʉ (v) answer. **Nʉ
tʉʔawekʉʉkạ.** Answer me.

tʉʔehkooiʔ W (n) walking cane, walking stick, rod, shepherd's crook. *See* **natsihtóoʔ.**

tʉʔekarʉ (v) paint something, anoint, grease something. **Kahni nʉʔ tʉʔekaruʔi.** I will paint the house. *See* **wihɪ tʉʔekarʉ.**

tʉʔekaʔ W (n) paint. *See* **turʉʔekaʔ.**

tʉʔíiʔ (n) sandpiper.

tʉʔinakʉrʉ (v) jerk meat for someone.

tʉʔinawʉnʉrʉ (v) have pneumonia. *See* **amawʉnʉtʉ.**

tʉʔiyaʔi wapɪ (n) watchman, watchdog.

tʉʔikatʉ (adj) resemble someone (appearance or personality). **Pʉ piaʔ u tʉʔikatʉ.** He is like his mother.

tʉʔnooʔ (n) travel carrier made of teepee poles, *travois* (for carrying children or bedding).

tʉʔoibʉkʉrʉ (v) be ill, suffer an illness.

tʉʔoikatʉ (adj) ill for a long time.

tʉʔoipʉ (n) long illness, invalid. *See* **wʉhmina nʉʉmʉ.**

tʉʔonaaʔ (n) weakness.

tʉʔọnaapʉ, tʉʔohnaabʉ (n) weak person or animal. **Itʉ tʉhʉʉyạ tʉʔonaabʉ.** This horse is weak.

X wehki'aɪ

tʉʔrʉkúuʔ

tʉʔrʉkúuʔ W, tʉrʉkúuʔ K (n), *acc* **tʉʔrikuuʔa,** *pl* **tʉʔrikúuʔnʉʉ** prairie dog. **Suʔana tʉrikúuʔnʉʉ sookʉnibaʔi̥.** There the prairie dogs had a town (3:1).

Tʉʔsinaʔ (name) Hanging-from-the-belt (ref. to items usually hung from the belt, such as tobacco, knife, or pick to make moccasins).

tʉʔʉyatʉ (v) frighten. **Sariia nʉʔ tʉʔʉyatʉ.** The dog will scare (a person).

U

u (pro, 3rd dist nom sg) he, she, it.

ubitakuhtsiʔa (adv man) slowly. **Nabukuwaa tsaʔ ubitakuhtsiʔa miʔarʉ.** The car moved slowly.

ubitʉkʉʉtʉ, ubitʉkʉrʉ (v) flirt (pursue opposite sex). **Naiʔbi tsaʔ ubitʉkʉʉtʉ.** The girl is chasing him (but he does not respond).

uhka (pro dem, dist acc sg) him, her, it.

uhoi kaʔwʉtʉ (v) congregate, crowd many people together. *See* **narahkaʔwitʉ.**

uhúntʉkʉ (adj) be ill, sickly.

umamiʔarʉ (v, pl) *sg* **tsakamiʔarʉ** lead.

umarhnitʉ (v) hurt someone.

unahrʉ (v) move across (be on the other side). **Hunuʔbi unahrʉ uʔ.** He is on the other side of the river.

urahkarʉ (v) learn something new (do something for the first time).

urarʉ (v), *pl* **uʔʉruhkʉrʉ** find something. **Wanʉseʔa uʔ urai.** She found a penny. *See* **maʔurarʉ.**

urii (pro dem, dist acc pl) them.

urʉ (pro dem, dist nom sg), he, she, it; *pl* **urʉʉ** they.

usúnɪ (adv) always, forever. **Usúnɪ nʉʔ sʉme suatʉ.** I always think like that.

usúʔuyaʔitʉ W, unisuʔuyaaʔaitʉ K (v) mock, deride, laugh at. *See* **tʉnį suʔuyaitʉ, nisuʔuyaitʉ.**

utʉkatʉ (v), *pl* **himikatʉ** give (something). **Pʉ tuaʔa hina utʉkatʉ.** She is giving her nephew one thing. **Pʉ tuaʔa uʔ kiano himikatʉ.** She is giving her nephew many things.

uwíhį (n), *acc* **uwihi** spear, sword (arch long knife). *See* **tahkanaʔ, tʉtsiwaiiʔ.**

ʉ

ʉbia (interj) oh! oh my! (exclamation of surprise used by women only). **Ʉbia, kimarʉ marʉ.** Oh my! They're coming. *See* **haʔii, yaa.**

ʉhpʉitʉ (v), *pl* **ʉhkooitʉ** sleep. **Ohnaa tsaʔ ʉhpʉikatʉ.** The baby is asleep. **Kahnikuhpatʉ tsaʔ sʉmʉ ʉhkoihkatʉ.** Everyone in the house is asleep. *See* **yuuʔʉhpʉitʉ.**

ʉhtaarʉ (v) stake down tightly (as a hide being stretched). **Pʉhi uʔ ʉhtaarʉ.** He is staking down the hide.

ʉhtaayuʔ (n) rawhide (being stretched). *See* **pahkipʉ.**

ʉhtamakʉʔatʉ (v) yawn. **Orʉ tsaʔ nʉʔ ʉhtamakʉʔetʉ.** That makes me yawn.

ʉhtaʔetʉ (adj) staked-down object.

ʉhtsumarʉ (v), *pl* **sʉmʉʉhtsumitʉ** close the eyes.

ʉhʉ (n) blanket (without fringes, as a beaver blanket). **Ma ʉhʉ nohinaʔsuyakinʉ.** Her blanket is beautiful.

ʉhʉkatʉ (v) cover oneself.

ʉhʉkʉrʉ (v) cover (someone). **Ma ʉhʉkʉ.** She covered him up.

ʉi (adv time) too late, past the time (beyond help). **Ʉi maʔ tsʉnipʉ.** It is too late.

ʉkʉ (adv time) recently (just now), still. **Ʉkʉ pitʉi maʔ.** He just now came in.

ʉkʉ- (pfx) young.

ʉkʉ nʉmʉ roopʉnʉ K (n) youngest generation.

Ʉkʉ tomopʉ (n) New Year's Day.

ʉkʉbitsį (adj) young. **Ʉkʉbitsį maʔ orʉ naiʔbi.** That girl is young.

Ʉkʉi yʉba mʉa (n) August (*lit* new fall month).

ʉkʉnaa (adv order) first. **Ʉkʉnaa ma iikʉ.** Let him in first.

ʉkʉnanakatʉ (adj) young, youthful. **Tuinʉhpʉʔ tsaʔ urʉ ʉkʉnanakatʉ.** The boy is just young.

ʉkʉ nʉmʉnʉʉ, ʉkʉ nʉmʉ roopʉ- nʉʉ (n) younger generation (generation of young Comanches). **Ʉkʉ nʉmʉnʉʉ tsaʔ hina tʉahwitʉ.** The younger generation expresses itself plainly. *See* **nʉmʉ rʉborapʉ.**

Ʉkʉ tooma mʉa (n) January (*lit* new year month).

ʉkʉsu (adv time) still, yet. **Ʉkʉsu uʔ karʉʉrʉ.** It is still sitting there.

ʉkwihkatʉ (v) sniff an odor, smell something. **Ma ʉʉkwiʔ.** Smell this (as one holds out a flower). **Totsiyaaʔa nʉʔ ʉkwihkatʉ.** I smell the flower.

ʉkwįsʉʔninitʉ K (v) sniff around, smell around (as a dog does). *See* **muwarʉ.**

ʉkwʉsʉʔnitʉ (v) smell something from a distance (get a whiff of something).

ʉmakahni, ʉmakʉni (n) rain shelter (lit rain house; summer shelter of buckskin hung outside the teepee to deflect rain from coming through the teepee top or opening). See yuʔa ʉmakʉni.

ʉmaarʉ (v) rain. Imarʉ maʔ. It's raining. Soo ʉmaarʉ. It's raining heavily. Ʉmahkʉti na puni nʉʔ. I see the rain coming.

ʉmahpaaʔ (n), obj ʉmahpai rain water, pond, lake. Ʉmahpai nʉʔ hibi. I drank some rainwater. Ʉmahpai nʉ puni. I see a pond.

ʉmapʉ (n) rain. Ʉmapʉ maʔ wʉesʉ. It already rained.

ʉnʉ (2nd pers sg dat pro) to you.

ʉnʉ bihnaa (n) honey [ʉnʉʉ insect + pihnaa sugar]. Ʉnʉ bihnaa urai nʉ. I found some honey.

ʉnʉ bihnaa kahni K (n) honeycomb (lit honey house).

ʉnʉʉʔ ruuʔ (n) honey sieve (to separate honey from honeycomb) [ʉnʉʉ insect + tuu- through].

ʉnʉì ʔ (n), pl ʉnʉʉʔ bug, insect, creature. Ʉnʉì ʔ tsaʔ tʉmarʉmá- atʉ. There are sure a lot of bugs.

ʉnʉʔa pʉnʉsʉ narʉnooʔkatʉ W (n) camel (lit creature that carries its own saddle). See tʉʉnoo ʉnʉʉʔ.

ʉpinakwʉ (adv loc) behind.

ʉra (adv) thank you. Ʉrahkokị. Thank you very much. See ahó.

Ʉrʉi mʉa (n) July (hot month).

urʉʉ (excl) ouch! it burns.

urʉʔ (adj, n) meek, kind, good-hearted. Ʉrʉ maʔ orʉ. She is a kind person. Orʉ tsaʔ ʉrʉʔ. That one (over there) is kind.

ʉrʉʔitʉ (n) dry season, drought, hot weather. Ʉhkitsi tabenima ʉrʉʔitʉ. Today is a hot day.

ʉsorokiitʉ (v) snore. Sarii tsaʔ ʉsorokiitʉ. The dog is snoring.

ʉsuaketʉ (v) breathe deeply in sleep. See nasuawʉhkitʉ.

ʉtsʉʔitʉ (adj, n) cold. Tʉbitsi ʉtsʉʔitʉ. It's really cold.

ʉʔaʔ, ʉʔe (n) wound, sore. Ʉʔe nʉʔ puni. I see a sore. Ʉʔakatʉ maʔ pʉ napekʉ. She has a sore on her feet.

ʉʔbʉiʔ (n) cocoon. Ori ʉʔbʉiʔnii puni. Look at those cocoons.

W

waa- (pfx) cedar. See waapi.

waahimarʉ (v), pl waanohiʔitʉ celebrate Christmas (lit to take a cedar tree).

waahimaʔ (n) Christmas.

Waahkusi okweʔ (n) Beaver Creek (lit gray flowing cedar creek; river which flows through present Wichita Falls, TX).

Waahunuʔbi (n) Canadian River (lit cedar creek; near Anadarko, OK).

waahuupi (n) teepee pole (made of cedar).

waaitʉ (v) dry up.

Waakakwa (name) Trotter (Laughing-John; person).

waakohno, waakʉne (n) cradle-board, day cradle (made of two cedar boards four inches wide, covered with buckskin sewed on with hood to cover the

baby's head; laced up in front).
Waakᵾno ma? waruhtarᵾ. The
baby is laced in the day cradle.
See **habikᵾno?.**

waakohno

waani K, waa?ne? W (n) fox.
Waani tsa? aimaiaa?arᵾ. The fox
is loping.

waapi (n), *acc* **waapita** cedar.
waapi huupi cedar trunk;
wahuupi cedar lumber. **Waapi
tsaa kwanarᵾ.** Cedar smells good.

waata, waahta (n), *pl* **waatanii**, *obj*
waate teepee pole (cedar- wood
teepee pole located apart from
the teepee). **Isa haka waatana?**
Whose poles are these?

waatsᵾ K (n), *acc* **waatsᵾna** rib. **Pᵾ
waatsi u? wᵾhkobaia.** She broke
her rib.

waa?akitᵾ (v) yell, wahoo. **Urii
wa?akikᵾ!** Yell at them!

waha- (pfx) two, double.

wahabahti (num) doubles (two
separate items, two pairs, two
groups). **Wahabahti nᵾ? wana
napᵾkatᵾ.** I have two pairs of

socks. **Wahabahkᵾ u? nᵾmihimi.**
He counted them out two-by-two.
See **wa?wa?.**

wahabisuatᵾ (adj) undecided,
doubtful (*lit* think two ways). **Uku
nᵾ? wahabisuatᵾ.** I can't decide
(am undecided) about that.

wahati, wahatᵾ (num) two. **Wahati
ma? tuakatᵾ.** She has two boys.

wahatomopᵾ K (n) two-year-old.
Itᵾ tsa? wahatomopᵾ. He is a
two-year-old. **Waha ma? tomopᵾ.**
The child is two years old. *See*
tomohtoopᵾ.

Wahi mᵾa, Wahima mᵾa (n)
December (evergreen month; a
memorial day celebrated before
the coming of the white man;
winter solstice celebration).

wahkami?arᵾ (v, pl) *sg* **aimi?arᵾ**
lope (as a horse with rider or a
pack load).

wahta (n) pole, club.

wahtóorᵾ (v) club someone,
something [**wahta** pole, club +
oo do]. *See* **wᵾhtokwᵾrᵾ.**

waikina, waikina (n) wagon, truck,
train, streetcar.

waikina nakwᵾᵾki (n) spokes (of
a wagon wheel; *lit* wagon spread-
like-a-fan).

waikina na?oomo (n) wagon wheel.
**Waikina naa?oomi tsa?sekwikᵾ
tsᵾkᵾkatᵾ.** The wagon wheel is
stuck in the mud.

waipa wananapᵾ (n) ladies hosiery.
See **wananapᵾ.**

wakarée? K, waka?ré?ee? W
(n) turtle. **Wakare?ee? tsa?
mahimi?ai.** Turtle went to war.
**Surᵾ kᵾse? wakare?ee?, 'Ke
nᵾ? tunehtsᵾwa?i naahkatᵾ,'**

waikina

me yu̱kwiiyu̱. That turtle said, 'I can't run' (9:9).

Wakaréʔe (name) Turtle (name of one of E. Canonge's daughters).

wakaru̱katu̱ (v) aim something (as a gun or arrow). **U wakaru̱katu̱ nu̱ʔ.** I am aiming at him.

waku̱ʔwu̱tu̱ (adj, n) zigzag, rickrack, jagged item. **Tu̱u̱pi̱ tsaʔ waku̱ʔwu̱tu̱.** The rock is jagged. **Waku̱ʔwu̱ti maʔ matsahku̱nai.** She sewed rickrack on it.

wana- (pfx) cloth. *See* **Wanapu̱.**

wana atsiʔ, waná atsiʔ (n), *acc* **waná atsiʔa** playing cards. **Waná atsikatu̱ nu̱ʔ.** I have playing cards.

wana buhihwi̱ (n), *acc* **wana buhiwita** paper money (*lit* cloth money: money for trade goods).

wana hu̱ K, wana u̱hu̱ W (n), *acc* **wana hi** cotton blanket, shawl.

wana kooʔ (n, arch) scissors (*lit* cloth cutter). *See* **tu̱kehkooʔ.**

wana kotse aawo (n) washtub.

wana kotse tsahparaaʔ K, wana kwiyaaʔ W (n) clothesline rope.

wana kotseʔ (n) soap [**wana** cloth + **kotse** washer].

wana napu̱ (n) stockings, socks. *See* **waipa wana napu̱.**

wana ramu̱, wana ramuna (n), *acc* **wana rame** thread, crochet thread (*lit* cotton sinew).

wana rohpetiru̱ (v) gamble, play cards (*lit* throw down yard goods). **Wana rohpetiʔetu̱ maʔ.** He gambles a lot. **Tenahpu̱ʔ tsaʔ wana rohpetiruʔi.** The man is going to gamble. *See* **nana ku̱huru̱, tu̱meru̱.**

wana̱ soona̱ (n), *acc* **wana soone** cotton quilt.

wana tsahku̱naʔ (n) needle [**wana** cloth + **tsahku̱na** sew].

wana tsihparaaʔ (n) bracing stick (holds up a cloth for shade).

wana tsiyaaʔ (n) flag [**wana** cloth + **tsiyai** hold on a pole].

wana tsiyaaʔa náhuupi̱ (n) flagpole.

wanama su̱apu̱ha pokopi̱ W, wana̱ sona pokóopi̱ K (n) cotton boll (*lit* cotton fruit).

wanapu̱ K (n), *acc* **wanapu̱ha, wanapha W** cloth, clothes, trade goods. **Wanapha̱ tu̱mu̱i hnu̱.** I brought some trade goods.

Wanarʉ (name) Quanah Parker's
daughter.

wanasihtaraaʔ W (n) lizard
(striped) [**wa-** reptile +
natsihtaraaʔ standing high].

wanatsihtaraaʔ (adj) striped, multi-
colored.

waraatsi̱ (n) sandals (fr. Span.
huarache). *See* **saaʔwʉnapʉ̱.**

warʉʔikatʉ (v) miss (fail to find
or locate), lack (fail to make
connections). **Nʉ ruaʔa nʉʔ
warʉʔikatʉ̱.** I am missing my
son (since his death). **Ke hina
warʉʔinu̱.** He did not lack
anything.

wasápe pʉmata kwʉhʉrʉʔ (n)
bear trap (used for bears or other
animals).

wasápeʔa tʉhkapʉ̱ (n) pear (*lit*
bear's food).

wasápe̱ (n), *acc* **wasápeʔa** bear.

wasʉpʉ̱ (n, pl), *sg* **tʉkʉwasʉʔ**
bagged game.

wasʉrʉ (v, pl), *sg* **pehkatʉ** kill.
Kokoráʔanii uʔ wasʉrʉ. He is
killing the chickens. **Wasápeʔa uʔ
pehkai.** He is killing a bear.

watasi̱ (n) ace (in game of cards).

watsi ikatʉ (v) sneak in. **Kahniku̱
watsi ikai uʔ.** He sneaked into
the house.

watsi iyarʉ (v) spy on someone
secretly (*lit* secretly watching).

watsi miʔarʉ (v) leave secretly,
sneak away.

watsi punitʉ (v) watch someone,
spy on someone. **watsih punikatʉ̱**
person spied upon. **Sitʉ kʉse̱ʔ
wakaréʔee u watsih punihka̱.**
This turtle is hiding watching him
(10:24). *See* **tʉpunitʉ.**

watsih nikwʉnʉrʉ (v) whisper,
speak softly.

watsih tekwarʉ (v) du
watsihtawʉkʉ whisper gossip,
tell (tip off someone). **Watsih
tʉawʉkʉi uʔ, ta miʔaruʔi.** He
whispered to him that we are
going.

watsikʉrʉ (v) lose something. **Hina
nʉʔ watsikʉi.** I lost something.
Nʉ wana napʉha nʉʔ watsikʉi.
My sock is lost.

watsikwarʉ (v) going to get lost.

watsitʉ, watsikatʉ (v, adj) lose
way, lost (become lost). **Huukuku̱
uʔ watsii.** He is lost in the woods.

watsitʉkitʉ K, **watsih tahtʉkitʉ** W
(v), *pl* **watsih tahniʔitʉ** hide (put
away secretly; *lit* cause to be made
secret). **Suhka pʉ kuʔina- pʉha
tsayumiʔi̱tsi u watsih tahniʔinu̱.**
Taking off that, his roasted meat,
(he) put it away in hiding (7–
8:39). **Nʉ puhwihtʉ nʉʔ watsih
tʉkituʔi.** I am going to hide my
money.

watsiʔarʉ (v) keep secret (*lit* hide
something in the mind). **watsi-
ʔaitʉ̱** secretive, secret. **Naya nʉʔ
hina watsiʔaitʉ̱.** I like to keep
things secret.

watsi̱ habiitʉ (v) hide, secret
oneself away. **Tʉeʔpʉ orʉ tsaʔ
watsi̱ habiitʉ.** The child is hiding.

waʔihpʉʔ (n) woman's female
kinsman. **Waʔihpʉʔ tsaʔ tʉmʉ-
miʔarʉ.** The woman is going
shopping. *See* **naʔwaʔihpʉʔ.**

waʔkooʔ W (n) clam, oyster (any
shellfish).

waʔkooʔ K (n) shell of any shellfish.

waʔooʔ, waʔóʔa (n) cat.

wa?ihpu?

wa?roo koyáa? (n), acc wa?ro
k̨uya?a. W crawfish, crawdad (lit
grabs and pinches).

Wa?sáasi? (n), pl Wa?sáasinuu
Osage people.

wa?wa? (n, du) twins, two-by-two,
two apiece. Wa?wahku numi
himii. They handed them out
two-by-two. See wahabahti.

weehtsitu (v), pl weeru go down, get
off (as of car or wagon). Weeka!
Get off! Suru k̨use? mak̨uhu
weehtsi, u yaanu. That one,
going down to it, took it (7:28).
Waikinabai uruu wee. They are
getting down off the wagon.

wehhari tuka?eety (n) fireman.

wehkinitu (v) search (look around
for). Hina unu wehkíniina?
What are you looking around for?
(15:6). See puhihwi wehki.

wehkitu (v) look for. Pu kwuhi ma?
wehkitu. He is looking for his wife.

wehuru?i (n) thin person, emaciated person. Nama? wehuru?ikatu
nu?. I am reducing.

wekubupu, wukububi (n)
bullroarer.

wekwiitu (v, pl), sg ikaru enter.

wekwimi?aru (v, pl) enter.

wenuaru (v), pl wekwenuaru
hang something. U kwasu?u tsa?
wehnuaty. Her dress is hanging
there.

wenu?nukimi?aru (v) run downhill,
get off running. See nuhkitu.

wepy̨kaitu (v) dangle, swing (swing
from side to side or back and
forth).

wesi- (pfx) burned, curled.

wesibaapi (n) curly hair [wesi-
burned + paapi hair].

wesibapi?aru (v) curl hair, wave
hair (give a permanent wave).

wesikaty (adj) burnt, scorched,
toasted, browned.

wesikitu, wesiketu (adj) curly,
curled. U paapi wesikety. Her
hair is curled.

wesikuru (v) burn something up,
scorch, toast bread, brown food.

we?haki? (n), acc wehari flame,
fire.

we?haru (v) burn, flame. wehha-
katu burn oneself; wehakuáru
burn someone. Ma? nu
wehahkaty. It's burning me.

we?kwiyanoru (adj v caus) shiny,
iridescent. Wanapy tsa? we?kwi-
yanoru. The cloth is iridescent.

we?kwiyanutu tuupi, wekwiyanu
ruupi (n) diamond (lit flashing
stone).

we?kwiyanuuty (v) gleam, shine,
flash. Kahniku we?kwiyanuuty.
The house is shining.

we?y̨uk̨u sohoobi K (n)
cottonwood. See tahpooku?.

wia? (n) mestizo (Native American having hispanic blood).

Wia?nʉʉ (n) Comanche band of Walters area (called Worn-away People by other bands).

wihirʉ (v) throw. **Tahkana? u? wihi.** He threw the spear. **Ma wihi!** Throw it (here)!

wihi (n) melted grease.

wihi tʉ?ekarʉ (v) lubricate, grease something. **Ta waikina na?omi wihi tʉ?ekʉ.** Grease the wagon wheels. *See* **tʉ?ekarʉ.**

wihi kamatʉ (v) taste oily or greasy.

wihnai mi?arʉ (v) walk lamely, limp (in walking; only hind legs of animals). **wihnai mi?arʉ** move along, walk limping. **Pʉ kahnibetu u? wihnai mi?arʉ.** He went home limping.

wihnaitʉ (adj) crippled. *See* **tatʉwetʉ.**

wihnu (adv time) then. **Urʉʉkʉhʉ u yuhuwehkipʉ wihnu surʉ pisikwanúu?inʉ.** Then that one, the fattest to be found of them, slid down (5:11).

wihtaitʉ (v) throw away. **Ika nʉ? tʉboopʉi?a wihtaitu?i.** I am going to throw this paper away. *See* **petihtarʉ.**

wihtekatʉ (v, adj) peep, peer through, peeping. **Tʉetʉ tsa? wihtekatʉ.** The child is peeping out. *See* **tasʉkʉpunitʉ.**

wihto?aitʉ (v, adj) disintegrate, disintegrated, worn out (wear out of own accord).

wihto?arʉ (v) wear something out. **wʉkwi?aitʉ** wear out clothes; **takwiarʉ** wear out shoes;

tsokwiarʉ wear out hat. *See* **wʉkwi?arʉ.**

wihtua? (n), *acc* **wihtuai** bucket, container. **Wihtuai u? wʉhtʉkwai.** He hit the bucket.

wihtʉ?eka? (n) cream, grease.

wiiyʉ (n) awl, ice pick, any sharp-pointed implement for punching holes through which sinews pass (as in making moccasins).

Witawoo?ooki (name) Barking-buttocks (person).

Witsapaai? (n), *pl* **Witsapaainʉʉ** Pawnee (ref. to tuft of hair on head or to witchcraft they practiced).

wiyaa? (n), *acc* **wiya?a** rope.

wi?hikoyo?itʉ (v) skip.

wi?nʉʉpi (n) plum bush (not the fruit). **Okʉ tsa? wi?nʉataitu ukika sʉ?kʉia humakwa.** There are a lot of plum trees over there; go and get some plums.

wobi (n) ref. to wood.

wobi aawo (n) trunk (container), box, chest (for personal belongings), barrel [**wobi** wood + **aawo** container].

wobi kahni, wobi kʉni (n) frame house [**wobi** wood + **kahni** house].

wobi muwo?ne? K (n) termite(s). *See* **muwo?ne?.**

wobi nakarʉ? (n) wooden bench, wooden chair. *See* **nakarʉ?.**

wobi narʉmʉ? (n) lumberyard (*lit* lumber store).

wobi pihnaa ʉnʉʉ? (n) honeybee. *Apis mellifera.*

wobi pihnaa? (n) K honey; W honeycomb [**wobi** wood + **pihnaa** sugar].

wobi puuku̱ (n) buggy, hack (*lit* wood horse). *See* **natsa?ani.**

wobi tohtaraki̱ K (n) woodpecker.

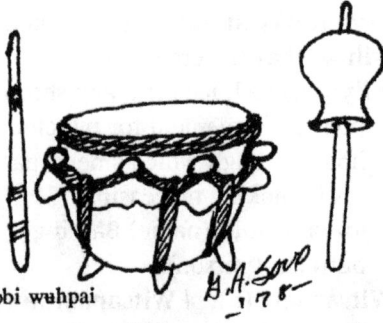

wobi wu̱hpai

wobi wu̱hpai K, wobi wihtua W (n) wooden drum (container), bucket.

wohho (n) ref. to enmity.

wohho namaka?muki?aru̱ (v) warpath (prepare for war).

wohho napu̱saru̱ (v) apply war paint.

wohho suaru̱ (v) deride, oppose.

wohho tu̱ikwu̱pitu̱ K (n) war songs, songs of victory.

wohhohpu̱? (n), *pl* **wohhonu̱u̱** enemy, rival provoking jealousy. **Nu̱ wohhonu̱u̱ tsa? kimaru̱.** My enemies are coming. *See* **tawohho.**

wohi?huu, wohihu̱ (n) mesquite. *See* **natsohkwe?.**

wohka?ni? (n) young unmarried man, bachelor.

wohtsawu̱kitu̱ (v) shake, bounce. **wohtsawiki mi?aru̱** go bouncing along.

wohtsa?wu̱tu̱ (adj) rough terrain, uneven land.

wohya (n) row (series of items lined up). **Nu̱ paapasi tsa? wohyaku̱ naru̱hnikatu̱.** My potatoes are planted in a row.

woinu (n) bugle, any wind instrument. *See* **aamuyake?.**

woko, wokóobi (n) pine. **wokóobi huupi̱** pine tree.

wokoohwi (n) tree squirrel (*lit* turns fast).

woko̱ huutsu̱ (n) parrot, parakeet (*lit* pine tree bird; parakeets used to be common in the wild in the U.S.).

woku̱ huupi̱ (n) thorn tree, honey locust. *Gleditschia triacanthos* (?) (thorns used as needles by early Comanches).

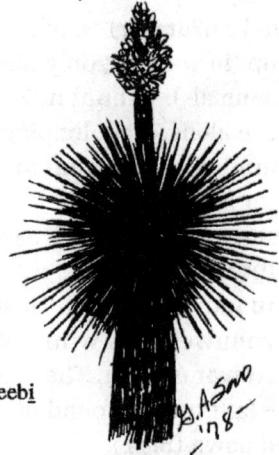

wokweebi̱

wokwe, wokweebi̱ (n) peyote plant or button, thorn, thistle. *Lophophora* Williamsii Lem. Coulter (peyote used strictly in religious ritual in curing or in conjunction with spirit power).

wokwe kahni (n) peyote teepee (used for peyote religious service).

wokwéesi (n) barrel cactus (commonly called *big-leaf cactus*; edible red berries). *Echinocereus Baileyi.*

wokwéesi (n) prickly pear cactus. *Opuntia* sp. (fruits eaten: burn off

thorns, then eat to stop diarrhea
[C & J]).

wokwekatʉ amakwooʔ (n)
pineapple (*lit* thorny apple).

wokwekatʉ huupi (n) thorn apple,
black haw (local term). *Crateagus*
sp. (sweet fruits eaten; inner bark
chewed as gum).

wokwesonipʉ (n) thorny weed
(general term), sunburst (a
specific thorny plant).

wokwetʉhkarʉ (v) eat peyote,
conduct a peyote meeting.

woobị (n) board, wood, lumber.

woohpʉnitʉ (v) howl, moan.

woorʉ (v) howl, moan. **U woona
nʉʔ nakai.** I heard it howling.

wooʔetʉ (n) a howl.

worʉrokʉ (n) esophagus, windpipe.

wosa aʔraʔ (n) grasshopper (large
species) [**wosa** bag + **aaʔraʔ** uncle].

wosạ (n), *acc* **wose** box, suitcase,
bag. *See* **tʉboopʉ wosa.**

woʔa-, woʔarʉ (pfx) wormy.

woʔaabị (n), *acc* **woʔabita** maggot,
worm.

woʔanatsuʔ (n) western ragweed
(*lit* dried worms). **Ambrosia
psilostachya** D.C. (used to
kill screw worms and to cure
influenza or bad cold [C & J]).

woʔarʉhkapʉ (n) rice (*lit* worm
food, because of resemblance to
larvae).

woʔataamạ (n), *acc* **woʔarami**
decayed tooth (*lit* wormy tooth).
woʔaramakatʉ have a decayed
tooth.

woʔnerʉ (v) perforate (make holes).

woʔnokatʉ (n) ditch. **Urʉ tsaʔ
tamumunakʉ woʔnokatʉ.** There
is a ditch in front of us.

woʔrohtsarʉ (adj) have a stiff neck.

woʔroorookị W, woʔrorai K (n)
windpipe.

woʔwoʔkitʉ (v) bark (as an animal
barks; *lit* say **woʔwo**).

wʉ- (pfx) flitter (nonhuman), force
(human).

wʉanuraitʉ K (v) run away from
something.

wʉapaʔarʉ (v) beat up.

wʉhabitʉ K, wʉkwaituʉ W (v)
parade. **Nʉmʉnuʉ tsaʔ wʉhabitʉ.** The Comanches are in parade.
See **namanahkeetʉ.**

wʉhbuikatʉ W, wʉhhwikatʉ K
(v) turn, turn away from. **Tʉhʉya
tsaʔ muhyupetu wʉhwikatʉ.**
The horse is turning around.
Kahnikụ nʉʔ pitsʉ wʉhhwi. I
turned back home.

wʉhhabiʔarʉ (v) defeat, force to lie
down wielding a weapon.

wʉhhanirʉ (v) cultivate, chop up
(with instrument).

wʉhhaʔwokarʉ (v) make hollow
(with instrument).

wʉhhomonutsaʔarʉ (v) crumble,
break into small pieces (with
instrument).

wʉhhorarʉ (v) dig (with hoe or
pick). *See* **tʉhorarʉ.**

wʉhhubinitʉ (v) hurt (cause to
groan or cry as by hitting).

wʉhibiʔ (n) cup, drinking glass, spoon.

wʉhkarʉ (v), *pl* **wʉhpomiʔitʉ** chop
down, cut down.

wʉhkikatʉ (v) shoot a gun, let an
arrow fly. *See* **tsatụkarʉ.**

wʉhkitsuʔtsukitʉ (v) rattle (make
rattling noise).

wʉhkitsuʔtsukiʔ (n) rattle (sound-
producing organ on rattlesnake).

wʉhki?arʉ (v) cut (as with a knife).

wʉhkobarʉ (v), *pl* **wʉhkobi?itʉ** break up (with instrument). **Huupita nʉ? wʉhkobi?itʉ.** I am breaking up the wood.

wʉhkonarʉ (v) chop a hole. **Huupita wʉhkonai.** He chopped a hole in the tree [**wʉh-** (instr) + **ko-** chop + **na-** do].

wʉhkuparʉ, wʉkuparʉ (v), *pl* **wʉhtokwetʉ** kill with a weapon. **Sariia wʉhkupa.** Kill that dog.

wʉhkurʉ (v) sight to shoot, aim a gun. **Ta?wo?i wʉhkurʉ urʉʉ.** They are shooting with a gun.

wʉhkuya?arʉ (v) frighten, scare. *See* **wʉ?yʉrʉhkikatʉ, wʉʉyoritʉ.**

wʉhkʉnai, wʉhkʉnʉkatʉ (adj) covered (any object).

wʉhkʉnarʉ (v) cover something (put its cover on a dish or other container). **Tʉhkapa nʉ? wʉhkʉnaru?i.** I will cover the food. **Aawe nʉ wʉhkʉnarʉ nʉ.** I am covering the dish. *See* **hʉhkʉnarʉ.**

wʉhkwabikʉrʉ (v) knock down (with instrument). **Huuma u wʉhkwikʉi.** He knocked them down with a stick.

wʉhkwarʉ?rʉkitʉ K (v) gargle. *See* **pakwarʉhtʉkitʉ.**

wʉhkwatubi (v) wind, wrap, or coil (something).

wʉhkwe?yarʉ (v) unscrew, unbolt.

wʉhkwinarʉ (v) swab out, clean the inner part.

wʉhkwitso?arʉ (v) rescue (save by using an instrument). *See* **kwitso?arʉ.**

wʉhkwitsunarʉ (v) wag (as to wag tail).

wʉhkwitubikatʉ (v) roll up to itself.

wʉhkwitunarʉ (v) wrap up, wrap around.

wʉhkwʉmarʉ (v) explode, open (come apart by force).

wʉhkwʉnetʉ (v) scrape outer side, dehair a hide, cut fat off surface. **Kaku tsa? wʉhkwʉneyʉ.** Grandma is dehairing it (the hide).

wʉhminanʉʉmʉ (n), *pl* **wʉ?mina?nʉʉmʉ** invalid. *See* **tʉ?oipʉ.**

wʉhpaaku?nerʉ (v) hit and push under water [**wʉh** (instr) + **paa** water **-ku** in + **ne-** push].

wʉhpararʉ (v) stretch out something, spread out something. **Wanapʉha u wʉhparai.** She spread out the cloth.

wʉhpa?itʉ (v, pl), *sg* **wʉhtʉkwarʉ** beat, hit repeatedly (with instrument). **Nʉʉpa?ima u wʉhpa?itʉ.** I am whipping with a whip.

wʉhpekwitʉ (v) bruise (raise a bump, cause to swell using an instrument).

wʉhpetsʉrʉ (v) wave (wave down; wave hand). **Pʉ haitsa u wʉhpetsʉrʉ.** He is waving to his friend.

wʉhpitʉ (v) overtake, catch up with, approach (reach a destination). **Na?ʉ nʉ ma wʉhpi- tʉ?i.** You will catch up some day (elder says to younger person). **Ʉ wʉhpitʉi nʉ?.** I caught up with you.

wʉhpiwokarʉ (v) drag by force. *See* **piwokarʉ.**

wʉhpohto?itʉ (v) strike out, pop (as crack a whip).

wʉhpomarʉ (v) cut down, mow. **Puhhipa nʉ? wʉhpomarʉ.** I am weeding the garden.

wuhpomiʔitu (v, pl), *sg* **wuhkaru** chop down, cut down.

wuhpoʔtseru K, **kwuhpoʔtseru** W (v) knock something, jerk something (with an instrument). **Huma nu? u wuhpoʔtse.** I knocked it with a stick.

wuhpukusuaru (v) unwind, uncoil something. *See* **purusuʔaru.**

wuhsibetu (v) shave (as shave face). *See* **siibetu, wusiberu.**

wuhtabaru (v) smash (break to pieces with an instrument).

wuhtakumiitu (v) partially sun-dry. **Tuhkapa inapu uru wuhtakumituʔi.** The jerked meat will be dried in the sun.

wuhtamaru (v) bundle together, tie something, bale something. **Wanapu wuhtamaru.** The cotton is baled.

wuhtamaʔ (n) string (any item with which to tie). *See* **tuuhtamaʔ.**

wuhtarakiitu (v) pound something, tap on something. **Pu inapa wuhtarakiitu.** He is pounding his meat (to keep it from spoiling).

wuhtaráaʔ (n) camp bed (framework of sticks covered by dry grass; nine forked sticks are pounded into ground, long crosspoles are placed through forks, and branches or grass are placed on frame).

wuhtiaru (v), *pl* **toʔwuʔwenitu** pour out, spill, dump into, empty into (pour into different containers). **Pai u wuhtiaai.** He poured out the water. **Situkwu kuse? puhu pomapuha toʔwuʔwenimiʔa.** These two kept dumping their pickings (115:7).

wuhtikuru, kwutikuru (v) shoot, fire on (fire a weapon, shoot at someone or something). **Arukaʔa kwuhtiku uru.** He is over there shooting a deer. **Tenahpuʔa u kwuhtii.** He shot at the man.

wuhtokaru (v) knock off something hanging (with instrument).

wuhtokweetu (v) kill with a weapon.

wuhtokweʔ (n, pl) clubbed ones (those that are clubbed to death).

wuhtokwuru, wuhtóoru (v) club someone or something. **Suru kuse? urii wuhtokwukina.** That one came clubbing them. *See* **wahtóoru.**

wuhtokwutu (v) club something.

wuhtopoʔnitu (v) wind into a ball.

wuhtopuʔnooru (v) tie in round bundle or round knot.

wuhtoʔyaru (v) turn loose, untie. **Ohka tuhuyu wuhtoʔyai.** She untied the horse.

wuhtsabeyaaʔ (n) gourd rattle (used in peyote ceremony).

wuhtsabeyakatu W, **wuhtsaya kwasinabooʔ** K (n) rattlesnake. *See* **kwasinaboo wuhkitsuʔtsuʔikatu.**

wuhtsamuhkitu (v) becalm (stop blowing). **Nuetu tsa? wuhtsamuhkitu.** The wind has stopped blowing.

wuhtsamuuhkikatu (adj) calm (wind or weather).

wuhtsanitu (v) hang up carelessly (throw over a line or pole).

wuhtsiboʔaru (v) peel off (using an instrument). **Huupita u wuhtsiboʔaru.** He is peeling bark off the tree.

wuhtsinetu (v) scrape (as in curing a hide; scrape inner side of flat object with instrument). **Pimoro?a puhi u wuhtsinetu.** He is scraping the hide.

wuhtsito?aru (v) pare, peel. **Nahuma paapasi wuhtsito?aru.** She is peeling the potato with a knife.

wuhtsi?aru (v) shave off, cut off pieces (with instrument). **Huupita u wuhtsi?aru?i.** He will cut off wood shavings.

wuhtsobokitu (v) blink, wink [**wuh-** eye + **tsoboki-** roll].

wuhtsohkuna? (n) bandana, scarf. *See* **tsokwukuuna?, yu?a korohko.**

wuhtsu?maru (v) scrape until clean, wipe off completely. **Nahuma nu? ma wuhtsumaru.** I am scraping it with a knife.

wuhtsukunaru (v) tie. **Wiya?a u wuhtsukunai.** He tied the rope.

wuhtuitu (v) wait (for someone or something to catch up from behind). **Si?ana pu?eku ma pia? ma wuhtúuihkatu.** Here somewhere in the trail his mother is waiting for him (83:31).

wuhtukaru K, **kwuhtukatu** W (v) extinguish a fire (put out a fire or flame). **Wehari nu? wuhtukaru.** I am putting out a fire. *See* **tukaru.**

wuhturu?aipu (n) windbreak (constructed outside teepees, of braided cane to protect from cold wind).

wuhturu?aru (v) make a windbreak.

wuhtubunitu (v) wake someone by pounding.

wuhtukwaitu (v) fall down.

wuhtukwaru (v), *pl* **wuhpa?itu** hit something, beat on someone. **Suru kuse? wihnu okuhu paa- kuhu wuhtui kwanu.** Then that one hit there in the water (5–6:12). **Wuhtukwaru?i nu?.** I am going to hit (beat) you.

wuhtumaru (v) fence up, bank up, clog up. *See* **tuuhtumaru.**

wuhtupukaru (v) button up, fasten, pin together.

wuhtupuka? (n) buckle, button.

wuhturoonitu (v) brace with something. **Huuma ma wuhturooni.** He braced it with a pole.

wuhturu?aru K (v) rip something. **Wanapa uk? wuhturu?ai.** She ripped the cloth. *See* **tohturu?aru.**

wuhu?neru (v) creep, scoot, crawl (stretched out on the stomach). *See* **mahu?netu, tahu?neru.**

wuhuwu?niitu (v) trim (to shape a tree), prune (to shape a tree). **Huupita u wuhuwu?niitu.** He is trimming (pruning) the tree. *See* **wu?yukwitu, kuhpomaru.**

wukutsaru (v) switch (as a tail).

wukutseru (v) crush, mash (with an instrument). **Paapsi nu? wukutse.** I mashed my potatoes.

wukweniitu K, **kwukwenitu** W (v) hang up. **Pia kwusu?e wukweni.** Hang up your coat.

Wukwiya, Wekwaa?a (name) Jesus-man (Comanche born around 1861).

wukwi?aru (v) wear out clothes. **Nu kwasui wukwiai.** I am wearing out my dress. *See* **wihto?aru.**

wukwubihkuru (v) beat on, rattle. **Huuma nu? wukwubihki.** I made noise with a stick.

wukwusaru (v) sprain a joint of the body. **Pu napi u wukwusai.** He sprained his ankle.

wumetu (v) overcome pain, bear pain. **Mohatsi nuutsikwari u wume.** He overcame severe pain.

wuminahkatu (adj) ill for a long time, invalid. **Monuʔohni uʔ wuminahkatu.** He was ill with tuberculosis for a long time.

wuminaru (v) break or reach something (with instrument). *See* **maʔwuminaru.**

wumiʔakuru K (v) force to go. **Nu wumiʔakui uʔ.** He made me leave (says woman because husband beat her). **Ma wumiʔakui nuʔ.** I made it go (as by winding a clock).

wumiʔaru W (v, inan obj) cause to run, move, go. **U wumiʔaru uʔ.** He is winding it.

wuminaaʔ (n) illness.

wuminatu (num) nine.

wumupusitu (v) cause to blow nose (by force, as by hitting) [**wu** force + **mupusi-** blow nose].

wumutsiakatuʔi (adj) keep sharpened.

wumutsiaru K (v) sharpen to a point (with instrument). **Pu wiiyu wumutsiai.** He is sharpening his pick.

wumuurihkatu (adj) turned over, shaped.

wumuuru (v) turn something over, shape or change something (with instrument). **Nu tasoni wumuuri.** I turned over my rug.

wunekuru (v) fan (as to fan the fire). **Ohka uʔ wehari wunekutu.** He is fanning the fire.

wunekutuʔ K (n) fan for fire. *See* **wuʔunenihkuʔ.**

wunikaru (v) insert into something.

wunoʔitu (v) chop down, cut. **Soonipa nuʔ wunoʔitu.** I am cutting the grass (roots and all).

wunoʔkaruru (v) hill up (as soil). *See* **maʔohtaʔaitu.**

wunoʔyaitu (adj) stirred. **Pu kooʔ tsaʔ wunoʔyaitu.** Her mush is stirred.

wunoʔyaru (v) stir. **U wunoʔyaai uʔ.** She stirred it.

wunuaru (v) sweep. **Pu tasooni wunuaru.** She is sweeping the floor.

wunutsaru (v) shatter, break into pieces (with instrument).

wunuhkaruru W (v) squat. *See* **kwanuʔitu, wutahkaruru.**

wunukutu (v) transplant (set out a plant). *See* **tsihtaboʔikutu.**

wunuru (adj) standing. **Inakwu tsaʔ sohobokooʔ wunuru.** In this direction a mulberry tree is standing.

wunuuhkuparu (adj) knocked down.

wunuukuparu (v) knock down by force.

wunuʔyuʔitu, wunuʔyuruʔitu (v) hit by surprise (causing a thud). **Oru ohko wunuʔyuʔtuʔi.** He is going to hit him by surprise (causing a thud).

wunu hupiitu (v), *pl* **tobooi hupiitu** stop movement toward something. **Hunaku wunuhupiitu uʔ.** He stopped in front. *See* **toboʔi hupiitu.**

wunukutu (v) tighten, turn, wind.

wupitapuʔni (n) war club, battle axe with flintstone handle.

wupitooru (v) tie a child to back.

wupiyaru (v) core something, remove item by item. **Amawoo?a wupiye u?.** He cored the apple.

wupunukeru (v) scrape (make smooth as to scrape a road).

wupuheru W, **wupheru** K (v), *pl* **wuyumi?itu** flail, knock off with an instrument, be thrown forcibly from a horse.

wupuhoikutu (v) prosper.

wupukaru (v) cut open.

wupukoi? (n) woodpecker (large species no longer native to Oklahoma). *Picidae*.

wuputsaru (v) cut open, perform surgery.

wura? (n) panther, mountain lion.

wusa?maru W, **wuhtsa?nakuru** K (v) protrude (stick out). **Huupi wusa?maaru.** The tree is sticking out (as when stripped of leaves). **Ma paapi wuhtsa?naku.** His hair is sticking out (every direction).

wusibepu (n) wood shaving.

wusiberu K (v) shave off, brush off. *See* **wuhsibetu, kwusiberu.**

wusibo?aru (v) skin an animal (take off hide when butchering). *See* **tsahkwuru?aru.**

wusi?kwaru (v) cut a strip.

wusóoru (v) hang a long object on a line.

wusuabetaitu (v) restore circulation (get feeling back after being numb).

wusukatu (v) experience something (feel in body or soul).

wusukwaru W, **wusu?waru** K (v) attempt to hit with a weapon.

wusuwarukiitu (v) give up waiting for someone.

wusu?naru (v) scrape (with instrument, as a hide with a knife).

wutahkaruru K (v) squat (sit on heels). *See* **wunuhkaruru.**

wutsupai (adj) witchy.

wutsu?mi (adj) full stomach (as a result of gluttony).

wutsu?mitu (adj) satisfied with sufficient food, filled up. *See* **pakwu?sumitu.**

wutsukaru (v) cut, shear, mow.

wutsukitu (v) crowd, shove. **U wutsuki u?.** He crowded him. adj tight, ill-fitting. **Pu nape wutsukitu.** His shoes are tight. *See* **ma?wikaru.**

wutsukunaru (v) tie a knot. **Nu napuna nu? wutsukunaru.** I am tying my shoes. **Situkwu kuse? ma napema ma wutsukui nanu.** These two tied it on his leg (9:12).

wutukwaru (v), *pl* **wuhpa?itu** beat.

wutubaru (v) crack something, break by dropping. **Kupita?a ma? wutubai.** He broke that lamp. *See* **tahparu.**

wutuki?netu (v) pound flat, smooth down (cause to be smooth). **Hanibitu wutuki?netu.** He is pounding the corn.

wuuyoritu, wuyoritu (v) disturb, startle, scare (causing to fly or jump up). **Huutsuni ma wiyori.** He scared up the birds (into flight). *See* **wuhkuya?aru.**

wuyakeetu W, **wuyakitu** K (n) songs of youth (special type sung at night by young Comanches going from camp to camp).

wuyaketu (v) cause to cry (by whipping, threatening, rattling something). **Wutsabiya? wuyakeyu.** He is rattling the gourd.

wuyaru (v) lift (with instrument, as a pole).

wuyumi?ipu (n) flailed material (as fruit or nuts knocked from tree).

wuyumi?itu (v, pl), *sg* **wupuheru** flail, knock off.

wuyupa?nitu (v) quiet down, calm down.

wu?aikuru (v) crank, row (with oars). *See* **ma?aikuru**.

wu?aniru (v) chop down, swat down. **Huupita u wu?ani.** He chopped down the tree.

wu?kuru (n) archery game (first man shoots arrow to place mark; each man shoots four arrows; closest to mark wins).

wu?ku?buu? (n) hummingbird [**wu-** flitter + **ku?buu?** say boo]. *Trochilidae.*

wu?kwuriaru (v) throw out of something.

wu?mina?nuumu (n, hum pl), *sg* **wuhminanuumu** invalids, handicapped persons.

wu?nikaru (v), *pl obj* W **wuwe-kwuru,** K **wukwekwuru** bolt down, screw in. **Meeku ma wu?niku.** Now bolt it together. **Pu nabukuwa?a ma? natsawe wukweku.** The doors are screwed on his car.

Wu?rabiahpu (name) Swift-moving (person).

wu?rabiaru (v) move quickly, act speedily.

wu?tsikwaru (adj) weary, tired of something. *See* **manuu?mai**.

wu?uraru (v) find something (with instrument). **Pu pokweti u wu?u-rai.** They found their canoe (with stick, poking in water).

wu?utsitu (v) pile up (cause to be lined up). **Huupita u wu?utsitu.** He is stacking his wood.

wu?uaru?aru (v) crack something (with an instrument). **Aawo huupima wu?uaruakatu.** He is cracking the cup with a stick.

wu?unenihku? W (n) fan for fire. *See* **wunekutu?**.

wu?wenitu K, **kwu?kwenitu** W (v) empty out, pour out. **U kwu?-kweni u.** He emptied it.

wu?yukwitu K, **kwu?yukwitu** W (v) trim, prune (as to shape a tree). **Tsaa u wu?yukwitu.** He is trimming it well. *See* **kuhpomaru, wuhuwu?niitu**.

wu?yuruhkikatu (adj) scared, afraid. *See* **makuya?aitu, kuya?akatu**.

wu?yuruhkitu (v) frighten someone with something, scare.

wuminaa kahni (n) hospital [**wuminaa** illness + **kahni** house]. *See* **natusu?u kahni**.

Y

yaa (interj) Oh! (used by women only). *See* **ha?ii, ubia**.

yaahuyaru (v), *pl* **yaahunitu** fetch, scrounge for.

yaakuru (v, sg obj), *pl obj* **himaki- tu** return an item, bring something back to someone.

yaapu (n) object or item taken.

yaaru (v, sg obj), *pl obj* **hima?aru** take one or several things. **Ihka yaa.** Take this.

yahihpu? (n) parent-in-law (of woman).

yahkatʉ (v) hold, have something in hand.

yahneetʉ (v), *pl* **naʔyʉnetʉ** laugh.

yahnena (n) laughter.

yaketʉ (v), *pl* **nawooʔi, nahwooitʉ** cry (make noise). *See* **muuyaketʉ, muyakeʔ.**

yakeyʉkarʉ (v) crying walking around (as mooing, bleating, etc.)

yanawoʔiʔ (n) cannon.

Yapai tʉhka (n), *pl* **Yapai nʉaʉ** Yap-eaters. (Shoshones name for Comanches—probably the last band to leave Shoshonean traditions; northernmost band located in Medicine Park, Meers, Elgin, Fletcher, Cyril, Apache, Boone counties of Oklahoma).

yee (interj) Oh, no! (used by men only, with appropriate negative intonation). Oh, good! (used by men only, with appropriate positive intonation).

yohyakatʉ K (v) hurry.

yohyaku (adv man) hastily, hurriedly (in a hurry).

yoka, yokapʉ (n) phlegm, juice (heavy liquid).

yokabahmʉ (n) chewing tobacco, snuff, tobacco [**yoka-** phlegm + **pahmʉ** smoke].

yokake, yokaketʉ (adj) spongy, soggy, soft.

yokanatsuʔu K (n) red false mallow (taboo term used only by medicine men). *See* **puhanatsu.**

yorimiʔarʉ (v, pl), *sg* **yʉtsʉrʉ** fly up, rise up.

yoʔmitsaitʉ (v) stir around, move around. **ʉ ʉnʉbihnaa yoʔmitsai-tʉ.** The honey bees are stirring around.

yubutsʉhkatʉ (v) stuck in the mud, bogged down. *See* **sekwi sʉhkai.**

yuhhu K (n) lard, grease, fat. **Sʉsʉmʉʔ kʉseʔ pʉmʉ u yuhukʉ u kwasʉi kʉnʉ.** Some (themselves) fried it in that fat (127:12). *See* **yuhukarʉka.**

yuhibitsipʉ K (n) buttermilk.

yuhnukarʉ (v) hold something (in a container).

yuhnunimiʔarʉ (v) carry something (in a container).

yuhu (n) ref to fat.

yuhu bitsipʉ (n) butter [**yuhu** lard + **pitsipʉ** milk].

yuhu bʉhkaitʉ (v) gain weight, fatten.

yuhu nohkopʉ (n) fried bread, frybread.

yuhu nohkorʉ (v) make frybread.

yuhu rʉkʉhmanipʉ (n) fried meat, meat.

yuhu wehkipʉ (n) fattest one. **Urʉʉkʉhʉ u yuhu wehkipʉ wihnu surʉ pisikwanúuʔinʉ.** Then that one, the fattest to be found of them, slid down (5:11).

yuhukarʉ (v) render lard. *See* **ku- ʔokwerʉ, kuhpitsʉniʔarʉ, kuhpawikʉʔitʉ.**

yuhukarʉka W (n) lard. *See* **yuhhu.**

yuhukarʉkarʉ (adj) rendered (as lard).

yukahnibarʉ (v) live unconcerned.

yukarʉrʉ (v), *pl* **yuuyʉkwitʉ** sit still.

yumarʉ (v, pl), *sg* **pahitʉ** fall, be born, drop off.

yunaharʉ (v) calm (continue having calm breeze or wind).

yunahkatʉ (adj) quiet, still (without movement). **Yunaahka̱!** Be still!

yunarʉ (v) separate milk from cream, skim from the surface. **Pitsiuyuhina atahpu u yunạ.** Skim the cream off.

yunirʉ, yuniitʉ (v) give something (in a container). **Aawokʉnụ u yuni nʉ?.** I gave it to her in a cup.

yunʉmitʉ (v), *pl* **yʉyʉkarʉ** live well, be well behaved (be good).

yupusia, yuposia (n) head louse. *See* **pusị?a.**

yupʉ (n) fat person.

yurahpetʉ (v) shrink, heal (stop swelling).

yusuatʉ, yuusua (adj) right (proper), normal (thinking good thoughts, *lit* fat-thinker). **Hakaniyuta ʉnʉ ke yuusua?** Why don't you think right?

yusʉhʉbi (n) weeping willow. *Salix* sp.

yusʉkʉ, yuu sʉkʉi (n) early plum (*lit* fat plum; fresh fruit eaten, dried fruit stored for use later). *Prunus* sp. *See* **parʉa sʉkʉi?, kusisʉkʉi.**

yuu sonipʉ (n) prairie clover, common grass. *Leguminosae.*

yuu habíitʉ (v), *pl* **yuu kwabitʉ** lie still.

yuu taibo? (n), *pl* **yuu taibonʉ** Mexican (*lit* fat white man).

yuu wʉnʉrʉ, yuu kwʉnʉrʉ (v), *pl* **yuutoborʉ** stand still (be unconcerned).

yuu ʉhpʉitʉ (v) sleep unconcerned. **Itʉʉ yu ʉhkoikʉ.** They slept on (in spite of noise). *See* **ʉhpʉitʉ.**

yu?a, yu?atʉ (adj) warm.

yu?a korohkọ (n) scarf (*lit* warm necktie). *See* **tsokwʉkʉʉna?, korohkọ.**

yu?a kwʉsu?u (n) sweater (*lit* warm blouse, shirt).

yu?a nakohtoo? (n) heater (*lit* warming stove).

yu?a namʉsoorʉ (v) wear warm clothing.

yu?a nʉe kahpi?nakwʉ (n) southwest.

yu?a ʉmakʉni (n) rain shelter for winter (a teepee lining made of buckskin or rawhide used to keep out cold and rain). *See* **ʉma kahni.**

yu?anee (n) south wind, summer wind.

yu?anʉbe nakwʉbụ (n) south (*lit* warm-wind direction).

yu?anʉe muhyʉnakwʉbu (n) southeast.

yu?a?itʉ (v) warm up.

yu?naitsi K, yu?nai tʉhtsi W (adv man) easy, easily. **Yu?naitsi ma nahaniitʉ.** It is easily made.

yʉba (n) fall season.

Yʉba mʉa (n) October (*lit* fall month).

yʉbarʉ (v) past the peak (movement in time).

Yʉba ʉhi mʉa (n) November (*lit* levelling-toward-winter month).

yʉhnʉ (n) porcupine. *See* **hʉʉnʉ?.**

yʉhnʉ wokweebi? (n) porcupine quill (*lit* porcupine thorn).

yʉihkạ (adv) this evening.

yʉihtʉhkatʉ (v) eat supper.

yʉihtʉhka? (n) supper (evening meal).

yʉitʉ (adj) evening.

yʉkarʉ (v, pl), *sg* **nʉmi** walk, move about.

yʉkwi kahni K (n) parlor (*lit* sitting room). *See* **pʉkʉra yʉkwi?enạ.**

yʉkwikʉ (v, pl), *sg* **karʉkʉrʉ** set up teepees.

yʉkwimiʔarʉ (v, pl), *sg* **karʉrʉ** sit down, stay. *See* **karʉkatʉ.**

yʉkwitʉ (v), *pl* **niwʉnʉrʉ** say. **Sʉme mayʉkwiitʉ.** He said it. *See* **tekwarʉ.**

yʉmʉhkitʉ (v) move, change position.

yʉrʉhkitʉ (v) startle, frighten. **Aawo pahitsi nʉ mayʉrʉhkinʉ.** The cup falling frightened me.

yʉtsʉrʉ (v), *pl* **yorimiʔarʉ** rise up, go up, fly up.

yʉtsʉʔ (n) airplane.

yʉwimiʔarʉ (v) descend, go down (go out of sight). **Tʉʔrikuu tsaʔ pʉ kahni taikʉkʉ yʉwimiʔai.** The prairie dog went down into his hole.

yʉwitʉ W (v) swallow something.

yʉyʉkarʉ (v, pl), *sg* **yunʉmitʉ** live well, be good, well behaved.

yʉʔbanaʔitʉ (v) sway, rocking way of walking (keep in time with music by body movement; chiefly said of women).

yʉʔyʉkarʉ (adj) be soft, softened. *See* **payʉʔyʉkatʉ.**

yʉʔyʉkarʉ (v) soften.

yʉʔyʉmuhkumiʔarʉ W (v) live, move around (keep moving). **Tsaaku mahpʉʉtu yʉʔyʉmuh-kumiʔa.** He is living this good life.

yʉʔyʉmuhkunạ (n) life.

yʉʔyʉmuhkuʔ W (n) movies, moving pictures.

yʉʔyʉturʉ (v) twitch, bodily jerk (with obligatory prefix indicating area of body jerking). **mayʉʔyʉ-tu** jerking hand.

Appendix A: Fauna

Animals

aruka? deer
awono?o? armadillo
ebimuura ya?ke? bullfrog
ekae?ree (W) swamp rabbit
ekakúura? buffalo calf
ekakuma? reddish brown horse, bay
ekapia? sorrel mare
ekatseena? red fox
ekaunuu?a tuhka?eetu anteater
esikuhma? gray male horse
esimuura? gray mule
esipia? slate gray mare
esiunuu? elephant
ewa kuupi? ground squirrel
ha?nii beaver
hooki hog
huuna? groundhog, woodchuck
hunubi pokaa? bat
huunu? porcupine
kaawosa fox, jackal
kaburuu? sheep
kaburuu?a tua lamb
kahuú? mouse
kuhtsu tubini? toad, horned toad
kuhtsu? cow, cattle

kusimuura donkey
kutsi?wobi? donkey
kuura pack rat
kuhtsaya?ya?ke? coyote
ku?kwuria? fox, coyote
ku?tseena fox, wolf, coyote
kwasi taiboo? monkey
kwipusiapu palomino horse
matusohpe? wildcat
ma?nu sarii? dachshund
motso sarii? poodle
mubi sarii? greyhound
munua? hog, pig
mupitsuha tunowapi camel
muura? mule
mu?kwipuna? elephant
naboohmatusohpe? (W) leopard
naboohmura? zebra
naboohroya ruhku? leopard
naki sarii? hound dog
narunookatu unuu camel
na?ahnia (K), na?ahnia (N)
   palomino, horse
na?nia buckskin horse
noyotso?me tabu? rabbit (Easter)
numamo?o? coon, raccoon
numu kuhtsu? buffalo
ohaahnakatu (W) fox, coyote

155

ohaeka?, ohaekapitu light brown horse, bay horse

otu kuma? (W) sorrel horse (male)

paa tsoko otter

pahtsi kaburuu? slickhaired goat

pahtsi kwasi possum

papiwui htama? otter, mink

paraimo?o mole

paruuku?, pa?ruhku? coon, raccoon

parua kuhma bull elk

pasawí?oo? frog

pa?a ruyu?, pa?a to?yo? giraffe

pa?arai mo?o woodchuck

pa?sunó?a? kangaroo

pa?wuhtakóo? tadpole

pa?wuhtuma? beaver

pia kahúa rat, field mouse

pia tseena? wolf

pimoroo?, pimoroo?a piabu cow

pimoroo?a kuhma bull

pimoroo?a tua? calf

pisuni?eeyu, pisuníi? skunk

pitsa naboo? (K) calico horse

pitsipu pimoróo? milk cow

pi?isutu pacer

pi?tohtsía? (W) white tailed deer

pohni?atsi skunk

pohpi kwáai? (W) frog

po?ro? pig, hog, swine

puku rúa? colt

pua watsi wild stallion

puhu kaburuu? sheep

puhu ku?kwe?ya? lion

sanahtu?re? snail

sarii? dog

ta?si?woo? buffalo

ta?wokinae?ree eka swamp rabbit

tosa naboo? paint horse, calico horse

tosa? white horse

toya ruhku? leopard

tseena? gray fox, coyote

tuhtseena? wolf

tupisi kuma? bay horse

tu?kina?, tabú?kina? rabbit

tue kahuu? mouse

tue tumakupa? bobcat

tuhuya horse (general)

tukwitsuna? elephant

tumahkupa? panther

tunookatu? (K) camel

tupusi kuma? sorrel horse

turayaa sarii bloodhound

tuunoo unuu? (K) camel

tu?rukúu? prairie dog

waani (K), waa?ne? (W) fox

wasápe bear

wa?oo? cat

wokoohwi tree squirrel

wura? panther, mountain lion

yuhnu, huunu? porcupine

Birds

ebihuutsuu? bluejay, bluebird

ebikuyuutsi? chaparral, roadrunner

ekabapi red headed buzzard

ekahuutsu? cardinal, redbird

hiitoo? (K, N) meadowlark

huhmara?, huumara? falcon

huutsúu bird (general)

kokáa? guinea fowl

kokorá?a chicken

kusikwa?aa? crane

kusikwi?ii? (W) type of bird

kusisai? small gray bird

kuyu?nii? turkey

kuyúutsi? quail

ku?e wóo? dove, pigeon

kukuburaakwa?si? scissortail, fork tailed flycatcher

kwihnai eagle

nohabitu̶ hen
nu̶ku̶ta goose
ohanu̶napu̶ (W) meadowlark, field lark
oʔooʔ horned owl
pakawkokoʔ, pakokokoʔ prairie chicken
pasahòo pigeon, dove, wren
paʔa toyokatu̶ huutsuuʔ crane, stork
pekwi tu̶hkaʔ kingfisher
pia huutsuuʔ eagle
pia kwihnai eagle
pitu̶su̶ nuʔyeʔ (W) woodpecker
pohkóoʔ burrowing owl
puhitóoʔ turkey/turkey gobbler
pu̶u̶yu̶ duck
soo yakeʔ mocking bird
su̶hu̶ mupitsu̶ screech owl
taibo huutsuuʔ pigeon
tosa kwiisuʔ black bird (white wings)
tosa nakaai hawk
turuawapi̶ laying hen, leghorn
tuwikaaʔ raven, crow, blackbird
tu̶e basuuʔ (W) quail
tu̶e kuyúutsi (K) partridge, quail (small)
tu̶nimanahke huutsuʔ (K) mockingbird
turu̶e basuu (K) quail
turu̶e kuʔyuutsi quail
tu̶ʔiiʔ sandpiper
wobi tohtaraki̶ (K) woodpecker
woko̶ huutsu̶ parrot, parakeet
wu̶pu̶koiʔ woodpecker (large sp.)
wu̶ʔku̶ʔbuuʔ hummingbird

Reptiles

ebimuutarooʔ mountain boomer
ebipabokoʔaiʔ (P) mountain boomer

ku̶htáa nuʔyaʔaʔ (W) racer snake
kwasi nu̶ru̶u̶ʔwu̶ʔ snapping turtle
kwasinaboo wu̶hkitsu̶ʔtsu̶ʔikatu̶ rattle snake
kwasinabooʔ snake (general)
naki̶ taiʔ, naki̶ tóone (N) long sp. lizard
nuhyaʔ snake, any species
nu̶mu̶ maʔtsaʔbahkiʔ clinging lizard
nu̶nu̶ʔyu̶wiʔ (W) alligator
pabokoʔai timber lizard
paʔboosiʔ water lizard, water dog
paʔkwaku̶me snapping turtle
pitsohka kwaba (W) alligator, snapping turtle
tuhparokooʔ water moccasin
tu̶pi pabokoʔai rock lizard
wakaréeʔ (K), wakaʔréʔeeʔ (W) turtle
wanatsihtaraaʔ (W) striped lizard
wu̶htsabeyakatu̶ (W) rattlesnake

Fish

hu̶ato fish (unknown sp.)
kwasinaboo pekwi eel
pekwi̶ fish
tahipu̶ pekwi flounder
tuumeʔso̶ young catfish
tuumoʔtsoʔ full grown catfish
tuʔreʔ leech
waʔroo koyáaʔ crawfish, crayfish

Insects

ahtakii grasshopper (small sp.)
ahtamuu jumbo grasshopper
ani̶kuuraʔ ant
animui̶ housefly

ekapusiʔa flea
ekaunuu red ant
kahni busiʔa bedbug
kaʔraʔáaʔ tick
kuna naʔmahpeeʔ lightning bug
kwasi tonaʔ scorpion
kwita maropona doodlebug, sowbug
mutsikwùʔaaʔ mosquito
muwoʔneʔ termite
ohahpiyaaʔ bumblebee
otu peena wasp
paka tuuʔruʔ dragonfly
pia animui horsefly
pihpi horsefly
puikuso redbug, chigger
pusiʔa head louse

puhu pusia crab louse
saabe busia body louse
soo moʔoʔ centipede
soo yakeʔ locust
teʔanimui biting fly
tosaraiʔ devil's horse
tuhmeko cricket
tuunuuʔ Junebug, black beetle
tuʔanikuuraʔ wood ant
tue anikuuraʔ sugar ant
tue esi unuu gnat
tupi simuhtaʔ moth (long sp.)
unúʔ bug, insect, creature
wobi muwoʔneʔ (K) termite
wobi pihnaa unuuʔ honeybee
wosa aʔraʔ grasshopper (long sp.)
yupusia head louse

Appendix B: Flora

Trees

ekamurora?i huupi redbud tree

etuhuupi osage orange, hedge apple, bois d'arc

huupi, huuhpi tree (general)

kunanatsu prickly ash, toothache tree

kuhtáa mubitai? hickory

kurahúu?, ku?ra?húu? hackberry

kwe?yuku sohóobi silver maple

mitsonaa? southern hackberry

mubitai, mu?bitai walnut

namabitsoo?ni mesquite

naséka persimmon

natsohkwe? mesquite

na?kuta?i? huuhpi pecan tree

ohahuupi osage orange, bois d'arc

ohasuhuubi willow, black

otu mitsonaa? soapberry tree

pahtsi mubitai hickory

parua, paruabi dogwood (rough leaf)

pa?sa ponii huupi oak

pihúura huupi catalpa

pimoroo?a korohko? elm, white elm

seyuyuki? ehyuyuki? ash tree

siba huupi dogwood (flowering variety)

soho bokopi hackberry

soho bo?koo? huupi mulberry tree

soho obi huupi cottonwood tree

suhuubi willow

suku?i huuhpi plum tree

tosa seyu?yuki? white ash

tosa tukanai huupi white oak

tubokóo huuhpi black haw (local term), thornapple

tuhmubitai black walnut

tuhnaséka Mexican persimmon

tuhuupi, tuhu huupi blackjack oak

tusohó? elm

tue amawoo? crabapple

tumaya huupi smooth sumac

waapi cedar

we?yuku sohoobi (K) cottonwood

wohi?huu mesquite

wokóobi pine

woku huupi thorn tree, honey locust

wokwekatu huupi thornapple, black haw

yusuhubi weeping willow

yusuku yuu sukui early plum

Plants

aakáa? devil's horn/devil's claw
anakwanare? gourd
atabitsunoi button snakeroot
ebitotsiya? Texas thistle
ekahkoni Indian breadroot
ekamitsaa? cactus
ekanatsu eriogonum root
ekapokopi yaupon holly
ekapo? mescal bean
ekasonipu little bluestem
ekatsiira? red pepper
ekawoni smartweed
esinuuhparabi loco weed
hani- maize, corn
hi?ookwana? sunflower
huutsú?a tuahkapu sumac
kabitsi cabbage
kahnitueka Indian paintbrush
kamúuta? sweet potato
kapisi namaya croton weed
kuhtsu pokàa? cocklebur, burr
kumiitsanatsu milkweed
kusinuuhparabi gray colored plant
kusiwuunu sage like shrub
kuhtsutsuu?ni? poisonous wild
  onion
kuriata yellow pond lily
kuru?atsi yellow lotus
kuukanaruhka?, kuuka wild onion
kwasinabo?a tuahkapu tomato,
  goat's rue
mumutsi? soapweed, yucca,
  beargrass
mutsi natsamukwe? wild grape
nakwusi? pumpkin
namabitsooni sonipu mesquite
  weed
natsaakusi sneeze weed
natsamukwe?a suuki grapevine
nayui wokwe cactus

numu rusaasi Indian perfume plant
ohahpokopi, ohahtukapu domestic
  carrot
ohapi watermelon, yellow
ohayaa? sunflower
paapasi wild potato
pahmo namahya sumac
pahmu tobacco
paiyapi wild plant with edible fruit
pakeeso purple prairie clover
pakuuka wild onion, swamp weed
panatsayaa? blackberry bush,
  raspberry bush
pasiwona puhubi silvery
  wormwood
pawahkapu herb (name unknown)
payaape aqueous wild tuber
pa?mutsi water lilylike plant
pa?puhi tuhka? celery
pa?sonipu weeds
pesotái buttonbush
pihtsamuu milky rooted plant
pihúraa bean plant
pisibuni? cattail
pitsa múu legume with edible
  tubers
pitsi tora prickly poppy
pohóobi sagebrush, quinine weed
poiya feverplant
poko ruhka? cucumber
po?aya?eetu thistle
puha natsu red false mallow
puhakatu heal all plant
puhi bihnáa? watermelon
puhi ta?ara? poison ivy
puhi topika bush
puhi tubi bush clover
puhi tuhkapu lettuce
puhi tumakwatubi? cigarette
  wrapper leaf
puhi turuhka? mistletoe
pui tsaseni rye grass

puewatsi kuuka wild onion
puhu natsu, puhu ru?saasi
  medicinal herb
saatotsiya flowering plant
sanaweha broomweed, mormon tea
siiko wild syacinth
simuihu? snakeroot, church root
soho kua?etu totsiyaa? morning
  glory
soko rahka?miitsa? cucumber
soko sikusa dandelion
soni bihnáa? sugar cane
soni narúa oats
soni wokweebi grass burrs
sonipu grass
suhu tsitsina? potato
tabetsotsiyaa fleabane daisy, clock
  flower
taibo bihnaa? cantaloupe
taibo suku?i domestic plum
tamutso?i greenbriar
tatsipuu sumac, skunkbush
tohpotsotsii nightshade
tohtía sonipu wheat plant
tohtía sonipuha taka? rye
toponibihuura? peas
tosa wahtsuki horseweed
totohtu edible tuber

to?roponii? beetlike tuber
tsapusiku sensitive briar
tsiira? chili pepper
tsunisu edible tuber
tuhbanatsaya blackberry bush
tukunu natsu purple coneflower
tunuhaa cymopterus plant
tutupipu wild tuber
tuwokwe goathead vine
tu?amowoo thornapple, blackhaw
tuahpi Chickasaw plum
tuetutaatu kuuka wild onion
tumakwatui? cigarette wrapper
  plant
tupi natsu medicinal plant
turanu breadroot, Indian bread
tusaasi Indian perfume plant, sage
tuunua broomgrass
tuunua? broom corn
wokweebi peyote plant, thorn,
  thistle
wokwesonipu thorny weed,
  sunburst plant
wokeéesi barrel cactus, prickly pear
wo?anatsu? western ragweed
yokanatsu?u red false mallow
yuu sonipu prairie clover, common
  grass

Appendix C: Body Parts

ahna side of chest, underarm, armpit
ahnapʉ pubic hair, underarm hair
ahnatukate armpit
ahrapʉ (Y, P) jaw
eeko̱ tongue
ekotʉwʉniʔ glottis
eʔrée forehead
hekwiʔ spleen
huhkʉ collarbone
hʉnʉpoʔaʔ human skin
kasa̱ wing
katsonakwʉ end, rear, back part
kaʔi forehead
kaʔibʉhʉ eyebrow
kiipʉ elbow
kohhiʔ small intestine, waist,
   abdomen
koobe̱ face
kotsana flank of living animal,
   hindquarter
kuitsi̱ throat
kuitsitʉkwʉni adam's apple
kupi̱si, kubi̱si brain
kutsiʔomo shin, shinbone
kʉʉtsi̱ wisdom tooth
kwahi back of person/animal
kwahi kupi̱si spinal cord (excluding
   bones)

kwahinupʉ spine
kwahiporopʉ spinal column
kwahitsuhni̱ vertebra (one)
kwahiwoʔoraa spine, backbone
kwahtsʉ (Y), kwahtsʉna rib
kwasi̱ tail of animal
kwiita buttocks
kwitatsi̱ large intestine
mahtokooʔ thumb
mahtuaʔ (K) little finger
mahtʉpi̱náaʔ (K) middle finger
makwe back of the hand, hand
mapaana̱ palm of hand
mapóʔaʔ human skin
mapʉhʉ hair on arm/wrist
masiito̱ fingernail
masʉwʉhkiʔ (K) fingers (including
   the thumb)
mawaatsa̱ rib
maʔwiítsa̱ wrist
miihtsi̱ ankle
mitʉkoʔo roof of mouth
motso̱ beard
moʔo moʔe hand
muubi̱ nose
naape̱ foot, lower leg
naki̱ ear
naki̱ kwiita̱ ear lobe, back of ear

natsimina? joint of the body
nʉnapʉ chest of the body
nʉʉhtoka?e? muscle
nʉʉmʉ liver
ohutuki flank of animal
oomo leg (from knee down)
paai vein
paapi, papi head (including face)
pabokohi large intestine
papi hʉnʉpo?a scalp of head
parʉʉtsi chin
pihi heart
pitsii?, pitsamʉ breast of woman
piwo?sa hip, lower back
pui eye
pui narʉso eyelid
puihtsara? (Y) flank of animal
puihtsita? (K) rib area of animal
pui? temple
puitʉsii eyelash
pu?i? gall bladder
pʉkapʉ lap
pʉʉra arm
sahpáana? side of stomach or
　abdomen
sapʉ stomach
sekwi bii? second stomach
　of a cow
sia feather
sihkupʉ (Y) collar bone
siikʉ navel
soo tuku flank of animal
soomo lung
so?o ruhkʉ gums of teeth
so?o tsuhni cheekbone
so?o cheek, cheekbone

taama tooth
tahpáana sole of foot
tahtokoo? big toe
tahtúa? little toe
tahtʉpinaa? middle toe
tamakwita roots of the teeth
tamaruhkʉ gums of the teeth
tamʉ sinew
tanapʉ knee
tana? kʉ?e kneecap
tapiko? heel of foot
tapʉ, tapʉhʉ hair of leg
tasakwʉʉhki? toes
tasiito toenail, claw, hoof
ta?ki? kidney
ta?wiitsa calf of the leg
tohoobe thigh, from the knee up
tookaatso toe
toyo tahka?miitsa sweetbreads
toyopʉ neck
tsoohpa tsuuni shoulder bone
tso?apʉ shoulder
tso?yaa? head of hair
tsuhnipʉ skull
tsuhni? bone
tuhhu shin/shinbone
tuhkohhi (Y) intestine
tuhkʉ body, flesh
tuhpui pupil of the eye
tʉpe mouth, lips
tʉrana bones of leg, marrow bones
tʉtsihtsuka? index finger
waatsʉ rib
worʉroku esophagus, windpipe
wo?rorooki (Y) windpipe
　múu lúf H

Appendix D: Months of the Year

January

Toh mʉa 'year month'
Ʉkʉrooma mʉa 'middle month'

February

Positsʉ mʉa 'sleet month'

March

Nanaʔbutitʉikatʉ mʉa 'hot or cold
    month'
Tahpookʉ mʉa 'cottonball month'

April

Tahma mʉa 'new spring month'

May

Totsiyaa mʉa 'flower month'

June

Puhi mʉa 'leaf month'

July

Pʉmata piabuhharaʔena mʉa
    'Fourth of July month'
Pia mʉa 'large month'
Ʉrʉi mʉa 'hot month'

August

Tahma ʉhʉyi, Tatsatʉ mʉa 'summer
    month'
Ʉkʉiyuba mʉa 'new fall month'

September

Tʉboo renahpʉmakwe kwiʔena
    mʉa 'paper man enters school'
Kwiʔena mʉa 'back to school
    month'

October

Yʉbamʉa 'fall month'

November

Yʉbaʉhi mʉa 'leveling toward
    winter month'
Aho tabenihtʉ mʉa 'Thanksgiving
    month'

December

Pia ʉtsʉʔi mʉa 'big cold month'
Pʉmata wahi mʉa, Pʉmata waa
    himaʔena mʉa 'gift month'
Wahimʉa 'evergreen month'
Pʉmata wanohiʔema mʉa
    'Christmas gift month'

Appendix E: Personal Names

Aruka paa? Deer water
Atakuni, Ata kahni Lone tipi
Atsabi? Creator, Holy Spirit
Eka kura Red buffalo
Ekamurawa Red crooked nose
Ekawokani Red young man
Esahibi Wolf drinking
Esatai Little wolf
Esihabiitu Gray streak, Gray flat
    lying object
Esikono Gray box
Esitami? Ase tammy
Esunapu Asenap
Hiitoo? Meadowlark
Huuhwiya Refuse to come
Huuwuhtukwa? Take a stick and
    hit someone
Hukiyani Carrying her sunshade
Huwuni Dawn
Hu?nipitu Hiccough daughter
Isananaka?, Isunanika Howling
    coyote, Echo of the wolf's howl
Isatekwa Liar, Lie talk
Isawura Crazy bear
Ishatai Coyote droppings
Kaatu, Katinu God
Kahpewai No bed

Kahúu nihku pipikure, Pipiku?
    Squeaky like a mouse
Ka?mutuhi?, Kamuru?i? Looking
    from side to side
Ke tokwe hina haniitu Satan
Kebakowe? Coyote
Kehaitsipaapi Bald
Ketse nab?bo Painted feather
Kiyu Horseback
Kohi Narrow gut
Kohitu se?tanuku Sitting bear
Kuhiyai Peeping from behind tree
Kuhtsu kwi?ta Cow dung
Kuhtsuna kwapipu Buffalo hump
Kuhtsunu kwahipu One who rides
    buffalo
Kuhtu Coals in a fire
Kukapu Cooks dried meat
Kurupitsoni Looks brown
Kutsukwipu Chew up
Kwahira Robe on his back
Kwana Quanah Parker
Kwasia Eagle tail feather
Kwihne tosabitu White eagle
Moo?wetu No hand
Mopai Owl
Mota, Tatseni Lee Motah
Mo?pi tsokopu Old owl

Mukwooru Spirit talker
Mura kwitapu Mule dung
Nabakwutiapu Christian
Narua, Nadua Cynthia Ann Parker
Narumi? Lord, Master
Naya Slope
Ninakaba?i? Refusing
Nookoni, Nocona, Peta Nokona Wanderer
Nuenuhkiki Wind running here
Nuetutsi Blowing wind
Numu ruibetsu She invites her relatives
Ohapia Bay mare
Ohapitu kwahi Yellow back
Ohawasápe Yellow bear
Ohawunu Yellow steps
Onawai Salt worn out
Otu kwasu Brown robe
Paa roponi *See* How deep the water is
Paa tsokotubutu Black otter
Paa tso?ko Otter
Pabopitu Light complexion
Pahtsi ketu Smooth
Pakawa Kills something
Pakekuni, Pake kahni Dry teepee
Paruwa kuma Bull elk
Paruwa sumuno Ten elks
Parua kuhma Bull bear
Pasawío Big green frog
Pia baa Big water
Pia nu?upai?i Big whip
Pia rutsima Big fall by tripping
Pia opu, Pi?opu Pia?opu
Piana buni?, Piana ronitu Big looking glass
Pipiku? Squeaky
Pisu kwá?na? Smeller
Pi?opu paroba tuyo, Peope Padiva, Taoyo, Tuyo Boy
Poo?aiku Blow it away

Pua paatsoko Medicine otter
Puhawi Medicine woman
Puku?a tua? Colt
Punitu Looking
Pu?ekatu Christian
Pu tua wuni kwai Been to see his son
Pu?na petu Only daughter
Sanah pia Sanahpia
Sanah pia ariba Sanahpia ariba
Santanta Santanta
Sata Tejas I, Saria Tuhka I Sata Tejas I
Sata Tejas II, Saria Tuhka II Sata Tejas II
Sihka tabe ke isopu This midday sun does not tell a lie
Soo pitenu Comes often
Tabe kwi?ne Sun eagle
Tabe nanika Hears the sunrise, Voice of the sunrise
Tabe wunuru Standing sun
Tahkapu Poor one
Tatsiwóo Buffalo
Ta?ahpu Our Father, Great Spirit
Tekwitsi Skinny and wrinkled
Tenebeka, Tunubeku Gets to be middle aged man
Tomo?a tua Sky child
Tope Tope
Topehtsi, Topache Pass it on
Topusana Flower
Tsaa tenayake? Good crier
Tsaa tsopa? Easy to break
Tsihtara Short dress
Tsuhni Bone
Tuhkwasi taiboo? Satan
Tu?paapi Black head
Tu?runaasu Straighter than straight
Tue buakutu Little medicine
Tue kuhtsu Little buffalo

Tʉhʉyana kwahipʉ Horseback

Tʉmʉbo, Timbo Son of bull bear

Tʉoyobisesʉ Chief Comanche dog soldiers

Tʉpanai Cliff

Tʉpi kʉniʔ Stonehouse

Tʉpi wʉnʉ Rocky creek

Tʉʔsinaʔ Hanging from the belt

Waakakwa Trotter (Laughing John)

Wakaréʔe Turtle

Wanarʉ Wanarʉ

Witawooʔooki Barking buttocks

Wʉkwiya, Wekwaaʔa Jesus man

Wʉʔrabiahpʉ Swift moving

Part II

English-Comanche Lexicon

English-Comanche Lexicon

A a

abandon someone nobʉahraitʉ
abdomen kohi̱
abdomen, side of stomach or sahpáana?
abdominal pain, suffer kohikamʉtʉ
able to walk nʉmirʉ
about, move yʉkarʉ
about, think sukwʉkitʉ
about something, think nasutamʉkatʉ tamai, su?atsitʉ, tʉsu?atsi̱katʉ
above everything oyo?rʉ ka?weki̱tʉ
_**above the horizon, stand just** tabe wʉnʉ?itʉ
accept someone, refuse to ninakabarʉ
accident, die in anitʉ
accident, hurt someone by tsahhuhyarʉ
accidentally, knock over and spill tsakwʉriarʉ
accidentally, spilled makwʉri?aikatʉ
accompany, allow women to notsa?kaarʉ

accord, open of its own natsahwi?etʉ
accord, spill of own nʉʉti?akatʉ
accord, split of own nʉʉhtsi?aitʉ
accord, unravel of own nʉʉpʉrʉsuarʉ
acculturate (as a Comanche) nʉmʉnaitʉ
accuse someone natsamarʉ
accuse someone falsely tʉbehyaarʉ
accuse someone of being gray-faced (in making fun of someone) etʉsikawo?arʉ W
ace (in game of cards) watasi̱
ache manʉʉtsikwa? W, nʉʉtsikwarʉ K
ache, have a head- papi̱kamaitʉ
ache, head- papi wʉnʉkatʉ
ache, stomach kohikamʉkatʉ, sapʉ nʉʉtsikwarʉ
ache tree, tooth- kunanatsu
ache in lower back piwo?sa wʉnarʉ
acid mohakamarʉ
acidic moha-, sʉʉkʉ
acorn pa?sa ponii
across saraa

across, drive tamanikarʉ
across, move unahrʉ
act angry tuhu rekwarʉ
act pretentious nasutsa akwarʉ K
act speedily wʉʔrabiarʉ
act without self-dignity eʔmʉarʉ
actions tʉyʉkwipʉ
adam's apple kuitsịtʉkwʉni, pia
  kuitsi?
address (speak to) niikwiitʉ
adhere sanarʉ, tsahpakịtʉ
admire nasuyaketʉ, tokwetʉtuarʉ
admire someone suʔakʉtʉ
admit tsaʔikarʉ
adobe house ohta kahni W
adopt a child toyarʉ, tʉetʉnabinarʉ
adopted daughter petʉ toyapʉ K,
  petʉboopʉ W
adopted son tua boopʉ W
adult kinsman nahnapʉ
adult male muʔwoo
adultery, commit naʔisahanitʉ W
advise naniʔʉrʉʔaitʉ, ninʉsuabitarʉ
  K, niʔatsiitʉ, tʉniʔatsitʉ, tʉsuʔʉrʉ
adviser tʉniʔatsikʉ
afflict makwihtserʉ
afraid kuyaʔakatʉ, wʉʔyʉrʉhkikatʉ
afraid, run away namanuhkitʉ
A-frame, meat-drying inakwata
after, go petsʉ pitarʉ
after, run miakʉrʉ
after another, sing one song
  nipʉyerʉ
afternoon tabe ʉhyʉh? K
again tʉasʉ
against someone, win in a contest
  tahniʔarʉ
against something, lean
  nʉʉbanịkatʉ
against something, rub pisuʔnetʉ
against something, rub head
  tsotsoʔneetʉ

**against something, scratch rear or
  back** pisuʔnetʉ
-against, Those-who-are-always
  Komanche
agent itsinạ, paraiboo?
agent, Indian itsinạ, nʉmʉ paraibo?
agnatic grandchild, man's kʉnu?
agnatic grandnephew, man's
  kʉnu?
agnatic grandchild, woman's
  huutsị
ago, long soo beʔsʉ
ago, many years soo beʔsʉ
agree to a proposal nihtsamuʔitʉ
agree to a statement tʉmahyokʉrʉ
agree with someone tokwetʉtuarʉ
agreeable tokwetʉkatʉ
agreement or contract, make an
  nanipuʔeʔaitʉ
agreement, nod the head in
  nihtsamuʔitʉ
ahead munakwʉ
ahead of, be munaikịyutʉ W
ahead, proceed muhnetʉ
aim (a gun) wʉhkurʉ
aim, miss awi-
aim (something) wakarʉkatʉ
airplane yʉtsʉ?
alcoholic beverage, drink hibikʉtʉ
align spine tahparaʔitʉ
alike sʉʉnitʉ
all oyo-
all, That's subeʔtʉ
all over, wrinkled takwikakwoʔapʉ
alligator nʉnʉʔyʉwi? W
allow to rest or cool off sua
  soyuraperʉ
allow women to accompany
  notsaʔkaarʉ
almost noha
alone, leave person kekʉnabeniitʉ
alone, one hill standing nookarʉrʉ

along (or away), drive
mahkʉsuwaitʉ

along, farther miibeʔtʉ

along, go nahaniitʉ

along, go moving noraʔwʉarʉ W

along, lead matsaaihkakurʉ,
tsakamiʔarʉ

along, roll anikwita miʔarʉ

along, take women notsaʔkaarʉ

along the edge of kʉmaʔ

along there suʔahri

alongside kʉmaʔrʉ

already pʉe

also tʉasʉ

always usúnḭ

-always-against, Those-who-are
Komanche

amazed tʉʉmoo|bi|r

amazed, be suwʉʔkai

amazing suwʉkaitʉ

ambush makamʉkarʉ, tʉkamʉrʉ

ambushed mahooikatʉ

ambusher tʉkʉmaʔaitʉʔ

Anadarko, Okla Tusokweʔ K

and tʉasʉ

angel kasaráibooʔ, nʉtʉhyoi wapḭ

anger tsahpisoʔarʉ

anger, feel tuhu suʔaitʉ

anger, jerk and slam things in
tuhu rekwarʉ

anger someone kʉpisoʔaitʉ K,
mahrubʉhkaitʉ

angered mabisoʔàitʉ, tapisoʔaitʉ W

angrily, stand pihisoʔaiwʉnʉrʉ

angry mabisoʔàitʉ, pihisoʔai,
pihisoʔaitʉ, piʔonʉ suakʉtʉ

angry, act tuhu rekwarʉ

angry, become (at a person)
tuhubʉkʉkatʉ

animal (or person), exhausted
namakweyaipʉ

animal, female piabʉ

animal, flank of puihtsaraʔ W, soo
tuku

animal, flank of living kotsana

animal, hobble an moʔo
wʉhtamarʉ

animal, lead a person or an
tsakarʉ

animal, male kuuma

animal, mean person or tuhupʉ

animal, leader, pack- tʉnoo wapḭ

animal, pack for an tʉnoopʉ W

animal, pen up taʔikʉrʉ

animal, rib area of puihtsitaʔ K

animal carcass, render an
tʉhtsohpeʔarʉ

animal, skin an pʉhʉ
tsahkweʔyarʉ, wʉsiboʔarʉ

animal, tame an masuyuʔikarʉ K

animal, trail a human or an
nayaarʉ

animal, unhitch an toʔyarʉ W

animal, water an hibikʉtʉ

animal, weak person or tʉʔǫnaapʉ

animal hide pimoroʔa pʉhi, pʉhʉʔ

animal hole itsaraitʉ ʉnʉa kahni

animal horn aa

animal horn comb aanatsihtuyeʔ

animal killed or butchered for
food tʉbehkapʉ

animal tail kwasi-, kwasḭ

animals, drive by force tamʉkurʉ

animals, drive in mahkʉkitʉ K

animals, drive up mahkʉrʉ W

ankle miihtsḭ

ankle, sprain naraminaitʉ K

announce tekwʉnitʉ, tʉnikʉkekitʉ K

annoy kʉpisoʔaitʉ K, nimʉsasuarʉ

anoint puha nabisarʉ, tʉʔekarʉ

another ata-

another, help one naruituahkarʉ

another, sing one song after
nipʉyerʉ

another one su?atu
another way, doing atapu
answer tu?awekuukaru
ant anikuura?
ant, red ekaunuu
ant, sugar tue anikuura?
ant, wood tu?anikuura?
anteater ekaunuu?a tuhka?eetu
Antelope Eaters Kwahari tuhka
any shellfish, shell of wa?koo? K
any species, snake of nuhya?
anything, more than oyo?ru ka?wekitu
Apaches, Eastern Nipanuu
apart, pull tsahka?aru, tsahpomi?itu
apart, take tsahpukusu?aru W
apiece, two wa?wa?
apparel namusoapu, oo?ru W
apart, tear tsahpako?aru
appear kunakuaru K, kuro?itu W, nabunitu, nakuakitu, to?itu
appear gray esinabuniitu
appear to be white tosa nabunitu
appearance, check over one's nabuihwunutu W
appearance, gray esitsunu?iitu
appease ninusupetitu
appetite, have an tsihasuaru
applaud (clap hands) tohtarakitu
apple amawóo
apple, crab ekaamawoo?, tue amawóo?
apple, hedge etuhuupi
apple, thorn tu?amowoo, wokwekatu huupi
apple, thorn- tubokóo
apple juice amawóo?a pàa
apple skin amawo?a? po?a?
apply medicine naru?ekaru
apply powder to oneself homonabisakatu
apply war paint wohho napusaru

applying pressure with the hands, rub masu?neru
approach wuhpitu
approach someone pitunu
approving tokwetukatu
April Tahma mua
apron pitsukwina?, tuku wuhpara? K
aqueous payaape
Arapaho Sarii Tuhka?
arbor soni huuki, tahuuki?aiku
arbor, brush huuki?aitu, puhi huuki, soni huuki, tahuuki?aiku
arbor, poles for constructing brush huukina huupi
arch potato suhu tsitsina?
archaic game na?nohne?eyu?
archery game wu?kuru
-are-always-against, Those-who Komanche
area, separated but in same general na?ata W
area, waist kohi
argue nani?wiketu W
argumentative nanitsuwakatu K
arise taayutsutu
arm puura
arm or hand, hair on lower mapuhu
arm, sprain or break hand or lower namaminaitu
arm, stretch out maruru?aru
arm, under- ahna, ana-
arm hair, under- anapuhu
arm to waist, under- ama-
armadillo awono?o?
armpit ahna, ana-, anatukate
arms, carry in toyaru
arms, carry in the kwabaru
arms or body, stretch narureru
army officer ekasahpana? paraiboo?
around, feel makwaru, tsakwatu

around, feel (with hand) mawa-

around, grope tsakwatʉ

around, kid kaasuarʉ

around, move nʉmirʉ, yoʔmitsaitʉ, yʉʔyʉmuhkumiʔarʉ W

around, roll maropoʔnarʉ

around, roll over or naʔanitʉ

around and play, run nohiʔnuraarʉ

around, scattered poohkatʉ

around something, slip a rope kuʔnikarʉ

around, smell muwarʉ W, ʉkwisʉʔninitʉ K

around, sneak hoʔaniitʉ

around, sniff ʉkwisʉʔninitʉ K

around, spin kwinuʔyarʉ, natsahkwinuʔitʉ

around, stir yoʔmitsaitʉ

around, turn koonitʉ, kooniʔetʉ, kwinuʔyarʉ

around quickly, turn pikwebuitʉ

around something, twist oneself nʉʉʔkwipunarʉ

around, walk nahnʉmiitʉ

around the neck, wear something korohkorʉ

around the waist, wear something kohinehkitʉ

around, wrap wʉhkwitunarʉ

around and around, wrap nʉʉhkwitubitʉ

arrest kwʉhʉrʉ

arrive pitʉnʉ

arrive (carrying something) noopitʉ

arrive home tsakʉbitʉkitʉ

arrow paakạ, siʔba?

arrow fly, let an wʉhkikatʉ

arrowhead tahka?

arrows, throwing naroʔtoneetsi?, tiroʔwoko

article of clothing, own an kwasuʔukatʉ K

Asenap Esʉnapʉ

Asetammy Esitami?

ash seyʉyuki?

ash, prickly kunanatsu

ash tree tosa seyuʔyuki?

ashes, color of (gray) kusi-

ashamed nasuʔaitʉ

ashes etʉsipʉ, kusipʉ

ashes, roast in kusiwʉhpima W

ashtray tusi aawọ

aside, tempt to turn tsapʉhesuwarʉ

ask nanimaaʔʉbʉʔikʉtʉ, niipuni-

ask a question tʉbinitʉ, tʉrʉbinitʉ

ask for help naníhtsawaʔitʉ

ask for something tʉrʉnirʉ

ask permission nanihtʉbinitʉ

asleep sʉsuʔnitʉ, tasʉsʉʔnitʉ

aspirin papịkamaka natʉsuʔu

assemble, dis- tohkweʔyarʉ

astray, lead tsakaʔuhrʉ

at, glare tsuhni bunitʉ

at, laugh suʔuyaaʔarʉ, tʉnịsuʔuyaitʉ, usúʔuyaʔitʉ W

at, look punitʉ, tʉpunirʉ

at oneself, look nabunitʉ

at a time, one sʉsʉmʉ?, sʉʔsʉmʉʔnʉku

at, peep kuhiyarʉ

at last haya kwasikʉ

at or to someone or something maaitʉ

at or to the left side ohininakwʉ

at this point siʔanetʉ

at top of teepee, ventilator natsihpara?

Athapascans Naboohnʉʉ

attach tsahpakʉkarʉ

attempt narahpunipʉ

attempt to hit with a weapon wʉsukwarʉ W

attention, listen with nakị hiikatʉ K

attention, pay tᵾnakiitᵾ
attentive nakamabitsiahkatᵾ,
  nakᵾkatᵾ
auger bit tᵾrohtᵾbᵾʔiʔ
augment in number suatᵾ
augmenting in quantity
  tᵾrakaʔaitᵾ
August Tahma ᵾhᵾyi, Tatsatᵾ mua,
  Ukᵾi yᵾba mua
aunt (father's sister) pahaʔ
aunt, maternal great kakuʔ
authority tᵾni-, tᵾsuʔatsipᵾ
authority, have tᵾsuʔatsᵢtᵾ
automatic pistol natsahkwineʔ
automobile naʔbukuwàaʔ
automobile tire naʔbukuwàaʔa
  narahpaana W
awaken tᵾbunitᵾ
awaken someone by shouting
  tayᵾtsᵾrᵾ
aware supᵢkaahkatᵾ
away, drive tahkᵾarᵾ
away (or along), drive
  mahkᵾsuwaitᵾ
away from (or off), fall tᵾpᵾherᵾ W
away, far manakwᵾ K
away, float okwehkwatᵾ, sᵾmᵾ
  okwetᵾ
away, force tahkᵾarᵾ
away, haul nookwarᵾ
away, kick something suᵾ potserᵾ
away, kicked suᵾhpotsᵾkatᵾ
away a wife, lead nᵾpetsᵾʔitᵾ
away, melt parᵾhwimiʔarᵾ
away, move nomiʔarᵾ, norawᵾʔaitᵾ
away (as a group), move sᵾmᵾ
  nomiʔarᵾ
away, push mahbotsetᵾ
away, put namabimarᵾ, tahtᵾkarᵾ,
  tᵾkarᵾ
away for safekeeping, put
  toʔnikarᵾ K

away, run nuhkitᵾ
away afraid, run namanuhkitᵾ
away from something, run
  wᵾanuraitᵾ K
away from somewhere, run pᵾa
  nuhkitᵾ
away one by one, run nunurawᵾtᵾ
away, secret oneself watsᵢ habiitᵾ
away, shoo manᵾkikᵾrᵾ
away, sneak watsi miʔarᵾ
away, store nabinaʔetᵾ
away something live, take
  tahtᵾkitᵾ
away, throw petihtarᵾ, wihtaitᵾ
away, to haul noorᵾ
away from, turn wᵾhbuikatᵾ W
away, walk natsihtóo miʔarᵾ
away, wipe tahtsukitᵾ
a while, once in susᵾʔana
awl wiiyᵾ
axe tᵾᵾhkaʔaʔ
**axe, battle (with flintstone
  handle)** wᵾpitapuʔni
axe, chisel or split with an
  tohtsiyuʔitᵾ
axe, double-bladed
  naʔbutikᵾmakatᵾ tᵾᵾhkaʔaaʔ

B b

baby ohnaʔaʔ
baby, wean a pitsi makatᵾ
baby bed ohnaʔa norᵾhnaaʔ
baby buggy naʔtsiʔaikᵾʔ
baby colic sapᵾ wᵾnᵾkatᵾ
baby crib ohnaʔa norᵾhnaaʔ
bachelor wohkaʔniʔ
back kwahi, pitᵾsᵾ
back, ache in lower piwoʔsa
  wᵾnarᵾ
back, carried on manookatᵾ

back, carry on nʉnoorʉ
back, carry on the kwahi nooru
back, come koʔitʉ
back, go pitsa miʔarʉ
back and forth, go (or from side to side) piʔnuʔa miʔarʉ
back, hunch- noʔwosarʉ
back on heels, kneel down sitting tanatookarʉtʉ
back, lie on paʔraihabiitʉ
back, lower piwoʔsa̲
back, on paʔarai
back, pull tsasinʉkaarʉ
back in place, put something tohtʉkiʔarʉ
-back, Robe-on-his Kwahira
back against something, scratch rear or pisuʔnetʉ
back to ease pain, stand on someone's tahparaʔitʉ
back and forth, swing natsakwenitʉ
back, tie a child to wʉpi̲toorʉ
-back, Yellow Ohapi̲tʉ kwahi
back of the hand makwe
back part (of ear cartilage) K naki̲ kwiita̲
back up hupi̲miʔarʉ, pimimiʔarʉ, pitsa ʉkwakatu kimarʉ
backache, have a piwoʔsa wʉnarʉ
backache, have a (in lower back) piwoʔsa wʉnʉkatʉ
backbone kwahinupʉ, kwahiporopʉ
backpack kwahi noorʉ
backward, step pimimiʔarʉ
backward, walk pimimiʔarʉ
backwards, come pitsa ʉkwakatu kimarʉ
backwards, go hupi̲miʔarʉ, piʔnuʔa miʔarʉ
bad aitʉ, tʉtsʉ-
bad odor, have kwanarʉ

bad tidings, upset people by niʔyʉsʉkaitʉ
badly nʉnʉmʉni̲ tʉhtsʉ
badly, piled pia utsaatʉ
bag narʉso̲, wosa̲
bag, nose puku rʉhka?
bag, war-bonnet tuna wosa
bag game tʉkʉh pehkarʉ
bagged game wasʉpʉ
bake tohtíaʔarʉ
bake biscuits nohkorʉ
bakery tohtía narʉmʉʉ?
baking biscuits, oven for nohko aawo̲
baking powder namahya?
Bald Kehaitsipaapi̲
bald head pahtsi kuʔe
bald headed pahtsi bapikatʉ K
bale something wʉhtamarʉ
baling wire soni nʉʉhtama? K, soni wʉhtʉma?
ball naʔmahpeʔeʔ, naʔsʉhpee?
ball, puff- mupitsʉha pisahpi̲ W
ball, roll into a tsahtopoʔnarʉ
ball, wind into a wʉhtopoʔnitʉ
ball bat tʉhpoʔtse?
ball game, Native-American naʔsʉhpeʔetʉ
ball-like toponi-
balloon mubohtohkipʉ
ban nihtoʔitʉ
banana aakaa?
band nʉʉpi̲tua?
band, Comanche Kwarʉ, Nokoni, Tʉtsanoo yehkʉ
band, Comanche (of Walters area) Wiaʔnʉʉ
band, rubber tuʔre?
Band, Water Horse Tasúra
bandana tsokwʉkʉʉna? W, wʉhtsohkʉna?
bank, creek tʉpána?

bank (financial) puhihwi kahni
bank, river ekatotsa̱
bank (of stream) ekatotsa̱
bank draft puhihwi tʉboopʉ
bank up wʉhtʉmarʉ
banker puhihwi paraiboo?
baptize pa?wʉtiarʉ
baptize by sprinkling ku?e naba
  wʉhtia
baptize someone nʉbawʉhtiarʉ
baptized mabáaku?neetʉ̱
baptized one Nabakwʉhtiapʉ
baptizer nʉbawʉhtiawapi̱, pawʉhtia
  wapi̱, tʉbawʉhtia wapi̱
barbecue kuhtu tʉkʉmanirʉ K,
  ku?inarʉ
barbecue grate ku?inawaata̱
barbed wire puhihwi tʉʉhtʉma?
barbed wire fence, put up a
  puhihwi tʉʉhtʉmarʉ
bare, thread- pupʉkatʉ
barely himataaka, pʉhimataka
bargain tohpunitʉ
bark po?a?, wo?wo?kitʉ
bark, tree huupi po?a?, huupita
  po?a
Barking-buttocks Witawoo?ooki
barley tohtía sonipʉha taka?
barrel huu aawo, wobi aawo̱
barrel cactus wokwéesi
barren oak tuhuupi
barrette papi̱ tsihtʉpʉ̱ka?
base tʉkwita
baseball nʉ?ʉhpee?
bashful nasu?aitʉ̱
basket sʉhʉ aawo
bat hʉnʉbi pokaa?
bat, ball- tʉhpo?tse?
bath, steam nakuhkwaraki? K
bath, take a steam kuhkwarʉkitʉ
bath, sweat nakuhkwaraki? K,
  nasukoo?i?

bathe pahabitʉ
bathe, steam nakuhkwarakitʉ,
  nasukoo?itʉ
bathed kuhkwarʉkitʉ
bathroom naro?ikahni K, pahabi̱
  kahni W
bathtub pahabi̱ aawo̱
batter kasamawʉrʉ
batter (allowed to become set)
  takoosahpʉ? W
battered kasamawʉrʉ
battered tree huupi kasamawʉ
battle axe with flintstone handle
  wʉpitapu?ni
battle with weapons nabitukʉrʉ
bay horse ekakʉma?, ohaeka? K,
  tupi̱si kʉma?
bay horse W ohaekapi̱tʉ
Bay-mare Ohapia
be ahead of munaiki̱yutʉ W
be amazed suwʉ?kai
be born pahitʉ, yumarʉ
be carried away by wind mabo?ayarʉ
be cold kwihnerʉ
be feverish kuhtsʉnitʉ̱
be good yʉyʉkarʉ
be hard and brittle koobetʉ̱
be ill tʉ?oibʉkʉrʉ, uhúntʉ̱kʉ̱
be in deep water kenawʉnʉrʉ
be in labor tuakatʉ
be made dizzy makwi?numaitʉ
be married kuumabaitʉ
be missing kehewa?itʉ
be night tukani̱tʉ
be sleepy-eyed puibʉʉtʉ̱
be soft yʉ?yʉkarʉ
be stiff tsihturuarʉ K
be straight kewesi̱ketʉ̱
be tempted masuyakerʉ
be well-behaved yunʉmitʉ
bead tsomo-
bead necklace tsomo korohko

bead something topᵾsarᵾ, tᵾropᵾsarᵾ

beaded naropᵾsarᵾ

beadwork tᵾropᵾsapᵾ?

bean pihúraa

bean, mescal ekapo?

bear wasápe̲

-bear, Sitting Kohitᵾ se?tanᵾkᵾ

-bear, Son-of-bull Tᵾmᵾbo

-bear, Yellow Ohawasápe

bear fruit pokopi tuarᵾ

bear offspring turuarᵾ

bear pain, to wᵾmetᵾ

bear trap wasápe pᵾmata kwᵾhᵾrᵾ?

beard motso̲

beard, pull own namutsono?itᵾ

beard, pull someone's mutsonoo?itᵾ

bearded white man motso taiboo?

beargrass mumutsi?

beat wᵾhpa?itᵾ, wᵾtᵾkwarᵾ

beat on totᵾbihkurᵾ, wᵾkwᵾbihkurᵾ

beat on someone wᵾhtᵾkwarᵾ

beat on someone (with watery object) pawᵾhpa?itᵾ

beat up wᵾapa?arᵾ

beaver ha?nii, pa?wᵾhtᵾma?

Beaver Creek Waahkusi okwe?

becalm wᵾhtsamᵾhkitᵾ

because suniyutᵾ

become naharᵾ

become angry at a person tuhubᵾkᵾkatᵾ

become calm nᵾemaitᵾ

become comatose sua watsikatᵾ

become insane sua watsitᵾ

become lazy nᵾᵾ?maitᵾ

become Spring tahma ro?itᵾ

bed kahpe, norᵾnapᵾ

bed, baby ohna?a norᵾhnaa?

bed, camp- wᵾhtaráa?

bed, make a nohrᵾnaarᵾ, norᵾnaarᵾ

bed, No- Kahpewai

bed, overflow the creek paru?itᵾ

bed, sheet for saabara

bedbug kahni busi̲?a

bedroom habikᵾni

bedsheet saabara, tosa kwana?hᵾ W

bedspring nasaa?wᵾ? W, nohrᵾna saawᵾ

bedstead nohrᵾna?

bee, bumble- ohahpiyaa?

bee, honey- wobi pihnaa ᵾnᵾᵾ?

Been-to-see-his-son Pᵾ tua wᵾni kwai

beer saah totsi baa

beetlike tuber to?roponii?

before hunakᵾ

before dawn ohahᵾkwᵾnikatᵾ, tosa hᵾwᵾnikatᵾma?

befriend tᵾsutaikatᵾ

beg marᵾᵾ?nitᵾ

beginning nabihtawᵾna

behaved, be well- yunᵾmitᵾ

behaved, well yᵾyᵾkarᵾ

behead toyo tsihka?arᵾ, toyo wᵾhka?arᵾ

behind pinakwᵾ, ᵾpinakwᵾ

behind, from pinai

behind, leave someone nobᵾahraitᵾ

behind oneself, look nabitᵾbunitᵾ

behind, pull something pitsákarᵾ

beige koropitᵾ

beige K otᵾ-, otᵾpitᵾ

belch akwarᵾtᵾ, akwarᵾ?

belief tokwᵾsuakᵾna

believe in someone tokᵾsuakᵾtᵾ

believe (something or someone) tokwᵾsuakᵾtᵾ

believe (pretend), make- nohitekwarᵾ

believer tᵾrokwᵾsuakᵾtᵾ

bell kawohwi̲?

bellows tꭎbuuhki?

belonging to hipꭎ

belongings (of any type) oo?rꭎ W

belongings, personal namahku

beloved kamakꭎna̱ W

belt kohinehki?, nehki̱ W,
   nꭎ?ꭎnehki̱ K

belt buckle nehki wꭎhtꭎpꭎka?,
   nꭎ?ꭎnehki?a nanꭎꭎtꭎpi̱ka? W

belted nꭎ?ꭎnehki̱katꭎ?

bench, wooden huunakarꭎ?, wobi
   nakarꭎ?

bend tsa?onutsarꭎ

bend down tumuurꭎ

bend (in river) paa mutsaa?

bend over mupi̱habirꭎ,
   muyꭎꭎ?wꭎrꭎ, nuhtsairꭎ

bent tsa?onutsai

bent down tumuukatꭎ

bent over mupi̱habiitꭎ, nuhtsapꭎ

berate someone ni?woso?arꭎ

berate someone falsely
   ni?he?bunitꭎ

berries pokopi̱

berries, picked pomapꭎ

berry, chippa- tubupokoo

berry, hack- kꭎrahúu? K, soho
   bokopi̱

berry, huckle- huwabo?kóo?

berry, soap- otꭎ mitsonaa?

berry, southern hack- mitsonaa?

berserk poosubꭎkꭎkaitꭎ

beseech nanimaa?ꭎbꭎ?ikꭎtꭎ

beside kꭎma?, kꭎma?kꭎ

bet on something narꭎbahkarꭎ

betray tsaka?uhrꭎ

betray someone kaanatsaka?uhturꭎ,
   natsaka?uhtu?etꭎ

betrayer natsaka?uhtu?etꭎ?

betrays, one who
   kaanatsaka?uhtupꭎ

between, go- nitꭎsu?nai wapi̱

between, two things, stuck tsꭎki̱katꭎ

beverage, drink alcoholic hibikꭎtꭎ

bewitch someone puha wꭎhtitꭎ

bias tape tꭎkꭎma?ai

Bible Puha rꭎboopꭎ

bicycle naraaikꭎ?, ta?aikꭎtꭎ

big pia

big doctoring piana huwai?

big toe tahtokoo?

Big-fall-by-tripping Pia rꭎtsima

Big-green-frog Pasawío

Big-looking-glass Piana buni?

Big-water Pia baa

Big-whip Pia nꭎ?ꭎpai?i

bill collector tꭎniwaitꭎ?

billy club tꭎhkupa?

bird huutsúu

bird, blue- ebihuutsuu?

bird, humming- wꭎ?kꭎ?buu?

bird, mocking- soo yake? W,
   tꭎnimanahke huutsu? K

bird, red- eka̱huutsu?

bird of its feathers, pick a no?itꭎ

bird (small gray) kusisai?

bird clean, pluck a pꭎhꭎ no?itꭎ

bird clean of feathers, pluck a
   pahtsi no?itꭎ

bird, small gray kusisai?

bird nest huutsú?a kàhni̱, huutsú?a
   pisoo?ni̱

birdcall, make a niyakekꭎtꭎ

birdhouse huutsú?a kàhni̱

birth, give tuakatꭎ

biscuit nohkopꭎ, nꭎmꭎ nohkopꭎ

biscuits, oven for baking nohko
   aawo̱

bit, auger tꭎrohtꭎbꭎ?i?

bit, bridle namutsora?, tꭎꭎyꭎ
   mutsora?

bit, little hꭎitsi

bit (used for boring holes)
   tꭎrohtꭎbꭎ?i?

bite kuhtsiaru, kunabenitu

bite into (and not turn loose)
kuhkarukatu

bite off kuhka?aru

bite off kuhpomi?itu K

bite to death kuhkobaru

bite together kuhkaru?itu,
kutsubakitu

biting fly te?animui

bitter moha-, mohakamaru

black tu-, tuhupi

black beetle tuunuu?

black bird (with white wings) tosa
kwiisu?

black cradle tuhkuni

black haw tubokóo, wokwekatu
huupi

Black Houses Tusa Kahni

black person tuhtaiboo? W

black walnut tuhmubitai

black willow ohasuhuubi

Black-head Tu?paapi

Black-otter Paa tsokotubutu

blackberry panatsayaa?

blackberry bush tuhbanatsaya

blackbird tuwikaa?

blackjack oak tuhuupi

blacksmith's blower tubuuhki?

blacktopped, paved a road
tuusanahpitu

blame manímuaru

bland otu kamaitu

blanket esiwana?uhu, uhu

blanket, buffalo ta?siwoo
wana?uhu W

blanket, cotton wana hu K

blanket, horse nahotsa?ma?

blanket, Mexican kusikwi?ii?

blanket, saddle kwahituki?,
nahotsa?ma?

blaspheme nani?emuahpu aitu

bleed puuokwetu

bless someone sutaaitu

blessed sutaitu

blind pui hwai, tubitabu?itu

blind, window nanabuni tsahpara?

blink wuhtsobokitu

blister ekawukwiapu

bloat pohtokitu

bloated pohtohkikatu

blond pabopitu

blood puu-, puuhpi

bloodhound turayaa sarii

bloom mubutsaakatu, totsiyaitu

blooming totsiyakatu

blossom out totsiyaitu

blow nuetu

blow away po?ayaahkwaru,
po?ayaakutu

blow (breath) puuhkitu

blow (dust) huhkukwunuru,
huukukwumuru, huukunatsiru,
huukunuetu

blow (hard) kuhtáanuetu

blow heat toward one kusuwetu

blow out (a tire) turaputsaru W

blow (the nose) mubisitu,
tsamukusitu

blower, blacksmith's tubuuhki?

Blow-it-away Poo?aiku

blowing, cease nuemaitu

Blowing-wind Nuetutsi

blown out puuhkikatu, puhtsapu

blown-away object po?oya?

blue ebi-, eebi

blue, dark tu?ebipitu K

blue, light ebipitu, kusipi W,
kusiebipitu K

blue-gray ebipitu

bluebird ebihuutsuu?

bluejay ebihuutsuu?

bluestem, little ekasonipu

board woobi

board, cradle- waakohno

board, ironing pᵾpaʔakura
tᵾrahkwᵾʔneʔenạ
board someone tᵾkiihkarᵾ
boast naníhpanaʔaitᵾ
boat pawobi puukụ W
bob a tail piʔtoʔarᵾ
bob up kunakᵾarᵾ K, kuroʔitᵾ W,
mᵾroʔitᵾ
bobby pin papị tsihtᵾpᵾka?
bobcat tᵾe tᵾmakupa?
bobtailed piʔto
bodily jerk yᵾʔyᵾturᵾ
body tuhkụ
body, break at joint of
narominaitᵾ, tominarᵾ
body, dead tᵾyaipᵾ
body, dry off pasarᵾ
body, powder the homopisarᵾ
body, rub medicine on mabararᵾ
body, sprain a joint of the
wᵾkwᵾsarᵾ
body, stretch arms or narurerᵾ
body (to draw out pain), suck on
musoopitᵾ
body on the ground, throw
kwanuʔitᵾ K
body, twist the kwitsunairᵾ
body louse saabe busia
body pain nᵾhtsikwarᵾ
bogged down yubutsᵾhkatᵾ
boil kuhnuʔitᵾ W, noʔyaikᵾtᵾ, saatᵾ
boil, cause to saaʔarᵾ
boil food karᵾkᵾrᵾ
boiled kuhnuʔitᵾ W
boiled food nasaapᵾ
boiled meat saapᵾ
bois d'arc tree ohahuupi
bois d'arc wood etᵾhuupi
**bois d'arc wood for archery
bows** eetᵾ
boll, cotton wanama sᵾapᵾha
pokopị W

bolt, un- wᵾhkweʔyarᵾ
bolt down wᵾʔnikarᵾ
bone tsuhni
Bone Tsuhni
bone, break nawᵾhkobaitᵾ,
nᵾᵾminaitᵾ
bone, break a kᵾminarᵾ, nasutamᵾ
wᵾmịnaitᵾ K
bone, cheek- soʔo tsuhnị, soʔọ
bone, collar huukụ, sihkupᵾ W
bone, shin or shin kutsiʔomo
bone, shin- tuhhu
bone, shoulder tsoohpa tsuuni W
bone, tail piwoʔsạ
bone marrow tuhhu rᵾhkapᵾ
bone marrow, congealed
tᵾᵾhtsohpe?
bone marrow, eat tuhhu rᵾhkarᵾ
bones, Comanche nᵾmᵾ tsuhni
bones, leg tᵾranạ
bones, marrow tᵾranạ
bones out of joint, pull tsahtokoʔarᵾ
bonnet, war pia tsoʔnika?
-bonnet bag, war tuna wosa
book, pocket- puhihwi narᵾsọ W,
puhihwi wosa K
book, story- nanáarᵾmuʔị tᵾboopᵾ,
narᵾmuʔi tᵾboopᵾ
boomer, mountain ebimuutaroo?,
ebipabokoʔai? P
boots, cowboy kuhtsu taibo napᵾ,
narakwᵾsakatᵾ napᵾ
boots, rubber tuuʔre napᵾ
bore nihtunetsᵾkatᵾe?
born tᵾbora
born, be pahitᵾ, yumarᵾ
born, Comanche- nᵾmᵾ ruaitᵾ
both sube?
bottle otᵾ aawọ, paboko aawo
bottom kwiita, tᵾkwita
bottom in water, sink to the
paʔikarᵾ

-bought food, store tʉkʉ tʉmʉʉpʉ
bounce wohtsawʉkitʉ
bouncy object, pull a tsahpoʔtsarʉ
bow (for shooting arrows) eetʉ
box koonǫ, wosạ
box, ice- tahka aawo
boy tuinʉhpʉʔ W
Boy Piʔopʉ parʉba tʉyo
boy, water tuuʔetʉ
boy friend tʉʉʔurapʉ W, K
boys pihiʔa W
brace marʉroonitʉ
brace (with something)
   wʉhtʉroonitʉ
braced marʉrooniitʉ K,
   tohtʉrooniitʉ W
bracelet maʔwitsohkǫ
bracing stick wana tsihparaaʔ
brag (on oneself) naníhpanaʔaitʉ
brag (on someone) nihpanaʔaitʉ
braid aawʉsipʉ, aawʉsitʉ, kwisikatʉ
   K, tʉkwʉsiitʉ
braided kwʉsipʉ W
brain kupịsi
brains, rub with kupịsiʔarʉ
branch mooka
branch, creek nabatai K
branch of a creek atahunubi
branch out mookʉsʉaitʉ
brand kohpoorʉ, nakohpoopʉ K,
   tʉkohpoopʉ
branding iron tʉkohpooʔ
brave tekwʉniwapị
brave, Indian tekwʉniwapị,
   tuibihtsiʔ, tʉetekwʉni wapị
brave young man tʉetekwʉni wapị
bread tohtíaʔ
bread, corn haninookopʉ
bread, fried yuhu nohkopʉ
bread, fry- yuhu nohkopʉ
bread, Indian tʉranʉ
bread, loaf of paanʉ

bread, make tohtíaʔarʉ
bread, sweet pihná nohkopʉ
bread, toast wesikʉrʉ
breadroot tʉranʉ
breadroot, Indian ekahkoni
breads, sweet toyo tahkaʔmiitsạ
break tahpomiʔitʉ, tsahpomiʔitʉ
break (a bone) kʉminarʉ, nasutamʉ
   wʉmịnaitʉ K
break (a horse) masuyuʔikarʉ K
break (a taboo) mahyarʉ
break (at joint of body)
   narominaitʉ, tominarʉ
break (at joint of foot)
   naraminaitʉ W
break (at the joint) taminaitʉ
break bone nawʉhkobaitʉ,
   nʉʉminaitʉ
break (by dropping) wʉtʉbarʉ
break, Easy-to- Tsaa tsopaʔ
break hand or lower arm, sprain
   or namaminaitʉ
break, wind- wʉhturuʔaipʉ
break in pieces, (cause to)
   tahtabaʔitʉ
break in pieces tahbaitʉ,
   tahporoorʉ
break into pieces tsanutsarʉ,
   wʉnutsarʉ
break into small pieces
   wʉhhomonutsaʔarʉ
break loose pihkaʔarʉ
break off tahkobarʉ, tsahkaʔarʉ,
   tsahkobarʉ
break off a piece tsanutsarʉ
break open mapʉtsarʉ, tapʉtsaitʉ
break open (with the teeth)
   kʉpʉtsarʉ
break or reach something
   wʉminarʉ
break or sever (with the teeth)
   kʉhkobarʉ

break something kᵾminarᵾ, tahparᵾ, tatᵾbarᵾ

break something down pihkobarᵾ

break something up tohkobi?itᵾ, tsahkokarᵾ

break up kohparᵾ, manutsa?arᵾ W, wᵾhkobarᵾ

break up (under own volition) na?rᵾbomitᵾ

break up (with the teeth) kᵾnutsarᵾ

breakfast, eat taarᵾhkarᵾ

breakfast for someone, prepare taamahkarᵾ

breaking it to pieces, sit on something pinutsarᵾ

Breaks Something Tsihkoba

breast, woman's pitsii?

breath sua, suahkenạ

breath odor sua kwanạ

breath, out of sua?su?maitᵾ

breathe suahketᵾ

breathe (deeply in sleep) ᵾsuaketᵾ

breathe (deeply while awake) nasuawᵾhkitᵾ K

breathe heavily hehékịtᵾ, sua?sua?miarᵾ

breathe through nose muhibitᵾ

breathe, unable to sua?su?maitᵾ

breathless sua?su?makatᵾ

breeze nᵾetᵾ

brew coffee huba aikᵾtᵾ

Briar Creek Tamutᵾso?ị hunu?bị

briar, sensitive tsapᵾsikᵾ

brick, red ekatᵾᵾpị

brick house, stone or tᵾpi kᵾni

bride narᵾahwᵾkᵾ, nᵾrᵾa?wekᵾ?

bridge posaaki

bridle arai, tᵾpe tsa?nika?

bridle a horse tᵾpe tsa?nikarᵾ

bridle bit namutsora?, tᵾᵾyᵾ mutsora? K

bridle reins narᵾmuhkᵾ

bright muhatsi, pahparatsihkweetᵾ W, tsaa marabetoikatᵾ K

bright red mohatsᵾkuekapịtᵾ

brim, filled to the ibu?itᵾ

bring back firewood kono honiitᵾ

bring in firewood konóorᵾ

bring out tsahto?irᵾ

bring something back (to someone) yaakᵾrᵾ

bristle sᵾroonitᵾ

broke financially tᵾtsu?mapᵾ

broken nuhtsapᵾ, pᵾhtsapᵾ

broken object kohpapᵾ, tahpapᵾ

broken up makoobikatᵾ, na?rᵾbomitᵾ

brooch natsihtᵾpᵾka?, nᵾna karᵾkᵾ? K

broom tᵾᵾnua?

broom corn tᵾᵾnua?

broom grass tᵾᵾnua

broomweed sanaweha

brother samohpᵾ?

brother, elder pabi?

brother, younger tami?

brother-in-law pᵾhᵾ re?tsị

brother-in-law, man's tetsị

brothers, dear little tamihtsi?benihtsi?

brother's child, woman's paha?

brown koropịtᵾ, otᵾ-, otᵾpịtᵾ W

brown, cook something otᵾ kwasᵾkᵾrᵾ

brown, looks- kurupitsoni

brown food wesikᵾrᵾ

brown sugar otᵾ pihnàa? W

brown the food otᵾ kwasᵾkᵾrᵾ

Brown-robe Otᵾ kwasu

brown-skinned otᵾhtᵾ mapo?akatᵾ

browned wesikatᵾ

bruise nᵾᵾkịtse?

bruise wᵾhpekwitᵾ

brush arbor huuki?aitu, puhi huuki, soni huuki, tahuuki?aiku

brush arbor, poles for constructing huukina huupi

brush, clothes oo?ru tutsihtu?ye? W

brush, hair- natsihtu?ye?

brush, horn aanatsihtuye?

brush, horse tuhuya natsihtu?ye?

brush, tooth- tamamatsuma?

brush, wire puhihwi natsihtu?ye?

brush off kwusiberu W, wusiberu K

brush something off (of oneself) nuuhta?neeru

bubble mubohtohkipu

bubble in water pamukwaru?rukitu

bubbles, make pamukwaru?rukitu

buck arukáa kuhma, aruka? nukuhma

buck off ku?e wunuru

bucket wihtua?, wobi wuhpai K

bucket, milk pitsipu wihtua

bucket (with spout) tupe wihtua?

buckle nanuuhtupuka?, nuna wuhtupuka?, wuhtupuka?

buckle, harness nuuhtupika?

buckle (or tighten something) tsanukuru

buckle (that is buckled) natsihpusa?

buckskin pikapu

buckskin clothing pika namusoopu

buckskin horse na?nia

buckskin jacket, man's pika kwasu?

bud mubora?itu

bud (of a plant or tree) murora?ipu W

bud, red- ekamurora?i huupi

buckle, belt- nehki wuhtupuka?, nu?unehki?a nanuutupika? W

buffalo numu kuhtsu?, ta?si?woo?

Buffalo Tatsiwóo

-buffalo, Red Eka kura

buffalo blanket ta?siwoo wana?uhu W

buffalo calf ekakúura?

Buffalo Eaters Kuhtsu tuhka

buffalo horn case na?aa

buffalo meat numu kutsu tuhkapu, ta?siwoo ruhkapu W

Buffalo-hump Kuhtsuna kwahipu

buffalo, One-who-rides- Kuhtsunu kwahipu

bug unú?

bug, doodle- kwita maropona

bug (of any kind), house kahni busi?a

bug, june tuunuu?

bug, lightning kuna na?mahpee?

bug, red- puikuso

bug, sow- kwita maropona

buggy pikwusii?, wobi puuku

buggy, baby na?tsi?aiku?

buggy, hitch up horses and nomohkaru

buggy, hook up doubletrees on nomohkaru

buggy, one-horse sumasu nooi K

buggy, single tue waikina

buggy, two-seated natsa?ani?

bugle woinu

build a fire kohtóoru

build a house kahni?aitu

build a nest pisona?aitu

builder, fire- kohtoo wapi

building tuboo kahni

bull pimoroo?a kuhma

-bull-bear, Son-of Tumubo

bull elk parua kuhma

Bull-bear Parua kuhma

Bull-elk Paruwa kuma

bullet nabaaka

bullfrog ebimuura ya?ke?

bullroarer wekubupu

bumblebee ohahpiyaa?
bumpy popʉtsanawʉtʉ
bunch up tsaʔookitʉ, tsaʔoorʉ
bunched up naraʔokatʉ
bundle or round knot, tie in round
    wʉhtopʉʔnoorʉ
bundle together wʉhtamarʉ
bureau ooʔrʉ taniʔi?
burial ceremony nʉpʉkarʉʉ?
burial mound nabʉkapʉ W
buried person or thing
    namʉsokoopʉ
burn kutsitonarʉ, weʔharʉ
burn down kuhtsuʔmarʉ
burn oneself nahweakʉtʉ W,
    nakʉwiyakʉrʉ K
burn oneself to death kuhtʉyarʉ
burn red ekawehaarʉ
burn something up kuhtsahwirʉ,
    wesikʉrʉ
burn to death accidentally
    kuhkuparʉ
burned wesi-
Burned Meat Ihtataʔo
burned out tree trunk kuwoʔnepʉ
burns, ouch! It ʉrʉʉ
burnt wesikatʉ
burp akwarʉtʉ, akwarʉ?
burr kuhtsu pokàa?
burr, grass soni wokweebi
burrow kahnitaikʉ
burrowing owl pohkóo?
burst pohtoʔitʉ, pʉhtsapʉ, pʉhtsarʉ,
    tsapʉtsarʉ
burst by pulling tsahpohtoorʉ
burst from overheating kupʉtsarʉ
burst, make tohpʉtsaʔitʉ
burst open mapʉtsarʉ, puhkarʉ
burst with the mouth kʉhpohtorʉ
bury pasokoʔarʉ, pʉka, tʉkarʉ
bury someone nʉpʉkarʉ
bus nʉmi nooʔetʉ

bush puhitopika
bush W puhi taitʉ
bush, blackberry tuhbanatsaya
bush, button- pesotái
bush clover puhi tubi
bush, plum wiʔnʉʉpi
bush, skunk- tatsipʉ
busy nanʉsoʔiitʉ W
butcher tʉhaniitu, tʉkwʉsʉrʉ
butcher an animal tʉbehkarʉ
butt mukwʉrʉ W
butter yuhu bitsipʉ
butter, Comanche tʉhtsohpeʔaipʉ
butter, Indian tʉʉtsohpepʉ
butter, make Comanche
    tʉhtsohpeʔarʉ
buttermilk nʉtsʉʔwʉpa pitsipʉ K,
    yuhibitsipʉ K
buttocks kwiita
button nanʉʉhtʉpʉka?,
    nʉʉhtʉpika?, wʉhtʉpʉka?
button, peyote plant or wokwe
button snakeroot atabitsʉnoi
button up wʉhtʉpʉkarʉ
buttonbush pesotái
buy tʉmʉʉrʉ
buy an article of clothing kwasuʔʉ
    tʉmʉʉrʉ
buy clothing oyorʉ tʉmarʉ
buy (for oneself) mahípʉrʉmʉrʉ
buy or otherwise receive groceries
    narʉhkaʔruarʉ
buy something marúmʉrʉ
buzzard, redheaded ekabapi
buzzing sound puuyaketʉ
by describing something, tempt
    nisuyakeetʉ
by force, take someone sutena betʉ
by going on foot, meet someone
    tamunaikʉmiʔarʉ
by hand, shell something
    tsahkítoʔarʉ

by pounding, soften tohparaarʉ W,
tsohkwe K
**by trampling on it, soften
something** tahpararʉ
-by-two, two waʔwaʔ
by someone, spilled taʔokitʉ
by a foot, torn tasiʔkwaitʉ
by speaking to someone, waken
nihtʉbuniorʉ
by cheating, win in a contest
kaakwakurʉ

C c

cabbage kabitsi̲
cache kuupʉ, kuurʉ
Cache, Okla Pisi narʉmʉʉ?
cactus ekamitsáa?, husi̲,
nayʉ́wokwe
cactus, prickly pear wokwéesi
Caddo people Tukanai
cake pihná nohkopʉ
calendar mʉarʉboopʉ
calf pimorooʔa tua?
calf, buffalo ekakúura?
calf (of leg) taʔwiitsa̲
calico horse pitsa naboo? K
call down nihmakwihtserʉ
call (to someone) nimaikatʉ
call together many people
sʉʉmaʔokarʉ
called one nimaihkana?
calm kesósoorʉ, tokoboʔniitʉ K,
wʉhtsamʉʉhkikatʉ, yunaharʉ
calm, become nʉemaitʉ
calm down tʉsuʔnarʉ, wʉyupaʔnitʉ
calm spirit tsʉmʉki̲katʉ
camel mupitsʉha tʉnowapi̲ W,
narʉnookatʉ ʉnʉʉ, tʉnookatʉ?,
tʉʉnoo ʉnʉʉ? K, ʉnʉʔa pʉnʉsʉ
narʉnooʔkatʉ W

camera kobe nabo? K, nʉmi booʔetʉ
W, pʉhtuku nʉmʉ, tʉbooʔetʉ W
camp (apart from the main group)
nokaʔitʉ
camp bed wʉhtaráa?
can narohtʉma?
can, coon soo tʉhimarʉ?
can, kick-the- soo tʉhimarʉ? **can,
milk** pitsipʉ wihtua
can opener kʉmapʉ, tʉrohtʉwa?
Canadian River Waahunuʔbi
cancer narʉʔʉyʉ ʉʉʔa?
cancerous moonʉʔʉakatʉ
candle tosahtuka? W, tosa yuhu
rukai? K
candy sucker mubi̲ tsooʔni?,
mukwite?
cane natsihtóo? K
cane, sugar huupi̲hnàa, soni
bihnáa?
cane, walk with natsihtóo noorʉ
cane, walking tʉʔehkooi? W
canned food tʉrohtʉmapʉ
canned goods narohtʉma?
cannon yanawoʔi?
canoe pawobi puukʉ W, sahki̲
canoe paddle panatsitoo?
cantaloupe taibo bihnaa?
canvas tent nʉʉsoo?
cap tʉmuihpaa? W
cap, fur pʉhʉ rʉmuihpaa?
cape, mourning kuʔnika?
cape, nurse kuʔhiboo?
captive kwʉhʉpʉ
capture kwʉhʉrʉ
**captured by the Comanches,
Mexicans** Esitoyanʉʉ
car, hand- kʉʔwonʉhʉbai
car or team, drive a (by hand)
tsahhanitʉ
car, railroad kunawaikinʉ,
kunawobipuukʉ

car, street- ohawaikịnạ, waikina

carcass, render an animal tʉhtsohpeʔarʉ

card deck, king in playing- ohahkuyaaʔ

card game, full house in manekihtʉʔ

cardinal ekạhuutsuʔ

cards, play wana rohpetirʉ

cards, playing wana atsiʔ

care for mabitsiarʉ, mananaaʔwaihkarʉ

care for (child) tʉrʉetʉsuarʉ

care for (needs of someone) tʉkiihkarʉ

care for (oneself) namabitsiapʉ

carefree supewaitʉ

carefully, listen tʉbitsịnakʉkʉrʉ K

carefully for, search puhwaaitʉ

carefully, set down tsakwʉnarʉ

carelessly, hang up wʉhtsanitʉ

carpenter's plane tʉsibeʔ

carpet pʉhʉ rasoonạ, tasoni, tasoonạ

carriage tuwaikịna

carried on back manookatʉ

carrier made of teepee poles, travel tʉʔnooʔ

carrot, domestic ohahpokopi K, ohahtʉhkapʉ

carry manoorʉ, toyaarʉkitʉ W

carry a container by the handle tsahimarʉ, tsayarʉ

carry a stick huuyaarʉ

carry (across) noomanitʉ, tsamanirʉ

carry (and put down) tohtaniʔitʉ

carry away nookwarʉ

carry (by the handle) natsayaarʉ

carry food tʉkʉ noorʉ

carry in himaʔikarʉ

carry in arms toyarʉ

carry in the arms kwabarʉ

carry in the claws taʔyaamiʔarʉ

carry load tʉnoorʉ

carry on back nʉnoorʉ

carry on the back kwahi noorʉ

carry on the head kuyaarʉ

carry someone behind on horseback piyarʉ

carry something tsiʔyarʉ, yuhnunimiʔarʉ

carry something on a stick tsihimarʉ

carry something on the head tsoʔyaarʉ

Carrying-her-sunshade Hʉkiyani

case, buffalo horn naʔaa

case, rawhide wardrobe natʉsakʉna

cash a check puhihwi yaarʉ

casino pepịkurʉ

casket tʉyaipʉ kohno

cat waʔooʔ

cat, wild- matʉsohpeʔ

cat's tail pisibuniʔ

catalpa pihúura huupi

catch kwʉhʉrʉ, tahhimaʔerʉ

catch something with the mouth kʉhtsakarʉ

catch up with tahtsaitʉ, wʉhpitʉ

catfish, fullgrown tuumoʔtsoʔ

catfish, young tuumeʔso̱

Catholic person Suabi puharaibo

cattail pisibuniʔ

cattle kuutsuʔ K

cattleman kuhtsu taiboʔ

caught tʉmuʔnikatʉ

cauldron saawihtua

cause to kiss tsamuhraikʉtʉ

cause to be killed nabehkakʉrʉ

cause to blow nose wʉmupʉsitʉ

cause to boil saaʔarʉ

cause to break in pieces tahtabaʔitʉ

cause to cry wʉyaketʉ

cause to hurry tsanamɨsohnitɨ
cause to protrude manakɨarɨ
cause to return tsahkoo?itɨ
cause to ring tsayaketɨ
cause to run wɨmi?arɨ W
cause to sneeze tsamupɨsitɨ W
cause to stop tsanɨnɨrɨ
cause to tangle kwisihkarɨ
cause to turn around and come back tsahkoo?itɨ
cause to turn something around tsakwɨhburɨ
caused to turn around tsakwɨhwitɨ
caused to worry tsamɨsasuakatɨ
cave kahni tai, taina
cease blowing nɨemaitɨ
cease doing pɨarɨ
cedar waa-, waapi
cedar, red ekawaapi
celebrate Christmas waahimarɨ
celery pa?puhi tɨhka?
cellar sekwikɨni, sokokɨni
cellar, cyclone (tornado) ohta kahni W
cellar, storm ohta kahni W, sekwikɨni, sokokɨni
cement mawo?a?aiyu
cemetery nɨpɨkɨ sokoobi
cemetery (or graveyard) nɨpɨkapɨ K, W, nɨpɨkɨ sokoobi
center tɨpɨnaatɨ
centipede soo mo?o?
cents, fifty sɨkweebi?
cereal taarɨhkapɨ
cereal, cooked kohtsáa?
ceremony, burial nɨpɨkarɨɨ?
ceremony, curing puha?aitɨ
ceremony (for someone), hold a curing puha?arɨ
ceremony, smoke during religious puha bahmu?itɨ

certain plant (with edible tuber) tsunisɨ
chain nabusa?
chain, watch tabe narɨmuhkɨ, tabe wenuakɨ?
chair nakarɨ? W
chair, rocking nabi?aaikɨnakarɨ K
chair, wooden wobi nakarɨ?
change clothes namɨsoarɨ
change from one position to another nuhyɨyukitɨ
change position yɨmɨhkitɨ
change something, shape or wɨmɨɨrɨ
channel water patsanuarɨ
chap tsi?wa?itɨ
chaparral cock ebikuyuutsi?
chapped tsi?wapɨ
charcoal kuhtuubi K
charcoal, cook over kuhtu tɨkɨmanirɨ K
chase miakɨrɨ, miakɨtɨ K
chase away tanuraakɨtɨ
chase on horseback tomakwɨyetɨ W
chase someone makwiyetɨ
chased makwiyetɨ
chatter tsaati tamakatɨ W
chatter, harass by nimɨsasuarɨ
chatter the teeth kɨɨhtarakiitɨ
chattering teeth saatitamakatɨ
cheat kaabehkarɨ, kaahaniitɨ, tɨtsikwɨsarɨ
cheat, intend to deceive or kaasuarɨ
cheater kaayɨkwitɨ
cheating, defeat by kaakwakurɨ
cheating, win in a contest by kaakwakurɨ
check puhihwi tɨboopɨ
check, cash a puhihwi yaarɨ
check over one's appearance nabuihwɨnɨtɨ W

cheek soʔo̲
cheekbone soʔo tsuhni̲, soʔo̲
cheese koʔabitsipu̲
cheese, cottage tumanuku?wetu
chest nunapu̲
chest, hairy puhu nunapu̲
chest, side of ahna, ama-
chest hair puhu nunapu̲
chest of drawers ooʔru taniʔi?
chest pain, suffer amawunutu
chestnut-brown horse otu̲ ku̲ma? W
chew kutsu̲kwetu̲, kuyuʔnetu
chew gum sanahkoo kuyuʔnetu
chew up fine W kuhpomiʔitu
Chew-up Kutsukwipu̲
chewing gum kutsu̲we?,
    sanahkoo? W
chewing tobacco yokabahmu̲
Cheyenne Sarii Tuhka?
Chickasaw plum tuahpi̲
chicken kokoráʔa
chicken, prairie pakawkoko?
chicken coop kokoráʔa kahni
chicken egg kokoráʔa nooyo̲,
    kokoráʔa atùapu̲
chicken hawk kokoráʔa
    aràhimaʔetu̲
chicken pox kokoráʔa tasiʔa
chicken wire kokoráʔa aruhtuma?
chief paraiboo?
Chief Comanche-dog-soldiers
    Tuoyobisesu
chief, peace paraibo
chief wife among multiple wives
    paraiboo?
chigger puiku̲so
child tuehpuʔru̲, tue?tu, turue,
    turuehpu children turuehpu
child, care for turuetu̲suaru
child, eldest nahnapu̲
child, keep an orphan as foster
    tahnikatu, tukiihkaru

child, rear a manu̲aru
-child, Sky Tomoʔa tua?
child to back, tie a wupi̲tooru
child, woman's brother's paha?
childbirth, labor in nuhtsikwaru
children turuehpu
children, have turuetuparu
chili pepper tsiira?
chill suutsunitu
chilly susuatu
chimney tukaʔa nakuʔe W
chimney, lamp tukaʔa nakuʔe W
chin paruutsi̲
Chinese Kuʔe kwu̲sih taibo?
chip, poker tuhhuu?
chip in tumaramiitu
chip off nuupearu, siʔaru
chippaberry tubupokoo
chips kunapi̲soʔni
chisel topu̲kaaru, tutsiyuʔi?
chisel or split with an axe
    tohtsiyuʔitu
chisel something tohpakuru
chisel wood tohtsiʔaru K
choke paabitsanitu, pitsanitu
choke out puhi tuyaitu
choke to death pitsanu̲ tuyaitu
choke to death by rope around the
    neck oihtuyaitu
choked makuhpu̲katu̲
choose nabinaru
chop kooʔitu, tuuhkaʔaru
chop a hole wuhkonaru
chop down wuhkaru, wuhpomiʔitu,
    wuno?itu, wuʔaniru
chop firewood kuhkeru
chop up wuhhaniru
chosen nabinaihkatu
Christian Nabakwuhtiapu̲, Puʔekatu
Christmas waahima?
Christmas, celebrate waahimaru
chronic moonu̲ʔuakatu

chronic sore naruʔuyʉ ʉʉʔaʔ
chuck, wood- huunaʔ, paʔarai moʔo
church puha kahni
church root itsa, timʉihʉʔ
church service puha niwʉnʉrʉʉ K
cider, hard saah totsi baa
cider, sweet amawóoʔa pàa
cigarette, marijuana nʉmi makwinumaʔetʉ pahmu
cigarette-wrapper plant tʉmakwatuiʔ
cigarettes, leaf wrappers for puhi tʉmakwatubiʔ
circles, go in mahoinitʉ
circular toponiweki
circulation, restore wʉsuabetaitʉ
circus nohihtaibooʔnʉʉ
circus people nohihtaibooʔnʉʉ
clabber nʉkuwʉmiʔarʉ, nʉkuʔwʉpʉ, pitsi pʉha nʉkuʔwʉpʉ
clabbered milk nʉtsʉʔwʉpa pitsipʉ K, pitsi pʉha nʉkuʔwʉpʉ
clack the teeth kʉhkwitsitʉ
claim it!, I aahe
clam waʔkooʔ W
clap hands tohtarakitʉ
claw tasiito
claw, devil's aakáaʔ
claw at something tsahkwanitʉ
claws, carry in the taʔyaamiʔarʉ
clean tutʉtsaai wahtʉ
clean, scrape until wʉhtsuʔmarʉ
clean the inner part wʉhkwinarʉ
clear kenanawatsitʉ, pabo-, pabokaʔaitʉ
clear a path puʔeʔarʉ
clear, crystal pabokopitʉ
clear stream pahtsi okweʔ
clear throat nanihkanuitʉ
cleaver tʉkʉ wʉhpomiʔ
clerk tʉrʉʔai wapi
click kʉtubarʉ W

cliff tʉbanaaʔ
Cliff Tʉpanai
climb down soho weerʉ
climb on horseback tʉhuya roʔitʉ
climb out kʉarʉ
climb up soho roʔitʉ
cling to tsahpakitʉ
clock tabe-
clock flower tabetotsiyaa
clog up wʉhtʉmarʉ
close marʉmarʉ, tsahtsukitʉ, tsahtʉmarʉ
close everyone's eyes sʉmʉ ʉhtsumitʉ
close someone's hand mahtsukitʉ
close the eyes ʉhtsumarʉ
close the hand mahtsokaitʉ
close the mouth kʉhtsuukarʉ
close up mamárʉmarʉ, tahtʉmarʉ
close up with hand marohtʉmarʉ
closed off tohtʉmapʉ
cloth matsumaʔ, wana-, wanapʉ K
cloth, dust- tʉmatsumaʔ W
cloth, table tʉkʉ soonạ
cloth, velvet pʉesúubeʔ K
cloth, wash- tʉehna matsumaʔ
cloth (edged with ribbon or lace) tʉkʉmaʔaitʉ
cloth (for wiping tʉmatsumaʔ) W
cloth cover sona, soonạ
cloth patch tʉkarʉkʉpʉ
clothes namahku, wanapʉ K
clothes, wear out wʉkwiʔarʉ
clothes brush ooʔrʉ tʉtsihtuʔyeʔ W
clothes closet ooʔrʉ kahni W
clothes hanger kwasuʔu sakweni, ooʔrʉ tohtsanaʔ W
clothesline tʉrohtsaniʔiʔ
clothesline pole ooʔrʉ tohtsaniʔiʔana huuhpi, tʉtsapara huupi
clothesline rope soni wiyaaʔ, wana kotse tsahparaaʔ K

clothing namɨsoapɨ, ooʔrɨ W
clothing, buckskin pika namɨsoopɨ
clothing, buy oyorɨ tɨmarɨ
clothing, buy an article of kwasuʔɨ
tɨmuurɨ
clothing, iron tɨrah kwɨʔnerɨ K
clothing, opening in kuruupe̱
clothing, own an article of
kwasuʔukatɨ K
clothing, wear warm yuʔa
namɨsoorɨ
cloud tomo-, tomopɨ 2
cloud up tomoʔakitɨ
clouds tomoobi̱
cloudy tomoakatɨ W
clover, bush puhi tubi
clover, prairie yuu sonipɨ
clover, purple prairie pakeeso
club kasamaarɨ, wahta
club, billy tɨhkupaʔ
club, war wɨpitapuʔni
club someone wahtóorɨ
club someone (or something)
wɨhtokwɨrɨ
club something wɨhtokwɨtɨ
clubbed ones wɨhtokweʔ
cluck kokoráʔa yaketɨ K
clump of grass K puhi taitɨ
clump of trees huukabatɨ
clumsily, waddle or move
masuʔwaʔnekitɨ
coal kutɨhuubi̱ W
coal mine kutɨhubihtaa ohweetɨ
coal oil tukaʔa nabaa
coal shovel kutɨhuyunaʔ W
Coals-in-a-wood-fire Kuhtu
coat kwasuʔɨ
coat, fur pɨhɨ kwɨsuʔɨ
coax someone nihpitɨkɨrɨ
cob, corn- haniwoʔora K
cock, chaparral ebikuyuutsiʔ
cocklebur kuhtsu pokàaʔ

cockscomb tsopekwiiyu W
coconut kwasi taibooʔa
naʔkɨhtabai, kwasi taibooʔa
tɨhkapɨ
cocoon ɨʔbɨiʔ
coffee huba, huubaʔ
coffee, brew huba aikɨtɨ
coffee, drink hubebitɨ
coffee, make huba aitɨ
coffeepot huba aawoʔ
coil maropoʔnarɨ
coil, or wɨhkwatubi
coil, un- pɨrɨsuʔarɨ
coil something, un- wɨhpɨkɨsuarɨ
coin purse puhihwi narɨso̱ W
coins ekapuhihwi, tosahpuhihwi̱
cold ɨtsɨʔitɨ
cold, be kwihnerɨ
cold, die of the sɨhtɨyaitɨ
cold feet, have tasɨkɨmitɨ
cold, shake from tsihturuarɨ W
cold, shiver from tsihturuarɨ W
cold, tremble [shiver] with
sɨɨtsɨnitɨ
cold, turn kwihnerɨ
colic, baby sapɨ wɨnɨkatɨ
collarbone huukɨ, sihkupɨ W
collect money tɨniwaitɨ
collector, bill tɨniwaitɨʔ
collector, tax tɨniwaitɨʔ
college pia tɨbookɨni
Colorado River Tahka hunuʔbi
color, dark tupi̱sibitɨ
color, gold ekahwi
color, red eka-
color, slate esipitɨ
color of ashes (gray) kusi-
color, yellow oha-
colored, cream tosa ohapi̱tɨ
colored, dust- koropitɨ
colored, multi- wanatsihtaraaʔ
colt puku rúaʔ

Colt Puku?a tua?

column, spinal kwahiporopʉ

Comanche, interpreter of nʉmʉ rekwakʉ wapi̱

Comanche band Kwarʉ, Nokoni, Tʉtsanoo yehkʉ

Comanche band of Walters area Wia?nʉʉ

Comanche bones nʉmʉ tsuhni

Comanche butter tʉhtsohpe?aipʉ̱

Comanche butter, make tʉhtsohpe?arʉ

Comanche man nʉmʉ renahpʉ?

Comanche perfume plant nʉmʉ rʉsaasi̱

Comanche young man nʉmʉ ruibihtsi?

Comanche-born nʉmʉ ruaitʉ

Comanches Parukaa

Comanches, Mexicans captured by the Esitoyanʉʉ

Comanches of Tejas), Proud People (Wichita name for Natai

comatose sua watsikʉ

comatose, become sua watsikatʉ**comb** natsihtu?ye?

comb natsihtu?ye?

comb, animal horn aanatsihtuye?

comb, curry- tʉhʉya natsihtu?ye?

comb, fine-toothed pusi?a natsihtu?ye?

comb, honey- ʉnʉ bihnaa kahni K, wobi pi̱hnaa? W

comb, metal puhihwi natsihtu?ye?

comb, side papi̱ tsi?nika?

comb, wooden huunatsihtu?ye?

comb hair natsihtu?yeetʉ, tsihtu?yerʉ

comb someone's hair matsíhtuyeetʉ P

come kimarʉ, sʉmʉ nokimarʉ

-come, Refuse-to Huuhwiya

come back ko?itʉ

come backwards pitsa ʉkwakatu kimarʉ

come moving along nokimarʉ

come onto someone nahabitʉtʉ

come open tʉhwaitʉ

come out kʉarʉ, to?itʉ

come out (at a particular place) kiahbitʉ, to?i̱bitʉ

come running nuraakitʉ

come slowly mahuinoorʉ

come this way ibʉniitʉ

come together na?akʉtʉ

come walking soko kimarʉ

Comes-often Soo pitenʉ

comfort an adult pʉhkaitʉniitʉ W

comforted pʉhkaikatʉ

command hani̱tʉni̱rʉ, ni?atsiitʉ

commander ni?atsiwapi?, tʉniatsi̱katʉ?

commit adultery na?isahanitʉ W

commit suicide nabakʉtʉ

common grass yuu sonipʉ̱

commotion nani?yʉsʉkaitʉ W

commotion, create a ni?yʉsʉkaitʉ

Communion pʉʉhibitu?itʉ, tohtía? rʉhkapʉ̱

Communion, partake of pʉʉhibirʉ

Communion wine pʉʉpi̱

compare (one thing with another) nahmakutʉ

compare with something ninʉkitʉ W

competition, gamble over some type of nararʉnarʉ

complain about someone natsamarʉ

complected, light- pabopi̱tʉ

complete namahka?mukitʉ, pʉpe?, sʉmʉ makʉkatʉ

completed tamarʉkʉ̱katʉ

completely (adv) sʉmʉ

completely, pound sʉmʉ rayu?nerʉ

completely, rip sᵻmᵻ sihwarᵻ
completely, torn up tsasikwaitᵻ
completely, wipe off wᵻhtsu?marᵻ
conceited nabana?aitᵻ
conduct a peyote meeting
  wokwetᵻhkarᵻ
coneflower, purple tukunᵻ natsᵿ
confess narᵻahwerᵻ
congealed bone marrow
  tᵻᵻhtsohpe?
congregate narahka?witᵻ,
  sᵻᵻma?aitᵻ, uhoi ka?wᵿtᵻ
congregate, invite to sᵻᵻma?okarᵻ
conscious suabetaikatᵻ
conscious, un- sua watsikᵻ
construct a house (or other
  building) kahni?aitᵻ
construct a road pu?e?arᵻ
constructing brush arbor, poles
  for hᵻᵻkina huupi̱
container aawo, awo-, koono̱,
  wihtua?
container, carry a (by the handle)
  tsahimarᵻ, tsayarᵻ
container, load into a to?nikarᵻ W
container, pull out of tsahpᵻyerᵻ
contest against someone, win in a
  tahni?arᵻ
contest by cheating, win in a
  kaakwakurᵻ
continue nahaniitᵻ, naharᵻ
continue along nayᵻkwiitᵻ
continue doing something
  naahkarᵻ
continue lying down naahábitᵻ
continue uncontrollably
  kenaninabenitᵻ
contract, make an agreement or
  nanipu?e?aitᵻ
control someone mᵻᵻrᵻ
convince someone tsasu?atsitᵻ
convulse esikooitᵻ, esitᵻyaitᵻ

cook karᵻkᵻrᵻ, kohtsáarᵻ, kwasᵻtᵻ
-cook corn soup, quick atakwá?sᵻ?
cook food tᵻkarᵻkᵻrᵻ
cook for someone tᵻkᵻ mahnitᵻ
cook, hired tᵻkᵻ maniwapᵿ
cook out marrow from bones
  tᵻrana?itᵻ
cook over charcoal kuhtu
  tᵻkᵻmanirᵻ K
cook something brown otᵿ
  kwasᵿkᵻrᵻ
cooked cereal kohtsáa?
cooked food kwasᵻkᵻpᵿ
cookie otᵿ tohtía?
cookies otᵿ nohkopᵿ W, pihná
  nohkopᵿ
cooking pot saawihtua
Cooks-dried-meat Kukapᵿ
cool sᵻsuatᵻ
cool, feel hᵻhtsawᵿkatᵻ
cool off hᵻᵻkatᵻ, hᵻᵻtsa?wetᵻ
cool off, allow to rest or sua
  soyuraperᵻ
coon paruuku?, pa?ruhku?
coon can soo tᵻhimarᵻ?
coop, chicken kokorá?a kahni
copper ohahpuhihwi
copy taka?arᵻ
cord, spinal kwahi kupi̱si̱
core something wᵻpiyarᵻ
corn hani-, haníibi̱
corn, broom tᵻᵻnua?
corn, ear of hani-, haníibi̱
corn, ground hanitusupᵿ
corn, Indian nᵻmᵻ hani
corn, parch kukᵿmerᵻ
corn, parched kukᵿmepᵿ
corn, pop- kuhmito?ai?, tahma
  yokake?
corn, quick-dried atakwa?sᵻ?aipᵿ
corn, roast atakwa?sᵻ?aitᵻ,
  hanikwasᵻkᵻrᵻ

corn, roasted atakwaʔsɨʔaipɨ
corn, squaw nɨmɨ hani
corn, toast hanikwasɨkɨrɨ
corn bread haninookopɨ
corn leaves hani buhipɨ
Corn People Hanitaibo
corn shucks hani buhipɨ
corn soup hanisahoba
corn soup, quick-cook atakwáʔsɨʔ
corncake, Indian nɨmɨ nohkopɨ
corncob haniwoʔora K
corner kii
cornmeal hanitusupɨ
cornmeal mush hanikotsapɨ, kooʔ
corpse tɨyaipɨ
cottage cheese tɨmanɨkuʔwetɨ
cotton blanket wana hɨ K
cotton boll wanama sɨapɨha
  pokopi W
cotton quilt wana soona
cottonwood soho obi, tahpookɨʔ,
  weʔyɨkɨ sohoobi K
cough ohnitɨ
cough, whooping tsɨɨʔtsɨkiʔ
cough hard tsɨʔtsɨkitɨ
council, hold kaʔwitɨ
counsel naniʔɨrɨʔaitɨ, tɨniʔatsitɨ,
  tɨsuʔɨrɨʔ
counsel, give tɨsuʔɨrɨ
counselor tɨniʔatsikɨ
count definite objects tɨtsɨrɨ
count something tɨrɨtsɨrɨ
country, foreign atɨsokoobi
country to settlement, open soko
  tsatɨwarɨ
couple, married nanakwɨhɨ W
cousin, same-sex haitsi
cover mamárɨmarɨ, marɨmarɨ,
  poʔaʔ, ɨhɨkɨrɨ
cover, cloth sona, soona
cover oneself ɨhɨkatɨ
cover over nɨɨkɨnarɨ

cover something hɨhkɨnarɨ,
  wɨhkɨnarɨ
cover something over W
  manaʔkoroomitɨ
cover the head K manaʔkoroomitɨ
cover up K tɨmarɨ
cover with earth pasokoʔarɨ
covered nabimarɨ, wɨhkɨnai,
  wɨhkɨnɨkatɨ
covered, earth- ohtakatɨ
covered, mud- sekwi nuyuʔitɨ
covered wagon nakɨnikatɨ waikina
covering naboʔaa W
**covering for teepees, skins or
  other** nɨmɨkɨni
covet kwahisiʔa, nasuyaketɨ
covetous person kwahisiapɨ
cow kuhtsuʔ W, kuutsuʔ K,
  pimorooʔ, pimorooʔa piabɨ
cow, milk pitsipɨ pimoróoʔ W
cow, milk a tɨmaʔokwetɨ
cow, second stomach of sekwi biiʔ
Cow-dung Kuhtsu kwiʔta
cow's cud pimorooʔa tɨyɨʔwipɨ
cowardly pihisiʔapɨ
cowboy kuhtsu taiboʔ, pimoroo
  taibooʔ
cowboy boots kuhtsu taibo napɨ,
  narakwɨsakatɨ napɨ
cowhide pimoroʔa pɨhi
cowhide, dried paakipɨ
coyote kɨhtsayaʔyaʔkeʔ,
  kɨʔkwɨriaʔ, kɨʔtseena,
  ohaahnakatɨ W, tseenaʔ K
Coyote Kebakoweʔ
Coyote-droppings Ishatai
crab piʔnuʔaʔ
crab apple ekaamawooʔ, tɨe
  amawóoʔ
crab louse pɨhɨ pusia, suhu posía
crack porokarɨ
crack knuckles tsahporakitɨ

crack something marátʉbaitʉ, tahparʉ, tapearʉ, wʉtʉbarʉ, wʉʔʉaruʔarʉ

crack something by sitting on it pitʉbarʉ

crack something with hands marʉbarʉ

crack with the teeth kʉtʉbarʉ

cracked of own accord tahpai

cracked skin tsiʔwapʉ W

cracker tosa rohtiya?

crackle kuhporákitʉ, kukʉbihkutʉ

cradle koonǫ, ohnáakʉno?

cradle, black tuhkʉni

cradle, day waakohno

cradleboard waakohno

cradleboard, day habikʉno?

cram tsinʉkʉrʉ

cram into limited space natsinʉhkʉrʉ

crammed into limited space tsinʉkʉ

cramp, have (in hand) maʔwʉtsa roʔonitʉ

cramp, have leg taʔitsaʔbʉrʉ W, taʔwitsa roponiitʉ K

cramp (or spasm), have muscle toponitʉ K

cramped hand maʔitsaʔbʉkatʉ

crane kusikwaʔaa?, paʔa toyokatʉ huutsuu? K

crank wʉʔaikʉrʉ

crave sweets pihná rʉhkarʉ

crawdad waʔroo koyáa?

crawfish waʔroo koyáa?

crawl wʉhuʔnerʉ

crawl like a snake nuhyimiʔarʉ W

crawl on hands and knees mahuʔnetʉ

crawl on knees tahuʔnerʉ

crazed poosubʉkʉkaitʉ

crazy poʔsa

crazy, go eʔmʉarʉ, poosubʉhkaitʉ

crazy person pooʔsa?

Crazy Warriors Pukutsi

Crazy-bear Isawʉra

creak kʉtsuʔtsuʔkitʉ

cream pitsipʉha poʔaa, wihtʉʔeka?

cream, face kobe kiihtʉʔeka? W

cream, separate milk from yunarʉ

cream colored tosa ohapitʉ

crease takwʉperʉ

crease with the hands makwipunarʉ K

create a commotion niʔyʉsʉkaitʉ

creation nʉmʉ rʉhorapʉ

Creator Atsabi?

creature ʉnú?

creek hunuʔbi, okwèetʉ

-creek, Rocky Tʉpi wʉnʉ

Creek, Sand Pasiwa huunuʔbi

Creek, Timber Huuhunuʔbi

creek bank tʉpána?

creek bed, overflow the paruʔitʉ

creek branch nabatai K

creep wʉhuʔnerʉ

cremate kuhkuparʉ

crib, baby ohnaʔa norʉhnaa?

cricket tuhmekǫ

crier, town tekwʉniwapi

crippled wihnaitʉ

criticize manímʉarʉ, tʉnimakwihtserʉ

croak tʉʉhkonarʉ

crochet thread wana ramʉ

crock tʉpi aawo

crook, shepherd's tʉʔehkooi? W

crooked onoʔitʉ

-crooked-nose, Red Ekamurawa

crop, garden tʉmʉsʉapʉ

crop, harvest a pomarʉ

crop, harvested pomapʉ

crops, plant tʉmʉsʉarʉ

crops, planted tʉrʉnapʉ

cross suaabe
cross over manitʉ
cross-eyed person pasapuni
crossing, river nagwee
crossing, wagon na?wee?, pu?e
nagwe
croton weed kupisinamaya
crow tuwikaa?
crowbar tʉhora?, tʉkʉh kwe?ya?
crowd wʉtsʉkitʉ
crowd many people together uhoi
ka?wʉtʉ
crowd of people sʉʉmʉ?okʉ
crowd with people tsʉhkikatʉ
crowded tsinʉkʉ
crowded into narrow place
tsʉkikatʉ
crowded together narahtsʉkikatʉ
crowded while standing tahtsʉkitʉ
cruel tʉtsʉ-
crumble homonutsaitʉ,
manutsa?arʉ W, tahnutsa?erʉ
K, tohhomonutsarʉ
W, tsahhomonutsarʉ,
wʉhhomonutsa?arʉ
crumble to powder mahomonutsarʉ
crumble to powder (with the foot)
tahhomonutsarʉ W
crumbled nuhtsaitʉ
crumbs tʉkʉ wesipʉ, tʉkʉ yumapʉ
crush pikʉtsekarʉ, tatsukwerʉ,
tayu?nerʉ, tsahhomonutsarʉ,
wʉkʉtserʉ
crush (in pieces)
tohhomonutsarʉ W
crush (or squash) tsakitsetʉ
crushed (into small pieces)
mabisukiitʉ
crutch natsihtóo? K
cry hubiyaarʉ, nawoo?i, yaketʉ
cry by hitting, make toyaketʉ
cry, cause to wʉyaketʉ

cry, imitate a niyakekʉtʉ
cry loudly hubiyaa piayakeetʉ
cry out hubinitʉ
crying, stop pʉhkai
crying (walking around)
yakeyʉkarʉ
crystal clear pabokopitʉ
cucumber poko rʉhka?, soko
rahka?miitsa?
cud, cow's pimoroo?a tʉyʉ?wipʉ
cultivate wʉhhanirʉ
cultivator puhí tsawoo?
cup aawo, awo-, hibikahti, wʉhibi?
cup, drinking hibiawo
cup, tin sʉʉ awo
cupboard aworahna
curdle nʉkuwʉmi?arʉ
cure partially through touch
marebunitʉ
curing ceremony puha?aitʉ
**curing ceremony (for someone),
hold a** puha?arʉ
curl hair wesibapi?arʉ
curled wesi-, wesikitʉ
curly wesikitʉ
curly hair wesibaapi
currant, wild huwabo?kóo?
curry animal fur tsihtu?yerʉ
currycomb tʉhʉya natsihtu?ye?
curse aikurekwatʉ, tsuhni tekwarʉ
curtain nanabuni wanapʉ K,
nanabuni wanatsahpara? W
cut ko-, natsahki?apʉ, tʉkʉrʉ,
wʉhki?arʉ, wʉno?itʉ, wʉtsʉkarʉ
nʉhki?apʉ
cut, hair- naraketorootʉ, nʉʉtsʉke?
cut, hair- (get a) nʉʉtsʉketʉ
cut a strip wʉsi?kwarʉ
cut down tʉrahnirʉ, wʉhkarʉ,
wʉhpomarʉ, wʉhpomi?itʉ
cut fat off surface wʉhkwʉnetʉ
cut in half tsapʉkarʉ

cut into pieces, object
tɨtsihpomiʔipɨ

cut off tɨtsihkaʔarɨ

cut off pieces wɨhtsiʔarɨ

cut off short piʔtoʔarɨ

cut on hand namahkiapɨ W

cut on the foot narahkiʔapɨ

cut oneself natsahkiʔarɨ, nɨɨkiʔaitɨ

cut open wɨpɨkarɨ, wɨpɨtsarɨ

cut out of the herd tahkaaitɨ

cut someone (to wound)
tsahkiʔaitɨ

cut something kiʔarɨ

cut someone down kuparɨ

cut up tɨtsihkaʔarɨ

cut up into pieces tsihpoma

cut up something kooʔitɨ

cut weeds or grass soni wɨhpomarɨ

cut with a knife tsihkaʔarɨ

cutter, wire tɨkɨh pomaʔ

cutting edge, sharpen a
tɨɨhkonarɨ

cyclone cellar ohta kahni W

cymopterus plant tunɨhaa

Cynthia Ann Parker Narua

D d

dab to wipe or erase tohpɨsakɨrɨ
K, tohtsomarɨ W

dachshund maʔnɨ sariiʔ

daisy, fleabane tabetotsiyaa

dam pawɨhtɨmapɨ

dam up paʔwɨtɨ

damages, payment of nanɨwokɨ

damp patsoʔitɨ

dampen pakwihtsikɨrɨ, paʔisokerɨ

dampened mabaʔisokitɨ

dance nɨhkana W, nɨhkarɨ, nɨkɨrɨ

dandelion soko sikɨsa

dandelion flower soko sikɨsatotsiyaʔ

dangerous narɨʔɨyapɨ

dangle wepɨkaitɨ

dark ketunabunitɨ, tu-, tukanikatɨ

dark blue tuʔebipitɨ K

dark color tupisibitɨ

darken ketunabunitɨ

dart kwiitsɨbaʔitɨ

date taibo naʔseekaʔ

daughter petɨʔ

daughter, adopted petɨ toyapɨ K,
petɨboopɨ W

**daughter or son (offspring),
grown** nahnapɨ

-daughter, Only Pɨʔna petɨ

daughter-in-law huutsi piahpɨʔ,
huutsi piahpɨ

dawn hɨwɨni, kɨhɨwɨnɨkatɨ,
taahkitɨ, tsaa nabuni, tsaa
nabunitɨ

dawn, before ohahɨkwɨnikatɨ, tosa
hɨwɨnikatɨmaʔ

dawn, early ohahɨkwɨnikatɨ

Dawn Hɨwɨni

day tabe-

day after tomorrow piʔnakwɨ
bɨetsɨ

day cradle waakohno

day cradleboard habikɨnoʔ

day, hot tabe kusɨwehkatɨ

day, late in the tabeʔehi

day, ration tɨhima rabeni

day, scorching tabe kusɨwehkatɨ

day, Sun Puha rabeni, Puha rakatɨ

daytime taahkatɨ

dead suaʔsuʔmaitɨ

dead body tɨyaipɨ

dead grass puhi kooʔipɨ, puhi
tɨyaitɨ

dead person kooipɨ

dead, play kaabehkarɨ

dead tree putsi waipɨ

deaf ketɨnakatɨ

deal, make a tohpunitʉ
dear friend haitsíi
dear little brothers
  tamihtsi?benihtsi?
death, choke to pitsanʉ tʉyaitʉ
**death, choke to (by rope around
  the neck)** oihtʉyaitʉ
death, drink oneself to
  nakʉhkuparʉ
death, eat oneself to nakʉhkuparʉ
death, freeze to sʉhtʉyaitʉ
death, prevent someone's
  makwitso?aitʉ
death, starve to tsiharʉyaitʉ
death, thirst to
  takuhtʉyaaihumi?arʉ
death, work someone to
  namakupakʉrʉ
death, worked to namakupʉkatʉ
death wail hubiya piayakeetʉ
deathbed, suffer on pisukwitarʉ
debts, pay tʉmakarʉ
decay e?bootsiarʉ, e?bootsia?
decayed tooth wo?ataamạ
deceitful emʉahkatʉ
deceive kaabehkarʉ, kaahaniitʉ
deceive, to emʉahkatʉ
deceive or cheat, intend to
  kaasuarʉ
December Pia ʉtsʉ?i mʉa, Pʉmata
  waahima?ena mʉa, Pʉmata
  wanohi?ema mʉa, Wahi mʉa
deceptive emʉahkatʉ
decide tʉbitsị suarʉ
decide, help tsasu?atsitʉ
decided, un- wahabịsuatʉ
deck, king in playing-card
  ohahkuyaa?
Decoration Day Pʉkʉra
  totsiyaa?ai?eka, Totsiyaaih
  tabenihtʉ W
decorative pin natsihtʉpʉka?

decoy duck pʉʉyʉ namanahkepʉ
deed soko bookʉtʉ
deed, title soko bookʉtʉ
deed or title to land nabinai
  tʉboopʉ
deep tuhkatʉ
deer arʉka?
deer, white-tailed pi?tohtsía? W
deer food K, O arʉkáa rʉhkapʉ
deer meat arʉka tuhku K, O, P,
  arʉkáa rʉhkapʉ, tahmai napʉ
Deer-water Arʉka páa?
defeat kwakurʉ K, tahni?arʉ,
  wʉhhabi?arʉ
defeat by cheating kaakwakurʉ
defecate naro?itʉ
deficient ketokwetʉ
defile mahyarʉ
definite noo
dehair a hide wʉhkwʉnetʉ
delay tsʉ?nitʉ
delayed mamamʉekatʉ
delicate health, person of takwipʉ
delouse nabusi?aketʉ, pusiaketʉ
demonstrate tʉmabunikʉrʉ
den itsaraitʉ ʉnʉa kahni
den of thieves tʉrʉkʉ kahni
dentures tamatsa?nika?
depend on someone nasupetitʉ
dependable nasutsawaitʉ W
dependable person nasupetipʉ K
dependable person, un-
  senihtʉhtsi?
deplete a supply tsahtsu?marʉ
deride su?uyaa?arʉ, usú?uya?itʉ W,
  wohho suarʉ
descend yʉwimi?arʉ
descendant na?nʉʉmʉ
descendants nʉhmabina
describing something, tempt by
  nisuyakeetʉ
desert pʉa nuhkitʉ, pʉah taitʉ

Desert-in-large-group Pᵾa kwarᵾ
deserve ta?urᵾkarᵾ W
desire suwaitᵾ
desire not to be disturbed
  pihiso?aiwᵾnᵾrᵾ
desk pᵾpa?akura tᵾbòo?ena W,
  tᵾboo rᵾhka?
destroy aibuniitᵾ
destruction], self-immolate [self-
  sacrifice or kuhtᵾyarᵾ
detained mamamᵾekatᵾ
device used for measuring, any
  tᵾmanahke?
devil Ketokwe hina haniitᵾ,
  Tuhkwasi taiboo?
devil's claw aakáa?
devil's horn aakáa?
devil's horse tosarai?
devil's snuffbox mupitsᵾha
  pisahpi W
devour sᵾmᵾ rᵾhkarᵾ
dew tosa nᵾᵾbaai?
diamond kiinaboo, nana?atahpu
  na?ha? rᵾᵾpi, pahparatsihkwetᵾ
  tᵾᵾpi, we?kwiyanutᵾ tᵾᵾpi
diaper pikwᵾrᵾpᵾka? W
diaper pin nahamuhkᵾ K
dice game awonohi?
die tᵾyaaitᵾ
die, to kooitᵾ
die in accident anitᵾ
die of the cold sᵾhtᵾyaitᵾ
die of thirst takuhtᵾyaaihumi?arᵾ
die out tukami?arᵾ
different ata-, atᵾrᵾ, ebu
different kinds nana?ataputᵾ,
  nanisusumatᵾ
different ways seni
differently, doing atapu
dig mahorarᵾ, tokwaitᵾ, tsahhorarᵾ,
  tsahtaikᵾtᵾ, tᵾhorarᵾ, wᵾhhorarᵾ
dig a fire hole kutᵾhorarᵾ

dig a hole horarᵾ, tᵾhhorarᵾ
dig a hole in the ground tohkonarᵾ
dig edible roots tᵾkᵾ ahwerᵾ
dig up awerᵾ
digger, posthole tᵾhora?
dignity, act without self- e?mᵾarᵾ
dinner tabe rᵾhkapᵾ W
dinner or lunch, eat tabe rᵾhkarᵾ K
direction, this ibu, inakwᵾ
directions, from all nano?onai
directions, from different
  nana?atanaiki
directions, various ebu
dirt ohta-, ohtapii
dirty nasᵾsᵾa?eetᵾ
dirty object tuhtsaipᵾ
disagreement, shake head in
  ka?witsetᵾ K
disassemble tohkwe?yarᵾ
discard tsahwitᵾ
discard something namaro?itᵾ
discarded by kicking sᵾᵾhpotsᵾkatᵾ
discarded thing namaro?ihkatᵾ
discharge a flash of lightning
  ekakwitse?erᵾ
disciple tᵾrᵾ?ai wapi
disconnect, to tsahtukarᵾ
discouraged ai?bihinᵾᵾsukatᵾ,
  nakᵾnᵾᵾ?maitᵾ, narahtokwetᵾ
disgust, expression of ai
dishes, wash awomakotserᵾ,
  tᵾmakotsetᵾ
dishonest person kaawosa
dishpan tᵾsoona
dishtowel awomatsuma?,
  tᵾmatsuma? W
dishwasher awomakotse
disintegrate wihto?aitᵾ
disintegrated wihto?aitᵾ
disjoint natsaminarᵾ, tsaminarᵾ,
  tsiminarᵾ
dislike kemabana?itᵾ

dislocate natsaminaitʉ

disobedient ketʉnakatʉ

disorderly in placement pia utsaatʉ

disown a friend haitsi̱ wihtaitʉ

display nasutsarʉ, nʉʉhtonitʉ

dispose of petihtarʉ

disrobe natsahkwe?yarʉ, tsahkwe?yarʉ

distance, separated by great namanakwʉ K

distance), smell something (from a ʉkwʉsʉ?nitʉ

distant soo naahkwetʉ

distraught kenaninabenitʉ

disturb ni?yʉsʉkaitʉ, wʉʉyoritʉ

disturbed pihiso?aitʉ

disturbed, desire not to be pihiso?aiwʉnʉrʉ

ditch wo?nokatʉ

dive mutsʉ?itʉ

divide na?rʉbomitʉ, tahkaaitʉ

divide in half tʉbinaa?werʉ

divided na?rʉbomitʉ

divided evenly na?nʉbe?

divided in half tʉbinaa?wekitʉ

divided into groups narahpomi?itʉ

divorced pʉah taikatʉ

dizzy kwinumakatʉ

dizzy, be made makwi?numaitʉ

dizzy, make kwinumarʉ

do hani̱tʉ

do something, fail to kemahpʉ?arʉ

do something, persuade someone to nitsʉbahikʉ?itʉ

do something, unable to kemahpʉ?arʉ, tsuhitʉ

do to mʉʉrʉ

do work tʉrʉ?aitʉ

doctor natʉsu?u puha raiboo? W

doctor, medical natsu̱ taibo? K

doctor, medicine puha tenahpʉ

doctor, witch tʉtsʉ puha?

doctoring, big piana huwai?

does-not-tell-a-lie, This-midday-sun- Sihka tabe ke isopʉ

dog sarii?

Dog Eaters Saria Tʉhka

Dog hero Makutabai

dog, hound- naki̱ sarii?

dog, prairie tʉ?rʉkúu? W

dog, watch- tʉ?iya?i wapi̱

dog, water pa?boosi?

dog paddle masu?wa?nekitʉ, paruhparʉ

dog-soldiers, Chief Comanche- Tʉoyobisesʉ

dogwood, flowering siba huupi

dogwood, rough-leafed parʉa

doing another way atapu

doing, cease pʉarʉ

doing something, continue naahkarʉ

doing, slow down what one is nʉnʉ?itʉ

doing differently atapu

doing, miss tsimi?akʉrʉ

doll nohitʉetʉ

doll up someone ma?yʉkwiitʉ

dollar, half- sʉkweebi?

domestic carrot ohahpokopi K, ohahtʉhkapʉ

domestic plum taibo sʉkʉ?i

domestic tree humasʉapʉ

domineer tahkoonitʉ

Don't! keta?

donkey kusimuura, kutsihpʉ?, kutsi?wobi?

doodlebug kwita maropona

door natsahtʉma? K

door, knock on tohtaraki?arʉ

door, screen nasaa?wʉ? K

doorway muhyʉ, namuhyʉ, natsahtʉma? K

double waha-

double, ride pihima, piyarʉ

double ball natsihtóoʔetʉ

double-bladed axe
na ʔbutikʉmakatʉ tʉʉhkaʔaa?

doubles wahabahti

doubletrees, hook up (on buggy)
nomohkarʉ

doubt the truth of a statement
tsuwíhnu

doubtful wahabị̲suatʉ̲

doubtless kewáhabahku

dough-like batter takoosahpʉ? W

dove kuʔe wóo?, pasahòo

down naʔʉyʉbuti W, tuhkatʉ̲

down, fall wʉhtʉkwaitʉ

down, force to sit sutena karʉrʉ

down, go weehtsitʉ, yʉwimiʔarʉ

down, help tsakwerʉ

down, hold (with hand) makʉnaitʉ

down, jerk tsapeherʉ

down (sitting back on heels),
kneel tanatookarʉtʉ

down, knock wʉhkwabikʉrʉ

down (by force), knock
wʉnʉʉkuparʉ

down, knock something tayuʔmarʉ

down, knocked wʉnʉʉhkuparʉ

down, lay something tʉkiitʉ K

down on something, lay the head
tsohtʉkikatʉ

down, lie haahpị̲tʉ 2, habiitʉ,
kwabitʉ

down and think, lie nasutamʉ̲
habitʉ

down, lying haahpị̲

down, nail tawʉnarʉ

down, pant with tongue hanging
hehekʉbʉniitʉ

down, press mabararʉ

down with hands to expel water,
press mabitsoorʉ

down, press something tatʉ̲keʔnerʉ

down, pressed manʉ̲kʉtʉ̲

down, pull tsahparʉ, tsapeherʉ

down, pull oneself natsahkupʉkatʉ

down in place, put tsahtʉkitʉ

down, put something tsaʔnikoorʉ

down something to sit on, put
pisoonarʉ

down, quiet tʉsuʔnarʉ,
wʉyupaʔnitʉ

down, set tsahtʉkitʉ

down carefully, set tsakwʉnarʉ

down, sit karʉkatʉ 1, nakarʉʔkarʉ,
yʉkwimiʔarʉ

down quickly, sit tsuhni karʉ

down, slide pisikwanúuʔitʉ

down (what one is doing), slow
nʉnʉʔitʉ

down, smooth wʉtʉ̲kịʔnetʉ

down, stake tawʉnarʉ

down tightly, stake ʉhtaarʉ

down object, staked- ʉhtaʔetʉ̲

down in, stuck tsʉhkarʉ

down, sun goes tabeʔikamiʔarʉ

down, swat wʉʔanirʉ

down, swing sitting
piʔweesuʔruʔitʉ

down, take tsayumiʔi

down a teepee, take tsahtʉ̲warʉ

down off of something, take
tsahpʉherʉ

down, tamp tanʉ̲kʉtʉ K, tonʉ̲kʉrʉ

down, tear tsahperʉ

down, throw tsayumarʉ

down a person, throw
tsahkwaʔnuʔitʉ

down, upside paʔarai

downhearted aiʔbihinʉʉsukatʉ̲,
narahtokwetʉ

downhill, run wenuʔnukị̲miʔarʉ

-downstream, Those-who-stay
Tinawa

downward na?ʉyʉbuti W, tuhkatʉ

downward, lying face- muparai habinitʉ K

draft, bank puhihwi tʉboopʉ

drag by force wʉhpiwokarʉ

drag something kʉwokarʉ, piwokarʉ, takwokarʉ W

drag something along piwokami?arʉ

drag something spread on flat surface pisunarʉ

dragging one foot, walk tasi?womi?arʉ

dragonfly paka tuu?ru?

drain tsa?okwetʉ

drain a liquid tsa?ohkwerʉ

draw line tsihpoorʉ

draw out pain, suck on body to musoopitʉ

draw water tuurʉ

drawer na?wosa, ooyorʉ tahna

drawer, dresser ooyorʉ tahna

drawing knife nahuu? W, nahhoo? K

drawknife huusibe?

dream nabʉsi?aipʉ, nabʉsi?aitʉ

dredge tsii?wʉweniitʉ

dress kwasu?ʉ, namʉsoarʉ

-dress, Short Tsihtara

dress, un- natsahkwe?yarʉ, tsahkwe?yarʉ

dresser, (chest of drawers) oo?rʉ tani?i?

dresser drawer ooyorʉ tahna

dribble kʉ?kwʉriarʉ

dribble from the mouth kʉ?okwetʉ

dried nara?okatʉ, tʉbitsi basapʉ

-dried corn, quick atakwa?sʉ?aipʉ

dried cowhide paakipʉ

dried meat esi inapʉ, tahmai napʉ

-dried meat, summer tahmai napʉ

dried plum natsomʉ, na?a?tsome?

dried pumpkin nakwʉsipʉ

drill a field tʉrahnai?itʉ

drill a hole with an instrument tohtʉbʉ?itʉ

drill in tahtʉkarʉ

drink hibitʉ

drink alcoholic beverage hibikʉtʉ

drink coffee hubebitʉ

drink oneself to death nakʉhkuparʉ

-drinking, Wolf Esahibi

drinking cup hibiawo

drinking glass paboko aawo, wʉhibi?

drip pahpatsohkitʉ

drip water paa kʉa?etʉ

drive tʉtsʉhanitʉ

drive a car or team by hand tsahhanitʉ

drive across tamanikarʉ

drive along or away mahkʉsuwaitʉ

drive animals by force tamʉkʉrʉ

drive away tahkʉarʉ

drive in animals mahkʉkitʉ K

drive out tahkʉarʉ

drive together ta?ookitʉ

drive up animals mahkʉrʉ W

driven into ground tawekwitʉ

driver, screw- tʉmabukwe?

drool pakʉsiiwʉnʉrʉ

droop takwitsoo?nimi?arʉ

drop peti-, tapʉherʉ

dropping, break by wʉtʉbarʉ

drop off pahitʉ, yumarʉ

drought tsihakooihkatʉ, ʉrʉ?itʉ

drown patʉrʉyaitʉ

drugstore natʉsu?ʉ narʉmʉʉ?, natʉsu?ʉ kahni

drum, wooden wobi wʉhpai K

drumming pihkarʉ

drunk hibipʉ, kwinumapʉ

drunk, made makwi?numaitʉ

drunk person hibipʉ

dry tʉbitsi basapʉ

dry (by heating) kupisarʉ

dry, hang meat up to ina?etʉ
dry, hang up to pasahtohtsanarʉ
-dry, partially sun wʉhtakʉmiitʉ
**dry it for jerky), roast meat over
   fire (or** ku?inarʉ
dry, set out to pasahtahtʉkitʉ W
dry, sit in sun to mabasahtʉkitʉ K
dry, sit in the sun to
   pasahtahtʉkitʉ W
dry goods tapi wanapʉ K,
   tarʉwanapi̱ W
dry object pasapʉ
dry off body pasarʉ
dry out pasarʉ
dry season ʉrʉ?itʉ
dry something pasakʉrʉ, tʉbitsi
   basarʉ
dry tea puhi huuba̱
dry up kuwaaitʉ, waaitʉ
Dry-teepee Pakekʉni
drying, A-frame, meat- inakwata
duck pʉʉyʉ
duck, decoy pʉʉyʉ namanahkepʉ
duck head under water paku?nerʉ
duck someone tsahpaaku?nikarʉ
dug (by man), hole nahorapʉ
dug (in soil), hole hoora
dull kʉmakwa?i, mutsiwahtʉ
dulled kemakʉmapʉ
dulled edge kemakʉmapʉ
dumb ketekwa
dump into to?wʉ?wenitʉ, wʉhtiarʉ
dun tʉniwaitʉ
dune, sand pasiwanoo? W
duplicate taka?aitʉ, taka?arʉ
during religious ceremony, smoke
   puha bahmu?itʉ
dusk tupi̱sinawoni?, tupʉsʉnarʉ
dust huhku-, huhkupʉ, huukupʉ
dust, raise huukʉhʉnʉrʉ
dust by walking, raise
   tahuhkuwʉnʉrʉ

dust, saw- huupita homoketʉ,
   huupita pisoni̱, huutusupʉ W
dust, stir up huukʉhʉnʉrʉ
dust off huukunatsirʉ
dust off by hand huukumatsumarʉ
dust storm huhkukwʉnʉrʉ,
   huukʉhʉnʉrʉ
dust-colored koropitʉ
dustcloth tʉmatsuma? W
dusty huukukatʉ
dwell nʉmʉnetʉ
dye tʉsaa?
dye something tʉsáarʉ
dying one sua?su?makatʉ
dynamite pʉhtsa?ctʉ?

E e

dying one sua?su?makatʉ
dynamite pʉhtsa?etʉ?
eagle kwihnai, pia huutsuu?, pia
   kwihnai
-eagle, Sun Tabe kwi?ne
-eagle, White Kwihne tosabitʉ
Eagle-tail-feather Kwasia
ear naki̱
ear cartilage, back part of K naki̱
   kwiita̱
ear lobe W naki̱ kwiita̱
ear of corn hani-, haníibi̱
ear, pierced naki̱ toonʉkatʉ K,
   nanaki̱tonapʉ
ear wax naki̱ oona̱
earache, have an naki̱ wʉnʉkatʉ
early nabʉesʉ, ohahʉkwʉnikatʉ,
   tosa hʉwʉnikatʉma?
early dawn ohahʉkwʉnikatʉ
early morning pʉetsʉku, tuka ʉhyʉi
early plum yusʉkʉ
earn something tahwikarʉ,
   tʉrahwikatʉ

earring naki̱ tsaʔnika?

ears, prick up the toʔyabaituₕearth sokoobi̱

earth sokoobi̱

earth, cover with pasokoʔaru

earth, paw the taʔsiʔwooru

earth, quake of soko yuʔyumuhkuru

earth, scratch up taʔsiʔwooru

earth [or earthquake], tremor of soko yuʔyumuhkuru

earth, wash out patowoʔneru

earth-covered ohtakatu̱

earthquake soko yuʔyumuhkutu̱

ease pain, stand on someone's back to tahparaʔitu

easily yuʔnaitsi K

east muhyu nakwu̱

east, north- kwihne muhyunakwu̱

east, south- yuʔanue muhyunakwu̱bu

Easter Tanoyoʔtsoʔmeʔe̱

Easter egg taabuʔkina noyo

Easter rabbit noyotsoʔme̱ tabu?

Eastern Apaches Nipanuu

easy yuʔnaitsi K

Easy-to-break Tsaa tsopa?

eat tuhkaru

eat K tuku yaaru

eat, take to W tuku yaaru

eat bone marrow tuhhu ruhkaru

eat breakfast taaruhkaru

eat dinner or lunch tabe ruhkaru K

eat most of something sumu ruhkaru

eat oneself to death nakuhkuparu

eat peyote wokwetuhkaru

eat supper yuihtuhkatu

eat up kuhtsuʔmaru, tuhkamaru

eaten food, partly naruhkapu̱

eaten up completely sumu kuhtsumai

Eaters, Sugar Pena tuhka, Penanuu

-eaters, Yap Yapai tuhka

eating, finish off by kuhtsuʔmaru

eating place tuku̱ kahni

Eating-tribe Maruhke

eavesdrop nakuhooru

eavesdropper nakuhoowaaitu̱

echo tuʔape nanakaru

edge tubanaa?

Echo-of-the-wolf-howl Isananaka?

edge tubanaa?

edge, dulled kemakumapu̱

edge, knife kumapu̱

edge, sharpen a cutting tuuhkonaru

edge, sharpen an makwumutsiaru

edge, sharpened kumapu̱

edged, cloth (with ribbon or lace) tukumaʔaitu?

edible fruit, plant with paiyapi̱

edible roots, dig tuku ahweru

edible tuber taʔwahkóo? W, totohtu

eel kwasinaboo pekwi

effort to remember, search the mind in suʔuraru

egg kokoráʔa pokopi̱, nooyo̱

egg, chicken kokoráʔa nooyo̱, kokoráʔa atùapu̱

egg, Easter taabuʔkina noyo

egg, want to lay an nohabi̱ suwaitu̱

egg yolk noyoʔna ohapi̱yuna

eggs, lay turuaru

eight namewatsukwi̱tu̱

either sex, kinsman of taʔka?

elbow kiipu̱

elder brother pabi?

elderly male tsukuhpu̱?

elderly man sukuupu̱

elderly woman hubi tsiitsi?, puetupu̱

eldest child nahnapu̱

eldest sister patsi?

elephant esiᵾnᵾᵾ?, mu?kwipuna?, tᵾkwitsuna?

elk, bull parᵾa kuhma

elm tusohó?

elm, white pimoroo?a korohko?

elocutionist tᵾnikepisa?

elves, little people similar to Nᵾnapi

emaciated person wehuru?i

emptily tsaana

empty into to?wᵾ?wenitᵾ, wᵾhtiarᵾ

empty out wᵾ?wenitᵾ K

encircle mahoinitᵾ

encounter someone nara?uraitᵾ

encourage kebisa?makarᵾ, natsᵾwitᵾmaka?eetᵾ

encourage to go on nihtunetsᵾ?itᵾ

end, stand hair on sᵾroonitᵾ

end of row or nerve sᵾkwerᵾ

enema, give an nariso?arᵾ W

enema, give oneself an natsinaro?ikᵾtᵾ

enemy wohhohpᵾ?

enemy tribe tawohho

engaged to be married, get nᵾpetsᵾ?itᵾ

enmity wohho

enough, not good ketokwetᵾ

enraged tapiso?aitᵾ W

enter wekwiitᵾ, wekwimi?arᵾ

enter by force sutena ikᵾrᵾ

entertain mananaa?waihkarᵾ, ma?yᵾneetᵾ

envy another person kwahisi?a

erase tahtsukitᵾ, tohpᵾsakᵾrᵾ K

erase, dab to wipe or tohpᵾsakᵾrᵾ K, tohtsomarᵾ W

eraser tᵾrahtsuki? K

eriogonum root ekanatsᵾ

erode patowo?nerᵾ

eroded soil patowo?nepᵾ

error in speech ni?watsᵾkatᵾ?

escape kᵾarᵾ

escape from somewhere namaro?itᵾ

escort a guest some place panimi?arᵾ

esophagus worᵾrokᵾ

ether nᵾmi tsa?ᵾbᵾikᵾ?eetᵾ

even sᵾᵾpetᵾ

even, un- ho?yopipᵾ, pihpokaarᵾ

even land, un- wohtsa?wᵾtᵾ

evenly divided na?nᵾbe?

evening tukaani, tupᵾsᵾnarᵾ, yᵾitᵾ

evening, this yᵾihkᵾ

event nahapᵾ

every time o?yᵾ?sᵾ

everyone sᵾmᵾ oyetᵾ

everywhere piapᵾ 2

evil aitᵾ

evil spirit pᵾe tᵾyaai?, tᵾtᵾsuana

evil spirit, have an poosubᵾhkaitᵾ

exact tokwetᵾ

exaggerate natsamarᵾ

examine puiwᵾnᵾrᵾ, tsasukarᵾ

examine oneself nabuihwᵾnᵾtᵾ W

excavate tokwaitᵾ

exchange narᵾma?erᵾ, narᵾmᵾᵾrᵾ

exchange gifts hinanahimitᵾ, nahimiitᵾ, na?uhturᵾ W

exchange one item for another mabihtᵾ?uyarᵾ

exchange several gift items na?oyorᵾmakarᵾ K

excite manᵾᵾsukaarᵾ, toyᵾsekaitᵾ

excitement, stir up toyᵾsekaitᵾ

exciting toyᵾsᵾkai

excrement kwitapᵾ

exhaust food supply tᵾkᵾ tsuhmarᵾ

exhaust oneself nananᵾᵾ?maitᵾ, narahkupaitᵾ

exhaust supply kehewa?itᵾ

exhausted, give up anitᵾ

exhausted person or animal namakweyaipᵾ

exit forcibly tohto?itʉ
expectorate tusitʉ
expel water, press down with hands to mabitsoorʉ
experience, know by masuabetaitʉ
experience, learn by masuabetaitʉ
experience something wʉsukatʉ
explain nimabunikʉtʉ, nitsʉbunikʉtʉ
explain something nisuabetarʉ K
explode pʉhtsarʉ, wʉhkwʉmarʉ
explode from heat kupʉtsarʉ
explore for oil tokwaitʉ
explosive pʉhtsa?etʉ?
expression of disgust ai
extend hospitality to a guest mananaa?waihkarʉ
extinguish murukarʉ, tukarʉ
extinguish, unplug to tsahtukarʉ
extinguish a fire wʉhtukarʉ K
extinguished puuhkikatʉ
extreme stomach pain sapʉ wʉnʉkatʉ
extremely greedy pihitsitʉyarʉ
eye pui
eye, pupil of tuhpui
eyebrow ka?ibʉhʉ
eyeglasses pui tsa?nika?
eyelash puitʉsii
eyelid pui narʉsoٖ
eyes, close everyone's sʉmʉ ʉhtsumitʉ
eyes, close the ʉhtsumarʉ
eyes water ohpeto?ikarʉ
eyes water heavily pa?okwetʉ

F f

face kobe
face, false kobe tsa?nika?
face, freckled tutʉsawʉ koobeٖ

face, gray esikakwo?a
face, make a wry sʉkʉbuninitʉ
face cream kobe kiihtʉ?eka? W
face- downward, lying muparai habinitʉ K
face powder homobi saapiٖ
face towel kobe matsuma?, nakobe matsuma?
fail to do something kemahpʉ?arʉ
fail to reach to?wʉminaitʉ
fail to reach something tsa?wʉminarʉ
faint esitʉyaitʉ, sua watsikatʉ, tsihkwinumai
faint, feel kwinumasuarʉ
faint repeatedly esikooitʉ
fairy story narʉkuyunapʉ
faith tokwʉsuakʉna
faith in someone, lose nasuwʉhkitʉ
faithful nanʉsutsawaitʉ, nasutsawaitʉ W
faithful person nasupetipʉ K
falcon huumara?
fall yumarʉ
fall using foot, make taperʉ
fall, snow- tahka?ʉmarʉ
fall, trip and nʉʉhkupatʉ, nʉʉhpisi?maitʉ
fall down wʉhtʉkwaitʉ
fall into something tʉyumarʉ
fall off pahitʉ, tʉpehemi?arʉ
fall off or away from tʉpʉherʉ W
fall plum kusisʉkʉi
fall season yʉba
fall short nasutamʉ wʉminaitʉ W, pihpokaarʉ, to?wʉminaitʉ
false nakaa?aitʉ
false face kobe tsa?nika?
false mallow, red puha natsu W, yokanatsu?u K
false teeth tamatsa?nika?
falsely, accuse someone tʉbehyaarʉ

families, three separate
pahibahtɨnɨnɨ

family nɨmɨ haahkana?

famine, have tsihakooihkatɨ

fan nɨɨhɨhtsaʔwɨ?, wɨnekɨrɨ

fan for fire wɨnekɨtɨ? K,
wɨʔɨnenihku? W

fantasy, (fairy story) narɨkuyunapɨ

far away manakwɨ K

farmer, white tɨtsakwoo raiboo?

farther along miibeʔtɨ

fast pɨhetɨ

fast, stuck pimɨnikatɨ

fast, walk pohyamiʔarɨ

fasten wɨhtɨpɨkarɨ

fasten on harness namuhkarɨ

fasten with shoelace napɨbosarɨ

fat yuhhu K

fat, cut off surface wɨhkwɨnetɨ

fat, fry out kuhpitsuniʔarɨ W

fat, ref to yuhu

fat person yupɨ

father ahpɨ?

Father, Our Taʔahpɨ

father's sister paha?

fatten yuhu bɨhkaitɨ

fattest one yuhu wehkipɨ

fault, find manímɨarɨ

fault, find (with someone)
tɨbehyaarɨ

fear, run to something through
namarunehtsɨrɨ

fearful nanakuyaʔarɨ

feather sia-, sie

-feather, Painted Ketse naʔbo

feather mattress sia sona rɨbaki?

feather pillow sia tsohpe

feathers, pick a bird of its noʔitɨ

feathers, pluck a bird clean of
pahtsi noʔitɨ

February Positsɨ mɨa

feces kwitapɨ

feed makaarɨ

feed, tell to makahtɨnikatɨ

feeding lot soni wɨhtɨmapɨ

feel masukaarɨ

feel anger tuhu suʔaitɨ

feel around makwarɨ, tsakwatɨ

feel around with hand mawa-

feel cool hɨhtsawɨkatɨ

feel faint kwinumasuarɨ

feel happy naʔokɨsuarɨ

feel numb sɨsɨʔnitɨ

feel pity mɨɨrɨʔikatɨ

feel rage tuhu suʔaitɨ

feel something tsasukarɨ

feel with foot tasukarɨ

feet, have cold tasɨkɨmitɨ

feet in water, paddle pawɨpaʔitɨ

feet, standing on hind
manawɨnɨkatɨ

feet, wash narakotserɨ, takotserɨ

feet, wipe tasuʔnetɨ

female animal piabɨ

female kinsman naʔnɨmɨ

female kinsman, man's
naʔwaʔihpɨ?

female kinsman, woman's
waʔihpɨ?

female teacher tɨboorɨɨ pia?

fence nɨɨhtɨma?, tɨɨhtɨmapɨ K

fence, hog mubi poʔroo
rɨhtɨma? W

fence, hog-pen hooki tɨɨhtɨmapɨ

fence, put up a barbed wire
puhihwi tɨɨhtɨmarɨ

fence of hog pen poʔro tɨhtɨmapɨ

fence something tɨɨhtɨmarɨ

fence staples tɨɨhtɨmapɨha
tɨrawɨna?

fence up wɨhtɨmarɨ

fenced pasture soni tɨhtɨmapɨ

fermented saahtotsitoʔikatɨ

festering pisi

fetch petsʉ miʔarʉ, yaahuyarʉ
fetch firewood kono miʔarʉ
fetch water tuuhuniitʉ W
fetch water for someone
  tuukʉmiʔarʉ
fever kuhtsʉniʔ
fever, typhoid narʉʔʉyʉ kuhtsʉniʔ
fever, yellow ohakuhtsʉni
feverish, be kuhtsʉnitʉ
fever plant poiya
few hʉitsi, hʉʉ
few times hʉʉsʉ
field, drill a tʉrahnaiʔitʉ
field, plowed tʉtsakwoopʉ
field lark hiitooʔ K, N,
  ohanʉnapʉ W
field mouse pia kahúa
Field-lark Hiitooʔ K, N
fifty cents sʉkweebiʔ
fight naʔarutʉ W
fight, fist naʔarurʉʉʔ
fight hand-to-hand narohparʉ
figures, group of tʉrʉtsʉpʉ
file tʉmatsuneʔ W
file a surface tʉmatsunarʉ
fill ibuʔikʉrʉ
fill something W tʉmarʉ
fill up muʔibuikʉrʉ
fill with people tsʉhkikatʉ
fill with water paa maʔibuʔikʉtʉ K,
  pawʉsaʔnaitʉ W
-filled, water paʔibuikatʉ
filled to the brim ibuʔitʉ
filled up wʉtsʉʔmitʉ
filled with water by drinking
  pakwʉʔsʉʔmitʉ
finally (or at last) haya kwasikʉ
financial bank puhihwi kahni
financially, broke tʉtsuʔmapʉ
find fault manímʉarʉ
find fault with someone
  tʉbehyaarʉ

find out sutuuʔarʉ
find out for oneself naraʔurakʉtʉ
find room for someone or
  something haakarʉ
find something urarʉ, wʉʔurarʉ
find something being looked for
  toʔurarʉ
find something with the hand
  maʔurarʉ
fine gravel pasi waapi
fine-toothed comb pusiʔa
  natsihtuʔyeʔ
finger, index tʉtsihtsukaʔ
finger, little mahtuaʔ,
  tʉehmahtuaʔ W
finger, middle mahtʉpináaʔ K,
  masʉwʉhkiʔ W
finger ring maʔnikaʔ, moʔo
  tsiʔnikaʔ
fingernail masiito
fingers masʉwʉhkiʔ
fingers, rip with tsahtʉrʉʔarʉ
fingers, snap mabohto
fingers, snuff fire with W
  tsahtukarʉ
finish marʉkarʉ, tsamarʉkarʉ,
  tsuʔma, tʉmarʉkarʉ
finish off by eating kʉhtsuʔmarʉ
finish telling nimarʉkaitʉ
finished item namarʉkapʉ
fire kohtoopʉ, nakuyaarʉ, weʔhakiʔ
fire, build a kohtóorʉ
fire, extinguish a wʉhtukarʉ K
fire, fan for wʉnekʉtʉʔ K,
  wʉʔʉnenihkuʔ W
fire, grass nakuyaarʉ
fire, heat of kohtoopʉ
fire, light a lamp or kupitarʉ
fire, prairie nakuyaarʉ
fire, quench a murukarʉ
fire (or dry it for jerky), roast
  meat over kuʔinarʉ

fire, set on kutsitonaru

fire with fingers, snuff W
tsahtukaru

fire, stir up kuma?omeru,
ma?omeru

fire, throw into the kuhtsahwiru

fire hole kutuhorapu W

fire hole, dig a kutuhoraru

fire on wuhtikuru

fire poker kutsani

fire-builder kohtoo wapi

fire-tender (in a peyote meeting)
momusaka

fireman kohtoo runahpu, wehhari
tuka?eetu

fireplace kutuhorapu W

firewood kono-, kuna-

firewood, bring back kono honiitu

firewood, bring in konóoru

firewood, chop kuhkeru

firewood, fetch kono mi?aru

firmly, speak ninabitsiaru

first ukunaa

fish ekwi, huato, pekwitu, tsahpi?eru

fish, to huaru

Fish Eaters Pekwi tuhka

fish hook hua? W

fish or fishing hua-

fish trap pekwi pumata huaru

fisherman huawapi

fishing pole huahuupi

fishnet saa?wu hua?

fist, hit with tohpa?itu

fist, hit with knuckle or W
tohtsi?aru

**fist or palm of hand, stop hitting
with** tohpuaru

fist, try or want to hit with
toso?waitu

fist fight na?aruruu?

fists, hit with na?arutu W

fit nunubetu

five mo?obe?

fix hanitu

fix up ma?yukwiitu

flag wana tsiyaa?

flagpole wana tsiyaa?a náhuupi

flail wupuheru W, wuyumi?itu

flailed material wuyumi?ipu

flame we?haki?, we?haru

flank ohútuki

flank of animal puihtsara? W,
soo tuku

flank of living animal kotsana

flap po?hibahpakitu

flap wings kasabipikuru

flash kuhtabearu, kwiitsuba?itu,
we?kwiyanuutu

flash, lightning ekakwitse?e

flash of lightning, discharge a
ekakwitse?eru

flashlight kupita?

flat tahi

flat, long and huyuba?atu

flat, pound wutuki?netu

flatiron turah kwu?ne?

flatten something maruki?netu

flattened suupetu

flea ekapusi?a

fleabane daisy tabetotsiyaa

flesh tuhku

flicker kwiitsuba?itu

flirt ubitukuutu

flirt, want to K na?isa suakutu

flirt with each other nana?isa
nayukwi tukwu

flirt with someone na?isa yukwitu K,
na?isa suakutu W

flitter wu-

float away okwehkwatu, sumu
okwetu

flood paruaitu

flood the riverbank paru?itu

floor napu soona, tasoni, tasoona

flounder tahipʉ pekwi
flour homo-, homopisarʉ, homopʉ
flour, packaged homorohtía?
flour, wheat pʉmata nookoina
flour sack tohtía narʉso
flour sifter tohtía tsasa?wʉki?,
  tsasa?wʉki? K
flow okweetʉ
flow, stop tohtʉmarʉ
flow, tears ohpeto?ikarʉ
flower totsiyaa?
Flower Topʉsana
flower, clock tabetotsiyaa
flower, dandelion soko
  sikʉsatotsiya?
flower, purple cone- tukunʉ natsu̱
flower, stamen of totsiyaa
  papihtsipʉ
flower, sun- ohayaa?
flower head, sun- hi?oopitaohayaa
flower salve, sun- hi?ookwana?
flower stalk or plant, sun- hi?oopi
flower petal totsiyaa patʉpi̱naatʉ
flower vase totsiyaa tsakwʉna?
flowering dogwood siba huupi
flowering plant saatotsiya
flowers, sun hi?oo-
flu ebi̱ wʉmi̱na?
flu, intestinal kohikamʉkatʉ
fly, horse- pia animui, pihpi̱
fly, house- ani̱mui
fly, let an arrow wʉhkikatʉ
fly spray ani̱mui wasʉ
fly up yorimi?arʉ, yʉtsʉrʉ
flycatcher, fork-tailed
  kʉkʉbʉraakwa?si?
flyswatter ani̱mui wʉhtokwe?a?
foam saahtotsito?i?
foaming saahtotsito?ikatʉ
fog pakʉ?nʉapʉ
foggy kwiisuatʉ W, pakʉnaikatʉ
fold tahkwatúubitʉ

fold, un- marʉpi̱su?arʉ W,
  tsahpʉkʉsu?arʉ W
fold over namakwatubiitʉ
folded makwatubiitʉ
folk, women- nanawa?ihpʉ?anʉ W
follow a road pu?eyarʉ
follow scent muwarʉ W
following someone, stop nʉnʉ?itʉ
food tʉhkapa, tʉhkapʉ, tʉhka?ena,
  tʉkʉ
food, animal killed or butchered for
  tʉbehkapʉ
food, boil karʉkʉrʉ
food, boiled nasaapʉ
food, brown wesikʉrʉ
food, brown the otʉ kwasʉkʉrʉ
food, canned tʉrohtʉmapʉ
food, carry tʉkʉ noorʉ
food, cook tʉkarʉkʉrʉ
food, cooked kwasʉkʉpʉ
food, deer K, O arʉkáa rʉhkapʉ
food (of any type), ground tʉkʉ
  tusupʉ
food, leftover kʉhtʉkʉto?ipʉ, tʉkʉ
  to?ipʉ
food, partly eaten narʉhkapʉ
food, pound tayu?nekarʉ
food, prepared hanipʉ
food, receive tʉkʉ himarʉ
food, roast kwasʉkʉrʉ
food, run out of tʉkʉ tsuhmarʉ
food, satisfied with sufficient
  wʉtsʉ?mitʉ
food, stew tʉkarʉkʉrʉ
food, stewed kohtsáa?, tʉkarʉkʉpʉ
food, store-bought tʉkʉ tʉmʉʉpʉ
food grinder tʉkʉ tusu?
food supply, exhaust tʉkʉ tsuhmarʉ
fool kaabehkarʉ, kaahaniitʉ
fool someone nohitekwarʉ
foot naape̱, ta-, tah-
foot, break at joint of naraminaitʉ W

foot, crumble to powder with the
tahhomonutsarʉ W

foot, cut on the narahki?apʉ

foot, feel with tasukarʉ

foot, go on (to look for)
takwainitʉ

foot, go on (to meet someone)
tamunaikʉmi?arʉ

foot, heel of the tapi̱ko?

foot, loosened by takwʉsarʉ

foot, make fall using taperʉ

foot, meet someone by going on
tamunaikʉmi?arʉ

foot, pack a load on tʉnoomi?arʉ

foot, rub with nara?worʉ K

foot, shake ta?wikitʉ

foot, shake the tahta?nitʉ

foot, sole of tahpáana̱

foot, tear with the tasi?kwairʉ

foot, torn by a tasi?kwaitʉ

foot, walk dragging one
tasi?womi?arʉ

foot and lower leg napʉ|b-|r

foot or lower leg nara-

foot wound narahki?apʉ

footprint nanapunipʉ, napʉ,
narapunipʉ

footstool tahtʉki?i?

footwear tried on narahpunipʉ

for, look ho?aniitʉ, puhwaaitʉ,
wehkitʉ.

for money, look puhihwi wehki

for, lust nasuyaketʉ

for, prepare maka?mukitʉ

for safekeeping, put away
to?nikarʉ K

for someone, prepare breakfast
taamahkarʉ

for, reach makwʉbʉtsʉrʉ W,
marurʉ?arʉ

for, scrounge yaahuyarʉ

for, search carefully puhwaaitʉ

for teepees, skins or other
covering nʉmʉkʉni

for someone, wait makamaitʉ

for, watch iyaa?itʉ

for, wish nasuyaketʉ

forbid nimoya?ekʉrʉ

force tahkʉarʉ

force, by (knock down)
wʉnʉʉkuparʉ

force, drag by wʉhpiwokarʉ

force, drive animals by tamʉkʉrʉ

force, enter by sutena ikʉrʉ

force, lead off by sutena betsʉmiarʉ

force, scatter by tohporoorʉ

force, stop someone by tahkoonitʉ

force, take someone by sutena
betʉ

force away tahkʉarʉ

force out tsahkʉarʉ

force to go wʉmi?akʉrʉ K

force to lie down wielding a
weapon wʉhhabi?arʉ

force to sit down sutena karʉrʉ

forced out tsahto?itʉ

forcefully sutena

forcibly exit tohto?itʉ

forcibly, open tohkwʉmarʉ

ford nagwee, na?wee?

forefathers pʉe nʉmʉ roopʉnʉʉ

forehead e?rée, ka?i

foreign country atʉsokoobi

foreigner atabitsi̱ W, atana?i 1

foreleg tohoobe̱

forest soo huuhpi̱

forever usúni̱

forget nasuwatsirʉ

forgive ni?tsu?narʉ, tʉsu?narʉ

forgotten nasuwatsipʉ

fork tʉhka?

fork of Red River, north Natʉmʉʉ
pa?i huna?

fork of a stream atahunubi

fork, pitch- soni tsiyaa?,
 sonitsiima?, tꞈtsiyaa? W
fork, table tꞈhka?
fork-tailed flycatcher
 kꞈkꞈbꞈraakwa?si?
form into a point manutsiarꞈ W
formed to a point mamámutsiakatꞈ
former friend haitsi ihtaipꞈ
forsake someone pꞈah taitꞈ
forth, swing back and natsakwenitꞈ
fortune, tell a nipꞈkarꞈ
fortunes, tell nꞈnipꞈkarꞈ
fortuneteller mapaana?,
 nipꞈkaa?eetꞈ, nꞈmi nipꞈka? K,
 tꞈnipꞈkawapi W
foster child, keep an orphan as
 tahnikatꞈ, tꞈkiihkarꞈ
four hayarokwetꞈ
four-wheeled hack natsa?ani?
Fourth of July Pia buha rabeni
fowl, guinea kokáa?
fox kaawosa, kꞈ?kwꞈria?, kꞈ?tseena,
 ohaahnakatꞈ W, waani K
fox, gray tseena? K
fox, red ekatseena?
frame house wobi kahni
frame, picture naboopꞈha
 naro?nika?, naboopꞈha narꞈso,
 naboopꞈha pꞈkꞈrato?nika?i?
freckled tutꞈsa?wꞈtꞈ W
freckled face tutꞈsawꞈ koobe
freckles tasi?a? W
freeze sꞈꞈkoitꞈ, tahka?imiarꞈ,
 tꞈ?asꞈitꞈ
freeze (or die of the cold)
 sꞈhtꞈyaitꞈ
freeze to death sꞈhtꞈyaitꞈ
freight train tꞈnoo kuna waikina K
frequently naiya
fret pisukwitarꞈ
fried bread yuhu nohkopꞈ
fried meat yuhu rꞈkꞈhmanipꞈ

friend notsa?ka?, tꞈi?
friend, dear haitsíi
friend, disown haitsi wihtaitꞈ
friend, former haitsi ihtaipꞈ
friends, girl- tꞈhtꞈi?
friend, same-sex haitsi
friendliness, un- nakahanupꞈ W
friendly, un- kwetꞈsapꞈ
frighten kuya?arꞈ, tahkuya?arꞈ,
 tꞈ?ꞈyatꞈ, wꞈhkuya?arꞈ, yꞈrꞈhkitꞈ
frighten someone with something
 wꞈ?yꞈrꞈhkitꞈ
frightened kuya?akatꞈ, makuya?aitꞈ
fringed nasꞈki?apꞈ
fringes na?sꞈkia?
fringes, shawl with na?sꞈkia?
frog pasawí?oo?, pohpi kwáai? W
frog, bull- ebimuura ya?ke?
**(from a distance), smell
 something** ꞈkwꞈsꞈ?nitꞈ
from a hide, scrape meat
 tohtsiyu?itꞈ
from a toothache, suffer
 tamanꞈꞈtsikwatꞈ
from, turn away wꞈhbuikatꞈ W
from all directions nano?onai
from behind pinai
from cold, shake tsihturuarꞈ W
from cold, shiver tsihturuarꞈ W
from different directions
 nana?atanaiki
from hands, release mabꞈarꞈ
from heat, shrivel up
 kuhtakwitsoo?nitꞈ W
from here sihkutꞈ
from now on sibe?nikiyutꞈ
from seated position, rise
 nꞈꞈ?nꞈarꞈ
from something, run away
 wꞈanuraitꞈ K
from somewhere, run away pꞈa
 nuhkitꞈ

from the surface, skim yunarʉ

(from place to place), wander noyʉkarʉ

front of, in hunakʉ, munakwʉ

frost tosa nʉʉbaai?, tosa nʉʉbaikatʉ

frothing at the mouth saahtotsito?ikatʉ

frown muhasuarʉ

frozen tahka?ikatʉ

fruit pokopi̱

fruit, bear pokopi tuarʉ

fruit, pick pomarʉ

fruit, plant with edible paiyapi̱

fry meat or vegetables kwasʉkurʉ

fry out fat kuhpitsʉni?arʉ W

frybread yuhu nohkopʉ

frybread, make yuhu nohkorʉ

fulfilled pʉpe?

full tʉtʉbetʉ

full and running over tʉhpetʉ

full house in card game manekihtʉ?

full stomach wʉtsʉ?mi

full strength, pull with tsahturerʉ

fullgrown catfish tuumo?tso?

funeral nʉpʉkarʉʉ?

funeral (burial ceremony) nʉpʉkarʉʉ?

fur, curry animal tsihtu?yerʉ

fur cap pʉhʉ rʉmuihpaa?

fur coat pʉhʉ kwʉsu?ʉ

fur hat pʉhʉ tso?nika?

fuss at someone nimakwihtsetʉ

futilely tsaana

fuzz, hair pʉhʉ?

G g

G-string kohinehki?, tsa?nika?

gag kuitsi̱tsi̱woirʉ W

gag oneself kuitsi̱kwaitʉ K

gain weight yuhu bʉhkaitʉ

gall bladder pu?i?

gall-bladder pain, suffer pu?i?wʉnʉrʉ

galloping sound, make totʉbihkurʉ

galoshes tuu?re napʉ

gamble nanakʉhurʉ, tʉmerʉ, wana rohpetirʉ

gamble over some type of competition nararʉnarʉ

game tʉkʉ wasʉ?

game, archaic na?nohne?eyu?

game, dice awonohi?

game, hunt tʉhoitʉ

game, Native-American ball na?sʉhpe?etʉ

games, play hand na?yʉwetʉ

game, stick for hand tuhhuu?

game, wheel aratsi?

garage na?bukuwáa? kahni̱

garbage tʉrokuriapʉ K, tʉtsakwʉʉriapʉ W

garden pokopi̱ masʉapʉ

garden, raise a tʉmʉsuarʉ

garden, vegetable narʉhka? sokoobi̱, tʉmʉsʉa sokobi K

garden crop tʉmʉsʉapʉ

garden patch tʉkʉ masʉa sokoobi̱ W, tʉmʉsʉa sokobi K

garden plot, vegetable tʉkʉ masʉa sokoobi̱ W

garden product tʉmʉsʉapʉ

garden product, home-grown masʉapʉ W

garden product, raise masʉarʉ W

gargle pakwarʉhtʉkitʉ W, wʉhkwarʉ?rʉkitʉ K

garter narawʉhtama?

gash natsahki?apʉ

gash oneself natsahki?arʉ

gasoline nabaa, na?bukuwàa?a nábaa

gather takwi?oobitʉ, tso?meetʉ

gather in tᵾbomarᵾ

gather together kaʔwitᵾ, narahkaʔwitᵾ, sᵾᵾmaʔaitᵾ

gathered, hand matsiʔokwᵾkatᵾ

geese nᵾkᵾta

general area, separated but in same naʔata W

generation, present nᵾmᵾ rᵾborapᵾ K, pᵾhkᵾra nahanᵾ W

generation, younger ᵾkᵾ nᵾmᵾnᵾᵾ

generation, youngest ᵾkᵾ nᵾmᵾ roopᵾnᵾ K

gentle kesósoorᵾ

geography soko rᵾboopᵾ

get puhihwi tuarᵾ

get a haircut nᵾᵾtsᵾketᵾ

get engaged to be married nᵾpetsᵾʔitᵾ

get, go to petsᵾ miʔarᵾ

get married nᵾpetsᵾʔitᵾ

get off weehtsitᵾ

get off running wenuʔnukimiʔarᵾ

get rations tᵾhimaʔetᵾ

Gets-to-be-middle-aged-man Tenebeka

ghost pᵾe tᵾyaaiʔ

giant mupitsi, piapᵾ

gift-exchanging partner hinanahimitᵾ waipᵾ

gifts, exchange hinanahimitᵾ, nahimiitᵾ, naʔuhturᵾ W

giraffe paʔa ruyuʔ

girl friends tᵾhtᵾiʔ

girth, saddle natsanᵾhkᵾʔ

give tsaʔrurᵾ, utᵾkatᵾ

give an enema narisoʔarᵾ W

give away moccasins napᵾ makarᵾ

give birth tuakatᵾ

give counsel tᵾsuʔᵾrᵾ

give money to someone puhihwimaka

give notice ninakᵾakᵾrᵾ W

give oneself an enema natsinaroʔikᵾtᵾ

give pain nᵾᵾtsikwarᵾ K

give sensation manᵾᵾsukaarᵾ

give several objects himiitᵾ

give something yunirᵾ

give up narahkupaitᵾ, nasutarᵾ

give up exhausted anitᵾ

give up waiting for someone wᵾsuwarᵾkiitᵾ

glare at tsuhni bunitᵾ

glass, drinking paboko aawo, wᵾhibiʔ

glass, looking nabuniʔ

gleam weʔkwiyanuutᵾ

glide puhyᵾnukitᵾ

glitter paratsihkweʔerᵾ

glory, morning soho kᵾaʔetᵾ totsiyaaʔ

glottis ekotᵾwᵾniʔ

glove moʔo narᵾso

glued matsᵾbakikatᵾ

gnat tᵾe esi ᵾnᵾᵾ

go miarᵾ, wᵾmiʔarᵾ W

go after petsᵾ pitarᵾ

go along nahaniitᵾ

go along, invite to petsᵾ kwarᵾ

go back pitsa miʔarᵾ

go back and forth or from side to side piʔnuʔa miʔarᵾ

go backwards hupimiʔarᵾ, piʔnuʔa miʔarᵾ

go crazy eʔmᵾarᵾ, poosubᵾhkaitᵾ

go down weehtsitᵾ, yᵾwimiʔarᵾ

go, force to wᵾmiʔakᵾrᵾ K

go hunting tᵾwoorᵾ

go in circles mahoinitᵾ

go live with in-laws nahyemiʔarᵾ

go moving along noraʔwᵾarᵾ W

go on tunehtsᵾrᵾ

go on foot to look for takwainitᵾ

go on foot to meet someone
tamunaikɨmiʔarɨ

go on vacation hɨɨtsaʔwɨ miʔarɨ

go on warpath mahimiʔarɨ

go out tukamiʔarɨ

go to get petsɨ miʔarɨ

go up yɨtsɨrɨ

go visiting kahni miʔa

go walking sokomiʔarɨ

go-between nitɨsuʔnai wapi

goat, slick-haired pahtsi kabɨrɨɨ?

goathead tuwokwe

God Kaatɨ

goes down, sun tabeʔikamiʔarɨ

going on foot, meet someone by
tamunaikɨmiʔarɨ

going to get lost watsikwarɨ

gold ekapuhihwi, puhihwi

gold color ekahwi

good tsaa, tsaatɨ

good, be yɨyɨkarɨ

good, leave someone for pɨa
miʔarɨ

good enough, not ketokwetɨ

good news tsaatɨ narɨmuʔipɨ

good, no nasɨsɨaʔeetɨ

good!, Oh, yee

good, taste tsaa kamarɨ

good thoughts, think suakɨtɨ

Good-crier Tsaa tenayake?

good-hearted ɨrɨ?

goods, canned narohtɨma?

goods, dry tapi wanapɨ K,
tarɨwanapi W

goods, household namahku

goods, trade wanapɨ K

goose nɨkɨta

gore mukwɨrɨ W

gore someone mukuhparɨ W

gospel tsaatɨ narɨmuʔipɨ

gossip isananarɨmuʔipɨ?,
nimɨɨmiʔarɨ W, tɨtsɨ narɨmiʔitɨ

gossip, whisper watsih tekwarɨ

gossips, one who isanaramuʔitɨ?

gourd anakwanare?

gourd rattle wɨhtsabeyaa?

gown, night- habikwasuugrab for
tsasukwarɨ

graduate tamarɨkarɨ

graduated person tamarɨkɨkatɨ

grammar tekwapɨ rɨboopɨ

grandchild, man's agnatic kɨnu?

grandchild, man's uterine toko?

grandchild, woman's agnatic
huutsi

grandchild, woman's uterine kaku?

granddaughter's husband
tsoʔaahpɨ?

grandfather, maternal toko?

grandfather, paternal kɨnu?

grandmother, maternal kaku?

grandmother, paternal huutsi

grandnephew, man's agnatic
kɨnu?

grandson's wife tsoʔapia?

grape, wild mutsi atsamukwe?,
natsamukwe?

grape juice natsamukweʔa paa

grapefruit ohápitɨɨʔa taka? W, pia
ohapitɨ K

grapevine natsamukweʔa sɨɨki

grasp matsarɨ W

grass ekasonipɨ, soni, sonipɨ

grass, broom tɨɨnua

grass, clump of puhi taitɨ K

grass, common yuu sonipɨ

grass, cut weeds or soni
wɨhpomarɨ

grass, dead puhi kooʔipɨ, puhi
tɨyaitɨ

grass, graze on soni toorɨ

grass, graze on turkey puhitookatɨ

grass, mow soni wɨhpomarɨ, soni
wɨtsɨkerɨ

grass, rye pui tsaseni
grass, turkey puhitóo?
grass burr soni wokweebi
grass fire nakuyaarʉ
grasshopper aatakíi?, aatamúu?, wosa a?ra?
grated object, pulverized or tusupʉ W
gratify ninʉsupetitʉ
grave nabʉkapʉ W, nʉpʉkapʉ K, N, W
gravel, fine pasi waapi
graveyard nʉpʉkapʉ K, W, nʉpʉkʉ sokoobi
gray esi-, esipitʉ, kusipi W
gray, appear esinabuniitʉ
gray appearance esitsʉnʉ?iitʉ
gray bird, small kusisai?
gray (color of ashes) kusi-
gray face esikakwo?a
gray-faced, accuse someone of being (used in making fun of someone) etʉsikawo?arʉ W
gray fox tseena? K
gray mare esipia?
gray mountain esitoyaabi
Gray-box Esikono
gray-colored plant kusinʉʉhparabi
Gray-flat-lying-object Esihabiitʉ
Gray-streak Esihabiitʉ
graze kʉnorʉ, toorʉ W, tʉhkanʉmiitʉ
graze (from place to place) tooniitʉ
graze (on grass) soni toorʉ
graze (on turkey grass) puhitookatʉ
grease wihtʉ?eka?, yuhhu K
grease, melted wihi
grease something tʉ?ekarʉ, wihi tʉ?ekarʉ
greasy, taste oily or wihi kamatʉ

great aunt, maternal kaku?
great distance, separated by namanakwʉ K
great grandchild tsoo?
great grandparent tsoo?
great uncle, paternal kʉnu?
Great Spirit Ta?ahpʉ
greater than ka?wekitʉ
greed pihitsinaina
greedy pihitsi
greedy, extremely pihitsitʉyarʉ
green pati-, patiwiaketʉ
greenbriar tamutso?i K
greyhound mubi sarii?
grief tabʉikatʉ
grill ku?inawaata
grin mu?yanesuarʉ
grind kʉhpitsoonitʉ, tusurʉ
grind, hand makitsarʉ
grind the teeth kʉhporokitʉ
grinder tʉkʉ tusu?
grinder, food tʉkʉ tusu?
grinding stone tʉsoyuni
grit the teeth kʉhkwitsitʉ, kʉhporokitʉ
groan hubinitʉ, nahúbiniitʉ
groceries narʉhka?, tʉkʉ tʉmʉʉpʉ
groceries, buy (or otherwise receive) narʉhka?ruarʉ
groceries, run out of narʉhka?tsu?marʉ
grope around tsakwatʉ
ground corn hanitusupʉ
ground, dig a hole in the tohkonarʉ
ground, driven into tawekwitʉ
ground, pound pillowsticks into tsohpe takwʉnarʉ
ground, rocky tʉpi sokoobi W
ground, throw body on the kwanu?itʉ K
ground food of any type tʉkʉ tusupʉ

ground meat tʉhkapa narʉsupʉ W
ground squirrel ekwakʉʉpi?, ewa kʉʉpi?
ground up object nasupʉ K
groundhog huuna?
grounds tusupʉ W
group of figures tʉrʉtsʉpʉ
group of people sʉʉmʉ?okʉ
groups, divided into narahpomi?itʉ
groups of people, three pahibahtʉnʉnʉ
groups, three separated pahibahtʉ
grow nahnami?arʉ, sʉatʉ
grow in height and health naanaarʉ
growing over, kill by puhi tʉyaitʉ
grown man mu?woo
grown son or daughter nahnapʉ
guess nʉnipʉkarʉ
guess-over-the-hill nanípʉka
guest, escort a (some place) panimi?arʉ
guest, extend hospitality to a mananaa?waihkarʉ
guest, take someone home as panimi?arʉ
guinea fowl kokáa?
gum sanahkoo? W
gum, chew sanahkoo kʉyu?netʉ
gum, chewing kʉtsʉwe?, sanahkoo? W
gums so?o ruhkʉ
gums of teeth tamaruhkʉ
gun tawo?i? K
gun, aim a wʉhkurʉ
gun, shoot a wʉhkikatʉ
gun repeatedly, shoot a ta?wo?ekarʉ
gun, shoot a repeating tsatʉka?karʉ
gun, shot- so?o narʉbaki?
gunny sack soni narʉso?

gunpowder nakutisi
gunshot ta?wo?i?

H h

hack tosa waikina, tuwaikina, wobi puukʉ
hack, four-wheeled natsa?ani?
hack oneself nʉʉhki?yu?itʉ
hackberry kʉrahúu? K, soho bokopi
hackberry, southern mitsonaa?
hail paho ʉmarʉ, pahoopi
hair tso?yaa?
hair, chest pʉhʉ nʉnapʉ
hair, comb natsihtu?yeetʉ, tsihtu?yerʉ
hair, comb someone's matsíhtuyeetʉ P
hair, curl wesibapi?arʉ
hair, curly wesibaapi
hair, head of tso?yaa?
hair, leg tapʉ K
hair, part natsihpe?akarʉ, tsihpe?akarʉ
hair on end, stand sʉroonitʉ
hair, tangled papi tsʉnʉ?itʉ
hair, underarm anapʉhʉ
hair, wave wesibapi?arʉ
hair fuzz pʉhʉ?
hair on lower arm or hand mapʉhʉ
hair tonic papi wihtʉ?eka?
hair-parter natsihpe?aka?
hairbrush natsihtu?ye?
haircut naraketorootʉ, nʉʉtsʉke?
haircut, get a nʉʉtsʉketʉ
-haired goat, slick pahtsi kabʉrʉʉ?
hairpin papi tsihtʉpʉka?
hairy chest pʉhʉ nʉnapʉ
hairy vegetation pʉhʉ?
half sʉkwerʉ

half-dollar sʉkweebiʔ
halter nakobe tsaʔnikaʔ
hammer tʉhraniitʉ K, tʉrʉhaniʔ W
hammer something tahhanitʉ
hand moʔo
hand, back of the makwe
hand, close someone's mahtsukitʉ
hand, close the mahtsokaitʉ
hand, close up with marohtʉmarʉ
hand, cramped maʔitsaʔbʉkatʉ
hand, cut on namahkiapʉ W
hand, find something with the
  maʔurarʉ
hand (or lower arm), hair on
  mapʉhʉ
hand, have cramp in maʔwʉtsa
  roʔponitʉ
hand, have something in yahkatʉ
hand, hired tʉrʉʔai wapi̱
hand, hold down with makʉnaitʉ
hand, hour tabe moʔo
hand, insert tʉmaʔniikarʉ K 2
hand or wrist, lose something
  from maʔkweʔyarʉ
hand, move by tsanuarʉ
hand, No- Mooʔwetʉ
hand, numb the masʉsʉʔnitʉ
hand, offer mahiyaitʉ
hand, open the makwʉsaitʉ
hand, palm of mapaana̱
hand, paralyzed maʔitsaʔbʉkatʉ
hand, plant by tʉrahnarʉ
hand games, play naʔyʉwetʉ
hand, polish by mapʉnukeerʉ
hand, quench by marukarʉ
hand, shell something by
  tsahkítoʔarʉ
hand, slap with palm of tohpaʔitʉ
hand or lower arm, sprain or
  break namaminaitʉ
hand, squeeze matsáhtsurʉ
hand, game, stick for tuhhuuʔ

hand, stop hitting with fist or
  palm of tohpʉarʉ
hand, tangled by makwʉsikʉkatʉ
hand, throw over- kwihitʉ
hand, touch lightly with the
  makwʉʔnetʉ
hand, wash namoʔo kotsetʉ
hand. wipe off with the
  makwineetʉ
hand gathered matsiʔokwʉkatʉ
hand grind makitsarʉ
hand jerk mayʉʔyʉrʉ
hand lotion makwʉrʉʔekaʔ W,
  moʔo kwitʉʔekaʔ K
hand-to-hand, fight narohparʉ
hand twitch mayʉʔyʉrʉ
handcar kʉʔwonʉhʉbai
handcar, railroad kʉʔwʉnʉbaaʔi̱,
  piʔyʉpu̱ káaʔi̱ W
handcuff a person moʔo wʉhtamarʉ
-handed, left ohinikatʉ
-handed, right tʉbitsikatʉ
handicapped persons
  wʉʔminaʔnʉʉmʉ
handkerchief namotʉsibeʔ
handkerchief, work-type
  pʉesúubeʔ K
handle tʉtsʉhanitʉ
handle, carry by the natsayaarʉ
handle, carry (a container by the)
  tsahimarʉ, tsayarʉ
hands, clap tohtarakitʉ
hands, crack something with
  marʉbarʉ
hands, crease with the
  makwipunarʉ K
hands and knees, crawl on
  mahuʔnetʉ
hands, hold moʔo tsaaitʉ
hands, loosen with mahkwʉmarʉ
hands, make a hole with
  tsahtaikʉtʉ

hands in the water, paddle
paruhparʉ

hands to expel water, press down
with mabitsoorʉ

hands, release from mabʉarʉ

hands, rub applying pressure with
the masuʔnerʉ

hands together, rub namʉsuʔnetʉ

hands, wring out with tsahpitsoorʉ

handsaw moʔo huutsihkaʔaʔ

hand saw, two-man huutsihkaaʔ

hang natsawenitʉ

hang a long object on a line wʉsóorʉ

hang (choke to death by rope
around the neck) oihtʉyaitʉ

hang meat up to dry inaʔetʉ

hang oneself nʉʉkwenitʉ

hang over something nʉʉsooʔetʉ

hang someone with a rope
ooibehkarʉ

hang something tsakwenitʉ,
tʉrohtsanitʉ, wenuarʉ

hang suspended tsanikatʉ

hang up totsʉbakitʉ, wʉkweniitʉ K

hang up carelessly wʉhtsanitʉ

hang up something tohtsanarʉ

hang up something on a nail or
hook tsaʔwenitʉ, tsahkwenitʉ W

hang up to dry pasahtohtsanarʉ

hanger natsaweniʔ

hanger, clothes kwasuʔu sakweni,
ooʔrʉ tohtsanaʔ W

hanging narohtsanarʉ,
natsahkweniitʉ

hanging, knock off something
wʉhtokarʉ

hanging down, pant with tongue
hehekʉbʉniitʉ

Hanging-from-the-belt Tʉʔsinaʔ

happen naharʉ

happen to be somewhere
nahabitʉtʉ

happening nahapʉ

happy tsaa nʉʉsukatʉ

happy, feel naʔokʉsuarʉ

harass by chatter nimʉsasuarʉ

hard kʉhtáatʉ, kʉtáatʉ

hard (and brittle), be koobetʉ

hard cider saah totsi baa

hard up nahawaruʔikatʉ

harness nabʉsa nabikapʉ,
narʉmuhkʉ

harness, fasten on namuhkarʉ

harness, leather nabikapʉ

harness buckle nʉʉhtʉpɨkaʔ

harness something nanoomanitʉ

harrow siibarʉ K, ɩsatʉsukitʉ,
tʉtsatʉkiʔ, tʉtsatʉsukitʉ

harrowed tʉtsatʉsukitʉ

harvest kohoʔaaitʉ, tsoʔmepʉ

harvest a crop pomarʉ

harvested crop pomapʉ

hastily yohyaku

hat soni tsoʔnikaʔ, tsoʔnikaʔ

hat, fur pʉhʉ tsoʔnikaʔ

hat, have a tsonikarʉ

hat, straw soni tsoʔnikaʔ

hat, wear a tsoʔnikarʉ

hatchet tsohpe tʉhkaʔaaʔ W

hateful tʉmabisoʔaitʉ

haul away nookwarʉ

haul away, to noorʉ

haul in noohkirʉ, noopitʉ

haul in a vehicle manoorʉ

haul off tsawehkwatʉ

haul sand pasiwanoorʉ

hauling noo-

have a backache piwoʔsa wʉnarʉ

have a backache in lower back
piwoʔsa wʉnʉkatʉ

have a hat tsonikarʉ

have a headache papɨkamaitʉ

have a husband kuumabaitʉ

have a sore throat kuitsɨsʉatʉ

have a stiff neck wo?rohtsarɨ
have an appetite tsihasuarɨ
have an earache nakị wɨnɨkatɨ
have an evil spirit poosubɨhkaitɨ
have authority tɨsu?atsịtɨ
have bad odor kwanarɨ
have children tɨrɨetɨparɨ
have cold feet tasɨkɨmitɨ
have cramp (in hand) ma?wɨtsa
  ro?ponitɨ
have famine tsihakooihkatɨ
have hope kɨ?urɨ
have leg cramp ta?itsa?bɨrɨ W,
  ta?witsa roponiitɨ K
have mercy sutaaitɨ
have money puhihwi tuarɨ
have moonlight mɨahtabeba?itɨ
have muscle cramp or spasm
  toponitɨ K
have odor kwanarɨ
have pneumonia tɨ?inawɨnɨrɨ
have power tɨsu?atsịtɨ
have something in hand yahkatɨ
have underwear on tsa?nikɨkatɨ
having a sibling taka?katɨ
having supernatural power
  puhakatɨ
haw, black tubokóo, wokwekatɨ
  huupi
haw, red tu?amowoo
hawk tosa nakaai
hawk, chicken kokorá?a
  aràhima?etɨ
hay rake tɨtsa?ooki?
he ma?, orɨ, surɨ, u, urɨ
head paapị, papị
head, carry on the kuyaarɨ
head, carry something on the
  tso?yaarɨ
head, cover the mana?koroomitɨ K
head, duck under water
  paku?nerɨ

head down (on something), lay
  the tsohtɨkikatɨ
head, lift tso?nɨarɨ
head in agreement, nod the
  nihtsamu?itɨ
head in disagreement, shake
  ka?witsetɨ K
head into something, poke
  tso?nikarɨ, tɨtso?nikarɨ
head, raise tso?nɨarɨ
head against something, rub
  tsotso?neetɨ
head no, shake the tso?wiketɨ
head, squeeze to a ma?okwerɨ
head lice, search for pusiaketɨ
head, sunflower hi?oopịtaohayaa
head, wipe something with the
  tsotsomarɨ
head louse pusị?a, yupusia
head of hair tso?yaa?
headache papị wɨnɨkatɨ
headache, have a papịkamaitɨ
headdress pia tso?nika?
-headed buzzard, red ekabapị
headwear, try on tsohponiitɨ
heal yurahpetɨ
heal-all plant puhakatɨ
health, improve in tebuunitɨ
health, person of delicate takwipɨ
healthy keho?yopịtɨ,
  kenama?ɨbɨ?itɨ
heap up pia wɨ?utsitɨ
hear nakarɨ W
hear or make noise in timber
  huukisaakitɨ
hear, over- nakɨhoorɨ
hear something tɨnakarɨ
hearer, place known by speaker
  and pɨkɨhu
hearing tɨnakatɨ
Hears-the-sunrise Tabe nanika
hearse tɨyai waikinạ K

hearse tᵤyaipᵤha nooʔeeʔtᵤ W

heart pihi-, pihinabooʔ, pihi̱

heart, sweet- notsaʔkaʔ, tᵤᵤʔurapᵤ W, K

hearted, good- ᵤrᵤʔ

heartily, laugh nanihkuparᵤ

hearth kutᵤhorapᵤ W

heat, explode from kupᵤtsarᵤ

heat, kill with kuhkuparᵤ

heat, radiate kusᵤwetᵤ

heat, shrivel up from kuhtakwitsooʔnitᵤ W

heat of fire kohtoopᵤ

heat something kuhtsᵤnikᵤrᵤ

heated rock nakutᵤkᵤnaʔ

heater yuʔa nakohtooʔ

heating, dry by kupisarᵤ

heavens tomobaʔatᵤ, tomoobi̱

heavily, pant hehekᵤbᵤniitᵤ

heavily, tread tanᵤʔyᵤkitᵤ

heavy pᵤhtᵤ

heavy shawl pohotᵤ naʔsᵤkíaʔ

hedge apple etᵤhuupi

heed naki̱ hiikatᵤ K

heel, rubber tuuʔre tahpikoʔ

heel of shoe tahpi̱koʔ

heel of the foot tapi̱koʔ

heels, kneel down sitting back on tanatookarᵤtᵤ

height and health, grow in naanaarᵤ

held matsokatᵤ

hello ahó

help, ask for naníhtsawaʔitᵤ

help decide tsasuʔatsitᵤ

help down tsakwerᵤ

help, offer someone masutsarᵤ

help one another naruituahkarᵤ

help someone tᵤituarᵤ

help someone walk tsamiʔakᵤrᵤ

help to mount tohkᵤarᵤ

help up matsáyᵤtsᵤrᵤ

help up from sitting to standing position matsákwᵤnᵤkᵤrᵤ

hem pihkᵤmaʔ K

hemmorhage pᵤᵤokwetᵤ

hen nohabitᵤ, turuawapi̱

hen, laying turuawapi̱

hen, setting nohabitᵤ

her ma, mahka, ohka, ohko, pᵤ, uhka

herb pawahkapᵤ

herb, medicinal pᵤhᵤ natsu, pᵤhᵤ rᵤʔsaasi

herd marᵤa, tahkoonikarᵤ

herd, cut out of the tahkaaitᵤ

here iki̱

here (at this point) siʔanetᵤ

here, from sihkutᵤ

here, right makᵤ

-here, Wind-running Nᵤenuhkiki

hiccough hᵤʔniipᵤʔ, hᵤʔniitᵤ

Hiccough-daughter Hᵤʔnipitᵤ

hickory kᵤhtáa mubitaiʔ, pahtsi mubitai, paatsi mubitaiʔ

hide tuhᵤpᵤ, tᵤhᵤbᵤ, watsitᵤkitᵤ K, watsi̱ habiitᵤ

hide, animal pimoroʔa pᵤhi, pᵤhᵤʔ

hide, cow pimoroʔa pᵤhi

hide, dehair a wᵤhkwᵤnetᵤ

hide, process of tanning a narᵤsoʔipᵤ

hide, raw- ᵤhtaayuʔ

hide ready to use, raw- pahkipᵤ

hide rope, raw- pahki̱ wiyaaʔ

hide, scrape meat from a tohtsiyuʔitᵤ

(hide oneself), secret oneself away watsi̱ habiitᵤ

hide, tan a kwiipᵤsiarᵤ, tᵤsoʔarᵤ

hide, tanned narᵤsoʔipᵤ, tᵤsoʔipᵤʔ

hide, tanned deer pikapᵤ

hide something namabimarᵤ

hide-and-seek naʔwekitᵤʔ

hides, pick for scraping
to?tsimuhpe?

high panihputʉ mabà?atʉ, pa?atʉ

high pitched putsi tʉnikwʉyʉ K

high pitched, sing putsi
kwʉtsʉbaitʉ

high up tsihtararʉ

hill keno, ku?ebi, noo-

hill, guess-over-the- nanípʉka

hill, one anáabi

hill standing alone, one nookarʉrʉ

hill, sand pasiwanoo? W

Hill People Ononʉʉ

hill up ma?ohta?aitʉ, wʉno?karʉrʉ

hillside keno

him ma, mahka, ohka, ohko, uhka

hind feet, standing on
manawʉnʉkatʉ

hindquarter kotsana, pabo tuhku,
tohoobe̠

hip piwo?sa̠

hips, walk swinging pi?weke mi?arʉ

hire naahkarʉ

hired cook tʉkʉ maniwapʉ

hired hand tʉrʉ?ai wapi̠

his pʉ

history narʉkuyunʉ rʉboopʉ

hit, attempt to (with a weapon)
wʉsukwarʉ W

-hit-someone, Take-a-stick-and
Huuwʉhtʉkwa?

hit and push under water
wʉhpaaku?nerʉ

hit by surprise wʉnʉ?yʉ?itʉ

hit repeatedly wʉhpa?itʉ

hit something wʉhtʉkwarʉ

hit with fist tohpa?itʉ

hit with fist, try or want to
toso?waitʉ

hit with fists na?a̠rutʉ W

hit with knuckle or fist
tohtsi?arʉ W

hitch, un- too?itʉ

hitch a horse, un- noro?yarʉ

hitch an animal, un- to?yarʉ W

hitch up mahkarʉ W

hitch up horses and buggy
nomohkarʉ

hitched namamohkarʉ

hitting, make cry by toyaketʉ

hitting with fist or palm of hand,
stop tohpʉarʉ

hobble mo?o wʉhtama?

hobble an animal mo?o wʉhtamarʉ

hobble for a horse tʉmo?o
wʉhtama?

hoe kuwʉhora?, muhpe?, puhi
yʉkwitʉ?

hoe soil puhi yʉkwitʉ

hog hooki̠, mubi̠ po?roo?, munua?,
po?ro?

hog fence mubi̠ po?roo rʉhtʉma? W

hog-pen fence hooki̠ tʉʉhtʉmapʉ

hog pen, fence of po?ro tʉhtʉmapʉ

hoggish pihitsi̠tʉyarʉ

hogs po?ropʉnʉʉ

hold yahkatʉ

hold a curing ceremony for
someone puha?arʉ

hold back information
niwatsi?aikʉ?itʉ

hold council ka?witʉ

hold down with hand makʉnaitʉ

hold hands mo?o tsaaitʉ

hold races narʉrʉnitʉ

hold something yuhnukarʉ

hole taaitʉ, taina

hole, animal itsaraitʉ ʉnʉa kahni

hole, chop a wʉhkonarʉ

hole, dig a horarʉ, tʉhhorarʉ

hole, dig a fire kutʉhorarʉ

hole, dig a (in the ground)
tohkonarʉ

hole digger, post- tʉhora?

hole, drill a (with an instrument)
tohtꜟbꜟ?itꜟ

hole, fire kutꜟhorapꜟ W

hole with hands, make a
tsahtaikꜟtꜟ

hole, smoke kahkuꜟ?e, kahni kuꜟ?e

hole dug by man nahorapꜟ

hole dug in soil hoora

holes saa?wꜟ

holey saa?wꜟtꜟ, tsahtaaikatꜟ

hollow ha?wo?itꜟ, kuwo?nepꜟ,
tꜟha?wokatꜟ

hollow, make wꜟhha?wokarꜟ

holly, yaupon ekapokopi

Holy Spirit Atsabi?

home kah-, kahni

home, (to) arrive tsakꜟbitꜟkitꜟ

home or room, invite into
ni?ika?itꜟ

home, own a nꜟmꜟnakarꜟ

home as guest, take someone
panimi?arꜟ

home-grown garden product
masꜟapꜟ W

homogeneous sꜟꜟnitꜟ

homogeneous throughout sꜟmꜟ
sꜟsꜟnitꜟ

hone tꜟmakꜟma?arꜟ

honey ꜟnꜟ bihnaa

Honey Eaters Pena tꜟhka

honey K wobi pihnaa?

honey locust wokꜟ huupi

honey sieve ꜟnꜟꜟ? ruu?

honeybee wobi pihnaa ꜟnꜟꜟ?

honeycomb ꜟnꜟ bihnaa kahni K,
wobi pihnaa? W

honor mabitsiarꜟ

honored maritsiakatꜟ

hoof tasiitꜟ, tosiite

hoofprints tꜟhꜟyena puni W

hook nanꜟꜟhtꜟpꜟka?, natsaweni?,
tꜟrohtsani?i?

hook, fish hꜟa? W

hook, shoe- napꜟbosa?

hook something muhkarꜟ W

hook up doubletrees on buggy
nomohkarꜟ

hoot muunanahwenurꜟ W

hope nasupeti?

hope, have kꜟ?urꜟ

hope in nasupetitꜟ

horizon, stand just above the tabe
wꜟnꜟ?itꜟ

horn aamuyake?

horn, animal aa

horn, devil's aakáa?

horn, saddle narꜟnoo bapi

horn, sounding of a muyake?

horn brush aanatsihtuye?

horned toad kuhtsu tꜟbini?

horse esikꜟhma?, puku, pꜟa watsi,
tꜟhꜟya, tosa naboo? K

horse, bay ekakꜟma?, ohaeka? K,
tupisi kꜟma?, W ohaekapitꜟ

horse, be thrown forcibly from a
wꜟpꜟherꜟ W

horse, break a masuyu?ikarꜟ K

horse, bridle a tꜟpe tsa?nikarꜟ

horse, buckskin na?nia

horse, calico pitsa naboo? K

horse, chestnut-brown otꜟ kꜟma? W

horse, devil's tosarai?

horse, hobble for a tꜟmo?o
wꜟhtama?

horse, lead a puku tsakꜟmi?arꜟ

horse, lead up a tsakꜟhunitꜟ

horse, mount a tꜟyato?yerꜟ

horse, palomino kwipꜟsiapꜟ,
na?ahnia K

horse, sorrel otꜟ kꜟma? W, tꜟpꜟsi
kꜟma?

horse, tie up a tꜟꜟtsꜟkꜟnarꜟ

horse, unbridle a tꜟpe
tsahkwe?yarꜟ

horse, unhitch a noro?yaru
horse, un- tsiperu
horse, unsaddle a narunoo?ro?yaru
Horse Band, Water Tasúra
horse, white tosa?
horse blanket nahotsa?ma?
horse brush tuhuya natsihtu?ye?
horse buggy, one- sumasu nooi K
horse tracks tuhuyena puni W
horse-drawn sulky sumasu nooi K
Horseback Kiyu, Tuhuyana kwahipu
horseback, carry someone behind
  on piyaru
horseback, chase on
  tomakwuyetu W
horseback, climb on tuhuya ro?itu
horseback, mount on nuuhto?itu
horseback, ride kuayuka?etu W,
  tuhuya karu
horsefly pia animui, pihpi
horses and buggy, hitch up
  nomohkaru
horseweed tosa wahtsuki
hosiery, ladies waipa wananapu
hospital natusu?u kahni, wuminaa
  kahni
hospitality, extend to a guest
  mananaa?waihkaru
hot day tabe kusuwehkatu
hot, turn red ekawehaaru
hot weather uru?itu
hound dog naki sarii?
hound, blood- turayaa sarii
hour hand tabe mo?o
house kah-, kahni, kahni
house, build a kahni?aitu
house, construct a (or other
  building) kahni?aitu
house, adobe ohta kahni W
house, bird- huutsú?a kàhni
house, frame wobi kahni
house, rooming kwaabih kahni

house, school tuboo kahni
house, Stone- Tupi kuni?
house, stone or brick tupi kuni
house, sweat nasukoo?i kahni
house, trailer kahni tubitsika? K
house bug (of any kind) kahni
  busi?a
house mouse kahúu?
house of thieves turuku kahni
house paint kahni ebi K
housefly animui
household goods namahku
housetop kahni ku?e
how many? huu
how many? how much? hipeka?i,
  hipetu
how? hakai, hakani
how, show tumabunikuru
how?, what way? hakaniiku
howl woo?etu
howl woohpunitu, wooru
Howling-coyote Isananaka?
huckleberry huwabo?kóo?
hug kwabaru, toyo kwabaru
human or an animal, trail a
  nayaaru
human skin hunupo?a?, mapó?a?
humble kesósooru
hummingbird wu?ku?buu?
hunchback no?wosaru
hung up narohtsanaru,
  natsahkweniitu
hunger tsihasuaru
hungry person, ravenously
  tsihasi?apu
hunt ho?aitu, tukeru
hunt game tuhoitu
hunting, go tuwooru W
hurriedly namusi, yohyaku
hurry tsanamusohnitu, yohyakatu K
hurry, cause to tsanamusohnitu
hurry up namusohitu

hurt tohhobinitʉ, wʉhhubinitʉ
hurt oneself nahohiyaitʉ,
  nahuhyaitʉ W, namarʉnitʉ K
hurt someone mawʉmerʉ,
  tsiyaketʉ, umarhnitʉ
hurt someone by accident
  tsahhuhyarʉ
husband kumahpʉʔ, mukwo,
  namuwoo
husband, granddaughter's
  (grandson-in-law) tsoʔaahpʉʔ
husband, have a kuumabaitʉ
husband, reject man as ninakabarʉ
husbands nanahtenanʉʉ
hush pʉhkai
hushed pʉhkaikatʉ
hyacinth, wild siiko
hymn hubiya?
hypocritical nakaaʔaitʉ

I i

I nʉ?
I claim it! aahe
ice tahkabi
ice or snow tahka-
ice pick wiiyu
icebox tahka aawo
icicle tahka weʔwenuka?
ignore kwetʉsuakʉrʉ W
ill hoʔyopitʉ, hoʔyopi
ill, be tʉʔoibʉkʉrʉ, uhúntʉkʉ
ill for a long time tʉʔoikatʉ,
  wʉminahkatʉ
illness hubʉhka?, wʉminaa?
illness, long tʉʔoipʉ
illness, recover from tebuunitʉ
illness, suffer an tʉʔoibʉkʉrʉ
imitate a cry niyakekʉtʉ
immediately kihtsi?, namʉsohi,
  subeʔsʉ

immerse oneself in water
  nabawʉhtiarʉ
-immolate (sacrifice/destroy), self
  kuhtʉyarʉ
implement for punching holes
  (through which sinews pass)
  wiiyu
important man namʉnewapi
imprison takwekwitʉ
imprisoned taʔikʉkatʉ
improve in health tebuunitʉ
in, gather tʉbomarʉ
in, haul noohkirʉ, noopitʉ
in a vehicle, haul manoorʉ
in, hope nasupetitʉ
in ashes, roast kusiwʉhpima W
in, screw wʉʔnikarʉ
in, screw something tsakwipunarʉ
in, share tʉmaramiitʉ
in, sneak watsi ikatʉ
in, stuck down tsʉhkarʉ
in agreement, nod the head
  nihtsamuʔitʉ
in disagreement, shake head
  kaʔwitsetʉ K
in front of hunakʉ, munakwʉ
in sun to dry, sit mabasahtʉkitʉ K
in the mud, stuck sekwi sʉhkai,
  yubutsʉhkatʉ
in the mouth, take something
  kʉhyaarʉ
in-law nanamʉsu?, naʔanampʉ
-in-law, brother pʉhʉ reʔtsi
-in-law, daughter huutsi piahpʉ?,
  huutsi piahpʉ
-in-law, parent yahihpʉ?
-in-law, sister paha piahpʉ
-in-law, son monahpʉ?
-in -law, sons nonanʉʉ
in-laws, go live with nahyemiʔarʉ
in place, put narʉkitʉ, tʉkarʉ
in place, set natsawʉnʉkatʉ

in place, set something
natsawʉnʉrʉ
in the sun to dry, sit
pasahtahtʉkitʉ W
in water, sink to the bottom
paʔikarʉ
in water, soak parʉkitʉ
in water, soak oneself naparʉkitʉ
incite to rear up manáawʉnʉʔetʉ
incline tʉpána?
increasing numerically
tʉrakaʔaitʉ
index finger tʉtsihtsuka?
Indian agent itsina̱, nʉmʉ paraibo?
Indian brave tekwʉniwapi̱,
tuibihtsi?, tʉetekwʉni wapi̱
Indian bread tʉranʉ
Indian breadroot ekahkoni
Indian butter tʉʉtsohpepʉ
Indian corn nʉmʉ hani
Indian corncake nʉmʉ nohkopʉ
Indian, non- taiboo?
Indian paintbrush kahnitʉeka
Indian perfume plant tʉsaasi̱
Indian store nʉmʉ narʉmʉʉ?
Indian tobacco tabahko
Indian-type saddle tʉmuhku
inexact hoʔyopipʉ
inexactly, mark nahoʔyopi̱kurʉ
infected pisi
infecting pisi miʔarʉ
infection pisi
inflate mubohtohkirʉ,
mubohtohkitʉ, pohtokʉrʉ
influenza ebi̱ wʉmi̱na?
inform ninʉsuabitarʉ K
information, hold back
niwatsiʔaikʉʔitʉ
inhale deeply through nose
muhibitʉ
ink pen parʉboo?
inquire nikwʉkitʉ

insane, become sua watsitʉ
insect ʉnʉ́?
insect, stinger of an tona?
insect sting tonarʉ
insert taʔnikʉtʉ, tsihtaboʔikʉtʉ
insert hand tʉmaʔniikarʉ K 2
insert into something tsiʔnikarʉ,
wʉnikarʉ
inspect tsaʔatsitʉ
instruct nimabunikʉtʉ,
nitsʉbunikʉtʉ
instrument, any wind woinu
instrument, drill a hole with an
tohtʉbʉʔitʉ
instrument, knock off with an
wʉpʉherʉ W
instrument, marking naboo? K
instrument, play mayaketʉ
instrument, play a wind
muuyaketʉ
instrument, scratch using an
tsahkiʔaitʉ
insult niʔheʔbunitʉ
intend tʉbitsi̱ suarʉ
intend to deceive or cheat
kaasuarʉ
intercede nani̱sutaikʉtʉ
interpret tekwakutʉ
interpreter tekwakʉwapi W
interpreter of Comanche nʉmʉ
rekwakʉ wapi̱
interrupt someone (because of
worry) pisukwitakʉrʉ
intestinal flu kohikamʉkatʉ
intestine tuhkohhi̱ W
intestine, large kwitatsi̱, paboko
intestine, small kohi̱
into, dump toʔwʉʔwenitʉ, wʉhtiarʉ
into, empty toʔwʉʔwenitʉ,
wʉhtiarʉ
into, load tʉrʉbakiʔarʉ
into a container, load toʔnikarʉ W

into small particles, mash
mahomonutsarʉ

into, peep tokwi̱tetʉ

into something, poke head
tsoʔnikarʉ, tʉtsoʔnikarʉ

into the mouth, put something
tʉroʔnikarʉ

into two parts, split tʉapakoʔitʉ

into the fire, throw kuhtsahwirʉ

into a ball, wind wʉhtopoʔnitʉ

intoxicated hibipʉ, makwiʔnumaitʉ

intoxicated person hibipʉ,
kwinumapʉ

introduce oneself nani̱suabetaʔaitʉ,
natsahpunitʉ

introduce someone nisuabetarʉ W

invalid tʉʔoipʉ, wʉhminanʉʉmʉ,
wʉminahkatʉ

invalids wʉʔminaʔnʉʉmʉ

invite into home or room
niʔikaʔitʉ

invite someone in nikwekwitʉ

invite to congregate sʉʉmaʔokarʉ

invite to go along petsʉ kwarʉ

-invites-her-relatives, She Nʉmʉ
ruibetsʉ

iridescent weʔkwi̱yanorʉ

Irish potato paapasi̱

iron tahkwʉʔnerʉ, tʉrah kwʉʔneʔ

iron, branding tʉkohpooʔ

iron, flat- tʉrah kwʉʔneʔ

iron clothing tʉrah kwʉʔnerʉ K

ironing board pʉpaʔakura
tʉrahkwʉʔneʔena̱

irrationally, speak niʔemʉabʉnitʉ

island paa tʉpʉnaatʉʔ W, sokobi
paa tʉbi̱naatʉ W

isolated toroʔihtʉkitʉ

it ma, mahka, maʔ, orʉ, surʉ, u,
uhka, urʉ

it is said that tʉa

It is worse! namanoke

itch pihnaketʉ, pihnaaketʉ

itch, scratch an natsawoʔnitʉ,
tsakwoʔnerʉ

item, exchange one for another
mabihtʉʔuyarʉ

item, finished namarʉkapʉ

item, jagged wakʉʔwʉtʉ

item, return an yaakʉrʉ

item by item, remove wʉpiyarʉ

item, sharpened namakʉmaʔaipʉ

item taken (or object) yaapʉ

item, tested marʉmabunipʉ

item, tried marʉmabunipʉ

item, two-year-old tomohtoopʉ W

items, exchange several gift
naʔoyorʉmakarʉ K

items, load tʉbakitʉ

its pʉ

itself, roll up to wʉhkwitubikatʉ

up with something, roll
tohtopoʔnarʉ

ivy, poison puhi taʔaraʔ

J j

jab tsisuʔwarʉ

jack ekakuyáaʔ, suutaʔ

jackal kaawosa̱

jacket, man's buckskin pika
kwasuʔ

jacket, yellow otʉ peena

jagged item wakʉʔwʉtʉ

jail narawekwi̱ kahni, tʉpi kʉni

January Tohmʉa, Ʉkʉ tooma mʉa

jar paboko aawo

jaw ahra, arapʉ

jealous tʉsuwaʔitʉ

jealousy, rival provoking
wohhohpʉʔ

jeer nisuʔuyaitʉ W

jeer at tʉni̱suʔuyaitʉ

jelly ekayʉ?yʉ?ka?

jelly, petroleum nʉʉhtʉ?eka?,
tsiikụwitehka? K, tsi?wụnʉʉ
tʉ?eka? W

jerk and slam things in anger tuhu
rekwarʉ

jerk, bodily yʉ?yʉturʉ

jerk, hand mayʉ?yʉrʉ

jerk down tsapeherʉ

jerk meat ina?etʉ

jerk meat for someone
tʉ?inakʉrʉ

jerk something wʉhpo?tserʉ K

jerk something toward oneself
tsahpo?tsarʉ

jerk the leg ta?yʉrʉhkitʉ K

jerk the lower leg tahta?yʉtʉ

jerked meat inapʉ, inarʉ

jerky esi inapʉ, inapʉ

jerky, meat inarʉ

**jerky), roast meat over fire (or dry
it for** ku?inarʉ

Jesus-man Wʉkwiya

jewelry nʉnatsi?nika?

jingles pisayu?ne?

jock strap tsa?nika?

join in tʉmaramiitʉ

joint natsimina?

joint, break at the taminaitʉ

joint. pull bones out of
tsahtoko?arʉ

joint of the body, sprain a
wʉkwụsarʉ

joke nohitekwarʉ

joker nayanohitekwarʉ?

jowl meat aratuhku

judge nanakukʉtʉ

judicial power tʉsu?atsipʉ

jug tʉpi aawo

jug, water pihpóo?

juice yoka

juice, grape natsamukwe?a paa

July Pia mʉa, Pʉmata pia buhha
ra?ena mʉa, Ʉrʉi mʉa

jump pohbitʉ

jumping rope nʉhpopi?

June Puhi mʉa

june bug tuʉnʉʉ?

juniper ekawaapi

just nah

just above the horizon, stand tabe
wʉnʉ?itʉ

K k

kangaroo pa?sʉno?a?

kebob, shish kutsiyaapʉ

keep an orphan as foster child
tahnikatʉ, tʉkiihkarʉ

keep quiet niwatsi?aikʉ?itụ

keep secret watsi?arʉ

keep sharpened wʉmutsiakatu?i

keep something tahtʉkarʉ

kerosene keto?kapaa, tuka?a nabaa

key tʉtsihtʉma?

khaki koropitụ

kick sʉʉ anirʉ, sʉʉhkwʉhtitʉ

kick off sʉʉta?ni?arʉ

kick something sʉʉhkwʉhtʉkurʉ

kick something away sʉʉ potserʉ

kick-the-can soo tʉhimarʉ?

kicked away sʉʉhpotsʉkatʉ

kicking, discarded by
sʉʉhpotsʉkatʉ

kid around kaasuarʉ

kidney ta?ki?

kill pehkarʉ, tʉkwụsʉrʉ, wasʉrʉ

kill by growing over puhi tʉyaitʉ

kill several persons nakwụsʉkʉrʉ

kill with a weapon wʉhkuparʉ,
wʉhtokweetʉ

kill with heat kuhkuparʉ

killed, cause to be nabehkakʉrʉ

Kills-something Pakawa
kind ʉrʉ?
kind thoughts tʉsu?ʉrʉ?
kinds, different nana?atapuṯʉ,
    nani̲susumatʉ
king tanisi? W
king in playing-card deck
    ohahkuyaa?
kingfisher pekwi tʉhka?
kinsman na?nʉʉmʉ
kinsman, adult nahnapʉ
kinsman, female na?nʉmʉ
kinsman, man's female na?wa?ihpʉ?
kinsman, male naabia, nahbi?a
kinsman, man's male narenahpʉ?
kinsman, woman's female
    wa?ihpʉ?
kinsman of either sex ta?ka?
Kiowa people Kaaiwanʉʉ
kiss muhraa?ipʉ
kiss, cause to tsamuhraikʉtʉ
kiss someone muhrarʉ
knead mabarʉ W, tʉmabarʉ
knee tana
kneecap tana? ku?e
kneel down sitting back on heels
    tanatookarʉtʉ
knees, crawl on tahu?nerʉ
knife nahuu? W, nahhoo? K
knife, cut with a tsihka?arʉ
knife, drawing nahuu? W,
    nahhoo? K
knife, draw- huusibe?
knife edge kʉmapʉ
knock down wʉhkwabikʉrʉ
knock down by force
    wʉnʉʉkuparʉ
knock off tokarʉ, wʉyumi?itʉ
knock off something hanging
    wʉhtokarʉ
knock off with an instrument
    wʉpʉherʉ W

knock on totʉbihkurʉ
knock on door tohtaraki?arʉ
knock over and spill accidentally
    tsakwʉriarʉ
knock something wʉhpo?tserʉ K
knock something down
    tayu?marʉ
knocked down wʉnʉʉhkuparʉ
knocked over mahuihkatʉ
knoll noo-
knot, tie a wʉtsʉkʉnarʉ
knot, tie in round bundle or round
    wʉhtopʉ?noorʉ
know by experience masuabetaitʉ
knowing supana?itʉ
knowledge of, lack kemabana?itʉ
knowledgeable supana?itʉ
known by speaker and hearer,
    place pʉkʉhu
knuckles, crack tsahporakitʉ

L l

labor, be in tuakatʉ
labor in childbirth nʉhtsikwarʉ
lace saa?wʉ tʉkʉma?ai?
lace, shoe- napʉ tsakwʉsa?,
    napʉbosa?
lace, un- tsahkwʉmarʉ
lace up tsakwʉsarʉ W
laced napʉ saarʉ
laced object natsakwʉsikʉ?
lack naromʉnitʉ
lack knowledge of kemabana?itʉ
lacrosse, play natsihtóo?itʉ
ladder huunaro?i?, naro?i?
ladies hosiery waipa wananapʉ
lady, old narutsa?i
lake ʉmahpaa?
lamb kabʉrʉʉ?a tua
lamely, walk wihnai mi?arʉ

lamp kupi̱ta?, natsayaa ruka? K,
tuka?, tʉka?

lamp or fire, light a kupi̱tarʉ

lamp chimney tuka?a naku?e W

lamp wick tuka?a nawanapi̱

lamppost tuka?a nahhuupi̱

land soko, sokoobi̱

land, deed or title to nabinai
tʉboopʉ

land, lease soko rʉmʉrʉ

land, quarter-section of soko
tsihka?apʉ

land, uneven wohtsa?wʉtʉ

language, sign mootekwo?pʉ

language, speak Wichita
tuhka?naai rekwarʉ

language, Speakers of Wichita
tuhka?naai? niwʉnʉ

lantern natsayaa ruka? K

lap pʉkapʉ

lap with the tongue ka?amoorʉ

lard yuhhu K, yuhukarʉka W

lard, render kuhpitsʉni?arʉ W,
ku?okwerʉ W, yuhukarʉ

large pia

large intestine kwitatsi̱, paboko

large object piapʉ 1

lariat moowi?

lark, field hiitoo? K, N,
ohanʉnapʉ W

lark, meadow- hiitoo? K, N,
ohanʉnapʉ W

lash kwibukitʉ

last kwasikʉ

late keyu K, keyu?u

late, stay tsʉ?nitʉ

late, too ʉi

late in the day tabe?ehi

late-summer plum parawa sʉkʉ

laugh na?yʉnetʉ, yahneetʉ

laugh at su?uyaa?arʉ,
tʉnisu?uyaitʉ, usú?uya?itʉ W

laugh heartily nanihkuparʉ

laughingstock nanʉsu?uyaatʉ,
su?uya?i?

laughter yahnena

lavender esiebipitʉ

lavender W kusiebipitʉ

law mahyarʉ

-law, in nanamʉsu?, na?anampʉ

-law, brother-in pʉhʉ re?tsi̱

-law, daughter-in huutsi piahpʉ?,
huutsi̱ piahpʉ

-law, parent-in yahihpʉ?

-law, sister-in paha piahpʉ

-law, son- in monahpʉ?

-law, sons-in nonanʉʉ

laws, go live with in- nahyemi?arʉ

lawman nʉmi hima?etʉ

lawnmower soni wʉtsʉke? K,
tʉʉtsʉke? W

Lawton, OK Soo kʉni?

Lawton, Okla Puha rʉpaanʉ

lawyer nani?ooki̱ taiboo?

lay an egg, want to nohabi̱ suwaitʉ

lay eggs turuarʉ

lay out tsakwʉnarʉ

lay something down tʉkiitʉ K

lay the head down on something
tsohtʉkikatʉ

layer, take off tsahkwʉrʉ?arʉ

laying hen turuawapi̱

lazy tsanʉmaitʉ

lazy, become nʉʉ?maitʉ

lead umami?arʉ

lead a horse puku tsaka̱mi?arʉ

lead a person or an animal tsakarʉ

lead along matsaaihkakurʉ,
tsakami?arʉ

lead astray tsaka?uhrʉ

lead away a wife nʉpetsʉ?itʉ

lead off by force sutena betsʉmiarʉ

lead others muhnemi?arʉ

lead up a horse tsakʉhunitʉ

leader namɨnewapi̱, nanohmɨnɨ wapi̱ K, nomɨnewapi̱ W

leader, pack-animal tɨnoo wapi̱

leaf puhi, puhipɨ

leaf mixture, mesquite- patso?

leaf wrappers for cigarettes puhi tɨmakwatubi?

leak pasiwɨnɨɨrɨ

lean against something nɨɨbani̱katɨ

lean on something mahtokwɨnaitɨ K

lean over something nɨɨsoo?etɨ

lean something namahtowɨnarɨ

learn nara?urakɨtɨ

learn by experience masuabetaitɨ

learn something new urahkarɨ

lease land soko rɨmɨrɨ

leather nabikapɨ, paakipɨ, pika, pikapɨ, taibo pikapɨ

leather harness nabikapɨ

leave a spouse pɨah kwarɨ

leave, order to nihto?itɨ

leave person alone kekɨnabeniitɨ

leave secretly watsi mi?arɨ

leave someone behind nobɨahraitɨ

leave someone for good pɨa mi?arɨ

leaves, corn hani buhipɨ

leaving a mark, scratch tsahtsi?arɨ

Lee Motah Mota

leech tu?re?

left ohinibetutɨ

left side, at or to the ohininakwɨ

left-handed ohinikatɨ

leftover piinaai

leftover food kɨhtɨkɨto?ipɨ, tɨkɨ to?ipɨ

leg bones tɨrana̱

leg, calf of ta?wiitsa̱

leg, foot and lower napɨ|b-|r

leg, foot or lower nara-

leg, fore- tohoobe̱

leg cramp, have ta?itsa?bɨrɨ W, ta?witsa roponiitɨ K

leg hair tapɨ K

leg, jerk the ta?yɨrɨhkitɨ K

leg, jerk the lower tahta?yɨtɨ

leg, lower naape̱, omo-

leg, raise one tahtsarɨ

legs out, spread po?arɨ

legume pitsa múu

leisurely supewaitɨ

lemon ohahpitɨ sɨkɨ?kamatɨ W, sɨkɨ ka?ma?

leopard naboohmatɨsohpe? W, naboohroya ruhku? K, toya ruhku?

lesion narɨ?ɨyɨ ɨɨ?a?

let an arrow fly wɨhkikatɨ

let out tahto?itɨ

letter tɨboopɨ

letter or package, mail a tɨhyetɨ

lettuce puhi tɨhkapɨ

level sɨɨpetɨ

level valley haapane

liar isapɨ, kaawosa̱, naya?isa?aitɨ

Liar Isatekwa

lice, search for head pusiaketɨ

lice eggs tatsii?

lick ekwɨsibeniitɨ

lid narohtɨma?, tɨmarɨma? K, tɨrohtɨma?

lie isapɨ, isa?aitɨ

lie down haahpitɨ, habiitɨ, kwabitɨ

lie down and think nasutamɨ habitɨ

lie down , force to (wielding a weapon) wɨhhabi?arɨ

lie on back pa?raihabiitɨ

Lie-talk Isatekwa

-lie, This-midday-sun-does-not-tell-a Sihka tabe ke isopɨ

life nɨmɨnaina?, yɨ?yɨmuhkuna̱

life, save someone's tsahkwitso?arɨ
life!, That's namami?akɨ
lift wɨyarɨ
lift from a prone position tsahnɨarɨ
lift head tso?nɨarɨ
lift up toyarɨ, tsahhɨkwɨ?niitɨ W
light kupita?, tuka?, tɨka?
light on something, throw a kupitarɨ
light a lamp or fire kupitarɨ
light blue ebipitɨ, kusipi W kusiebipitɨ K
light, flash- kupita?
light meat pabo tuhku
light-complected pabopitɨ
lighted, un- tukanikatɨ
lightly, rub makwɨ?netɨ
lightly with the hand, touch makwɨ?netɨ
lightning bug kuna na?mahpee?
lightning, discharge a flash of ekakwitse?erɨ
lightning flash ekakwitse?e
lightweight tahi
lightweight shawl tapi na?sɨkia?
-like-a-mouse, Squeaky Kahúu nihku pipikurę
like someone su?akɨtɨ
lily, plant similar to water pa?mutsi
lily, yellow pond kɨriata
limb, tree huupita mooka
limited space, cram into natsinɨhkɨrɨ
limited space, crammed into tsinɨkɨ
limp matɨwetɨ, pitɨwetɨ, tatɨwetɨ, wihnai mi?arɨ
line, clothes- tɨrohtsani?i?
line, draw tsihpoorɨ
line, hang a long object on a wɨsóorɨ

lion pɨhɨ ku?kwe?ya?
lion, mountain wɨra?
lips tɨpe, tɨɨpe
liquid, drain a tsa?ohkwerɨ
liquid, spit out pai tusi?itɨ K
liquid tea puhi tuhpaa W
listen nakɨhitɨ, tokwetɨparɨ, tɨnakarɨ, tɨnakiitɨ
listen carefully tɨbitsinakɨkɨrɨ K
listen to someone tɨmahyokɨrɨ
listen with attention naki hiikatɨ K
listening nakɨkatɨ
little tɨe
little bit hɨitsi
little bluestem ekasonipɨ
little finger mahtua?, tɨehmahtua? W
little one tɨe?tɨ
little people similar to elves Nɨnapi
little toe tahtúa?, tɨeh tahtua?
Little-buffalo Tɨe kuhtsu
Little-medicine Tɨe buakɨtɨ
Little-wolf Esatai
live kahtɨ, yɨ?yɨmuhkumi?arɨ W
live separately, move off to noka?itɨ
live, take away something tahtɨkitɨ
live somewhere nɨmɨnetɨ
live unconcerned yukahnibarɨ
live well yunɨmitɨ, yɨyɨkarɨ
live with in-laws, go nahyemi?arɨ
liver nɨɨmɨ
Liver Eaters Taninɨɨ
livingroom pɨkɨra yɨkwi?enạ W
lizard naki tai?, nɨmɨ ma?tsa?bahki?, paboko?ai, wanasihtaraa? W
lizard, rock tɨpi paboko?aai W
lizard, water pa?boosi?
load noona K

load, carry tɨnoorɨ
load into tɨrɨbaki?arɨ
load into a container to?nikarɨ W
load items tɨbakitɨ
load on foot, pack a tɨnoomi?arɨ
load, un- tsahpɨherɨ, tsapɨyetɨ, tsayumi?i
load up tɨnookɨrɨ
loaf of bread paanɨ
lobe, ear W nakị kwiitạ
locate something ta?wairɨ
location, throughout a oyo?rɨtu
lock tɨtsihtɨma?
lock, pad- natsihtɨma?
lock something, pad- tɨtsihtɨrɨ
lock, un- tsihtɨwarɨ
lock up someone ta?ikɨrɨ
locked up ta?ikɨkatɨ
loco weed esinɨɨhparabi
locust soo yake? W
locust, honey wokɨ huupị
loincloth tsa?nika?
lollypop mukwite?
Lone-tipi Atakɨni
long pa?a-, pa?atɨ
long ago soo be?sɨ
long and flat huyuba?atɨ
long illness tɨ?oipɨ
long time, ill for a tɨ?oikatɨ, wɨminahkatɨ
look at punitɨ, tɨpunirɨ
look at oneself nabunitɨ
look behind oneself nabitɨbunitɨ
look for ho?aniitɨ, puhwaaitɨ, wehkitɨ
look for, go on foot to takwainitɨ
look for money puhihwi wehki
look over puiwɨnɨrɨ
Looking Punitɨ
looking glass nabuni?
Looking-from-side-to-side Ka?mɨtɨhi? W

Looks-brown Kurupitsoni
loose hagwoitɨ W, ha?wo?itɨ
loose, break pihka?arɨ
loose, turn pɨarɨ, wɨhto?yarɨ
loose tooth saatitamakatɨ
loosen takwɨsaitɨ, tsahkwɨmarɨ
loosen with hands mahkwɨmarɨ
loosened by foot takwɨsarɨ
lope aimi?arɨ, wahkami?arɨ
lope, make tsa?aikɨrɨ
Lord Narɨmi?
lose way watsitɨ
lose faith in someone nasuwɨhkitɨ
lose something nasuwatsi, watsikɨrɨ
lose something from hand or wrist ma?kwe?yarɨ
lost watsitɨ
lost, going to get watsikwarɨ
lot, feeding soni wɨhtɨmapɨ
lotion, hand makwɨrɨ?eka? W, mo?o kwitɨ?eka? K
lotus, yellow kɨrɨ?atsị
loud pia
Loud, Talk Pibia nịwɨnɨ?nɨɨ
loudly piapɨ
loudly, cry hubiyaa piayakeetɨ
loudly, sing pia rɨnikwɨtɨ
louse, body saabe busia
louse, crab pɨhɨ pusia, suhu posía
louse, de- nabusi?aketɨ, pusiaketɨ
louse, head- pusị?a, yupusia
love kamakɨrɨ
loved one kamakɨnạ W
lover nɨmɨ?ara?, tɨɨ?urapɨ W, K
lower arm, sprain or break hand or namaminaitɨ
lower back piwo?sạ
lower leg naape̩, omo-
lower leg, foot and napɨ|b-|r
lower leg, foot or nara-
lubricate wihị tɨ?ekarɨ

lukewarm pakuyu?atʉ
lumber woob<u>i</u>
lumberman huuyʉkkwi?
lumberyard huunarʉmʉʉ?, wobi narʉmʉ?
lunatic emʉahkatʉ
lunch tabe rʉhkapʉ W, tʉkʉ noopʉ
lunch or dinner, eat tabe rʉhkarʉ K
lung soom<u>o</u>
lust nasúyake? K
lust for nasuyaketʉ
lye isawasʉ wanakotse?
lying down haahp<u>i</u>
lying down, continue naahábitʉ
lying face-downward muparai habinitʉ K
lying in prone position muparai habinitʉ K
lying somewhere haahp<u>i</u>tʉ

M m

machine, sewing tʉtsahkʉna?
machine, washing tʉkotse? K
machine oil, sewing tʉtsakʉnaha yuhu
made drunk makwi?numaitʉ
made of teepee poles, travel carrier tʉ?noo?
made to trot poyohkarʉ
maggot wo?aab<u>i</u>
mail a letter or package tʉhyetʉ
mailbox tʉboopʉ wosa W
mailman tʉboo tahni?, tʉboo hima?eetʉ K
maize hani-, haníib<u>i</u>, nawohani, nʉmʉ hani
maize, toasted kukʉmepʉ
make kwisihkarʉ
make lope tsa?aikʉrʉ

make a bed nohrʉnaarʉ, norʉnaarʉ
make a bird nest huupiso?na?aitʉ
make a birdcall niyakekʉtʉ
make a deal tohpunitʉ
make a hole with hands tsahtaikʉtʉ
make a mark on something tsahporʉ
make a plan nimaka?mukitʉ, su?atsitʉ
make a windbreak wʉhturu?arʉ
make a wry face sʉkʉbuninitʉ
make (an agreement or contract) nanipu?e?aitʉ
make bread tohtía?arʉ
make bubbles pamukwarʉ?rʉkitʉ
make burst tohpʉtsa?itʉ
make coffee huba aitʉ
make Comanche butter tʉhtsohpe?arʉ
make cry by hitting toyaketʉ
make dizzy kwinumarʉ
make fall using foot taperʉ
make frybread yuhu nohkorʉ
make galloping sound totʉbihkurʉ
make hollow wʉhha?wokarʉ
make music muuyaketʉ
make noise, pull to matsáapikaarʉ
make noise yelling hubiyairʉ
make pointed mamutsiarʉ
make popping noise kuhporákitʉ
make round with the mouth kʉhtoponarʉ W
make something rattle tsatsʉbipʉkurʉ
make swim tapʉhabi
make threatening movements tahkuya?arʉ
make up oneself nap<u>i</u>sarʉ
make up someone pisarʉ
make-believe nohitekwarʉ
male kuhma

male, adult muʔwoo
male, elderly tsukuhpʉʔ
male animal kuuma
male kinsman naabia, nahbiʔa
male kinsman, man's narenahpʉʔ
male teacher tʉboo wapi
mallet, wooden huutʉrohpakoʔiʔi
mallow, red false puha natsu W,
   yokanatsuʔu K
mallet, wooden huutʉrohpakoʔiʔi
mallow, red false puha natsu W,
   yokanatsuʔu K
man kuhma, tenahpʉʔ W
man, bearded white motso taibooʔ
man, brave young tʉetekwʉni wapi
man, Comanche nʉmʉ renahpʉʔ
man, Comanche young nʉmʉ
   ruibihtsiʔ
man, elderly sukuupʉ
man, grown muʔwoo
man, hole dug by nahorapʉ
man, important namʉnewapi
man, marry a kuumarurʉ
man, medicine puha raibooʔ W,
   puha tenahpʉ
man, old narabʉ
man, pay medicine mabekakʉrʉ W
man, pay something to medicine
   tʉmabekarʉ
man, police nʉmi himaʔetʉ,
   tʉʉhtamʉh raiboʔ
man, post- tʉboo tahniʔ, tʉboo
   himaʔeetʉ K
-man, Red-young Ekawokani
man as husband, reject ninakabarʉ
man, spokes- tekwawapi,
   tʉnikepisaʔ
-man hand saw, two huutsihkaaʔ
man, watch- tʉʔiyaʔi wapi
man, white huuyʉkkwiʔ, pabo
   taibooʔ
man, work- tʉrʉʔai wapi

man, young tuibihtsiʔ
man, young unmarried wohkaʔniʔ
man's agnatic grandchild kʉnuʔ
man's agnatic grandnephew kʉnuʔ
man's brother-in-law tetsi
man's buckskin jacket pika kwasuʔ
man's female kinsman
   naʔwaʔihpʉʔ
man's male kinsman narenahpʉʔ
man's moccasin taʔseʔyukuʔ,
   taʔsiʔyuki?
man's shirt tenahpʉʔa kwasuʔu
man's uterine grandchild tokoʔ
manage tʉtsʉhanitʉ
mane ania
manner sinihku
manually, operate mamiʔakʉtʉ,
   nʉʉmiʔakʉrʉ
many soo, sootʉ, tʉmarʉʉmaatʉ
many?, How hʉʉ
many?, How (how much?)
   hipekaʔi, hipetʉ
many tears, shed paʔokwetʉ
many years ago soo beʔsʉ
map soko naboopʉ W, soko rʉboopʉ
maple, silver kweʔyʉkʉ sohóobi
March Nanaʔbutitʉikatʉ mʉa,
   Tahpookʉ mʉa
mare, gray esipiaʔ
mare, sorrel ekapiaʔ
marijuana nʉmi makwinumaʔetʉʔ
marijuana cigarette nʉmi
   makwinumaʔetʉ pahmu
mark, scratch leaving a tsahtsiʔarʉ
mark inexactly nahoʔyopikurʉ
mark off tsahporʉ
mark on something, make a
   tsahporʉ
mark something tsihpoorʉ
marked naboo-
marking naboʔ
marking instrument nabooʔ K

marriage, propose kwᵾhᵾniwaitᵾ

marriage, separate in pᵾah kwarᵾ

marriage, separated in pᵾah
taikatᵾ

marriage of uncle and niece
arakwᵾ?ᵾtᵾ

married kwᵾᵾhtᵾkatᵾ W, K

married, be kuumabaitᵾ

married, get nᵾpetsᵾ?itᵾ

married, get engaged to be
nᵾpetsᵾ?itᵾ

married couple nanakwᵾhᵾ W

marrow tᵾrana?ipᵾ

marrow, bone tuhhu rᵾhkapᵾ

marrow, cook out (from bones)
tᵾrana?itᵾ

marrow, eat bone tuhhu rᵾhkarᵾ

marrow bones tᵾrana̠

marry kuhmaru, kwᵾᵾhturᵾ

marry a man kuumarurᵾ

marry each other nanakwᵾᵾhtᵾ

marry someone nanakwᵾᵾrᵾ

marvel nani̠suwᵾkaitᵾ

marvelous nanaarᵾᵾmoa,
nani̠suwᵾkaitᵾ

mash maki̠tsarᵾ, makᵾtserᵾ,
pikᵾtsekarᵾ, tatsukwerᵾ,
wᵾkᵾtserᵾ

mash in the mouth kᵾhkihtserᵾ K

mash into small particles
mahomonutsarᵾ

mash up something mapi̠tserᵾ

mashed maki̠tsetᵾ

mask kobe tsa?nika?

massage mabararᵾ, narᵾ?ekarᵾ

Master Narᵾmi?

match huukuna?

material, flaile wᵾyumi?ipᵾ

material possessions
tarᵾwanapi̠ W

material, printed nakohpoopᵾ W,
soo naboo?

maternal grandfather toko?

maternal grandmother kaku?

maternal great aunt kaku?

matter!, no natsa

mattock kuwᵾhora?, to?tsimuhpe?

mattress sona rᵾbaki?

mattress, feather sia sona rᵾbaki?

May Totsiyaa mᵾa

maybe kia, sᵾᵾkᵾtsa?noo

me nᵾe

meadowlark hiitoo? K, N,
ohanᵾnapᵾ W

Meadowlark Hiitoo? K, N

meal tᵾkᵾ manipᵾ

meal, corn- hanitusupᵾ

mean kesuatᵾ, narᵾ?ᵾyapᵾ, tᵾtsᵾ-

mean person or animal tuhupᵾ

mean things, say nimakwihtsetᵾ

measles ekatasia

measure manahkerᵾ, tamanahkerᵾ

measure oneself namanahkitᵾ

measure something tᵾmanahketᵾ

measure, tape tᵾmanahke?

measuring, any device used for
tᵾmanahke?

meat ta?oo?, tuhkᵾ, tᵾhkapa,
tᵾhkapᵾ, yuhu rᵾkᵾhmanipᵾ

**meat (animal killed or butchered
for food)** tᵾbehkapᵾ

meat bag oyóotᵾ?

meat, boiled saapᵾ

meat, buffalo nᵾmᵾ kutsu tᵾhkapᵾ,
ta?siwoo rᵾhkapᵾ W

meat, deer arᵾka tuhku K, O, P,
arᵾkáa rᵾhkapᵾ, tahmai napᵾ

meat, dried esi inapᵾ, tahmai napᵾ

meat, fried yuhu rᵾkᵾhmanipᵾ

meat (or vegetables), fry
kwasᵾkᵾrᵾ

meat, ground tᵾhkapa narᵾsupᵾ W

meat up to dry, hang ina?etᵾ

meat, jerk ina?etᵾ

meat, jerk (for someone)
tʉ?inakʉrʉ

meat, jerked inapʉ, inarʉ

meat jerky inarʉ

meat, jowl aratuhku

meat, light pabo tuhku

meat, pound tʉrayu?nerʉ

meat, pounded tʉrayu?nepʉ

meat, roast tʉkwʉsʉkʉrʉ

**meat over fire (or dry it for jerky),
  roast** ku?inarʉ

meat, roasted ku?inapʉ,
  tʉkwʉsʉkʉpʉ?

meat from a hide, scrape
  tohtsiyu?itʉ

meat, summer-dried tahmai napʉ

meat, thigh pabo tuhku

meat-drying A-frame inakwata

meatball tʉrahyapʉ

meatball preparation tʉrahyarʉ

mediator nitʉsu?nai wapi

medical doctor natsʉ taibo? K

medicinal herb pʉhʉ natsu, pʉhʉ
  rʉ?saasi

medicinal plant tʉpi natsu

medicine natʉsu?ʉ, puha

medicine, apply narʉ?ekarʉ

medicine, prepare puha?arʉ

medicine, prepared puha?aitʉ

medicine on body, rub mabararʉ

Medicine Bluff Puha rʉpanaabi

medicine doctor puha tenahpʉ

medicine man puha raiboo? W,
  puha tenahpʉ

medicine man, pay mabekakʉrʉ W

medicine man, pay something to
  tʉmabekarʉ

medicine outfits puha
  namaka?mukipʉ

Medicine-otter Pua paatsoko

Medicine-woman Puhawi

meek ʉrʉ?

meekness tʉsutaibitsi

meet nara?uraitʉ, na?akʉtʉ

meet someone ta?urarʉ, to?urarʉ

meet someone by going on foot
  tamunaikʉmi?arʉ

meet someone, go on foot to
  tamunaikʉmi?arʉ

meet to suggest something
  nanika?witʉ

meeting, conduct a peyote
  wokwetʉhkarʉ

**meeting, pallet used during
  peyote** pisóona

melon, water- ohapi, puhi bihnáa?

melt paruhwitʉ

melt away parʉhwimi?arʉ

melt something kuhpawikʉ?itʉ

melted kuhparʉ

melted grease wihi

Memorial Day Totsiyaaih
  tabenihtʉ W

men tenahpʉ? W

men, mud- sekwitsipuhitsi

menfolk nanahtenanʉʉ

meningitis tsotsoo?ni

menopausal woman
  tsihhabʉhkamapʉ

menstruate tsihhabʉhkamarʉ

mercy tʉsutaibitsi

mercy, have sutaaitʉ

merit ta?urʉkarʉ W

mescal bean ekapo?

mesh saa?wʉ?

mesquite namabitsoo?ni,
  natsohkwe?, wohi?huu

mesquite weed namabitsooni
  sonihpʉ

mesquite-leaf mixture patso?

messenger nʉtʉhyoi wapi

mestizo wia?

metal, tin or other shiny
  pisayu?ne?

metal comb puhihwi natsihtuʔye?

Mexican yuu taibo?

Mexican blanket kusikwiʔii?

Mexican persimmon tuhnaséka

Mexicans captured by the Comanches Esitoyanuu

midday tokwetabeni

-midday-sun-does-not-tell-a-lie, This Sihka tabe ke isopu

middle tubinaaʔweki̱, tupu̱naatu̱

middle finger mahtupi̱náa? K, masuwuhki? W

middle toe tahtupinaa?

middle-aged woman hubi

midget nunu pu̱hi?

mildew eʔbootsiaru, eʔbootsia?

mile soko rutsupu̱

milk pitsipu̱

milk a cow tuma?okwetu̱

milk bucket pitsipu̱ wihtua

milk, butter- nutsuʔwu̱pa̱ pitsipu̱ K, yuhibitsipu̱ K

milk, clabbered nutsuʔwu̱pa̱ pitsipu̱ K, pitsi pu̱ha nuku?wu̱pu̱

milk from cream, separate yunaru

milk can pitsipu̱ wihtua

milk cow pitsipu̱ pimoróo? W

milk something ma?okweru

milkweed kumiitsanatsu

Milky Way Esitohi?

milky-rooted plant pihtsamuu

mill, wind- patsahtoʔi?

mind sua

mind in effort to remember, search the suʔuraru

mine, coal kutu̱hubihtaa ohweetu̱

mink papi̱ wu̱htama?

miracle nani̱suwu̱kaitu

mirror nabuni?

mischievous emuahkatu̱, po?sabihiʔa

miss waru̱ʔikatu

miss aim awi-

miss doing tsimiʔakuru

missing, be kehewaʔitu

mistletoe puhi turuhka?

misunderstand statement nanawatsikaru

mix mabaru W

mix takoosahpu̱? W

mixture, mesquite-leaf patso?

moan woohpu̱nitu̱, wooru

moccasin numu napu̱

moccasin, man's taʔseʔyuku̱?, ta?siʔyuki?

moccasins, give away napu̱ makaru

moccasin (snake), water tuhparokoo?

mock nisuʔuyaitu̱ W, tuni̱suʔuyaitu̱, usúʔuya?itu̱ W

mockingbird soo yake? W, tunimanahke huutsu? K

moisten in the mouth kuhparoʔaitu K

moistened mabáaʔaitu̱

molasses huupi̱hnàa

mole paraimoʔo

money ekapuhihwi, puhihwi

money, collect tuniwaitu

money, give (to someone) puhihwimaka

money, have puhihwi tuaru

money, look for puhihwi wehki

money, paper wana buhihwi̱

money, pay with narumakaru

money, silver tosahpuhihwi̱

money, spend su?makutu̱

monkey kwasi taiboo?

month mua

moo muu yakenitu

moon mua

moonlight muakatu

moonlight, have muahtabebaʔitu

mop pawu̱nua?

more than anything oyoʔrɨ
kaʔwek̲i̲t̲ɨ

mormon tea sanaweha

morning pɨetsɨ̲kunakwɨ̲sa, taa-,
taahkatɨ, tabén̲i̲

morning, early pɨetsɨ̲ku, tuka
ɨhyɨi

morning glory soho kɨaʔetɨ
totsiyaaʔ

mortar huaawo, huu aawo

mosquito mutsikwàʔaaʔ

mosquito net muhpoo kahni
wanapɨ K

moth tɨp̲i̲ simuhtaʔ

mother pia

mother, step- paraibooʔ

mother's sister pia

motion, move in slow aimiʔarɨ

motor oil naʔbukuwàaʔa nahyɨ̲,
tɨhyu

mound, burial nabɨkapɨ̲ W

mount a horse tɨyatoʔyerɨ

mount, help to tohkɨarɨ

mount on horseback nɨɨhtoʔitɨ

mountain toya

mountain, gray esitoyaab̲i̲

Mountain, Navaho Naboohroyaʔ N

mountain boomer ebimuutarooʔ,
ebipabokoʔaiʔ P

mountain lion wɨraʔ

mountains east of El Paso, Texas
Esitoyaʔ

mourning cape kuʔnikaʔ

mouse tɨe kahuuʔ

mouse, field pia kahúa

mouse, house kahúuʔ

-mouse, Squeaky-like-a Kahúu
nihku pip̲i̲kur̲e̲

mousetrap kahúu pɨmata hɨarɨʔ

mouth tɨpe, tɨɨpe

mouth, catch something with the
kɨhtsakarɨ

mouth, close the kɨhtsuukarɨ

mouth, dribble from the
kɨʔokwetɨ

mouth, frothing at the
saahtotsitoʔikatɨ

mouth, make round with the
kɨhtoponarɨ W

mouth, mash in the kɨhkihtserɨ K

mouth, moisten in the
kɨhparoʔaitɨ K

mouth wide, open pia kɨsarɨ

mouth, open the kɨsarɨ

mouth, pop with the kɨhpohtorɨ

mouth, put something into the
tɨroʔnikarɨ

mouth, roll in the kɨhkwatuubirɨ K

mouth, roof of mitɨkoʔo

mouth, take something in the
kɨhyaarɨ

mouth, throw with nose or
muhwitɨ K, mukwɨbɨarɨ W

**mouth, unwrap something with
the** kɨhtoʔyarɨ K

move wɨmiʔarɨ W, yɨmɨhkitɨ

move about yɨkarɨ

move across unahrɨ

move around nɨmirɨ, yoʔmitsaitɨ,
yɨʔyɨmuhkumiʔarɨ W

move away nomiʔarɨ, norawɨʔaitɨ

move away as a group sɨmɨ
nomiʔarɨ

move by hand tsanuarɨ

move clumsily, waddle or
masuʔwaʔnekitɨ

move from place to place
noonɨmiʔarɨ

move from side to side tohtsatsarɨ

move in slow motion aimiʔarɨ

move nervously pisukwitaitɨ

move off to live separately
nokaʔitɨ

move on nayɨkwiitɨ

move over nuaru
move quickly wu?rabiaru
move slowly puhyunukitu
move something tanuaru
move something with the mouth
    kunuaitu
movement toward something,
    stop wunu hupiitu
movements, make threatening
    tahkuya?aru
movie nunura?wu?, tupuuni
    yu?yumuhku? K
movies yu?yumuhku? W
moving, rope someone or
    something while ku?nikakuru
-moving, slow nanahbiso?aitu
-moving, Swift Wu?rabiahpu
moving pictures yu?yumuhku? W
mow wuhpomaru, wutsukaru
mow grass soni wuhpomaru, soni
    wutsukeru
mower, lawn- soni wutsuke? K,
    tuutsuke? W
much soo, sootu, tumaruumaatu
much?, How many?, How
    hipeka?i, hipetu
much worse nasu?ana
mud sekwi, sekwipu
mud, stuck in the sekwi suhkai,
    yubutsuhkatu
mud-covered sekwi nuyu?itu
mud-men sekwitsipuhitsi
mulberries pahtsi kwasi tukahpu
mulberry huwabo?kóo?, soho
    bo?koo? W
mule esimuura?, muura?
Mule-dung Mura kwitapu
multi-colored wanatsihtaraa?
mumble esipipikuuru
mumps tubekwipu
murmur esipipikuuru
muscle nuuhtoka?e?

muscle cramp or spasm, have
    toponitu K
mush koo?
mush, cornmeal hanikotsapu, koo?
mushroom mupitsuha pisahpi W,
    pasawi?oo?a huki?ai?
music, make muuyaketu
music (of any kind) muyake?
mutilate oneself nuuhki?yu?itu
mutton kaburuu tuhkapu
my nu
my!, Oh, ha?íi
my!, Oh! Oh ubia

N n

nail turawuna? K, turohtsani?i?
nail, shoe napu narawuna?, napu
    rurawuna?
nail, toe- tasiito
nail down tawunaru
nail something ta?nikutu,
    turawunaru K
naked paputsipitu
name nahnia
name for the Comanches of Tejas),
    Proud People (Wichita Natai
name someone nahnia makaru,
    nihakuru
nap tabe uhpuitu
napkin namo?o matsuma?
Narrow-gut Kohi
narrow place, crowded into
    tsukikatu
nasty nasusua?eetu
nations sokoba?aihtu
Native-American ball game
    na?suhpe?etu
natural windbreak huukono?itu
Navaho Mountain Naboohroya? N
Navaho people Naboohnuu

navel siikṵ

near miitṵtsi

nearly noha

neck toyo, toyopṵ

neck, have a stiff woʔrohtsarᵾ

neck, wear something around the korohkǫrᵾ

necklace, bead tsomo korohko

necktie korohkǫ

need suwaitᵾ

needle wana tsahkᵾna?

needy nahawaruʔikatᵾ

negative ke-

neighbor kahtᵾi?

nerve, end of row or sᵾkwerᵾ

nervously, move pisukwitaitᵾ

nest pisuʔni?

nest, bird huutsúʔa kàhnị, huutsúʔa pisooʔnị

nest, build a pisonaʔaitᵾ

nest, make a bird huupisoʔnaʔaitᵾ

net, fish- saaʔwᵾ hᵾa?

net, mosquito muhpoo kahni wanapᵾ K

never Kesᵾ

new, learn something urahkarᵾ

New Year's Day ᵾku tomopᵾ

news, good tsaatᵾ narᵾmuʔipᵾ

newspaper narᵾmuʔi tᵾboopᵾ

next time kwasikᵾ

nibble kᵾʔkwiyarᵾ

niece, marriage of uncle and arakwᵾʔᵾtᵾ

night tuka ᵾhyᵾi, tukaanị

night, be tukanịtᵾ

nightgown habikwạsuu

nightshade tohpotsotsii

nine wᵾmịnatᵾ

nits tatsii?

no ke-

no!, Oh yee

no good nasᵾsᵾaʔeetᵾ

no matter! natsa

No-bed Kahpewai

No-hand Mooʔwetᵾ

no to someone, say nimamᵾsukᵾtᵾ

no, shake the head tsoʔwiketᵾ

nod the head in agreement nihtsamuʔitᵾ

noise (in timber), hear or make huukisaakitᵾ

noise, make popping kuhporákitᵾ

noise yelling, make hubiyairᵾ

noise, pull to make matsáapikaarᵾ

noisy tᵾnisuatᵾ

non-Indian taiboo?

noon tokwetabeni

north kwihnenakwᵾ

north fork of Red River Natᵾmᵾᵾ paʔi huna?

north star kemiʔarᵾtatsino

northeast kwihne muhyᵾnakwᵾ

northwest kwihne kahpinakwᵾ

nose mu-, muhbi

nose, blow the mubịsitᵾ, tsamukụsitᵾ

nose, cause to blow wᵾmupᵾsitᵾ

nose, inhale deeply through muhibitᵾ

nose, poke out munakᵾaitᵾ

-nose, Red-crooked Ekamurawa

nose, suck through simuhtarᵾ

nose or mouth, throw with muhwitᵾ K, mukwᵾbᵾarᵾ W

nosebag puku rᵾhka?

not good enough ketokwetᵾ

not-tell-a-lie, This-midday-sun-does Sihka tabe ke isopᵾ

nothing kehe

notice sutuuʔarᵾ

notice, give ninakᵾakᵾrᵾ W

November Ahotabenihtᵾ mᵾa, Yᵾba ᵾhi mᵾa

now (or at this point) siʔanetᵾ

now on, from sibeʔnikiyutu
now, right meeku, namusohi
now kihtsiʔ, tsuh
nudge matsuru
Nueces River Sumonu kuhtsu paa
numb susuʔnitu, tasusuʔnitu, tsasusuʔnikatu
numb, feel susuʔnitu
numb the hand masusuʔnitu
number turutsupu
number, augment in suatu
numbness susuʔnikatu
numerically, increasing turakaʔaitu
nun Suabi puharaibo
nurse cape kuʔhibooʔ
nursling puesúubeʔ W
nuts pokopi

O o

oak paʔsa ponii huupi
oak, blackjack tuhuupi
oak, white tosa tukanai huupi
oar panatsitooʔ
oath, take mahiyaru
oath, take an narabeeʔaitu
oats soni narúaʔ
obedient tunakatu
obey tumayokuru
obey orders tokwetuparu
object, broken kohpapu, tahpapu
object cut into pieces tutsihpomiʔipu
object, dirty tuhtsaipu
object, dry pasapu
object, ground up nasupu K
object (on a line), hang a long wusóoru
object, laced natsakwusikuʔ
object, large piapu

object, old tsukuhpuʔ
object, pull a bouncy tsahpoʔtsaru
object, pulverized or grated tusupu W
object, round maropoʔniʔipu
object, sharp-pointed mutsipu
object, side of an sukwe naisu
object, staked down - uhtaʔetu
object, torn sihwapi
object, unwrap an tsahpekoʔaru
object (or item) taken yaapu
objects, count definite tutsuru
objects, give several himiitu
objects, pick up several himaʔaru
objects, take several himaʔaru
oblong huyubaʔatu, mahuyubakatu, pia huyubatu
ocean pia baa
October Puhipuha puma oha toʔiʔena mua, Yuba mua
odd nanakuyaʔaru, natsuwukai
odor, breath sua kwana
odor, have kwanaru
odor, have bad kwanaru
odor, sniff an ukwihkatu
of two of them mahru
of us two taa
of you two muhu
off, drop pahitu, yumaru
off, dust huukunatsiru
off, dust (by hand) huukumatsumaru
off, fall pahitu, tupehemiʔaru
off (or away from), fall tupuheru W
off, get weehtsitu
off running, get wenuʔnukimiʔaru
off, haul tsawehkwatu
off, kick suutaʔniʔaru
off, knock tokaru, wuyumiʔitu
off, knock something hanging wuhtokaru
off, knock (with an instrument) wupuheru W

off by force, lead sutena betsumiaru

off, mark tsahporu

off, peel kwuru?aru, tokiaru,
wuhtsibo?aru

off skin, peel kibo?aru

off, pitch ku?e wunuru

off, pull tokaru, tsahto?aru K

off or out, pull something
tsahkwe?yaru

off, rub toso?netu

off, scrape siibetu, toso?netu

off, shake something nuu?wikeetu,
suuta?ni?aru

off, shave wuhtsi?aru, wusiberu K

off, show nasutsa akwaru K

off, snap tahkobaru, tsahkobaru

off, strip makwiteeru

off of something, take down
tsahpuheru

off, take mabo?ayaru, tohkwe?yaru

off a shoe, take tahkwe?yaru

off layer, take tsahkwuru?aru

off, tear sumu sihwaru

off, tip ninakuakuru W

off completely, wipe wuhtsu?maru

off with the hand. wipe
makwineetu

off, wipe something tahtsumaru K

offer hand mahiyaitu

offer someone help masutsaru

office, post tuboopu kuni

officer nanohmunu wapi K,
nomunewapi W, paraiboo?

officer, army ekasahpana?
paraiboo?

offspring, bear turuaru

offspring (son or daughter),
grown nahnapu

often naiya

Oh, good! yee

Oh, my! ha?íi

Oh, no! yee

Oh! yaa

oh! oh my! ubia

oil nabaa, nahyu

oil, coal tuka?a nabaa

oil, explore for tokwaitu

oil, motor na?bukuwàa?a nahyu,
tuhyu

oil, sewing machine tutsakunaha
yuhu

oil well nabaai tokwaaitu, tuka?a
nabaa

oily or greasy, taste wihi kamatu

ointment, personal nuuhtu?eka?

-old, two-year wahatomopu K

-old item, two-year tomohtoopu W

old, two years tomohtootu W

old lady narutsa?i

old man narabu

old object tsukuhpu?

Old-owl Mo?pi tsokopu

on back pa?arai

on, fire wuhtikuru

on, go tunehtsuru

on foot, go (to look for) takwainitu

on foot, go (to meet someone)
tamunaikumi?aru

on, have underwear tsa?nikukatu

on, knock totubihkuru

on door, knock tohtaraki?aru

on, move nayukwiitu

on, pour tokwuriaru

on, pour water payunitu

on a sled, ride seated pisiko?i

on deathbed, suffer pisukwitaru

on fire, set kutsitonaru

on purpose, spill something
tokwuriaitu

on, tried marahpunihkatu

on, urge nihtunetsu?itu

on, wait mananaa?waihkaru

on opposite side pa?arai

on shoes, put tahtooru

on someone or something, with or maa

on something, lean mahtokwʉnaitʉ K

on something, pull tsanuarʉ

on something, rest mahtokwʉnaitʉ K

on something, suck mukwihterʉ

on something, tap wʉhtarakiitʉ

on top of kuʔe

on trousers, put pitsohkorʉ

on vacation, go hʉʉtsaʔwʉ miʔarʉ

on warpath, go mahimiʔarʉ

on what? hipaʔa

on what?, with what? himakʉ

once sʉmʉsʉ

once in a while sʉsʉʔanạ

one sʉmʉ, sʉmʉʔ

one, dying suaʔsuʔmakatʉ

one, fattest yuhu wehkipʉ̣

one, little tʉeʔtʉ

one another, help naruituahkarʉ

one, loved kamakʉnạ W

one another, sell to narʉmʉʉrʉ

one, that suhkapʉ

one, wrong atʉrʉ

one at a time sʉsʉmʉʔ, sʉʔsʉmʉʔnʉku

one by one, run away nunurawʉtʉ

one hill anáabi

one hill standing alone nookarʉrʉ̣

one is doing), slow down (what nʉnʉʔitʉ

one leg, raise tahtsarʉ

one song after another, sing nipʉ̣yerʉ

one or several things, take yaarʉ

one to sin, tempt tʉrape suwaitʉ

one foot, walk dragging tasiʔwomiʔarʉ

one time sʉmʉsʉ

one who betrays kaanatsakaʔuhtupʉ̣

one who gossips isanaramuʔitʉʔ

one-horse buggy sʉmasʉ nooi K

One-who-rides-buffalo Kuhtsunu kwahipʉ

oneself pʉnʉsʉ

oneself, cut natsahkiʔarʉ, nʉʉkiʔaitʉ

oneself, examine nabuihwʉnʉtʉ W

oneself, exhaust nananʉʉʔmaitʉ, narahkupaitʉ

oneself, gag kuitsịkwaitʉ K

oneself, gash natsahkiʔarʉ

oneself, hack nʉʉhkiʔyuʔitʉ

oneself, hang nʉʉkwenitʉ

oneself, hurt nahohiyaitʉ, nahuhyaitʉ W, namarʉnitʉ K

oneself, immerse (in water) nabawʉhtiarʉ

oneself, introduce nanịsuabetaʔaitʉ, natsahpunitʉ

oneself, jerk something toward tsahpoʔtsarʉ

oneself, look at nabunitʉ

oneself, look behind nabitʉbunitʉ

oneself, make up napịsarʉ

oneself, measure namanahkitʉ

oneself, mutilate nʉʉhkiʔyuʔitʉ

oneself, paint napịsarʉ

oneself, prepare namakaʔmukitʉ

oneself down, pull natsahkupʉkatʉ

oneself up, pull natsahtoʔitʉ

oneself with something, puncture nabisoʔarʉ

oneself, scratch natsahtsiaitʉ

oneself away, secret watsị habiitʉ

oneself, shave namotʉsibetʉ

oneself in water, soak naparʉkitʉ

oneself, tire nananʉʉʔmaitʉ

oneself, twist nʉʉkwitsʉnarʉ

oneself around something, twist nʉʉʔkwipunarʉ

oneself, watch naʔiyaitʉ

oneself, wound natsahki?aru

onion, poisonous wild
kuhtsutsuu?ni?

onion, wild kuukanaruhka?,
kuuka̠, pakuuka̠, puewatsi kuuka̠,
tuetutaatu kuuka̠

Onion Creek, Texas Kuna?itu?

only pu?une W

Only-daughter Pu?na petu

**onto someone or something, up to
or** maatu

open tsahwitu, wuhkwumaru

open, break maputsaru, taputsaitu

open, break (with the teeth)
kuputsaru

open, burst maputsaru, puhkaru

open, come tuhwaitu

open, cut wupukaru, wuputsaru

open, pound on to tohkwumaru

open, pry tohkwumaru,
tsihto?aru W

open, split peko?aru

open, wide pia tsatuakatu

open country to settlement soko
tsatuwaru

open forcibly tohkwumaru

open mouth wide pia kusaru

open of its own accord
natsahwi?etu

open something matuhwaru,
tohtuwaru, tsahtuwaru, tuhwaru

open something wide pia tsatuaru

open the hand makwusaitu

open the mouth kusaru

opened mahuruhwakatu

opener, can kumapu, turohtuwa?

opening in clothing kuruupe̠

openly maihtuku̠

operate manually mami?akutu,
nuumi?akuru

operation, surgical nuuputsapu̠

opossum pahtsi kwasi

oppose wohho suaru

oppose something tso?wiketu

opposite-sex sibling-in-law haipia?

opposite side, on pa?arai

or tuanóo

or coil wuhkwatubi

orally, reminded ninusutamakutu

orange ekaohapitu̠, ohaekapitu̠,
ohapi̠tuu

orange, osage etuhuupi, ohahuupi

orchard pokopi̠ masuapu̠

order hani̠tuniru, ni?atsiitu

order sternly ninabitsiaru

order to leave nihto?itu

orders, obey tokwetuparu

originated tubora

ornery tumabiso?aitu̠

orphan as foster child, keep an
tahnikatu, tukiihkaru

osage orange etuhuupi, ohahuupi

Osage people Wa?sáasi?

other ata-

other, marry each nanakwuuhtu

**other covering for teepees, skins
or** numukuni

other shiny metal, tin or
pisayu?ne?

other, with each naha-

others aturuu

others, lead muhnemi?aru

others, separated from
toro?ihtukitu̠

otter paa tsoko, papi̠ wúhtama?

Otter Paa tso?ko

ouch! aná

ouch! it burns uruu

our numu, tahu

Our Father Ta?ahpu

out. come (at a particular place)
kiahbitu, to?i̠bitu̠

out, drive tahkuaru

out, dry pasaru

out, empty wɥʔwenitɥ K
out, find sutuuʔarɥ
out, find (for oneself) naraʔurakɥtɥ
out, force tsahkɥarɥ
out. forced tsahtoʔitɥ
out, go tukamiʔarɥ
out, lay tsakwɥnarɥ
out, let tahtoʔitɥ
out, pick nabinarɥ
out something, pluck noʔitɥ
out something, point muruahwɥnɥrɥ
out nose, poke munakɥaitɥ
out, pour wɥhtiarɥ, wɥʔwenitɥ K
out, pull tsahpiʔerɥ
out of breath suaʔsuʔmaitɥ
out of container, pull tsahpɥyerɥ
out of joint, pull bones tsahtokoʔarɥ
out, reach mahiyaitɥ
out and touch, reach maʔwɥminarɥ
out of food, run tɥkɥ tsuhmarɥ
out of groceries, run narɥhkaʔtsuʔmarɥ
out, rust nasaanutoʔitɥ
out, set tsihtaboʔikɥtɥ
out to dry, set pasahtahtɥkitɥ W
out, shovel tsiiʔwɥweniitɥ
out, sing nihtoʔitɥ
out, snuff marukarɥ
out on something, spill tokwɥriarɥ
out, spit W kɥhkihtserɥ
out liquid, spit pai tusiʔitɥ K
out, spread legs poʔarɥ
out something, spread tsahpararɥ, wɥhpararɥ
outer side, scrape wɥhkwɥnetɥ
out something, strain tsasoʔarɥ
out, stretch haahpitɥ 2
out arm, stretch maruruʔarɥ
out something, stretch wɥhpararɥ

out, stretch something tsahturɥ
out, strike wɥhpohtoʔitɥ
out pain, suck on body to draw musoopitɥ
out, swab wɥhkwinarɥ
out, take tsahkɥarɥ, tsahtoʔirɥ
out of something, throw wɥʔkwɥriarɥ
out, tire kweʔyɥkatɥ, nɥɥʔmaitɥ
out, try kɥhpunitɥ, tohpunitɥ
out, wash- patowoʔnepɥ
out earth, wash patowoʔnerɥ
out clothes, wear wɥkwiʔarɥ
out shoes, wear tawiarɥ W
out, wear something wihtoʔarɥ
out, worn wihtoʔaitɥ
out, worn- napatawiʔaitɥ
out with hands, wring tsahpitsoorɥ
outfits, medicine puha namakaʔmukipɥ
outrun someone naromɥnitɥ
outside hunakɥ, hunakɥ
oval huyuni
oven nohko aawoʔ K, pɥkɥra nohkoʔena̱ W
oven for baking biscuits nohko aawo̱
over, cross manitɥ
over, fold namakwatubiitɥ
over, kill by growing puhi tɥyaitɥ
over, knock (and spill accidentally) tsakwɥriarɥ
over, knocked mahuihkatɥ
over something, lean nɥɥsooʔetɥ
over, look puiwɥnɥrɥ
over. move nuarɥ
over, pushed mahuihkatɥ
over fire (or dry it for jerky), roast meat kuʔinarɥ
over something, step tasarɥ
over, turn natsamɥritɥ

over, turn something tsamᵿrikarᵿ, wᵿmᵿᵿrᵿ

over, turned wᵿmᵿᵿrihkatᵿ

over someone, win kwakurᵿ K

over, wrinkled all takwikakwo?apᵿ

overcome tahni?arᵿ

overcome pain wᵿmetᵿ

overflow ata?okwetᵿ, muru?itᵿ

overflow the creek bed paru?itᵿ

overflowing tᵿhpetᵿ

overhand, throw kwihitᵿ

overhear nakᵿhoorᵿ

overheating, burst from kupᵿtsarᵿ

overtake tahtsaitᵿ, wᵿhpitᵿ

overworked namakupᵿkatᵿ

owl o?oo?

Owl Mopai

owl, burrowing pohkóo?

owl, Old- Mo?pi tsokopᵿ

owl, screech sᵿhᵿ mupitsᵿ

own hipᵿkatᵿ

own accord, open of its natsahwi?etᵿ

own accord, spill of nᵿᵿti?akatᵿ

own accord, split of nᵿᵿhtsi?aitᵿ

own accord, unravel of nᵿᵿpᵿrᵿsuarᵿ

own a home nᵿmᵿnakarᵿ

own an article of clothing kwasu?ukatᵿ K

own beard, pull namutsono?itᵿ

own something ta?urᵿkarᵿ K

owned hipᵿ

oyster pisi wa?kóo? W, pisi wa?rokóo? K, wa?koo? W

P p

pace pisᵿtᵿkitᵿ

pacer pi?isᵿtᵿ

pack norᵿbakᵿtᵿ

pack a load on foot tᵿnoomi?arᵿ

pack for an animal tᵿnoopᵿ W

pack rat kuura

pack-animal leader tᵿnoo wapi

package, mail a letter or tᵿhyetᵿ

packaged flour homorohtía?

packed in tightly manᵿkᵿtᵿ

packsaddle narᵿnoo?

pact nanihpu?e?aikᵿpᵿ K

paddle, canoe panatsitoo?

paddle, dog masu?wa?nekitᵿ, paruhparᵿ

paddle feet (in water) pawᵿpa?itᵿ

paddle hands (in the water) paruhparᵿ

paddle water masu?wa?nekitᵿ

padlock natsihtᵿma?

padlock something tᵿtsihtᵿrᵿ

pain manᵿᵿtsikwa? W

pain, body nᵿhtsikwarᵿ

pain, extreme stomach sapᵿ wᵿnᵿkatᵿ

pain, give nᵿᵿtsikwarᵿ K

pain, overcome wᵿmetᵿ

pain, stand on someone's back to ease tahpara?itᵿ

pain, suck on body to draw out musoopitᵿ

pain, to bear wᵿmetᵿ

pain, suffer abdominal kohikamᵿtᵿ

pain, suffer chest amawᵿnᵿtᵿ

pain, suffer gall-bladder pu?i?wᵿnᵿrᵿ

paint tᵿrᵿ?eka?, tᵿ?eka? W

paint, house K kahni ebi

paint oneself napisarᵿ

paint something tᵿrᵿ?ekarᵿ, tᵿ?ekarᵿ

painted tᵿrᵿ?ekarᵿ

Painted-feather Ketse na?bo

paintbrush, Indian kahnitᵿeka

pajamas habikwᵿsuu

pale pink esiekapi̲tu̲

pallet used during peyote meeting pisóona̲

palm of hand mapaana̲

palm of hand, slap with tohpaʔitu̲

palm of hand, stop hitting with fist or tohpu̲aru̲

palm reader mapaanaʔ

palomino horse kwipu̲siapu̲, naʔahnia K

pan tu̲soona

pancake tohtíaʔ

pancakes taaru̲hkapu̲

pant hehéki̲tu̲, suaʔsuaʔmiaru̲

pant heavily heheku̲bu̲niitu̲

pant with tongue hanging down heheku̲bu̲niitu̲

panther tu̲mahkupaʔ, wu̲raʔ

paper tu̲boopu̲

paper, sand- tu̲maku̲maʔaaiʔ, tu̲pi tu̲matsuneʔ

paper, wall- kahni̲ tu̲boopu̲, tu̲banaa ru̲bopu̲

paper money wana buhihwi̲

parade namanahkeetu̲ W, wu̲habitu̲ K

parakeet woko̲ huutsu̲

paralyzed su̲kwe tu̲yai

paralyzed hand maʔitsaʔbu̲katu̲

paralyzed person su̲kwe tu̲yaipu̲

parch corn kuku̲meru̲

parched corn kuku̲mepu̲

pardon tu̲suʔnaru̲

pare wu̲htsitoʔaru̲

parent-in-law yahihpu̲ʔ

parfleche oyóotu̲ʔ

Parker, Quanah Kwana

Parker's daughter, Quanah Wanaru̲

Parker's wife, Quanah Tope

parlor pu̲ku̲ra yu̲kwiʔena̲ W, yu̲kwi kahni K

parrot woko̲ huutsu̲

part namabeʔahkapu̲, pekoʔaru̲

part, clean the inner wu̲hkwinaru̲

part hair natsihpeʔakaru̲, tsihpeʔakaru̲

partake of Communion pu̲u̲hibiru̲

parted mabeʔakatu̲ W, naʔbekoʔaru̲

parter, hair- natsihpeʔakaʔ

partially sun-dry wu̲htaku̲miitu̲

particles, mash into small mahomonutsaru̲

particular noo

partly eaten food naru̲hkapu̲

partner notsaʔkaʔ

partner, gift-exchanging hinanahimitu̲ waipu̲

partners tu̲htu̲iʔ

partridge tu̲e kuyúutsi K

parts, split into two tu̲apakoʔitu̲

pass word on nimu̲u̲miʔaru̲ W

Pass-it-on Topehtsi

past the peak yu̲baru̲

past the time u̲i

paste, tooth- tamakotseʔ

pasted matsu̲bakikatu̲

pasture soni sokoobi, soni wu̲htu̲mapu̲

pasture, fenced soni tu̲htu̲mapu̲

patch, cloth tu̲karu̲ku̲pu̲

patch, garden tu̲ku̲ masu̲a sokoobi̲ W, tu̲mu̲su̲a sokobi K

patch something tu̲karu̲ku̲ru̲

paternal grandfather ku̲nuʔ

paternal grandmother huutsi̲

paternal great uncle ku̲nuʔ

path puʔe̲

path, clear a puʔeʔaru̲

pave a road tuusanahpi̲tu̲

paved a road (blacktopped) tuusanahpi̲tu̲

paw the earth taʔsiʔwooru̲

Pawnee Witsapaaiʔ

pay attention tɨnakiitɨ
pay debts tɨmakarɨ
pay medicine man mabekakɨrɨ W
pay something to medicine man
    tɨmabekarɨ
pay with money narɨmakarɨ
payment of damages nanɨwokɨ
pea toponibihuura?
pea, sensitive huutsú?a kàhnị
peace chief paraibo
Peace River Kutsiokwe
peaceful spirit tsɨmɨkịkatɨ
peach pɨhɨsɨ?kɨị
peak ku?ebi
peak, past the yɨbarɨ
pear wasápe?a tɨhkapɨ
pear, cactus, prickly wokwéesi
Pease River Mura hunu?bi
pecan kɨhtabai, nakkɨtaba?i
pecker, wood- pitụsɨ nu?ye? W,
    wobi tohtarakị K, wɨpɨkoi?
Pecos River Kusiokwe
pedal ta?aikɨtɨ
Pedernales River Pai pakạ pia
    huna?
peel wɨhtsito?arɨ
peel off kwɨrɨ?arɨ, tokiarɨ,
    wɨhtsibo?arɨ
peel off skin kibo?arɨ
peel something tsahkíto?arɨ
peeling tool huusibe?
peep tasɨkɨpunitɨ, wihtekatɨ
peep at kuhiyarɨ
peep into tokwịtetɨ
peeping wihtekatɨ
Peeping-from-behind-tree Kuhiyai
peer through wihtekatɨ
peeved pihiso?ai
pen, ink parɨboo?
pen up animal ta?ikɨrɨ
pencil naboo? K, tɨboo?
penned up tawekwitɨ

penniless tɨtsu?mapɨ
pensively, rest, nasutamɨ habitɨ
people nɨmi, sɨmɨ?
people, Caddo Tukanai
people, Corn Hanitaibo
people, circus nohihtaiboo?nɨɨ
people, crowd of sɨɨmɨ?okɨ
people, crowd with tsɨhkịkatɨ
people, fill with tsɨhkịkatɨ
people, group of sɨɨmɨ?okɨ
People, Hill Ononɨɨ
people, Kiowa Kaaiwanɨɨ
people similar to elves, little
    Nɨnapi
people, Navaho Naboohnɨɨ
people, Osage Wa?sáasi?
(people), Pawnee Witsapaai?
People, Proud (Wichita name for
    the Comanches of Tejas) Natai
people, Sioux Papitsimina?, Suhta?
people, three groups of
    pahibahtɨnɨnɨ
People, Timber Huuh?inɨɨ
people by bad tidings, upset
    ni?yɨsɨkaitɨ
people, Wichita Tuhka?naai?
pepper tɨkɨ mahya?
pepper, chili tsiira?
pepper, red ekatsiira?
perceptive supịkaahkatɨ
perforate wo?nerɨ
perform surgery wɨpɨtsarɨ
perfume plant, Indian tɨsaasị
perhaps kia, sɨɨkɨtsa?noo
permission, ask nanihtɨbinitɨ
perplexed mɨɨwarɨ?itɨ
persecute makwihtserɨ
persimmon naséka
persimmon, Mexican tuhnaséka
persistent natsanahaatɨ
person alone, leave kekɨnabeniitɨ
person, black tuhtaiboo? W

person, covetous kwahisiapɨ
person, crazy poo?sa?
person, cross-eyed pasapuni
person, dead kooipɨ
person, dependable nasupetipɨ K
person, dishonest kaawosa̱
person, drunk hibipɨ
person, emaciated wehuru?i
person, envy another kwahisi?a
person, faithful nasupetipɨ K
person, fat yupɨ
person, graduated tamarɨkɨkatɨ
person, handcuff a mo?o wɨhtamarɨ
person, intoxicated hibipɨ,
    kwinumapɨ
person, paralyzed sɨkwe tɨyaipɨ
person, poor takahpɨ
person, ravenously hungry
    tsihasi?apɨ
person, reject a nakabarɨ
person, rejected ninakaba?itɨ
person, sickly nama?abɨ, takwipɨ
person, sneaky nakɨhoowaaitɨ
person, sore namakɨnɨmapɨ
person, stingy nahkɨepɨ K
person, stubborn sutenapɨ
person, thin kanabɨɨtsi?, wehuru?i
person, throw down a
    tsahkwa?nu?itɨ
person, tired namakɨnɨmapɨ
person, tongue-tied ekotɨyaipɨ
person, undependable senihtɨhtsi?
person or animal, weak tɨ?o̱naapɨ
person, white taiboo?
person, wounded kwɨhti?
person of delicate health takwipɨ
person or thing, buried
    namɨsokoopɨ
person or animal, exhausted
    namakweyaipɨ
person or an animal, lead a
    tsakarɨ

person or animal, mean tuhupɨ
personal belongings namahku
personal ointment nɨɨhtɨ?eka?
persons, handicapped
    wɨ?mina?nɨɨmɨ
persons, kill several nakwɨsɨkɨrɨ
perspiration takwɨsipɨ
perspire taku̱sito?itɨ
persuade someone to do
    something nitsɨbahikɨ?itɨ
pester by talk nimɨsasuarɨ
pester someone nihtunetsarɨ
pesticide isawasɨ?
pestle tsohkwe?
pestle, pound with a tayu?nerɨ
pestle, wooden tɨrayu?ne?
pet nisutaitɨ, tohtarakiitɨ
pet or stroke tohtaraki?arɨ
petal, flower totsiyaa patɨpi̱naatɨ
petroleum jelly nɨɨhtɨ?eka?,
    tsiikṵwitehka? K, tsi?wɨ̱nɨɨ
    tɨ?eka? W
peyote, eat wokwetɨhkarɨ
peyote meeting, conduct a
    wokwetɨhkarɨ
peyote meeting, pallet used
    during pisóona̱
peyote plant or button wokwe
peyote teepee puha kahni, wokwe
    kahni
phlegm yoka
physically, strong natsṵwitɨ
piano mayake?
pick mutsimuhpe?, tso?meetɨ
pick a bird of its feathers no?itɨ
pick for scraping hides
    to?tsimuhpe?
pick fruit pomarɨ
pick, ice wiiyṵ
pick out nabinarɨ
pick up several objects hima?arɨ
picked berries pomapɨ

picture naboopʉ, tʉpuuni
picture frame naboopʉha
naroʔnikaʔ, naboopʉha narʉso,
naboopʉha pʉkʉratoʔnikaʔiʔ
pictures, moving yʉʔyʉmuhkuʔ W
pie noʔa nohkopʉ
piece, break off a tsanutsarʉ
pieces nakooʔipʉ
pieces, break in tahbaitʉ,
tahporoorʉ
pieces, break into tsanutsarʉ,
wʉnutsarʉ
pieces, break into small
wʉhhomonutsaʔarʉ
pieces, crush in
tohhomonutsarʉ W
pieces, crushed into small
mabisukiitʉ
pieces, cut off wʉhtsiʔarʉ
pieces. cut up into tsihpoma
pieces, object cut into
tʉtsihpomiʔipʉ
**pieces, sit on something breaking
it to** pinutsarʉ
pierce tonarʉ
pierced ear nakị toonʉkatʉ K,
nanakịtonapʉ
pig mubị poʔrooʔ, munuaʔ, poʔroʔ
pigeon kuʔe wóoʔ, pasahòo, taibo
huutsuuʔ
piker pihisiʔapʉ
pile high pia wʉʔutsitʉ
pile up wʉʔutsitʉ
piled badly pia utsaatʉ
pillow tsohpẹ
pillow, feather sia tsohpẹ
pillowsticks tsohpe tawʉnaʔ
pillowsticks into ground, pound
tsohpe takwʉnarʉ
pimple mohtoʔa K
pin nahamuhkụ K
pin, bobby- papị tsihtʉpʉkaʔ

pin, decorative natsihtʉpʉkaʔ
pin, diaper nahamuhkụ K
pin, hair- papị tsihtʉpʉkaʔ
pin, safety nahamuhkụ K,
naʔhʉmuhkụ W
pin, straight- piitsʉnʉaʔ
pin together tsihtʉpʉkarʉ,
wʉhtʉpʉkarʉ
pincer tʉkʉh pomaʔ
pincers tʉkʉh kweʔyaʔ
pincers, wire tʉkʉh kaʔaʔ
pinch masitotsarʉ W, matsurʉ
pine woko
pineapple wokwekatʉ amakwooʔ
pink ekaʔotu, tosa ekapịtʉ W
pink, pale esiekapịtʉ
pipe toʔị
pipe stem omotoi
piper, sand- tʉʔíiʔ
pistol tawoʔiʔ K
pistol, automatic natsahkwineʔ
pitch tokwʉkiʔarʉ
pitch off kuʔe wʉnʉrʉ
pitched, high putsi tʉnikwʉyʉ K
pitchfork soni tsiyaaʔ, sonitsiimaʔ,
tʉtsiyaaʔ W
pitied tʉtaatʉ
pitiful senihtʉhtsiʔ
pity tʉsutaibitsị, tʉsutaikatʉ
pity, feel mʉʉrʉʔikatʉ
place, eating tʉkʉ kahni
place, put down in tsahtʉkitʉ
place, put in narʉkitʉ, tʉkarʉ
place, put something back in
tohtʉkiʔarʉ
place, resting koonọ
place, set in natsawʉnʉkatʉ
place, set something in
natsawʉnʉrʉ
**place known by speaker and
hearer** pʉkʉhu
place to place, graze from tooniitʉ

place to place, move from
noonumi?aru

place to place, wander from
noyukaru

placed narukitu

plain kenanawatsitu

plainly maihtuku

plan, make a nimaka?mukitu,
su?atsitu

plane, carpenter's tusibe?

plane, wood huusibe?

plane something smooth tusibetu

plant turunaru

plant by hand turahnaru

plant, certain (with edible tuber)
tsunisu

plant, cigarette-wrapper
tumakwatui?

plant, Comanche perfume numu
rusaasi

plant, cymopterus tunuhaa

plant, fever poiya

plant, flowering saatotsiya

plant, gray-colored kusinuuhparabi

plant, heal-all puhakatu

plant, Indian perfume tusaasi

plant, medicinal tupi natsu

plant, milky-rooted pihtsamuu

plant (or button), peyote wokwe

plant, potted saatotsiyapu

plant, stem of totsiyaa?a suuki

plant, sunflower stalk or hi?oopi

plant, wheat tohtía sonipu

plant crops tumusuaru

plant seed tuhtukitu, turuni?itu

plant seeds tahnaaru

plant similar to water lily pa?mutsi

plant with edible fruit paiyapi

planted crops turunapu

planter turuna?

plaster ebikahni

plaster W kahni ebi

plate tusoona

play nohitu

play, run around and nohi?nuraaru

play a wind instrument muuyaketu

play cards wana rohpetiru

play dead kaabehkaru

play hand games na?yuwetu

play instrument mayaketu

play lacrosse natsihtóo?itu

play poker pokaru

playground swing pi?wesurúu?i?

playing-card deck, king in
ohahkuyaa?

playing cards wana atsi?

plaything nohi?

plead nanimaa?ubu?ikutu,
tunihpararu

please someone tsaa manusuru

pleased tsaa manusu?itu

pliers tukuh kwe?ya?

plot, vegetable garden tuku masua
sokoobi W

plow tutsa?woo? K

plow soil tutsa?woru

plowed field tutsakwoopu

pluck tsanooru

pluck a bird clean puhu no?itu

pluck a bird clean of feathers
pahtsi no?itu

pluck out something no?itu

plug to extinguish, un- tsahtukaru

plum parua sukui?, suku?i

plum, (Chickasaw) tuahpi

plum, domestic taibo suku?i

plum, dried natsomu, na?a?tsome?

plum, early yusuku

plum, fall kusisukui

plum, late-summer parawa suk

plum bush wi?nuupi

plum tree parua sukui?

pneumonia, have tu?inawunuru

pocket amawosa

pocketbook puhihwi narɨso W,
puhihwi wosa K

point mutsi-, muutsi̠, tsihtɨʔawerɨ

point, form into a manutsiarɨ W

point, formed to a mamámutsiakatɨ

point, sharpen to a tomotsiarɨ W,
wɨmutsiarɨ K

point, sharpened to a
mamutsiakatɨ

point out something
muruahwɨnɨrɨ

pointed mutsi-

pointed, make mamutsiarɨ

-pointed object, sharp mutsipɨ

poison isawasɨ?

poison ivy puhi taʔara?

poisonous wild onion
kɨhtsɨtsɨɨʔni?

poke tsisuʔwarɨ

poke head into something
tsoʔnikarɨ, tɨtsoʔnikarɨ

poke out nose munakɨaitɨ

poker chip tuhhuu?

poker, fire kutsani

poker. play pokarɨ

pole wahta

pole, clothesline ooʔrɨ
tohtsaniʔiʔana huuhpi, tɨtsapara
huupi

pole, fishing hɨahuupi̠

pole, flag- wana tsiyaaʔa náhuupi̠

pole, teepee huutsiyaa?, waahuupi̠,
waata̠

pole, telephone puhihwi
tekwapɨhana huupi

**poles, travel carrier made of
teepee** tɨʔnoo?

poles for constructing brush arbor
hɨɨkina huupi̠

policeman nɨmi himaʔetɨ,
tɨɨhtamɨh raibo?

polish tapɨnukeerɨ W

polish by hand mapɨnukeerɨ

pond ɨmahpaa?

pond lily, yellow kɨriata

ponder suʔurarɨ

pony tail kuwikɨsii

poodle motso sarii?

poor person takahpɨ

Poor-one Tahkapɨ

pop kukɨbihkutɨ, pipóhtorɨ,
wɨhpohtoʔitɨ

pop, soda pihná baa

pop on someone kuhpuruʔairɨ

pop with the mouth kɨhpohtorɨ

popcorn kuhmitoʔai?, tahma
yokake?

poppy, prickly pitsi tora

porch kahni nahɨɨki

porcupine hɨɨnɨ?, yɨhnɨ

porcupine quill yɨhnɨ wokweebi?

pork mubi̠ poʔroo rɨhkapɨ W, poʔro
tɨhkapɨ K

pork rind mubi̠ poʔroʔa poʔaa W

position, change yɨmɨhkitɨ

**position, change (from one to
another)** nuhyɨyukitɨ

**position, help up from sitting to
standing** matsákwɨnɨkɨrɨ

position, lift from a prone
tsahnɨarɨ

position, lying in prone muparai
habinitɨ K

position, prone haahpi̠

position, rise from seated
nɨɨʔnɨarɨ

possess hipɨkatɨ, huuyaarɨ,
mahípɨrɨmɨrɨ, mahípɨrɨmɨtɨ

possess sticks huuhimarɨ

possessed hipɨ

possession, regain makoʔitɨ

possessions, material tarɨwanapi̠ W

post, trading ekanarɨmɨɨ?, nɨmɨ
narɨmɨɨ?

post office tᵾboopᵾ kᵾni
posthole digger tᵾhora?
postman tᵾboo tahni?, tᵾboo
hima?eetᵾ K
pot, cooking saawihtua
potato, arch sᵾhᵾ tsitsina?
potato, Irish paapasi̱
potato, sweet kamúuta?
potato, wild paapasi̱
potted plant saatotsiyapᵾ
pound narayaakᵾpᵾ, tᵾhraniitᵾ K
pound completely sᵾmᵾ rayu?nerᵾ
pound flat wᵾtᵾki̱?netᵾ
pound food tayu?nekarᵾ
pound meat tᵾrayu?nerᵾ
pound on something tahhanitᵾ
pound on to open tohkwᵾmarᵾ
pound pillowsticks into ground
tsohpe takwᵾnarᵾ
pound something wᵾhtarakiitᵾ
pound with a pestle tayu?nerᵾ
pounded nara?okatᵾ
pounded meat tᵾrayu?nepᵾ
pounding, soften by tohparaarᵾ W,
tsohkwe K
pounding, wake someone by
wᵾhtᵾbunitᵾ
pour on tokwᵾriarᵾ
pour out wᵾhtiarᵾ, wᵾ?wenitᵾ K
pour water on payunitᵾ
powder homo-, homopᵾ, pisahpi̱
powder (apply to oneself)
homonabi̱sakatᵾ
powder, crumble to
mahomonutsarᵾ
powder, crumble to (with the
foot) tahhomonutsarᵾ W
powder, face homobi saapi̱
powder, gun- nakuti̱si̱
powder, talcum homoroso?yoki?
powder something homopisarᵾ
powder the body homopisarᵾ

powdery homoketᵾma?
power tᵾsu?atsipᵾ
power, have tᵾsu?atsi̱tᵾ
power, having supernatural
puhakatᵾ
power, judicial tᵾsu?atsipᵾ
power, supernatural puha̱
powwow nᵾhkana W
pox, chicken kokorá?a tasi?a
pox, small- narᵾ?ᵾyᵾ tasi?a̱,
tasi?a? W
practice something namabunitᵾ
prairie nᵾmᵾwahtᵾ, pᵾhᵾwahtᵾ
prairie chicken pakawkoko?
prairie clover yuu sonipᵾ
prairie clover, purple pakeeso
prairie dog tᵾ?rᵾkúu? W
prairie fire nakuyaarᵾ
praise panaaitᵾ
praise someone nihpana?aitᵾ
pray nani̱sutaitᵾ
pray for someone nani̱sutaikᵾtᵾ
prayer of thanks ahotabeni̱htᵾ
preach puha rekwarᵾ W
preacher puha raiboo? W
precede someone muhnetᵾ
pregnant no?a-
preparation, meatball tᵾrahyarᵾ
prepare breakfast for someone
taamahkarᵾ
prepare for maka?mukitᵾ
prepare medicine puha?arᵾ
prepare oneself namaka?mukitᵾ
prepared namahka?mukitᵾ
prepared food hanipᵾ
prepared medicine puha?aitᵾ
present generation nᵾmᵾ rᵾborapᵾ
K, pᵾhkᵾra nahanᵾ W
press tahkwᵾ?nerᵾ
press down mabararᵾ
press down with hands to expel
water mabitsoorᵾ

press something down tatᵾke?nerᵾ
pressed down manᵾkᵾtᵾ
pressure with the hands, rub applying masu?nerᵾ
pretend kaasuarᵾ, nohitekwarᵾ
(pretend) make-believe nohitekwarᵾ
pretentious, act nasutsa akwarᵾ K
pretty nananisuyake
prevent someone's death makwitso?aitᵾ
prick someone with something piso?arᵾ
prick up the ears to?yabaitᵾ
prickly ash kunanatsu
prickly pear cactus wokwéesi
prickly poppy pitsi tora
priest Suabi puharaibo
primp nama?yᵾkwitᵾ
print, foot- nanapunipᵾ, napᵾ, narapunipᵾ
printed material nakohpoopᵾ W, soo naboo?
prints, hoof- tᵾhᵾyena puni W
prison narawekwi kahni, tᵾpi kᵾni
prize, win a tᵾrahwikatᵾ
probe tsikwainitᵾ
proceed ahead muhnetᵾ
process of tanning a hide narᵾso?ipᵾ
procreated by us nᵾmᵾ rᵾborarᵾ
produce pomapᵾ
product, garden tᵾmᵾsᵾapᵾ
product, home-grown garden masᵾapᵾ W
product, raise garden masᵾarᵾ W
prohibit makᵾetᵾ W, namamᵾsurᵾ, nimoya?ekᵾrᵾ, ninakaba?ikᵾtᵾ
prohibited mamᵾsuakatᵾ K
promise sutsamurᵾ
prone position haahpi
prone position, lift from a tsahnᵾarᵾ

prone position, lying in muparai habinitᵾ K
propel tsatᵾkarᵾ, tᵾkwᵾrᵾ
proper tokwetᵾ
prophet ta?ahpᵾ?a tekwawapi K, tᵾrᵾ?awe wapi W
propose marriage kwᵾhᵾniwaitᵾ
prosper wᵾpᵾhoikᵾtᵾ
protrude kunakᵾarᵾ K, kuro?itᵾ W, wᵾsa?marᵾ W
protrude, cause to manakᵾarᵾ
protruding nakᵾahkatᵾ
proud panaaitᵾ
Proud People (Wichita name for the Comanches of Tejas Natai
provoking jealousy, rival wohhohpᵾ?
prune kᵾhpomarᵾ, kᵾmakoorᵾ, tuhnatso?me?, wᵾ?yᵾkwitᵾ K
pry open tohkwᵾmarᵾ, tsihto?arᵾ W
pry up tsahto?arᵾ K
puff up pohtokitᵾ
puffball mupitsᵾha pisahpi W
pull tsah-, tsanoorᵾ
pull a bouncy object tsahpo?tsarᵾ
pull apart tsahka?arᵾ, tsahpomi?itᵾ
pull back tsasinᵾkaarᵾ
pull bones out of joint tsahtoko?arᵾ
pull down tsahparᵾ, tsapeherᵾ
pull off tokarᵾ, tsahto?arᵾ K
pull on something tsanuarᵾ
pull oneself down natsahkupᵾkatᵾ
pull oneself up natsahto?itᵾ
pull out tsahpi?erᵾ
pull out of container tsahpᵾyerᵾ
pull own beard namutsono?itᵾ
pull someone's beard mutsonoo?itᵾ
pull something behind pitsákarᵾ
pull something off or out tsahkwe?yarᵾ
pull to make noise matsáapikaarᵾ

pull up tsahkɨarɨ, tsahtoʔirɨ
pull with full strength tsahturerɨ
pulled up tsahtoʔitɨ
pulling, burst by tsahpohtoorɨ
pulverized or grated object
  tusupɨ W
pump patsaʔaikɨ, tsaʔaikɨrɨ
pump water patsahtoʔitɨ
pump, water patsahtoʔiʔ,
  patsaʔaikɨ
pumpkin nakwɨ̲si?
pumpkin, dried nakwɨ̲sipɨ̲
punch tohpaʔitɨ
punch repeatedly (or slap)
  tohtɨkwarɨ
puncture a tire tɨrapɨ̲tsarɨ W
puncture oneself with something
  nabisoʔarɨ
punctured napi̲soʔakatɨ̲
puny nɨɨsukatɨ
pupil of eye tuhpui
pure tutɨ̲tsaai wahtɨ̲
purple tukaʔyuwɨ W
purple coneflower tukunɨ natsu̲
purple prairie clover pakeeso
purple W tuʔebipi̲tɨ̲
purpose, spill something on
  tokwɨriaitɨ
purr soroʔrokitɨ
purse, coin puhihwi narɨ̲so̲ W
purse, woman's puhihwi wosa K
pus pisi
push maʔwikarɨ, tanuarɨ,
  taperɨ, toh-
push away mahbotsetɨ
push someone under water
  tsahpaakuʔnikarɨ
push something that rolls
  maʔaikɨrɨ, tsiʔaikɨrɨ
push under water, hit and
  wɨhpaakuʔnerɨ
pushed over mahuihkatɨ̲

pushed under water
  tohpaakuʔnetɨ W
put away namabimarɨ, tahtɨkarɨ,
  tɨkarɨ
put away for safekeeping
  toʔnikarɨ K
put down in place tsahtɨkitɨ
put down something to sit on
  pisoonarɨ
put in place narɨkitɨ̲, tɨkarɨ
put on shoes tahtoorɨ
put on trousers pitsohkorɨ
put something back in place
  tohtɨkiʔarɨ
put something down tsaʔnikoorɨ
put something into the mouth
  tɨroʔnikarɨ
put up a barbed wire fence
  puhihwi tɨɨhtɨmarɨ

Q q

quail kuyúusi?, tɨe basuu? W, tɨe
  kuyúutsi K, tɨrɨe kuʔyuutsi, tɨrɨe
  basuu K
quake of earth soko yɨ̲ʔyɨmuhkurɨ
Quanah Parker Kwana
Quanah Parker's daughter
  Wanarɨ
Quanah Parker's wife Tope
quantity, augmenting in
  tɨrakaʔaitɨ
quantity, small tɨtaatɨ
quarrel naniʔwiketɨ W
quarrel with someone niʔwiketɨ̲
quarreling, stop kekɨnabeniitɨ
quarrelsome nanitsu̲wakatɨ̲ K
quarter section soko rɨmanahkepɨ̲
quarter-section of land soko
  tsihkaʔapɨ̲
quarters, sleeping habikɨ̲ni

queer nanakuya?arʉ
quench a fire murukarʉ
quench by hand marukarʉ
question, ask a tʉbinitʉ, tʉrʉbinitʉ
question someone tʉbinarʉ,
   tʉbinitʉ
quick pʉhetʉ
quick-cook corn soup atakwá?sʉ?
quick-dried corn atakwa?sʉ?aipʉ
quickly namʉsi
quickly, move wʉ?rabiarʉ
quickly, sit down tsuhni karʉ
quickly, turn around pikwebuitʉ
quiet kebayʉmʉkitʉ, tokobo?niitʉ K,
   yunahkatʉ
quiet by speech ni?tsu?narʉ
quiet down tʉsu?narʉ,
   wʉyupa?nitʉ
quiet, keep niwatsi?aikʉ?itʉ
quiet someone niyukarʉrʉ W
quiet spirit tsʉmʉkikatʉ
quill, porcupine yʉhnʉ wokweebi?
quilt pisóonạ, soonạ
quilt, cotton wanạ soonạ
quilt top sona bo?a
quinine weed pohóobi
quit something pʉarʉ
quiver kʉhkwibikitʉ, sʉhkwibitʉ

R r

rabbit tabú?kina?
rabbit, Easter noyotso?mẹ tabu?
rabbit, swamp ekae?ree W,
   ta?wokinae?ree eka K
raccoon nʉmamo?o?, paruuku?,
   pa?ruhku?
race, run a nanarʉna?itʉ,
   narubunitʉ
racer narʉbuni?etʉ?
racer snake kʉhtáa nu?ya?a W

races, hold narʉrʉnitʉ
radiate heat kusʉwetʉ
rage, feel tuhu su?aitʉ
ragweed, western wo?anatsu?
railroad car kunawaikinʉ,
   kunawobipuukụ
railroad handcar kʉ?wʉnʉbaa?i̱,
   pi?yʉpụ káa?i̱ W
railroad tracks kunawaikina pu?e
rain ʉmaarʉ, ʉmapʉ
rain shelter ʉmakahni
rain shelter for winter yu?a
   ʉmakʉni
rain water ʉmahpaa?
rainbow pisi ma?rokóo?
raining, stop pʉhkitʉ
raise a garden tʉmʉsʉarʉ
raise dust huukụhʉnʉrʉ
raise dust by walking
   tahuhkuwʉnʉrʉ
raise garden product masʉarʉ W
raise head tso?nʉarʉ
raise one leg tahtsarʉ
raise someone manʉarʉ
rake tsahtʉ?oki? K, tʉtsanua?
rake, hay tʉtsa?ooki?
rake something tʉtsahtʉ?oorʉ
rake together manuarʉ W,
   marʉ?okitʉ K, tanuarʉ
rake up tsa?oorʉ
rash on skin tasi?a? W
rasp tʉmatsune? W
rasp a surface tʉmatsunarʉ
raspberry panatsayaa?
rat pia kahúa
rat, pack kuura
ration day tʉhimạ rabeni
rations tʉhimana W
rations, get tʉhima?etʉ
rattle wʉhkitsu?tsukitʉ,
   wʉhkitsu?tsuki?, wʉkwʉbihkurʉ
rattle, gourd wʉhtsabeyaa?

rattle, make something
tsatsᵾbipᵾkurᵾ
rattled tsatsubihkurᵾ
rattlesnake kwasinaboo
wᵾhkitsu?tsu?ikatᵾ,
wᵾhtsabeyakatᵾ W
rattling tsatsubihkurᵾ
rattrap kahúu pᵾmata hᵾarᵾ?
rave ni?emᵾabᵾnitᵾ, tuhu yᵾkwiitᵾ
ravel, un- pᵾrᵾsu?arᵾ
ravel of own accord, un-
nᵾᵾpᵾrᵾsuarᵾ
ravel, something, un-
nᵾᵾpᵾrᵾsuanᵾpurᵾ
raven tuwikaa?
ravenously hungry person
tsihasi?apᵾ
raw skin tuhᵾpᵾ
rawhide ᵾhtaayu?
rawhide ready to use pahkipᵾ
rawhide rope pahki wiyaa?
rawhide wardrobe case natᵾsakᵾna
reach, fail to to?wᵾminaitᵾ
reach something, fail to
tsa?wᵾminarᵾ
reach (or break) something
wᵾminarᵾ
reach for makwᵾbᵾtsᵾrᵾ W,
marurᵾ?arᵾ
reach out mahiyaitᵾ
reach out and touch ma?wᵾminarᵾ
read nihakᵾrᵾ, tᵾhnearᵾ W
reader, palm mapaana?
ready tsuh
ready to use, rawhide pahkipᵾ
really tᵾbitsi
rear katsonakwᵾ
rear a child manᵾarᵾ
rear or back against something,
scratch pisu?netᵾ
rear up, incite to manáawᵾnᵾ?etᵾ
reared up manawᵾnᵾkatᵾ

reason sukwᵾkitᵾ
rebuke nihmakwihtserᵾ
recall su?urarᵾ
recede pasanuarᵾ
receive food tᵾkᵾ himarᵾ
recently ᵾkᵾ
recognize suabetaitᵾ
recover kwitso?aitᵾ
recover from illness tebuunitᵾ
red ekapi, tuka?ekapitᵾ
red, shine ekakuhtabearᵾ
red ant ekaᵾnᵾᵾ
red brick ekatᵾᵾpi
red cedar ekawaapi
red color eka-
red false mallow puha natsu W,
yokanatsu?u K
red fox ekatseena?
red haw tu?amowoo
red hot, turn ekawehaarᵾ
red pepper ekatsiira?
Red River Ekahohtᵾpahi hunu?bi,
Pia pasi hunu?bi
Red River, north fork of Natᵾmᵾᵾ
pa?i huna?
red rock ekatᵾᵾpi, ekwipisa?
red soil ekahuukupᵾ, ekasokoobi
red store ekanarᵾmᵾᵾ?
Red-buffalo Eka kura
Red-crooked-nose Ekamurawa
Red-young-man Ekawokani
redbird ekᵾhuutsu?
redbud ekamurora?i huupi
redbug puikᵾso
redheaded buzzard ekabapi
ref to fat yuhu
refrigerator tahka aawo
refuse makᵾetᵾ W, nimamᵾsukᵾtᵾ
refuse to accept someone
ninakabarᵾ
Refuse-to-come Huuhwiya
refused nahkaba?itᵾ

Refusing Ninakaba?i?
regain possession mako?itʉ
reins, bridle narʉmuhkʉ
reject kemabana?itʉ,
  kwetʉsuakʉrʉ W
reject a person nakabarʉ
reject man as husband ninakabarʉ
reject someone kemenikwitʉ W,
  nimakabaitʉ
rejected kemenikwitʉ W,
  nahkaba?itʉ
rejected person ninakaba?itʉ
rejoice na?okitʉ
rejoice verbally nanina?ukitʉ
rejoicing tsaa nʉʉsukatʉ
relate narʉmu?ikatʉ
relatives nʉmʉ haahkana?
-relatives, She-invites-her Nʉmʉ
  ruibetsʉ
relax sua yurahpitʉ
relaxed kesósoorʉ
release tsahparʉ W, tsahpʉarʉ W
release from hands mabʉarʉ
religious ceremony, smoke during
  puha bahmu?itʉ
remember nasutamʉkatʉ tamai
remember, search the mind in
  effort to su?urarʉ
remind someone nasutamakʉrʉ W
reminded orally ninʉsutamakʉtʉ
remnant saved piinaai
remove tohkwe?yarʉ, tsayumi?i
remove item by item wʉpiyarʉ
render an animal carcass
  tʉhtsohpe?arʉ
render lard kuhpitsʉni?arʉ W,
  ku?okwerʉ W, yuhukarʉ
rendered yuhukarʉkarʉ
renter tʉrʉ?ai wapi
repair hanitʉ
repeatedly, faint esikooitʉ
repeatedly, hit wʉhpa?itʉ

repeatedly, shoot a gun
  ta?wo?ekarʉ
repeatedly, slap (or punch)
  tohtʉkwarʉ
repeating gun, shoot a
  tsatʉka?karʉ
request (ask for something)
  tʉrʉnirʉ
request something naníhtsawa?itʉ,
  nigwaitʉ K
rescue kwitso?arʉ, makwitso?aitʉ,
  wʉhkwitso?arʉ
resemble someone tʉ?ikatʉ
respect mabitsiarʉ
respect, treat with pahna?aitʉ
respect someone marʉhnikatʉ
respected maritsiakatʉ
rest sua yurahpitʉ
rest, allow to (or cool off) sua
  soyuraperʉ
rest on something
  mahtokwʉnaitʉ K
rest pensively nasutamʉ habitʉ
restaurant tʉkʉ kahni
resting place koono
restore circulation wʉsuabetaitʉ
return ko?itʉ, pitsa mi?arʉ
return (an item_ yaakʉrʉ
return, cause to tsahkoo?itʉ
return, send word to someone to
  nʉníhkoonirʉ
return (from warpath) mahiko?itʉ
revived suabetaikatʉ
rheumatic tsuhni wʉminahkatʉ
rheumatism tsuhni wʉminakatʉ?
rib kwahtsʉ W, mawaatsa, waatsʉ K
rib area of animal puihtsita? K
ribbon tʉkʉma?ai
rice wo?arʉhkapʉ
rich tsaa naahkatʉ
riches tsaanahapʉ
rickrack wakʉ?wʉtʉ

ride double pihima, piyarʉ
ride horseback kʉayʉka?etʉ W,
  tʉhʉya karʉ
ride seated on a sled pisiko?i
-rides-buffalo, One-who Kuhtsunu
  kwahipʉ
ridicule nohitʉ, tʉnimakwihtserʉ
ridiculous nanʉsu?uyaatʉ
rifle tawo?i? K
right yusuatʉ
right, to the tʉbitsi petutʉ
right here makʉ
right now meeku, namʉsohi
right side tʉbitsinakwʉ
right something tsahkarʉkʉrʉ
right-handed tʉbitsikatʉ
rind, pork mubi po?ro?a po?aa W
ring kawohwitʉ
ring (a bell) pihkarʉ
ring, cause to tsayaketʉ
ring, finger- ma?nika?, mo?o
  tsi?nika?
ring something tu?tsayaketʉ
Rio Frio Kwana pekwasʉ
Rio Grande Kwana kuhtsu paa?
riot naniyo?naitʉ K
rip completely sʉmʉ sihwarʉ
rip something puhkarʉ, tohtʉrʉ?arʉ
  W, wʉhtʉrʉ?arʉ K
rip with fingers tsahtʉrʉ?arʉ
ripe kwasʉpʉ
ripped puhkapʉ
ripsaw mo?o huutsihka?a?
rise atabaro?itʉ, paro?ikitʉ,
  pohtokitʉ
rise from seated position nʉʉ?nʉarʉ
rise up yorimi?arʉ, yʉtsʉrʉ
ritually, smoke nakatsʉhetʉ
rival provoking jealousy
  wohhohpʉ?
River, north fork of Red Natʉmʉʉ
  pa?i huna?

River, Nueces Sʉmonʉ kuhtsu paa
River, Peace Kutsiokwe
River, Pease Mura hunu?bi
River, Pecos Kusiokwe
River, Pedernales Pai pakạ pia
  huna?
River, Red Ekahohtʉpahi hunu?bi,
  Pia pasi hunu?bi
river, small okwèetʉ
river, up obutʉma?
River, Washita Tusoho?ọkwe?
river bank ekatotsạ
riverbank, flood the paru?itʉ
river crossing nagwee
road pu?ẹ
road, construct a pu?e?arʉ
road, follow a pu?eyarʉ
road, pave a tuusanahpitʉ
road, paved a- (blacktopped)
  tuusanahpitʉ
road, surfaced tʉpi pu?e
roadrunner ebikuyuutsi?
roam noyʉkarʉ
roamer noyʉka?
Roamers Noyʉhkanʉʉ
roast corn atakwa?sʉ?aitʉ,
  hanikwasʉkʉrʉ
roast food kwasʉkʉrʉ
roast in ashes kusiwʉhpima W
roast meat tʉkwʉsʉkʉrʉ
**roast meat over fire (or dry it for
  jerky)** ku?inarʉ
roast on a stick kuhtsiyarʉ
roast on sticks ku?tsiyaarʉ
roasted corn atakwa?sʉ?aipʉ
roasted meat ku?inapʉ,
  tʉkwʉsʉkʉpʉ?
Robe-on-his-back Kwahira
rock tʉpi, tʉʉpi
rock, heated nakutʉkʉna?
rock, red ekatʉʉpi, ekwipisạ?
rock lizard tʉpi paboko?aai W

rocking chair nabiʔaaikɨnakarɨ K

rocking way of walking yɨʔbanaʔitɨ

rocky ground tɨpi sokoobi W

Rocky-creek Tɨpi wɨnɨ

rod tɨʔehkooiʔ W

rodeo kuhtsu taibo nohhiitɨ W, tukumakwɨyetɨʔ W

roll, un- tsahkwɨmarɨ, tsahpɨkɨsuʔarɨ W

roll along anikwita miʔarɨ

roll around maropoʔnarɨ

roll in the mouth kɨhkwatuubirɨ K

roll into a ball tsahtopoʔnarɨ

roll over or around naʔanitɨ

roll to start something toʔaikɨrɨ

roll up namakwatubiitɨ, tɨmakwatɨbiʔetarɨ

roll up to itself wɨhkwitubikatɨ

roll up with something tohtopoʔnarɨ

rolled matsobokɨkatɨ

rolled up makwatubiitɨ

rolls, push something that maʔaikɨrɨ, tsiʔaikɨrɨ

roof of mouth mitɨkoʔo

room kah-, kahni, kahni tai, taina

room, find (for someone or something) haakarɨ

room, invite into home or niʔikaʔitɨ

room, living- pɨkɨra yɨkwiʔena W

rooming house kwaabih kahni

roomy pia wekitɨ

rooster kokoráʔa kuhma W

root tɨrana

root, church itsa, timɨihɨʔ

root, eriogonum ekanatsɨ

root, snake itsa, timɨihɨʔ

root, tree huupita tɨrahna

root, up tsahtobarɨ

root around ahweniitɨ, muwainitɨ K

roots, dig edible tɨkɨ ahwerɨ

roots of the teeth tamakwita

rope wiyaaʔ

rope, clothesline soni wiyaaʔ, wana kotse tsahparaaʔ K

rope, hang someone with a ooibehkarɨ

rope, jumping nɨhpopiʔ

rope, rawhide pahki wiyaaʔ

rope around something, slip a kuʔnikarɨ

rope someone or something while moving kuʔnikakɨrɨ

rosin huupitan pihnàa

rot eʔbootsiarɨ, eʔbootsiaʔ, papɨsitɨ

rotate nuhyɨyukitɨ

rotten papɨsipɨ

rotting papoosinɨ

rouge ekawɨpisi K, ekapisaʔ

rough kesuatɨ

rough, talk tuhu rekwarɨ

rough skin tsiʔwapɨ W

rough terrain wohtsaʔwɨtɨ

rough-leafed dogwood parɨa

round tohtoponitɨ, topohtɨ

round bundle or round knot, tie in wɨhtopɨʔnoorɨ

round object maropoʔniʔipɨ

round up tahkoonikarɨ, taʔookitɨ

round with the mouth, make kɨhtoponarɨ W

rouse tsayoritɨ

row maʔaikɨrɨ, wohya, wɨʔaikɨrɨ

row or nerve, end of sɨkwerɨ

rub tasitotsarɨ W

rub against something pisuʔnetɨ

rub applying pressure with the hands masuʔnerɨ

rub feet tasuʔnetɨ

rub hands together namɨsuʔnetɨ

rub head against something tsotsoʔneetɨ

rub lightly makwu?netu

rub medicine on body mabararu

rub off toso?netu

rub the wrong way masu?naitu K,
masuroonitu

rub with brains kupisi?aru

rub with foot nara?woru K

rubber band tu?re?

rubber boots tuu?re napu

rubber heel tuu?re tahpiko?,

rug puhu rasoona, tasoni, tasoona

rule tuni-

ruler tumanahke?

rump katsonakwu

run nuhkitu

run a race nanaruna?itu, narubunitu

run after miakuru

run around and play nohi?nuraaru

run away nuhkitu

run away afraid namanuhkitu

run away from something
wuanuraitu K

run away from somewhere pua
nuhkitu

run away one by one nunurawutu

run, cause to wumi?aru W

run downhill wenu?nukimi?aru

run out of food tuku tsuhmaru

run out of groceries
naruhka?tsu?maru

run short kehewa?itu

run slowly pohyami?aru

run to something tunehtsuru

run to something through fear
namarunehtsuru

runner, road- ebikuyuutsi?

running, come nuraakitu

running, get off wenu?nukimi?aru

running over, full and tuhpetu

-running-here, Wind Nuenuhkiki

rust nasaanuto?itu, nasanopi K

rust out nasaanuto?itu

rustle tahkoonikaru

rye tohtía sonipuha taka?

rye grass pui tsaseni

S s

sack naruso

sack, flour tohtía naruso

sack, gunny soni naruso?

sack, tow soni naruso?

sacrifice or destroy oneself, self-
immolate kuhtuyaru

saddle pa?mutsi?

saddle, Indian-type tumuhku

saddle, pack- narunoo?

saddle a horse, un- narunoo?ro?yaru

saddlebag tunoo?

saddle blanket kwahituki?,
nahotsa?ma?

saddle girth natsanuhku?

saddle horn narunoo bapi

saddle strap nakwusi tsa?nika?,
narunoo? namuku

saddle up narunoo?rukitu

sadness tabuikatu

safekeeping, put away for
to?nikaru K

safety pin nahamuhku K,
na?humuhku W

sage esipohoobi, tusaasi

sagebrush pohóobi

said that, it is tua

sailor pa?ekusahpana?

saliva huutsipu, kupisi?, tusi

saloon po?sa baa kahni

salt ona-, onaabi

salt something ona?aitu

Salt-worn-out Onawai

salve, sunflower hi?ookwana?

same general area, separated but
in na?ata W

same-sex cousin haitsi̱
same-sex friend haitsi̱
sand pasi waapi̱
sand, haul pasiwanooru
Sand Creek Pasiwa huunuʔbi
sand dune pasiwanoo? W
sand hill pasiwanoo? W
sandals saaʔwu̱ napu̱, waraatsi̱
sandpaper tu̱maku̱maʔaai?, tu̱pi
tu̱matsune?
sandpiper tu̱ʔíi?
sap sanahkena W
sash nu̱u̱pi̱tua?, nu̱ʔu̱nehki̱katu̱?
**Sata Tejas I (Dog Eaters chief cir.
1689-1693)** Sarua Tu̱hka I, Sata
Tejas I
**Sata Tejas II (Dog Eaters chief cir.
1873-1889)** Sarua Tu̱hka I, Sata
Tejas II
Satan Ketokwe hina haniitu̱,
Tuhkwasi taiboo?
satisfied pihikaru
satisfied with sufficient food
wu̱tsu̱ʔmitu̱
Saturday Tu̱eh buha rabeni
saucer nakwiita̱
sauna nasukooʔi?
sausage tuhku tsaʔnikapu̱, tu̱ku̱
tusupu̱
save kwitsoʔaru, nabinaʔetu̱,
tsihakwitsoʔaru
save someone makwitsoʔaitu
save someone's life tsahkwitsoʔaru
saved, remnant piinaai
saw, hand- moʔo huutsihkaʔa?
saw, rip- moʔo huutsihkaʔa?
saw, see- naʔatsiyaa?, naʔtsiyaa?
saw, two-man hand- huutsihkaa?
saw something with a saw
huutsikaʔaru
sawdust huupita homoketu̱, huupita
pisoni̱, huutusupu̱ W

say yu̱kwitu̱
say mean things nimakwihtsetu̱
say no to someone nimamu̱suku̱tu̱
say that, they tu̱a
scaffold paʔwu̱htaràa?
scale narayaaku?
scalp kuʔe tsasimapu̱, papi̱
hu̱nu̱poʔa, papi̱ kuʔe̱
scalp someone kuʔe tsasimaru
scar pihka̱
scare wu̱hkuyaʔaru, wu̱u̱yoritu̱,
wu̱ʔyu̱ru̱hkitu̱
scared kuyaʔakatu̱, wu̱ʔyu̱ru̱hkikatu̱
scarf tsokwu̱ku̱u̱na? W,
wu̱htsohku̱na?, yuʔa korohko̱
scatter by force tohporooru
scatter something tsahpoʔaru
scattered tsahpetitu̱
scattered around poohkatu̱
scent, follow muwaru W
school house tu̱boo kahni
scissors tu̱keh koo?, wana koo?
scissortail ku̱ku̱bu̱raakwaʔsi?
scold nihmakwihtseru
scold someone niʔwikeru
scoop tsiiʔwu̱weniitu̱
scoop up mahoraru
scoot wu̱huʔneru
scorch wesikuru
scorched wesikatu̱
scorching day tabe kusu̱wehkatu̱
scorpion kwasi tona?
scrape tsasinu̱kaaru, tsasuʔneru,
wu̱htsinetu̱, wu̱pu̱nukeru,
wu̱suʔnaru
scrape meat from a hide
tohtsiyuʔitu̱
scrape off siibetu̱, tosoʔnetu̱
scrape outer side wu̱hkwu̱netu̱
scrape until clean wu̱htsuʔmaru
scraping sibepu̱
scraping hides, pick for toʔtsimuhpe?

scraps tʉkʉ wesipʉ

scratch naraʔworʉ K,
   natsahkupʉkatʉ, tasitotsarʉ W

scratch an itch natsawoʔnitʉ,
   tsakwoʔnerʉ

scratch leaving a mark tsahtsiʔarʉ

scratch oneself natsahtsiaitʉ

scratch rear or back against
   something pisuʔnetʉ

scratch someone tahtsiarʉ

scratch up earth taʔsiʔwoorʉ

scratch using an instrument
   tsahkiʔaitʉ

screech owl sʉhʉ mupitsʉ

screen, window nanabuni saawʉʔ,
   nasaaʔwʉʔ W

screen door nasaaʔwʉʔ K

screening saaʔwʉʔ

screw tʉmatsukiʔ, tʉtsipʉsaʔ

screw, un- wʉhkweʔyarʉ

screw in wʉʔnikarʉ

screw something in tsakwipunarʉ

screwdriver tʉmabukweʔ

scrounge for yaahuyarʉ

scrub pawʉnuarʉ

scythe soni wʉtsʉkeʔ K,
   tʉʉtsʉkeʔ W

seal something, un- tsahtoʔarʉ K

sealed matsʉbakikatʉ

search wehkinitʉ

search carefully for puhwaaitʉ

search for head lice pusiaketʉ

search the mind in effort to
   remember suʔurarʉ

season, dry ʉrʉʔitʉ

season, fall yʉba

season, summer taatsa̱

seat, un- tsiperʉ

seat, wet pihpárʉbʉʔai

seated on a sled, ride pisikoʔi

seated position, rise from
   nʉʉʔnʉarʉ

-seated buggy, two natsaʔaniʔ

second stomach of cow sekwi biiʔ

secret, keep watsiʔarʉ

secret oneself away watsi̱ habiitʉ

secretly, leave watsi miʔarʉ

secretly, spy on someone watsi
   iyarʉ

section, quarter soko
   rʉmanahkepʉ

section of land, quarter- soko
   tsihkaʔapʉ

see punitʉ

See-how-deep-the-water-is Paa
   roponi

seed pehe

seed, plant tʉhtʉkitʉ, tʉrʉniʔitʉ

seeder tʉrʉnaʔ

seeds, plant tahnaarʉ

seeds, sow tahnaarʉ

seek anahabiniitʉ

seek, hide-and- naʔwekitʉʔ

seesaw naʔatsiyaaʔ, naʔtsiyaaʔ

self-immolate (sacrifice/destroy)
   kuhtʉyarʉ

sell to one another narʉmʉʉrʉ

send kʉmiʔakʉrʉ

send something or someone
   tʉhyetʉ

send word to someone to return
   nʉníhkoonirʉ

sensation, give manʉʉsukaarʉ

sense suapʉ

senseless suapʉwahtʉ

sensitive briar tsapʉsikʉ

sensitive pea huutsúʔa kàhni̱

separate families, three
   pahibahtʉnʉnʉ

separate in marriage pʉah kwarʉ

separate milk from cream yunarʉ

separated naʔbekoʔarʉ

separated but in same general
   area naʔata W

separated by great distance
namanakwᵤ K

separated from others
toroʔihtᵤkitᵤ

separated groups, three pahibahtᵤ

separated in marriage pᵤah taikatᵤ

separately, move off to live
nokaʔitᵤ

September Tᵤboo renahpᵤ makwe
kwiʔena̱ mᵤa, Kwiʔena̱ mᵤa

servant tᵤrᵤʔai wapi̱

service, church puha niwᵤnᵤrᵤᵤ K

set down tsahtᵤkitᵤ

set down carefully tsakwᵤnarᵤ

set in place natsawᵤnᵤkatᵤ

set on fire kutsi̱tonarᵤ

set out tsihtaboʔikᵤtᵤ

set out to dry pasahtahtᵤkitᵤ W

set something in place
natsawᵤnᵤrᵤ

set the table awotsawᵤniʔitᵤ

set up karᵤkᵤrᵤ, maʔyᵤkwiitᵤ

set up straight tsayᵤkwikᵤ

set up teepees yᵤkwikᵤ

set upright tsahkarᵤkᵤrᵤ

setting hen nohabitᵤ

settlement, open country to soko
tsatᵤwarᵤ

seven taatsᵤkwi̱tᵤ

sever, or break (with the teeth)
kᵤhkobarᵤ

several objects, pick up himaʔarᵤ

several objects, take himaʔarᵤ

several,persons, kill nakwᵤsᵤkᵤrᵤ

several things, take one or yaarᵤ

sew tsahkᵤnarᵤ, tᵤtsahkᵤnarᵤ

Sewers Tᵤtsakana

sewing machine tᵤtsahkᵤna?

sewing machine oil tᵤtsakᵤnaha
yuhu

sex, kinsman of either taʔka?

-sex sibling-in-law, opposite haipia?

-sex cousin, same haitsi̱

-sex friend, same haitsi̱

shade hᵤkikᵤ, hᵤᵤki̱

shade, night- tohpotsotsii

shaded hᵤkitᵤ

shadow hᵤhkiapᵤ, hᵤᵤkia?, tuhani̱

shake wohtsawᵤkitᵤ

shake foot taʔwikitᵤ

shake from cold tsihturuarᵤ W

shake head in disagreement
kaʔwitsetᵤ K

shake something kᵤʔwikeetᵤ,
tsaʔwikiitᵤ

shake something off nᵤᵤʔwikeetᵤ,
ṣuutaʔniʔarᵤ

shake the foot tahtaʔnitᵤ

shake the head no tsoʔwiketᵤ

shake vigorously tsobokitᵤ

shallow paʔasᵤ

shaman nipᵤkaaʔeetᵤ, puhaʔaitᵤ

shame nasuʔaitᵤ?

shape or change something
wᵤmᵤᵤrᵤ

shaped wᵤmᵤᵤrihkatᵤ

share in tᵤmaramiitᵤ

**sharp-pointed implement for
punching holes (through which
sinews pass)** wiiyᵤ

sharp-pointed object mutsipᵤ

sharpen tahkᵤmaʔaitᵤ

sharpen a cutting edge tᵤᵤhkonarᵤ

sharpen an edge makwᵤmutsiarᵤ

sharpen something tᵤmakᵤmaʔarᵤ

sharpen to a point tomotsiarᵤ W,
wᵤmutsiarᵤ K

sharpened makᵤmaʔaitᵤ

sharpened edge kᵤmapᵤ

sharpened item namakᵤmaʔaipᵤ

sharpened, keep wᵤmutsiakatuʔi

sharpened to a point mamutsiakatᵤ

shatter tahporoorᵤ, wᵤnutsarᵤ

shave siibetᵤ, wᵤhsibetᵤ

shave off wᵤhtsiʔarᵤ, wᵤsiberᵤ K
shave oneself namotᵤsibetᵤ
shave someone mutᵤsiberᵤ
shaving sibepᵤ
shaving, wood wᵤsibepᵤ
shavings, wood kunapiso?ni̱
shawl wana hᵤ K
shawl, heavy pohotᵤ naʔsᵤkía?
shawl, lightweight tapi naʔsᵤkia?
shawl with fringes naʔsᵤkia?
she maʔ, orᵤ, surᵤ, u, urᵤ
She-invites-her-relatives Nᵤmᵤ
   ruibetsᵤ
shear wᵤtsᵤkarᵤ
shed kweʔyarᵤ
shed many tears paʔokwetᵤ
sheep kabᵤrᵤᵤ?, pᵤhᵤ kabᵤrᵤᵤ?
sheep wool kabᵤrᵤᵤ?a pᵤhᵤ
sheer tapi̱tᵤhtsi
sheet for bed saabara
sheet, bed- saabara, tosa
   kwanaʔhᵤ W
shell of any shellfish waʔkoo? K
shell something by hand
   tsahkíto?arᵤ
shellfish, shell of any waʔkoo? K
shelter, rain ᵤmakahni
shelter for winter, rain yuʔa
   ᵤmakᵤni
shepherd kabᵤrᵤʔa tahkoni wapi̱,
   narahkooni wapi̱ W
shepherd's crook tᵤʔehkooi? W
sheriff nᵤmi himaʔetᵤ, tᵤᵤhtamᵤh
   raibo?
shield naʔyᵤnehtᵤ? W, topᵤ, toʔpᵤ
shimmer paratsihkweʔerᵤ
shin or shin bone kutsiʔomo
shinbone tuhhu
shine weʔkwi̱yanuutᵤ
shine red ekakuhtabearᵤ
shingle kahni nasiyuuki? K,
   naboʔaa W

shiny ekahwi, pahparatsihkweetᵤ
   W, weʔkwi̱yanorᵤ, tsaa
   marabetoikatᵤ K, tsihtsirahputᵤ
shirt kwasu?ᵤ
shirt, man's tenahpᵤʔa kwasu?ᵤ
shirt, under- tuhkanaai kwasu?ᵤ
shish kebob kutsiyaapᵤ
shiver sᵤhkwibitᵤ, sᵤhtorokitᵤ W
shiver from cold tsihturuarᵤ W
[shiver] with cold, tremble
   sᵤᵤtsᵤnitᵤ
shoe napᵤ
shoe, heel of tahpi̱ko?
shoe, take off a tahkweʔyarᵤ
shoe nail napᵤ narawᵤna?, napᵤ
   rᵤrawᵤna?
shoe polish napᵤ rᵤʔeka?
shoe sole napᵤ rahpaana̱,
   narahpaana̱
shoehook napᵤbosa?
shoelace napᵤ tsakwᵤsa?,
   napᵤbosa?
shoelace, fasten with napᵤbosarᵤ
shoes napᵤ|b-|r
shoes, put on tahtoorᵤ
shoes, sole of tahpanaʔaarᵤ
shoes, try on tahpunitᵤ
shoes, wear out tawiarᵤ W
shoestring napᵤ tsakwᵤsa?
shoo tanᵤkikᵤtᵤ
shoo away manᵤkikᵤrᵤ
shoot tsakwᵤkatᵤ, tsatᵤkarᵤ,
   tᵤkwᵤrᵤ, wᵤhtikᵤrᵤ
shoot, sight to wᵤhkurᵤ
shoot a gun wᵤhkikatᵤ
shoot a gun repeatedly taʔwoʔekarᵤ
shoot a repeating gun tsatᵤkaʔkarᵤ
shoot something kwᵤᵤhtikᵤrᵤ
short paʔitsiʔwᵤnᵤrᵤ, paʔi̱tᵤhtsi?
short, cut off piʔtoʔarᵤ
short, fall nasutamᵤ wᵤmi̱naitᵤ W,
   pihpokaarᵤ, toʔwᵤmi̱naitᵤ

short, run kehewaʔitʉ

Short-dress Tsihtara

shot, gun- taʔwoʔiʔ

shotgun soʔo narʉbakiʔ

shot, sling- taʔkʉbuuʔ W

shoulder tsoʔapʉ

shoulder bone tsoohpa tsuuni W

shout pia pʉku rekwarʉ, pia rekwa

shouting, awaken someone by
tayʉtsʉrʉ

shove maʔwikarʉ, wʉtsʉkitʉ

shovel kusiyunaʔ, tsiyunarʉ,
tʉtsiyunaʔ

shovel, coal kutʉhuyunaʔ W

shovel out tsiiʔwʉweniitʉ

shovel something tʉtsiyunarʉ

show how tʉmabunikʉrʉ

show off nasutsa akwarʉ K

show someone something
tsahpunitʉ

shrink yurahpetʉ

shrivel up from heat
kuhtakwitsooʔnitʉ W

shrub kusiwʉʉnʉ

shucks, corn hani buhipʉ

shrunken paihtsi

shyster kaawosa̱

sibling samohpʉʔ

sibling, having a takaʔkatʉ

sibling-in-law, opposite sex
haipiaʔ

sick, be tʉʔoibʉkʉrʉ, uhúntʉkʉ

sickle soni wʉhpomaʔ

sickly hoʔyopi̱, hoʔyopitʉ,
nʉʉsukatʉ, uhúntʉkʉ

sickly person namaʔabʉ, takwipʉ

side comb papi̱ tsiʔnikaʔ

side of an object sʉkwe naisʉ

side of chest ahna, ama-

side of stomach or abdomen
sahpáanaʔ

side, on opposite paʔarai

side, right tʉbitsi̱nakwʉ̱

side, scrape outer wʉhkwʉnetʉ

**side to side, go from (or back and
forth)** piʔnuʔa miʔarʉ

side-to-side, looking from
kaʔmʉtʉhiʔ W

side to side, move from tohtsatsarʉ

siding naboʔaa W

sieve saaʔwʉʔ, tsasaʔwʉkiʔ K

sieve, honey ʉnʉʉʔ ruuʔ

sieze tsasukwarʉ

sift tsasaʔwʉkitʉ

sifter tʉsoyuni

sifter, flour tohtía tsasaʔwʉkiʔ,
tsasaʔwʉkiʔ K

sigh nahuahtsitʉ, nasuawʉhkitʉ K

sight to shoot wʉhkurʉ

sign language mootekwoʔpʉ

silver tosa-, tosahwi̱ , tosapi̱ ,
tosahpuhihwi̱

silver maple kweʔyʉkʉ sohóobi

silver money tosahpuhihwi̱

silvery wormwood pasiwona
pʉhʉbi

similar to elves, little people
Nʉnapi

similar to water lily, plant
paʔmutsi

sin aihinahanitʉ

sin, tempt one to tʉrape suwaitʉ

since then subeʔsʉ

sinew tamu

sing a song nihtoʔitʉ, tʉnikwʉrʉ

sing a song for someone
nahubiyaarʉ

sing high pitched putsi kwʉtsʉbaitʉ

sing loudly pia rʉnikwʉtʉ

sing one song after another
nipʉyerʉ

sing out nihtoʔitʉ

single buggy tʉe waikina̱

singletree pihtsakʉ huupi̱

sink to the bottom in water
paʔikarʉ
sinner tʉrapehekatʉ
Sioux people Papitsimina?, Suhta?
sister samohpʉ?
sister, eldest patsi?
sister, father's paha?
sister, mother's pia
sister, younger nami?
sister-in-law paha piahpʉ
sit kahtʉ
sit down karʉkatʉ 1, nakarʉ?karʉ,
yʉkwimi?arʉ
sit down, force to sutena karʉrʉ
sit down quickly tsuhni karʉ
sit in sun to dry mabasahtʉkitʉ K
sit in the sun to dry
pasahtahtʉkitʉ W
sit on, put down something to
pisoonarʉ
sit on something (breaking it to pieces) pinutsarʉ
sit still yukarʉrʉ
sit straight tsayʉkwitʉ
sitting back on heels, kneel down
tanatookarʉtʉ
Sitting-bear Kohitʉ seʔtanʉkʉ
sitting down, swing
piʔweesuʔruʔitʉ
sitting on it, crack something by
pitʉbarʉ
situated haahpitʉ 1, natsawʉnʉkatʉ
six naabaitʉ
size, small tʉtaatʉ
sizzle kukʉbihkutʉ
skate tahkitemiʔarʉ,
tasikoʔiʔmiʔarʉ
skillet kukʉmeʔawe
skim from the surface yunarʉ
skin hʉnʉpoʔaʔ, kiboʔarʉ, poʔaʔ,
tsasinʉkaarʉ, tsahkʉrʉ?arʉ
skin, animal tsahkwʉrʉ?arʉ

skin an animal pʉhʉ tsahkweʔyarʉ,
wʉsiboʔarʉ
skin animal tsahkwʉrʉ?arʉ
skin, cracked tsiʔwapʉ W
skin, human hʉnʉpoʔaʔ, mapóʔaʔ
skin, peel off kiboʔarʉ
skin, rash on tasiʔaʔ W
skin, raw tuhʉpʉ
skin, rough tsiʔwapʉ W
skin, tear nʉʉsihwaʔitʉ
skin something kiboʔarʉ
skinned, brown- otʉhtʉ mapoʔakatʉ
Skinny-and-wrinkled Tekwitsi M
skins or other covering for teepees
nʉmʉkʉni
skip wiʔhikoyoʔitʉ
skull tsuhnipʉ
skunk pisuníi? K, pisuniʔeeyʉ,
pohniʔatsi
skunkbush tatsipʉ
sky tomo-, tomobaʔatʉ
Sky-child Tomoʔa tua?
slam things in anger, jerk and
tuhu rekwarʉ
slander moyaʔitʉ
slanting nahʉyatʉ, naʔʉyatʉ
slap (or punch repeatedly)
tohtʉkwarʉ
slap (with palm of hand) tohpaʔitʉ
slate color esipitʉ
slave naʔraiboo?
sled, ride seated on a pisikoʔi
sleep habiitʉ, ʉhpʉitʉ
sleep unconcerned yuu ʉhpʉitʉ
sleeping quarters habikʉni
sleepy mitsokokʉkatʉ, puibʉʉtʉ,
puibʉʉtʉtʉ
sleepy-eyed, be puibʉʉtʉ
sleet paasitsi
sleeve makwʉsà?
slender huutubuʔitʉ W,
huutunaakatʉ K

slender, tall and kanaba?aitʉ, kʉbʉráatạ

slice koo?itʉ, tsihpoma

slick pahtsi, patsiketʉ, puhnuketʉ

slick-haired goat pahtsi kabʉrʉʉ?

slide nuarʉ, pisikwanúu?i?

slide down pisikwanúu?itʉ

slide standing up tahkitemi?arʉ

slingshot ta?kʉbuu? W

slip a rope around something ku?nikarʉ

slip standing up tahkitemi?arʉ

slippery puhnuketʉ

slobber kʉ?okwetʉ

Slope Naya

sloping nahʉyatʉ, na?ʉyatʉ

slow napiso?aitʉ

slow down (what one is doing) nʉnʉ?itʉ

slow motion, move in aimi?arʉ

slow-moving nanahbiso?aitʉ

slowly ubitakuhtsi?a

slowly, come mahuinoorʉ

slowly, move puhyʉnukitʉ

slowly, run pohyami?arʉ

small tʉe

small gray bird kusisai?

small intestine kohị

small particles, mash into mahomonutsarʉ

small quantity tʉtaatʉ

small river okwèetʉ

small size tʉtaatʉ

smaller than inaarʉ

smallpox narʉ?ʉyʉ tasi?ạ, tasi?a? W

smartweed ekawoni

smash tatsukwerʉ, wʉhtabarʉ

smell around muwarʉ W, ʉkwịsʉ?ninitʉ K

smell something ʉkwihkatʉ

smell something (from a distance) ʉkwʉsʉ?nitʉ

Smeller Pisu kwá?na?

smile mu?yạnesuarʉ

smoke kwipʉ

smoke during religious ceremony puha bahmu?itʉ

smoke hole kahku?e, kahni ku?e

smoke ritually nakatsʉhetʉ

smooth makwʉ?nikʉtʉ K, pahtsi, patsiketʉ, puhnuketʉ, tsasu?nerʉ

Smooth Pahtsi ketʉ

smooth down wʉtʉkị?netʉ

smooth, plane something tʉsibetʉ

smooth sumac tʉmaya huupi

snagged patʉ tsanitʉ

snail sanahtu?re?

snake kwasinaboo?

snake, crawl like a nuhyimi?arʉ W

snake, racer kʉhtáa nu?ya?a W

snake, rattle- kwasinaboo wʉhkitsu?tsu?ikatʉ, wʉhtsabeyakatʉ W

(snake), water moccasin tuhparokoo?

snake of any species nuhya?

snake root itsa, timʉihʉ?

snakeroot, button atabitsʉnoi

Snakes Idahi

snap kʉtubarʉ W, porokitʉ

snap fingers mabohto

snap off tahkobarʉ, tsahkobarʉ

snapping turtle kwasi nʉrʉʉ?wʉ?, pa?kwakʉme

snatch tsasukwarʉ

sneak around ho?aniitʉ

sneak away watsi mi?arʉ

sneak in watsi ikatʉ

sneaky person nakʉhoowaaitʉ

sneeze aakwʉsitʉ, tsa?akʉsitʉ K

sneeze, cause to tsamupʉsitʉ W

sneezeweed natsaakʉsi, tʉrʉkwobamʉ

sniff an odor ʉkwihkatʉ

sniff around ɨkwisɨʔninitɨ K
snore ɨsorokiitɨ
snort suhurɨkitɨ
snow tahkabi
snow, ice or tahka-
snowfall tahkaʔɨmarɨ
snuff yokabahmu
snuff fire with fingers W
  tsahtukarɨ
snuff out marukarɨ
snuffbox, devil's mupitsɨha
  pisahpi W
soak in water parɨkitɨ
soak oneself in water naparɨkitɨ
soak through parɨbɨɨʔitɨ
soaked paʔisoketɨ
soaked thoroughly papoosinu
soap wana kotse?
soapberry otɨ mitsonaa?
soapweed mumutsi?
socks wana napɨ
soda pop pihná baa
soft yokake
soft, be yɨʔyɨkarɨ
soften tsasuʔnerɨ, yɨʔyɨkarɨ
soften (by pounding) tohparaarɨ
  W, tsohkwe K
**soften (something by trampling
  on it)** tahpararɨ
softened payɨʔyɨkatɨ, yɨʔyɨkarɨ
softly, speak watsih nikwɨnɨrɨ
soggy yokake
soil ohta-, ohtapii
soil, eroded patowoʔnepɨ
soil, hoe puhi yɨkwitɨ
soil, hole dug in hoora
soil, plow tɨtsaʔworɨ
soil, red ekahuukupɨ, ekasokoobi
soldier ekasahpana?, taibo
  ekɨsahpana?
soldiers, Chief Comanche- dog-
  Tɨoyobisesɨ

sole of foot tahpáana
sole of shoes tahpanaʔaarɨ
sole, shoe napɨ rahpaana,
  narahpaana
some sɨsɨmɨ?
someone sɨmɨ?
someone, club wahtóorɨ
someone (or something), club
  wɨhtokwɨrɨ
someone, doll up maʔyɨkwiitɨ
someone, duck tsahpaakuʔnikarɨ
someone, encounter naraʔuraitɨ
someone, fetch water for
  tuukɨmiʔarɨ
**someone (or something), find
  room for** haakarɨ
someone, flirt with naʔisa yɨkwitɨ
  K, naʔisa suakɨtɨ W
someone, fool nohitekwarɨ
someone, forsake pɨah taitɨ
**someone, frighten (with
  something)** wɨʔyɨrɨhkitɨ
someone, fuss at nimakwihtsetɨ
someone, give money to
  puhihwimaka
someone, give up waiting for
  wɨsuwarɨkiitɨ
someone, go on foot to meet
  tamunaikɨmiʔarɨ
someone, gore mukuhparɨ W
someone, hang (with a rope)
  ooibehkarɨ
someone, help tɨituarɨ
someone walk, help tsamiʔakɨrɨ
**someone, hold a curing ceremony
  for** puhaʔarɨ
someone, hurt mawɨmerɨ,
  tsiyaketɨ, umarhnitɨ
someone, hurt (by accident)
  tsahhuhyarɨ
**someone, interrupt (because of
  worry)** pisukwitakɨrɨ

someone, introduce nisuabetaru W

someone in, invite nikwekwitu

someone, jerk meat for tu?inakuru

someone, kiss muhraru

someone behind, leave nobuahraitu

someone for good, leave pua mi?aru

someone, like su?akutu

someone, listen to tumahyokuru

someone, lock up ta?ikuru

someone, lose faith in nasuwuhkitu

someone, make up pisaru

someone, marry nanakwuuru

someone, meet ta?uraru, to?uraru

someone by going on foot, meet tamunaikumi?aru

someone, name nahnia makaru, nihakuru

someone help, offer masutsaru

someone, outrun naromunitu

someone to do something, persuade nitsubahiku?itu

someone, pester nihtunetsaru

someone, please tsaa manusuru

someone, pop on kuhpuru?airu

someone, praise nihpana?aitu

someone, pray for nanisutaikutu

someone, precede muhnetu

someone, prepare breakfast for taamahkaru

someone with something, prick piso?aru

someone, question tubinaru, tubinitu

someone, quiet niyukaruru W

someone, raise manuaru

someone, refuse to accept ninakabaru

someone, reject kemenikwitu W, nimakabaitu

someone, remind nasutamakuru W

someone, resemble tu?ikatu

someone, respect maruhnikatu

someone or something while moving, rope ku?nikakuru

someone, save makwitso?aitu

someone, say no to nimamusukutu

someone, scalp ku?e tsasimaru

someone, scratch tahtsiaru

someone, send something or tuhyetu

someone to return, send word to nuníhkooniru

someone, shave mutusiberu

someone something, show tsahpunitu

someone, sing a song for nahubiyaaru

someone, spilled by ta?okitu

someone, spy on kuhiyaru, watsi punitu

someone secretly, spy on watsi iyaru

someone, stone tupi táhparu

someone, stop following nunu?itu

someone by force, stop tahkoonitu

someone, strangle kuitsimarukutu

someone, surrender manusuta?aitu

someone by force, take sutena betu

someone home as guest, take panimi?aru

-someone, Take-a-stick-and-hit Huuwuhtukwa?

someone into something, talk nitsubahiku?itu

someone, talk to niwunuru, tekwaru

someone something, teach nisuabetaru

someone, teach something to tunisuabetaru

someone, tempt or test mabunihkaru

someone, tickle pinakɯtsɯrɯ

someone or something, toward mawakatu

someone, train suabetaikɯrɯ

someone, trip tanɯɯhkupaitɯ

someone, trust tokɯsuakɯtɯ

someone, understand nahkɯsuaberɯ

someone or something, up to or onto maatu

someone, wait for makamaitɯ

someone, wake tsahtɯbunitɯ

someone by pounding, wake wɯhtɯbunitɯ

someone, wake up tsayoritɯ

someone, waken by speaking to nihtɯbuniorɯ

someone, watch watsi punitɯ

someone, win in a contest against tahni?arɯ

someone, win over kwakurɯ K

someone or something, with or on maa

someone to death, work namakupakɯrɯ

someone's death, prevent makwitso?aitɯ

someone's beard, pull mutsonoo?itɯ

someone's life, save tsahkwitso?arɯ

someone's back to ease pain, stand on tahpara?itɯ

some place, escort a guest panimi?arɯ

somersault nakkuminoorɯ

something wahtóorɯ

something carried in the claws ta?yaahkana? W

something, club wɯhtokwɯtɯ

something, drag kɯwokarɯ, piwokarɯ, takwokarɯ W

something, drag along piwokami?arɯ

something, drag (spread on flat surface) pisunarɯ

something, dry pasakɯrɯ, tɯbitsi basarɯ

something, dye tɯsáarɯ

something, earn tahwikarɯ, tɯrahwikatɯ

something, eat most of sɯmɯ rɯhkarɯ

something, experience wɯsukatɯ

something, explain nisuabetarɯ K

something, fail to do kemahpɯ?arɯ

something, fall into tɯyumarɯ

something, feel tsasukarɯ

something, fence tɯɯhtɯmarɯ

something, fill tɯmarɯ W

something, find urarɯ, wɯ?urarɯ

something, find (being looked for) to?urarɯ

something, find (with the hand) ma?urarɯ

something (or someone), find room for haakarɯ

something, flatten marɯki?netɯ

something, grease tɯ?ekarɯ, wihi̱ tɯ?ekarɯ

something, hammer tahhanitɯ

something, hang tsakwenitɯ, tɯrohtsanitɯ, wenuarɯ

something, hang over nɯɯsoo?etɯ

something, hang up tohtsanarɯ

something, hang up (on a nail or hook) tsa?wenitɯ, tsahkwenitɯ W

something, harness nanoomanitɯ

something in hand, have yahkatɯ

something, hear tɯnakarɯ

something, heat kuhtsɯnikɯrɯ

something, hide namabimarɯ

something, hit wɯhtɯkwarɯ

something, hold yuhnukarɯ

something, hook muhkarʉ W

something, insert into tsiʔnikarʉ, wʉnikarʉ

something, jerk wʉhpoʔtserʉ K

something, jerk (toward oneself) tsahpoʔtsarʉ

something, keep tahtʉkarʉ

something, kick sʉʉhkwʉhtʉkurʉ

something away, kick sʉʉ potserʉ

something hanging, knock off wʉhtokarʉ

something, knock wʉhpoʔtserʉ K

something down, knock tayuʔmarʉ

something down, lay tʉkiitʉ K

something, lay the head down on tsohtʉkikatʉ

something, lean namahtowʉnarʉ

something, lean against nʉʉbanikatʉ

something, lean on mahtokwʉnaitʉ K

something, lean over nʉʉsooʔetʉ

something new, learn urahkarʉ

something, locate taʔwairʉ

something, lose nasuwatsi, watsikʉrʉ

something from hand or wrist, lose maʔkweʔyarʉ

something, make a mark on tsahporʉ

something rattle, make tsatsʉbipʉkurʉ

something, mark tsihpoorʉ

something, mash up mapitserʉ

something, measure tʉmanahketʉ

something, meet to suggest nanikaʔwitʉ

something, melt kuhpawikʉʔitʉ

something, milk maʔokwerʉ

something, move tanuarʉ

something (with the mouth), move kʉnuaitʉ

something, nail taʔnikʉtʉ, tʉrawʉnarʉ K

something, open matʉhwarʉ, tohtʉwarʉ, tsahtʉwarʉ, tʉhwarʉ

something wide, open pia tsatuarʉ

something, oppose tsoʔwiketʉ

something, own taʔurʉkarʉ K

something, padlock tʉtsihtʉrʉ

something, paint tʉruʔekarʉ, tʉʔekarʉ

something, patch tʉkarʉkurʉ

something, peel tsahkítoʔarʉ

something, persuade someone to do nitsʉbahikʉʔitʉ

something smooth, plane tʉsibetʉ

something, pluck out noʔitʉ

something, point out muruahwʉnʉrʉ

something, poke head into tsoʔnikarʉ, tʉtsoʔnikarʉ

something, pound wʉhtarakiitʉ

something, pound on tahhanitʉ

something, powder homopisarʉ

something, practice namabunitʉ

something down, press tatʉkeʔnerʉ

something, prick someone with pisoʔarʉ

something, pull on tsanuarʉ

something behind, pull pitsákarʉ

something off or out, pull tsahkweʔyarʉ

something, puncture oneself with nabisoʔarʉ

something that rolls, push maʔaikʉrʉ, tsiʔaikʉrʉ

something back in place, put tohtʉkiʔarʉ

something down, put tsaʔnikoorʉ

something into the mouth, put tʉroʔnikarʉ

something to sit on, put down pisoonarʉ

something, quit pᵤarᵤ
something, rake tᵤtsahtᵤʔoorᵤ
something, request naníhtsawaʔitᵤ,
  nigwaitᵤ K
something, rest on
  mahtokwᵤnaitᵤ K
something, right tsahkarᵤkᵤrᵤ
something, ring tuʔtsayaketᵤ
something, rip puhkarᵤ,
  tohtᵤrᵤʔarᵤ W, wᵤhtᵤrᵤʔarᵤ K
something, roll to start toʔaikᵤrᵤ
something, roll up with
  tohtopoʔnarᵤ
something while moving, rope
  someone or kuʔnikakᵤrᵤ
something, rub against pisuʔnetᵤ
something, rub head against
  tsotsoʔneetᵤ
something, run away from
  wᵤanuraitᵤ K
something, run to tunehtsᵤrᵤ
something through fear, run to
  namarunehtsᵤrᵤ
something, salt onaʔaitᵤ
something with a saw, saw
  huutsikaʔarᵤ
something, scatter tsahpoʔarᵤ
something, scratch rear or back
  against pisuʔnetᵤ
something in, screw tsakwipunarᵤ
something or someone, send
  tᵤhyetᵤ
something in place, set
  natsawᵤnᵤrᵤ
something, shake kuʔwikeetᵤ,
  tsaʔwikiitᵤ
something off, shake nᵤᵤʔwikeetᵤ,
  sᵤᵤtaʔniʔarᵤ
something, shape or change
  wᵤmᵤᵤrᵤ
something, sharpen
  tᵤmakᵤmaʔarᵤ

something by hand, shell
  tsahkítoʔarᵤ
something, shoot kwᵤᵤhtikᵤrᵤ
something, shovel tᵤtsiyunarᵤ
something, show someone
  tsahpunitᵤ
something breaking it to pieces,
  sit on pinutsarᵤ
something, skin kiboʔarᵤ
something, slip a rope around
  kuʔnikarᵤ
something, smell ᵤkwihkatᵤ
something (from a distance),
  smell ᵤkwᵧsᵤʔnitᵤ
something by trampling on it,
  soften tahpararᵤ
something, spill out on tokwᵧriarᵤ
something on purpose, spill
  tokwᵤriaitᵤ
something, split tohpakurᵤ
something, spread out tsahpararᵤ,
  wᵤhpararᵤ
something, stake tᵤrawᵤnarᵤ K
something, step over tasarᵤ
something, stop movement
  toward wᵤnᵤ hupiitᵤ
something, straighten kᵤhpararᵤ
something wrinkled, straighten
  tahtunaabarᵤ
something, strain out tsasoʔarᵤ
something, stretch out wᵤhpararᵤ
something out, stretch tsahturᵤ
something, suck on mukwihterᵤ
something, support tsihtᵤroorᵤ
something, swallow tᵤyuwarᵤ,
  yᵤwitᵤ W
something, sweep tᵤᵤnuarᵤ
something live, take away tahtᵤkitᵤ
something, take down off of
  tsahpᵤherᵤ
something in the mouth, take
  kᵤhyaarᵤ

something, talk someone into
nitsꭒbahikꭒ?itꭒ

something, tangle tokwꭒsikꭒtꭒ,
tsakwꭒ?ikꭒrꭒ W

something, tap on wꭒhtarakiitꭒ

something, teach someone
nisuabetarꭒ

something to someone, teach
tꭒnisuabetarꭒ

something, tear puhkarꭒ, sihwarꭒ,
tosi?kwarꭒ, tsai?warꭒ K

something, tear at tsahkwanitꭒ

something, tempt by describing
nisuyakeetꭒ

something, test natsahpunitꭒ

something, think about
nasutamꭒkatꭒ tamai, su?atsitꭒ,
tꭒsu?atsꭒkatꭒ

something, throw a light on
kupꭒtarꭒ

something, throw at tahtꭒkwarꭒ

something, throw out of
wꭒ?kwꭒriarꭒ

something, tie wꭒhtamarꭒ

something, tire of manꭒꭒ?maitꭒ

something, tired of
nakꭒnꭒꭒ?maitꭒ, wꭒ?tsikwarꭒ

something, toward someone or
mawakatu

something, trail tꭒnahyarꭒ

something over, turn tsamꭒrikarꭒ,
wꭒmꭒꭒrꭒ

something, twist tsakwipunarꭒ

something, twist oneself around
nꭒꭒ?kwipunarꭒ

something, unable to do
kemahpꭒ?arꭒ, tsuhitꭒ

something, uncoil wꭒhpꭒkꭒsuarꭒ

something, unravel
nꭒꭒpꭒrꭒsuanꭒpurꭒ

something, unseal tsahto?arꭒ K

something, unwrap tahkwꭒmarꭒ

something with the mouth,
unwrap kꭒhto?yarꭒ K

something, up to or onto someone
or maatu

something, water payunitꭒ

something, wear natsa?nikarꭒ

something around the neck, wear
korohkorꭒ

something around the waist, wear
kohinehkitꭒ

something out, wear wihto?arꭒ

something, weigh narayaakꭒrꭒ

something off, wipe tahtsumarꭒ K

something with the head, wipe
tsotsomarꭒ

something, with or on someone
or maa

something, wrinkle
takwikakwo?arꭒ

sometimes sꭒsꭒ?ana

somewhere i?a

somewhere, escape from
namaro?itꭒ

somewhere, happen to be
nahabitꭒtꭒ

somewhere, live nꭒmꭒnetꭒ

somewhere, lying haahpitꭒ 1

somewhere, run away from pꭒa
nuhkitꭒ

son tua?

son, adopted tua boopꭒ W

son-in-law monahpꭒ?

Son-of-bull-bear Tꭒmꭒbo

son or daughter (offspring),
grown nahnapꭒ

song hubiya?

song, sing a nihto?itꭒ, tꭒnikwꭒrꭒ

song after another, sing one
nipꭒyerꭒ

song for someone, sing a
nahubiyaarꭒ

songs, war wohho tꭒikwꭒpitꭒ K

songs of victory wohho tᵾikwᵾpitᵾ K

songs of youth wᵾyakeetᵾ W

sons-in-law nonanᵾᵾ

soon kemarᵾkwisᵾ

sore ᵾ?a?

sore, chronic narᵾ?ᵾyᵾ ᵾᵾ?a?

sore person namakᵾnᵾmapᵾ

sore throat, have a kuitsisᵾatᵾ

sorrel horse otᵾ kᵾma? W, tᵾpᵾsi kᵾma?

sorrel mare ekapia?

soul sua, suana

sound tah ta-

sound, buzzing puuyaketᵾ

sound, make galloping totᵾbihkurᵾ

sounding of a horn muyake?

soup saa huubᵾ

soup, corn hanisahoba

soup, quick-cook corn atakwá?sᵾ?

sour moha-, sᵾkᵾ-, sᵾᵾkᵾ

sour, taste mohakamarᵾ

south yu?anᵾbe nakwᵾbᵾ

south wind yu?anee

southeast yu?anᵾe muhyᵾnakwᵾbu

southern hackberry mitsonaa?

southwest yu?a nᵾe kahpi?nakwᵾ

sow seeds tahnaarᵾ

sowbug kwita maropona

space, cram into limited natsinᵾhkᵾrᵾ

space, crammed into limited tsinᵾkᵾ

spade tuhpihhínaboo?, tuhtahkanaboo?, tᵾtsihpeti?, tᵾtsiyuna? K

sparkling tsihtsirahputᵾ

spasm, have muscle cramp or toponitᵾ K

speak tekwarᵾ

speak firmly ninabitsiarᵾ

speak irrationally ni?emᵾabᵾnitᵾ

speak softly watsih nikwᵾnᵾrᵾ

speak to niikwiitᵾ

speak Wichita language tuhka?naai rekwarᵾ

speaker tekwawapi

speaker and hearer, place known by pᵾkᵾhu

Speakers of Wichita language tuhka?naai? niwᵾnᵾ

speaking tayᵾtsᵾrᵾ

speaking to someone, waken by nihtᵾbuniorᵾ

spear tahkana?, tᵾtsiwaii? K, uwíhi

species, snake of any nuhya?

speech ni-, tekwapᵾ

speech, error in ni?watsᵾkatᵾ?

speech, quiet by ni?tsu?narᵾ

speech, tremble in nihkwibihbikitᵾ

speedily, act wᵾ?rabiarᵾ F

spend money su?makᵾtᵾ

spherical tohtoponitᵾ, topohtᵾ

spider pᵾhᵾ re?tsi

spill kᵾ?kwᵾriarᵾ, pi?wᵾ?wenitᵾ, wᵾhtiarᵾ

spill accidentally, knock over and tsakwᵾriarᵾ

spill of own accord nᵾᵾti?akatᵾ

spill out on something tokwᵾriarᵾ

spill something nᵾᵾti?arᵾ, pi?wᵾriarᵾ, tahkwᵾriarᵾ

spill something on purpose tokwᵾriaitᵾ

spilled narohkwᵾri?etᵾ

spilled accidentally makwᵾri?aikatᵾ

spilled by someone ta?okitᵾ

spin around kwinu?yarᵾ, natsahkwinu?itᵾ

spinal column kwahiporopᵾ

spinal cord kwahi kupisi

spine kwahinupᵾ

spine, align tahpara?itᵾ

spinner kuʔe kwʉsiʔ
spirit nanisuwʉkaitʉ
spirit, calm tsʉmʉkịkatʉ
spirit, evil pʉe tʉyaaiʔ, tʉtʉsuana
spirit, have an evil poosubʉhkaitʉ
spirit, peaceful tsʉmʉkịkatʉ
spirit, quiet tsʉmʉkịkatʉ
spirit, unclean tʉtʉsuana
Spirit-talker Mukwoorʉ
spirited nanisuwʉkaitʉ
spit tusitʉ
spit out liquid pai tusiʔitʉ K
spit out kʉhkihtserʉ W
spittoon tusi aawo̜
splash into water pakwaʔnuarʉ
splash water on pakwihtsikʉrʉ
splash with water pawʉhpaʔitʉ
splatter kuhpuruʔairʉ, puruarʉ
splattered kuhpuruʔaitʉ
spleen hekwiʔ
splice nanakatsoʔarʉ
splinter tsatsiaʔ
split tabakoitʉ, topʉkaarʉ,
 tsahpakoʔarʉ, tsapʉkarʉ
split into two parts tʉapakoʔitʉ
split of own accord nʉʉhtsiʔaitʉ
split open pekoʔarʉ
split something tohpakurʉ
spoke of wheel naʔomo̜ nasʉwʉhkiʔ
spokes waikina nakwʉʉkị
spokesman tekwawapi̜, tʉnikepisa?
sponged mabaʔisokitʉ
spongy yokake
spoon tʉe aawo, wʉhibiʔ
spoon, table- pia rʉʔewo
spotless tutʉtsaai wahtʉ
spotted naboo-
spouse notsaʔkaʔ
spouse, leave a pʉah kwarʉ
sprain a joint of the body
 wʉkwʉsarʉ
sprain ankle naraminaitʉ K

sprain or break hand or lower arm
 namaminaitʉ
sprained makwʉsetʉ
spray, fly animuị wasʉ
sprayed with water pawʉʔweʔniitʉ
spread a tablecloth tʉkʉ soonarʉ
spread legs out poʔarʉ
spread out something tsahpararʉ,
 wʉhpararʉ
spring parʉtsohpeʔ
Spring, become tahma roʔitʉ
spring water parʉtsohpeʔ
sprinkle pasibunarʉ, paʔisokerʉ,
 piʔwʉʔwenitʉ
sprinkled tohpaʔịsokitʉ W
sprinkling, baptize by kuʔe naba
 wʉhtia
sprout paʔmukʉsʉʔarʉ
spun natsahkwinuʔitʉ
spur natsiwekwaʔ
spy on hoʔaniitʉ
spy on someone kuhiyarʉ, watsi
 punitʉ
spy on someone secretly watsi iyarʉ
squash makịtsarʉ
squash, or crush tsakịtsetʉ
squashed makịtsetʉ
squat kwanuʔitʉ K, wʉnʉhkarʉrʉ
 W, wʉtahkarʉrʉ K
squaw corn nʉmʉ hani
squeak kahúu pipịkuniitʉ,
 kʉtsuʔtsuʔkitʉ
Squeaky Pipịkuʔ
Squeaky-like-a-mouse Kahúu nihku
 pipịkure̜
squeeze kwabarʉ
squeeze hand matsáhtsurʉ
squeeze to a head maʔokwerʉ
squeezed tight tsinʉkʉ
squint tasʉkʉpunitʉ
squirm pisukwitaitʉ,
 pʉhkwinuʔitʉ W

squirrel, ground ekwakɨɨpi?, ewa kɨɨpi?

squirrel, tree wokoohwi

stab tonarɨ

stable puku kahni

staff natsihtóo? K

stagger when walking tsimɨami?arɨ

stairs huunaro?i?, naro?i?

stake tɨrawɨna? K

stake down tawɨnarɨ

stake down tightly ɨhtaarɨ

stake something tɨrawɨnarɨ K

staked-down object ɨhta?etɨ

stalk or plant, sunflower hi?oopi

stalked mahooikatɨ

stall nanamɨ?aitɨ K

stallion, wild pɨa watsi

stamen of flower totsiyaa papihtsipɨ

stand tobo?ikatɨ

stand angrily pihiso?aiwɨnɨrɨ

stand hair on end sɨroonitɨ

stand in the sun tabe wɨnɨ?itɨ

stand just above the horizon tabe wɨnɨ?itɨ

stand on someone's back to ease pain tahpara?itɨ

stand still yuu wɨnɨrɨ

stand tall kanaba?aitɨ

stand waiting tahkamɨrɨ

standing wɨnɨrɨ

standing, crowded while tahtsɨkitɨ

standing alone, one hill nookarɨrɨ

standing on hind feet manawɨnɨkatɨ

standing position, help up from sitting to matsákwɨnɨkɨrɨ

standing up, slide tahkitemi?arɨ

standing up, slip tahkitemi?arɨ

Standing-sun Tabe wɨnɨrɨ

staples, fence tɨɨhtɨmapɨha tɨrawɨna?

star tatsinuupi

star, north kemi?arɨtatsino

start nabihtawɨna, to?aikɨrɨ

start something, roll to to?aikɨrɨ

startle wɨɨyoritɨ, yɨrɨhkitɨ

starve to death tsiharɨyaitɨ

starving ketsihanabenitɨ

statement, misunderstand nanawatsikarɨ

stationary karɨɨrɨ

stay karɨkatɨ 1, yɨkwimi?arɨ

-stay-downstream, Those-who Tinawa

stay late tsɨ?nitɨ

steak tɨhkapa nakoopɨ

steal sikusarɨ, tɨrɨhkarɨ

steam no?yaikɨtɨ

steam bath nakuhkwaraki? K

steam bath, take a kuhkwarɨkitɨ

steam bathe nakuhkwarakitɨ, nasukoo?itɨ

steel tool tɨɨhko?ne?

steeple puha kahni muutsi

stem (of plant) totsiyaa?a sɨɨki

stem, pipe omotoi

step backward pimimi?arɨ

step over something tasarɨ

stepmother paraiboo?

-steps, Yellow Ohawɨnɨ

sternly, order ninabitsiarɨ

stew kohtsáarɨ

stew food tɨkarɨkɨrɨ

stewed food kohtsáa?, tɨkarɨkɨpɨ

stick hu-

stick, bracing wana tsihparaa?

stick, carry a huuyaarɨ

stick, carry something on a tsihimarɨ

stick, roast on a kuhtsiyarɨ

-stick-and -hit-someone, Take-a
Huuwᵾhtᵾkwaʔ

stick, walking tᵾʔehkooiʔ W

stick for hand game tuhhuuʔ

stick to sanarᵾ

sticks, pillow- tsohpe tawᵾnaʔ

sticks, possess huuhimarᵾ

sticks into ground, pound pillow-
tsohpe takwᵾnarᵾ

sticks, roast on kuʔtsiyaarᵾ

stiff, be tsihturuarᵾ K

stiff neck, have a woʔrohtsarᵾ

still ᵾkᵾ, ᵾkᵾsᵾ, yunahkatᵾ

still, lie yuu habíitᵾ

still, sit yukarᵾrᵾ

still, stand yuu wᵾnᵾrᵾ

sting, insect tonarᵾ

stinger of an insect tonaʔ

stingy otᵾ suakatᵾ

stingy person nahkᵾepᵾ K

stir wᵾnoʔyarᵾ

stir around yoʔmitsaitᵾ

stir up dust huukᵾhᵾnᵾrᵾ

stir up excitement toyᵾsekaitᵾ

stir up fire kumaʔomerᵾ, maʔomerᵾ

stirred wᵾnoʔyaitᵾ

stirrup narahtᵾkiiʔ, taʔnikaʔ W

stock, laughing- nanᵾsuʔuyaatᵾ,
suʔuyaʔiʔ

stockings wana napᵾ

stomach sapᵾ, sapᵾ

stomach ache kohikamᵾkatᵾ, sapᵾ
nᵾᵾtsikwarᵾ

stomach, extreme pain in sapᵾ
wᵾnᵾkatᵾ

stomach, full wᵾtsᵾʔmi

stomach of cow, second sekwi biiʔ

stomach or abdomen, side of
sahpáanaʔ

stomp tanᵾʔyᵾkitᵾ

stone tᵾmakᵾmaʔaaiʔ, tᵾpi, tᵾᵾpi

stone, grinding tᵾsoyuni

stone, whet- tᵾmakᵾmaʔaaiʔ, tᵾpi
tᵾmatsuneʔ

stone or brick house tᵾpi kᵾni

stone someone tᵾpi táhparᵾ

Stonehouse Tᵾpi kᵾniʔ

stool tahtᵾkiʔiʔ

stool, foot- tahtᵾkiʔiʔ

stoop nuhtsairᵾ, tumuurᵾ

stooped tumuukatᵾ

stop toboʔihupiitᵾ, tᵾtsanᵾnᵾʔitᵾ

stop, cause to tsanᵾnᵾrᵾ

stop crying pᵾhkai

stop flow tohtᵾmarᵾ

stop following someone nᵾnᵾʔitᵾ

stop hitting with fist or palm of
hand tohpᵾarᵾ

stop movement toward something
wᵾnᵾ hupiitᵾ

stop quarreling kekᵾnabeniitᵾ

stop raining pᵾhkitᵾ

stop someone by force tahkoonitᵾ

stop suddenly tsuhni kwᵾnᵾrᵾ K

stop talking nihpᵾʔaitᵾ

stopped up tohtᵾmapᵾ

store narᵾmᵾᵾʔ

store, drug- natᵾsuʔᵾ narᵾmᵾᵾʔ,
natᵾsuʔᵾ kahni

store, Indian nᵾmᵾ narᵾmᵾᵾʔ

store, red ekanarᵾmᵾᵾʔ

store away nabinaʔetᵾ

store-bought food tᵾkᵾ tᵾmᵾᵾpᵾ

stories, tell off-color tᵾtsᵾ
narᵾmiʔitᵾ

stork paʔa toyokatᵾ huutsuuʔ K

storm kᵾhtáanᵾetᵾ

storm, dust huhkukwᵾnᵾrᵾ,
huukᵾhᵾnᵾrᵾ

storm, wind nᵾepi

storm cellar ohta kahni W,
sekwikᵾni, sokokᵾni

story narᵾmuʔipᵾ

story, fairy narᵾkuyunapᵾ

storybook nanáarumu?i tuboopu, narumu?i tuboopu
stove nakohtóo?
straight kewesịkatu, tuna
straight, be kewesịketu
straight, set up tsayukwiku
straight, sit tsayukwitu
straight pin piitsunua?
straighten tsahtunaabaru
straighten something kuhpararu
straighten something wrinkled tahtunaabaru
straighter-than-straight tu?runaasu
Straighter-than-straight Tu?runaasu
strain out something tsaso?aru
strained natsamarunitu
strange nanakuya?aru, natsuwukai
stranger. kuukume?
strangle tsa?okuru
strangle on water paabitsanitu
strangle someone kuitsịmarukutu
strangled kuitsịmarukitu, makuhpukatu, tsa?oibehkatu
strap, jock tsa?nika?
strap, saddle nakwusi tsa?nika?, narunoo? namuku
straw hat soni tso?nika?
strawberry ekapokopi
stream hunu?bị, okwèetu
stream, bank of ekatotsa
stream, clear pahtsi okwe?
stream, fork of a atahunubi
street kawonokatu
streetcar ohawaikịna, waikina
strength natsuwi
strength, pull with full tsahtureru
strengthen kebisa?makaru, natsuwitumaka?eetu
stretch tsahtureru, turetu
stretch arms or body narureru
stretch out haahpịtu

stretch out arm maruru?aru
stretch out something wuhpararu
stretch something out tsahturu
stretched pohitu, tsahtunehtu
strike out wuhpohto?itu
string tuuhtama?, wuhtama?
string, G- kohinehki?, tsa?nika?
string, shoe- napu tsakwusa?
strip, cut a wusi?kwaru
strip off makwịteeru
striped naboo-, nawo?oru, wanatsihtaraa?
stroke nisutaitu, tohtarakiitu
stroke, pet or tohtaraki?aru
strong kuhtáatu, kutáatu
strong physically natsuwitu
strung napu saaru
strut nuuhtonitu
stubborn person sutenapu
stuck between two things tsukịkatu
stuck down in tsuhkaru
stuck fast pimunịkatu
stuck in the mud sekwi suhkai, yubutsuhkatu
stumble tahtsanitu
stump huupita turahna
stump, tree huupita kwiita
stupid suapuwahtu
stutter nigwatsukatu
suck mubị tsoo?nitu
suck on body (to draw out pain) musoopitu
suck (on something) mukwihteru
suck through nose simuhtaru
sucker (candy) mubị tsoo?ni?, mukwite?
suddenly, stop tsuhni kwunuru K
suffer abdominal pain kohikamutu
suffer an illness tu?oibukuru
suffer chest pain amawunutu
suffer from a toothache tamanuutsịkwatu

suffer gall-bladder pain
pu?i?wᵾnᵾrᵾ
suffer on deathbed pisukwitarᵾ
suffer temptation masuyakerᵾ
sufficient food, satisfied with
wᵾtsᵾ?mitᵾ
sugar pihnáa? W
sugar, brown otᵾ pihnàa? W
sugar ant tᵾe anikuura?
sugar cane huupi̱hnàa, soni
bihnáa?
Sugar Eaters Pena tᵾhka, Penanᵾᵾ
suggest something, meet to
nanika?witᵾ
suicide, commit nabakᵾtᵾ
suitcase wosa̱
sulky pikwᵾsii?
sulky, horse-drawn sᵾmasᵾ
nooi K
sumac huutsú?a tᵾahkapᵾ, pahmo
namahya, tatsipᵾ
sumac, smooth tᵾmaya huupi
summer plum, late- parawa sᵾkᵾ
summer season taatsa̱
summer wind yu?anee
summer-dried meat tahmai napᵾ
summertime tatsatᵾ
summit ku?e
sun tabe-
sun goes down tabe?ikami?arᵾ
sun-dry, partially wᵾhtakᵾmiitᵾ
sun to dry, sit in mabasahtᵾkitᵾ K
sun to dry, sit in the
pasahtahtᵾkitᵾ W
sun, stand in the tabe wᵾnᵾ?itᵾ
-sun, Standing Tabe wᵾnᵾrᵾ
-sun-does-not-tell-a-lie, This-
midday Sihka tabe ke isopᵾ
Sun-eagle Tabe kwi?ne
Sunday Puha rabeni, Puha rakatᵾ
sunflower ohayaa?
sunflower head hi?oopi̱taohayaa

sunflower salve hi?ookwana?
sunflower stalk or plant hi?oopi̱
sunflowers hi?oo-
-sunrise, Voice-of-the Tabe nanika
supernatural power puha̱
supernatural power, having
puhakatᵾ
supper yᵾihtᵾhka?
supper, eat yᵾihtᵾhkatᵾ
supply, deplete a tsahtsu?marᵾ
supply, exhaust kehewa?itᵾ
supply, exhaust food tᵾkᵾ
tsuhmarᵾ
support something tsihtᵾroorᵾ
supported marᵾrooniitᵾ K,
tohtᵾrooniitᵾ W
sure noo
surely kewáhabahku, tᵾbitsi
surface, file a tᵾmatsunarᵾ
surface, rasp a tᵾmatsunarᵾ
surface, skim from the yunarᵾ
surfaced road tᵾpi̱ pu?e
surgery nᵾᵾpᵾtsapᵾ
surgery, perform wᵾpᵾtsarᵾ
surgical operation nᵾᵾpᵾtsapᵾ
surprise, hit by wᵾnᵾ?yᵾ?itᵾ
surprised tᵾᵾmoo
surrender manᵾsutarᵾ, nasutarᵾ
surrender someone
manᵾsuta?aitᵾ
suspended, hang tsanikatᵾ
suspenders hapiana?
swab out wᵾhkwinarᵾ
swallow, to ku?nuitᵾ
swallow something tᵾyuwarᵾ,
yᵾwitᵾ W
swamp pamᵾpᵾtso?ni
swamp rabbit ekae?ree W,
ta?wokinae?ree eka K
swamp weed pakᵾᵾka̱
swat down wᵾ?anirᵾ
sway yᵾ?bana?itᵾ

swear mahiyarʉ, tabéʔaitʉ
sweat takʉsitoʔitʉ, takwʉsipʉ
sweat bath nakuhkwarakiʔ K,
nasukooʔiʔ
sweater yuʔa kwʉsuʔu
sweathouse nasukooʔi kahni
sweep wʉnuarʉ
sweep something tʉʉnuarʉ
sweet, taste pihnákamarʉ
sweet bread pihná nohkopʉ
sweet cider amawóoʔa pàa
sweet potato kamúutaʔ
sweetbreads toyo tahkaʔmiitsa̱
sweetheart notsaʔkaʔ,
tʉʉʔurapʉ W, K
sweets pihnáaʔ W
sweets, crave pihná rʉhkarʉ
swell atabaroʔitʉ, paroʔikitʉ,
pekwitʉ
swell up pohtokitʉ
Swift-moving Wʉʔrabiahpʉ
swim pahabitʉ
swim, make tapʉhabi
swim dog paddle masuʔwaʔnekitʉ,
paruhparʉ
swindle tʉtsikwʉsarʉ
swine poʔroʔ
swing natsawenitʉ, wepʉkaitʉ
swing, playground piʔwesurúuʔi̱ʔ
swing back and forth
natsakwenitʉ
swing sitting down
piʔweesuʔruʔitʉ
swinging hips, walk piʔweke
miʔarʉ
switch kwibukitʉ, sʉʉki̱,
tʉkwibukiitʉ, wʉkʉtsarʉ
switches parʉkwihtsipʉ
swollen pekwipʉ
sword tʉtsiwaiiʔ K, uwíhi̱
sympathize suakʉtʉaitʉ
syrup huupi̱hnàa

T t

table, set the awotsawʉniʔitʉ
table fork tʉhkaʔ
tablecloth tʉkʉ soona̱
tablecloth, spread a tʉkʉ soonarʉ
tablespoon pia rʉʔewo
taboo mamʉsuakatʉ K,
nabiʔatsikatʉ
tadpole paʔwʉhtakóoʔ
tail, animal kwasi-, kwasi̱
tail, cat- pisibuniʔ
tail, cat's pisibuniʔ
tail, pony kuwikʉsii
tail, scissor- kʉkʉbʉraakwaʔsiʔ
tailbone piwoʔsa̱
-tailed deer, white piʔtohtsíaʔ W
take a steam bath kuhkwarʉkitʉ
take an oath narabeeʔaitʉ
take apart tsahpʉkʉsuʔarʉ W
take away something live
tahtʉkitʉ
take down tsayumiʔi
take down a teepee tsahtʉwarʉ
take down off of something
tsahpʉherʉ
take oath mahiyarʉ
take off maboʔayarʉ, tohkweʔyarʉ
take off a shoe tahkweʔyarʉ
take off layer tsahkwʉrʉʔarʉ
take one or several things yaarʉ
take out tsahkʉarʉ, tsahtoʔirʉ
take, over- tahtsaitʉ, wʉhpitʉ
take several objects himaʔarʉ
take someone by force sutena
betʉ
take someone home as guest
panimiʔarʉ
take something in the mouth
kʉhyaarʉ
take to eat W tʉkʉ yaarʉ
take women along notsaʔkaarʉ

Take-a-stick-and-hit-someone
Huuwʉhtʉkwa?

taken, object (or item) yaapʉ

talcum powder homoroso?yoki?

tale narʉkuyunapʉ, narʉmu?ipʉ

Talk Loud Pibia n̲i̲wʉnʉ?nʉʉ

talk, pester by nimʉsasuarʉ

talk rough tuhu rekwarʉ

talk someone into something
nitsʉbahikʉ?itʉ

talk to someone niwʉnʉrʉ, tekwarʉ

talk tough nimakwihtsetʉ

-talker, Spirit Mukwoorʉ

talking, stop nihpʉ?aitʉ

tall panihputʉ mabà?atʉ, tsihtararʉ

tall, stand kanaba?aitʉ

tall and slender kanaba?aitʉ,
kʉbʉráatḁ

tame kesósoorʉ

tame a wild thing manʉsu?narʉ W

tame an animal masuyu?ikarʉ K

tamed, un- pʉewatsi

tamp down tanʉkʉtʉ K, tonʉkʉrʉ

tan koropi̲tʉ

tan a hide kwiipʉsiarʉ, tʉso?arʉ

tangle kwisikatʉ K, sakwʉsikʉtʉ,
takwʉsiskʉrʉ, tsakwʉsikʉkatʉ K

tangle, cause to kwisihkarʉ

tangle something tokwʉsikʉtʉ,
tsakwʉ?ikʉrʉ W

tangled kwisihka, kwʉsipʉ W

tangled by hand makwʉsikʉkatʉ

tangled hair papi̲ tsʉnʉ?itʉ

tangled up tomʉsiketʉ K

tanned deer hide pikapʉ

tanned hide narʉso?ipʉ, tʉso?ipʉ?

tanning a hide, process of narʉso?ipʉ

tap on something wʉhtarakiitʉ

tape, bias tʉkʉma?ai

tape measure tʉmanahke?

tar tusanahpi̲

tarantula pia pʉhʉ re?tsi

tardy keyu K

taste kamatʉ, kʉhpunitʉ, kʉsukarʉ,
kʉ?kwiyarʉ

taste good tsaa kamarʉ

taste oily or greasy wihi̲ kamatʉ

taste sour mohakamarʉ

taste sweet pihnákamarʉ

taunt ni?he?bunitʉ

tax collector tʉniwaitʉ?

taxi nʉmi noo?etʉ

tea, dry puhi huubḁ

tea, liquid puhi tuhpaa W

tea, mormon sanaweha

teach suabetaikʉrʉ

teach someone something
nisuabetarʉ

teach something to someone
tʉnisuabetarʉ

teacher tʉboo bia?, tʉnisuabetai
wapi̲ W

teacher, female tʉboorʉʉ pia?

teacher, male tʉboo wapi̲

tear masi?warʉ 1, ohpepʉ

tear apart tsahpako?arʉ

tear at something tsahkwanitʉ

tear down tsahperʉ

tear off sʉmʉ sihwarʉ

tear skin nʉʉsihwa?itʉ

tear something puhkarʉ, sihwarʉ,
tosi?kwarʉ, tsai?warʉ K

tear with the foot tasi?kwairʉ

tear with the teeth kʉsi?kwarʉ

tears, shed many pa?okwetʉ

tears flow ohpeto?ikarʉ

teaspoon tʉe aawo

teatowel awomatsuma?

teepee kah-, kahni, nʉmʉkʉni

teepee, peyote puha kahni, wokwe
kahni

teepee, take down a tsahtʉwarʉ

teepee, ventilator at top of
natsihpara?

teepee pole huutsiyaa?, waahuupi̱, waata̱

teepee poles, travel carrier made of tʉ?noo?

teepees, set up yʉkwikʉ

teepees, skins or other covering for nʉmʉkʉni

teeter-totter na?atsiyaa?, na?tsiyaa?

teeth, break up with the kʉnutsarʉ

teeth, chatter the kʉʉhtarakiitʉ

teeth, chattering saatitamakatʉ

teeth, clack the kʉhkwitsitʉ

teeth, crack with the kʉtʉbarʉ

teeth, false tamatsa?nika?

teeth, grind the kʉhporokitʉ

teeth, grit the kʉhkwitsitʉ, kʉhporokitʉ

teeth, gums of tamaruhkʉ

teeth, roots of the tamakwita̱

teeth, sever (or break) with the kʉhkobarʉ

teeth, tear with the kʉsi?kwarʉ

Tejas), Proud People (Wichita name for Comanches of Natai

telegram namʉsi buhihwi tekwapʉ

telephone puhihwi tekwapʉ

telephone pole puhihwi tekwapʉhana huupi

tell narʉmu?ikatʉ, tʉ?a̱wetʉ, watsih tekwarʉ

tell a fortune nipʉkarʉ

tell-a-lie, This-midday-sun-does-not- Sihka tabe ke isopʉ

tell fortunes nʉnipʉkarʉ

tell off-color stories tʉtsʉ narʉmi?itʉ

tell to feed makahtʉnikatʉ

teller, fortune- mapaana?, nipʉkaa?eetʉ, nʉmi nipʉka? K, tʉnipʉkawapi̱ W

telling, finish nimarʉkaitʉ

temple pui?

tempt (by describing something) nisuyakeetʉ

tempt one to sin tʉrape suwaitʉ

tempt (or test someone) mabunihkarʉ

tempt to turn aside tsapʉhesuwarʉ

temptation, suffer masuyakerʉ

tempted, be masuyakerʉ

ten sʉʉmarʉ

Ten-elks Paruwa sʉmʉno

tenant na?raiboo?

tent, canvas nʉʉsoo?

tent pin tʉrawʉna? K

termite wobi muwo?ne? K

termites muwo?ne?

terrain, rough wohtsa?wʉtʉ

terrible nasu?ana

test tohpunitʉ

test something natsahpunitʉ

test (or tempt someone) mabunihkarʉ

test someone, tempt or mabunihkarʉ

tested marahpunihkatʉ

tested item marʉmabunipʉ

than, smaller inaarʉ

thank you ahó, ʉra

thanks, prayer of ahotabeni̱htʉ

thanksgiving ahotabeni̱htʉ

that one suhkapʉ

that way suni

That's all sube?tʉ

That's It Tasúra

That's life! namami?akʉ

their marʉʉ, pʉʉ

them marii, urii

them, two of mahri

them, of two of mahrʉ

then wihnu

then, since sube?sʉ

these two itʉkwʉ, sitʉkwʉ

they urʉ

they say that tʉa
thick pohotatʉ
thief tʉrʉhka?
thieves, den of tʉrʉkʉ kahni
thieves, house of tʉrʉkʉ kahni
thigh tohoobe̲
thigh meat pabo tuhku
thin hʉnʉketʉ, tahi, tapi̲tʉhtsi
thin person kanabʉʉtsi?, wehuru?i
thing hihini
thing, discarded namaro?ihkatʉ
thing, play- nohi?
thing, tame a wild manʉsu?narʉ W
things, say mean nimakwihtsetʉ
things, stuck between two tsʉki̲katʉ
things, take one or several yaarʉ
think suatʉtʉ
think, lie down and nasutamʉ habitʉ
think about sukwʉ̲kitʉ
think about something nasutamʉ̲katʉ tamai, su?atsitʉ, tʉsu?atsi̲katʉ
think good thoughts suakʉtʉ
thinness hʉnʉ-
thirst takʉsuaitʉ
thirst, die of takuhtʉyaaihumi?arʉ
thirst to death takuhtʉyaaihumi?arʉ
this ihka, isʉ, itʉ
this direction ibu, inakwʉ
this evening yʉihka̲
This-midday-sun-does-not-tell-a-lie Sihka tabe ke isopʉ
thistle po?aya?eetʉ, wokwe
thistle, Texas ebitotsiya?
thorn wokwe
thorn apple tu?amowoo, wokwekatʉ huupi
thorn tree wokʉ̲ huupi̲
thornapple tubokóo

thorny weed wokwesonipʉ
thorough sʉmʉ makʉkatʉ
thoroughly sʉmʉ
thoroughly, soaked papoosinʉ
those ehka, etʉʉ, setʉʉ, surʉʉ
Those-who-are-always-against Komanche
Those-who-stay-downstream Tinawa
thought sua, suapʉ
thoughts suana
thoughts, kind tʉsu?ʉrʉ?
thoughts, think good suakʉtʉ
thread wana ramʉ
thread, crochet wana ramʉ
threadbare pupʉkatʉ
threatening movements, make tahkuya?arʉ
three pahihtʉ
three groups of people pahibahtʉnʉnʉ
three separate families pahibahtʉnʉnʉ
three separated groups pahibahtʉ
thresh tusurʉ
throat kuitsi̲
throat, clear nanihkanuitʉ
throat, have a sore kuitsi̲suatʉ
through nana-
through, peer wihtekatʉ
through, soak parʉbʉʉ?itʉ
through nose, suck simuhtarʉ
throughout nana-
throughout a location oyo?rʉtu
throw takwʉ̲kitʉ, tokwʉ̲ki?arʉ, wihirʉ
throw a light on something kupi̲tarʉ
throw at something tahtʉkwarʉ
throw away petihtarʉ, wihtaitʉ
throw body on the ground kwanu?itʉ K

throw down tsayumaruh

throw down a person
tsahkwaʔnuʔituh

throw into the fire kuhtsahwiruh

throw out of something
wuhʔkwuriaruh

throw overhand kwihituh

throw with nose or mouth
muhwituh K, mukwubuaruh W

throwing arrows naroʔtoneetsiʔ,
tiroʔwoko

thrown (forcibly from a horse)
wupuheruh

thumb mahtokooʔ

thunder tomoyaketuh

thus sunihku

tick kaʔraʔáaʔ

tickle someone pinakutsuruh

tidings, upset people by bad
niʔyusukaituh

tie wuhtsukunaruh

tie, un- wuhtoʔyaruh

tie a child to back wupitooruh

tie a knot wutsukunaruh

tie in round bundle or round knot
wuhtopuʔnooruh

tie something wuhtamaruh

tie up a horse tuutsukunaruh

-tied person, tongue ekotuyaipu

tied up nuutsukunaruh

tied up, wrapped and nuuhtamiʔituh

ties tuuhtamaʔ

tight kuhtáatu, kutáatu, matsukikatu

tight, squeezed tsinuku

tighten wunukutu

tightly kuhtáaku

tightly, packed in manukutu

tightly, stake down uhtaaruh

till tsatusukitu

Timber Creek Huuhunuʔbi

Timber People Huuhʔinuu

time, day- taahkatu

time, next kwasiku

time, one sumusu

time, one at a susumuʔ,
suʔsumuʔnuku

time, past the ui

time, summer- tatsatu

time, winter kwihneʔ

times, few huusu

tin cup suu awo

tin or other shiny metal pisayuʔneʔ

tip off ninakuakuru W

tire makwuʔniku W, narahpanaʔ

tire, automobile naʔbukuwàaʔa
narahpaana W

tire, (blow out a) turaputsaru W

tire, puncture a turaputsaru W

tire of something manuuʔmaitu

tire oneself nananuuʔmaitu

tire out kweʔyukatu, nuuʔmaitu

tired of something nakunuuʔmaitu,
wuhʔtsikwaruh

tired person namakunumapu

title (or deed to land) nabinai
tuboopu

title deed soko bookutu

to, speak niikwiitu

to deceive emuahkatu

to die kooitu

to dry, sit in sun mabasahtukitu K

to dry, sit in the sun
pasahtahtukitu W

to disconnect tsahtukaru

to fish huaru

to haul away nooru

to swallow kuʔnuitu

to the right tubitsi petutu

to trap huaru

to turn aside, tempt tsapuhesuwaru

to you unu

toad, horned kuhtsu tubiniʔ

toast bread wesikuru

toast corn hanikwasukuru

toasted wesikatʉ

toasted maize kukʉmepʉ

tobacco pahmu, yokabahmʉ

tobacco, chewing yokabahmʉ

tobacco, Indian tabahko

today tabéni̱

toe tookaatso̱

toe, big tahtokoo?

toe, little tahtúa?, tʉeh tahtua?

toe, middle tahtʉpinaa?

toenail tasiito̱

toes tasa̱kwʉʉhki?

together naha-, nahma?ai, sʉʉ

together, come na?akʉtʉ

together, crowded narahtsʉkikatʉ

together, drive ta?ookitʉ

together, gather ka?witʉ, narahka?witʉ, sʉʉma?aitʉ

together, pin tsihtʉpʉkarʉ, wʉhtʉpʉkarʉ

together, rake manuarʉ W, marʉ?okitʉ K, tanuarʉ

together, rub hands namʉsu?netʉ

tomato kwasinaboo?a tʉahkapʉ

tomb (burial mound) nabʉkapʉ W

tomorrow, day after pi?nakwʉ bʉetsʉ

tongue eko-

tongue, lap with the ka?amoorʉ

tongue hanging down, pant with hehekʉbʉniitʉ

tongue-tied person ekotʉyaipʉ

tonic, hair papi̱ wihtʉ?eka?

tool (any sharp-pointed implement for punching holes through which sinews pass) wiiyu̱

tool, peeling huusibe?

tool, steel tʉʉhko?ne?

too late ʉi

tooth taama̱, tama-

tooth, decayed wo?ataama̱

tooth, loose saatitamakatʉ

tooth, wisdom kʉʉtsi̱

toothache, suffer from a tamanʉʉtsi̱kwatʉ

toothache tree kunanatsu

toothbrush tamamatsuma?

toothpaste tamakotse?

top ku?e

top, house- kahni ku?e

top of, on ku?e

top, quilt sona bo?a

top of teepee, ventilator at natsihpara?

Tope Tope

torment aibuniitʉ

torn puhkapʉ

torn by a foot tasi?kwaitʉ

torn object sihwapi̱

torn up completely tsasikwaitʉ

tornado nʉepi̱

tortilla tohtía?

-totter, teeter na?atsiyaa?, na?tsiyaa?

touch marʉkitʉ, masukaarʉ, tasukarʉ

touch, cure partially through marebunitʉ

touch (lightly with the hand) makwʉ?netʉ

touch, reach out and ma?wʉminarʉ

tough, talk nimakwihtsetʉ

toward someone or something mawakatu

toward something, stop movement wʉnʉ hupiitʉ

towel awomatsuma?, kobe matsuma?

towel, face kobe matsuma?, nakobe matsuma?

town narʉmʉʉ?, sookʉni

town crier tekwʉniwapi̱

towsack soni narʉso?

toy nohi?

toy wagon nohiwaikinʉ

tracks, horse tʉhʉyena puni W

tracks, railroad kunawaikina puʔe

trade narʉmʉʉrʉ, tʉmʉʉrʉ

trade goods wanapʉ K

trading post ekanarʉmʉʉʔ, nʉmʉ narʉmʉʉʔ

tradition nanihpuʔeʔaikʉpʉ K, puʔeʔaikʉpʉ W

trail napʉ, napʉhu, napʉhu miʔarʉ, puʔe̜

trail a human or an animal nayaarʉ

trail something tʉnahyarʉ

trailer pitsakaʔ, tʉbiyaakʉʔ W

trailer house kahni tʉbitsikaʔ K

train kunawaikinʉ, kunawobipuukʉ, waikina

train, freight tʉnoo kuna waikina̜ K

train someone suabetaikʉrʉ

traitor natsakaʔuhtuʔetʉʔ

trampling on it, soften something by tahpararʉ

transparent pabo-, pabokopi̱tʉ

transplant tsihtaboʔikʉtʉ, wʉnʉkʉtʉ

trap hʉarʉʔ

trap, to hʉarʉ

trap, bear wasápe pʉmata kwʉhʉrʉʔ

trap, fish pekwi pʉmata hʉarʉ

trap, mouse kahúu pʉmata hʉarʉʔ

trap, rat- kahúu pʉmata hʉarʉʔ

trapper hʉawapi

trash tʉtsakwʉ̱riapʉ K

travel carrier made of teepee poles tʉʔnooʔ

tread heavily tanʉʔyʉkitʉ

treasure puhihwi ta ahweetʉ, tsaanahapʉ

treat mʉʉrʉ

treat with respect pahnaʔaitʉ

treaty mahyarʉ, nanihpuʔeʔaikʉpʉ K

tree hu-, huu-

tree, ash tosa seyuʔyuki?

tree, bois d'arc ohahuupi

tree, cottonwood soho obi̱, tahpookʉʔ, weʔyʉkʉ sohoobi K

tree, dead putsi waipʉ

tree, domestic humasʉapʉ

-tree, Peeping-from-behind Kuhiyai

tree, plum parʉa sʉkʉi?

tree, silver maple kweʔyʉkʉ sohóobi

tree. single- pihtsakʉ huupi̱

tree, thorn wokʉ huupi̱

tree, toothache kunanatsu

tree bark huupi poʔaʔ, huupita poʔa

tree limb huupita mooka

tree root huupita tʉrahna̱

tree squirrel wokoohwi

tree stump huupita kwiita

tree trunk owóora

tree trunk, burned out kuwoʔnepʉ

trees, clump of huukabatʉ

tremble kwibihpikitʉ W, sʉhkwibitʉ

tremble in speech nihkwibihbikitʉ

tremble with cold sʉʉtsʉnitʉ

tremor of earth soko yʉʔyʉmuhkurʉ

tribe, Eating- Marʉhke

tribe, enemy tawohho

tributary atahunubi, nabatai K

trick kaabehkarʉ

tried item marʉmabunipʉ

tried on marahpunihkatʉ

trim kʉhpomarʉ, kʉmakoorʉ, wʉhʉwʉʔniitʉ, wʉʔyʉkwitʉ K

trip and fall nʉʉhkupatʉ, nʉʉhpisiʔmaitʉ

trip someone tanʉʉhkupaitʉ

triplets paʔabeʔnʉʉ

troll nɨnɨ pɨhi?

trolley ohawaikina̲

trot aimi?arɨ, pohyami?arɨ

trot, made to poyohkarɨ

Trotter Waakakwa

troublesome tɨmabiso?aitɨ

trough, water puku hibikɨ?

trousers pitɨsohko̲?

trousers, put on pitsohkorɨ

truck tɨnoona bukuwa?, tɨnoo waikina̲, waikina

true tɨbitsiyu

trunk wobi aawo̲

trunk, tree owóora

trunk, tree (burned out) kuwo?nepɨ

trunk of a white putsi waipɨ

trust tɨmayokɨrɨ

trust someone tokɨsuakɨtɨ

truth, doubt the (of a statement) tsuwíhnu

try nani?ookitɨ

try on headwear tsohponiitɨ

try on shoes tahpunitɨ

try or want to hit with fist toso?waitɨ

try out kɨhpunitɨ, tohpunitɨ

tub, wash- wana kotse aawo

tuber ahwepɨ

tuber, edible ta?wahkóo? W, totohtɨ

tuber, wild payaape̲, tutupitɨ

tuberculosis monɨ ohni

tug-of-war natsaaturu?itɨ?

tunnel kahnitaikɨ

turkey kuyu?nii, puhitóo? K

turkey grass puhitóo?

turn wɨhbuikatɨ W, wɨnɨkɨtɨ

turn around koonitɨ, kooni?etɨ, kwinu?yarɨ

turn around (and come back), cause to tsahkoo?itɨ

turn around, caused to tsakwɨhwitɨ

turn around quickly pikwebuitɨ

turn aside, tempt to tsapɨhesuwarɨ

turn away from wɨhbuikatɨ W

turn cold kwihnerɨ

turn loose pɨarɨ, wɨhto?yarɨ

turn over natsamɨritɨ

turn red hot ekawehaarɨ

turn something around, cause to tsakwɨhburɨ

turn something over tsamɨrikarɨ, wɨmɨɨrɨ

turned nakɨmɨɨ?etɨ W

turned over wɨmɨɨrihkatɨ

turtle pitsohka kwaba W, wakarée? K

Turtle Wakaré?e

turtle, snapping kwasi nɨrɨɨ?wɨ?, pa?kwakɨme

twig sɨɨki̲

twigs, willow sɨhɨ tsitsina?

twine soni wiyaa?

twins wa?wa?

twist kwipunarɨ, makwipunarɨ K

twist oneself nɨɨkwitsɨnarɨ

twist oneself around something nɨɨ?kwipunarɨ

twist something tsakwipunarɨ

twist the body kwitsunairɨ

twitch yɨ?yɨturɨ

twitch, hand mayɨ?yɨrɨ

two waha-, wahati̲

two apiece wa?wa?

two of them mahri

two of them, of mahrɨ

two, of us taa

two, of you mɨhɨ

two, these itɨkwɨ, sitɨkwɨ

two, you mɨkwɨ

two years old tomohtootɨ W

two-by-two wa?wa?

two-man handsaw huutsihkaa?
two parts, split into tʉapako?itʉ
two-seated buggy natsa?ani?
two things, stuck between tsʉkikatʉ
two-year-old wahatomopʉ K
two-year-old item tomohtoopʉ W
-type handkerchief, work pʉesúube? K
typewriter mo?o rʉboo?
typhoid fever narʉ?ʉyʉ kuhtsʉni?

U u

ugly tʉtsʉ-
umbrella hʉkiai, hʉʉki?ai?
unable mʉnitʉ
unable to breathe sua?su?maitʉ
unable to do something kemahpʉ?arʉ, tsuhitʉ
unbolt wʉhkwe?yarʉ
unbridle a horse tʉpe tsahkwe?yarʉ
uncle ara?
uncle and niece, marriage of arakwʉ?ʉtʉ
uncle, paternal great kʉnu?
unclean spirit tʉtʉsuana
uncoil pʉrʉsu?arʉ
uncoil something wʉhpʉkʉsuarʉ
unconcerned, live yukahnibarʉ
unconscious sua watsikʉ
uncontrollably, continue kenaninabenitʉ
undecided wahabisuatʉ
undependable person senihtʉhtsi?
under water, hit and push wʉhpaaku?nerʉ
under water, pushed tohpaaku?netʉ W
underarm ahna, ana-
underarm hair anapʉhʉ

underarm to waist ama-
undershirt tuhkanaai kwasu?ʉ
understand someone nahkʉsuaberʉ
understood kenanawatsitʉ
undertaker K tʉyaipʉha noo?ee?tʉ
underwear tsa?nika?
underwear on, have tsa?nikʉkatʉ
undress natsahkwe?yarʉ, tsahkwe?yarʉ
uneven ho?yopipʉ, pihpokaarʉ
uneven land wohtsa?wʉtʉ
unfold marʉpisu?arʉ W, tsahpʉkʉsu?arʉ W
unfriendliness nakahanupʉ W
unfriendly kwetʉsapʉ
unhitch too?itʉ
unhitch a horse noro?yarʉ
unhitch an animal to?yarʉ W
unhorse tsiperʉ
unlace tsahkwʉmarʉ
unlighted tukanikatʉ
unload tsahpʉherʉ, tsapʉyetʉ, tsayumi?i
unlock tsihtʉwarʉ
unmarried man, young wohka?ni?
unplug to extinguish tsahtukarʉ
unravel pʉrʉsu?arʉ
unravel of own accord nʉʉpʉrʉsuarʉ
unravel something nʉʉpʉrʉsuanʉpurʉ
unroll tsahkwʉmarʉ, tsahpʉkʉsu?arʉ W
unsaddle a horse narʉnoo?ro?yarʉ
unscrew wʉhkwe?yarʉ
unseal something tsahto?arʉ K
unseat tsiperʉ
untamed pʉewatsi
untie wʉhto?yarʉ
unwind pʉrʉsu?arʉ, tsahkwʉmarʉ, tsahkwʉnunúukitʉ, wʉhpʉkʉsuarʉ
unworthy tʉtaatʉ

unwrap mahkwʉmarʉ, tsahkwʉmarʉ
unwrap an object tsahpeko?arʉ
unwrap something tahkwʉmarʉ
unwrap something with the mouth kʉhto?yarʉ K
up, dry kuwaaitʉ, waaitʉ
up, fill mu?ibuikʉrʉ
up, filled wʉtsʉ?mitʉ
up, fix ma?yʉkwiitʉ
up, fly yorimi?arʉ, yʉtsʉrʉ
up, give narahkupaitʉ, nasutarʉ
up exhausted, give anitʉ
up, go yʉtsʉrʉ
up, heap pia wʉ?utsitʉ
up, help matsáyʉtsʉrʉ
up, help (from sitting to standing position) matsákwʉnʉkʉrʉ
up, high tsihtararʉ
up, hill ma?ohta?aitʉ, wʉno?karʉrʉ
up, hitch mahkarʉ W
up, hitch (horses and buggy) nomohkarʉ
up, hung narohtsanarʉ, natsahkweniitʉ
up, hurry namʉsohitʉ
up, lace tsakwʉsarʉ W
up a horse, lead tsakʉhunitʉ
up, lift toyarʉ, tsahhʉkwʉ?niitʉ W
up, load tʉnookʉrʉ
up someone, lock ta?ikʉrʉ
up, locked ta?ikʉkatʉ
up something, mash mapitserʉ
up animal, pen ta?ikʉrʉ
up, penned tawekwit
up several objects, pick hima?arʉ
up, pile wʉ?utsitʉ
up the ears, prick to?yabaitʉ
up, pry tsahto?arʉ K
up, puff pohtokitʉ
up, pull tsahkʉarʉ, tsahto?irʉ
up, pull oneself natsahto?itʉ

up, pulled tsahto?itʉ
up, rake tsa?oorʉ
up, reared manawʉnʉkatʉ
up, rise yorimi?arʉ, yʉtsʉrʉ
up, roll namakwatubiitʉ, tʉmakwatʉbi?etarʉ
up to itself, roll wʉhkwitubikatʉ
up with something, roll tohtopo?narʉ
up, rolled makwatubiitʉ
up, round tahkoonikarʉ, ta?ookitʉ
up, saddle narʉnoo?rʉkitʉ
up, scoop mahorarʉ
up earth, scratch ta?si?woorʉ
up, set karukʉrʉ, ma?yʉkwiitʉ
up straight, set tsayʉkwikʉ
up teepees, set yʉkwikʉ
up from heat, shrivel kuhtakwitsoo?nitʉ W
up, slide standing tahkitemi?arʉ
up, slip standing tahkitemi?arʉ
up dust, stir huukʉhʉnʉrʉ
up excitement, stir toyʉsekaitʉ
up fire, stir kuma?omerʉ, ma?omerʉ
up, stopped tohtʉmapʉ
up, swell pohtokitʉ
up, tangled tomʉsiketʉ K
up a horse, tie tʉʉtsʉkʉnarʉ
up, tied nʉʉtsʉkʉnarʉ
up completely, torn tsasikwaitʉ
up, use tsu?ma
up, wake tʉbunitʉ
up someone, wake tsayoritʉ
up, warm yu?a?itʉ
up, wrap tʉmakwatʉbi?etarʉ, wʉhkwitunarʉ
up, wrapped and tied nʉʉhtami?itʉ
up to or onto someone or something maatu
upright, set tsahkarʉkʉrʉ
upriver obutʉma?

uproot tsahtobarʉ
upset people by bad tidings
 niʔyʉsʉkaitʉ
upside down paʔarai
upward tukuhputʉ
urge on nihtunetsʉʔitʉ
urinate siitʉ
urine siipʉʔ
us nʉmi, tai
us two, of taa
us, procreated by nʉmʉ rʉborarʉ
use, rawhide ready to pahkipʉ
use up tsuʔma
used to noha
using an instrument, scratch
tsahkiʔaitʉ
uterine grandchild, man's tokoʔ
uterine grandchild, woman's
kakuʔ

V v

vagabond noyʉkaʔ
valley, level haapane
various directions ebu
various ways seni
vase paboko aawo, totsiyaa aawo̲
vase, flower totsiyaa tsakwʉnaʔ
vegetable garden narʉhkaʔ
sokoobi̲, tʉmʉsʉa sokobi K
vegetable garden plot tʉkʉ masʉa
sokoobi̲ W
vegetables, fry meat or kwasʉkʉrʉ
vegetation, hairy pʉhʉʔ
vehicle, haul in a manoorʉ
vein paai
velvet cloth pʉesúubeʔ K
ventilate tsihpʉrarʉ
ventilator at top of teepee
natsihparaʔ
verbally, rejoice naninaʔukitʉ

vertebra kwahitsuhni̲
very mohatsi̲, nohi
vessel aawo, awo-
vessel, wooden huu aawo
vexed pihisoʔai
victory, songs of wohho
tʉikwʉpitʉ K
vigorously, shake tsobokitʉ
village sookʉni
vine totsiyaaʔa sʉʉki̲
vine, grape- natsamukweʔa sʉʉki̲
visit kahni miʔa, puni kwarʉ
visiting, go kahni miʔa
voice tʉʔaape̲
Voice-of-the-sunrise Tabe nanika
vomit ooʔitʉ

W w

waddle or move clumsily
masuʔwaʔnekitʉ
wag wʉhkwitsunarʉ
wagon tʉnoo waikina̲, waikina
wagon, covered nakʉnikatʉ
waikina̲
wagon, toy nohiwaikinʉ
wagon crossing naʔweeʔ, puʔe
nagwe
wagon wheel waikina naʔoomo̲
wahoo waaʔakitʉ
wail hubiyaa piayakeetʉ
wail, death hubiya piayakeetʉ
waist area kohi̲
waist, underarm to ama-
waist, wear something around the
kohinehkitʉ
wait wʉhtuitʉ
wait for someone makamaitʉ
wait on mananaaʔwaihkarʉ
waiting for someone, give up
wʉsuwarʉkiitʉ

waiting, stand tahkamᵾrᵾ
wake someone tsahtᵾbunitᵾ
wake someone by pounding
  wᵾhtᵾbunitᵾ
wake up tᵾbunitᵾ
wake up someone tsayoritᵾ
waken tahtᵾbunitᵾ
waken by speaking to someone
  nihtᵾbuniorᵾ
walk yᵾkarᵾ
walk, able to nᵾmirᵾ
walk around nahnᵾmiitᵾ
walk away natsihtóo miʔarᵾ
walk backward pimimiʔarᵾ
walk dragging one foot
  tasiʔwomiʔarᵾ
walk fast pohyamiʔarᵾ
walk, help someone tsamiʔakᵾrᵾ
walk lamely wihnai miʔarᵾ
walk swinging hips piʔweke miʔarᵾ
walk with cane natsihtóo noorᵾ
walking around, crying
  yakeyᵾkarᵾ
walking, come soko kimarᵾ
walking, go sokomiʔarᵾ
walking, raise dust by
  tahuhkuwᵾnᵾrᵾ
walking, rocking way of
  yᵾʔbanaʔitᵾ
walking, stagger when
  tsimᵾamiʔarᵾ
walking cane tᵾʔehkooiʔ W
walking stick tᵾʔehkooiʔ W
wall kahni tᵾbanaa, tᵾbanaaʔ
wallet puhihwi narᵾso̱ W
wallow naʔanitᵾ
wallpaper kahni̱ tᵾboopᵾ, tᵾbanaa
  rᵾbopᵾ
walnut mubitai
walnut, black tuhmubitai
wander (from place to place)
  noyᵾkarᵾ

Wanderer Nookoni
Wanderers Noyᵾhkanᵾᵾ
want suwaitᵾ
want to flirt K naʔi̱sa suakᵾtᵾ
want to hit with fist, try or
  tosoʔwaitᵾ
want to lay an egg nohabi̱
  suwaitᵾ
war nabitᵾkᵾrᵾ
-war, tug-of natsaaturuʔitᵾʔ
war bonnet pia tsoʔnikaʔ
war club wᵾpitapuʔni
war paint, apply wohho napᵾsarᵾ
war songs wohho tᵾikwᵾpitᵾ K
war-bonnet bag tuna wosa
wardrobe case, rawhide
  natᵾsakᵾna
warm kusuatᵾ, yuʔa
warm, luke- pakuyuʔatᵾ
warm clothing, wear yuʔa
  namᵾsoorᵾ
warm up yuʔaʔitᵾ
warn ninakabaʔikᵾtᵾ
warpath wohho namakaʔmukiʔarᵾ
warpath, go on mahimiʔarᵾ
warpath, return from mahikoʔitᵾ
wart kuʔmiitsa̱, taʔkaʔmiitsaʔ
wash dishes awomakotserᵾ,
  tᵾmakotsetᵾ
wash feet narakotserᵾ, takotserᵾ
wash hand namoʔo kotse̱tᵾ
wash out earth patowoʔnerᵾ
washcloth tᵾehna matsumaʔ
washing machine tᵾkotseʔ K
Washita River Tusohoʔo̱kweʔ
washout patowoʔnepᵾ
washtub wana kotse aawo
wasp otᵾ peena
waste aibuniitᵾ
wasted tuʔrᵾmetᵾ
watch tᵾpunirᵾ
watch, wrist- tabe-

watch chain tabe narᴜmuhkụ, tabe wenuakᴜ?

watch for iyaa?itụ

watch oneself na?iyaitᴜ

watch someone watsi punitᴜ

watchdog tᴜ?iya?i wapị

watchman tᴜ?iya?i wapị

water pa- W, paa, pai, tuu-, tuupụ

water an animal hibikᴜtᴜ

water, be in deep kenawᴜnᴜrᴜ

water boy tuu?etᴜ

water, channel patsanuarᴜ

water dog pa?boosi?

water, draw tuurᴜ

water, drip paa kᴜa?etᴜ

water, duck head under paku?nerᴜ

water, eyes ohpeto?ikarᴜ

water, fetch tuuhuniitᴜ W

water, fetch (for someone) tuukᴜmi?arᴜ

water, fill with paa ma?ibu?ikᴜtᴜ K, pawụsa?naitᴜ W

water, filled with (by drinking) pakwᴜ?sᴜ?mitᴜ

water heavily, eyes pa?okwetᴜ

water, hit and push under wᴜhpaaku?nerᴜ

water, immerse oneself in nabawᴜhtiarᴜ

water, paddle masu?wa?nekitᴜ

water, paddle feet in pawᴜpa?itᴜ

water, paddle hands in the paruhparᴜ

water lily, plant similar to pa?mutsi

water on, pour payunitᴜ

water, press down with hands to expel mabitsoorᴜ

water, pushed under tohpaaku?netᴜ W

water, rain ᴜmahpaa?

-water-is, *See-* how-deep-the Paa roponi

water, sink to the bottom in pa?ikarᴜ

water, soak in parᴜkitᴜ

water, soak oneself in naparᴜkitᴜ

water, splash into pakwa?nuarᴜ

water on, splash pakwihtsikᴜrᴜ

water, splash with pawᴜhpa?itᴜ

water, sprayed with pawᴜ?we?niitᴜ

water, spring parᴜtsohpe?

water, strangle on paabitsanitᴜ

Water Horse Band Tasúra

water jug pihpóo?

water lizard pa?boosi?

water moccasin tuhparokoo?

water pump patsahto?i?, patsa?aikᴜ

water something payunitᴜ

water trough puku hibikᴜ?

water well pahorapụ

water-filled pa?ibuikatụ

watered mabáa?aitụ

watermelon ohapị, puhi bihnáa?

wave po?hibahpakitᴜ, wᴜhpetsᴜrᴜ

wave hair wesibapi?arᴜ

wax, ear nakị oonạ

wax, weed hi?oosanahkòo

way, doing another atapu

way, lose watsitᴜ

way of walking, rocking yᴜ?bana?itᴜ

way, rub the wrong masu?naitᴜ K, masᴜroonitᴜ W

way, that suni

way? how?, what hakaniiku

ways, different seni

ways, various seni

we nᴜnᴜ

weak kenatsụwitᴜ, tsihkwinumai

weak person or animal tᴜ?ọnaapụ

weakness tᴜ?onaa?

wean a baby pitsi makatᴜ

weaned pitsimai

weapon, attempt to hit with a
wʉsukwarʉ W

weapon, force to lie down wielding a wʉhhabiʔarʉ

weapon, kill with a wʉhkuparʉ, wʉhtokweetʉ

wear a hat tsoʔnikarʉ

wear out clothes wʉkwiʔarʉ

wear out shoes tawiarʉ W

wear something natsaʔnikarʉ

wear something around the neck
korohkọrʉ

wear something around the waist
kohinehkitʉ

wear something out wihtoʔarʉ

wear warm clothing yuʔa
namʉsoorʉ

weary wʉʔtsikwarʉ

weather, hot ʉrʉʔitʉ

weave tʉkwʉsiitʉ

wedge tʉroh pakuʔiʔ

weed, croton kupisinamaya

weed, horse- tosa wahtsuki

weed, loco esinʉʉhparabi

weed, mesquite namabitsooni
sonihpʉ

weed, quinine pohóobi

weed, smart- ekawoni

weed, sneeze- natsaakʉsi,
tʉrʉkwobamʉ

weed, soap mumutsiʔ

weed, swamp pakʉʉkạ

weed, thorny wokwesonipʉ

weed wax hiʔoosanahkòo

weeds paʔsonipʉ

weeds, cut (or grass) soni
wʉhpomarʉ

weeping willow yusʉhʉbi

weigh something narayaakʉrʉ

weight, gain yuhu bʉhkaitʉ

well kenamaʔʉbʉʔitʉ, pahorapʉ,
tsaa

well, live yunʉmitʉ, yʉyʉkarʉ

well, oil nabaai tokwaaitʉ, tukaʔa
nabaa

well, water pahorapʉ

well behaved yʉyʉkarʉ

well-behaved, be yunʉmitʉ

west kahpinakwʉ, tabeʔikʉnakwạʔ

west, north- kwihne kahpinakwʉ

west, south- yuʔa nʉe kahpiʔnakwʉ

western ragweed woʔanatsuʔ

wet patsoʔitʉ, paʔisoketʉ

wet seat pihpárʉbʉʔai

what way? how? hakaniiku

what? hina, hini

what? On hipaʔa

what? on what?, with himakụ

(what one is doing), slow down
nʉnʉʔitʉ

what place?, where? hakʉ

wheat tohtía masʉaʔ

wheat flour pʉmata nookoina

wheat plant tohtía sonipʉ

wheel makwʉʔnikʉ W, naʔomọ

wheel, spoke of naʔomọ
nasʉwʉhkiʔ

wheel, wagon waikina naʔoomọ

wheel game aratsiʔ

when? hipeʔ

where? hakʉseʔ

where? what place? hakʉ

whetstone tʉmakʉmaʔaaiʔ, tʉpi
tʉmatsuneʔ

which?, who? hakarʉ

which way? where to? hakaapu

while, once in a sʉsʉʔanạ

**while moving, rope someone or
something** kuʔnikakʉrʉ

whip kwibukitʉ, tʉkwibukiitʉ

whir kasabipikurʉ

whisky poʔsa baa

whisper watsih nikwʉnʉrʉ

whisper gossip watsih tekwarʉ

whistle huuk<u>u</u>muyake?,
kusitekwar<u>u</u>, tsuhni muyake?
white tosa-
white, appear to be tosa nabunit<u>u</u>
white, trunk of a putsi waip<u>u</u>
white elm pimoroo?a korohko?
white farmer t<u>u</u>tsakwoo raiboo?
white horse tosa?
white man huuy<u>u</u>kkwi?, pabo
taiboo?
white man, bearded motso taiboo?
white oak tosa tukanai huupi
white person taiboo?
White-eagle Kwihne tosabit<u>u</u>
white-tailed deer pi?tohtsía? W
who? which? hakar<u>u</u>
-who-are-always-against, Those
Komanche
who betrays, one
kaanatsaka?uhtup<u>u</u>
who gossips, one isanaramu?it<u>u</u>?
who-rides-buffalo, One- Kuhtsunu
kwahip<u>u</u>
-who-stay-downstream, Those
Tinawa
whole keho?yop<u>i</u>t<u>u</u>
whom hahka
whoop tsu?tsukit<u>u</u>
whoop, woman's katakakit<u>u</u> W
whooping cough tsuu?tsuki?
why? hakani?y<u>u</u>
Wichita language, speak
tuhka?naai rekwar<u>u</u>
Wichita language, Speakers of
tuhka?naai? niw<u>u</u>n<u>u</u>
Wichita people Tuhka?naai?
wick, lamp tuka?a nawanap<u>i</u>
wicked ait<u>u</u>
wide pia wek<u>i</u>t<u>u</u>
wide open pia tsatuakat<u>u</u>
wide, open mouth pia k<u>u</u>sar<u>u</u>
wide, open something pia tsatuar<u>u</u>

widely piap<u>u</u>
wife kw<u>u</u>h<u>u</u>?, n<u>u</u>petsu?
wife, chief (among multiple
wives) paraiboo?
wife, grandson's (granddaughter
-in-law) tso?apia?
wife, lead away a n<u>u</u>petsu?it<u>u</u>
wig pap<u>i</u> tsa?nika?
wigwam mutsik<u>u</u>ni
wild p<u>u</u>ewatsi
wild currant huwabo?kóo?
wild grape mutsi atsamukwe?,
natsamukwe?
wild hyacinth siiko
wild onion k<u>uu</u>kanar<u>u</u>hka?, k<u>uu</u>k<u>a</u>,
pak<u>uu</u>k<u>a</u>, p<u>u</u>ewatsi k<u>uu</u>k<u>a</u>,
t<u>u</u>et<u>u</u>taat<u>u</u> k<u>uu</u>k<u>a</u>
wild onion, poisonous
k<u>u</u>htsutsu<u>u</u>?ni?
wild potato paapas<u>i</u>
wild stallion p<u>u</u>a watsi
wild thing, tame a man<u>u</u>su?nar<u>u</u> W
wild tuber payaap<u>e</u>, tutup<u>i</u>t<u>u</u>
wildcat mat<u>u</u>sohpe?
will suana, t<u>u</u>su?atsip<u>u</u>
willow s<u>u</u>h<u>u</u>
willow, black ohas<u>u</u>h<u>uu</u>bi
willow, weeping yus<u>u</u>h<u>u</u>bi
willow twigs s<u>u</u>h<u>u</u> tsitsina?
wilt takwitsoo?nimi?ar<u>u</u>
win a prize t<u>u</u>rahwikat<u>u</u>
win in a contest against someone
tahni?ar<u>u</u>
win in a contest by cheating
kaakwakur<u>u</u>
win over someone kwakur<u>u</u> K
wind n<u>u</u>ena, n<u>u</u>et<u>u</u>, w<u>u</u>hkwatubi,
w<u>u</u>n<u>u</u>k<u>u</u>t<u>u</u>
Wind N<u>u</u>ena
wind, be carried/blown away by
mabo?ayar<u>u</u>
wind, south yu?anee

wind, summer yuʔanee
wind, un- pɨrɨsuʔarɨ,
  tsahkwɨmarɨ, tsahkwɨnunúukitɨ,
  wɨhpɨkɨsuarɨ
wind into a ball wɨhtopoʔnitɨ
wind instrument, any woinu
wind instrument, play a
  muuyaketɨ
wind storm nɨepi
Wind-running-here Nɨenuhkiki
windbreak wɨhturuʔaipɨ
windbreak, make a wɨhturuʔarɨ
windbreak, natural huukonoʔitɨ
windmill patsahtoʔiʔ
window nanabuniʔ
window blind nanabuni tsahparaʔ
window screen nanabuni saawɨʔ,
  nasaaʔwɨʔ W
windpipe worɨrokɨ, woʔrorookɨ W
wine ekapaa, natsamukweʔa paa
wine, Communion pɨɨpi
wing kasa
winged kasakatɨ
wings, flap kasabipikurɨ
wink puih tsahtsurɨ, wɨhtsobokitɨ
winnow poʔhimarɨ
winter tomoorɨ, tomopɨ 2
winter, rain shelter for yuʔa
  ɨmakɨni
wintertime kwihneʔ
wipe matsumarɨ, tahkwinerɨ W
wipe away tahtsukitɨ
wipe, dab to (or erase)
  tohpɨsakɨrɨ K, tohtsomarɨ W
wipe feet tasuʔnetɨ
wipe off completely wɨhtsuʔmarɨ
wipe off with the hand makwineetɨ
wipe something off tahtsumarɨ K
wipe something with the head
  tsotsomarɨ
wiping, cloth for tɨmatsumaʔ W
wire soni wɨhtɨmaʔ

wire, barbed puhihwi tɨɨhtɨmaʔ
wire fence, put up a barbed
  puhihwi tɨɨhtɨmarɨ
wire, chicken kokoráʔa arɨhtɨmaʔ
wire brush puhihwi natsihtuʔyeʔ
wire cutter tɨkɨh pomaʔ
wire pincers tɨkɨh kaʔaʔ
wisdom tɨsuʔɨrɨʔ
wisdom tooth kɨɨtsi
wish for nasuyaketɨ
witch doctor tɨtsɨ puhaʔ
**(Wichita name for the Comanches
  of Tejas), Proud People** Natai
witchy wɨtsɨpai
with a saw, saw something
  huutsikaʔarɨ
with brains, rub kupisiʔarɨ
with each other naha-
with fingers, rip tsahtɨrɨʔarɨ
with fingers, snuff fire W tsahtukarɨ
**with fist or palm of hand, stop
  hitting** tohpɨarɨ
with fist, try or want to hit
  tosoʔwaitɨ
with foot, rub naraʔworɨ K
with full strength, pull tsahturerɨ
with something, prick someone
  pisoʔarɨ
with something, puncture oneself
  nabisoʔarɨ
with something, roll up
  tohtopoʔnarɨ
with sufficient food, satisfied
  wɨtsɨʔmitɨ
with fringes, shawl naʔsɨkiaʔ
with palm of hand, slap tohpaʔitɨ
with water, splash pawɨhpaʔitɨ
with water, sprayed pawɨʔweʔniitɨ
with the foot, tear tasiʔkwairɨ
with the teeth, tear kɨsiʔkwarɨ
with the hand, touch lightly
  makwɨʔnetɨ

with respect, treat pahnaʔaitʉ
with cold, tremble sʉʉtsʉnitʉ
**with the mouth, unwrap
something** kʉhtoʔyarʉ K
with cane, walk natsihtóo noorʉ
with the hand. wipe off
makwineetʉ
with the head, wipe something
tsotsomarʉ
with hands, wring out tsahpitsoorʉ
with or on someone or something
maa
with what? on what? himakʉ
wither kʉhtakwitsooʔnitʉ W,
takwitsooʔnimiʔarʉ
wolf kʉʔtseena, pia tseenaʔ,
tuhtseenaʔ
Wolf-drinking Esahibi
wolf-howl, Echo-of-the- Isananakaʔ
woman, elderly hʉbi tsiitsiʔ,
pʉetʉpʉ
woman, menopausal
tsihhabʉhkamapʉ
woman, middle-aged hʉbi
woman, working tʉrʉʔai waipʉ
woman, young naiʔbi
woman's agnatic grandchild
huutsi
woman's breast pitsiiʔ
woman's brother's child pahaʔ
woman's female kinsman
waʔihpʉʔ
woman's purse puhihwi wosa K
woman's uterine grandchild kakuʔ
woman's whoop katakakitʉ W
women nanawaʔihpʉʔanii
women along, take notsaʔkaarʉ
womenfolk nanawaʔihpʉʔanʉ W
wonder at suyoroʔarʉ
wonderful nanaarʉʉmoa,
nanisuwʉkaitʉ, suyoroʔakapʉ
wood hu-, huu-, wobi, woobi

wood, bois d'arc etʉhuupi
wood, chisel tohtsiʔarʉ K
wood, cotton- soho obi, tahpookʉʔ,
weʔyʉkʉ sohoobi K
**wood for archery bows (bois
d'arc)** eetʉ
wood ant tuʔanikuuraʔ
wood plane huusibeʔ
wood shaving wʉsibepʉ
wood shavings kunapisoʔni
woodchuck huunaʔ, paʔarai moʔo
wooden bench huunakarʉʔ, wobi
nakarʉʔ
wooden chair wobi nakarʉʔ
wooden comb huunatsihtuʔyeʔ
wooden drum wobi wʉhpai K
wooden mallet huutʉrohpakoʔiʔi
wooden pestle tʉrayuʔneʔ
wooden vessel huu aawo
woodpecker pitʉsʉ nuʔyeʔ W, wobi
tohtaraki K, wʉpʉkoiʔ
woods huukabatʉ, soo huuhpi
word tekwapʉ
word on, pass nimʉʉmiʔarʉ W
word to someone to return, send
nʉníhkoonirʉ
work tʉrʉʔaipʉʔ
work, do tʉrʉʔaitʉ
work someone to death
namakupakʉrʉ
work-type handkerchief
pʉesúubeʔ K
worked to death namakupʉkatʉ
working woman tʉrʉʔai waipʉ
workman tʉrʉʔai wapi
worm woʔaabi
wormwood (silvery) pasiwona
pʉhʉbi
wormwood, silvery pasiwona
pʉhʉbi
wormy woʔa-
worn out wihtoʔaitʉ

wornout napatawi?aitʉ
-worn-out, Salt- Onawai
worried tsamʉsasuakatʉ
worry musasuarʉ, pisukwitarʉ
worry, caused to tsamʉsasuakatʉ
worse nahaya?ni
worse!, It is namanoke
worse, much nasu?ana
worthy, un- tʉtaatʉ
wound ʉ?a?
wound, cut someone to tsahki?aitʉ
wound, foot narahki?apʉ
wound oneself natsahki?arʉ
wounded person kwʉhti?
wrap namakwatubiitʉ, wʉhkwatubi
wrap, un- mahkwʉmarʉ,
   tsahkwʉmarʉ
wrap an object, un- tsahpeko?arʉ
wrap something, un- tahkwʉmarʉ
wrap something with the mouth,
   un- kʉhto?yarʉ K
wrap around wʉhkwitunarʉ
wrap around and around
   nʉʉhkwitubitʉ
wrap up tʉmakwatʉbi?etarʉ,
   wʉhkwitunarʉ
wrapped and tied up nʉʉhtami?itʉ
wrapper plant, cigarette-
   tʉmakwatui?
wrappers for cigarettes, leaf puhi
   tʉmakwatubi?
wren pasahòo
wrestle narohparʉ
wriggle pʉhkwinu?itʉ W
wring out with hands tsahpitsoorʉ
wrinkle kuhtakwitsoo?nitʉ W
wrinkle something takwikakwo?arʉ
-wrinkled, Skinny-and Tekwitsi M
wrinkled, straighten something
   tahtunaabarʉ
wrinkled all over takwikakwo?apʉ
wrist ma?wiitsa̱

wrist, lose something from hand
   or ma?kwe?yarʉ
wristwatch tabe-
write tʉboorʉ
wrong nʉnʉmʉni tʉhtsʉ
wrong one atʉrʉ
wrong way, rub the masu?naitʉ K,
   masʉroonitʉ W
wry face, make a sʉkʉbuninitʉ

Y y

Yap-eaters Yapai tʉhka
yard, lumber- huunarʉmʉʉ?, wobi
   narʉmʉ?
yarn aawʉʉtama?, tʉʉhtama?
yaupon holly ekapokopi
yawn ʉhtamakʉ?atʉ
year toh-, tomopʉ, tomopʉ
-year-old, two wahatomopʉ K
-year-old item, two tomohtoopʉ W
years ago, many soo be?sʉ
years old, two tomohtootʉ W
yell waa?akitʉ
yell noisily hubiyaarʉ
yelling, make noise hubiyairʉ
yellow ohapi̱
yellow color oha-
yellow fever ohakuhtsʉni
yellow jacket otʉ peena
yellow lotus kʉrʉ?atsi̱
yellow pond lily kʉriata
Yellow-back Ohapitʉ kwahi
Yellow-bear Ohawasápe
Yellow-steps Ohawʉnʉ
yes haa, tsuh
yesterday kʉtu
yet ʉkʉsʉ
yolk, egg noyo?na ohapi̱yuna
you mʉi, mʉmi, mʉnʉ, si?ana
you, thank ahó, ʉra

you, to ʉnʉ
you two mʉkwʉ̧
you two, of mʉhʉ
young pʉesúube? W, ʉkʉ-, ʉkʉbitsi̧,
   ʉkʉnanakatʉ̧
young catfish tuume?so̧
young man tuibihtsi?
young unmarried man wohka?ni?
young woman nai?bi
younger brother tami?
younger generation ʉkʉ nʉmʉnʉʉ
younger sister nami?
younger than inaarʉ

youngest generation ʉkʉ nʉmʉ
   roopʉnʉ̧ K
your mʉmʉ, mʉʉ, mʉʉ
youth, songs of wʉyakeetʉ̧ W
youthful ʉkʉnanakatʉ̧
yucca mumutsi?

Z z

zebra naboohmura?
zigzag wakʉ?wʉtʉ̧
zipper natsakwʉ̧sa?

Part III

Comanche Grammar

Comanche Grammar

The format for the following description of the Comanche language conforms in broad outline to that used by Langacker in his *Overview of Uto-Aztecan Grammar* (1977). Comanche did not play a role in the workshop leading to the series *Studies in Uto-Aztecan Grammar,* of which Langacker's work was the first volume, nor is the present grammar sketch a part of that series. Nevertheless, it was felt that the sketch could have the most value, particularly to those already familiar with the structure of another Uto-Aztecan language and the series referred to above, if Langacker's descriptive framework were adopted in large part. Our debt to him will be obvious to all those who know his work.

Choice of orthography has been influenced by the fact that the majority of Comanches are readers and speakers of English as a first language. This is due, of course, to government policy and not to personal choice, as the Comanche language was not taught in the schools and, in fact, children were not allowed to speak Comanche in school. Thus, the majority of Comanches today are not fluent in the Comanche language.

Many of the changes in the Comanche language in the past thirty years are due to the influence of English, since Comanche children have studied English exclusively in public schools or Indian schools. One way the English influence shows up is in loanwords. Aside from English, there are various loanwords from Spanish, Kiowa, and Siouan.

Some examples of loanwords are listed in (1).

(1) *waraatsi* from Spanish *huarache* 'sandal', with wider meaning 'shoe'
     papaasi   from Spanish *papa* 'potato'
     hooki   from English 'hog'

waikina	from English 'wagon'
kabitsi̱	from English 'cabbage'
haa	from Kiowa and Chiwere 'yes'
ahó	from Kiowa and Chiwere 'hello; thanks'

Comanche had contact with Spanish both in the United States and from early raids into Mexico, bringing back Mexican captives who became integrated into tribal life. This contact brought loanwords chiefly in reference to material culture, fauna, and flora. In Oklahoma, aside from English, closest contact seems to have been with the Kiowa and the Siouan (Chiwere), from which more words have been borrowed than from other languages.

1

Phonology

Given the various audiences for whom this work is intended, some compromise on notation had to be reached. The orthography used in both the dictionary and the grammar reflects actual pronunciation fairly closely, but the grammar reflects the abstract phonological analysis given in (2). Where the underlying phonological form of a particular grammatical morpheme differs from the surface form cited in example sentences, the underlying form is often presented in the text set off by diagonals.

(2)

	bilabial	dental	palatal	velar	rounded velar	glottal
stop	p	t, c		k	kw	?
fricative		s				
nasal	m	n				
glide			y		w	H, h
vowel			i	ʉ	u	
			e	a	o	

This is not the place for an exhaustive treatment of Comanche phonology. We briefly describe some major aspects of pronunciation having to do with consonants, vowels, and stress.

1.1. Consonants. Given the English-language background of most Comanche readers, and in conformity with Canonge's *Comanche Texts*, source of most of our illustrative examples, we treat /c/ and /kʷ/ as clusters /ts/ and /kw/, respectively. Our orthography does not reflect the fact that /y/ is often

309

pronounced as **[dž]** (*ma yaa* **[ma džaa]** 'takes it') nor that /kw/ is often voiced *nʉ kwʉhʉ* (**[nʉ gwʉhʉ]** 'my wife'). We do not write the predictable glottal stop **?** at the begining of vowel-initial words such as *okwe* **[?okwe]** 'to flow', but we do write it within a word, as in *sʉmʉ?okwe* 'to flow completely'.

Comanche exhibits a pattern of consonant gradations brought about by important processes affecting stops whenever they are within a breathgroup (i.e., not preceded by a pause), and a pattern of metathesis.

Spirantization. When preceded by a vowel, /p/ is a voiced bilabial fricative *b* **[ƀ]** : *pabi?* **[paƀi?]** 'brother', but *nʉ babi?* **[nʉ ƀaƀi?]** 'my brother'. Similarly, /t/ is a voiced tap *r* **[r]** , but only when preceded by one of the nonfront vowels /ʉ u a o/: *toyabi* 'mountain', *nʉ royabi* 'my mountain', but *esitoyabi* 'grey mountain'. An intervening /h/ or /?/ does not block spirantization of either /p/ or /t/: *puiba?a* 'on the eye' (/puih/ 'eye'), *tua?ba?a'on* the son', *tua?ruhka* 'under the son' (but *puituhka* 'under the eye').

Preaspiration. If /H/ precedes a stop, spirantization does not occur and /H/ surfaces as **[h]** , i.e. preaspiration of the stop. Consider the instrumental prefix /wʉH/ 'with body, sideways': *wʉhpitʉ* 'to reach a destination', *wʉhtokwe'to* kill with a weapon', *wʉhtsito?a* 'to peel', *wʉhkoba* 'to break'. If /H/ occurs in any other context, it has no surface manifestation or effect: *wʉsibo?a* 'to shave off', *wʉnʉ?yʉ?i* 'to make a heavy noise, thud', *wʉhabi* 'to march in formation', *wʉ?ani* 'to chop down'. /H/ also fails to surface if the following syllable has an organic voiceless vowel (§1.2): *nanaHkwʉhʉ* → *nanakwʉhʉ* 'married couple'.

Nasalization. Historically, Comanche exhibited a process similar to preaspiration, but involving nasals rather than surface *h*. As currently spoken, the language does not retain syllable-final surface nasals, but /n/ is still systematically present, in that it blocks spirantization before being deleted: *ʉn panpi* → *ʉ papi* 'your head'.

Metathesis. A fairly regular process permutes the sequence $CV1hV2$ to $hCV1V2$, where C is voiced. The process applies only sporadically if C is voiceless. If the two vowels are identical, they merge as a single short vowel. Metathesis is most common in pronominal forms such as *otʉnhʉh* → *orʉhʉ* → *ohrʉ* 'they (dual)', but is also seen elsewhere: *naniha* → *nahnia* 'name', *tsaHwihi* → *tsahwi* 'to open, turn over'.

Historically, all stops were voiceless and unaspirated, aside from preaspiration as indicated by *h*. As early as the forties, and probably before, some speakers had aspirated stops arising through loss of voiceless vowels (§1.2). Thus, older *nʉnʉpʉhi* 'midget', elicited by Canonge in the Yapai area, is some thirty years later given as *nʉnʉpʰi* in the Kwahare-speaking area around

Cache. Similarly, *pitsipᵿha* 'milk (A)' is replaced by *pitsipʰa*. Historical change has also affected preconsonantal *ʔ* and *h*, which many speakers omit. In place of preaspiration, a long vowel is found (*aakaaʔ* for *ahkaaʔ* 'devil's horn'), or preaspiration is used in free variation with the long vowel.

1.2. Vowels. The distinction between vowels such as /a/ vs. /ᵿ/ and /o/: vs. /u/ is often reduced or lost phonetically. The details vary between dialects, but careful pronunciation of the deictic roots with distance ranking *(i, o, ᵿ)*, for example, preserves the systematic distinction in many pronouns, demonstratives, and adverbials.[1]

Many occurrences of the vowel *e* derive historically from the cluster *ai* as seen by comparison with Shoshone cognates: SH *ekon* 'tongue', C *eko,* SH *enka* 'red, C *eka;* but SH *aisen* 'gray', C *esi.*[2] Morphophonemic changes in certain forms also give rise to *e,* as in the postpositions *waka* 'toward' and *wahketᵿ* 'away from'. The two forms *ai* and *e* cannot be used interchangeably in Comanche since they stand in contrast in certain forms: *aiʔmiʔa'to* lope, trot (SG SUBJ)', *eʔmᵿa* 'be without self-dignity, crazy'; *aitᵿ* 'bad, wicked', *etᵿ'bow,* gun', *etᵿᵿ* 'those scattered'.

Aside from such matters, the major processes affecting vowels are devoicing and lengthening. There are two forms of devoicing, so-called organic and inorganic.

Organic devoicing. Phonemic /s/ and /h/ always devoice a preceding unstressed short vowel that is not part of a cluster: *sitᵿsuʔa* 'this one also', *wanaʔᵿhᵿ* 'cloth blanket', but *sitᵿᵿsuʔa* 'these ones also', *tᵿasᵿ* 'and, again, also'. Vowel quality other than voicing is generally preserved, except that voiceless *a* shifts to *ᵿ* unless a glottal stop *ʔ* precedes it: *miʔahtsi* → *miʔɑtsi* 'having gone', but *kimahtsi* → *kimᵿtsi* 'having come'. As these examples also show, consonant deletion (§1.1) removes /h/ except before a vowel, so that the conditioning factor for organic devoicing is often not apparent. Two adjacent syllables cannot both have organic voiceless vowels. In such a situation the second vowel does not devoice: *nakihkah* → *nak̲ika* 'at the ear'. Note that preaspiration /H/ does not induce devoicing: *nanaHtena* → *nanahtena* 'male kinsmen'.

---

[1]See Wistrand Robinson (1989) for the corresponding Cashibo set and discussion relating Pano-Tacanan to Uto-Aztecan. An example of the phonetic overlap of /u/ and /o/ can be seen in the prefixes *koh-* and *kuh-*, both meaning 'of fire, by means of fire'. The unstressed form preceding a stressed, stem-initial syllable is *koh-,* while the stressed form is *kuh. koh-to* 'to build a fire', *koh-tsáaʔ* 'cooked or stewed food', *kuh-te* 'chop firewood', *kuh-kwarᵿki* 'take a steam bath'. Unstressed *koh* 'by fire' must be distinguished from *koh* 'break, broken', of different origin.

[2]Shoshone forms are retranscribed from Miller 1972:105.

Inorganic devoicing. A short vowel that is not part of a cluster is optionally devoiced at the end of a breath group. Vowel quality other than voicing is generally preserved and a preceding preconsonantal /H/ is not deleted: *kasạ* 'wing', *tunehtsụ* 'to run', *uhtụ* 'to give'. Inorganic devoicing may apply even if the preceding vowel has undergone organic devoicing *pitsipụhạ* 'milk (A)', *pụetsụkụ* 'in the morning'. An inorganic voiceless vowel conditions optional lengthening of a voiced penultimate vowel if there is no intervening /H/: *kaasạ* 'wing', *oomọ* 'leg'.

1.3. Stress rules. Comanche has alternating stress according to the number of syllables in a word or compound. Monosyllabic words are without stress or pitch; others have stress on the first or second syllable. Normal initial stress is on the first syllable of a two-syllable word. Acute accent will be used here for primary stress; grave accent for secondary stress. A preconsonant aspirate (h) or glottal (?) usually groups in the syllable with its respective consonant, but it may at times phonologically group with the vowel preceding it.

(3)   kú.ʔè   'top'   pí.ʔtò   'bob-tailed'
        tó.sà   'white'   ká.hpè   'bed'
        tó.sàʔ   'white horse'   tá.ʔòoʔ   'dried meat'
        wí.hnù   'then'   sú.nì   'that way'

The compound-forming, proclitic form of a noun is basic, having a short vowel. The first vowel of an isolation or citation form of a noun is often lengthened under primary stress and the vowel of the second syllable is voiceless, which is to say, it often undergoes inorganic devoicing.

(4)   wapi-   wáapị   'cedar'
        awo-   áawọ   'cup'
        tama-   táamạ   'tooth'

Possessive pronouns, which serve as phonological proclitics to the noun, do not change root or stem-initial stress. These are seen especially with nouns which require possessive pronouns such as body parts and kinship terms.

(5)   ʉ + nákị   'your ear'   nʉ + námi   'my sister'
        ʉ + púi   'your eye'

Diphthongs *ai, oi,* and *ui* act as one vowel with one mora of time.

(6)   nái.ʔbì   'young woman'   wói.nù   'bugle, music'
        ái.tʉì   'bad'   púi.kʉ.sò   'chigger'

Initial stress falls on the first syllable of three-syllable words; normal secondary stress falls on the third syllable.

(7) tá.pị.kò?   'heel' (of foot)   ná.kwụ.sì?   'pumpkin'
     tú.hụ.bụ̀ỉ   'hide, raw skin'   má.kwụ.sà?   'sleeve'

In three-syllable words which are two-syllable words with an added prefix or suffix, the second syllable does not become voiceless, or may be voiceless if the main stress moves to the second noun of a compound noun.

(8) tá.si + ?à   'smallpox, freckles'   pù + sí + ?à   'head louse'
     pò + sáa.ki   'bridge'   à.ma + wóo   'apple'
     àa.ta + kîi   'grasshopper'   tù.nụ + háa   'cymopterus plant'

Words of four, five, and six syllables have normal alternating stress when nouns of a compound are coequal, or the root or stem has a one-syllable suffix. Examples with four syllables are:

(9) á.ni.mùi   'housefly'   á.ta + bì.tsị   'foreigner'
     yú.pu.sì.a   'louse'   ná.na + bù.ni   'window'
     wụh + tú.pụ.kà?   'buckle, button'   tụ̀ỉ.rụ + è + tụ   'child'

Words or compounds of five syllables also have primary stress on the first syllable and secondary stress on the third syllable.

(10) ká.wo + nò.ka.tụ   'street'   nó.hi + tụ̀ỉ.e tụ   'doll'
     ná.tsa + mù.kwe?   'grapes'   só.ni + nà.rụ.so?   'towsack'

Words or compounds of six syllables have primary stress on the first and secondary stress on the fourth syllable.

(11) kú.?i.na.kụ̀ỉ.?e.tụ   'roasts for'
     ná.ro.htsa.nì.?i.ku   'as hanging'
     tụ̀ỉ.kwụ.sụ kụ̀ỉ.e.yu   'cooks on coals for'
     ná.mụ.so.hì.htsi   'hurrying up'

Again, a prefix or enclitic which is not stem-changing does not receive initial stress, so that the alternating stress begins on the second syllable as in the following words of six syllables, following the pattern of five-syllable words:

(12) wụ.hká.?a.mì.?a.nụ   'went to cut down'
     wụ.sú.wa.rụ̀ỉ.ki.nụ   'began to miss'

When a form may seem to have stress on the third syllable, as marked in Canonge's Comanche Texts, what is marked as primary stress (apparently) is secondary stress, except in cases when both a proclitic and prefix are used.

(13)   *kú.tsị.tò.na.nụ*   'set on fire'
        há.bị + hu.píi.tụ   'stopped and lay down'
        ká.rụ + hu.píi.tụ   'stopped and sat'
        wà.ka + ré?ee?   'turtle'

A three-syllable word with an added one-syllable suffix or enclitic retains the stress form of the main word, in spite of the added fourth syllable.

(14)   *tsú.hnì.pụ*   + ha   'bone (A)'
        káa.be.hkà + nụ   'cheated'
        tú.ne.htsù + nụ   'ran'

In narratives, verbs often exhibit stylistic stress shift when occurring at the end of a breath group. Stress moves one syllable to the right if that syllable is voiced; otherwise, it skips over the voiceless vowel to the next syllable.

(15)   *pohpínụ*   'jumped'   *norụnákụnụ*   'made a bed'
        tụhká?eeyụ   'would eat'   *tsatụwánụ*   'opened'

2

The Simple Sentence

Here and in following sections, the syntax of the various forms of simple sentences is discussed, with chief divisions according to mood—declarative mood, interrogative mood, imperative mood, and their corresponding subdivisions. Other types of modality and nondistinct argument phenomena follow. First, however, a few comments concerning interjections and other discourse phenomena need to be made.

An interjection may stand alone or occur preceding a sentence. A number of common interjections are listed in (16) and an interjection with following sentence is illustrated in (17).

(16)   *aahe*   'I claim it!'   *yaa*   'oh' (used by women)
       ahó   'thank you'   *yee*   'oh no!' (disapproval by
       ai   'I'm disgusted'   men)
       anḋa   'ouch! (physical pain)'   *ʉbiaʻ*   oh; oh, my!' (surprise by
       haa   'yes'   women)
       haʔii   'oh, my!'   *ʉra*   'thank you'
       kee   'no'   *ʉrʉʉ*   'ouch!' (It burns!)

(17)   haa   *tsaatu*   *u?*
       yes   good^NOM   D4NS[3]
       Yes, it is good.   (78:13)[4]

An extended treatment of Comanche discourse phenomena is beyond the scope of this sketch, but a few morphemes which function at the highest levels of narrative form are introduced in this section.

The quotative morpheme *tua* occurs in the initial sentence of all but three of the narratives in *Comanche Texts*. It can be translated 'they say, it is said', or more colloquially 'the story goes'. The following sentences illustrate its use.

(18)   *soobe?su*   *-kutsa?*   *rua*   *kuyuníi?-nuu*   *bisikwanúu?i-buni*
       much^MEAS   EVID-DECL   QUOT   turkey-Np   slide-AUG
       Long ago, they say, (some) turkeys were doing a lot of sliding.   (5:1)

(19)   *soobe?su*   *nunu*   *tua*   *tu-híma-?ee-yu*
       much^MEAS   1xNp   QUOT   food-take-REP-DUR
       Long ago, they say, we would get rations.   (129:1)

Another quotative morpheme, *me(h),* marks embedded direct discourse introduced by a verb of saying or thinking (which may be covert). It appears in final position as meh; elsewhere as me.

(20)   *suru* *-ku-se?*   *wihnu*   *tanu*   *hakanih-ku* *ma*   *hani* *me*   *yukwii-yu*
       D4   EVID-CTR   then   1piN   how-A   D2A   do   QUOT   say-DUR
       Then that one said, "What shall we do with him?"   (6:19)

(21)   *suru* *-ku-se?*   *anáa*   *meh*
       D4   EVID-CTR   ouch!   QUOT
       That one said, "Ouch!"   (6:13)

---

[3]The rich deictic system of Comanche which underlies pronouns and demonstrative adjectives is presented in detail in §12.1. Note here, however, that four degrees of distance from the place of the speech act are abbreviated in illustrations by D1, D2, D3, and D4, respectively, and that plural referents may be designated as D5 to denote that they are in some respect scattered. Pronouns and adjectives may be further marked for case as nominative (N), genitive (G), accusative (A), locative (L), or manner (M), and for number as singular (S) or plural (P).

[4]In examples, references are to page and sentence number in *Canonge's Comanche Texts* unless otherwise noted. Examples given without references are from Comanche-speaking consultants.

Enclitic *kʉ-kʉ* is an evidential, which indicates remote past or speaker un-involvement. Given these conditions, its occurrence is obligatory in second position for the initial sentence of each successive paragraph of a discourse. Another narrative enclitic, *-se?*, marks successive paragraphs of a discourse, again occurring in second position and following *-kʉ* if that is also present. See *Comanche Texts* for extensive use of these morphemes in context. They occur in sentences (20) and (21) and in many other sentences throughout this sketch.

The temporal conjunctions *wihnu* 'then' and *sube?* 'then' reinforce the temporal relationship between a prior event and a subsequent one, as in (22) and (23).

(22) *setʉ -se?   nʉʉmʉ   suhka tabeni ukʉhu   sʉmʉ-no-kima-?e-tʉ*
      D5   CTR   Comanche   D4As   day   D4ˆatˆto all-haul-come-REP-PROG

      no-bitʉ-?ee-yʉ   wihnu   tʉeh-buha-rabeni   pʉetsʉku-sʉ
      haul-arrive-REP-DUR   then   small-power-day   agoˆA-INTENS

      tʉ-hima-?ee-yʉ
      foodˆtake-REP-DUR
      That day various Comanches, having moved there would camp and
      then early Saturday morning (they) would get rations.   (129:5, 6)

(23) *mia-ru?   nʉ?   me   yʉkwii-yʉ   surʉ   -kʉ-se?   wihnu*
      goˆUNR   1xNs   QUOT   say-DUR   D4   EVID-CTR   then

      hunu?bʉ-hoi-kị   nuhkị-nụ
      creek-around-at   run-PST
      "I will go," (he) said. Then he ran off around the creek.   (6:22, 23)

The adverb *si?anetʉ* 'at this place' functions equally as a locative and a temporal adverb. In narrative it might be translated as 'at this point' or 'meanwhile at another location', indicating a change in location or scenery, depending upon whether reference to time or location is intended. In (24), this adverb marks a change back to an earlier scene.

(24) *sitʉ   -kʉ-se?   u   kumahpʉ?   si?ane-tʉ   uhri   kuhíya-mi?a-nụ*
      D1   EVID-CTR   D4G   husband   D1L-from   D4Ad   spy-go-PST
      At this point, her husband went to spy on them.   (105:22)

Note that the usual position for these elements is after the first major constituent of a clause following the modal enclitic, although they occasionally occur between a demonstrative and the rest of a subject.

(25) *suru*   *-ku̲-se?*   *si?ane-tu̲*   *oha?ahnakatu̲*   *nuhkí-nu̲*
      D4   EVID-CTR   D1L-from   coyote   run-PST
      At this point, coyote ran away.   (23:31)

2.1. The declarative mood. The second-position enclitic -tsa? marks declarative sentences in conversational speech and sets the dramatis personae
on stage in narrative structure. In this manner, the mood is made explicit
to begin narrative. In subsequent narrative clauses, mood is not explicitly
marked until a change of mood is made.

(26) *nai?-bi*   *-tsa?*   *ubitu̲ku̲u̲-tu̲*
      girl-ABS   DECL   flirt-PROG
      The girl is flirting with him.

If the evidential -ku̲ (remote past) occurs with -tsa? (declarative), the evidential precedes the declarative morpheme, as in (27).

(27) *su̲mu̲-?* *-ku̲-tsa?*   *raiboo?*   *waahpi-hta*   *wu̲hká?a-mi?a-nu̲*
      one-NS   EVID-DECL   white^man   cedar-A   chop-go-PST
      A white man went to chop down a cedar tree.   (27:1)

2.2. Nonverbal sentences. The basic, or neutral, word order for sentences
which predicate prototypically nonverbal notions by means of a predicate
nominal or predicate adjective is S (MODAL) P,[5] with the modal being enclitic to
the subject noun phrase.

(28) *i*   *-tsa?*   *nu̲*   *kahni*
      D1   DECL   1xG   house
      This is my home.   (38:22)

(29) *u̲*   *tua?-nu̲u̲*   *-tsa?*   *tahu̲*   *haitsi̲-nu̲u̲*
      2sG   son-NP   DECL   1diG   friend-Np
      Your sons are our friends.   (Canonge 1949)

(30) *nu̲*   *kwu̲hu̲* *-tsa?*   *ke-sua-tu̲*
      1xG wife   DECL   NEG-want-NOM
      My wife is mean.   (38:23)

---

[5]Where P stands for PREDICATE.

(31) *i*   *-tsa?*   *pueh-tu-pu*
      D1   DECL   ago-NOM-ABS
      She is elderly.

There are a number of BE-verbs in Comanche, but these occur in contexts other than simple nonverbal sentences, primarily with intransitive verbs such as *naahka* 'live, become', *karu'sit,* live', *wunu* 'stand', and *habi* 'lie'.

2.3. Intransitive sentences. The basic, or neutral, word order for intransitive sentences is S (MODAL) V. Verbs of this intransitive type take full tense/aspect suffixation.

(32) *itu*   *-tsa?*   *tahu*   *napuhu*   *ukusu*   *kima-ru-tuku*
      D1   DECL   1diG   trail   still   come-PROG-same
      This one is still coming on our trail.   (42:21)

(33) *suruu*   *tuku-tsi*   *yuu-?uh-kooi-nu*
      D4Np   eat-SS   quiet-eye-die-PST
      Having eaten, they slept unconcerned.   (8:46)

(34) *ibu*   *nu?*   *mia-ru?i*
      D1DIR   1xNs   go-UNR
      I will go this way.   (43:24)

(35) *wahah-tu-kwu*   *wasáasi?-tena-nu-kwu*   *nu-waka*   *bitu-?i*
      two-NOM-d   Osage-man-NOM-d   1xA-toward   arrive-REAL
      Two Osage men arrived by me.   (105:21)

2.4. Transitive sentences. The basic, or neutral, word order for transitive sentences in full form, where new information is being introduced, is S (MODAL) O V. Full forms of tense/aspect are used with the verb.

(36) *suruu*   *-se?*   *hani-bi-hta*   *tu-runi?i-nu*
      D4Np   CTR   corn-ABS-A   INDEF-put^away-PST
      They planted corn.

Various temporal, locative, or other adverbial elements may also occur, normally falling after the S, although only a limited number of grammatical elements may fall between the subject and the verb.

(37) *situkwu*   *wihnu*   *puhu*   *ina-na*   *maruka-nu*
      D1Nd   then   COGd   jerk-NOM   finish-PST
      Then these two finished their jerking.   (112:24)

(38) *situkwu*   *si-hkutu*   *puhu*   *kahni-ku-hu*   *nuraa-nu*
      D1Nd   D1-to^from   COGD   house-at-to   run-PST
      These two ran from here to their house.   (116:13)

(39) *situ*   *-ku-se?*   *pu*   *paka-maku*   *tsah-tunehtsu-nu*
      D1   EVID-CTR   COGS   arrow-on^A   INSTR-run-PST
      He stretched (it) with his arrow.   (100:15)

Accusative pronouns precede verbs as proclitics. An indirect object follows a direct object, in the order S O IO V.

(40) *situu*   *kwasinaboo?-nuu*   *ma*   *ma-nuki-ku-nu*
      D1Np   snake-Np   D2A   INDEF-run-CAUS-PST
      These snakes chased her.   (52:21)

(41) *maruu*   *nanah-tena-nuu*   *-ku-se?*   *tai*   *makaa-ka*   *me*   *urii*
      D2Gp   RECIP-man-Np   EVID-CTR   1iAp   feed-!p   QUOT   D4Ap

      niikwii-yu
      say-DUR
      Their menfolk said to them, "Feed us."   (128:16)

Simple, nonemphatic subject pronouns, without added enclitics, are themselves enclitic. They regularly move out of first position and into the sentence to the right of the second constituent, with which they are pronounced as one word. This second constituent may be as small as a word or as large as an entire phrase.

(42) *noha*   *u?*   *nu*   *kwuhuru?i*
      nearly   D4Ns   1xA   catch^UNR
      He nearly caught me.   (105:28)

(43) *soobe?su*   *nunu*   *tua*   *tu-hima-?ee-yu*
      long^ago   1xNp   QUOT   f   ood-take-REP-DUR
      Long ago, they say, we would get rations.   (129:1)

(44) *waikinu-ba?a*   *-ku*   *urukwu*   *mi?a-?i*
      wagon-on   EVID   D4Nd   go-REAL
      They went by wagon.   (115:2)

(45) *wasápeʔ-a*   *kobe*   *nɨʔ*   *puni-tuʔi*
     bear-G   face   1xNs   see-UNR
     I'll see the bear's face.

Note that if the verb is in second postion with no other grammatical element intervening, the subject when moved is in sentence-final position.

(46) *mia-ruʔi*   *nɨʔ*
     go-UNR   1xNs
     I'll go.   (96:20)

Because a pronoun object is a proclitic on the verb, these two elements cannot be separated by moving a subject pronoun into second position. Hence, the verb ends up out of final position, with the order O V S.

(47) *ma*   *buni-tuʔi*   *nɨʔ*
     D2A   see-UNR   1xNs
     I will see it.

(48) *tai*   *wɨh-tokwɨ-ki-tɨ*   *maʔ*
     1iAp   INSTR-club-come-PROG   D2Ns
     He is coming clubbing us.   (4:15)

Movement of subject pronouns rightward into the sentence imparts no special significance semantically. However, movement of some constituent leftward into initial position is a syntactic means of emphasizing that constituent. The sentence topic can be shifted to make it more prominent. Indirect object is brought into focus in (49).

(49) *pɨɨ*   *kah-tɨì iʔ-nii*   *surɨ*   *u*   *kwɨhɨ ke*   *u*   *pitɨ-na*
     COGp   house-friend-Ap   D4Np   D4G   wife   NEG   D4G   arrive-NOM

     narɨmuʔi-kɨ–nu
     tell-CAUS-PST
     His wife told their neighbors of his not having arrived.   (28:13)

In (50), the manner constituent is brought into focus.

(50) *sunih-ku*   *surɨɨ*   *usúni*   *hani-mia-ʔee-yu*
     D4M-A   D4N   always   do-go-REP-DUR
     They always go on doing like that.   (130:14)

There is also a type of postposing, involving either an object or an adverbial element as complement of a verb of motion. This takes place either because the two positions preceding the verb are occupied by other grammatical material, to make a verb more prominent, or to lend definiteness to an object.

(51)	sitʉkwʉ	-kʉ-seʔ	siʔane-tʉ	miʔa-nʉ	pʉʉ	kahni-kʉ-hʉ
	D1Nd	EVID-CTR	D1L-from	go-PST	COGp	house-at-to

These two, at this point, went to their house.   (125:12)

2.5. HAVE **sentences.** Although there is no independent verb meaning 'have', there are two verbalizing suffixes that express this meaning (§8.2).

(52)	suhka	na-hnía-ba-ʔị		toya-ma	karʉʉ-rị
	D4As	REFL-name-have-REAL		mountain-on	sit-PROG^A

(He) had that name, Sits-on-mountain.   (72:35)

2.6. DO sentences. DO sentences are of four types. The most neutral of the verbs in this semantic range is *mʉʉ* 'do, treat (someone), work (something)'. It is used in a generic and referential sense, referring to actions named more specifically in prior discourse, or understood in context.

(53)	surʉ	-kʉ-seʔ	wihnu	suni	uhka	bʉi	-hka	mia-ruʔi
	D4	EVID-CTR	then	D4M	D4As	COAp	do-DS	go-UNR

	nʉʔ	me	yʉkwii-yʉ
	1xNs	QUOT	say-DUR

When they had done thus to him, that one said, "I'll go."   (6:22)

The suffix -*ʔai* 'do, make, create' forms numerous verbs from noun stems.

(54)	nah	ranʉ	ke	kahni-ʔai-waʔị-tʉ-ʉ
	just	1iNp	NEG	house-make-UNR-PROG-P

Let's just not make a house.   (111:3)

Other examples of this form are *isaʔai* 'tell a lie', *puʔeʔai* 'make an agreement', *hubaʔai* 'make coffee', and *puhaʔai* 'prepare medicine'.

Two additional verbs expressing 'do' are *naha* 'happen, continue' and *naahka* 'continue, become'.

(55) *hakani*   *ɨnɨ*   *nahá-nu̱*
      how?   2Ns   happen-PST
      What happened to you?   (6:14)

(56) *suni -kɨ-seʔ*   *urii*   *naha-miʔa-ku*   *ata-bitsi̱-nɨɨ*   *urɨɨ-ma*   *pahí-nu̱*
      D4M EVID-CTR   D4Ap   happen-go-DS   other-ABS-Np   D4Np-on   fall-PST
      As they continued on that way, non-Comanches attacked them. (41:3)

The verbalizing suffix -tu/-ru expresses the meaning 'do so as to have', as in kuhmaru 'marry (of a woman)'.

3

Interrogative Mood

3.1. Yes/No questions. Questions anticipating a 'yes' or 'no' response are formed by the interrogative enclitic -ha in the second, modal position of a sentence.

(57)　　*nʉ*　　*kahni*　　*-ha*　　*tsaa-yʉ*
　　　　1xG　　　house　　QUES　　good-VB
　　　　Is my house good?　　　　　　　　　　　　　　　　　(Canonge 1949)

(58)　　*nʉ*　　*-ha*
　　　　1x　　QUES
　　　　Me?　　　　　　　　　　　　　　　　　　　　　　　　(5:9)

(59)　　*ʉ*　　*-takʉ*　　*-ha*　　*nʉmii-yʉ*
　　　　2Gs　　alone　　QUES　　move-DUR
　　　　Is it only you moving around?　　　　　　　　　　　　　(95:7)

3.2. Alternative questions. An alternative question is a special type of yes/no question which employs the interrogative enclitic -*ha* in second position, but which also provides alternatives to choose between.

(60)　　*ʉnʉ*　　*-ha*　　*pihi-ʔa-nii*　　*tʉanoo*　　*tʉrʉe-waʔihpʉ-ʔa-nii*　　*puni*
　　　　2Ns　　QUES　　boy-?-Ap　　or　　little-woman-?-Ap　　see
　　　　Did you see boys or girls?

(61)　　*nʉnʉ*　　*-ha*　　*pimoróoʔ-a*　　*pehka-ʔi*　　*tʉanoo*　　*arʉkaʔ-a*
　　　　1xNp　　QUES　　cow-A　　kill-REAL　　or　　deer-A
　　　　Did we kill a cow or a deer?

3.3. Information questions. An information question requests information and is introduced by a question word in initial position, which for Comanche begins with the syllables *hi-* or *ha-*. Other constituents can precede the question word for emphasis. A number of forms distinguish subject from object and singular from plural.

(a) hini 'what? (subject)'. The underlying form of this nominative form of the question word is /hinin/, final *n* blocking the spirantization of a following stop before being deleted (§1.1).

(62)　　*u-sʉ*　　　　　　　*hini*　　　　*pahí-nʉ*
　　　　D4-INTENS　　　　what?^N　　　fall-PST
　　　　What is that that fell?　　　　　　　　　　　　　　　　　　　(17:30)

(63)　　*i-sʉ*　　　　　　　　*ʉ*　　　　*hinị*
　　　　D1-INTENS　　　　　2Gs　　　what?^N
　　　　What is this of yours?　　　　　　　　　　　　　　　(Canonge 1949)

(64)　　*hini-paʔi*　　　　*ʉnʉ*
　　　　what?^N-have　　　2Ns
　　　　What do you have?　　　　　　　　　　　　　　　　(Canonge 1949)

(b) hina 'what? (object)'. This is the accusative form of the question word.

(65)　　*hina*　　　　　　　*ʉnʉ*
　　　　what?^A　　　　　　2Ns
　　　　What do you want?　　　　　　　　　　　　　　　　　　　(31:7)

(66)　　*hina*　　　*ʉnʉ*　　*ʉ-pi-nakwʉ-ku*　　*yaa-hkạ*
　　　　what?^A　　2Ns　　2As-INSTR-DIR-A　　take-ST
　　　　What are you taking behind you?　　　　　　　　　　　　(82:17)

(67)　　*hina*　　　*ranʉ*　　*taa*　　*tʉrʉeʔ-tii*　　*tʉhká-kʉ-hu-tuʔị*
　　　　what?^A　　1INp　　1iGi　　child-Ap　　eat-CAUS-INDEF-UNR
　　　　What are we going to feed our children?　　　　　　　　(119:3)

When the word for 'what?' occurs as object of a locational postposition, it takes the shortened form *hi*.

(68)　　*hi-paʔa*　　　*tanʉ*　　*yʉkwi-hka*
　　　　what?-on　　　1iNi　　sit-ST
　　　　What are we sitting on?　　　　　　　　　　　　　　　　(60:19)

(69) *hi-tuhka-ti*   *u?*   *wuhka?a-buni*
   what?-under-at D4Ns   chop-AUG
   What is he chopping a lot under?

(c) hipe 'when?'

(70) *hipe*   *suuru* *mi?a-hu-tu?i*
   when?   D4Ns go-INDEF-UNR
   When will he go?   (Canonge 1949)

(71) *hipe*   *unu* *kima-nu*
   when?   2Ns come-PST
   When did you come?   (Canonge 1949)

(d) hipeka?i 'how big?' is a compound verb *hipeka* 'what size have?' Compare *Nu batsi? tsa? u pabi? betu* 'My sister is the size of your brother' (Osborn and Smalley 1949). Its presumed underlying structure is /hin-pe-?-kan-?ih/ 'what-MEAS-Ns-have-REAL'.

(72) *hipeka?i*   *u* *tua?*
   what^size 2Gs son
   How big is your son?   (Canonge 1949)

(e) hakaru 'who?/which? (Ns)', *hakaruu* 'who?/which? (Np)'. These forms consist of the root haka followed by suffixes *-tun* (nominal) and *-u* (plural).

(73) *u-su*   *hakaru* *hibi-hka*
   D4-INTENS who?^Ns drink-ST
   Who is that (who is) drinking?   (59:7)

(74) *hakaru* *maruhu-mati* *u* *hii-pu*
   who?^Ns D2d-PART^A   2Gs thing-ABS
   Which of the two is yours?   (Canonge 1949)

(75) *i-su*   *hakaruu*
   D1-INTENS who?^Np
   Who are these?   (Canonge 1949)

(f) hahka 'whom?' The underlying form of this nonnominative question word is /ha-Hka/ 'QUES-As'.

(76)   *hahka*   *ʉnʉ*   *tʉrʉʔai*
        whom?   2Ns   work
        For whom do you work?'   (Canonge 1949)

(77)   *hahka̱*
        whom?
        To whom?   (Canonge 1949)

(78)   *i-sʉ*   *hahka*   *petʉ̱*
        D1-INTENS   whom?   daughter
        Whose daughter is this?   (Canonge 1949)

   (g) hakai 'how? (state of being)'. This form consists of the root *haka* and the
verbal suffix *-i* (be).

(79)   *hakai*   *ʉnʉ*   *nʉʉ-suka?*
        how?   2Ns   REFL-feel
        How do you feel?   (Canonge 1949)

   (h) hakani 'how?'. This manner interrogative consists of the root *haka* and
the suffix /-niH/ (manner).

(80)   *mʉnʉ*   *esi-ʔahtamúu?-nʉʉ*   *hakanih-ku*   *nananisuyake-ku*   *naboo-hka̱*
        2Np   gray-grasshopper-Np   how?-A   beautifully-A   design-ST
        How are all you gray grasshoppers designed so beautifully?   (33:20)

(81)   *hakani*   *-kia*   *ʉnʉ*   *nahá-nʉ̱*
        how?   INFER   2Ns   happen-PST
        (I) wonder what happened to you?   (105:20)

   (i) *hakaniʔyutʉ̱* 'why?' The interrogative of purpose is made up of
the root *haka* and suffixes /-niH/ (manner), /-yun/ (verbalizer), /-tʉn/
(nominal).

(82)   *hakaniʔyutʉ̱*   *ʉnʉ*   *yake-nʉ̱*
        why?   2Ns   cry-PST
        Why did you cry?   (Canonge 1949)

(83)   *hakaniʔyutʉ̱*   *ʉnʉ*   *sinih-ku*   *tai*   *hani-tʉ̱i̱ ni̱*
        why?   2Ns   D1M-A   1iAp   do-tell
        Why are you telling us to do (it) this way?   (75:25)

(j) *haku* 'where?'. This locative interrogative has the underlying form /ha-kah/ 'QUES-at'.

(84)   *haku*   *suru*   *poko-pi*   *u*   *tu?awe-na*
        where?   D4N   fruit-ABS   2Gs   tell-NOM
        Where is that fruit you told of?   (16:12)

(85)   *haku*   *-se?*   *u*   *kuma-hpu?*
        where?   CTR   2Gs   husband-ABS
        Where is your husband?   (104:14)

(86)   *haku-ku*   *u*   *sarii?*   *tuhkaa-yu*
        where?-A   2Gs   dog   eat-DUR
        Where is your dog eating?   (Canonge 1949)

(k) *hakahpu* 'to/from where?'. This directional interrogative has the form /hakaH-pun/ 'QUES-DIR'.

(87)   *hakahpu*   *u*   *pia?*   *mi?aa-yu*
        where?   2Gs   mother   go-DUR
        Where is your mother going?   (Canonge 1949)

(88)   *hakahpu*   *noo*   *nu?*
        where?   NEC   1xNs
        Where must I [go]?

(l) *huu* 'how many?'.

(89)   *huu*   *u*   *a-hpu?-a*   *tomo-pu*
        how^many? 2   Gs   father-ABS-G   year-ABS
        How old is your father?   (Canonge 1949)

4

Imperative Mood

4.1. Positive imperative. The singular positive imperative form is the simple verb stem.

(90) *kima*   *habi-kị*
      come   lie-come
      Come lie down!   (48:20)

(91) *ihka*   *buni*   *tɨi-h*
      D1As   see   friend-VOC
      Look at this, friend!   (41:7)

Dual and plural imperatives are indicated by the simple verb stem with a second-position coreferential pronoun showing number agreement. Dual imperative is indicated by *pɨhɨ* or *pɨkwɨ*.

(92) *ɨhkooi*   *bɨhɨ*
      sleep   COd
      You two, sleep!   (Canonge 1949)

(93) *nɨ*   *ramiʔa*   *bɨkwɨ*   *buunị?*
      1xG   brother   COd   see
      You two, look at my brother!   (Osborn and Smalley 1949)

Plural imperative is indicated by -ka (!p) suffixed to the simple stem when only the verb is used, or in second position following any other sentence-initial element.

(94) muʉ   taʔwoʔiʔ-a -ka   makaʔmuki
      2Gp   gun-A   !p   getˆready
      All of you, get your guns ready!					(122:9)

(95) ohka   -ka   kwasinabooʔ-a   wuhkuupạ
      D3As   !p   snakeˆA   kill
      All of you, kill that snake!					(51:8)

(96) namʉsohi-htsi   -ka   namʉsi   tuhkandáiʔ-niwʉnʉ
      hurry-NOM   !p   quickly   Wichita-speak
      Hurrying, all of you, quickly speak Wichita!					(78:15)

The pronoun nʉʉʔ (second-person nominative) may occur in second position as the pronoun of address and subject of an imperative when needed for reference or emphasis in the singular. Dual and plural suffixes follow nʉʉʔ in their respective uses.

(97) tai   tʉkʉhmanị-bʉni   nʉʉʔ
      1iAp   cookˆfood-AUG   2N
      You (sg), cook a lot for us!					(81:3)

(98) nʉkʉ-tsi   nʉʉʔ   -ka   nahma   moʔo-tsaai-htsi
      dance-SS   2N   !p   together   hand-hold-NOM

      sʉmʉ--ʔʉhtsumi- hki-nạ
      one-closeˆeyes-come-CONT
      All of you, dancing, holding hands with each other, keep coming with your eyes tightly closed.					(3:11)

Other pronouns sometimes, though rarely, serve as overt subjects of imperatives.

(99) ʉnʉ   ma kumahpʉʔ-a wekị-kwa
      2sN   D2G husband-A seek-go
      You, go look for her husband!					(104:17)

4.2. Hortatory. Comanche expresses the hortatory by combining an obligatory first-person dual or an overt plural subject and a simple verb stem

optionally inflected for unrealized (=future) aspect. Since these forms overlap entirely with simple declaratives, context is crucial for understanding
them as exhortations.

(100) *meeku*   *rakwʉ*   *ma-baʔatu*   *nararʉʉnạ*
       now   1diN   D2-over   gamble
       Now let's (us two) gamble over it.   (9:8)

(101) *kima*   *orʉʉ-kʉhu*   *tanʉ*   *raibooʔ-nʉʉ-kʉhu*   *nuraa*
       come   D3-PART   1piN   white^man-P-to   run
       Come. Let's (pl) run to those white people.   (60:11, 12)

(102) *mia*   *ranʉ*
       go   1piN
       Let's (pl) go!   (29:30)

5

Polarity

5.1. Affirmation. As seen previously, the word for 'yes' is *haa*, frequently pronounced with nasalization on the lengthened vowel, although this is not indicated in our transcription. This form is also used as a greeting.

There are two known forms of emphasis in addition to the preposing considered earlier. Some of the personal pronouns have special forms used in contrastive or emphatic environments.

(103)   *sitʉ*   *tsuhni-pʉ*   *-kʉ-seʔ*   *ke*   *marʉ*   *nʉe*   *tʉʔʉya-tʉ-ʉ*
       D1N   bone-ABS   EVID-CTR   NEG   D2Np   1xAs   fear-PROG-p

          ʉmi   *marʉʉ*   *ʉkwi-hka-tʉ*   *tahi*   *tʉʔʉya-tʉ-ʉ*   *me*   *yʉkwii-yʉ*
          2As   D2Gp   smell-ST-PROG   1iAd   fear-PROG-p   QUOT   say-DUR
          This skull said, "They are not afraid of me, but smelling you, they are
          afraid of us."   (43:31, 32)

Besides the special emphatic pronouns, the postposition *-masʉ*, from /-man/ 'on' and /-sʉn/ (intensifier), can be added to an element for emphasis.

(104)   *poʔsa*   *pimoróoʔ*   *nʉ-ma-sʉ*   *ʉ*   *kaa-bekʉ-tsi*   *ʉ*   *tʉ-behka-nu*
       crazy   cow   1x-on-INTENS   2As   deceit-kill-SS   2As   food-kill-PST
       Crazy cow, cheating you, I have killed you.   (20:27)

5.2. Negation. As seen in §2.1, the word for 'no' is *kee* in its free form. The shortened form *ke* (/ken/) marks negation within sentences, and usually occurs directly before the predicate. In sentences with *ke*, the verb takes the aspectual suffix -*wa?į* (unrealized) rather than -*tu?į* (unrealized).

(105) *tena-hpu? -tsa? ke   tu-ru-?ai-tu*
man-ABS DECL NEG   RDP-INDEF-do-PROG
The man doesn't work.   (Canonge 1949)

(106) *sarii?   -tsa?   ke   u   suwai-tu*
dog   DECL   NEG   D4A want-PROG
The dog doesn't like him.   (Canonge 1949)

The negative imperative marker keta? (/ken-ta?/) always occurs in initial position. Negative imperatives do not occur with a simple verb stem, but with one of the variants, according to number, of /-tun/ (progressive).

(107) *keta?   nu   kuya?a-ku-tu*
NEG!   1xAs fear-CAUS-PROG
Don't be afraid of me.   (96:18)

(108) *keta?-ka   mu-bisi-tu-u*
NEG-!p   INSTR-blow-PROG-p
Don't blow your noses.   (127:7)

The verbalizing suffix -*wai* means 'be without, lack', indicating negative possession.

(109) *situ   kwasinaboo?   kwasi-waai-tu*
D1   snake   tail-lack-PROG
This snake lacks a tail.   (36:14)

In the verb *kehewa* 'be all gone, no longer have', -*wa* combines with the negative *ke* (cf. *kehena* 'nothing').
The verb *muni* 'fail to do, be unable to do' indicates negative ability.

(110) *puu   muhyi urii   muni-hka-ku-su   suru oha?ahnakatu*
COGp   door^A D4Ap unable-ST-DS-INTENS D4   coyote

sooti   wuh-tókwe-nu
much^A   INSTR-kill-PST
They still being unable to do their door, Coyote clubbed many. (4:17)

6

Other modality

Three forms which mark modal notions are presented in this section. The form witsa (obligation) occurs in the second position, usually reserved for a mood marker, with otherwise normal declarative sentence syntax.

(111)   *tanʉ*   *-witsa*   *nah*   *paa-kʉ-hu*   *ma*   *wihi-nʉ*
         1iNi   NEC   just   water-in-to   D2As   throw-PST
         We ought to just throw him in the water.   (6:20)

(112)   *ʉnʉ*   *-witsa*   *nʉ*   *naki̱-ma*   *tsaai-mi?a-rʉ*
         2Ns   NEC   1xGs   ear-on   hold-go-PROG
         You ought to go holding onto my ear.   (20:17)

Normal declarative syntax is again used with the inferential mood enclitic *-kia* 'I wonder if, I guess'.

(113)   *sitʉ*   *-kʉ-se?*   *pia-rʉrahyapʉ*   *ʉnʉ*   *-kia*   *si?ana*   *habii-yʉ*
         D1   EVID-CTR   big-meatball   2Ns   INFER   D1L   lie-DUR

            me   *u*   *niikwii-yʉ*
            QUOT   D4A   say-DUR
         This big meatball said to him, "(I) guess you're lying here?"   (21:12)

(114) *suru* *-ku-seʔ*   *suhka* *bu*   *tueʔti*   *sumu-ʔ* *-kia*   *u-paʔa-tu*
       D4   EVID-CTR   D4As   COG   child^A   one-NS   NFER   2As-on-along

       tusí-nu   *me-ku*
       spit-PST   QUOT-EVID
       That one said to her child, "I wonder if one spit on you?"   (13:8)

The form *noo* (evidential necessity), meaning 'must', occurs in second position following either a word or a phrase. The following example shows that *noo* and *-kia* (inferential) may occur together as a unit in modal position.

(115) *suru*   *noo* *-kia*   *hini*   *huhtsúuʔ* *ma*   *ra-puhe-htsi*   *tai*
       D4   NEC   INFER   what?   bird   D2A   INSTR-drop-SS   1iAp

       tsaah-tuhka-ku-nu
       good-eat-CAUS-PST
       I guess some kind of bird, dropping it, must have caused us to eat
       well.   (18:35)

7

Nondistinct Argument Phenomena

A predication normally entails reference to persons or objects which stand in particular grammatical relations to a predicate as its ARGUMENTS. There are cases, however, in which one or more such referents is either unknown and, therefore, unspecifiable or is for some reason left indefinite. There are also cases in which a single referent stands in more than one grammatical relation to the same predicate. Such phenomena are treated together as NONDISTINCT ARGUMENTS under the headings UNSPECIFIED SUBJECTS, UNSPECIFIED OBJECTS, REFLEXIVES/PASSIVES, and RECIPROCALS.

7.1. Unspecified subject. A semantically unspecified subject is indicated by *ta*. This form distinguishes neither person nor number.

(116) *so-ko   ra   sooh-kahni-bai-hku   uru-u-ku   no-bitu-nu*
      D3-at   UNSPˆA much-house-have-DS   D4-p-at   haul-arrive-PST
      There where they had many teepees, (those ones) camped among
      them.   (106:34)

Ta is frequently used to form neologisms, such as *ta ukwiʔena* 'ether' (lit. what one smells), *puku ra nohkoʔena* 'oven' (lit. place in which one bakes [biscuits]), and *pupaʔaku ra turahkwiʔneʔena* 'ironing board' (lit. place on which one irons).

7.2. Unspecified object. An unspecified object is indicated by one of two verbal prefixes, either *ma-*, having to do with some object related to activity by the hand, or *tu-*, having to do with some object's lower end or foot.

339

(117) *ma-kwinuma*   'make one dizzy/drunk'
       ma-kwitso?ai   'save someone'
       ma-tsųbaki   'glue/stick something to'
       tɨh-tɨki   'plant something (pointed end down)'
       tɨ-boo   'write something'
       tɨ-?eka   'paint something'

7.3. Reflexive/Passive. The verbal prefix *na-* marks a reflexive or passive sense.

(118) *na-maka?muki*   'get one's self ready'
       na-marɥni   'hurt oneself'
       na-buni   'look at oneself'
       na-suwatsi   'lose one's mind'
       na-ropɥsa   'be beaded'
       na-rohtsana   'be hung up/hanging'
       na-rɨhka?   'groceries (that which is bought to be eaten)'

Special semantic constraints distinguish which occurrences of *na-* are reflexive and which reference an inanimate object. This lies partially in the final syllable of the stem *-ki/-ni/-tsi/-i* 'being' or *-sa/-na/-ka/-a* 'doing', respectively.

(119) *surɨ* *-kɥ-se?*   *na-marɥni-?*   *nɨ?* *me* *yɥkwi-htsi* *nahúbinii-yɥ*
       D4   EVID-CTR   REFL-hurt-REAL   1xNs QUOT say-SS   groan-DUR
       That one saying "I hurt myself," was groaning.   (6:14)

(120) *tsaa*   *nɨ?* *na-boo-ri*   *kwasu?-i* *suwaai-tɨ*
       good   1xNs   REFL-draw-NOMˆA   coat-A   want-PROG
       I want a nice designed coat. (32:8)

7.4. Reciprocal. The verbal prefix /nanah-/ (reciprocal) may be a reduplicated form of *na-* (reflexive).

(121) *nana-kwɨhɨ*   'marry (each other)'
       nana-buni?   'window (thing for seeing each other)'
       nana-watsi   'misunderstand (lose each other)'

8

Derivational Morphology

While the distinction between derivational processes and inflection is not always sharp, this section presents those more clearly derivational principles by which nouns, verbs, and adjectives are formed by the addition of affixes to various stems. Inflectional noun suffixes are discussed in §9.

8.1. Noun morphology. While some nouns are not made up of smaller units, others can be analyzed as stems plus derivational affixes. These stems and affixes are of several types. They are discussed below in terms of whether they are derived from underlying nouns or verbs.

One class of affixes derives nouns from stems that are themselves nominal. The suffixes *-htsi?* and *-wee?* are affective in that they carry the notions DIMINUTIVE and ENDEARMENT,which generally, although not always, overlap in each of the two suffixes.

(122) *tuibi-htsi?*   'young man, brave'
       sitɨ-htsi?   'this little one'
       tɨe?tɨ-htsi?   'dear child'
       nɨmi wɨ?yɨrɨhki-htsi?   'scares people' (name of a quail)

(123) *tɨtaa-tɨ*   *nɨ*   *rua?*   *tɨ?ɨya-tɨ-wee?*
       little-NOM   1xGs   son   fear-NOM-DIM
       My poor little son is afraid.   (83:29)

The suffix *-htsi?* may also have a pejorative sense, as in the noun *senihtɨ-htsi?* 'one of an inferior kind'.

The prefix *na-* derives nouns from nominal stems, designating a part-whole relationship, as in *na-?omo* 'wagon wheel', *na-rohtɨma?* 'lid' (lit. its stopper), na-rɨnoo?*a saddle' (lit. its loader).

The prefix *naʔ-* derives nonspecific kinship relationships from general terms referring to humans.

(124)   *naʔ-waʔihpʉʔ*   'female kinsman'
        naʔ-renahpʉʔ   'male kinsman'
        naʔ-nʉmʉ   'kinsman'

Other suffixes derive nouns from verbal stems. The suffix *-tʉ* (/-tʉn/) forms an imperfective participle indicating the person or thing which performs an action or possesses a quality.

(125)   *ohaʔahnaka-tʉ*   'coyote' (lit. one who has yellow underneath)
        kokoráʔaʔarahimaʔe-tʉ   'chicken hawk' (lit. one who steals chickens)
        tosapi-tʉ   'white (color)'
        poyohka-rʉ   'trotter'
        namamohka-rʉ   'hitched animal or object'
        nawoʔo-rʉ   'striped object'
        takwʉsa-rʉ   'item loosened (by foot)'

The suffix *-pʉ* (perfective participle), with underlying form /-Hpʉh/, marks nouns derived from verbs through completed process or change. The nouns name those things that result from the activity of the verb, or less frequently those things that are simply acted upon through the verbal activity. The noun resulting from an adjective stem with the suffix *-pʉ* indicates 'one who has the quality of being'.

(126)   *tekwa-pʉ*   'word' (lit. that which is spoken)
        ahwe-pʉ   'tuber' (lit. that which has been dug up)
        naboo-pʉ   'picture' (lit. that which is drawn/sketched)
        kwʉhʉ-pʉ   'a captive' (lit. one who has been captured)
        pia-pʉ   'giant person' (AJ stem)

The suffix *-na* (continued action) derives a range of nouns in relation to the continued action named by the intransitive or transitive verb with nonspecific or cognate object. Some of the nouns refer to physical objects related to the verbal activity as instrument or object, and some refer to more abstract notions.

(127)   *poma-na*   'picking'
        nʉhka-na   'dancing, dance'
        pitʉ-na   'arriving, arrival'
        tʉhkaʔe-na   'food'
        yʉhkwihka-na   'seat'
        yahne-na   'laughing, laughter'

The suffix *-wapi̱* (agentive), from /-wapih/, may more rightfully be termed a compound-forming noun with agentive meaning. It marks the person or animal that carries out the action of a verb.

(128) *tʉnoo-wapi̱*   'pack animal'
       hʉa-wapi̱   'fisherman'
       tʉni̱suabetai-wapi̱   'teacher'
       tʉe-tekwʉni-wapi̱   'Indian brave'

A person named by such a noun does not just occasionally carry out the named activity, but is, rather, a professional, a specialist, or one paid to carry it out. Thus, a term with the suffix *-wapi̱* has honorific overtones.

The suffix *-ʔ* (nominal) derives nouns and pronouns from verbs and demonstrative elements.

(129) *tuka-ʔ*   'light, lamp'
       kwasinaboo-ʔ   'snake' (that whose tail is striped)
       narʉmʉʉ-ʔ   'town, store'
       kwʉhti-ʔ   'victim' (one who is shot)
       taʔwoʔi-ʔ   'gun'
       nʉ-ʔ   'I'
       u-ʔ   'he, she, it' (remote distal)

8.2. Verb morphology. While many verbs are not reducible to smaller parts, others consist of a stem and a verbalizing suffix. The suffix *-ʔi* (temporary state), for example, has the meaning 'being in the state or condition of' or may reference quality.

(130) *esi-tʉyaʔi-*   'faint' (esi-tʉyaitʉ 'unconscious')
       esi-tsʉnʉʔi-   'gray in appearance'
       haʔwoʔi-   'hollow, loose'
       papi̱-tsʉnʉʔi-   'having tangled hair'
       pʉhʉ-noʔi-   'pluck hair/eyebrows' (cause to be taken away)

The examples of (130) name temporary conditions and require either *-tuʔi* (unrealized) or *-tʉ* (progressive) as aspect marker; otherwise the forms might be confused with those having the suffix *-i* (realized). The presence of the suffix *-ʔi* (temporary state) can be determined by adding *-tuʔi*, as in *pʉhka-ʔi-tuʔi* 'will (temporarily) stop crying'. These forms do not have *-i* (realized); they only state that a condition will be present *(-ʔi-tuʔi)* or is temporarily present *(-ʔi-tʉ)*.

Postpositions have forms with an added *-i* meaning 'be' in some locative constructions. Such postpositions include *-paʔai* 'be over', *-kuhpai* 'be inside', *-kabai* 'be in or among', and *-nai* 'side' or 'direction'.

(131) situkwʉ   -ku-seʔ   pʉ-hʉ   ina-pʉh-a   pʉ-hʉ   ina-wata-paʔa-i-ki̱
       D1d   EVID-CTR   CO-Gd   jerk-NOM-A   CO-Gd   jerk-pole-on-VB-at

       roh-tsániʔi-nʉ
       INSTR-hangˆup-PST
       These two hung their jerked meat over their meat poles.   (112:25)

The verbalizing suffix *-nai* 'become' derives compound verbs from nouns.

(132) situ -kʉ-seʔ siʔahru   marʉʉ-kʉ-hu   toʔi-nʉ   pʉ   kwasuʔ-i
       D1   EVID-CTR   D1Lˆalong   D2p-at-to   goˆup-PST   COGs   dress-A

       sʉmʉ-sihwapʉ-nai-hkʉ
       one-torn-became-DS
       This one along here went up to them, her dress having become completely torn.   (53:24)

The verbalizing suffix *-pai* 'have' with an inanimate noun shows possession of the item named by the noun. The noun is not grammatically marked as accusative.

(133) *puhihwi-pai*   'have money'
       pianohkoʔawo-bai   'have a large biscuit oven'
       kahni-bai   'have a teepee/house'

Possession of a noun referring to the personal characteristics of an animate being is marked by the suffix *-ka* 'have' (as personal characteristic).

(134) *puʔe-ka*   'be a Christian' (lit. have a road/path)
       ohaʔahna-ka   'Coyote' (lit. have yellow underarms)
       turʉeʔtʉ-ka   'have children'

The verb suffix *-ʔa* indicates 'do, make' forming a verb from a basic noun.

(135) *piso-ʔa-*   'stick someone, puncture'
       nariso-ʔa-   'give an enema'
       puʔe-ʔa-   'make/construct a road'

The suffix (/-yun/) -yu (verbalizer), possibly related to -yu (durative aspect [§13.7]), forms a verb stem from an adjective root or quantifier.

(136)   soo-yo   'be many' (cf. *soo* 'much')
        tʉmarʉʉmoa-yu   'be a lot' (cf. *tʉmarʉʉmoa* 'much')

8.3. Adjective morphology. As with nouns and verbs, adjectives are simple or derived by a derivational suffix. In many instances this suffix is identical to those found in nouns, particularly the imperfective participial suffix -tʉ/-rʉ and the perfective participial suffix -pʉ. Certain adjectives cannot occur as free forms without the addition of one of these suffixes, although they may be combined with other elements to form compounds without them.

A few stems which take the imperfective participial suffix -tʉ/-rʉ are listed in (137).

(137)   tʉeʔ-tʉ   'small'
        sʉmʉ-rʉ   'one' (and other numerals)
        tʉtaa-tʉ   'small'
        nʉʉtsʉkʉna-rʉ   'tied up'
        sʉʉhpe-tʉ   'level, flat'
        paʔitsiʔwʉnʉ-rʉ   'short' (stand short)
        taʔoki-tʉ   'spilled'
        pihpokaa-rʉ   'uneven' (as a hem)

The perfective participial suffix -pʉ forms adjectives which reference completed action, as in (138).

(138)   pia-pʉ   'big, large'   papʉsi-pʉ   'rotten'
        yuu-pʉ   'fat'   pasa-pʉ   'dry'
        nuhtsa-pʉ   'bent, stooped'   namʉsokoa-pʉ   'buried'

Reduplicated adjectives indicate duality or plurality, whether in immediate succession or habitually.

(139) soobeʔsʉ   -kʉ-tsaʔ   rʉa   suʔana   u   toya-kʉmaʔ-kʉ
       long^ago   EVID-DECL   QUOT   D4L   D4G   mountain-edge-at

           pʉ-bʉeh-tʉ-ʉ   kahní-bai
           RDP-ago-NOM-p   house-have
       Long ago, they say, somewhere there beside that mountain, people of
       long ago had a camp.   (69:1)

(140) *nɨ-*   *bia?*   *-se?*   *pi-bia-pɨh-i*   *waa-wata-yɨkwi-?ee-yu̱*
       1xGs   mother   CTR   RDP-big-ABS-A   cedar-pole-setˆup-REP-DUR
       My mother would set up long cedar poles.   (109:2)

Numerals are never reduplicated, except for *sɨmɨ?* 'one', which has a reduplicated form *sɨsɨmɨ?* 'some' (§4.6).

(141) *su?ana* *-kɨ-tsa?*   *-rɨa*   *sɨ-sɨmɨ?-nɨɨ*   *nɨmɨ-nɨɨ*   *nobitɨ-nu̱*
       D4L   EVID-DECL   QUOT   RDP-one-Np   Comanche-Np   camp-PST
       Somewhere there, they say, some Comanches camped.   (73:1)

Similarly, the nonnumeric quantifiers *soo* 'much, many' and *tɨmarɨɨmoa*
'much, many' are never reduplicated.

Adjectives dealing with certain qualities and properties are modified in
terms of extent or degree. This may be through the use of separate lexical
items, such as *nohi?* 'very' or *tɨbitsi* 'really', or through the use of the intensifying suffix /-hɨn/.

(142) *nohi?*   *tɨh-tɨtaa-tɨɨ*   *tɨ-rɨehpɨ?-rɨɨ*   *tai*   *tsaah-tɨhka-ku-nu̱*
       very   RDP-little-NP   RDP-child-Np   1iAp   good-eat-CAUS-PST
       Very little children fed us well.   (75:28)

(143) *surɨ*   *-se?*   *tɨbitsi*   *tsaa*   *sanahkóo-?*   *kama-nu̱*
       D4N   CTR   really   good   gum-Ns   taste-PST
       That tasted like really good gum.   (110:20)

(144) *su?ana*   *pia-pɨ-hɨ*   *pimoróo-?*   *paa-kɨma?-ru*   *kimaa-yu̱*
       D4L   big-ABS-INTENS   cow-Ns   water-edge-along   come-DUR
       Somewhere there, a big cow was coming along the edge of the
       water.   (19:1)

9

Noun Inflection

Nouns have different forms depending on their function in sentences or as isolated words.

9.1. Absolutive. Quoting Langacker, "Absolutive suffixes are one of the more distinctive and characteristic features of [Uto-Aztecan] grammar. An absolutive suffix, in UA terms, is an ending with no apparent semantic value that appears in citation forms but may drop when a noun is subjected to various morphological processes, such as affixation, compounding, or reduplication" (1977:77). This general statement for UA is true for Comanche.

Although no constant semantic value can categorically be given to any particular absolutive suffix in Comanche, there are small classes of nouns which have a certain semantic cohesiveness. The absolutive ending *-pi*, for example, seems to mark a class of mass or collective nouns.

(145) *toya-bi*   'mountain'   *hani-bi*   'corn'
       ona-bi   'salt'   *hunu?-bi*   'creek, river'
       waah-pi   'cedar tree'   *huuh-pi*   'tree, stick'
       tɨah-pi   'chickasaw plum'   *poko-pi*   'berries, nuts'

The suffix *-pi̱* marks a class of color nouns.

(146) *oha-pi̱*   'yellow'   *tuhu-pi̱*   'black'
       otɨ-pi̱   'brown'   *tosa-pi̱*   'white'

A set of kinship terms has the suffix *-hpɨ?*.

347

(147) *a-hpʉʔ*   'father'   *waʔi-hpʉʔ*   'woman'
       samo-hpʉʔ   'sibling'   *tuinʉ-hpʉʔ*   'boy'
       tʉe-hpʉʔ   'child'   *tena-hpʉʔ*   'man'
       kuma-hpʉʔ   'husband'

Absolutive suffixes are often absent when a noun is followed by a postposition or is part of a compound.

(148) *huu-ma* 'with the stick'   *waa-watayʉkwi* 'set up cedar poles'

A form homophonous with the perfective participial suffix *-pʉ* (§8.3) functions as an absolutive suffix.

(149) *soni-pʉ*   'grass'   *puhi-pʉ*   'weeds, leaves'
       soni-tu   'through the grass'   *puhi-kabaiki*   'through the weeds'

9.2. Dual and plural number. Nouns other than proper, mass, color, and collective nouns may be inflected for number by the suffixes (-*nʉ-hʉh* →) -*nʉhʉ* (dual), (*nʉ-wʉh* →) -*nʉkwʉ* (dual), or -*nʉʉ* (plural). These distinctions of number are usually not marked for nonhuman nouns, except in contexts where number is emphasized or in narratives where it is used rhetorically to personify an otherwise inanimate object. Where context makes number clear, forms unmarked for number predominate. The two forms for dual number are used interchangeably. A simple noun, a derived noun with *-pʉ* (perfective participle), and a derived noun with final glottal are presented in (150) to illustrate formation of dual and plural forms.

(150) **Singular**   **Dual**   **Plural**
       kahni   *kahni-nʉhʉ*   *kahni-nʉʉ*   'house'
       hibi-pʉ   *hibipʉ-nʉkwʉ*   *hibipʉ-nʉʉ*   'drunk'
       hʉarʉʔ   *hʉarʉʔ-nʉhʉ*   *hʉarʉʔ-nʉʉ*   'trap'

Derived nouns with *-tʉ/-rʉ* (imperfective participle) omit the *-nʉ* portion of dual and plural suffixes, resulting in the shortened forms *-hʉ/-kwʉ* (dual) and *-ʉ* (plural).

(151) **Singular**   **Dual**   **Plural**
       ohaʔahnakatʉ   *ohaʔahnakatʉ-hʉ*   *ohaʔahnakatʉ-ʉ*   'coyote'
       ooʔrʉ   *ooʔrʉ-kwʉ*   *ooʔrʉ-ʉ*   'clothing'

Nouns derived from adjectives show reduplication of their first syllables in dual and plural forms.

(152)

Singular	Dual	Plural	
tʉtaatʉ	tʉh-tʉtaatʉkwʉ	tʉh-tʉtaatʉ-ʉ	'child'
mutsipʉ	mu-mutsipʉ-nʉhʉ	mu-mutsipʉ-nʉʉ	'sharp one'

Some kinship nouns add -*a* before dual and plural suffixes.

(153)

Singular	Dual	Plural	
tuibihtsiʔ	tuibihtsiʔ-a-nʉhʉ	tuibihtsiʔ-a-nʉʉ	'brave'
waʔihpʉʔ	waʔihpʉʔ-a-nʉkwʉ	waʔihpʉʔ-a-nʉʉ	'woman'

9.3. Accusative. Comanche nouns are overtly marked for only three cases—genitive, accusative, or vocative. In subject position, for example, a noun may be inflected for number or may have an absolutive ending; but it has no nominative ending associated directly with its syntactic function as subject. Accusative, on the other hand, is overtly marked on nouns functioning as direct or indirect objects, as well as on those functioning as subjects of certain subordinate clauses (§15.2). Singular nouns are marked for accusative case by -*i* or -*a*. For singular nouns ending in voiced, high *u* or *ʉ*, -*i* replaces that final vowel. In the examples which follow, forms listed as nominative are, as indicated above, actually unmarked by a case ending.

(154)

Nominative	Accusative	
puku	puki	'horse'
ʉhʉ	ʉhi	'blanket'
tʉehpʉʔrʉ	tʉehpʉʔri	'child'
ohaʔahnakatʉ	ohaʔahnakati	'coyote'

For nonderived singular nouns ending in low vowels *a* or *o*, -*i* replaces that vowel and lowers to -*e* (actually coalescence of *ai* or *oi* to *e*).

(155)

Nominative	Accusative	
moʔo	moʔe	'hand'
paka	pake	'arrow'

Singular nouns ending in phonemic *h* add -*a* (accusative).

(156)

Nominative	Accusative	
animui	animuih-a	'fly'
haitsi̱	haitsi̱h-a	'friend'
pitsipʉ	pitsipʉh-a	'milk'
tʉnoowapi̱	tʉnoowapi̱h-a	'pack animal'

Singular nouns ending in glottal also add -*a* (accusative).

(157)   **Nominative**   **Accusative**
    taiboo?   *taiboo?-a*   'stranger'
    kwasinaboo?   *kwasinaboo?-a*   'snake'

Singular nouns ending in -*pi*, -*bi*, or -*wi* require -*hta* (accusative).

(158)   **Nominative**   **Accusative**
    huuhpi   *huuhpi-hta*   'stick'
    wobi   *wobi-hta*   'board'
    puhihwi   *puhihwi-hta*   'money'

Many singular nouns do not follow the above rules for formation of the accusative case. Known exceptions have been indicated in the dictionary, but there are undoubtedly many exceptions of which we are unaware.

(159)   **Nominative**   **Accusative**
    kahni   *kahni*   'teepee'
    po?a   *po?a-i*   'bark, skin'
    woinu   *woinu-i*   'horn'
    motso   *motso-i*   'beard'

Note, in particular, that derived nouns ending in -*na* have no special accusative form.

(160)   **Nominative**   **Accusative**
    pomana   *pomana*   'picking'
    pitʉna   *pitʉna*   'arriving'

Dual nouns are inflected for accusative case by adding the suffix -*i*. Stem-final *h* is deleted and, by vowel harmony, preceding vowels ʉ also become *i*. (Dual suffixes -*nʉkwʉ* and -*kwʉ* do not occur in accusative forms.)

(161)   **Nominative**   **Accusative**
    ahpʉ?nʉhʉ   *ahpʉ?nihi*   'fathers'
    tʉhtʉtaatʉhʉ   *tʉhtʉtaatihi*   'children'

Similarly, plural nouns are inflected for accusative case by adding the suffix -*i*. By vowel harmony, preceding vowels ʉ also become *i*, and the cluster is reduced to *ii*.

(162) **Nominative**   **Accusative**
       nɨmɨnɨɨ   nɨmɨnii   'Comanches'
       tɨrɨeʔtɨɨ   tɨrɨeʔtii   'children'

9.4. Genitive. A noun or pronoun functioning as possessor precedes its head noun, some being distinctively marked as genitives but others not. Singular derived nouns ending in (underlying) /-tɨn/, for example, occur with -a (genitive) when functioning as possessors, as do other nouns having a final *n*.

(163) tɨehpɨʔrɨn-a nohiʔ   'child's toy'
       ohaʔahnakatɨn-a kwasi   'Coyote's tail'
       atɨhɨn-a ahpɨʔ   'stranger's father'
       uʔahrɨn-a moʔo   'anyone's hand'

Other singular nouns functioning as possessors are marked by -a or -hta (accusative) (§9.3).

(164) animuih-a kobe   'fly's face'
       wasápeʔ-a kwɨhɨ   'bear's wife'
       huuhpi-hta moka   'tree's branch'

Dual nouns add -ɨ (genitive). Plural nouns have no special genitive form but like other possessors they precede the possessed noun.

(165) wasápeʔnɨh-ɨ kahni   '(two) bears' house'
       tɨhtɨtaatɨɨ nohiʔ   'children's toy'

9.5. Vocative. Kinship terms used as forms of address or in calling have special vocative forms. Most of the known examples involve an *h* substituting for stem-final glottal.

(166) **Nominative**   **Vocative**
       piaʔ   piah   'mother'
       tɨiʔ   tɨih   'friend'

Derived-noun kinship terms ending in -pɨʔ undergo regular phonological changes when the vocative -h substitutes for the final glottal.

(167) **Nominative**   **Vocative**
       ahpɨʔ   apɨ   'father'

Other dual and plural nouns have no special vocative form.

10

Postpositions

Postpositions are a rich and varied class, expressing locative, directional, instrumental, and other notions. While most postpositions are enclitic and can occur only in association with a head noun or pronoun, a few are free forms that can also occur alone. Many postpositions combine with each other and some have different forms depending on phonological considerations or on the type of verb with which they occur. Most postpositions reference semantic ranges of location or direction.

10.1. Locative. Several postpositions, such as *-ka/-ku̱* 'in, at, on', locate a referent spatially.[6]

(168) pu̱   *tu̱ʔrikúuʔ-kwasu̱-ku̱-pu̱-ka*   *pitu̱-nu̱*
      COG   prairieˆdog-cook-CAUS-NOM-at   arrive-PST
      (He) arrived at his cooked prairie dog.   (10:20)

The vowel of the postposition often assimilates to a preceding deictic root, as (169) shows.

(169) *so-ko̱*   *ma*   *ku̱ʔe-ku̱*   *marii*   *bitu̱-hka*
      D3-at   D2G   top-at   D2Ap   arrive-DS
      ... as they arrived there at the top of it.   (28:25)

Other locative postpositions include those of (170).

---

[6]The first form occurs following a voiceless vowel; the second after a voiced vowel.

353

(170)   *-hi/-ti*   'in, at'   *-miihtsi?*   'near'
        -hoi   'around'   *-munakwʉ*   'in front of'
        -kaba   'among'   *-pa?a*   'over, above, on'
        -kuhpa   'inside, within'   *-pinakwʉ*   'behind'
        -ku?eku   'on top of'   *-tuhka*   'under'
        -kʉma?   'beside'   *-tʉbinaa?(weki)*   'in the middle of'
        -ma   'on'   *-yahne*   'at/on the other side of'

The postposition *-hi/-ti* may, in fact, be considered an agreement marker in that its distribution is severely restricted by a verb of movement.

(171)   ʉ   *manaa?-nakwʉ-hi*   *ma-sukaa*
        2Gs   further-side-at   UNSPEC-feel
        Feel on your further side!   (61:30)

(172)   *sʉmʉ-?*   *-kʉ-se?*   *tena-hpʉ?*   *hunu?-betu-ti*   *buni-nu*
        one-Ns   EVID-CTR   man-ABS   creek-toward-at   see-PST
        One man looked toward the creek.   (122:14)

10.2. Allative. The general allative postposition is *-ku* 'to, into'. It occurs in clauses with verbs of motion.

(173)   *paa-ku*   *-kʉ-se?*   *surʉ*   *kima-nu*
        water-to   EVID-CTR   D4Ns   come-PST
        That one came to the water.   (93:5)

Other directional postpositions include those of (174). Of these, *-metʉ* 'at' deserves special mention in that it is apparently limited to occurrence with verbs of laughing.

(174)   *-hu*   'to, into'   *-petu*   'toward'
        -kahtu   'into'   *-tu*   'through, along'
        -metʉ   'at'   *-tʉ*   'from'
        -nai   'from'   *-waka*   'toward'
        -nakwʉ   'side, direction'

10.3. Instrumental. The postposition *-ma* 'with, by' marks an instrument involved in an action.

(175)   *sitʉu*   *kuyunii?-a*   *pʉʉ*   *wasʉ-?i-ma*   *tsihá-kwitso?ai-nu*
        D1Np   turkey-A   COGp   kill-REAL-INSTR   hunger-save-PST
        They were saved from starvation by turkeys they killed.   (120:21)

10.4. Partitive. There are two postpositions signalling that part of an object or group of items is being referred to, rather than the whole object or group of items. These partitive postpositions are /-kᵤhu/ and /-mantᵤn/.

(176) sᵤmᵤ-ʔ   urᵤᵤ-matᵤ   ma-waka   nahá-biitᵤ
       one-Ns   D4Np-PART   D2A-toward   happen-arrive
       One of them happened onto him.   (86:18)

(177) urᵤᵤ-kᵤhu   u   yuhu-wehki-pᵤ   wihnu   surᵤ   pi-sikwanúuʔi-nu
       D4N-PART   D4 fat-search-NOM   then   D4Ns   INSTR-slide-PST
       Then that one, the fattest of them to be found, slid down.   (5:11)

These two postpositions occur with -i (accusative) when the noun or pronoun they mark is functioning as an object.

(178) situ-   kᵤ-seʔ   ma   piaʔ   u-kᵤhi   yaa-ʔe-tᵤ   ma-rii
       D1   EVID-CTR   D2G   mother D4-PART^A   take-REP-PROG D2-Ap

       himi-miʔa̱
       give-go
       Taking some of it, her mother went to give it to them.   (73:8,9)

(179) u-mati   nᵤᵤʔ   noo-htsi   miʔa-nu
       D4-PART^A   2N   haul-ss   go-PST
       Carrying some of it, you go.   (97:27)

10.5. Miscellaneous. Several other postpositions express diverse concepts. Simple coordination of two nominal elements is marked by /-maʔaiн/ 'with' following the second element. More generally, this postposition expresses the notion of accompaniment.

(180) ...sᵤmᵤ--ʔ rena-hpᵤʔ   pᵤ kwᵤhᵤ-maʔai   pᵤ-hᵤ   tᵤeʔtᵤ-maʔai
       ...one-Ns   man-ABS   COGs wife-with   CO-GD   child-with

       no-miʔa-nu̱
       haul-go-PST
       ...a man, his wife, and their children moved away.   (99:1)

Coordination of two elements from one clause to another is indicated by -suʔa 'and' in a second clause.

(181) *sitʉ*   *-suʔa*   *-kʉ-seʔ*   *ma*   *haitsi*   *suʔah-ru*   *ku-roʔi-nʉ*
       D1   and   EVID-CTR   D2G   friend   D4L-along   INSTR-goˆup-PST
       His friend also bobbed up along there.   (58:17)

There is a qualifier -taka 'just, only' and two intensifiers -sʉ and -tuku, the latter often translatable as 'same'.

(182) *nah*   *nʉkwʉ*   *u*   *tohobe-mati*   *-taka*   *tʉ-tsih-kaʔa-ruʔi*
       just   1xNd   D4G   hindquarter-PARTˆA only   food-INSTR-cut-UNR
       We will cut off only part of its hindquarter.   (97:29)

(183) *yee*   *surʉ-sʉ-tuku*   *ʉnʉ*   *nʉ*   *kaa-behka-noo-rʉ*
       oh   D4-INTENS-INTENS   2Ns   1xAs   deceit-kill-haul-PROG
       Oh, you are the same one who is moving along cheating me. (23:30)

Finally, similarity of conditions is marked by the postposition -waʔi 'like, similar to'.

(184) *ihka*   *buni*   *pʉ-waʔi*   *tahʉ*   *naah-kwabi-ka-tuʔih-a*
       D1As   see   COs-like   1iGd   continue-lie-ST-UNR-A
       Look at this which we will continue to lie like.   (41:8)

10.6. Ordering. Postpositions may combine to form complex forms. It is useful to distinguish first-order postpositions, second-order postpositions, and so forth, in the structure of these complex forms. A second-order element can follow a first-order element, a third-order can follow a second-order, and so on. Not all possible combinations actually occur, and the exact limits are unknown. Most of the simple forms are first-order elements, and therefore are not listed here. Other orders are as listed in (185).

(185) Second order: *-tu/-ru*   'through, along' /-tun/
                       -ka/-kʉ   'at'   /-kah/
       Third order: *-hu*   'into'   /-hun/
                       -ku   'to'
       Fourth order: *-tʉ*   'from'   /-tʉh/
       Fifth order: *-hi/-ti*   'in, at'
       Sixth order: *-taka*   'just'
                       -tuku   (intensifier)

(186) ...*paa-kʉmaʔ-ru*   *kimaa-yʉ*
          water-edge-along   come-DUR
       ...was coming along the edge of the water.   (19:1)

(187)   ...*hunu?-ma-tu*   *pohpí-nu̱*
        creek-on-along   jump-PST
        ...jumped into the creek.   (52:15)

(188)   ...*paa-ku̱-hu*   *ma*   *wihi-nu̱*
        water-in-to   D2   throw-PST
        ...throw him into the water.   (6:20)

Postpositions, whether simple or complex, directly follow a noun or pronoun to form postpositional phrases. With a few minor exceptions, the noun
in such a phrase is otherwise unmarked for case. As two exceptions, the two
postpositions -*ku̱ma?* 'beside' and -*tu̱bi̱naa?(weki̱)* 'in the middle of' follow a
noun optionally marked as genitive. A pronoun in a postpositional phrase is
usually a normal nominative form less any -*?* nominalizer, but again there are
a few exceptional forms, as indicated in (189).

(189)   *tamu̱*   1i (with postposition)
        mu̱mu̱   2p (with postposition)
        pu̱   sˆREFL (with postposition)

Demonstrative adjectives or other elements that modify a noun marked by a
postposition are themselves also marked by a copy of that same postposition.

(190)   ...*sii-ma*   *pia-huu-ma*   *ma*   *wu̱h-kúpa-nu̱*
        D1-INSTR   big-wood-INSTR   D2A   INSTR-kill-PST
        ...killed him with this big club.   (17:23)

(191)   ...*si-ku̱-hi*   *taitu̱-ku̱-hi*   *ma*   *puni-hka*
        D1-at-toˆA   cave-at-toˆA   D2A   see-DS
        ...as he looked into this cave.   (91:9)

11

Noun Modifiers

11.1. Demonstrative adjectives. Demonstrative elements reflect a spatial ranking from the point of view of the speaker. There is a three-way distinction between PROXIMAL, DISTAL, and SCATTERED—the last of these encompassing both spatial scattering and type scattering in the sense of the word 'various'—and within the first two categories a further distinction between IMMEDIATE and REMOVED. The demonstrative stems are listed in (192).

(192)		PROXIMAL	DISTAL	SCATTERED
	IMMEDIATE	*i-*	*o-*	
				e-
	REMOVED	*ma-*	*u-*	

Demonstrative adjectives may be simple, as in (192), or may be derived by the suffix *-tʉ/-rʉ* (imperfective participle), and can be further marked for dual or plural number. Since number distinctions are generally optional, derived demonstrative adjectives may appear unmarked for number, as *itʉ* (immediate proximal) and *orʉ* (immediate distal), or marked for plural number, as *itʉʉ* (immediate proximal plural) and *orʉʉ* (immediate distal plural), and similarly for *-e* (scattered). The forms **etʉhʉand *etʉkwʉ* which would encode SCATTERED DUAL are semantically anomalous and do not occur.

All vowel-initial demonstrative adjectives may also occur with initial *s* (*si-, so-,* etc.) to indicate that the speaker presupposes the hearer to have prior knowledge of the thing or person referred to.

(193) *setʉʉ*   *waʔihpʉʔa-nʉʉ*   *kohtoo-htsi*   *tʉkʉh-manii-yʉ*
       D5NP   woman-Np   make^fire-SS   food-prepare-DUR
       The various women, making fire(s), were preparing food.   (56:16)

(194) *surʉ -kʉ-seʔ*   *tena-hpʉʔ*   *hina*   *mʉkwʉ me*   *uhri*   *niikwii-yʉ*
       D4   EVID-CTR   man-ABS   what?^A   2Nd   QUOT D4Ad say-DUR
       That man asked those two, "What do you two want?"   (57:3)

A demonstrative adjective may be inflected for accusative or genitive case. In the accusative case, dual and plural derived forms have the vowel *i* common to other nouns and adjectives with the derivational suffix *-tʉ/-rʉ* (imperfective participle). Singular derived forms, however, are marked with the special accusative ending /-Hka/ that occurs elsewhere only in *hahka* 'whom?'. Genitive dual and plural forms are identical to the corresponding nominative forms, while genitive singular forms are identical to accusative singular forms, as indicated in (195) and (196).

(195)

		As	Ad	Ap
IMMED^PROX	(D1)	*(s)ihka*	*(s)itʉhi*	*(s)itii*
REM^PROX	(D2)	*mahka*	*mahri*	*marii*
IMMED^DIST	(D3)	*(s)ohka*	*(s)ohri*	*(s)orii*
REM^DIST	(D4)	*(s)uhka*	*(s)uhri*	*(s)urii*
SCATTERED	(D5)	*(s)ehka*	———	*(s)etii*

(196)

		Gs	Gd	Gp
IMMED^PROX	(D1)	*(s)ihka*	*(s)itʉhʉ*	*(s)itʉʉ*
REM^PROX	(D2)	*mahka*	*mahrʉ*	*marʉʉ*
IMMED^DIST	(D3)	*(s)ohka*	*(s)ohrʉ*	*(s)orʉʉ*
REM^DIST	(D4)	*(s)uhka*	*(s)uhrʉ*	*(s)urʉʉ*
SCATTERED	(D5)	*(s)ehka*	———	*(s)etʉʉ*

A demonstrative adjective precedes the noun it modifies. An adjective or possessive pronoun occurs between the demonstrative and the noun. Any element that may move to the second, modal position of the sentence may interrupt these constituents. A demonstrative adjective may occur alone, with an overt head noun following it.

(197) *sitʉ -kʉ-seʔ*   *ma*   *piaʔ*   *pʉ-hi*   *muhne-htsi*   *miʔa-nʉ*
       D1   EVID-CTR   D2G   mother   CO-Ad   precede-SS   go-PST
       His mother went, leading them.   (81:9)

(198) *urɨ-tuku*   *maʔ*   *na-rɨʔɨya-tɨ*   *kwasinabooʔ*
      D4-INTENS   D2Ns   REFL-fear-NOM   snake
      It's that same dangerous snake.   (28:21)

11.2. Nonnumeric quantifiers. There is no particular form characteristic of nonnumeric quantifiers. Some are free forms, others bound; some are derived from more basic forms, others are not. A few such quantifiers are listed in (199). Most are unmarked for case, but three have special accusative forms and one a genitive form as well.

(199)   *sɨɨhpeʔsɨ*   'all together'
        oyetɨ   'everyone'
        -etɨ   'each one'
        oʔyɨsɨ   'every time'
        tɨmarɨɨmoa, tɨmarɨɨmoaku (A)   'much'
        soo(-tɨ), sooti/sooko (A), *sootɨna* (G)   'many, much'
        soobeʔsɨ   'long ago'
        sɨsɨmɨʔ, sɨsɨmɨʔ-nɨɨ (Np), *sɨsɨmɨʔ-nii* (A)   'some'

(200)   *suʔana*   *sɨ-sɨmɨʔ-nɨɨ*   *kahní-baʔi*
      D4L   RDp-one-Np   house-have
      Some people had a camp there.   (85:1)

A quantifier normally precedes the noun it modifies, but some may also occur alone, without a noun.

(201)   *soo*   *maʔ*   *hibi-hka-tɨ*
      much   D2Ns   drink-ST-PROG
      She has drunk a lot.   (56:21)

(202)   *sɨɨhpeʔsɨ*   *u*   *kwɨtɨkú-nɨ*
      together   D4A   shoot-PST
      They all shot it at the same time.   (28:21)

(203)   *sitɨ*   *-kɨ-seʔ*   *tɨmarɨɨmoa-ku*   *tomoa-nɨ*
      D1   EVID-CTR   much-A   cloud-do-PST
      It clouded up a lot.   (51:2)

A few quantifiers may be verbalized by /-yun/, the vowel of which harmonizes to *o* following *soo*.

(204) *situ̲u̲   -ku̲-seʔ   u   pu̲etsu̲-ku   soo-yo-tu̲*
      D1Np   EVID-CTR   D4G   early-A   much-VB-PROG
      There were many of them that morning.   (29:24)

(205) *suru̲   -ku̲-seʔ   paa   tu̲maru̲u̲moaa-yu̲*
      D4   EVID-CTR   water   much-VB
      That was a lot of water.   (93:3)

A type of partitive construction exists with certain quantifiers. In this construction, the quantifier may precede both a demonstrative adjective and the
noun, occur between them, or follow them both.

(206) Q   D   H
      tu̲maru̲u̲moa-ku   *sihka*   *ku̲ru̲ʔatsi̲h-a*   *ahwé-nu̲*
      much-A   D1As   lily-A   dig-PST
      (They) dug up lots of these water lily roots.   (127:6)

(207) D   Q   H
      suru̲u̲   -seʔ   su̲-su̲mu̲ʔ-nu̲u̲   waʔihpu̲ʔa-nu̲u̲   suhka   wanakotseʔ-a
      D4Np   CTR   RDP-one-Np   woman-Np   D4As   soap-A

      petihtai-ʔee-yu̲
      drop-REP-DUR
      Some of those women would throw away that soap.   (129:7)

(208)   D   H
      wihnu   maru̲u̲   nanawaʔihpu̲ʔa-nu̲u̲   sehka   kuyuníiʔ-a
      then   D2Gp   women^folk-Np   D5As   turkey-A

      Q
      soo-ko   kwasu̲i -ku̲-nu̲
      many-A   cook-CAUS-PST
      Then their womenfolk would cook many of those various turkeys.
                                                               (120:20)

There are no special existential quantifiers for indefinite quantification,
but the question words *hini* 'what? (NOM)' and *hina* 'what? (ACC)' function
in this role (cf. §3.3). There is, in addition, a derived nominal form *uʔahru̲*
'anyone' (NOM), with accusative and genitive forms *uʔahri* and *uʔahru̲na*,
respectively, which appear to be restricted to negative clauses; but this is
not certain.

(209)   *o-bo-ti-ka*   *hunu?-ru-ti*   *noo*   *hina*   *tu-hani̱-ki-ti*
        D3-DIR-at-!p creek-along-at NEC what?ˆA   black-do-come-PROGˆA

        okwe-hki-ti   *puhwai-hbu̱u̱ni̱*
        flow-come-PROGˆA   look-AUG
        Look along the creek for some blackish thing coming floating down
        toward us over there!   (6:24)

(210)   *keta?* *kwasi-ku̱* *si-nih-ku* *u?ahru̱n-a* *atu̱hu̱n-a* *nohi?-a* *yaa-ru̱*
        NEG! tail-at D1-M-A anyone-G stranger-G toy-A take-PROG
        Next time, do not take any stranger's toy like this!   (83:32)

11.3. Numerals. Little information is available concerning the numeri-
cal system. The stem *su̱mu̱-* 'one' also expresses notions of completeness
and totality (§13.3). The form *hayarokwe* 'four' is analyzable as *haya* 'two
times' (?) plus *tokwe* 'exact' and *mo?obe?* 'five' is clearly *mo?o* 'hand' plus
-be? (measure).

The suffix *-?* marks *su̱mu̱?* 'one' as a derived noun or adjective. Similarly,
the stem *waha-* 'two' may appear in derived form with *-tu̱/-ru̱* (imperfective participle), where it is in addition marked overtly with the dual
suffix, as *wahahtu̱hu̱* or *wahahtu̱kwu̱*. Other numerals can be marked as
plural forms, all making use of this same *-tu̱/-ru̱* plus *-u̱* for plural. All
derived numerals are marked as genitive or accusative in appropriate
contexts.

The suffix *-bah* can be added to at least some numeral stems to express
separateness (i.e., the items are not a natural set) or distribution over two or
more items.

(211)   *suru̱*   *-ku̱-se?*   *suhri* *bihi?a-nih* *waha-bah-tih* *na-ropu̱si?i-tih*
        D4   EVID-CTR D4Ad boy-Ad   two-SEP-Ad   REFL-bead-Ad

        uhri   *napu̱-máka-nu̱*
        D4Ad   shoe-give-PST
        She gave each of the two boys a pair of beaded moccasins.   (74:19)

Other processes are hinted at, but how productive these are is not known.
Reduplication of *su̱mu̱?* 'one' yields *su̱su̱mu̱?* 'some', and *su̱su̱?ana* 'sometimes'.
Addition of the intensifier *-su̱* to the same basic form yields *su̱mu̱su̱* 'once, one
time'.

Finally, there are two ways to express 'half'. The form *su̱kwee-bi* originally has to do with working down a row but not returning. The postposition
tu̱bi̱naa?(weki̱) means both 'half' and 'in the middle'.

A numeral normally precedes the noun it modifies. Genitive pronouns are proclitic to nouns and, therefore, follow numerals. The postposition *tʉb̲inaa?(weki̲)* 'half' naturally follows its noun.

(212)   Q   H
         wahah-tʉkwʉ̲   *ta?wo?i?-nʉkwʉ̲*   *na-mahtowʉnʉ̲-ka̲*
         two-Nd   gun-Nd   REFL-lean-ST
         Two guns stood leaning (against the wall).   (92:12)

(213)   Q   PO   H
         sʉmʉ-?   *u*   *tʉi?*   *toya-ma-tu*   *poma-mi?a-nʉ̲*
         one-Ns   D4G   friend   mountain-on-along   pick-go-PST
         Her friend went up into the mountain to pick.   (111:10)

12

Pronouns

In general, the pronoun system distinguishes three persons (speaker, spoken to, spoken about) and three numbers (singular, dual, plural). The system further distinguishes inclusive and exclusive forms for nonsingular first person—inclusive pronouns including person(s) addressed, exclusive pronouns excluding them. Third-person pronouns exhibit another embellishment of the system in distinguishing the same spatial ranking of third persons as is found in demonstrative adjectives (§12.1). Nominative forms of pronouns are introduced first, followed by accusative, genitive, and reflexive forms, in that order.

12.1. Nominative pronouns. Nominative forms of pronouns occur primarily as main clause subjects. First-person nominative pronouns are listed in (214). There are two singular forms, the second of which is emphatic and occurs only rarely. There are three dual forms, one exclusive (x) of a second person and two inclusive (i) of a second person, the two inclusive forms being used interchangeably. There are two plural forms, one exclusive and one inclusive.

(214) *nɨʔ, nɨɨ*   (1xNs)
       nɨkwɨ   (1xNd)
       nɨnɨ   (1xNp)
       tahɨ, takwɨ   (1iNd)
       tanɨ   (1iNp)

The second-person nominative pronouns are listed in (215). The two dual forms are interchangeable. The second-person form *nɨɨʔ* (2Ns/p) occurs

365

exclusively in imperatives (§4.1) when addressing a single or plural number of persons, but not two persons.

(215)   *ʉnʉ*   (2Ns)
        mʉhʉ, mʉkwʉ   (2Nd)
        mʉnʉ   (2Np)

Third-person pronouns are based on demonstrative adjective roots (§11.1) and distinguish four of the five spatial categories of the demonstrative system—IMMEDIATE PROXIMAL, REMOTE PROXIMAL, IMMEDIATE DISTAL, and REMOTE DISTAL. Third-person-singular nominal pronouns add the suffix -*ʔ* to a demonstrative root, while dual and plural forms add the suffix -*tʉ/-rʉ*, as indicated in (216). There are two interchangeable endings for each of the dual forms.

(216)

		3Ns	3Nd	3Np
IMMEDˆPROX	(D1)	*iʔ*	*itʉhʉ, itʉkwʉ*	*itʉʉ*
REMˆPROX	(D2)	*maʔ*	*mahrʉ, marʉkwʉ*	*marʉʉ*
IMMEDˆDIST	(D3)	*oʔ*	*ohrʉ, orʉkwʉ*	*orʉʉ*
REMˆDIST	(D4)	*uʔ*	*uhrʉ, urʉkwʉ*	*urʉʉ*

12.2. Accusative pronouns. Accusative forms of pronouns occur in main clauses as direct or indirect objects, and in subordinate clauses marked by -*ka*, -*ku*, or -*tsi* as either subjects or objects (§15.2).

First-person accusative pronouns are listed in (217). As with nominative forms, there is a second, emphatic form of the first-singular accusative pronoun.

(217)   *nʉ, nʉe(tʉ)*   (1xAs)
        nʉhi   (1xAd)
        nʉmi   (1xAp)
        tahi   (1iAd)
        tai   (1IiAp)

Second-person-singular accusative pronouns are listed in (218). The second singular form is emphatic, but the two plural forms are interchangeable.

(218)   *ʉ, ʉmi*   (2As)
        mʉhi   (2Ad)
        mʉi, mʉmi   (2Ap)

Third-person accusative pronouns are listed in (219). The singular pronouns are identical to corresponding nominative forms, except that they lack the derivational suffix *-ʔ* of nominatives. Dual and plural accusative pronouns have the ending *-i* common to many other accusative forms (§9.3).

(219)

		3AS	3AD	3AP
IMMED^PROX	(D1)	*i*	*itʉhi*	*itii*
REM^PROX	(D2)	*ma*	*mahri*	*marii*
IMMED^DIST	(D3)	*o*	*ohri*	*orii*
REM^DIST	(D4)	*u*	*uhri*	*urii*

12.3. Genitive pronouns. A genitive pronoun occurs primarily as the possessor constituent of a noun phrase, with the genitive form preceding the head noun. There are five first-person genitive pronouns, as listed in (220). All but the singular form end in an underlying *n* which prevents spirantization of a following stop (§1.1).

(220)

nʉ	(1xGs)
nʉhʉ	(1xGd)
nʉmʉ	(1xGp)
tahʉ	(1iGd)
taa	(1iGp)

There are four second-person genitive pronouns, distinguishing the three number categories, but with two competing plural forms, as indicated in (221). All four have an underlying final *n*.

(221)

ʉ	(2Gs)
mʉhʉ	(2Gd)
mʉʉ, mʉmʉ	(2Gp)

Third-person genitive pronouns are listed in (222). These also have an underlying final *n*.

(222)

		3Gs	3Gd	3Gp
IMMED^PROX	(D1)	*i*	*itʉhʉ*	*itʉʉ*
REM^PROX	(D2)	*ma*	*mahrʉ*	*marʉʉ*
IMMED^DIST	(D3)	*o*	*ohrʉ*	*orʉʉ*
REM^DIST	(D4)	*u*	*uhrʉ*	*urʉʉ*

(223)

nah	*nʉʔ*	*mʉʉ*	*kahni-kʉ-hu*	*ʉ*	*tsa-wee-hkwa-tuʔi*
just	1xNs	2Gp	house-at-to	2As	INSTR-descend-go-UNR

I'll just haul you off to your camp. (39:35)

(224) nʉ   kwʉhi   nʉ?   nʉ   rʉrʉeʔ-tii   puni-tuʔį   ʉkʉnaa
       1xGs   wifeˆA   1xNs   1xGs   child-Ap   see-UNR   first
       I'll see my wife and my children first.   (39:25)

An IMPERSONAL GENITIVE form (*tan* →) *ta* 'one's, our, people's' does not distinguish either person or number.

12.4. Coreferential pronouns. Nondistinct argument phenomena were discussed in §7, where forms designating unspecified subjects, unspecified objects, reflexives, passives, and reciprocals were discussed. There is also a set of coreferential pronouns that serve an intensifying function in apposition with other pronouns or full nominal forms. These forms make no distinction as to person, but do distinguish singular, dual, and plural number, as well as case, as indicated in (225). Competing forms are separated by comma (,). Genitive forms have underlying final *n* and are used within an object noun phrase when the possessor of the object noun is also the subject of the sentence or is included in the subject.

(225)   COS   COD   COP
       N   pʉnʉ   pʉhʉ, pʉkwʉ   pʉmʉ
       A   pʉmi   pʉhi   pʉi, pʉmi
       G   pʉ   pʉhʉ   pʉʉ

(226) (sitʉ-kwʉ)   su-kʉ-hu   bʉʉ   kahni-kʉ-hu   urii   bʉa-htsi   pʉkwʉ miʔa-nʉ
       D1Nd   D4-at-to   COGp   house-in-to   D4Ap   leave-ss   CONd go-PST
       Leaving them there in their teepee, (these two) themselves went.
                                                                       (103:4)

(227) su-sʉmʉʔ   -kʉ-seʔ   pʉmʉ   u   yuhu-kʉ   u   kwasʉi -kʉ-nʉ
       RDP-one   EVID-CTR   CONp   D4   fat-in   D4   cook-CAUS-PST
       Some of them fried it in the fat.   (127:12)

13

Verbs

13.1. Verb stems. Each verb stem occurs in two forms, an unmodified form and a combining form. In general, the combining form of a verb stem is identical to the unmodified form except that it has either a final voiceless vowel or triggers an added *-h*. There are regular phonological patterns reflected in these forms, but these will not be considered here.

The unmodified form of a verb occurs in isolation as a citation or elicitation form. It can also take various suffixes. The combining form never occurs alone. It must have one of a special set of suffixes or be part of certain types of compounds. Since the special suffixes are scattered through several sections of this grammar summary, they are listed together in (228) for the sake of convenience.

(228) *-ka*   'stative'
       -ka   'dependent clause (different subject)'
       -ki   'motion toward (come)'
       -kwa   'motion away (go)'
       -kwai   'motion around, back and forth'
       -puni   'much'
       -tsi   'dependent clause (same subject)'
       -tuki   'begin'
       -tuni/-runi   'tell'

Many verbs are irregular in the sense that the stem used in the singular is different from that used in the dual and the plural. There is never a distinction between dual and plural in verb stems. In all cases, suppletion is determined by the number of the subject for intransitive verbs and by the number of the object for transitive verbs. Each form is alphabetized separately in the dictionary, but with the other form supplied as well. Thus, one can find *tʉyaai* as the singular stem for 'die', with the nonsingular form *kooi* also given; or one can find *kooi* as the nonsingular stem, with the singular stem *tʉyaai* also given.

Suppletion is widespread, with several phonological patterns distinguishing the singular and nonsingular stems, but space does not permit discussion of these here. However, it was noted in section §9.2 that it is common for nominal elements not to be overtly marked for number, particularly if context makes clear the number involved. Suppletion in verbs can now be seen as one device available to the speaker for an indirect indication of number, whether of subject or object. In example (229), the object is not overtly marked as plural, yet *tʉkʉwasʉ* 'kill (PL OBJ) for food' rather than *tʉkʉhpehka* 'kill (SG OBJ) for food' provides sufficient indication of number for the object.

(229) soobe?sʉ   nʉnʉ   su-nih-ku   puhitóo?-a   rʉkʉ-wasʉ-?e-tʉ-ʉ
       longˆago   1xNp   D4-M-A   turkey-A   food-kill-REP-PROG-P
       Long ago we killed turkeys for food in that way.   (119:9)

(230) sitʉ   -kʉ-se?   ma   wʉh-kúpa-nʉ
       D1   EVID-CTR   D2A   INSTR-kill-PST
       He clubbed it to death.   (125:8)

(231) tai   wʉh-tokwʉ-ki-tʉ   ma?
       1iAp   INST-kill-come-PROG   D2Ns
       He's coming clubbing us to death.   (4:15)

Note that in (232) and (233), the verb is chosen on the basis of the subject even though there is an object in the sentence. *Yʉkwi/niwʉnʉ* 'say' is intransitive in the sense that it cannot take an indirect object; suppletion is controlled by the number of the subject.

(232) surʉ -kʉ-se?   oha?ahnakatʉ   taa   haitsi   na-marʉni-nʉ   me
       D4   EVID-CTR coyote   1iGp   friend   REFL-hurt-PST QUOT

       yʉkwii-yʉ
       say-DUR
       Coyote said, "Our friend hurt himself."   (6:18)

(233) surʉʉ   -kʉ-se?   na-kwʉsʉ-?i-tuku   marʉkwʉ   me   niwʉnʉʉ-yʉ
       D4Np   EVID-CTR   REFL-kill-REAL-same D2Nd   QUOT   say-DUR
       Those ones said, "They killed each other."   (94:18)

While not common, reduplication in certain verb stems can be used to signal a number of actions performed by subjects acting individually rather than as a group. The known examples are almost all verbs of motion or have an adjective as their first element.

(234) *surʉʉ*   *-kʉ-seʔ*   *pʉʉ*   *kahni-kʉ-hu*   *tu-runehtsʉ-nʉ*
       D4Np   EVID-CTR   COGp   house-at-to   RDP-run-PST
       They ran to their houses.   (4:16)

(235) *marʉʉ*   *ooʔrʉ*   *tʉa-sʉ*   *marʉʉ*   *kahni*   *o-ʔokwenu-nạ*
       D2Gp   clothes   QUOT-INTENS   D2Gp   house   RDP-flow-CONT
       Their clothing and teepees are floating.   (122:19)

13.2. Instrumental prefixes. A prominent feature of many verbs is the incorporation of an initial, usually instrumental, element. Most instrumental prefixes relate to body parts, but a few relate to other notions such as 'mind', 'speech', and 'fire'. Several of the prefixes have two or three different forms depending on phonological considerations, but each has been alphabetized in such a way that related forms fall together in the dictionary. Examples of prefixes follow, with illustrative sentences below.

(236) *hu-*   'with back'   *to(h)-*   'with violent motion of hand'
       ki-   'with elbow'   *tsa(h)-* 'with inward, upward motion
                                                      of hand'
       ku-   'with head'   *tsi(h)-* 'with sharp pointed instrument'
       kʉ(h)-   'with teeth'   *tso(h)-* 'with head'
       ma-   'with hand'   *wʉ(h)-*   'with body/sideways'
       mu-   'with nose'   *ku(h)-*   'with heat'
       pi(h)-   'with buttocks'   *ni-*   'with speech'
       sʉʉ(h)- 'with feet'   *su-*   'with mind'
       ta(h)-   'with foot/leg'

(237) *nʉ-mati-tʉ*   *sʉmʉ-sʉ*   *pia-kʉh-kaʔa*
       1sAs-PART-Ns   one-INTENS   big-INSTR-cut
       Take one big bite of me!   (22:14)

(238) *sitʉ* *-kʉ-seʔ* *waʔihpʉʔ* *pʉ*   *tʉeti*   *soko-ko*   *ma-hbé-nʉ*
       D1   EVID-CTR   woman   COG   child^A   earth-on   INSTR-drop-PST
       This woman dropped her child to the ground.   (61:32, 33)

(239) *situ*   *-ku̠-seʔ*   *u*   *suuh-poʔtse-nu̠*
       D1   EVID-CTR   D4A   INSTR-jerk-PST
       She kicked it.   (41:7, 8)

(240) *situ*   *-ku̠-seʔ*   *ma*   *kwuhu*   *ma*   *ku-ʔina-nu̠*
       D1   EVID-CTR   D2G   wife   D2A   INSTR-jerk^meat-PST
       His wife roasted it.   (126:14)

13.3. Temporal prefixes. Other, noninstrumental, prefixes are generally temporal in nature. These include *uku-* 'still, just', *namu̠si-* 'quickly',
and *sumu* 'completely, thoroughly'. There is also an augmentative *pia-*
'big, loud'.

(241) *me*   *u*   *uku-yukwi̠-ka*   *pia-woinu*   *pi-piku̠u-yu̠*
       QUOT   D4A   just^now-say-DS   big-horn   RDP-sound-DUR
       Just as he had spoken, a big bugle sounded.   (85:13)

(242) *namu̠sohi-htsi-ka*   *namu̠si-tuhkanáaiʔ-niwunu*
       hurry-SS-!p   quickly-Wichita-talk
       Hurry and quickly speak Wichita!   (78:15)

(243) *situ*   *-ku̠-seʔ*   *siʔah-ru*   *maruu-ku̠-hu*   *toʔi-nu̠*   *pu*
       D1   EVID-CTR   D1L-along   D2p-at-to   go^up-PST   COG

       kwasuʔi   *sumu̠-sihwapu̠-nai-hku̠*
       dress^A   one-torn/become-BE-DS
       This one came up to them along here, her dress having become all
       torn.   (53:24)

(244) *suru*   *-ku̠-seʔ*   *wihnu*   *ohaʔahnakatu*   *pia-yake-nu̠*
       D4   EVID-CTR   then   Coyote   big-cry-PST
       Then Coyote cried loudly.   (6:18)

13.4. Number agreement. Syntactic marking in verbs is limited to number
agreement and various subordinating suffixes. Verbs optionally take suffixes
to mark them as agreeing with their subjects. This marking option is most often realized with dual subjects, less often with plural. In both circumstances,
number agreement is a type of emphasis.

With *-tu/-ru* (progressive aspect), agreement is by addition of the dual suffix
-hu̠ or *-kwu̠,* used interchangeably, or the plural suffix *-u.* These verbs therefore look like derived nouns (§8.1) or adjectives (§8.3).

(245) **Singular**   **Dual**   **Plural**
    tɨhka-rɨ   *tɨhka-rɨ-hɨ*   *tɨhka-rɨ-ɨ*   'eat'
    wihi-tɨ   *wihi-tɨ-kwɨ*   *wihi-tɨ-ɨ*   'throw'

In verbs not marked with progressive aspect, optional agreement is by the dual suffix *-nɨhɨ* or *-nɨkwɨ*, used interchangeably, and the plural suffix *-nɨɨ*. These verbs therefore look like nonderived nouns (§9.2).

(246) **Singular**   **Dual**   **Plural**
    nɨhkaʔi   *nɨhkaʔi-nɨhɨ*   *nɨhkaʔi-nɨɨ*   'danced'
    nɨkɨbɨni   *nɨkɨbɨni-nɨkwɨ*   *nɨkɨbɨni-nɨɨ*   'dance much'

Whether or not a speaker chooses to mark number overtly by adding an agreement suffix, number is sometimes indicated through verb-stem suppletion or reduplication (§13.1). Thus *ɨhpɨi* 'sleep (SG SUBJ)' is distinct from *ɨhkooi* 'sleep (PL SUBJ)', and *okwe* 'flow' (with no subject indication) is distinct from *oʔokwe* 'flow' (with reduplication showing that several subjects are acting as individuals and not collectively).

13.5. Causative/Benefactive. Many verbs are inherently causative or benefactive, such as *tsaka* 'lead by the hand/reins' or *maka* 'feed'. Other noncausative or benefactive verbs can be made such by the addition of the suffix *-kɨ* (causative). In terms of sentence structure, this suffix normally makes an intransitive verb transitive, and a transitive verb ditransitive. As (247) and (248) show, the subject of the originally intransitive verb may become the object of the causative verb marked with *-kɨ*. In (248), the benefactive *kohtookɨ* 'build a fire for' accepts an object where originally no object would have been permitted (because *kohtoo* 'build a fire' is intransitive).

(247) *surɨ*   *-kɨ-seʔ*   *u*   *kwasɨ-hka*   *pɨ*   *tɨ-rɨeʔ-tii*   *nimai-nɨ*
    D4   EVID-CTR   D4A   cook-DS   COG   RDP-child-Ap   call-PST
    When it had cooked, he called his children.   (7:30)

(248) *sitɨ*   *-kɨ-seʔ*   *wakaréʔeeʔ*   *moʔobe-tii*   *tɨʔrikúuʔ-nii*   *kwasɨ-kɨ-bɨni*
    D1   EVID-CTR   turtle   five-Ap   prairie^dog-Ap   cook-CAUS-AUG
    This turtle cooked (transitive) five prairie dogs.   (9:1)

(249) *sɨmɨ-ʔ*   *ruibihtsi-ʔ*   *pɨi*   *kohtóo-kɨ-nɨ*
    one-Ns   young^man-Ns   COAp   make^fire-CAUS-PST
    One young man built a fire for them.   (70:16)

At times the syntactic structure in which verbs with and without -*kʉ* occur is more complex. For example, *tuhubʉhka* 'get angry' takes a human subject and no object, but *tuhubʉhkakʉ* 'get angry about' takes the same human subject plus a direct object noun phrase which expresses the source of anger.

(250) *sitʉ*   -*kʉ-seʔ*   *ohaʔahnakatʉ*   *tuhú-bʉhka-nʉ*   *pʉ-metʉ*
       D1   EVID-CTR   Coyote   black-hush?-PST CO-at

       u   *yahne-na*   *ruhú-bʉhka-kʉ-nʉ*
       D4G   laugh-NOM   black-hush?-CAUS-PST
       Coyote got angry, got angry at her laughing at him.   (16:15)

13.6. Motion. Some of the adverbial suffixes expressing motion are shown below, along with related independent verbs. The suffixes without an asterisk (*) never attach to the combining form of a verb (§13.1). Those marked with an asterisk can occur with the combining form or with the unmodified verb stem. With these suffixes, a difference in meaning is expressed by choosing the combining form over the unmodified form. The combining form expresses the notion of action either followed by the indicated motion or occurring simultaneously with the indicated motion, while the unmodified form of the stem expresses the notion of indicated motion resulting in or for the purpose of the named action.

(251) -*miʔa*   'unspecified motion' (*miʔa* 'go')
       -*nii*   'motion around, from place to place (SG)'
       -*yʉhka*   'motion around, from place to place (PL)', (*yʉka*
                      'move about, walk (PL)')
       -ki   'motion toward' (*kima* 'come')
       -kwa   'motion away'
       -kwai   'motion around, back and forth'

(252) *sitʉ*   -*kʉ-seʔ*   *yʉtsu-miʔa-rʉ*
       D1   EVID-CTR   fly-go-PROG
       This one goes flying.   (31:6)

(253) *hini*   *u-waka-tu*   *kasá-bi-pi̱ku-hki-na̱*
       what?^N   D4-toward-along   wing-RDP-beat-come-CONT
       Something kept coming toward him making wing noises.   (27:3)

(254) *sitʉʉ*   -*sihka*   *raibooʔ-a*   *noo-nʉ-kwa̱*
       D1Np   D1As   white^man-A   haul-PST-go
       These ones carried off this white man.   (28:23)

(255)   *setʉ*   *ma*   *noo-pʉh-a*   *hima-hkwai-tʉ*
       D5   D2G   haul-NOM-A   take-back^and^forth-PROG
       These various ones come and go taking his load.   (97:34)

As the above examples show, the adverbial suffixes expressing motion can occur with aspect markers (§13.7). These suffixes are sometimes used redundantly, so that the indicated motion is doubly indicated.

(256)   *kima*   *habi-kị*
      come   lie^down-come
      Come! Come and lie down!   (48:20)

Three other adverbial affixes will be mentioned here. The suffix *-etʉ* 'each one' indicates identical or similar action distributed over several subjects. The suffix *-pʉni/-bʉni* 'much' is augmentative, indicating that a good deal of the action named by the verb is going on. It takes the combining form of the verb (§13.1). Of these two suffixes, only the second can occur with a singular subject. Finally, the proclitic numeral **sʉmʉ-** 'one' indicates that the action named by the verb is done completely or thoroughly.

(257)   *sitʉʉ*   *pʉʉ*   *kahni-kʉ-ku*   *kohtoo-?etʉ-tsi*   *sihka*   *pʉʉ*
       D1p   OGp   house-at-A   make^fire-each^one-SS   D1As   COGp

       ahwe-pʉh-a   *tʉkʉh-mani-nʉ*
       dig-NOM-A   food-prepare-PST
       Each making a fire in her home, they cooked their diggings. (127:10)

(258)   *sitʉ*   *-kʉ-se?*   *si?ana*   *wʉnʉ-rʉ*   *na-buih-wʉnʉ-bʉni*
       D1   EVID-CTR   D1L   stand-PROG   REFL-eye-stand-AUG
       This one stands here and examines himself a lot.   (32:11)

(259)   *nʉkʉ-tsi*   *nʉʉ?-ka*   *sʉmʉ-?ʉ?-tsumi-hki-na*
       dance-SS   2N-!p   one-eye?-disappear-come-CONT
       Dancing, keep coming with your eyes completely closed.   (3:11)

13.7. Aspect. There are apparently no tense markers as such, but a rich array of aspect markers. Tense refers to specification of when, in the flow of time, an event takes place. Aspect does not place an event in time, but rather focuses on other features of the event—its beginning or ending, whether it is ongoing or not, whether it is to be considered as an action or as a state, and so on.

A common possibility is for the verb stem to occur in uninflected form. This is clearly the semantically neutral or unmarked state, where context is sufficient to make intended meanings clear, and the addition of specific aspect suffixes is dependent on the judgment of the speaker as to the ability of the hearer to keep up with the flow of information. Considerations of emphasis may of course dictate the addition of one or another aspect marker even when one is not otherwise required.

(260) *suruu*   *-ku̱-se?*   *na-rah-ka?wi̱-tsi*   *nuku̱-bui̱ ni̱*
       D4Np   EVID-CTR   REFL-INSTR-gather-SS   dance-AUG
       Those ones, having gathered together, were dancing a lot.   (3:2)

(261) *surukwu̱* *-ku-se?*   *tena-nukwu̱* *tsaa-tu*   *ma?*   *me*   *niwu̱nu̱*
       D4d   EVID-CTR   man-Nd   good-NOM   D2Ns   QUOT   say
       Those two men said, "It's good."   (111:5)

Inceptive. There are two verb markers that focus on the beginning of a named event, /-tuki/ and /-pitu̱/. The first marker may be related to the independent verb *tuki* 'place, put'; the second is clearly related to the independent verb *pitu̱* 'arrive'.

(262) *suruu*   *-ku̱-se?*   *wihnu*   *uruu*   *wobi-wihtua*   *piku̱-rui̱ uki̱*
       D4p   EVID-CTR   then   D4Gp   wood-bucket   beat-begin
       Those ones then began beating their drum.   (70:19)

(263) *su̱mu̱?*   *uruu-matu̱*   *ma-waka*   *nahá-biitu̱*
       one^Ns   D4p-PART   D2-toward   happen-arrive
       One of them happened onto him.   (86:18)

(264) *situ̱*   *-ku̱-se?*   *umu̱-hú-piitu̱*
       D2   EVID-CTR   rain-INDEF-arrive
       It began to rain. (51:4)

As (264) shows, *-piitu̱* may be preceded by /-hun/ (indefinite), the two elements appearing as *-hupiitu̱*. Both forms are sometimes translated 'suddenly', suggesting that there may be an element of spontaneity or unexpectedness present. Notice also that *-tuki* takes the combining form of the verb, *-piitu̱* takes the unmodified form of the stem.

Completive. The suffix *-ma* (completive) focuses on the coming to completion of an event that is presupposed to have been ongoing. It attaches to the unmodified form of a verb stem. The suffix *-?i* (realized) is similar to *-ma* in dealing with the completion of an event, but -ʔi states that the event is over and done while -ma specifies more closely the coming to be over and done. It also attaches to the unmodified form of the stem.

(265) *sitɨ*   *-kɨ-seʔ*   *suhka*   *tɨhka-rɨ*   *wihnu*   *tɨhká-ma-nɨ*
       D1   EVID-CTR   D4As   eat-PROG   then   eat-COMPL-PST
       This one was eating that, and then finished eating.   (39:30)

(266) *wahah-tɨkwɨ*   *wasáasiʔ-tena-nɨkwɨ*   *nɨ-waka*   *bitɨ-ʔi*
       two-Nd   Osage-man-Nd   1xA-toward   arrive-REAL
       Two Osage men arrived where I was.   (105:21)

(267) *sitɨɨ*   *-kɨ-seʔ*   *ma*   *pitɨ-ʔi-ma-tu*   *na-ʔoki-tɨ*
       D1p   EVID-CTR   D2G   arrive-REAL-on-along   REFL-rejoice-PROG
       These ones are rejoicing over her return.   (40:43)

As (267) shows, a verb marked with -ʔi may serve as the stem to which post-positional elements can be attached. As such, it may be possible to analyze -ʔi as a nominalizer. The ramifications of this analysis will not be pursued here.

Stative. The suffix /-kan/ (stative) focuses on events as states rather than actions, expressing the notion that such-and-such a state exists. The suffix attaches to the combining form of the verb. The stative forms are often translatable as 'be X-ing' or 'be X-ed'.

(268) *surɨ*   *-kɨ-seʔ*   *sɨmɨ-bekwi̠-ka̠*
       D4   EVID-CTR   one-swell-ST
       That one was all swelled up.   (28:17)

(269) *sitɨɨ*   *-kɨ-seʔ*   *sehka*   *taʔsiwóoʔ-a*   *soni-too-hka-ku*   *marɨɨ-kɨ-hu*
       D1p   EVID-CTR   D5As   buffalo-A   grass-graze-ST-Ds   D2p-at-to

       kɨa-hu-piitɨ
       come^up-INDEF-arrive
       As the buffalo were grazing, they came up to them.   (69:6, 7)

Repetitive. The suffix -ʔe marks repeated action. It occurs with the unmodified verb stem. Since -ʔe contains no indication of how frequently an event is repeated, it can be used for a variety of contexts. In (270), repeated action over a short time span is expressed. In (271), the sense is more along the lines of habitual activity, presumably over an indefinitely long time period.

(270) *situ*   *-ku̱-se?*   *u*   *tsuhni-pu̱h-a*   *u̱mah-paa-ku̱-hu*   *wihí-?ee-yu̱*
     D1   EVID-CTR   D4G   bone-ABS-A   rain-water-in-to   throw-REP-DUR
     This one threw its bones in the lake.   (10:22)

(271) *suru̱u̱*   *-ku̱-se?*   *ma-nakwu̱-hi*   *tuu-?ee-yu̱*
     D4p   EVID-CTR   beyond?-side-at   fetchˆwater-REP-DUR
     They would get water far away.   (81:2)

Continuative. The suffix *-na* (continuative) focuses on the continuation of an event and attaches to the unmodified form of the verb stem. The suffix *-mi?a* 'go' (§13.6) has apparently been extended to have much the same sense. It sometimes occurs with a preceding *-hu* (indefinite). Both markers might be translated 'keep on X-ing'.

(272) *si?ana*   *-ku̱-se?*   *pi-bia-kwasinaboo-?*   *ma-waka-tu*
     D1L   EVID-CTR   RDP-big-snake-Ns   D2-toward-along

     pa-kwabi-hkwai-na̱
     water-lie-backˆandˆforth-CONT
     Here big snakes were swimming around toward her.   (52:18)

(273) *tukani̱-hu-mi?a-ru̱*   *ma?*
     night-INDEF-go-PROG   D2Ns
     It is about to get dark.   (82:13)

(274) *nu̱nu̱*   *-se?*   *paa-ku̱*   *wihnu*   *u*   *kotsé-mia-?ee-yu̱*
     1xNp   CTR   water-in   then   D4A   wash-go-REP-DUR
     We would then go wash it in water.   (110:17, 18)

Progressive. The suffix /-tu̱n/ (progressive) focuses on an event as being in progress. The distinction between progressive and continuative is often subtle. Continuative expresses the idea that the event keeps on going, while the progressive says nothing about continuation but merely reports that the event is occurring. This suffix attaches to the unmodified form of the verb stem.

(275) *nu̱*   *na?-nu̱mu̱-nii*   *nu̱?*   *nu̱e*   *no-bu̱a-hrai-kwu̱-ka*
     1xGs   kin-Comanche-Ap   1xNs   1xAs   haul-leave-final-go-Ds

     uru̱u̱   *napu̱-hu*   *mi?a-ru̱*
     D4Gp   foot-to   go-PROG
     My relatives having abandoned me, I am following their trail. (38:14)

(276)   *suru*   *-se?*   *pia-nohko-?awo-baai-tu*
      D4   CTR   big-bake-vessel-have-PROG
      She had a big oven.   (109:8)

Unrealized. The suffixes /-tu?ih/ and /-wa?ih/ (unrealized) mark an event as not having taken place although potentially capable of taking place. They attach to the unmodified form of a verb stem, with *-tu?i* occurring in an affirmative clause and *-wa?i* occurring if *ke* (negative) is in the same clause. The suffix *-hu* (indefinite) often occurs preceding *-tu?i* (never before *-wa?i*). Both suffixes can take a following *-tu* (progressive) to express ongoing potentiality, and both are often translatable as the English future.

(277)   *...ke*   *tamu-ma-tu*   *musa-sua-wa?i-tu*
      NEG   1INd-on-along   ?-think-UNR-PROG
      ...will not be concerned about us.   (78:14)

(278)   *situ*   *-ku-se?*   *ma*   *petu?*   *ru?uya-na*   *pu*   *ahpu?-a*   *pu*
      D1   EVID-CTR   D2G   daughter   fear-CONT   COGs   father-A   COGs

        turuhka-ru?ih-a   *ke*   *su-waai-ku*
        steal-UNR-A   NEG   INSTR-lack-Ds
      Her daughter is afraid, because her father does not want her to steal.
                                         (66:20, 21)

(279)   *noha*   *u?*   *nu*   *kwuhu-ru?i*
      nearly   D4Ns   1sAs   catch-UNR
      He almost caught me.   (105:28)

Other. In this section the suffixes /-nuh/ and *-yu* will be mentioned, although their exact status remains unclear. Each of these attaches to the unmodified verb stem. /-nuh/ most often occurs in contexts where English uses the past tense. It appears to express the notion of a relatively short-lived event. On the other hand, *-yu* expresses the idea of a longer-lived event (here glossed DURATIVE). These suffixes thus contrast with each other, although they are compatible with the *-ma* (completive). /-nuh/ is incompatible with *-?e* (repetitive).

(280)   *uhka*   *orii*   *wuh-pa?i-ku*   *-se?*   *u*   *pia?*   *yake-nu*
      D4As   D3Ap   INSTR-beat-Ds   CTR   D4G   mother   cry-PST
      When they beat him, his mother cried.

(281) *uhka*   *orii*   *wuh-paʔi-ku*   *-seʔ*   *u*   *piaʔ*   *yakee-yu*
       D4As   D3Ap   INSTR-beat-Ds   CTR   D4G   mother   cry-DUR
       When they beat him, his mother was crying.

(282) *situ*   *-ku-seʔ*   *pitu-su*   *pitu-nu*
       D1   EVID-CTR   back-INTENS   arrive-PST
       This one arrived back.   (105:24)

(283) *nohiʔ*   *tsaa*   *na-buni-yu*   *nuu*
       very   good   REFL-see-DUR   1xNs
       I look very nice.   (32:12)

Note that of the two suffixes under discussion, verbs of saying *(niikwi, yukwi, niwunu)* regularly take *-yu* and apparently never /-nuh/.

Summary. Since the preceding examples of aspect markers do not adequately illustrate their sequential possibilities, these are summarized as follows.

As noted it is common for a verb to be marked with no overt aspect suffix. For verbs taking *-ma* (completive), *-tuki* (inceptive), *-pitu* (inceptive), *-miʔa* 'go', and *-ka* (stative), there is usually no further indication of aspect. The combination *-ka* + *-tu* (temporary state) occurs frequently enough, however, that it deserves special mention. Also note that *-nu* (short-lived) falls before the motion suffixes *-ki* and *-kwa* (§13.6), even though it would seem that it should follow them.

(284)   **Aspect sequences**

Repeated	**Motion**	**Realized**	**Other**
-ʔe	*-ki*	*-ʔi*	*-tu*
-nu	*-kwa*	*-tuʔi/-waʔi*	*-na*
			-yu

14

Adverbs

Apart from their linking function between successive clauses in discourse, adverbial elements are of various types and play varying roles within the sentence. Temporal, locative, manner, directional, and other adverbials may be individual lexical items, nominals, postpositional phrases, or entire subordinate clauses. Whenever a clause contains two or more adverbials of the same type (temporal, locative, etc.), the normal order is from more general to more specific. Adverbs of degree precede the elements they modify.

(285)   *nohi?*   *tʉh-tʉtaa-tʉʉ*   *tʉ-rʉe-hpʉ?-rʉʉ*   *tai*   *tsaah-tʉhka-kʉ-nʉ*
       very   RDP-little-Np   RDP-small-ABS-Np   1iAp   good-eat-CAUS-PST
       Very small children caused us to eat well.   (75:28)

14.1. Temporal adverbs. Temporal adverbs include *kwasikʉ* 'next time', *ʉkʉnaa* 'first', *meeku* 'now', *ʉkihtsi?* 'now', *kʉtu* 'yesterday', *pʉetsʉku* 'in the morning', *pʉetsʉkusʉ* 'early in the morning', and others. When noun phrases are used as temporal adverbs, they are in the accusative case.

(286)   *setʉ*   *-se?*   *suhka*   *tabe-ni*   *u-kʉ-hu*   *no-bitʉ-?ee-yʉ*
       D5   CTR   D4As   sun-?   D4-at-to   haul-arrive-REP-DUR
       That day, they would camp there.   (129:5)

14.2. Locative adverbs. Locative adverbs include *kʉma?kʉ* 'beside', *kʉma?ru* 'alongside', *uhtu* 'along there', *una?ru* 'along the other side', *hunaiki* 'outside', and many others.

(287) *situ*   *-ku-se?*   *ma*   *kwuhu*   *hunai-ki*   *punu*   *numii-yu*
       D1   EVID-CTR   D2G   wife   outside-at   CONs   move-DUR
       His wife herself was moving about outside.   (48:19)

14.3. Directional adverbs.

Directional adverbs include *kuma?ku* 'to the edge of' and *pitusu* 'back'. With verbs of motion, directional adverbs distinguish between motion toward and motion away from, as in *hunakuhu* '(toward) outside' and *hunakwuhi* '(from) outside'.

(288) *si?ane-tu*   *situhu*   *pitu-su*   *mia-hu-tu?i*
       D1L-from   D1Nd   back-INTENS   go-INDEF-UNR
       At this point, these two are about to go back.

(289) *situ*   *-ku-se?*   *uh-tu*   *to?i-kwa*   *e-ku-hu*   *huna-ku-hu*   *to?i-nu*
       D1   EVID-CTR   D4-along   go^up-go   D5-al-to   outside-at-to   go^up-PST
       He went up through there and climbed outside there.   (92:17)

(290) *sumu-?*   *-ku-se?*   *wa?i-hpu?*   *hu-nakwu-hi*   *ke*   *bu-ku-hu*
       one-Ns   EVID-CTR   woman-ABS   out-side-at   NEG   CO-at-to

       to?i-wa?i   *na-naka-ku*   *-ku-se?*   *suru*   *nu*   *-tsa?*
       go^up-UNR   REFL-hear-Ds   EVID-CTR   D4   1xNs   DECL

       to?i-tu?i   *me*   *yukwii-yu*
       go^up-UNR   QUOT   say-DUR
       Sounding from outside like a place not to go out to, one woman said,
       "I'll go out."   (52:11)

14.4. Demonstrative adverbs.

Demonstrative adverbs are based on the same roots and conceptual scheme as demonstrative adjectives (§11.1), consisting of a demonstrative root plus an additional element. As might be expected, the patterns for locative and directional demonstrative adverbs are the most elaborate.

Locative and allative demonstrative adverbs. Three locative adverbs consist of a demonstrative root plus the general locative postposition /-kah/ 'in, at, on'. In these simple forms the vowel of /-kah/ is always devoiced and assimilates to that of the preceding root vowel.

(291) *i-ki*   'here (D1)'
       o-ko   'there (D3)'
       u-ku   'there (D4)'

Further semantic material in the form of other postpositions may be added. One set, formally allative and not strictly locative, overlaps with the above in distribution. This set uses the same three roots and the postposition /-kah/ (locative), but in addition has the postposition -hu 'into'. With the stem o (immediate distal), the postposition -hu appears as -ho. These forms can be used as locatives or allatives.

(292) *i-kᵾ-hu*   '(to) here (D1)'
       o-kᵾ-ho   '(to) there (D3)'
       u-kᵾ-hu   '(to) there (D4)'

Another set of allative demonstratives consists of a demonstrative root plus -bu 'way, direction'. After the stem o-, the vowel of -bu harmonizes to o.

(293) *i-bu*   'this (D1) way'
       o-bo   'that (D3) way'
       u-bu   'that (D4) way'
       e-bu   'various (D5) ways'

All these forms may occur with initial consonant s, indicating presupposed prior knowledge of the location or direction on the part of the hearer. These and other possible forms are illustrated in (294)–(296).

(294) *surᵾ* *-kᵾ-seʔ*   *o-kᵾ-ho*   *hunuʔ-baʔa-tu*   *toʔi-nᵾ*
       D4   EVID-CTR   D3-at-to   creek-on-along   goˆup-PST
       She came out over there along the creek.   (37:7)

(295) *su-kᵾ-hu*   *sitᵾ*   *tᵾmarᵾᵾmoa-ku*   *urii*   *kᵾhtá-nᵾe-nᵾ*
       D4-at-to   D1Ns   much-A   D4Ap   hard-blow-PST
       The wind blew hard on them there.   (53:26)

(296) *pᵾᵾ*   *omo-mᵾ-sᵾ*   *surᵾᵾ*   *u-kᵾ*   *bitᵾ-nᵾ*
       COGp   leg-on-INTENS   D4Np   D4-at   arrive-PST
       They arrived there on foot.   (119:10)

There are also three indefinite locative adverbs based on demonstrative roots and the suffix -ʔa which mean 'somewhere', having the same spatial ranking scheme as that underlying demonstrative adjectives. As with adjectives, initial s indicates that a location, even though indefinite, is presupposed to be a part of the hearer's knowledge.

(297)   *(s)i-ʔa*   'somewhere (D1)'
        (s)o-ʔa   'somewhere (D3)'
        (s)u-ʔa   'somewhere (D4)'

Three suffixes can occur with these stems: *-na* 'at somewhere' marks a narrowly focused location. (/ʔah-tun/) *-ʔahru* along/through somewhere', a variant of the postposition *-tu,* marks a location characterized as having span. *-netʉ,* a fusion of *-na* and *i* (verbalizer), with the postposition *-tʉ* 'from', signals change from one location to another or (in discourse) from one scene to another, either in location or time.

(298)   *surʉ*   *-kʉ-seʔ*   *so-ʔa-na*   *bʉ*   *tʉ-rʉeʔ-tʉʉ-kʉ*   *bitʉ-nʉ*
        D4   EVID-CTR   D3-L-at   COGS   RDP-small-Np-at   arrive-PST
        That one arrived somewhere there among his children.   (6:23)

(299)   *sitʉ*   *-kʉ-seʔ*   *ohaʔahnakatʉ*   *si-ʔah-ru*   *toʔi-ki*
        D1   EVID-CTR   Coyote   D1-L-along   go^up-come
        Coyote comes up along here somewhere.   (10:23)

(300)   *sitʉ*   *-kʉ-seʔ*   *si-ʔa-ne-tʉ*   *toʔi-nʉ*
        D1   EVID-CTR   D1-L-at-from   go^up-PST
        At this point, he came out.   (20:26)

Temporal demonstrative adverbs. Temporal demonstratives consist of a demonstrative root with presuppositional *s, -be* (measure), the suffix *-ʔ* (nominalizer), and usually with /-sʉn/ (intensifier). The variety of forms characteristic of locatives and allatives is not found. The two known forms are listed in (301).

(301)   *si-beʔ-sʉ*   'at this time, now (D1)'
        su-beʔ-sʉ   'at that time, then (D4)'

As (302) and (303) show, these forms can be used to express temporal notions extending beyond the purely punctual.

(302)   *su-beʔ-sʉ*   *-kʉ-seʔ*   *sʉ-sʉmʉʔ*   *kwasinabooʔ*   *piʔtoʔ-naʔi*
        D4-MEAS-INTENS   EVID-CTR   RDP-one   snake   bobtailed-become
        Since then, some snakes are bobtailed.   (36:16)

(303) *puhihwi-kahni-k*ʉ   *ra-kw*ʉ   *ta-h*ʉ   *puhiwi-hta*   *si-be?-ni-k*i*-yu-t*ʉ
       money-house-in   1i-ND   1i-GD   money-A   D1-MEAS-M-in-VB-from

       *tahni?i-?e-tu?*i̲
       put-REP-UNR
       From now on, let's put our money in the bank.   (49:33)

There are two indefinite temporal adverbs, *hipe?s*ʉ 'at some time' and
*sus*ʉ*?ana* 'sometimes'. The former is related to the question word *hipe?* 'when?'

Manner demonstrative adverbs. Manner demonstratives consist of a demonstrative root and *-ni* (manner), the root always occurring with either initial *s* indicating the referent is presupposed to be known to the hearer or
with a definite referent. Little elaboration is observed, forms apparently being
limited to the those listed in (304).

(304) *si-ni*   'in this (D1) way, thus'
       so-ni   'in that (D3) way, thus'
       su-ni   'in that (D4) way, thus'
       se-ni   'in various (D5) ways'

(305) *keta?*   *kwasi-k*ʉ   ʉ   *puhiwi-hta*   *suni*   *m*ʉʉ*-r*ʉ
       NEG!   tail-in   2Gs   money-a   D4M   do-PROG
       Next time, do not treat your money like that.   (49:33)

In constructions where these manner adverbials relate to objects, they are
optionally marked with the accusative adverbial ending *-ku*.

(306) *sur*ʉʉ   *wihnu*   *su-hku-t*ʉ   *mi?a-n*ʉ   *sunih-ku*   *uhri*   *buni-hts*i̲
       D4Np   then   D4-at-from   go-PST   D4M-A   D4Ad   see-SS
       They then went from there, having seen them like that.   (94:19)

One additional manner demonstrative adverb is mentioned here, although
it does not contain any of the demonstrative stems that figure in the forms
considered above. This adverb is *s*ʉ*-me* 'thus', used in contexts of saying or
thinking. The first element of this form may be a demonstrative stem that no
longer occurs elsewhere in the language. The second element is the quotative
particle *me(h)* which was discussed in §2.

(307) *s*ʉ*-me*   *-k*ʉ*-se?*   *u*   *y*ʉ*kwi-hka*   *si?ana*   *oha?ahnakat*ʉ   *kimaa-y*ʉ
       ?-QUOT   EVID-CTR   D4A   say-Ds   D1L   Coyote   come-DUR
       As she thus spoke, somewhere here Coyote was coming.   (19:4)

15

Complex Sentences

The following sections treat complex sentences—those involving coordination, clausal complements, and relative clauses.

15.1. Coordination. We here distinguish between 'and', 'but', and 'or'. The most common expression of 'and' in coordinate sentences is simply by a succession of constituents, that is, by no overt conjunction. These constituents may be of any size up to an entire phrase or clause.

(308) *nʉ*   *kwʉhi*   *nʉ?*   *nʉ*   *rʉrʉeʔ-tii*   *puni-tuʔi̠*   *ʉkʉnaa*
      1xGs   wifeˆA   1xNs   1xGs   child-Ap   see-UNR   first
      I'll see my wife and my children first.   (39:25)

(309) *mahrʉ*   *natsaʔaniʔ*   *muh-paʔaraih-tu*   *wʉh-tʉi̠kwa-nʉ*   *mahri*
      D2Gd   buggy   INSTR-inverted-along   INSTR-hit-PST   D2Ad

      ma-naʔkoroomi-nʉ̠
      UNSP-coverˆup-PST
      Their buggy fell upside down and covered them up.   (57:14)

The word (*tʉa-sʉn* 'QUOT-INTENS' →) *tʉasʉ* 'and, also' can be used to emphasize the notion of conjunction. It occurs between the elements being conjoined.

(310) nʉ   rʉʉhkaʔaʔ-a   tʉasʉ   nʉ   kukʉmeʔawe-tʉku   nʉʔ
       1xGs   axe-A   and   1xGs   skillet^A-same   1xNs

       na-su-watsiʔ
       REFL-INSTR-lose
       I forgot my axe and my skillet.   (123:20)

(311) su-kʉ-hu   sitʉ   tʉmarʉʉmoa-ku   urii   kʉhtá-nʉe-nʉ   pahoopi-ma
       D4-at-to   D1   much-A   D4Ap   hard-blow-PST   hail-with

       tʉasʉ   urii   ʉma-nʉ
       and   D4Ap   rain-PST
       It blew hard on them there, and also hailed on them.   (53:26)

In contrastive environments where English would use 'but', the realization
of conjunction is zero.

(312) sitʉ   -kʉ-seʔ   tena-hpʉʔ   sihka   mahrʉ   tʉ-noo-pʉh-a
       D1   EVID-CTR   man-ABS   D1As   D2Gd   UNSP-haul-NOM-A

       tsa-pʉhe-su-waai-tʉ   u   mʉni-nʉ
       INSTR-drop-INSTR-lack-PROG   D4   fail-PST
       This man tried to throw off their packs, but couldn't.   (96:22)

(313) sitʉ   -kʉ-seʔ   tʉkani-nʉ   tsaa   mʉah-tabe-baʔi
       D1   EVID-CTR   night-PST   good   moon-sun-have
       Night fell, but there was good moonlight.   (59:4)

The word for 'or' is tʉanoo, from tʉa (quotative) and noo (necessitative). It
separates two equal constituents.

(314) orʉ   -tsaʔ   rena-hpʉʔ   hube   tʉa-noo   pitsi-pʉh-a   hibi-tʉʔi
       D3   DECL   man-ABs   coffee^A   QUOT-NEC   milk-ABs-A   drink-UNR
       That man will drink coffee or milk.

(315) pihiʔa-nii   tʉa-noo   tʉrʉeʔ-waʔihpʉʔa-nii   nʉnʉ   puniʔi
       boy-Ap   QUOT-NEC   small-woman-Ap   1xNp   see-REAL
       We saw boys or girls.

15.2. Complement clauses. Complement clauses are marked with one of
three subordinating suffixes and take subjects marked as accusative. The major distinctions are whether an event occurs simultaneously with the event of

the next higher clause (or is overlapped temporarily by it), or whether subordinate and main clause subjects are different or identical.

No simultaneity or overlap. The subordinate suffix is -*ka* if the subject of the subordinate clause is different from that of the next higher clause. If the subjects are identical, the subordinate clause suffix is -*tsi* and its subject does not occur overtly. Both -*ka* and -*tsi* can attach to the combining form of the verb, and -*ka* can also be preceded by the inceptive marker -*hupitʉ* and either -*tuʔi* or -*waʔi* (unrealized).

(316) u   yʉi-hka   -kʉ-seʔ   marʉʉ   nanah-tena-nʉʉ
     D4A   evening-Ds   EVID-CTR   D2Gp   RECIP-man-Np

       soo-kʉni-kʉ-hu   hibi-miʔa-nʉ
       much-house-at-to   drink-go-PST

When it had gotten evening, their menfolk went into town to drink.
(59:3)

(317) hunakwʉ   mahri   toboʔi-hu-pitʉ-ka   -kʉ-seʔ   u   kwʉhʉ
     outside   D2Ad   stand-INDEF-arrive-Ds   EVID-CTR   D4G   wife

       mahrʉ-waka-tu   toʔi-nʉ
       D2Nd-toward-along   goˆup-PST

When the two had come to a stop outside, his wife came out towardthem.
(39:26)

(318) surʉʉ   tʉkʉ-tsi   yuu-ʔʉh-kooi-nʉ
     D4Np   eat-SS   quiet-eye?-die-PST

Having eaten, they slept undisturbed.
(8:46)

(319) suhka   u   tʉiʔ-a   bʉa-htsi   uhri   miʔa-ku   -kʉ-seʔ
     D4As   D4G   friend-A   leave-ss   D4Ad   go-DS   EVID-CR

       taʔsiwóoʔ   nu-nura-wʉ-na
       buffalo   RDP-run-?-CONT

As they went, having left her friend, buffalo ran off.
(43:30)

There is a restriction having to do with -*tsi* (same subject) and -*tuʔi*/-*waʔi* (unrealized). Since UNREALIZED cannot occur syntactically with -*tsi*, there is a problem in sentences having identical main and subordinate clause subjects with unrealized aspect in the subordinate clause. The solution is to choose -*ka* as the subordinate clause in a special way to indicate that it is identical to the next higher subject. The special subject marking involves coreferential pronouns *pʉ* (singular), *pʉhi* (dual), and *pʉi* (plural).

(320) soo-beʔ-sʉ   nʉmʉ-nʉʉ   pʉi   puhihwʉ-hima-ruʔi-ka
      much-MEAS-INTENS   Comanche-Np   COAp   money-take-UNR-DS

        nʉmʉ-na-rʉmʉʉʔ-nʉʉ-kʉmaʔ-kʉ   no-bitʉ-nu
        Comanche-REFL-trade-Np-edge-at   haul-arrive-PST
        Long ago when Comanches were about to receive money, they camped
        near Comanche trade stores.   (59:1)

Simultaneity or overlap. The subordinate clause suffix is *-ku*, which attaches to the unmodified verb or is preceded by *-ka* (stative) or *-ʔe* (repetitive). If the next higher subject is different from the subordinate subject, the structure is straightforward.

(321) urii   kima-noo-ko   suʔana   urʉʉ-mu-nakwʉ   pia-ʔʉmah-paa-baʔi
      D4Ap   come-haul-DS   D4L   D4p-INSTR-side big-rain-water-have
      As they came traveling, there ahead of them was a big lake.   (93:2)

If the subjects of the two clauses are identical, the coreferential pronouns mentioned above are used in the lower clause. The subjects of the clauses can be identical since *-tsi* does not allow a preceding *-ka* (stative). Instead, *-ku* is found along with a coreferential pronoun in the complement.

(322) sitʉ   -kʉ-seʔ   tʉtaati wihtue   pʉ   tsa-yaa-hka-ku   u   boma-nʉ
      D1   EVID-CTR littleˆA bucket-A COGs   INSTR-take-ST-DS D4A pick-PST
      As she is carrying a little bucket, she picked it.   (73:4, 5)

Finally, note the following construction involving the word *kesʉ* 'before' (*ke* 'not' + *-sʉ* 'still').

(323) sitʉ   -kʉ-seʔ   kesʉ   pʉ   waikina   u   wʉh-pitʉʉ-ku   u
      D1   EVID-CTR before   COGs   wagonˆA   D4A INSTR-arrive-DS D4A

      kʉh-tsía-nʉ
      INSTR-bite-PST
      Before he could reach his wagon, this one bit him.   (27:9)

Subject and object. Both subjects and objects of complement clauses are marked syntactically as accusative. For accusative case-marking nouns, see §9.3. The accusative form of pronouns is presented in §12.2. Since only a single accusative pronoun can be proclitic to the verb, in a complement clause with both pronominal subject and object in OSV order, the first pronoun is stranded in nonproclitic position.

(324) suni   urii   tai   mʉʉ-hka -se? taa   nanah-tena-nʉʉ oh-to
       D4M   D4Ap   1iA   do-DS   CTR   1iGp   RECIP-man-Np   D3-along

    tobo?i-hu-tu?i
    stand-INDEF-UNR
    When we have done thus to them, our menfolk will stand along
    there.   (119:18)

(325) urii   urii   maka-hka -kʉ-se? urʉʉ pia?   nohi? tsaa-ku
       D4Ap   D4Ap   feed-DS   EVID-CTR D4Gp mother very   good-A

    mʉnʉ nʉ   rʉrʉe?-tii maka-nu
    2Np   1Gs child-Ap   feed-PST
    When they had fed them their mother said, "You fed my children very
    good."   (74:15)

Whenever a third-person-singular pronoun object would be stranded before another pronoun in a complement clause, a demonstrative (in the accusative case) substitutes for it. Third-person-singular accusative pronoun forms can occur only directly before the verb.

(326) meeku-ka na-maka?mʉʉki uhka rai   buni-kwa-tu?i-ka
       now-!p   REFL-getˆready D4As 1iAp see-go-UNR-DS
    Get ready now, so we can go see him!   (7:36)

(327) uhka   u   wʉh-ka?a-bʉni-ku   -kʉ-se?   hini
       D4As   D4A   INSTR-chop-AUG-DS   EVID-CTR   what?ˆN

    kasá-bi-piku-hki-na
    wing-RDP-beat-come-CONT
    As he was chopping it, something was coming making wing noises.
                                                              (27:3)

Coreferential forms. If the subject of a higher clause is also the object of a complement clause, a coreferential pronoun (§12.4) is used in the complement clause.

(328) situ̲   -ku̲-se?   wakaré?ee? suni pu̲mi u   mu̲u̲-mi?a-ku
       D1   EVID-CTR   turtle   D4M   COA   D4A do-go-DS

       ma-hoi-ki̲   nu̲u̲?-kwipu-nu̲-kwa̲
       D2-around-at   REFL-wrap-PST-go

This turtle, when he (the snake) treated him (the turtle) in that way,
he (the turtle) went off wrapping himself around [some weeds].

(36:12)

Similarly, if the main clause subject is included in the subject or the object
of a complement clause, then the latter will be a coreferential form.

(329) suru̲   -ku̲-se?   suni uhka bu̲i   mu̲u̲-hka mia-ru?i̲ nu̲?   me
       D4   EVID-CTR   D4M   D4As COAp do-DS   go-UNR   1xNs QUOT

       yu̲kwii-yu̲
       say-DUR

When they treated him that way, he said, "I'll go."   (6:22)

(330) situ̲   -ku̲-se?   ma   pia?   pu̲hi   muhne-htsi   mi?a-nu̲
       D1   EVID-CTR   D2G mother COAd   lead-SS   go-PST

His mother, leading them, went.   (81:9)

15.3. Relative clauses. The most common type of relative clause has a
verb marked with the suffix *-a*. The verb takes either the suffix *-?i̲* (realized) or
one of the suffixes *-tu?i̲/-wa?i̲* (unrealized). Both subjects and objects of relative clauses are marked as genitives (§§9.4 & 12.3). Relative clauses normally
directly follow the nouns they modify, but may sometimes precede them.

(331) nu̲   buhiwi-hta nu̲? [narohtu̲ma-ku̲ nu̲ ru̲ki-?ih-a] watsi-ku̲-?i̲
       1Gs money-A   1xNs can-in   1Gs put-REAL-A lose-CAUS-REAL

       I lost my money that I had put in a can.   (49:27)

(332) su̲mu̲-? -ku̲-tsa?   raiboo? [pu̲-ma-ku bu̲u̲   waahima-ru?ih-a]
       one^Ns EVID-CTR   man   CO-on-a   COGp Christmas-UNR-A

       waah-pi-hta   wu̲h-ká?a-mi?a-nu̲
       cedar-ABS-A   INSTR-chop-go-PST

A white man went to cut down a cedar tree with which they would
celebrate Christmas.   (27:1)

It is common for a noun modified by a relative clause to be present only semantically and not syntactically. Even if a noun is not overt, however, a demonstrative adjective may be present.

(333)   *u-mati*   *takwu̧*   *[taa*   *tu̧hka-ru?ih-a]*   *pomaa-kwa̧*
       D4-PART^A   1iNd   1iGp   eat-UNR-A   pick-go
       Let's go pick from it what we will eat.   (16:10)

(334)   *situ̧*   *-ku̧-se?*   *[suru̧u̧*   *pihi?a-nu̧u̧*   *pu̧mu̧*   *ai?-ku*   *hani-?ih-a]*
       D1   EVID-CTR   D4Gp   boy-Gp   COGp   bad-A   do-REAL-A

         nasúwatsi-nu̧
         forget-PST
       He forgot what bad things those boys had done.   (80:30)

(335)   *situ̧u̧*   *-ku̧-se?*   *taiboo?-nu̧u̧*   *sehka*   *[bu̧u̧*   *toh-ku̧a-?ih-a]*
       D1p   EVID-CTR   man-Np   D5As   COGp   INSTR-go^up-REAL-A

         su̧u̧-ma-tu   *tso?mȩ-tsi*   *u*   *ku-tsi̧tóna-nu̧*
         one-on-along   gather-SS   D4A   INSTR-set^fire-PST
       These white men, gathering together that which they had blown out, set it on fire.   (29:29)

(336)   *situ̧*   *-ku̧-se?*   *tuibihtsi?*   *suhka*   *[pu̧na?-wa?i-hpu̧?-a*
       D1   EVID-CTR   young^man   D4As   COG   kin-woman-ABS-G

         tu̧hka-ru?ih-a]   *hima-nu̧*
         eat-UNR-A   take-PST
       This young man got that which his woman would eat.   (71:27)

As in complement clauses, if a relative clause has pronominal subject and object, the order is OSV. A proclitic third-person-singular pronoun cannot stand as an object in this structure, so a demonstrative in genitive case substitutes for it. Note also that the use of coreferential pronouns in relative clauses is identical to that used in complement clauses.

(337)   *...[mahka*   *pu̧*   *tu̧ku̧-hima-ku̧-?ih-a]*   *ma*   *maka-nu̧*
         D2GS   COG   food-take-CAUS-UNR-A   D2A   feed-PST
       ...fed her what he had taken for her to eat.   (71:28)

Selected Bibliography

Armagost, James L. 1982. The temporal relationship between telling and happening in Comanche narrative. *Anthropological Linguistics* 24:193–200.

Armagost, James L. 1984. The Grammar of Personal Pronouns in Comanche. In David S. Rood (ed.), *1983 Mid-America Linguistics Conference Papers,* 25–35. Boulder, CO: University of Colorado.

Baker, Theodor. 1882. Über die musik der nordamerikanischen wilden. In Songs of the Comanche, 10–13, 37–41, 50–51, 59–79.

Beals, Ralph L. 1943. *The aboriginal culture of the Cahita Indians.* Volume 19. Berkeley and Los Angeles.

Becker, W. J. 1936. The Comanche Indian and his language. *Chronicles of Oklahoma* 14:328–342.

Becker, W. J. 1951. The compounding of words in the Comanche Indian anguage: A Thesis. M.A. thesis, University of Oklahoma, Norman, Oklahoma.

Canonge, Elliott D. 1949. Comanche Frames. Unpublished manuscript.

Canonge, Elliott D. 1957. Voiceless vowels in Comanche. *International Journal of American Linguistics* 23:63–67. Rev.: D. Hymes in *Language* 35:370–371 (1959); Tovar in *Word* 16:407–409 (1960).

Canonge, Elliott D. 1958. *Comanche texts.* (Repub. 1962, 1974.) Norman, Oklahoma: Summer Institute of Linguistics of the University of Oklahoma. (Coyote tales, fables, histories, food preparation. Includes vocabulary of about 1,300 entries.)

Carlson, Gustav A. and Volney H. Jones. 1939. Some notes on the uses of Plants by the Comanche Indians. *Papers of the Michigan Academy of Science, Arts and Letters* 25:517–542.

Casagrande, Joseph B. 1948. Comanche baby language. *International Journal of American Linguistics* 14:11–14.

Casagrande, Joseph B. 1954. Comanche linguistic acculturation I. International *Journal of American Linguistics* 20:140–151.

Casagrande, Joseph B. 1954. Comanche linguistic acculturation II. *International Journal of American Linguistics* 20:217–237.

Casagrande, Joseph B. 1955. Comanche linguistic acculturation III. *International Journal of American Linguistics* 21:8–25.

Chomsky, Noam and Morris Halle. 1968. *The sound pattern of English.* New York: Harper & Row.

Espinosa, Aurelio Macedonio, ed. 1907. Los Comanches. *University of New Mexico Bulletin, (Language Series I)* 1:1–46.

Fehrenbach, Theodore R. 1974. *Comanches: The destruction of a people.* New York: Knopf.

García Rejón, M. 1866. *Vocabulario del idioma Comanche.* Mexico.

Gilles, Albert S., Sr. 1974. *Comanche Days.* Dallas: Southern Methodist University Press.

Gladwin, Thomas Favill. 1948. Comanche kin behavior. *American Anthropologist* 50:73–94.

Hale, Kenneth. 1958. Internal diversity in Uto-Aztecan: I. *International Journal of American Linguistics* 24:101–107.

Hale, Kenneth. 1959. Internal diversity in Uto-Aztecan: II. *International Journal of American Linguistics* 25:114–121. (Comanche on p. 116).

Hoebel, E. Adamson. 1939 Comanche and Hekandika Shoshone relationship systems. *American Anthropologist* 41:440–457.

Hale, Kenneth. 1940. Political organization and law-ways of the Comanche Indians. *American Anthropologist Memoir 54 (supplement).*

Hoffman, W. J. 1886. Remarks on Indian tribal names. *Papers of the American Philosophical Society* 23:299–301.

Lanacker, Ronald W., ed. 1977. *An overview of Uto-Aztecan grammar. Studies in Uto-Aztecan grammar.* Summer Institute of Linguistic and the University of Texas at Arlington Publications in Linguistics 56. Dallas: Summer Institute of Linguistics and the University of Texas at Arlington.

Marcy, Randolph B. [with remarks by W. W. Turner]. 1853. Vocabularies of words in the languages of the Comanches and Wichitas. U.S. Senate Doc. Ex. No. 666 (Exploration of the Red River of Louisiana.), Appendix H, pp. 307–311. Washington.

McLaughlin, John E. 1982. From aspect to tense, or what's -*nuh* in Comanche. *1982 Mid-America Linguistics Conference Proceedings,* 412–427. Lawrence, Kansas: University of Kansas.

Miller, Wick. 1972. Newe natekwinappeh: Stories and dictionary. *University of Utah Anthropological Papers 94.* Salt Lake City: University of Utah.

Neighbors, Robert S. 1852. Comanche (Nauni) vocabulary. In Henry Rowe Schoolcraft (ed.), *Information respecting the history, conditions and prospects of the Indian tribes of the United States* 2:494–505. Philadelphia.

Osborn, Henry and William A Smalley. 1949. Formulae for Comanche stem and word formation. *International Journal of American Linguistics* 15:93–99.

Richardson, Rupert N. 1929. The culture of the Comanche Indians. *Texas Archeological and Paleontological Society Bulletin* 1:58–73.

Osborn, Henry and William A Smalley. 1933. *The Comanche barrier to South Plains Settlement.* Glendale, California.

Riggs, Venda. 1949. Alternate phonemic analyses of Comanche. *International Journal of American Linguistics* 15:229–31.

Shimkin, Demitri Boris. 1940. Shoshone-Comanche origins and migrations. *Proceedings of the 6th Pacific Science Congress* 4:17–125.

Shimkin, Demitri Boris. 1941. The Uto-Aztecan System of Kinship Terminology. *American Anthropologist* 43:223–245.

Smalley, William A. 1953. Phonemic rhythm in Comanche. *International Journal of American Linguistics* 19:297–301.

Tilghman, Zoe A. 1938. Quanah: *The eagle of the Comanches.* Oklahoma City: Harlow.

Voegelin, Florence M. and Kenneth L. Hale. 1962. Typological and Comparative Grammar of Uto-Aztecan: I (Phonology). *Indiana University Publications in Anthropology and Linguistics,* Memoir No. 17.

Wallace, Ernest and E. Adamson Hoebel. 1952. *The Comanches: Lords of the Southern Plains.* Norman: University of Oklahoma.

Wistrand-Robinson, Lila. 1976. Sample cognate list and preliminary sound correspondences toward a North and South American Indian language relationship. Paper read at Southeastern Conference on Linguistics XXVIII Meetings, University of Maryland at College Park, April 8, 1983.

Wistrand-Robinson, Lila. 1985. Bi-directional movement in historical change Shoshone: Comanche. Paper read at the 1985 Annual Meetings, American Anthropological Association, Washington, D.C.

Wistrand-Robinson, Lila. 1991. Uto-Aztecan affinities with Panoan of Peru I: Correspondences, in Mary Ritchie Key, (ed.), Language change in South American Indian languages. Philadelphia: University of Pennsylvania Press.

SIL International Publications
Additional Releases in the **Publications in Linguistics** Series

147. The Kifuliiru Language, Volume 2: A descriptive grammar, by Roger Van Otterloo, 2011, 612 pp., ISBN 978-1-55671-270-8

146. The Kifuliiru language, Volume 1: Phonology, tone, and morphological derivation, by Karen Van Otterloo, 2011, 512 pp., ISBN 978-1-55671-261-6

145. Language death in Mesmes, by Michael B. Ahland, 2010, 155 pp., ISBN 978-1-55671-227-2

144. The phonology of two central Chadic languages, by Tony Smith and Richard Gravina, 2010, 267 pp., ISBN 978-155671-231-9

143. A grammar of Akoose: A northwest Bantu language, by Robert Hedinger, 2008, 318 pp., ISBN 978-1-55671-222-7

142. Word order in Toposa: An aspect of multiple feature-checking, by Helga Schröder, 2008, 213 pp., ISBN 978-1-55671-181-7

141. Aspects of the morphology and phonology of Kɔnni, by Michael C. Cahill, 2007, 537 pp., ISBN 978-1-55671-184-8

140. The phonology of Mono, by Kenneth Olson, 2005, 311 pp., ISBN 978-1-55671-160-2

139. Language and life: Essays in memory of Kenneth L. Pike, edited by Wise, Headland, and Brend, 2003, 674 pp., ISBN 978-1-55671-140-4

138. Case and agreement in Abaza, by Brian O'Herin, 2002, 304 pp., ISBN 978-1-55671-135-0

137. Pragmatics of persuasive discourse in Spanish television advertising, by Karol J. Hardin, 2001, 247 pp., ISBN 978-1-55671-150-3

SIL International Publications
7500 W. Camp Wisdom Road
Dallas, TX 75236-5629

Voice: 972-708-7404
Fax: 972-708-7363
publications_intl@sil.org
www.ethnologue.com/bookstore.asp

www.ingramcontent.com/pod-product-compliance
Lightning Source LLC
Chambersburg PA
CBHW071009140426
42814CB00004BA/170